Costa Rica

2nd Edition

Travel better, enjoy more

ULYSSES

Travel Guides

Offices

CANADA: Ulysses Travel Guides, 4176 Rue St-Denis, Montréal, Québec, H2W 2M5, ☎ (514) 843-9447 or 1-877-542-7247, Fax: (514) 843-9448, info@ulysses.ca, www.ulyssesguides.com

EUROPE: Les Guides de Voyage Ulysse SARL, BP 159, 75523 Paris Cedex 11, France, ☎ 01 43 38 89 50, Fax: 01 43 38 89 52, voyage@ulysse.ca, www.ulyssesguides.com

U.S.A.: Ulysses Travel Guides, 305 Madison Avenue, Suite 1166, New York, NY 10165, ☎ 1-877-542-7247, Fax: (514) 843-9448, info@ulysses.ca, www.ulyssesguides.com

Distributors

CANADA: Ulysses Books & Maps, 4176 Saint-Denis, Montréal, Québec, H2W 2M5, ☎ (514) 843-9882, ext.2232, 800-748-9171, Fax: 514-843-9448, info@ulysses.ca, www.ulyssesguides.com

GREAT BRITAIN AND IRELAND: World Leisure Marketing, Unit 11, Newmarket Court, Newmartket Drive, Derby DE24 8NW, ☎ 1 332 57 37 37, Fax: 1 332 57 33 99, office@wlmsales.co.uk

SCANDINAVIA: Scanvik, Esplanaden 8B, 1263 Copenhagen K, DK, ☎ (45) 33.12.77.66, Fax: (45) 33.91.28.82

SPAIN: Altaïr, Balmes 69, E-08007 Barcelona, ☎ 454 29 66, Fax: 451 25 59, altair@globalcom.es

SWITZERLAND: Havas Services Suisse, ☎(26) 460 80 60, Fax: (26) 460 80 68

U.S.A.: The Globe Pequot Press, 246 Goose Lane, Guilford, CT 06437 - 0480, ☎1-800-243-0495, Fax: 800-820-2329, sales@globe-pequot.com

Other countries , contact Ulysses Books & Maps, 4176 Rue Saint-Denis, Montréal, Québec, H2W 2M5, ☎ (514) 843-9882, ext. 2232, 800-748-9171, Fax: 514-843-9448, info@ulysses.ca, www.ulyssesguides.com

Cataloguing-in-Publication Data (see page 8)
© January 2001, Ulysses Travel Guides.
All rights reserved
Printed in Canada
ISBN 2-89464-292-X

Vivían en valles verdiazules,
con cielos transparentes
y aires olorosos a cedro.
Entre esplendores de selvas
y augustas soledades.

Cary Sagot Salazar de Carmiol
Cuando Lala enloquecia

They lived in the green and blue valleys
where the skies were clear
and the air was scented with cedars.
Between the splendours of the forest
and an imposing solitude.

Authors
Stéphane G. Marceau
Francis Giguère
Yves Séguin
Collaboration
François Brodeur
Marie-Josée Guy
Maxime Soucy

Editor
Daniel Desjardins

Publisher
Pascale Couture

Copy Editing
Anne Joyce
Eileen Connolly
Editing Assistance
Dena Duijkers
Isabelle Lalonde

Page Layout
Typesetting
Dena Duijkers
Isabelle Lalonde
Visuals
Anne Joyce

Translation Coordination
Jacqueline Grekin

Translation
Traci Williams
Christina Poole
Sarah Kresh
Danielle Gauthier
Suzanne Murray
Tracy Kendrick
Janet Logan
Francesca Worrall

Cartography
André Duchesne
Patrick Thivierge
Yanik Landreville
Bradley Fenton

Photography
Cover Page
Margaret Mead/
Image Bank
Inside Pages
Claude-Hervé Bazin
Stéphane G. Marceau
Roger Michel
Didier Raffin

Design
Patrick Farei
(Atoll Direction)

Illustrations
Myriam Gagné
Lorette Pierson
Marie-Annick Viatour
Richard Serrao
Josée Perreault
Laura Zuckerman

Thanks to: Béatrice Passot, Didier Raffin, María Exiria Jara Campos, Manfred Quesada, Luis Arguedas, Mariette Daignault, Natalie Ewing, Marc Fournier, Edgar Neidhardt, Elizabeth Newton, Pierre Perron, Manfred Gutierrez, Jeff Crandall, Loic Dervieu, Daisy Arroyo Sanchez, Estela Fuentes Alvarado, Edgar Neidhardt, Luis F. Quesada, Maria Amalia Revelo and Ireth Rodriguez.

We acknowledge the financial support of the Government of Canada through the Book Publishing Industry Development Program (BPIDP) for our publishing activities.

We would also like to thank SODEC (Québec) for its financial support.

Table of Contents

Map List

Map Symbols

❶	Tourist Information	☕	National Parks	✉	Post Office
✚	Hospital	◆	Wildlife Sanctuary	⛪	Cathedral
✈	Airport, Airfield	▲	Volcano	✝	Church
🚌	Bus Terminal	▲	Mountain	- - - - -	Unpaved Road
🚗	Car Ferry	☀	Lookout	———	Footpath
🚢	Passenger Ferry	◎	Beach		
🚶	Pedestrian Walkway	▲	Camping		

Symbols

🛥	Ulysses's favourite
☎	Telephone number
⇄	Fax number
≡	Air conditioning
⊗	Fan
♯	Screen
≈	Pool
ℜ	Restaurant
⊕	Whirlpool
ℝ	Refrigerator
K	Kitchenette
▣	In-room safe
△	Sauna
⊘	Fitness Centre
tv	Colour television
ctv	Cable television
hw	Hot water
cw	Cold water
pb	Private bathroom
sb	Shared bathroom
fb	Full board (lodging + 3 meals, usually quoted for one person)
½ b	Half board (lodging + 2 meals, usually quoted for one person)
bkfst incl.	Breakfast Included

ATTRACTION CLASSIFICATION

★	Interesting
★★	Worth a visit
★★★	Not to be missed

The prices listed in this guide are for the admission of one adult.

HOTEL CLASSIFICATION

$	$15 or less
$$	$15 to $25
$$$	$25 to $50
$$$$	$50 to $75
$$$$$	$75 to $120
$$$$$$	$120 or more

The prices in this guide are for one standard room,
double occupancy in high season.

RESTAURANT CLASSIFICATION

$	$5 or less
$$	$5 to $10
$$$	$10 to $20
$$$$	$20 to $40
$$$$$	$40 or more

The prices in the guide are for a meal for one
person, not including drinks and tip.

All prices in this guide are in U.S. dollars.

Cataloguing-in-Publication Data

Guimont-Marceau, Stéphane, 1969-

    Costa Rica

    2nd ed.
    (Ulysses travel guide)
    Translation of: Costa Rica.
    Includes index.

    ISBN 2-89464-292-X

    1. Costa Rica - Guidebooks I. Title. II. Series.

F1543.5.S4313 2000   917.28604'5   C00-941751-6

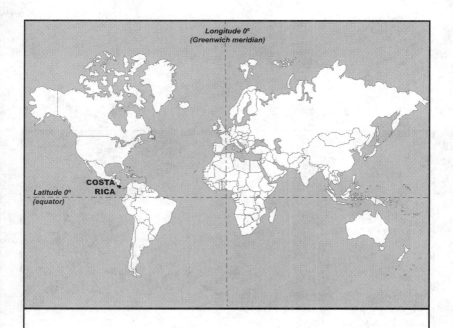

Longitude 0°
(Greenwich meridian)

Latitude 0°
(equator)

COSTA RICA

Where is
Costa Rica ?

Costa Rica
Capital: San José
Area: 50,700km² (19,570 sq mi)
Population: 3,500,000 inhab.
Languages: Spanish, English, Creole
Currency: colón

Gulf of Mexico

Atlantic Ocean

Mexico

Cuba

Dominican Republic

Haiti

Belize

Jamaica

Guatemala   Honduras

El Salvador

Caribbean Sea

Nicaragua

COSTA RICA

Panama

Venezuela

Pacific Ocean

Colombia

©ULYSSES

Ecuador   Peru

Brazil

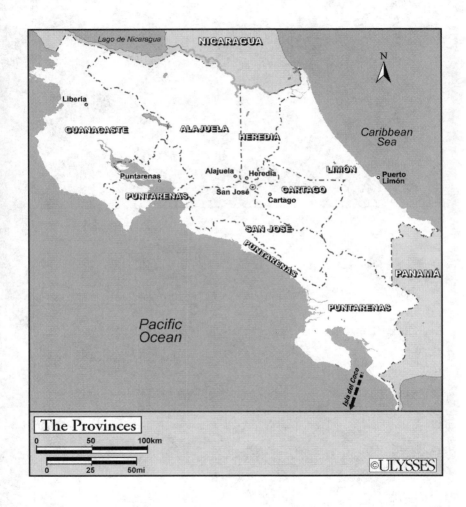

The Provinces

Portrait

How do you
describe Costa Rica, a country with so many natural treasures? Perhaps the best way to start would be with its name, which means "the rich coast."

As the first word in its name, "Coast" attests to this part of Central America's position, bordered by two long, sinuous coasts with kilometres of idyllic beaches. The eastern side is bathed by the Caribbean Sea with its many coral reefs, while the western side by the calm, vast Pacific Ocean.

And the region between these coasts can only be described as "rich." Since it's located on the isthmus separating the Americas, Costa Rica is the natural habitat for many species of flora and fauna found in both northern and southern continents. The microclimates of its mountains and rivers, valleys and plains, and dry tropical and rainforests favour the existence and continual

growth of this abundant plant and animal life. In its lush vegetation, you can smell the heady scent of flowers, hear the birds whose songs are as enchanting as their plumage, see multicoloured butterflies fluttering through the fields, and glimpse endangered species in the forest: Costa Rica's natural beauty is mesmerizing. However, its culture and people are just as fascinating and the warm and welcoming

Ticos have contributed greatly to Latin American society.

No matter how long you stay, this rich coast is sure to seduce you!

Geography

Although Costa Rica has an area of only 50,700km² (19,577 sq mi), it is not the smallest country in Central America; it is larger than both El Salvador (21,040km² or 8,124 sq mi) and Belize (22,960km² or 8,866 sq mi). The area of Costa Rica is comparable to that of the states of Vermont and New Hampshire combined (49,079km² or 18,951 sq mi), the Midi-Pyrenees region of France (45,602km² or 17,608 sq mi), Denmark (43,070km² or 16,631 sq mi) or Switzerland (41,288 km² or 15,943 sq mi). And with its high plateaus, stable political system and abolished army (1949), Costa Rica is dubbed the "Switzerland of Central America." Costa Rica is 380km (236mi) at its longest point and 270km (168mi) at its widest. Its narrowest point between the two coasts measures only 120km (74.6mi). With its many bays, coves and two peninsulas (Nicoya and Osa), the Pacific Coast is 1,016km (631mi) long. The Atlantic Coast is far shorter, only 212km (132mi) long.

Costa Rica is bordered on the north by Nicaragua and on the south by Panama. The Interamericana Highway runs 534km (332mi) north to south through Costa Rica,

from the Nicaraguan border (Peñas Blancas) to the Panamian border (Paso Canoas). Costa Rica is located between 8° and 11° latitude north and between 82° and 86° longitude west. Isla del Coco (25km² or 9.7 sq mi), 500km (311mi) off the Pacific Coast (5 30' N. and 87 05' W.), belongs to Costa Rica and is also a national park.

Costa Rica is divided into seven provinces: San José, Heredia, Cartago, Alajuela, Limón, Puntarenas and Guanacaste. Each province has the same name as its capital city, except Guanacaste, whose capital is Liberia. The provinces of San José, Heredia, Alajuela and Cartago are all found in the Central Valley. The other three provinces are divided according to their geographic location in relation to the Central Valley (one on both coasts and one in the north).

With a population of 330,000, at an altitude of 1,150m (3,773ft), and in the middle of Costa Rica and the Central Valley, San José is not only the largest city, but also the capital.

Sea and Mountains

No matter where you are in the country, warm, salty water (Caribbean Sea or Pacific Ocean) is often less than an hour away, and rarely more than three.

Agricultural Exchanges

Did you know that before the Spanish arrived in America, sugar cane and coffee didn't grow here? On the other hand, potatoes, cocoa, corn, tomatoes, vanilla, hot peppers, peanuts, tobacco and cotton are all crops that, in the beginning, existed only in America. Long live exchanges!

Thus, you can spend the morning in the mountains (exploring volcanoes, hiking, rafting, bird-watching, etc.) and the afternoon by the sea (swimming, scuba diving, surfing, fishing and so on).

The mountain range, or cordilleras, divides Costa Rica into two distinct regions: the Caribbean (Atlantic) and Pacific. The slopes on the Atlantic side are less steep than those of the Pacific side where summits rise between 1,500m (16,146ft) to 3,819m (12,530ft) in altitude. It's possible to see the typical vegetation of the lower, middle and higher mountains on the western slopes.

The long mountain range, stretching across the country from the northwest (Nicaragua) to southeast (Panamá), is made up of four distinct mountain chains: Guanacaste, Tilarán, Central and Talamanca. In the north, the newer **Guanacaste Cordillera** consists of young volcanic rock and has several active volcanoes including Orosí (1,487m or 4,879ft), Rincón de la Vieja (1,895m or 6,217ft), Santa María (1,916m or 6,286ft) and Miravalles (2,028m or 6,654ft). To the south, near Arenal Lake, the **Tilarán Cordillera** is home to the Arenal Volcano (1,633m or 5,358ft), one of the most active volcanos in the world, and one of the most popular attractions in the country. At nightfall, from a safe distance, you can hear the volcano rumbling and admire the red lava flowing from it.

In the middle of the country, the **Central Cordillera** has some of the highest and most accessible volcanos in Costa Rica. The Poás (2,704m or 8,871ft), Barva (2,906m or 9,534ft), Irazú (3,432m or 11,260ft) and Turrialba (3,328m or 10,919ft) volcanos are a complete change of scenery, and a sight to behold only 60km (37.3mi) from the capital. The Central Cordillera shelters part of the Central Valley (Valle Central or Meseta Central), which ranges from 800m (2,625ft) to 1,600m in height. With 3,500km² (1,351 sq mi) of fertile land, this valley is blessed with a temperate climate— cooler and less humid than on the coasts— and has quickly become the place to enjoy the "good life." It's no wonder that almost two-thirds of the Costa Rican population lives in this mountainous region, where most of the major cities are found, including the country's capital, San José (pop. 330,000), located at an altitude of 1,150m (3,773ft).

In the south, the **Talamanca Cordillera** is a plicated rock mass of limestone and igneous rock. It boasts Cerro Chirripó (3,819m or 12,530ft), the highest point in Costa Rica, and more than a dozen summits over 3,000m (9,843ft) high, including Urán (3,600m or 11,811ft), Terbi (3,720m or 12,205ft), Ami (3,295m or 10,810ft), Ena (3,126m or 10,256ft), Cabécar (3,030m or 9,941ft), Eli (3,097m or 10,161ft) and Dúrika (3,280m or 10,761ft).

Although Costa Rica has many impressive mountains and volcanos, there are also lower-lying areas. The largest plain is on the northeast coast, along the Caribbean Sea. This immense, often swampy area extends from the Nicaraguan border to the city of Limón, covering 20% of the country.

On the Pacific side, the mountains are much closer to the coast, alternately forming capes, cliffs, bays and creeks. There are also two large gulfs: in the north, the Gulf of Nicoya with a peninsula bearing the same name; and in the south, the Golfo Dulce and the Osa Peninsula. These two gulfs bathe the shores of the province of Puntarenas, where there are many highly prized tourist attractions, the biggest towns being Jacó, Quepos and Montezuma.

Costa Rica has very few natural freshwater lakes. Apart from small lakes, such as Cachi (San José), Astillero (Heredia) and Caño Negro (Alajuela), the country's only lake of any significant size is Arenal (Guanacaste). This incredible body of clear water (39km by 5km or 24.2mi by 3.1mi) lies just west of the famous Arenal Volcano. Highly valued by swimmers and fishers alike (especially for its rainbow perch, called *guapote*), Lake Arenal is also a paradise for windsurfers who come from all over to tackle its winds.

Although it's a country of mountains—some of them very high—Costa Rica also harbours many waterways, some emptying into the

Pacific, others zigzagging towards the Caribbean Sea. There are about fifteen major rivers, the most popular being the Tempisque, Sarapiquí, Reventazón and Pacuare. The last two have earned an international reputation for great rafting and kayaking.

Geological Formation

Costa Rica's current territory only came into being three million years ago. A million years before the formation of the actual land mass, the sea still occupied this region between North and South America. At this time, however, a string of volcanic islands on the Pacific side already existed, as evidenced by volcanic rock and sediment dating back about 100 million years that were discovered on the Nicoya Peninsula in this century.

The relatively sudden appearance of Costa Rica three million years ago was due to tectonic forces, which caused the Cocos plate to begin drifting eastward and collide with the Antillean plate, sliding under it at a rate of 10cm (4in) a year. The friction between the two plates raised the bedrock, causing numerous volcanic eruptions. This formed a land bridge between the two continents. At that point, Costa Rica was made up of about

100 volcanoes, but most have levelled off, leaving only about a dozen perfectly conically shaped ones, mostly in the northwest and centre of the country.

Costa Rica lies on the Pacific "Rim of Fire," which consists of approximately 60 volcanoes, seven of which are still active in Costa Rica. Some of the most active volcanoes—Poás (2,704m or 8,871ft), Rincón de la Vieja (1,895m or 6,217ft) and especially Arenal (1,633m or 5,358ft)—have become major tourist attractions.

The collision of the Cocos and Caribbean plates has also caused a number of earthquakes. Though most have been minor, some earthquakes, such as the one that occurred in April 1991, measuring 7.4 on the Richter Scale, warn of the ever-present potential for a natural disaster.

Climate

Costa Rica has a tropical climate with two seasons: the dry season and the rainy (or green) season . Several microclimates also exist, depending on the region and altitude. Basically, four climatic zones can be discerned The Caribbean Coast's is wet and has the highest rate of precipitation year round. On

the Pacific Coast, Guanacaste province and the Nicoya Peninsula have an arid climate and weeks can pass during the dry season before it rains. The reverse is true for the mountains where it can rain two out of three days during the rainy season. In the Central Valley and San José, it's spring year round, with steady temperatures averaging between 22°C (72°F) and 25°C (77°F).

The rainy season lasts from May to November. Costa Ricans call this wet season *invierno* (winter), which is nothing like the snowy, intensely cold winter in North America and Europe. The rainy season is referred to as the "green season" by Costa Ricans because this is when plants begin to sprout. Most people prefer to visit the country during the rainy season for the incredible blossoming flora, the reduced number of tourists and the significantly lower prices. The dry season lasts from December to April and is known as *verano* (spring). March and April are generally the warmest months.

Temperatures don't tend to fluctuate in Costa Rica, except between altitudes. On the coasts, the mercury regularly rises above 35°C (95°F). On the Caribbean Coast, these high temperatures can be attributed to the humidity, whereas on the Pacific Coast, particularly in the province of Guanacaste, they're the result of the very dry and arid climate. Some parts of this province might not see a single drop of rain between January and May!

The higher you go, the cooler it gets (temperatures drop by 1°C or 34°F for every 150m or 492ft in altitude). At the top of the highest mountains, such as Mount Chirripó (3,819m or 12,530ft), temperatures can fall to the freezing point. The coldest temperature ever recorded was -9°C (16°F), on Mount Chirripó.

For the past few years, climatic conditions have been irregular and unpredictable, probably due to deforestation and El Niño. But since Costa Rica is a small country with many climates, every tourist will find some place that matches his or her comfort level. People who don't like very hot and humid weather should stay in the Central Valley, where it rains less than in other regions and where the temperature is almost always cool and comfortable.

Flora and Fauna

Approximately three million years ago, the two American subcontinents (North America

and South America) were connected by a narrow strip of land, creating a land bridge or isthmus. This bridge has been crossed not only by humans, but also by the flora and fauna from both subcontinents. Thus, Costa Rica, with its varied climates and location between the two land masses, is a natural "biodome" with a diverse plant and animal life.

Flora

According to a vegetation classification system devised by the biologist L.H. Holdridge in 1947, there are some 116 life zones on earth. These observations are based on the different types of climates, temperature changes, precipitation and seasonal changes. Due to the great diversity in climatic conditions and the very rugged terrain of Costa Rica, 12 life zones and eight transition zones have been identified. Lagoons, marshes, herbaceous zones, mangroves, plains, tropical dry forest and high-altitude subalpine plains (*páramos*) make up the Costa Rican landscape, depending on the altitude or region. The country's high mountains have the some of the lowest temperatures in Central America and their rivers flow into the Atlantic and Pacific Oceans.

Although Costa Rica represents only 0.03% (3/10,000ths) of the Earth's surface, it's home to 5% of all existing vegetation and animal species. Therefore, approximately 10,000 species of plants and more than 1,000 tree species live side by side with 1,400 orchid species, including the national flower, *guaria morada*, a lilac-coloured "Cattleya" orchid.

The Tropical Dry Forest

The tropical dry forest has practically disappeared in Central America. Only 2% of its original area is left, most of it in Costa Rica, in the northwestern province of Guanacaste.

Where the forests of Guanacaste once proudly stood, there are now huge cleared tracts of land and pastures. The former open woodland and savannah cannot be replaced because deforestation has impoverished the soil so it can no longer retain water. This intensified the dry and rainy seasons, making the dry season, which runs from December to April, a truly desert-like climate, where rain is almost unheard of. This drought, which can last for several months, has forced trees to adapt by shedding their leaves.

Heliconia

The rainy season brings relief and makes this desert bloom again. The grass becomes green, flowers try to outdo each other with their brilliant displays of colour, the trees blossom with white, yellow, red or pink flowers. Even the majestic *guanacaste* (*Enterolobium cyclocarpum*), Costa Rica's national tree for which its northwestern province is named, shows off its white flowers and green foliage.

The Tropical Rainforest

The tropical rainforest is extremely diverse in Costa Rica, both on the Atlantic (Caribbean Sea) and the Pacific coast, and even in the centre of the country. It's called "rainforest," because, like the Amazon, at least 200cm (79in) of rain falls there every year, sometimes as much as 600cm (236in), especially in

the province of Limón on the Atlantic coast. Humidity is also very high, and the annual temperature is almost steady with an average of approximately 24°C (75°F).

A constant supply of clean water is therefore essential to the survival of the tropical rainforest. Also, since the tropical rainforest recycles 75% of its water through evaporation, it sucks up plant and animal nutrients from the soil. Termites and mushrooms then decompose the dead vegetation so the trees can replenish it with the lost nutrients through their roots.

Altitude also affects the rainforest's vegetal composition. Vegetation gets sparser the higher you go. Between 1,000m (3,281ft) and 3,000m (9,843ft), the forest is extremely dense with mosses, lichens, lians, vines, bushes and trees whose canopy is shrouded in mist. Between 3,000m (9,843ft) and 4,000m (13,123ft), another type of vegetation grows, which is characteristic of the cold and wet high plains: the *páramo*. The northern end of the Andean *páramo* is in Costa Rica. Here, only vegetation that can adapt to the harsh climate grows, such as stunted bushes. You can see this type of vegetation by climbing

above the tree line in the high mountains of the Talamanca Cordillera, especially on the Chirripó (*cerros*) (3,819m or 12,530ft) and Muerte (3,491m or 11,453ft) mountains.

Deforestation

Before the Spanish conquistadors set foot on its shores in the 16th century, Costa Rica was almost entirely made up of rich natural forests. Only small sections had been deforested by Indigenous People to grow corn and cassava, among other crops. When the Spanish colonized the country, they began clearing forested areas to make way for towns and later for crops like bananas and coffee, or for pastures.

Deforestation proceeded at a relatively moderate rate until the mid-20th century when it took off at a drastic pace. In 1950, 75% of Costa Rica was still forested; in 1978, this percentage dropped to close to 35%, and to 26% in 1985. In 1993, the percentage of forested areas was less than 20%. If this trend continues, the rainforest may completely disappear. Thus, it's extremely important to protect the existing forests and implement an efficient reforestation policy. If not, the deforestation of tropical rainforest will cause an ecological disaster and it will take tens, if not hundreds, of years before anything can grow again.

Deforestation has done more than just deface some of the most beautiful natural landscapes in Costa Rica. Soil erosion has actually created deserts in the province of Guanacaste, where the average temperature has increased by approximately 10°C (50°F). During the dry season, water for domestic and industrial consumption becomes scarcer. Some rivers dry up, endangering much of their flora and fauna. During the rainy season, floods cause the most extensive damage.

Environmental Conservation

Starting in the 1960s, many grassroots environmental movements sprang up worldwide to counteract mass deforestation, realizing the importance of protecting natural resources. These groups viewed the United States National Park System as the basic model for conservation. However, since the population of tiny Costa Rica doubled within 20 years (1950-1970) and was distributed evenly throughout the country, the forest conservation project was seen as a threat to the prosperity of farmers and breeders. Therefore, environmentalists had to find a

good reason for the population to cooperate in protecting the forest, while maintaining their livelihood. Tourism was the answer. Tourism and farming were seen as more profitable than farming alone and, blending the two could better protect nature. These economic activities were thus combined in long-term resource management or "sustainable development," in which most of the population of Costa Rica is involved.

And so, since the 1970s, protecting nature has become a national priority. Almost 25% of the territory is now protected (through parks and reserves), which corresponds to the percentage of uncleared or unused territory. Costa Rica is ranked first in the world for having the highest percentage of protected land and is one of the first countries in the world to have practiced ecotourism.

Fauna

Because of its microclimates and geographical location on the Central American isthmus, Costa Rica has the greatest variety of animal species in the world. Biodiversity (the variety of animal species), is measured by counting the number of species per 10,000km² (6,214 sq mi). Thus,

according to the *World Resources Institute* (1995), Costa Rica is the biodiversity capital of the world, with 615 species (mammals and birds) identified in 10,000km² (6,214 sq mi). Even a country as large as the United States (104 species) has six times fewer varieties of animal species in a given territory than Costa Rica.

Because of this, you don't have to go too far in Costa Rica to observe animals fully adapted to and thus thriving in their environment. In this tiny corner of the planet, you can discover some of the 15,000 species of butterflies, 850 species of birds (a true birdwatchers' paradise), 208 species of mammals, 220 species of reptiles, 34,000 species of insects, 130 species of freshwater fish and 160 species of amphibians. Some of these species are indigenous to Costa Rica: 41 species of amphibians, 24 species of reptiles, 16 species of freshwater fish, six species of birds and five species of mammals.

Some of the many animals that you may see in Costa Rica include monkeys (white-faced capuchins, howler monkeys and spider monkeys), sloths, agoutis, coatis, white-tailed deer, iguanas, lizards, toads, vermillon-coloured poison dart frogs, crocodiles and caimans.

Timid mammals like coyotes, anteaters, tapirs and large felines (jaguars, pumas, ocelots) flee at the sight of humans, but sometimes leave their tracks behind. The country also has several species of snakes, including vipers, boa constrictors and the fearsome "spearhead," known as *terciopelo* in Costa Rican.

Jaguar

Four species of sea turtles visit the beaches: the leatherback turtle, the largest sea turtle in the world; Ridley's turtle; Hawksbill turtle and the Pacific green turtle. It's fascinating to watch a female leatherback turtle lay her eggs on the Playa Grande of the Parque Nacional Marino Las Baulas (Guanacaste).

Just like tourists, several bird species from North America head south to Costa Rica for the winter; including swallows, warblers, bunting and thrushes.

Costa Rica has so many birds that new species are identified each year. Toucans and par-

akeets come in all shapes and sizes, and their colourful plumage is dazzling. The saffron toucanet and majestic scarlet macaws are some of the most beautiful birds in the world and are easy to spot in certain regions of the country. But the bird that turns the most heads is the gorgeous quetzal. Indeed, many of the world's ornithologists travel to Costa Rica just to observe it.

This relatively large bird (almost 35cm or 13.8in tall), with its long emerald tail measuring up to 60cm (23.6in), lives high up in the canopy of the rainforest, such as in the Monteverde region.

History

The Pre-Columbian Period

When one imagines pre-Columbian settlements in Central America, what comes to mind most often are the Mayan pyramids of the Yucatan Peninsula, or the pomp and circumstance surrounding the Aztec ruler in the

capital of Tenochtitlan (Mexico). The empires built up by these civilizations were located in territories much further north than Costa Rica. However, this doesn't mean that Costa Rica didn't have any great civilizations before the arrival of the Spaniards—in fact, quite the contrary is true.

Humans first settled in what is now Costa Rica over 10,000 years ago. Different Indigenous civilizations with their own social and economic structure came from either north or south (via what is now Nicaragua and Panamá), and gradually settled in the area. Nomadic hunters roamed the east coast, while sedentary groups settled in the interior and on the west coast. These last people practised agriculture and acquired advanced craftsmanship techniques, especially those in the interior, as is evidenced by pottery, metal and gold objects found during 20th-century excavations. In fact, there were goldsmiths in Costa Rica 1,000 years before the Spaniards had even discovered gold!

These groups were never very numerous and there were barely more than 20,000 Indigenous people by the time the Europeans arrived. This low population was probably due to the nature of the

Important Historical Dates

September 18, 1502   Arrival of Christopher Columbus on his fourth voyage to the Americas at the Bay of Cariari on the Caribbean Coast.

1524   Founding of the territory's first colony at Villa Bruselas in the Golfo de Nicoya.

1540   Creation of the Gobernación de Cartago at the beginning of colonization.

1564   Founding of the city of Cartago by Vásquez de Coronado.

September 15, 1821   After long negotiations, the Provincia de Guatemala, of which Costa Rica is a member, declares its independence from Spain.

1824   Creation of Las Provincias Unidas de Centro America which includes, other than Costa Rica, Guatemala, Honduras, El Salvador and Nicaragua.

November 14, 1838   President Braulio Carillo declares Costa Rica free and independent, but the country remains part of the República Federal de Centroamerica.

August 31, 1848   Declaration of total independence, founding of the República de Costa Rica.

1856-1857   War at the Nicaraguan–Costa Rican border against William Walker, an invader from the United States, won by the Central American countries thanks to Costa Rican hero Juan Santamaría.

November 7, 1889   Birth of democracy; after 50 years of corruption in the electoral system and a series of 10 constitutions, the population revolts to demand universal suffrage.

1885-1948   Consolidation of the welfare state though a series of liberal measures including separation of Church and State, a reformed, mandatory universal system of education and reformed labour laws.

1948   Civil war caused once again by dissatisfaction with corruption. José Figueres Ferrer takes power after the crisis, nationalizes the banks and hydroelectricity and abolishes the army. A new constitution adopted in 1949 is still in effect today.

1987   President Oscar Arias Sanchez (1986–1990) wins the Nobel Peace Prize for his efforts to reestablish peace in neighbouring Central American countries.

land: at times moun-
tainous, at times
swampy, it didn't make
Costa Rica a very hos-
pitable environment to
support a large popula-
tion. Geographical fea-
tures also explain why
there was almost no
mixing between the
populations of the
north and south of this
part of the Central
American isthmus.

Unfortunately, little else
is known about these
pre-Columbian civiliza-
tions, nor is there any
trace of written records
or conflicts that could
have led one tribe to
defeat another and set
up the basis for an
empire. Therefore,
retracing these people's
way of life is more a
task for archeologists
than for historians, and
a matter of speculation
rather than narrative.

The country's most
interesting archeologi-
cal site, Monumento
Nacional Guayabo (see
p 129), is about 50km
(31mi) from San José.
The site contains the
remains of an ancient
city, that existed many
centuries before the
common era and was
first inhabited by one
or more nomadic
groups, then the
Corobicis, and finally
by the most advanced
society of the Nahuatl,
who came from Mex-
ico. At its peak, the city
had a population of
10,000.

Archeologists are puz-
zled by the different-
sized, perfectly shaped

granite spheres found
lying on the ground in
the southwest of the
country, particularly on
Isla del Caño and in the
Palmar region (see p ?
and ?). Although some
claim that they're the
work of the Chibchas
(a group that lived in
the southern part of the
Pacific coast), no one is
entirely sure of their
origin or purpose.

Archeological findings
in the northwestern
part of the country,
more particularly in the
Nicoya peninsula,
reveal that the local
population traded with
the more northerly
civilizations well before
the common era.

The development of
trade inevitably led to
the settlement of this
area by Costa Rica's
largest Indigenous civi-
lization, the
Chorotegas. Their cul-
ture is similar to that of
the Aztecs and Mayas,
and not surprisingly so,
since the Chorotegas
fled from southern
Mexico around 1325
(*chorotegas* means "run-
away"). They practised
agriculture and grew
mainly legumes, corn
and squash, but unlike
Costa Rica's previous
civilizations, the
Chorotega had a writ-
ten language as well as
a calendar. They also
had a complex social
system in which priests
and nobles formed the
ruling class. At the very
bottom of the social
scale were slaves
snatched from neigh-

bouring tribes who
were forced to perform
hard labour or, even
worse, used as human
sacrifice. Chorotega art
is among the country's
most interesting,
known particularly for
its stylized jade pieces.
Many of these have
been preserved and
most are on display in
San José's jade museum
(see p 80).

After Christopher Columbus

After being commis-
sioned by King
Ferdinand and Queen
Isabella of Spain to find
a westward passage to
the orient and all of its
riches, Christopher Co-
lumbus accidentally
discovered the Amer-
icas when he landed in
the Caribbean in 1492.
In 1502, while on his
fourth expedition, a
storm damaged his rig
and forced him land at
Cariari Bay, near
present-day Puerto
Limón.

This is how Central
America and Costa Rica
were "discovered,"
though Indigenous
people had been here
for a thousand years
preceding the arrival of
the Spanish. Columbus
was surely impressed
by the lush vegetation,
since he baptized the
country *Huerta*, which
means "garden" in
Spanish. The coastal
Indigenous peoples
gave him a warm wel-
come and showered
him with gifts of a cer-
tain precious yellow

metal coveted by Europeans: gold.

Ferdinand of Spain decided to colonize the new territories and convert the natives to Christianity in order to procure their gold. In 1506, he named Diego de Nicuesa governor of the new colony and put him at the head of a new expedition. However, things took a turn for the worse the minute Nicuesa and his men landed in Panamá. They had to head north, across impossible terrain and through inhospitable climate. Their morale fell quickly and many troops either mutinied or died of tropical diseases. To make matters worse, relations between the Indigenous people and Spaniards worsened, and the latter were subject to repeated surprise attacks. Spain did not gain anything from Nicuesa's efforts, other than the realization that this region of Central America would be difficult to overcome.

In 1522, Gil González Davila tried to conquer and colonize the region. At first, his expedition met with more success than Nicuesa's because he managed to find gold. Convinced that he had discovered Eldorado, he changed the country's name from La Huerta to *Costa Rica*, the "rich coast." However, Davila was unable to colonize the area because disease and hardship claimed the lives of many of his men.

These failed early expeditions caused the Spanish conquistadors to lose interest in Costa Rica for a while. Instead, they colonized the empire's other possessions, which they deemed Eldorados; namely Peru and Mexico. Colonizing Costa Rica only resumed in the second half of the 16th century, when King Philip II of Spain sent missionaries to convert the Indigenous peoples to Christianity. However, this proved to be no easy task, since the Indigenous population had decreased significantly during the Spanish absence from Costa Rica. Defenceless against the viruses brought over by the Europeans, they had been decimated by smallpox and tuberculosis. Those who managed to survive fled to the valleys hidden deep in the interior. In fact, only the Chorotegas of the Nicoya Peninsula remained when Costa Rica's new governor, Juan Vásquez de Coronado, arrived in 1562.

Coronado

Juan Vásquez de Coronado showed more interest in Costa Rica than his predecessors. He explored the country's interior and discovered the Central Valley, which he decided to colonize because of its better climate and fertile volcanic soil. Thus, in 1563, he built Cartago, Costa Rica's first town.

The priests accompanying Coronado were not the only people frustrated by the lack of inhabitants, whom they sought to convert. The soldiers also needed more slave labour to make lands granted to them under the *Encomienda* system profitable. Because they couldn't find enough people to work the land and were far from the slave markets, the governor and settlers had to work the land themselves. They practiced subsistence agriculture, unlike the thriving plantations of neighbouring colonies.

The Coronado colony was also very isolated geographically. In other regions of Central America, the Spanish were concentrated along the coasts, which provided trade routes. Costa Ricans, on the other hand, lived in the country's interior, several hours or days from the coast. Mountains and forests further hindered contact with the outside world. This isolation even forced the settlers to use cocoa beans as currency for some time. The Spaniards soon discovered that, unlike other New World colonies, Costa Rica had very few precious metals in its soil.

Not surprisingly, the colony grew slowly. In fact, it was to take over 250 years for its population to reach 70,000. Once again, Spain lost interest in Costa Rica and abandoned its flock of settlers in the midst of the jungle. Cut off from the outside world, Costa Ricans developed their own society, more egalitarian than those of other Spanish colonies. This was primarily the result of having no social classes, since almost everyone in the Central Valley made a living from farming. While other regions in Central and South America eventually achieved the status of intendants (*intendencias*) under the Spanish crown, Costa Rica remained under the rule of the Captaincy-General of Guatemala and of the Bishopric of León in Nicaragua. Just to show how isolated these settlers were, for over a century and a half, Cartago was the only town in the Central Valley!

Gradually, however, other towns were established. Heredia and Cubujuquie were founded in 1717, and San José 20 years later. Alajuela was not established until 1782.

The coastal regions of Costa Rica experienced a somewhat different development. On the west coast, Nicaragua directly controlled Guanacaste. This allowed large agricultural plantations, similar to those in colonies further north, to be set up. On the Caribbean coast, settlers grew cocoa and then tobacco. These very profitable crops could have made the region rich, but harvests had to be exported, which became impossible in 1665, when Spain closed down all the region's ports in an attempt to discourage piracy. The result was exactly the opposite of what was intended, since the coast was then clear for pirates and smugglers to thrive.

The 19th Century

Sparsely populated, difficult to access, and with no riches to speak of, Costa Rica never really interested colonial authorities, be they from Guatemala, Mexico, or Madrid. Costa Rica's towns were thus left to the country's elite to govern. This relative indifference did not bother settlers, who never really made a formal demand for independence. There was not even much excitement in the streets of San José when the news spread of the liberation of Spanish colonies starting on September 15, 1821. Costa Rican settlements were still so isolated that the news, brought by mule, was only heard a month later.

The initial response of Heredia and Cartago to the liberation movement was to join the new empire of Mexico. But, in 1823, the other former colonies of Central America opted for the creation of a federation with Guatemala City as its capital. The issue of joining the empire became a hot debate in Costa Rica. In San José and Alajuela, a Republican party called for joining the new federation. Heredia and Cartago opposed this. Talks broke down and a civil war broke out the same year, from which the Republicans in Ochomogo emerged victorious. The towns of Costa Rica therefore joined the federation, but remained fully autonomous. The Republicans chose San José as the capital of the new province, putting an end to Cartago's two-and-a-half century reign. A year later, Guanacaste separated from Nicaragua and joined Costa Rica.

The first head of the new province, Juan Mora Fernández, ruled for 12 years, during which he ushered in peace and laid the foundations for Costa Rican independence. To stimulate the local economy, Fernández took a risk in growing coffee and managed to attract foreign buyers, particularly from Great Britain. However, an uprising in 1835 pitted San José against the province's other towns. The capital city, headed by a new dictator, Braulio Carillo, won. In 1838, he led Costa Rica to independence. Carillo was not the head of state for long, since he was ousted by Honduran General Francisco Morazán in 1842. The latter turned out to be even less fortunate than his predecessor; his military ambitions led to his overthrow and execution less than a year later.

In the meantime, Costa Rican coffee was successfully breaking into the market and the response was exceptionally good. The development of the country's ports on both the Pacific and the Caribbean coasts was necessary to export the coffee harvest. The coffee bean was seen as the *grano de oro*, or "golden bean," and coffee plantations sprang up all over the country. The success of the coffee industry led to the modernization of Costa Rica. However, it also made the coffee barons, or *cafetaleros*, so powerful that they were able to seize political control of the country, replacing Costa Rica's first elected president, José Maria Castro, with one of their own, Juan Rafael Mora.

It is argued that it was only during President Mora's second mandate that Costa Rica really assumed its national identity. This was precipitated by a very bizarre crisis: the excessive ambition of an adventurer from the United States named William Walker, who tried to conquer Central America (see p 24). President Mora was not any more successful than Morazán, whom Costa Ricans remember with resentment. Instead of dealing with the cholera epidemic that killed one out of every 10 Costa Ricans, Mora tampered with ballot boxes to stay in power. But when he attempted to break the coffee barons' monopoly on the nation's finances, they ran him out of power and executed him when he attempted to regain it.

Shortly thereafter, rivalry for political control of the country broke out between the coffee barons. In April 1870, General Tomás Guardia seized power and held onto it for 12 years. His dictatorship was considered very beneficial for Costa Rica because he managed to curb the coffee barons' power by taxing them and using that money toward the common good. Guardia was also responsible for social innovations; most notably, he abolished the death penalty and made primary schooling free and compulsory for everyone. Thus, it became

evident to Costa Ricans that peace brought prosperity.

Guardia also wanted to build a railway between the Central Valley and the Caribbean Sea to replace transportation by mule. However, such a large-scale project was beyond the country's finances, and foreign capital was sought.

The project interested Henry Meigg, a financier from the United States who raised the necessary funds to begin construction of the railway. Due to a lack of local manpower, cheap labour was imported from China, Italy and Jamaica. Despite these efforts, Meigg could not complete the project: climate, topography, dense forests and wild animals stood between the central plateau and the coast. In addition, the state found itself heavily in debt. Construction stopped until Meigg's nephew, Minor C. Keith, arrived on the scene and proposed an innovative solution. He paid off the government's debt in exchange for land along the railway, which finally opened in 1890. But what did he do with this land? The answer—bananas! Keith used the land to plant bananas, which quickly became Costa Rica's second most valuable export.

Portrait

The Era of William Walker

Of all the people who played major roles in Central American history, few have gained as much notoriety as William Walker. Academically gifted, Walker attended universities in the United States and Europe. He became a lawyer, a doctor, and then a gold prospector. Around 1850, he finally found his true vocation—as a mercenary. During this era, disagreements between slave-owners and abolitionists were tearing the United States apart. Walker sided with the former, and set out to conquer territories where he would legalize slavery to reinforce the position of the states of the Union, where this practice was tolerated.

He first conquered the Baja Peninsula in Mexico, where he declared himself president. He remained there for a year, but soon returned to the United States, where he was arrested for violating the peace with Mexico.

However, thanks to friends in high places, he was acquitted.

He re-established contact with his sponsors, this time for an even more daring plot: to conquer Central America and build a canal in southern Nicaragua, which would link the Atlantic and Pacific Oceans. Eventually, the conquered territories were to be annexed to the United States. The idea of opening a canal won him the support of President Buchanan and financier Cornelius Vanderbilt.

Walker landed in Nicaragua in 1855 with approximately 50 men. Things got off to a bad start, and he had to wait for reinforcements from California before succeeding in conquering the country and declaring himself its president. President Mora of Costa Rica saw the invasion as a threat to the young country's independence. He was

not alone in his thinking, and within a week, 5,000 men from various backgrounds answered his call to arms with old rifles, machetes, and pickaxes. Though they were not trained soldiers, they reached Guanacaste after two weeks and defeated 200 Americans at the Hacienda Santa Rosa, on March 20, 1856. The militia then pursued Walker through Nicaragua. Cornered, Walker finally found asylum aboard an American warship.

Walker didn't stay in exile for long, however, and attempted to conquer Honduras in 1860. This time his luck completely ran out. The Hondurans put an end to his career—and his life. William Walker is still reviled throughout Central America—his enormous ambition resulted in the deaths of nearly 200,000 people.

Minor C. Keith founded the United Fruit Company, notorious for its economic and political role throughout Central America. His and several other major international corporations quickly bought up the entire banana market, creating stiff competition for small local producers.

The 20th Century

There is one event that singlehandedly changed political behaviour in Costa Rica before the turn of the century: in 1889, Joaquín Rodríguez won the national elections fair and square, but the outgoing president, Bernardo Soto, refused to give up his seat. The people took to the streets in protest and Soto relinquished his position. For the first time in the country's history, democracy had been achieved in its truest form. But democracy wasn't Rodríguez's strongest point, nor was it that of his immediate successors, Rafael Iglesias and González Visquez. They had the habit of dissolving the legislature, appointing their successor and exiling their rivals— anything for the *presidente* to stay in power longer.

The first real "test" of democracy occurred in 1913, when none of the candidates acquired a majority in the elections through direct suffrage.

Consequently, the legislative assembly appointed Alfredo González Flores as president, even though he was not a candidate. General Federico Tinoco Granados wouldn't hear of this and seized power in 1917. His dictatorship quickly rendered him unpopular, and even the United States refused to recognize his authority. The army and the navy successfully overthrew him in 1919.

Democracy prevailed again when Rafael Calderón Guardia became president in 1940. He approved a new labour code, improved the social system and managed to expand industry for the war effort. However, like his predecessors, he became power-hungry. The elections saw Teodoro Picado, a weaker candidate, come to power—probably through a setup. In 1948, Calderón lost the election and claimed electoral fraud, but he couldn't prove it because a fire destroyed the ballots and Picado nullified the results.

The controversy over the 1948 elections sparked a short but bloody civil war, which claimed the lives of several thousand people. This was the opportunity that "Don Pepe" José Figueres Ferrer, Calderón's long-time opponent, was

waiting for. Don Pepe overthrew his rival and proclaimed himself president. He used his presidency to improve the democratic system by adopting new social measures: nationalization of the banks, universal right to vote and company taxes, among other things. Tired of having the army interfere in politics and disturb the general peace, he abolished it. Military barracks were transformed into fine-arts museums, and the army's budget was reallocated to education. Once his reforms were implemented, he gave back power to the real elected president, Otilio Ulate. Like any good democrat, he waited to run for president in the 1953 elections. He won and was even re-elected a second time (1970-1974). He died a national hero in 1990.

The Civil War of 1948 allowed Costa Rica to consolidate its democracy after decades of abuse. Calderón took this opportunity to run for a second presidency in 1962. He lost, however, because the electorate was from a newer generation.

More stable, the Costa Rican government was able to play a greater role in the country's social and economic affairs. The government set up a welfare state system based on that of other democracies. This steered the country in the right direction economically during the 1960s and 1970s, but Costa Rica made the same mistake as its Latin American neighbours by borrowing foreign money for its national development projects.

Costa Rica was doubly hard hit by the second oil crisis of the 1970s, which caused coffee and banana prices to fall drastically. An agricultural crisis ensued and the government, heavily in debt, could no longer afford to keep up its overinflated bureaucracy.

At the same time, Central American peace was rapidly collapsing. Costa Rica's neighbours were swept up by a wave of political turmoil and terrorism. Each time a government was overthrown by a military junta in either Nicaragua, Guatemala or El Salvador, refugees poured into Costa Rica. The country simultaneously welcomed certain guerilla groups to use its soil as a training ground. President Luis Alberto Monge's policy of neutrality became very strained and, in 1985, Costa Rica even froze diplomatic relations with Nicaragua.

The following year, Oscar Arias Sánchez, a political scientist, became president. He immediately began working on a solution to the problems plagu-ing his country and this region of the Americas. He proposed a peace plan to his neighbours in February 1987, which they reluctantly accepted. It came into affect in August 1987. Shortly thereafter, Sánchez received the Nobel Peace Prize for his treaty.

Economically, Costa Rica was not recovering very well from the recession brought on by the oil crises of the 1970s. Sanchez temporarily suspended payments on the debt, which hovered around $5 billion US and asked his creditors to restructure the repayment schedule.

As the 21st century dawns, Costa Rica is a well-established democracy despite its still fragile economy. In the spring of 2000, the population proved this in no uncertain terms by mass protests, including strikes and demonstrations, against a government bill privatizing the national electricity company, ICE; a bill that eventually had to be abolished. Costa Ricans used this occasion to express their dissatisfaction with the extremely difficult economic situation that has plagued them for several years. This mobilization of a large part of the population, a phenomenon that is becoming increasingly rare on the planet, emphasizes that democ-racy is still one of this people's most important values.

Political Administration

Although Costa Rica is a small country, it has seven provinces: San José, Alajuela, Cartago, Heredia, Limón, Puntarenas and Guanacaste. These provinces are subdivided into cantons, which are further subdivided into districts. The provinces have very limited powers and cannot levy taxes, and are headed by a governor, appointed by the president. Therefore, Costa Rica is considered to be a strongly centralized federation.

Costa Rica has a presidential government system. Every four years, a president of the republic, two vice-presidents and 57 representatives who'll make up the legislative assembly are elected. In order to prevent potentially explosive situations such as the ones that occurred in 1948 and keep any political party from getting too powerful, the president can't run for a second term immediately after a first. In fact, there is very little difference in ideology between the two major parties who alternately take control: the PLN (Partido de Liberación Nacional) is a type of social democratic party, and the

PUSC (Partido Unidad Social Cristiana) is a Christian democratic party.

The Costa Rican constitution is based on the principle of separating the powers of government between the executive, legislative and judiciary. As in most western democracies, there is much friction between the executive and legislative branches of the state. According to the constitution, the legislative assembly adopts laws, controls the budget and has the power to veto presidential decisions with a two-thirds majority vote. As a result, many presidents have had to rule by decree as a last resort in order to govern effectively. The advantage of such a system is that it forces the parties to work on solutions together.

The legislative assembly also appoints 24 judges to Costa Rica's supreme court. A judge has an eight-year mandate, which is automatically renewed at the end of the term unless the assembly votes against it. In turn, these judges name magistrates to the lower courts.

In Costa Rica, one out of four employed persons works for the government. The country's public employees are well known for their love of bureaucratic red tape. Having to line up at a series of counters can try tourists' nerves. To avoid this problem, hire a *despachante*, a person who is very familiar with the workings of government bureaucracy and who'll take your place and stand in the right lines for you. Corruption is still a real problem, but one that is slowly declining in severity.

Since its very beginnings, Costa Rica has worked toward the democratic ideal, even though it's been a bumpy ride. The country's main advantage over its neighbours is that the distinctions between the different social classes are not as evident. Whereas other Spanish colonies exploited the population by establishing overlords and enslaving the poor, Costa Rican society has been a place where everyone has had to earn his or her own lot. However, this gap between the rich and the poor has widened increasingly in recent years, as is true almost everywhere in the world.

Costa Rica also differs from its neighbours because it was the first Latin American country to abolish slavery and establish a democracy right after obtaining its independence in 1838. Fifty years later, honest and free elections were held It will be years before the neighbouring republics can make a similar claim. Thanks to mandatory elections held every four years in February (the next take place in February 2002), two main political parties alternate in power: the PUSC (Partido Unidad Social Cristiana) whose colours are red and blue, and the PLN (Partido Liberación Nacional) whose colours are white and green. They're trailed by several opposition parties, the largest of which, Fuerza Democrática, has three elected deputies. Since February 1998, the country has been run by Manuel Rodríguez and his party, the PUSC (Partido Unidad Social Cristiana).

Economy

Its political system, society, history and economy have made Costa Rica the country with the most egalitarian distribution of wealth in Latin America. Costa Rica's social security system is the most elaborate in Central America and is so efficient that the country's life expectancy rate is the highest in the region: 72 years for men and 77 for women.

Each region of Costa Rica has a different economic activity: the coffee industry is concentrated in the Central Valley, the banana industry on the Caribbean coast, cattle rearing for meat production (which accounts for a modest percentage of Costa Rican exports) in the province of Guanacaste and palm oil in the southern part of the Pacific coast. Consumer goods, such as clothing, ornamental plants and cut flowers are mostly produced in the urban areas of the Central Valley.

The Flower Industry

The flowers and ferns that decorate the bouquets sold at florists in North America and Europe probably came from Costa Rica. Indeed, these plants usually grow on the mountainsides at altitudes too high for coffee cultivation. These dense crops, grown in greenhouses covered in green and black tarpaulins to protect them, can be seen on the road to the Poás Volcano.

The coffee industry is not dominated by a few large coffee-producing corporations; it is mostly carried out by many small coffee farmers. In fact, over half of the coffee producers are small family operations. This is in stark contrast with the banana industry, which is run by a few big multinationals. Bananas and coffee still represent over 40% of Costa Rica's exports.

Costa Rica's foreign currency revenues fluctuate greatly due to the limited range of export products. Markets are very volatile in the country's vital sectors (i.e. banana and coffee growing). It's a buyers' market in which suppliers have very little impact on the prices. This is why Costa Rica's national debt reached almost $5 billion US at the end of the 1980s: a fortune with respect to the country's ability for repayment.

For the last few decades, the country has been trying to diversify its economy. Although mineral resources are abundant, lots of capital is needed to exploit them. As of yet, only small deposits have been tapped into. Christopher Columbus's dreams of mountains of gold seem to be just that—dreams.

Forests are still being cut down at an alarming rate. Today, only one-third of the original forest remains, the area having been cleared primarily for pasture and agricultural purposes. Deforestation has had a serious impact on the country's climate. In Guanacaste, for example, the dry season is getting progressively longer and more severe.

Despite deforestation, Costa Rica harbours an incredible wealth of natural ecosystems. Over 5% of the world's biodiversity is found here. In the last 20 years, many officials have become more aware of the importance of protecting the country's many waters and green spaces. Forests, marshes, nesting areas for endangered species, coral seabeds and other ecosystems are now rigorously protected.

Thanks to these efforts, ecotourism has really taken off in Costa Rica and is developing at about the same rate as leisure tourism. Vacationers mostly come for the beaches: Costa Rica has about 1,200km (746mi) of coastline and the water is reportedly always warm and pleasant in both the Pacific Ocean and Caribbean Sea. Therefore, it's not surprising that every region in the country is undergoing a boom in tourism. In 1999, one million tourists visited Costa Rica.

Moreover, because leisure tourism developed later than in some other countries of the region, it benefitted from the experience and know-how that was painstakingly acquired by its neighbours. Tens of thousands of North Americans who've moved to

The "Dollarization" of the Economy

Costa Rica may well adopt the U.S. dollar as legal tender in the next few years, just like Panamá did in 1934. The country would then lose the power to devaluate or re-evaluate its currency as an economic strategy, but it would protect itself from speculation, which is always possible when money is in low supply. The central bank of Costa Rica is currently studying this proposal.

Costa Rica have also contributed to this steadily developing market based on the country's wonderful climate. The ICT (Instituto Costaricense de Turismo) is presently trying to turn ecotourism into a sustainable development.

Costa Rica is also trying to improve its economic ties with other countries. Costa Rica's main trading partner is the United States, for both exports and imports. However, so as not to become entirely dependant on this trading partner and to expand its markets, Costa Rica signed a free-trade agreement with Mexico in 1995. Moreover, Costa Rica is currently holding talks with Canada, the other Central American countries, and even with member countries of the OAS, that are aimed at the free trade of goods and services. This opening of borders won't occur seamlessly, making this an interesting issue to follow.

Finally, the Costa Rican government has begun to exploit another priceless resource: its population. Costa Rica's education system has created a well-educated and highly skilled work force. And because Costa Ricans are willing to work for less than their North American and European counterparts, they're being increasingly sought out by major companies that are changing the world economy, such as Intel the communications technologies company. Other markets are also being developed, including recycling: tests are currently being conducted to transform banana- and palm-tree leaves into paper products.

One day, Costa Rica will see the fruits of its economic endeavours, but this day has to come soon: Costa Rica must quickly find a way to balance its trade deficit (more imports than exports), or its social welfare system, which has been painstakingly developed for over a century, could collapse.

People and Religion

Population

Costa Rica has a population of approximately 3,500,000 people, over half (50.2%) of which is urbanized. Costa Rica's ancestry is very different from that of other Central American countries: 80% are of European descent (mainly from Spain), 15% are *mestizo* (a mix of European and Indigenous ancestry), 3% are African-Caribbean (found mostly on the Caribbean coast, in the Province of Limón) and 2% are Asian. Indigenous people make up less than 1% of the population: they number about 15,000, are scattered in 22 communities and are isolated from large urban centres and mainstream society.

Tico Tico

Along with the rest of Latin Americans, Costa Ricans call themselves *Tico* and *Tica*. This endearing nickname comes from the fact that in speaking they often add the ending *tico* or *tica* to a word to mark the diminutive. For example, *chico* (small) becomes *chiquitico* (even smaller)!

With 69 inhab./km² (178.7 inhab./sq mi), Costa Rica has the third highest population density in Central America after El Salvador (275.5 inhab./km² or 713.5 inhab./sq mi) and Guatemala (100.4 inhab./km² or 260 inhab./sq mi). Its population density is much higher than that in Canada (2.98 inhab./km² or 7.7 inhab./sq mi) and the United States (28.8 inhab./km² or 76.6 inhab./sq mi), but lower than France's (106.6 inhab./km² or 276 inhab./sq mi). Approximately 60% of the population lives in the Central Valley, where the largest cities in the country are located (San José, Cartago, Heredia and Alajuela).

Spanish is the most widely spoken language in the country. Because elementary education is free and compulsory, under 10% of the population is illiterate today, ranking Costa Rica with industrialized countries. Lastly, life expectancy of Costa Ricans is 76.3 years, one of the highest in the world.

Religion

Catholicism is still the most practiced religion (95%), followed by Protestantism in a distant second place (3%). Although Catholicism is the state religion (the Catholic Church is still funded by public money), religious tolerance was made official by the 1873 constitution.

Architecture and Landscaping

Costa Rica is still building itself architecturally. Costa Rican buildings (hotels, houses, clinics, commercial spaces, office buildings) are set up in such a way as to bring the outdoors inside, even more so in the countryside. Urban residential dwellings, especially the more traditional ones, often have "closed yards," with the living room facing a small atrium.

Urban planning is rather simple, especially in the oldest parts of the city. In the middle of the city, there's a central plaza laid out with green spaces, which serves as a social meeting place and is surrounded by a church and administrative and commercial buildings. Streets follow a consistent grid-like pattern (city blocks of 100m or 328ft), making it easy to find your way around. Instead of numbered addresses, addresses are given by intersections or by distances of metres from a certain landmarks.

The landscaping of the central square follows a standard design: an architectural structure at the centre of the park reserved for shows and festivities, a French garden around it (geometrical, with formal separation of spaces) spreads all the way to the street with numerous benches, paved surfaces for strolling and green spaces for rest and relaxation. Certain streets around this park may be closed to traffic during festivities. Parks confer a certain charm upon Costa Rica's lively town centres, but the construction of North-American-style shopping centres outside the downtown core is threatening the traditional way of life by luring Costa Ricans away from the central plazas.

Apart from San José, which has a handful of high-rises, most cities in

Costa Rica are of modest size. Due to the social system, there are few if any shantytowns, but many places reflect their lack of prosperity in their simple architecture and poor landscaping. Plus, elaborate architecture may not be such a big concern in Costa Rica because of the many earthquakes that have destroyed much of the country's architectural heritage (which is the case for Cartago). But there are still many beautiful things to discover.

In certain areas, land that was once jungle has been turned into farmland for grazing and agriculture. So don't expect to walk out of the Liberia airport and into lush tropical forest! In Guanacaste, you have to travel for miles for this—but it's well worth the trip!

Like many countries in the world, Costa Rica is being largely urbanized. The number of cars is constantly growing. The government is trying to deal with these new realities as best it can. For now, the highway system is still in its initial stages and concentrated around the capital, whereas the rest of the roads in the country are of varying condition, from the relatively well-maintained two-lane highway (which is primarily the Interamericana) all the way down to the dirt

Greetings

A little guide to help ensure that you'll be well received:

¡Buenos días!, is said in the morning; *¡Buenas tardes!* replaces *¡Buenos días!* from noon until sunset; *¡Buenas noches!* is used the rest of the time!
In case of doubt, you can use *¡Buenas!* alone, but you should know that it is more informal.

The use of *¡Hola!*, which corresponds to "Hi," is always appropriate, of course.

When leaving, *¡Adios!*, is the equivalent of "Goodbye."

¡Hasta luego!, "See you soon," is also frequently used as a farewell, even between strangers.

Also, you will undoubtedly be graced at times with *¡Que le vaya bien!* or *¡Que Díos le acompañe!*. These expressions are actually wishes that your path be blessed.

Finally, the air-kiss (only one, and on the right cheek) is exchanged quite frequently, both between women and between men and women, except perhaps in business relationships, but sometimes even then!

road linking a hotel, a park or a village, which is often impassable during the rainy season. Sometimes you have to ford a river or cross a waterway on an incredibly narrow bridge (sometimes single lane). City roads are not necessarily any better—so watch out!

Art and Culture

Costa Ricans' fondness of art and culture is evident in the many cultural centres and museums found throughout the country, especially in San José. These include the Museo Nacional (see p 80), the Museo de Arte Costarricense (see p 78), and the basement level of the Plaza de la Cultura (see p 82). Costa Rica has a rich Latin American and *Tican* artistic and cultural scene, and immersing yourself in it is a great way of getting to know the country and region. The Costa Rican Department of Culture contributes (despite its budget constraints) to the development of cultural activities by funding most forms of art (theatre, music, opera, dance, literature, poetry, sculpture, painting, cinema and so on).

Musically, Costa Rica has all the warm, steamy rhythms of Latin-American music—salsa, merengue, cumbia, reggae and Latino rock—so you can let loose! Costa Rica has also carved out its place in classical music with the great 19th century tenor, Melicio Salazar. Since then, classical music has grown in popularity and the country even has two symphony orchestras that became internationally renowned in the 1970s: the National Symphony Orchestra and the National Youth Orchestra.

Costa Rica has produced some famous names in the literary world, such as poets Roberto Brenes Mesén, Carmen Naranjo and Eunice Odio; writers Carlos Gagini, Quince Duncan and José León Sánchez; authors Manuel González Zeledón and Pio Víquez in *costumbrismo* (short stories based on local legends) and Carmen Lyra for children's stories. Their works are widely available in bookstores throughout the country.

Because of centuries of isolation during the colonization of Latin America, Costa Rica has produced an original style of painting and sculpture, which is reflected in the works of artists Luisa González de Saenz, Enrique Echandi and Juan Rafael Chacón.

Language

Costa Rican Spanish is the same as that spoken all over Latin America, but with a different accent and expressions unique to the country. Neverthe-

Some Useful Terms...

Pura vida: this is the favourite *tica* expression. It is a very positive expression, used when things are going well, similar to "wonderful" or "great."

Tico, *Tica*: short for *Costariccense*, which is the colloquial term for Costa Ricans.

Tuanis: is the second most popular expression, and is used to express appreciation, happiness, etc. For instance, if a place is *tuanis*, it comes highly recommended.

Mae (or *Maje*): means "man." Young people use it all the time.

Jale: means "let's go!"

Upe: what you would call out in an empty building or area, similar to "is anyone there?"

Tucán: like in Canada, where one-dollar coins are often called "loonies" after the bird that is engraved on them, *Ticos* sometimes call 5,000 *colones* coins *"tucán"*; you can see why....

Vos: In Costa Rica, *vos* is most often used when speaking to people. It refers to the second person singular ("you") and should be conjugated as such.

less, people here will still understand you if you speak the Spanish from one of the regions of Spain. If you don't speak Spanish, Costa Rica has several language schools where you can learn it.

Some people speak English, which is taught as a second language in high school, mainly in the tourist areas. In this guide, we've tried to point out places where you can be understood in English.

If you'd like to give your Spanish a try, refer to the small conversation guide at the end of this book on p 397.

Table of distances (km/mi)

Via the shortest route

1 mile = 1.62 kilometres
1 kilometre = 0.62 mile

	Ciudad Quesada	Golfito	Jacó	Liberia	Nicoya	Paso Canoas (Southern Border)	Peñas Blancas (Northern Border)	Puerto Limón	Puerto Viejo de Sarapiquí	Puntarenas	Quepos	San Isidro de El General
Golfito	385/239											
Jacó	146/91	272/169										
Liberia	186/115	465/288	193/120									
Nicoya	212/131	442/274	162/100	83/51								
Paso Canoas (Southern Border)	389/241	53/33	284/176	470/291	452/280							
Peñas Blancas (Northern Border)	221/137	524/325	263/163	77/48	160/99	536/332						
Puerto Limón	181/112	447/277	243/151	345/214	331/205	448/278	425/264					
Puerto Viejo de Sarapiquí	57/35	393/244	184/114	272/169	264/164	402/249	383/237	126/78				
Puntarenas	111/69	334/207	79/49	136/84	118/73	355/220	211/131	246/153	173/107			
Quepos	119/74	195/121	78/48	265/164	243/151	209/130	334/207	337/209	254/157	154/95		
San Isidro de El General	213/132	186/115	251/156	351/218	336/208	186/115	428/265	264/164	205/127	249/154	329/204	
San José	76/47	309/192	114/71	220/136	202/125	321/199	306/190	130/81	67/42	118/73	192/119	130/81

Example: The distance between Liberia and Puntarenas is 136km/84mi.

Practical Information

This chapter contains all the information you need to plan your trip to Costa Rica, and to make the most of your trip once you are there.

Entrance Formalities

To enter Costa Rica, citizens of Canada, the United States and the European Union only need a passport that is valid for the length of their stay. No visas are necessary for stays of under 90 days. Citizens of other countries are advised to consult the nearest Costa Rican embassy or consulate. Because entrance requirements can change without notice, it's a good idea to get the most up-to-date information before you leave.

Officials can ask to see your passport or tourist card at any time during your stay. It is therefore a good idea to keep a photocopy of the key pages of your passport and other important papers, and to write down your passport number and its expiry date. This way, the documents will be much easier to replace if they are lost or stolen. If this should oc-

cur, contact your country's consulate or embassy to have a new passport issued.

Departure Tax

Each person leaving Costa Rica must pay a departure tax of US$17. The tax is collected at the airport when you check in for your return flight. Remember to have this amount in cash, because credit cards are not accepted.

Embassies and Consulates

In Costa Rica

All embassies in Costa Rica are in San José.

Australia
Plaza Polanco Torre B, Col. Los Morales, Mexico D.F.
☎395-9092.

Austria
Avenida 4, Calle 36/38
☎255-3007

Canada
Calle 3, Avenida 1
☎296-4149

Germany
Rohrmoser
☎*232-5533 or 232-5450*
⇄*231-6403*
www.embajada-alemania.org

Great Britain
Edificio Centro Colón, Paseo Colón, Centro Colón
☎*258-2025*
⇄*233-9938*

Italy
White house on the corner, 5th entrance of the Barrio Los Yoses
☎*234-2326*
⇄*225-8200*
www.ambitcr.com

Netherlands
Los Yoses
☎*234-0949*

Panama
San Pedro
☎*257-3241*
⇄*257-5067*

Spain
Calle 32, between Avenida 2 and Paseo Colón
☎*222-1933 or 222-5745*

Sweden
La Uruca
☎*232-8549*

Switzerland
Centro Colón
☎*233-0052*

United States
Apartado 920-1200 Pavas
☎*220-3939 or 220-3137*
⇄*220-2305*

Costa Rican Embassies and Consulates Abroad

Australia
30 Clarence Street, Sidney NSW 2000, mailing address; PO Box 2513 NSW 2001 Sidney
☎*(612) 9261-1177*
⇄*(612) 9261-2953*

Austria
Schloeglgasse 10A-1120 Vienna
☎*(431) 804-0537*
⇄*(431) 804-9071*

Belgium
489 Avenida Louise, Box 13, 1050 Brussels
☎*(02) 640-5541*
⇄*(02) 648-3192*

Canada
325 Dalhousie, suite 407 Ottawa, Ontario
K1N 7G2
☎*(613) 562-2855*
⇄*(613) 562-2582*

Consulate
1425 Boulevard René-Lévesque Montréal, Québec
☎*(514) 393-1057*
⇄*(514) 393-1624*

Germany
Langenbachstrasse 19, 53113 Bonn
☎*(228) 54.00.40*
⇄*(228) 54.90.53*

Great Britain
Flat 1, 14 Lancaster Gate, London W2 3L
☎*(441) 71-706-8844*
⇄*(441) 71-706-8655*
www.embcrlon.demon.co.uk

Italy
Via Bartolomeo Eustachio 22 Roma 00161
☎*(6-4) 425-1046*
☎*(6-4) 425-1042*
⇄*(6-4) 425-1048*
www.mix.it/utenti/embcosta

Netherlands
Laan Copes Van Cattenburch 46 2585 G.B. Den Haag
☎*(31) 070-354-0780*
⇄*(31) 070-358-4754*

Norway and Sweden
Skippergart 33, N-0154 Oslo, Norway
☎*(22) 425-823*
⇄*(22) 330-408*

Spain
Paseo de la Castellana 164, 17-A 28046 Madrid
☎*(91) 345-9622*
⇄*(91) 353-3709*

Switzerland
Schwartzentorstrasse 11, 3007 Berne
☎*(31) 372-7887*
⇄*(31) 372-7334*

United States
2112 "S" Street NW, Washington, DC 20008
☎*(202) 328-6628*
☎*(202) 234-2945*
⇄*(202) 265-4795*

Getting There

By Plane

Airports

Costa Rica has two international airports: the Aeropuerto Internacional San Juan Santamaría and the Aeropuerto Daniel Oduber.

Aeropuerto Internacional Juan Santamaría
☎*441-4737*
The Aeropuerto Internacional Juan Santamaría is the country's main airport. Located in the middle of Costa Rica, it is near

the capital and receives flights from most major international airlines.

The airport has been undergoing a huge facelift during the year 2000 to update it to a world-class facility. The administrative buildings as well as the arrival and departure terminals have been entirely re-done. Once a pleasant little airport, Aeropuerto Juan Santamaría is now an international air-traffic centre. Of course, all the required services will be here, such as restaurants, foreign exchange offices, car rental companies and so on. These renovations will certainly make travelling easier during busy periods; however, the work may not be finished by the beginning of 2001, so a little patience might be necessary.

The airport is located on the General Cañas Highway which leads directly to San José, the country's capital, which is only about 20km (12.4mi) to the southeast. The airport is well-linked to the country's major transportation routes, so you can also easily access the beaches on the central Pacific coast to the west via this highway, or head directly to Guanacaste province on the Inter-American Highway. Taxis are always available: the fare to San José is about US$10. Hotel shuttle buses pick up

passengers upon arrival. You can also take the bus *($0.50)* that frequently stops in front of the airport on its way into town. Things generally run smoothly, and you'll be able to clear customs and get out into the Costa Rican sunshine with no major hassles.

Aeropuerto Daniel Oduber
every day from 6am to 9pm
☎*667-0199 or 667-0032*
≈*667-0000*
The Aeropuerto Daniel Oduber is smaller and located in the country's northwest, in Guanacaste. It is only 17km (10.5mi) south of the region's capital, Liberia, along the Santa Cruz highway. The airport has all the standard features (customs, narcotics inspection, bank services, etc.). Some airlines have connecting flights from the Aeropuerto Internacional Juan Santamaría in the Central Valley. Some chartered flights from North America also land here, which saves travel time for visitors who only come for the beaches in this area.

Other Airports

Costa Rica has several other landing strips used mostly by domestic flights. The **Tobias Bolaños** Airport *(☎232-8049)* in Pavas, a suburb of San José, is one of these, but there are several others near cities in remote areas (such as the Golfito

Airport in the south) or popular bathing areas along the coast (such as Playa Carrillo, near Playa Sámara in Guanacaste). These airfields are listed in the chapters of the regions in which they are located.

Airlines

LACSA
Calle 1, Avenida 5, Edificio Numar
☎*257-9444 or 296-0909*
≈*232-3372*
The sales offices of LACSA Airlines, the national airline, are located near the intersection of Calle 1 and Avenida 1 in San José. This company flies to the major international destinations.

Major International Airlines in San José

American Airlines
Edificio Centro Cars, Calle 42 Avenida 5
☎*257-1266*
≈*223-5213*

British Airways
Avenida 7, Calle 7
☎*223-5648*
≈*223-4863*

Continental Airlines
200m (656ft) south, 300m(984ft) east, and 50m (164ft) north of the American embassy
☎*296-4911*
≈*296-4920*

Copa
Calle 1, Avenida 5
☎*222-6640*
≈*221-6798*

KLM
Edificio Oficentro Ejecutivo
50m (164ft) south of the
Contraloría
☎220-4111
≈220-3092

Mexicana
Calle 5, Avenida 7/9
☎257-6334
≈257-6338

Taca
Calle 40, Avenida 3
☎222-1790
≈223-4238

United Airlines
Sabana Sur, 50m (164ft) south
of the Contraloría
☎220-4844
≈220-4855

Major Domestic Airlines

Two large airlines handle most domestic flights in Costa Rica: **Sansa** *(Calle 24, Avenida Ctl/1,* ☎221-9414, ≈255-2176) is state-owned and uses the international airport, while **Travel Air** *(Terminal Internacional, Tobias Bolaños Airport,* ☎220-3054, ≈220-0413) is a private enterprise and flies out of the smaller Tobias Balaños Airport, in the suburbs west of the capital. Both companies have reasonable rates for visitors who want to travel around the country quickly. **Aero Costa Rica** *(west side of the Juan Pablo Segundo bridge, La Uruca,* ☎296-1111, ≈290-5848), **Aero Costa Sol** *(Juan Santamaría airport,* ☎441-0922 *or* 441-1444, ≈441-2671) and **Aerotour** *(Tobias Bolaños Airport,* ☎323-

1248, ≈232-9192) also offer domestic flights.

Luggage

The maximum luggage weight allowed into an airplane varies from one airline to the next. On chartered flights, it is restricted to a minimum, and charges are applied for excess weight. Remember that you are usually only allowed one piece of hand luggage on the plane, and it must fit under the seat in front of you.

Be sure to securely fasten all bags and suitcases and to carefully wrap all packages, since they could get damaged by the trolley's mechanism as they go into or come out of the baggage hold. Some airlines and airports supply sturdy plastic bags for backpacks, boxes and other pieces of luggage.

Before boarding the plane, you might be asked whether or not you left your luggage unattended, or if you packed it yourself. The reason for this is to prevent strangers from slipping illegal merchandise into your bags, which you would then unknowingly carry with you.

You are not allowed to bring dangerous objects, such as knives and pocketknives, into the plane; these items can, however, be kept in luggage that will be

put in the baggage hold. Outdoor enthusiasts should note that oxygen tanks cannot be carried into airplanes and that bicycle tires must be deflated. If you are travelling with unusual items, it is best to inquire with the airline before packing.

By Boat

Costa Rica has major ports in each of its coastal regions. On the Pacific coast, the port of Caldera is 8km (5mi) south of Puntarenas. Limón is the main port on the Caribbean coast. Yacht owners can also dock at various other marinas along the coast.

By Car

Travelling by car is the most feasible form of transportation, since you don't have to plan around bus schedules and can always get exactly where you want to go.

Costa Rica has a good network of roads, even though there are few highways once you get further away from the capital. The secondary roads usually have two lanes, which occasionally merge as the road crosses a bridge. Other roads are often in poor condition, especially in villages, parks, and around the beaches, so it's important to drive with caution.

Keep in mind that it's necessary to calculate considerably more travel time than you usually do. If it takes 1hr to 1.5hrs to go 100km (62mi) on a highway in North America, you can count on it taking twice as long in Costa Rica, whether travelling by car or by bus. This is due to the state of the roads (see below), which can make driving dangerous, especially in the mountains, as well as vehicles such as trucks which often block the one lane available.

The **Inter-American Highway** (Carretera Interamericana) runs north and south through the country. This road begins on the west coast, but veers inland around San José. It is much used and well maintained.

Road conditions are variable: sometimes whole roads are unpaved, sometimes only sections are. Also, heavy downpours during the rainy season can affect the road surface and levelling, and road conditions can deteriorate rapidly. As a result, many roads become impassable. Take note that when a road is in bad condition, it's in terrible condition. Deep holes, bumps and obstacles can obstruct even paved roads. Drive carefully and remember that tourist vehicles can't go everywhere.

Entrances to tourist attractions are not always easily visible from the road: you'll have to watch for them carefully. The same can be true for popular hotels and parks, whose signs are sometimes poorly indicated, or which may be accessed by small, nondescript paths.

Keep in mind that "traffic" can include many different things in Costa Rica—not just cars! You might well find yourself sharing the road with a cow, or perhaps a whole herd of cows, as well as sheep, people on horseback, cyclists and other unexpected companions. People often walk along the road, even on the shoulder of major thoroughfares. Also, watch for vehicles stopping suddenly right in front of you: buses often pick up passengers along roads, including highways. Be careful if you decide to stop somewhere along the way yourself (to admire the view or stretch your legs), since there are usually no shoulders or rest areas beside the road.

If possible, avoid driving at night. The streets are not lit, and destinations are poorly indicated.

Service stations are sometimes scarce in certain villages. Therefore, it's a good idea to fill up your tank when you can!

Driving and the Highway Code

You will notice frequent signs along the road that warn *"Puente angosto adelante"* (narrow bridge ahead), so be careful! Also, respect all *"Ceda el paso"* (yield the right of way) and *"No hay paso"* (do not enter) and stop signs. One-way streets are indicated by arrows painted onto the pavement in the cities.

The word *"escuela"* (school) frequently appears on signs in villages, and is often accompanied with the added warning *"despacio"*, or slow down.

Direction signs are not always consistent. They might suddenly discontinue, or appear right at the last minute. The numerous holes in the Inter-American Highway are not necessarily well indicated, either.

It is rare for cities to have special signs to indicate their names, so watch for the blue ICE signs which have the name of the town, as well as directions to public telephones or other regional means of communication, written on them.

Parking

Try to park in busy, well-lit areas. In San José, however, take a taxi (very affordable) or park your car in one of the many *parqueos publicos* (public parking areas). Be careful, though: some are open 24hrs a day, while others are not. Also, prices can vary from place to place.

Many hotels and restaurants, especially in San José, provide patrolled parking areas. It is standard to tip the guard about 200 colons.

When parking your car, even for a short time, make sure all the doors are well locked and don't leave anything visible inside. A coat or jacket may invite a thief to check for a wallet in one of the pockets. Stealing from cars is frequent, so do be careful.

Renting a Car

Renting a car in Costa Rica is easy, and you can even do so at the airport as soon as you arrive. During the holidays, however (Christmas, Easter, etc. see p 55), it is important to reserve well in advance, especially for four-wheel drive vehicles. The legal driving age is 18, but most agencies will only rent to people 21 years old or more. Many agencies ask for an added $1,500 deposit (generally through your credit card). Note as well that the government requires you to buy a minimum amount of daily insurance when you rent a car. Even if you have a Gold credit card that insures you

Car-Rental Agencies in San José

Alamo	☎233-7733
Avis	☎293-2222
Budget	☎223-3284
Discovery	☎293-2866
Hertz	☎221-1818
National	☎233-4044
Prego	☎221-8680
Thrifty	☎257-3434
U-Haul	☎257-8283

automatically, you're still required to pay for this insurance.

Which vehicle you should choose depends on the length and nature of your trip. For example, if you take a two-week trip to remote and difficult to access areas, a vehicle with high suspension and good shock absorbers and traction (ideally, four-wheel drive) is essential. If you are only going between cities and stay on the better roads, a regular car will do.

If you want to switch cars along the way, you don't need to return to San José. You can have the rental agency deliver a car to you for a fee between $45 and $110, depending on where you are in the country.

Lastly, note that on the windshield of a rental car there is a sticker with the car's registration number. In the case of a traffic violation, police are supposed to hand out a ticket with this number on it and never your name. You can make arrangements with the rental company to pay the fine. This measure is supposed to eliminate the corruption that sometimes victimizes tourists.

By Train

Train travel was discontinued in Costa Rica in 1991, because of earthquakes and financial difficulties.

By Bus

The public transportation system is efficient (though sometimes slow), well-maintained and much used in Costa Rica. Bus service runs from the cities to even the smallest towns, and there are many departures daily. The buses are usually quite comfortable, even if they are sometimes so crowded that they seem ready to burst!

For a list of the routes, pick up a copy of *Costa Rica Today*, published annually.

Usually, you can go directly to the bus terminal and purchase your ticket just prior to your departure. Each city has a central bus depot, but San José has several, so check beforehand which one your bus departs from (see p 74). Here is a list of bus companies that run from San José to the country's major cities:

Autotransportes Blanco
to Puerto Jiménez
Calle 12, Avenida 9
☎771-2550)

Autotransportes Ciudad Quesada
to Ciudad Quesada
Coca Cola bus depot
☎255-4318

Autotransportes Mepe
to Bribrí, Cahuita and Sixaola
Calle Ctl., Va. 9/11
☎221-0524

Coopelimon
to Puerto Limón
Avenida 3, Calle 19/21
☎223-7811

Empresa Alfaro
to Nicoya, Santa Cruz and Filadelfia as well as Sámara and Tamarindo
Calle 14, Avenida 3/5
☎222-2750

Empresarios Unidos de Puntarenas
to Puntarenas
☎222-0064

Pulmitan
to Playa del Coco and Liberia
Calle 14, Avenida 1/3
☎222-1650

Sacsa
to Cartago
Calle 5, Avenida 18
☎233-5350

Tracopa
to Ciudad Neily, Palmar, Norte, Golfito and San Vito
Avenida 18, Calle 4
☎221-4214

Tracopa Empresa Alfaro
to San Vito
Calle 14, Avenida 3/5
☎222-2750

Tralapa
to Playa Flamingo
Calle 20, Avenida 3
☎221-7202

Transportes La Cañera
to Cañas
Calle 16, Avenida 1/3
☎222-3006

Transportes Morales
to Quepos and Manuel Antonio
☎223-5567

Transportes Musoc
to San Isidro and El General
Calle 16, Avenida 1/3
☎222-2422

Transtura
to Turrialba
Avenida 16, Calle 13
☎556-0073

Tuasa
to Alajuela
Avenida 2, Calle 12
☎222-5325

Tuasur
to San Isidro and El General
☎222-9763

On Foot

Costa Rica's urban layout is quite easy to understand: almost every town has a central park surrounded by many public and commercial establishments, such as churches, hotels, banks, restaurants and shops. For the most part, the idea of putting large commercial centres at the peripheries of a city has not caught on yet in Costa Rica. Street blocks are usually 100m (328ft) long, making it easy to use distances in giving directions and addresses. For more on the system of addresses, see p 50.

Be careful when exploring the cities on foot, since they were often not built with pedestrians in mind. You will come across sidewalks in all kinds of conditions, and the traffic lights are often difficult to see.

By Taxi

Taxis are easy to spot: they're all painted red! There are plenty of taxis around, even in small villages, but the cars are in various conditions. You can nearly always hail one in the street, even at night. In fact, it often takes less time to hail a cab than to call for one and wait for it to arrive. Taxi stands can also be found, mostly near busy places like parks, public squares and even hotels and bars.

Taking a taxi is inexpensive. In San José, cab fare shouldn't cost more than $5, although the trip to the airport costs about $10.

Tourist Information

Great efforts are being made to improve Costa Rica's tourist infrastructure. The **Instituto Costarricense de Turismo** (**ICT**) *(Apartado postal 777-1000, San José,* ☎*223-1733 or 800-343-6332 from Canada and the United States,* ⇌*223-5452)* tries hard to provide tourists with information and a warm welcome. The government plans to open tourist information offices in the country's most frequently visited areas at the beginning of 2001. In the meantime, there isn't much in the way of public tourist information. Private companies have taken advantage of this lack and have set up what they call tourist information offices, but it's difficult to get objective information here. They, of course, steer you to their establishments and organizations. Be cautious at these offices, but don't hesitate to use them. Also, certain serious associations are grouping together now, as is the case in the northern part of the country, where numerous enterprises provide tourist services and in this way publicize themselves. If you have any questions, however, talking to the locals is still the best way to learn about

a place and to meet people!

Also, many organizations, both public and private, publish information about all sorts of sites and activities that could interest tourists. Hotel receptions often have several of these useful brochures available. Some of the more popular hotels can give you good advice; it is worthwhile to consult them.

If you want a guided visit of a national park, city or region, here are a few suggestions of agencies in and around San José that offer guided tours or outdoor activities throughout the country. You can make arrangements over the phone with most companies, saving yourself the trip to their offices. Also, most San José hotels have numerous brochures and can make reservations for you.

Aventuras Naturales
Avenida Central, Calle 33/35
☎**225-3939**
⇌**253-6934**
Aventuras Naturales offers rafting excursions on the Río Pacuare and the Río Reventazón.

Calypso Tours
Avenida 2, Calle 1/3, in the Las Arcadas building, Oficina 11
☎**256-2727**
⇌**233-0401**
Since 1975, Calypso Tours has been organizing very popular boating excursions (aboard the catamarans *Calypso* or *Manta Raya*)

on the Gulf of Nicoya, and particularly to Isla Tortuga.

Costa Rica Expeditions
every day 5:30am to 9pm
souvenir shop
Calle Central, Avenida 3
☎**257-0766 or 222-0333**
⇌**257-1665**
costaric@expeditions.co.cr
A quick stop at Costa Rica Expeditions, right in the middle of downtown San José, should be enough to convince you that Costa Rica has become one of the world's top destinations for ecotourism and adventure-tourism. This agency, generally thought of as having pioneered nature tourism in Costa Rica, provides very professional service. Whether you go on a half-day, one-day or overnight excursion (hiking, rafting, canopy tours, horseback riding, birdwatching, sightseeing and more), you will be accompanied by experienced and qualified naturalist guides.

Costa Rica Sun Tours
Avenida 7, Calle 5/7
☎**255-3418**
⇌**255-4410**
Costa Rica Sun Tours offers a host of guided tours in and around the greater Central Valley region, and manages the Arenal Observatory Lodge and the Tiskita Lodge.

Ecole Travel
Calle 7, Avenida Central/1
☎**223-2240**
⇌**223-4128**
Ecole Travel offers guided tours (Isla

Tortuga, Manuel Antonio, Monteverde, Arenal, Corcovado, Tortuguero, etc.) for budget travellers.

Ecoscape Nature Tours
☎297-0664
⇌297-0549
and
Marbella Travel & Tours
☎259-0055
⇌259-0065
These agencies will take you on a one-day tour of the Volcán Poás and Braulio Carrillo parks, as well as the Río Sarapiquí, Cataratas La Paz and Selva Verde Lodge.

Expediciones Tropicales
Calle 3B, Avenida 11/13
☎257-4171
⇌257-4124
Expediciones Tropicales offers guided tours of the Central Valley's main volcanoes (Irazú, Poás, Barva, Orosí).

Geotur
☎/⇌227-4029
Geotur takes visitors on tours of the Parque Nacional Braulio Carrillo and the Reserva Biológica Carara.

Horizontes
Calle 28, Avenida 1/3
☎222-1848
⇌255-4513
Horizontes offers rafting on the Rió Pacuare and the Rió Reventazón, as well as guided family tours.

Agencia de Viajes La Cruz
☎679-9276
⇌226-5581
Agencia de Viajes La Cruz is managed by Ricardo Bolaños, a

first-rate tour guide. The agency organizes trips throughout the country, but specializes in the Guanacaste region, particularly the northern part of the province. Visits to this region's parks and reserves (Rincón de la Vieja, Santa Rosa, etc.) as well as sea excursions such as snorkelling and outings to beaches, are offered. The talkative Ricardo, who speaks English, will be happy to answer your questions—at great length!

Maguines Travel Service
☎/⇌283-4510
manfredg@racsa.co.cr
Run by Manfred Gutiérrez, Maguines Travel Service organizes customized packages of short and extended stays in various regions of the country for gay travellers (hotel and car reservations plus all kinds of activities).

Ríos Tropicales
Calle 38, Avenida ct 1/2
☎233-6455
⇌255-4354
www.riostropicales.com
Ríos Tropicales specializes in rafting, as well as river and sea kayaking.

Swiss Travel Service
☎282-4896
⇌282-4890
and
Fantasy Tours
☎326-8279 or 220-2126
⇌220-2393
Both organize many different guided tours (San José, volcanoes, rafting, Isla Tortuga,

etc.) in the greater Central Valley region.

Tikal Express
Calle 7, Avenida 9/2
☎223-2811
⇌223-1916
Tikal Tours specializes in ecotourism and offers guided tours of several regions of the country.

Vesa Tours
☎387-8372
⇌220-2779
vesatour@racsa.co.cr
Since 1985, Vesa Tours has been organizing expeditions that explore the country's natural, as well as cultural and historical, attractions. Among these, the guided tour of San José is particularly interesting, and will introduce you to the production of coffee and handicrafts, take you on various outdoor excursions like rafting and horseback riding and, of course, visit the national parks. The staff is experienced and conscientious.

Climate and Packing

Climate

Costa Rica's various microclimates can undoubtedly be considered among the country's many riches (see also p 14), and have helped shape its rich and diverse fauna and flora. Generally, the Caribbean coast and the southern part of the Pacific coast have a humid, tropical climate with high temperatures and plenty of rainfall. The central area of the country has a more temperate climate, with cooler temperatures the higher you go. Guanacaste and the Nicoya Peninsula have a hot, dry climate with very little precipitation during the dry season.

Costa Rica has two seasons: the dry season from December to April, and the rainy or "green" season, from May to November, which has plenty of precipitation, especially from September onwards.

What to Pack

Given the many different climates of Costa Rica, what you pack will depend on which regions you are planning to visit. In the mountains and volcanic regions a windbreaker will come in handy, and a set of warm clothes is indispensable if you want to do some hiking in these areas. On the other hand, pack light cotton clothes if you are staying on the coast, and don't forget a hat and sun screen. It's "eternal spring" in the Central Valley, which lies at an elevation that is between these two regions. Here, it becomes quite cool in the evenings, and it might even seem chilly if you're coming from the coast. If you visit dur-

ing the rainy season, be sure to bring along a good umbrella, as sudden downpours are frequent.

Insurance

Health Insurance

Health insurance is the most important type of insurance for travellers and should be purchased before your departure. A comprehensive health insurance policy that provides sufficient coverage to pay for hospitalization, nursing care and doctor's fees is recommended. Keep in mind that health care costs are rising quickly everywhere. The policy should also have a repatriation clause in case the required care is not available in Costa Rica. As patients are sometimes asked to pay for medical services up front, find out what provisions your policy makes in this case. Always carry your health insurance policy with you when travelling to avoid problems if you are in an accident, and get receipts for any expenses incurred.

Cancellation Insurance

This type of insurance is usually offered by your travel agent when you purchase your airplane ticket or tour package. It covers any non-refundable pay-

ments to travel suppliers such as airlines, and must be purchased at the same time as initial payment is made for air tickets or tour packages. This insurance allows you to be reimbursed for the ticket or package deal if your trip must be cancelled due to serious illness or death. This type of insurance can be useful, but weigh the likelihood of your using it against the price.

Theft Insurance

Most residential insurance policies in North America protect some of your goods from theft, even if the theft occurs in a foreign country. To make a claim, you must fill out a police report. Usually the coverage for a theft abroad is 10% of your total coverage. If you plan on travelling with valuable objects, check your policy or with an insurance agency to see if additional baggage insurance is necessary. European visitors should take out baggage insurance.

Health

Hospitals and medical centres are generally well-equipped in Costa Rica, thanks to the large sums of money pumped into health care over the last few years. Doctors and health workers are competent, and usually take the time to understand your problem. Of course, medical services outside the big centres might seem more modest. In tourist areas, you can usually find an English-speaking doctor. If you need a blood transfusion, make sure that the blood has been tested and is safe.

Health care costs are much lower in Costa Rica than in most of North America and Europe, and there are many private medical clinics and pharmacies. Your country's consulate can best advise you where to turn should you need medical services. You can also consult the *Costa Rica Guide*, published yearly by the *Tico Times*, which can recommend clinics to treat most health problems.

Insufficiently treated water, which can contain harmful bacteria, is the cause of most of the health problems you are likely to encounter, such as stomach upset, diarrhea or fever. Although the drinking water in most cities and towns in Costa Rica is treated and presumably safe, always ask about it before you drink it. Signs posted at the entrance of many cities and towns indicate whether the water is safe to drink or not. Drinking only bottled water, which is available in stores and restaurants throughout the country, is the best way

to avoid catching anything. Make sure the bottle is well-sealed when you buy it. In addition, fresh fruits and vegetables that have been washed but not peeled can also pose a health risk. Make sure that the vegetables you eat are well-cooked, and peel your own fruit. Remember: cook it, peel it, or forget it.

If you do get diarrhea, soothe your stomach by avoiding solids; instead, drink carbonated beverages, bottled water, or weak tea (avoid milk) until you recover. As dehydration can be dangerous, drinking sufficient quantities of liquid is crucial. Pharmacies sell various preparations for the treatment of diarrhea, with different effects. Pepto Bismol and Imodium will stop the diarrhea, which slows the loss of fluids, but they should be avoided if you have a fever as they will prevent the necessary elimination of bacteria. Oral rehydration products, such as Gastrolyte, will replace the minerals and electrolytes which your body has lost as a result of the diarrhea. In a pinch, you can make your own rehydration solution by mixing one litre of pure water with one teaspoon of sugar and two or three teaspoons of salt. After, eat easily digested foods like rice to give your stomach time to adjust. If symp-

toms become more serious (high fever, persistent diarrhea), see a doctor as antibiotics may be necessary.

Nutrition and climate can also cause problems. Pay attention to the food's freshness (especially fish and meat) and the cleanliness of the preparation area. Good hygiene (wash your hands often) will help avoid undesirable situations.

It is best not to walk around bare-foot as parasites and insects can cause a variety of problems, the least of which is athlete's foot.

Costa Rica is a wonderful country to explore; however, travellers should be aware of and protect themselves from a number of health risks associated with the region, such as malaria, typhoid, diphtheria, tetanus, polio and hepatitis A. Cases of these diseases are rare but there is a risk. **Travellers are therefore advised to consult a doctor (or travellers' clinic) for advice on what precautions to take.** Remember that it is much easier to prevent these illnesses than it is to cure them and that a vaccination is not a substitute for cautious travel.

Illnesses

Please note that this section is intended to provide general information only.

Malaria

Malaria (paludism) is caused by a parasite in the blood called *Plasmodium sp.* This parasite is transmitted by anopheles mosquitoes, which bite from nightfall until dawn. Hardly any cases of malaria have been reported in Costa Rica in the last few years. The risk is minimal and anti-malaria drugs are not necessary. It is nevertheless a good idea to take measures to prevent mosquito bites (see below).

The symptoms of malaria include high fever, chills, extreme fatigue and headaches as well as stomach and muscle aches. There are several forms of malaria, including one serious type caused by *P. falciparum.* The disease can take hold while you are still on holiday or up to 12 weeks following your return; in some cases the symptoms can appear months later.

Hepatitis A

This disease is generally transmitted by ingesting food or water that has been contaminated by faecal matter. The symptoms include fever, yellowing of the skin, loss of appetite and fatigue, and can appear between 15 and 50 days after infection. An effective vaccination by injection is available. Besides the recommended vaccine, good

hygiene is important. Always wash your hands before every meal, and ensure that the food and preparation area are clean.

Hepatits B

Hepatitis B, like hepatitis A, affects the liver, but is transmitted through direct contact of bodily fluids. The symptoms are flu-like, and similar to those of hepatitis A. A vaccination exists but must be administered over an extended period of time, so be sure to check with your doctor several weeks in advance.

Typhoid

This illness is caused by ingesting food that has come in contact (direct or indirect) with an infected person's stool. Common symptoms include high fever, loss of appetite, headaches, constipation and occasionally diarrhea, as well as the appearance of red spots on the skin. These symptoms will appear one to three weeks after infection. Which medication you take (it exists in two forms, oral and by injection) will depend on your trip. Once again, it is always a good idea to visit a travellers' clinic a few weeks before your departure.

Diphtheria and Tetanus

These two illnesses, against which most people are vaccinated during their childhood, can have serious consequences. Thus, before leaving, check that your vaccinations are valid; you may need a booster shot. Diphtheria is a bacterial infection that is transmitted by nose and throat secretions or by skin lesions on an infected person. Symptoms include sore throat, high fever, general aches and pains and occasionally skin infections. Tetanus is caused by a bacteria that enters your body through an open wound that comes in contact with contaminated dust or rusty metal.

Other Health Tips

Cases of illnesses like Hepatitis B, AIDS and certain venereal diseases have been reported; it is therefore a good idea to be careful.

Remember that consuming too much alcohol, particularly during prolonged exposure to the sun, can cause severe dehydration and lead to health problems.

Mosquitoes

A nuisance common to many countries, mosquitoes are no strangers to Costa Rica. They are particularly numerous during the rainy season. Protect yourself with a good insect repellent. Repellents with DEET are the most effective. The concentration of DEET varies from one product to the next; the higher the concentration, the longer the protection. In rare cases, the use of repellents with high concentrations (35% or more) of DEET has been associated with convulsions in young children; it is therefore important to apply these products sparingly, on exposed surfaces, and to wash it off once back inside. A concentration of 35% DEET will protect for four to 6hrs, while 95% will last from 10 to 12hrs. New formulas with DEET in lesser concentrations, but which last just as long, are available.

To further reduce the possibility of getting bitten, do not wear perfume or bright colours. Sundown is an especially active time for insects. When walking in wooded areas, cover your legs and ankles well. Insect coils can help provide a better night's sleep. Before bed, apply insect repellent to your skin and to the headboard and baseboard of your bed. If possible, get an air-conditioned room, or bring a mosquito net.

Lastly, since it is impossible to completely avoid contact with mosquitoes, bring along a cream to soothe the bites you will invariably get.

Snakes and Insects

Among a country's rich and diverse fauna, there are bound to be some species that are less congenial than others. Accordingly, Costa Rica is home to several kinds of snakes, some of which are poisonous. There is no need to get too alarmed, as you are unlikely to cross paths with one during your visit. Nevertheless, it is important to keep your eyes open and watch where you step. In the forest, look around before you lean against something or sit down somewhere. When hiking, be careful as you part the foliage that sometimes hangs across the path, and check the shores as well as the surface of the water if you go swimming in a river. Some people think they are faster than a snake and tease it, or poke it to see if they can make it move; needless to say, this is not a good idea! The presence of snakes should not prevent you from exploring everything that Costa Rica has to offer. Like most wild animals, snakes avoid contact with humans as much as possible.

The Sun

Its benefits are many, but so are its harms. Always wear sunscreen (SPF 15 for adults and SPF 30 for children) and apply it 20 to 30min before exposure. Many creams on the market do not offer adequate protection; ask a pharmacist. Too much sun can cause sunstroke (dizziness, vomiting, fever, etc.). Be careful, especially the first few days, as it takes time to get used to the sun. Take sun in small doses and protect yourself with a hat and sunglasses.

First-Aid Kit

A small first-aid kit can prove very useful. Bring along sufficient amounts of any medications you take regularly as well as a valid prescription in case you lose your supply; it can be difficult to find certain medications in the small towns. Other medications such as anti-malaria pills and Imodium (or an equivalent), can also be hard to find. Finally, don't forget self-adhesive bandages, disinfectant cream or ointment, analgesics (pain-killers), antihistamines (for allergies), an extra pair of sunglasses or contact lenses, contact lens solution, and medicine for upset stomach. Though these items are all available in Costa Rica, having them on

Practical Information

hand can certainly make life easier.

Safety and Security

Costa Rica hasn't had an army since the 1940s, but the police is still very powerful and has a strong presence, especially on the roads outside the cities. Also, there is a kind of private militia whose main purpose is to combat the drug trade and prevent illegal immigrants from entering the country.

They operate mainly along the borders with Panama and Nicaragua. You can recognize them by their insignia of crossed rifles, and it is not advisable to bother them for nothing, since they mean business.

Theft is common, especially in the cities, and every establishment with any kind of a reputation to uphold has its own parking lot attendant, often armed with a bat.

Generally, the country is really quite safe. By taking the usual precautions, you shouldn't run into any problems, even in San José. Nevertheless, avoid walking by yourself through dimly lit areas after dark. Remember, the sun sets at about 6pm! On the Caribbean coast (see p 145) the crime rate is higher. Theft is more frequent, but this shouldn't stop you from enjoying this beautiful region, as long as you're careful.

Money and Banking

Currency

The currency in Costa Rica is the *colon*.

Since the value of the colon can change rapidly, prices in this guide are given in US dollars. Some restaurants and hotels also choose to advertise their rates in US dollars.

Banks

The Banco de Costa Rica and the Banco Nacional are the country's most important financial institutions. Both banks have at least one outlet in every city.

Exchange Rates*

$1 US	= 315.19 colones	100 colones	= $0.32 US
$1 US	= $1.55 CAN	$1 CAN	= $0.65 US
$1 US	= £0.70	£ 1	= $1.43 US
$1 US	= $1.93 AUS	$1 AUS	= $0.52 US
$1 US	= $2.53 NZ	$1 NZ	= $0.40 US
$1 US	= 1.77 SF	1 SF	= $0.56 US
$1 US	= 1.17 Euro	1 Euro	= $0.86 US
$1 US	= 47.00 BF	10 BF	= $0.21 US
$1 US	= 2.28 DM	1 DM	= $0.44 US
$1 US	= 193.86 PTA	100 PTA	= $0.52 US
$1 US	= 2,255.94 ITL	1000 ITL	= $0.44 US
$1 US	= 2.57 fl	1 fl	= $0.39 US

*Samples Only—Rates Fluctuate

As in North America, banks are open Monday to Friday, from 9am to 3pm.

Credit Cards

Most credit cards, especially Visa (blue card), MasterCard, and American Express (in that order) are accepted in a large number of businesses, including hotels and restaurants. While the main advantage of credit cards is that they allow you to avoid carrying large sums of money, using a credit card also makes leaving a deposit for a rental car much easier. In addition, the exchange rate with a credit card is usually better.

Credit cards also let you avoid service charges when exchanging money. By overpaying your credit card (to avoid interest charges), you can then withdraw against it. You can thus avoid carrying large amounts of money or traveller's cheques.

Withdrawals can be made directly from an automated teller if you have a personal identification number (PIN) for your card.

Automated Teller Machines (ATMs)

Several banks have automated tellers for withdrawing cash, and A Toda Hora (ATH)

machines are also available on some streets. Most of the bank machines have Cirrus and Plus so visitors can make withdrawals directly from their personal accounts. You use your bank card as usual, but you'll receive *colones* while the equivalent amount is deducted from your account. And this takes no more time than if you were at your own bank! This being said, the system occasionally encounters communication problems, meaning you won't get any money. If your transaction is refused, try your luck at another bank. However, take care not to find yourself empty-handed.

Traveller's Cheques

It is always best to keep a certain amount of money in traveller's cheques, which are accepted in some restaurants, hotels and shops (those in American dollars are most widely accepted). They are also easy to cash in at banks and exchange offices. Always keep a copy of the serial numbers of your cheques in a separate place; that way, if the cheques are lost, the company can replace them quickly and easily. Do not rely solely on traveller's cheques, always carry some cash.

Telecommuni-cations

Costa Rica's telecommunications system is still being developed. Seven-digit telephone numbers were introduced a few years ago to increase the network's capacity. The country code is **506**, and there are no regional codes. To call Costa Rica, dial the number for the international operator (011 in Canada and the United States, for example), followed by 506 and the number you want to reach.

There are two types of public telephones in the country: rotary dial phones accept 5, 10 and 20 colon pieces, while the touch-tone telephones require a special phone card that you can buy. The latter have a small screen that explains how to use them; the instructions will appear in English if you press the right buttons.

Important Phone Numbers

Dial ☎*911* for all emergencies. For a Red Cross ambulance, call ☎*128*; in case of fire, dial ☎*118*.

Practical Information

There are two kinds of pre-paid telephone cards: one has various amounts on the card and works very well; the other gives you an identification number to dial in order to make a call. This second system is definitely less efficient.

To make an international call from Costa Rica, dial **00**, followed by the country code, the area or city code (if needed), and the number of the person you want to reach.

For instance, to call **Canada** or the **United States**, dial 00-1, the area code, and the number. Canada Direct (☎*0-800-015-1161*) is a free service that connects you with a Canadian operator. If you are using a public telephone, you will still have to insert a phone card or money to get a dial tone.

To contact a telephone operator at:
AT&T
☎*800-011-4114*

Sprint
☎*800-013-0123*

MCI
☎*800-012-2222*

Internet

At the moment, a national company, Racsa, has the monopoly for the country's Internet communications: all e-mail addresses based in the country end with

Some Interesting Web Sites

www.tourism-costarica.com
This is the Web site of the Instituto Costariciense de Tourismo, the government agency in charge of tourism.

www.tourism.co.cr
This is the Web site of Canatur, another organization responsible for tourism.

www.costarica.com
Another general site.

www.nacion.co.cr
For those who read Spanish, this is the site of one of the large, daily newspapers.

www.ticotimes.net
Local newspaper published in English.

There are many other Web sites that can give you information and ideas, so feel free to surf!

@racsa.co.cr (there used to be a "sol." before the "racsa"). The Internet works very well in Costa Rica and most businesses have up-to-date Web sites. Communicating with them is easy and you can even reserve your hotel room this way. Also, once you're in Costa Rica, you shouldn't have a problem accessing your messages. Most of the larger cities have cybercafés with accessible hours and prices. If you can't find one, ask at your hotel reception if you can use their computer.

Mail

Apart from numbered PO Boxes (*apartado*

postal), the country uses an address system based on geographic orientation from a specific point, such as an intersection, important building, central plaza or park. Thus, the postal address of a hotel might be: 100m south and 300m west of the central park. The government is currently working out the details of a costly shift to the more commonly used international system, with numbered buildings. Some buildings are marked with a number, but addresses are not officially designated this way yet. Currently, addresses are given as: Calle 4, Avenida 3/4 or Avenida 4, Calle 2. This means that the place is located on Fourth Street, between Third and Fourth Avenues, or on Fourth Avenue, near Second Street. You might also encounter postal addesses refering to a post office box number, or *apartado postal*.

Traditional addresses have not been provided in this guide for the small villages in order to make the text more clear and concise. To write to one of these places, simply indicate the name of the establishment, the name of the city or town and the name of the region, followed by the name of the country, of course. This is all the information needed for your letter to arrive!

Postage is inexpensive in Costa Rica: sending a letter to Europe only costs 32¢, while mailing a postcard costs 5¢ less.

Media

Newspapers

La Nación includes a calendar of cultural activities around the country (movies, performances and art shows). *La República*, *El Día* and *La Prensa Libre* are national newspapers published in Spanish.

The *Tico Times* is an English-language newspaper published by Costa Rica's English-speaking community. It deals with political issues similar to those in *La Nación* and *La*

Prensa Libre. A section on cultural activities and movie listings is also included.

Magazines

Costa Rica Today is a bilingual English and Spanish magazine published with tourists in mind. It is sold at stands, but you can pick up a free copy at most hotels and airports. It contains a calendar of events.

Guide is also targeted at tourists, and is distributed at airports.

In addition to tourist publications, Costa Rica also has its own special interest magazines for women, businesspeople, etc. *Gente 10* is a local gay publication that can be found at various locations throughout the country.

Radio

There are radio stations for all tastes, especially if you're staying in the Central Valley. In the regions on the other side of the mountains, however, you might have difficulties picking up the FM broadcasts without an antenna (i.e. on the car).

For music from the 1960s and beyond, tune in to **Radio 2** at 99.5 FM; the DJs speak in both English and Spanish.

For classical music, turn your dial to 96.7 FM, **Radio Universidad**.

Latin (Latin-American or Spanish) and North-American music can be found on **Estereo Azul**, at 99.9 FM.

Accommodations

There are several types of accommodations in Costa Rica, from luxury hotels with a wide array of services, to small, charming bungalows with a more local feel.

Prices listed in this guide are for one double-occupancy room in high season:

$	less than US$15
$$	$15 to $25
$$$	$25 to $50
$$$$	$50 to $75
$$$$$	$75 to $120
$$$$$$	more than $120

The 13% general tax is included in the price of the hotel room, but a tourist tax of about 3% (rate varies) is not.

Types of Accommodations

Hotels

Small, inexpensive hotels usually have a room with a bed, and no extra amenities. Bathrooms are often shared, and do not always have running water. This type of hotel costs under $15.

The big luxury hotels at the other end of the scale have seemingly limitless facilities. Designed for wealthy tourists, business people and celebrities, they are often (but not always) vast complexes with spacious grounds and many services, such as casinos, large restaurants, bars, swimming pools, refrigerators in the rooms, etc.

CST

For the country's hotels, the three letters CST mean a lot. In fact, they are the acronym of a government program set up to foster lasting and respectful development of the tourist industry. In order to display these precious letters, establishments must prove that their economic development is in balance with the natural, social and cultural environments. They must take concrete steps to encourage this equilibrium and to preserve, while still developing, the country's resources. To find the hotels that have already been recognized, call ☎*255-0841* or *800-343-6332*, or visit the Web site *www.turismosostenible.co.cr*.

All beaches belong to the state, so no one can claim the exclusive right to any specific stretch of the coast. Sometimes, however, a beach can only be accessed through private property. Thus, certain hotels have taken advantage of this so their guests can enjoy a serene seaside experience.

Because tourism has grown so quickly in Costa Rica, there wasn't enough time for accommodations between these two categories to develop until recently. Gradually, more mid-range establishments are opening their doors, offering travellers a variety of services at a moderate price.

Patios and other outdoor areas attached to a room are not necessarily private. Most hotels have small safes available to store your valuables. Most bathrooms only have showers.

"*Cabinas*" are an alternative to the traditional hotel room. They are small, detached bungalows which usually consist of only one room, and sometimes have a private bathroom. Occasionally they come with a kitchenette and small livingroom. This type of lodging is also known as "*habitación*."

Hotel rooms in the mid- and higher-range

categories often have private bathrooms with hot water (although sometimes only in the shower), but bathtubs are very rare. Usually these hotels also have air-conditioning or a ceiling fan, a safe in the room or at the reception, a service organizing excursions, laundry services and secure parking.

Apart-hotels

Apart-hotels are like hotels in that they offer all the services, but like apartments because rooms include kitchenettes equipped with dishes and utensils. This is a very economical option for longer stays.

Lodges

One kind of accommodation that's popular in Costa Rica is the lodge. However, a lodge can mean quite different things, so make sure you understand what you're reserving. Usually, a lodge is a charming rustic establishment in the countryside, where nature can be experienced and savoured. It could also be located on a huge stretch of land by the sea, by a river or in the heart of the jungle where accommodations have been built for visitors (the comfort level varies) and all meals are provided (the formula varies). This option gives guests the opportunity to enjoy the countryside and

Holy Week

In Costa Rica, Holy Week often corresponds to the last few days of summer. Moreover, during the week leading up to Easter, most workers are on vacation. While many take the opportunity to renew their spiritual ties, more than a few take off and use these last sunny vacation days to enjoy the beaches instead. If you're travelling during that week, always keep in mind that most businesses and offices across the country will be closed and the beaches and hotels on the coast will be jammed! That said, you can take the opportunity to admire the beautiful processions that parade during this period!

many outdoor activities. As well, a lodge often specializes in a certain activity like bird-watching, rafting, horseback riding and so on.

Bed and Breakfasts

Bed and breakfasts, where you stay with a family in their home, are very popular, and the atmosphere is much warmer than in a hotel! However, the charm of staying at a bed and breakfast lies primarily in the decor and the friendliness of the welcome, which can vary from place to place. The owners can often help you plan your excursions in an informal way, and help you out with any problems you might encounter during your stay.

Staying in someone's home is the perfect way to fully experience life in another country, with everything this may entail. Although Costa Ricans are known for their hospitality, living conditions vary from one place to the next. You will also be living with the daily habits of your hosts; the incessant sounds of the television or radio are not uncommon. Also, Costa Ricans tend to go to bed early. Inquiring about these details beforehand can make the difference between an "okay" vacation and the one of your dreams. In addition to the establishments listed in this guide, language schools, some churches, classified advertisements or chat-

ting with people at the University of Costa Rica can all be sources of information about interesting bed and breakfasts.

Camping

You can camp in several parks in the country. Facilities are rustic, but there are often washrooms nearby. See the descriptions of the parks or the "Accommodations" section of each chapter for more detailed information about specific sites. There are few official campgrounds to speak of, but many hotels allow travellers to camp on their grounds. Inquire about this possibility at the local tourist offices. Alternatively, you can join Costa Rican campers who pitch their tents under the trees along the beach. Of course, no services are available here. Should you choose this option, make sure to respect the natural surroundings.

Wilderness camping is possible in most parks, but you must reserve in advance.

Restaurants and Food

Costa Rica has different types of cuisine, thanks to the numerous waves of immigration, all of which have contributed to its variety. You will, for example, find some

Chinese restaurants around. However, apart from the large cities in the Central Valley, it is still difficult to find upscale restaurants or non-Costa Rican specialized–cuisine. You can find some real gems in the country-side, but these are quite sparse, especially if you stay in remote areas where tourism is just beginning to take hold. In these areas, the restaurants found in hotels are your best bet.

Breakfasts and lunch are the main, and most substantial, meals of the day. Some of the smaller restaurants close early in the evening.

International restaurant chains are no strangers to Costa Rica: Pizza Hut, MacDonald's and the like have franchises here. However, fans of these commercial giants should note that these restaurants are found only in the large cities of the Central Valley. On the other hand, some kinds of fast food abound throughout the country. **Pop's** and **Wall's** restaurants, specializing in ice cream, and **AS**, a 24hr chain that serves light meals, are among these. There are also slightly more upscale chains, like **Rosti Pollos**, where you can have Costa Rican–style chicken at the counter or in a sit-down dining room. Another notable chain is the **Musmanni** bakery and pastry shops. They sell differ-

ent kinds of bread and goodies, as well as snacks like turnovers and pizzas. Of course, don't expect high-class cuisine, but their products are usually quite good. Furthermore, there's a branch in al-most every town.

Most menus are in Spanish and English. The bill usually in-cludes a 10% tip *(propina)* and the 13% tax.

There is no such thing as a non-smoking sec-tion in Costa Rican restaurants, though some vegetarian estab-lishments prohibit smoking altogether.

Prices (in $US) listed in this guide are for a meal (drinks not in-cluded) for one person:

$	less than $5
$$	$5 to $10
$$$	$10 to $20
$$$$	$20 to $40
$$$$$	over $40

Types of Restaurants

A *soda* is a small neigh-bourhood restaurant that generally serves local cuisine and fast food (hamburgers, sandwiches, etc.). At lunch, they often serve a *plato del día* (daily special), sometimes referred to as the *ejecutivo* or *comida corrida*.

A *pulpería* is something like a small corner store. These are found

in even the smallest villages and provide a slew of basic necessi-ties: canned goods, beverages, toiletries, bread, milk, and some-times sandwiches and other quick snacks.

Panaderías (bakeries) and *pastelarías* (pastry shops) sometimes serve small meals, sand-wiches and drinks in addition to their usual wares.

Local **cafés** are much the same as those found elsewhere: small establishments where you can relax, chat or read while enjoying a coffee or a light meal in a laid-back atmosphere.

Vegetarian restaurants are popular in Costa Rica, especially in San José. They prepare tasty meals that really let you savour the many fruits and vegetables that grow here! Also, the meals are usually quite inexpensive.

Costa Rican Cuisine

Contrary to what you'd expect if you've only ever had Mexican food, not all Latin American cuisine is spicy! Costa Rican cooking is gener-ally quite mild, and while hot peppers are often served on the side, they are rarely used in food prepara-tion. Fresh coriander, on the other hand, is used in almost every-thing!

For a start, the **tortilla** is literally the bread of Latin America. Tortillas are round thin pancakes, made of cornmeal and cooked in a frying pan. Traditionally cooked by hand on a wood stove, today they are prepared in factories and are increasingly made with white flour. They should not be confused with Spanish tortillas, which are made with eggs and potatoes.

Gallo pinto is Costa Rica's national dish. A mixture of fried rice and red or black beans, it is often served with eggs, meat or vegetables. It can be served for any meal of the day, or for all three! **Casado** is the traditional dish that a wife served her husband in bygone days, thus its name (married). This dish can still be found in restaurants serving *tica* food. It is a combination of various dishes served in generous helpings. Inevitably, there is rice as well as red or black beans along with meat: for example, **picadillo** is a plate of vegetables and minced meat served with one or two salads (cold slaw, potato, etc).

Ceviche is raw white fish or seafood marinated only in lemon juice and seasoned with onions and coriander.

Chicken, or **pollo**, is very popular. Prepared in many different ways, it is the mainstay of many restaurants.

Tamales are small cornmeal pastries stuffed with meat and vegetables. They are usually served at Christmas.

When you order a drink, especially an alcoholic one, you'll be served **bocas** or appetizers. One of these may be a *Ticos* favourite: fried pork rind or **chicharrones**.

Tres leches cake is an incredibly smooth, creamy, sweet indulgence; **arroz con leche** (rice pudding) is another popular dessert.

Freshly squeezed fruit juices (**frescos** and **jugos**), mixed with water or milk, are very popular and are sold everywhere. Made with sun-ripened fruits, these drinks are a real treat!

Wine, Beer and Spirits

Costa Rica is neither a wine producer nor a big importer of wine. Nevertheless, you shouldn't have any difficulty finding a bottle of red or white wine (*vino tinto, vino blanco*). Larger restaurants, especially those specializing in French cuisine, all have a good selection of vintages.

The country's national alcoholic beverage is **guaro**, made from sugar cane. Quality rum and coffee liqueurs are also produced here.

Beer

If you order a beer, you might be surprised to find that it is served on ice! This only makes it cooler and more refreshing, though. Home-brewed beer is also popular: it generally tastes like light, blond American beers.

Entertainment

Most of the nightlife is found in the Central Valley, especially in San José, where bars, nightclubs, theatres, cinemas, and other diversions abound. You shouldn't have any problems finding things to do in the other regions, either. Although cinemas and theatres are rarer in the outlying areas, you will be hard pressed to find a place that doesn't have a bar or a dance club! Bars sometimes serve *bocas* with your drink.

Gambling is also common in Costa Rica, and you can find casinos just about everywhere, especially in San José. Some casinos are located in hotels.

Festivals and Public Holidays

Costa Rica has many holidays, both civil and religious. In addition, there are several regional festivals that are only celebrated in certain parts of the country.

Public Holidays

New Year's Day
January 1

Semana Santa
April 17 to 23, 2000
April 9 to 15, 2001

Festival of Juan Santamarína
April 11

Labour Day
May 1

Anniversary of the Annexation of Guanacaste Province
July 25

Mother's Day
August 15

Independence Day
September 15

All Souls Day
November 2

Christmas Day
December 25

Major Festivals

January
Fiesta Patronales
(Alajuela);
Fiestas de Santa Cruz
(Santa Cruz);

February
Agricultural Fair (San Isidro de El General)

March
Book Fair (San José)
Festival Internacional Los Artes (San José);

April
Festival of Juan Santamarína (Alajuela);

May
Oxcart Parade (Escazú and San Isidro de El General);

July
Guanacaste Festival (Liberia and Santa Cruz): folk dances, music and rodeos;
Festival Internacional de Música (☎282-7724, *national*)

August
Festival Internacional de Música (☎282-7724, *national*);
Festival of the Virgin of Los Angeles (Cartago, Aug 2): religious procession;

Holy Week Processions

Holy Week is a religious holiday in Latin America, sometimes more celebrated than Christmas. In Costa Rica, masses, processions and many dramatizations animate towns and villages during the entire week before Easter. Seated on a bench in a *parque central*, you may be surprised by a multi-coloured parade in which statues are lofted in upraised arms. The Virgin Mary and Mary Magdalene for example, are represented by participants wearing colourful costumes who play leading roles in the celebrations. The festivities themselves sometimes take surprising turns. San Joaquin de Las Flores

in the province of Heredia, for example, is known for extremely realistic renditions of the Stations of the Cross and the Crucifixion in which men submit to genuine torture!...

But in most parishes, these enactments are more restrained and most interesting to watch. Good Friday is the liveliest day. From 9am on, the Stations of the Cross and the Crucifixion are staged pretty much everywhere. Three o'clock signals the death of Jesus and the burial takes place at 4pm. Don't worry, Sunday morning will be much more cheerful, as the resurrection is joyfully celebrated.

September
Independence Day
(national, Sep 15): parades, fireworks and all kinds of celebrations;

October
Puerto Limón Carnival: parades, dances;
Día de la Raza (Oct 12): commemorates Christopher Columbus's arrival in America;

November
All Souls Day (Nov 2): religious processions, pilgrimages;
Festival Internacional de Teatro (San José): theatre performances, street theatre, and other entertainment;

December
Fiesta de Los Negritos (Boruca, Dec 8): costumed dances;
Immaculada Concepción (national, Dec 8): fireworks;
Fiesta de la Yeguita (Nicoya, Dec 12): processions, fireworks, concerts;
Las Posadas (national, Dec 15);
Fiestas de fin de año (San José, Dec 26): procession of horses, parades.

Shopping

Bringing back souvenirs and gifts is certainly one of the many joys of travelling. However, be careful about what you buy. If possible, find out how the item was made so as not to encourage abuse; in some countries, it is still possible to purchase objects made from endangered

animal or vegetable species, even though many international agreements forbid this type of commerce.

Remember that objects made of ivory, coral, tortoiseshell and snakeskin are some of the things you should avoid purchasing.

Some restrictions on importing products derived from animals or plants exist in order to prevent the introduction of non-native species and diseases. Fruit, vegetables, plants and animals, among others, cannot be brought across the border without special authorization.

You can find almost everything in Costa Rica, especially in the Central Valley. Specialty stores, department stores and more can be found in all urban centres. Few of the large international chains have opened stores in Costa Rica, though you might come across some familiar North American names in the shopping centres that have recently opened in the San José area. Every town has a *pulpería* (see p 54), a type of convenience store.

There are people selling fruit, clothing and knick-knacks along the road, even though this is officially prohibited in Costa Rica, at least on the larger routes. Note that bargaining is

not customary in Costa Rica.

Here are some of the main stores you will find in Costa Rica:

Mas X Menos (More or Less) is a very popular chain of supermarkets. There are locations throughout the country, but most are found in the Central Valley (in San José, there is one on Paseo Colón, corner of Calle 26).

The **Automercado** is a supermarket similar to Mas X Menos. One of its locations is in San José on Calle 3, between Avenida 4 and 5.

La Gloria is a large chain store. The San José outlet is somewhat run down, but other locations are clean and modern.

Every urban centre has its own **central market** (*mercado central*). This is a great place to walk around and mingle with the locals to get a taste of what everyday life is like in the country—and of the food, as well!

It is illegal to buy Pre-Columbian artifacts and goods made from animals that are on the endangered species list. If someone offers to sell you either of these, they are either illegal or fake.

The 13% sales tax is included in the prices marked on items.

What to Bring Back

Colourful **summer clothing** (T-shirts, dresses, blouses) and **accessories** (scarves, hats) with lively patterns make charming souvenirs.

Reproductions of Pre-Columbian objects also make great gifts.

Wood carvings are wonderful mementos. They come in all shapes and sizes, and can be bought retail, wholesale, or directly from artisans. Sarchí (see p 117) is a town in the Central Valley that is particularly renowned for its wood carvings.

Costa Rican coffee is practically a must, whether you buy the beans, ground coffee, coffee liqueur (Café Rica), or coffee essence. It is available just about everywhere, but some specialized souvenir shops carry all of the above under one roof.

Several shops in San José specialize in imported cigars.

Paper made from banana, coffee or tobacco leaves is more and more common and particularly attractive. Writing paper, notebooks and diaries are made of this paper, which comes in various colours.

Time Change

Costa Rica is 6hrs behind Greenwich Mean Time (Britain), and 7hrs behind the rest of Europe. It is in the Central Time Zone (Chicago, Houston, Winnipeg), 1hr behind the Eastern Time Zone (Montréal, Toronto, New York). It does not observe daylight savings time.

Business Hours

Banks are open Monday to Friday from 9am to 3pm. Government offices are open Monday to Friday from 9am to 4pm, while private offices are usually open until 6pm.

Stores are usually open Monday to Saturday from 9am to 6pm, and are closed Sundays.

The Other Culture

Culture Shock

You will soon visit a new country, meet interesting people, taste different flavours, smell unknown aromas, see surprising things... in short, discover a culture unlike your own. This experience will most probably be a positive one, but it could also unsettle you more than you expect. Culture shock can hit anyone and anywhere, even when you're not that far from home.

This is why you should be sensitive to the symptoms of culture shock when travelling to a foreign country. Faced with a lifestyle that is different than yours, your usual reference points will probably become obsolete. Indeed, you might not understand the language, have a hard time comprehending local beliefs and habits, and have difficulty approaching people; some things might even seem unacceptable to you at first. But don't panic: humans have a great ability to adapt. All you need are the right tools.

Remember that cultural diversity is a richness! You shouldn't necessarily try to find your usual reference points; rather, try to live as the people around you do and understand their lifestyle. If you remain courteous, modest and sensitive, they will certainly be more willing and able to help you. Respect is the key that will make any situation better, but remember that it is not enough to simply tolerate what seems different to you; respect is much more. Who knows, discovering new cultures could become one of your favourite aspects of travel!

The Responsible Traveller

Travelling will probably be an enriching experience for you. But will it be the same for your hosts? The question of whether or not tourism is good for a host country is controversial. On one hand, tourism brings many advantages, such as the economic development of a region, the promotion of a culture and intercultural exchange; on the other hand, tourism can have negative impacts: increase in crime, deepening of inequalities, environmental destruction, etc. But one thing is for sure: your journey will have an impact on your destination.

This is rather obvious when we speak of the environment. You should be as careful not to pollute the environment of your host country as you are at home. We hear it often enough: we all live on the same planet! But when it comes to social, cultural and even economic aspects, it can be more difficult to evaluate the impact of our travels. Be aware of the reality around you, and ask yourself what the repercussions will be before acting. Remember that you may make an impression that is much different than the one you wish to give.

Regardless of the type of travelling we choose, it is up to each and every one of us to develop a social conscience and to assume responsibility for our actions in a foreign country. Common sense, respect, altruism, and a hint of modesty are useful tools that will go a long way.

Laws and Traditions in Foreign Countries

Obviously, it is not necessary to memorize all the laws of the country you will be visiting. However, you should know that when you are in a foreign land, you are subject to its laws—even if you are not a citizen of that country. Therefore, never assume that something that is allowed in your country will be allowed elsewhere, and don't forget to take cultural differences into account. When travelling abroad, certain gestures or attitudes that may seem insignificant to you could actually get you into hot water... Therefore, the best way to prevent misunderstandings is to be sensitive to the traditions of your host country.

Travellers with Disabilities

Tourist facilities everywhere are becoming more and more responsive to the needs of travellers who have difficulties getting around, and Costa Rica is no exception. However, aside from establishments that cater specifically to tourists, buildings and public spaces are not really designed with these considerations in mind.

A non-profit organization, FAUNA (Fundación para el Acceso Universal a la Naturaleza—Foundation for Universal Access to Nature), has been established specifically to make the country's beautiful sites accessible to everyone. For more information, E-mail Monic Chabot (*chabote@racsa.co.cr*).

Travelling with Children

Travelling with children, however young they may be, can be a pleasant experience. A few precautions and ample preparation are the keys to a fun trip.

Aboard the Airplane

A good reclining stroller will allow you to bring an infant or small child everywhere you go and will also be great for naps, if needed. In the airport, it will be easy to carry with you, especially since you are allowed to bring the stroller up to plane's gates.

Travellers with children can board the plane

first, avoiding long line-ups. If your child is under the age of two, remember to ask for seats at the front of the plane when reserving your tickets since they offer more room and are more comfortable for long flights, especially if you've got a toddler on your lap. Some airlines even offer baby cribs.

If you are travelling with an infant, be sure to prepare the necessary food for the flight, as well as an extra meal in case of a delay. Remember to bring enough diapers and moist towels, and a few toys might not be a bad idea!

For older kids who might get bored once the thrill of taking off has faded, books and activities such as drawing material and games will probably do the trick.

When taking off and landing, changes in air pressure may cause some discomfort. In this case, some say that the nipple of a bottle can soothe infants, while a piece of chewing gum will have the same effect for older children.

In Hotels

Many hotels are well equipped for children, and there is usually no extra fee for travelling with an infant. Many hotels and bed and breakfasts have cribs; ask for one when reserving your room. You may have to pay extra for children, however, but the supplement is generally low.

Car Rentals

Most car rental agencies rent car seats for children. They are usually not very expensive. Ask for one when making your reservation.

The Sun

Needless to say, a child's skin requires strong protection against the sun; in fact, it is actually preferable not to expose toddlers to its harsh rays. Before going to the beach, remember to apply sunscreen (SPF 25 for children, 35 for infants). If you think your child will spend a long time under the sun, you should consider purchasing a sunscreen with SPF 60.

Children of all ages should wear a hat that provides good coverage for the head throughout the day.

Swimming

Children usually get quite excited about playing in the waves and can do so for hours on end. However, parents must be very careful and watch them constantly; accidents can happen in a matter of seconds. Ideally, an adult should accompany children into the water, especially the younger ones, and stand farther out in the water so that the kids can play between the beach and the supervising adult. This way, he or she can quickly intervene in case of an emergency.

For infants and toddlers, some diapers are especially designed for swimming, such as "Little Swimmers" by Huggies. These are quite useful when having fun in the water!

Women Travelling Alone

Women travelling alone should not encounter any problems. For the most part, people are friendly and not aggressive. Generally, men are respectful toward women, and harassment is uncommon, although Costa Rican males do have a tendency to flirt. Of course, a certain level of caution should be exercised; avoid making eye contact, ignore any advances or comments and do not walk around alone in poorly lit areas at night.

Gay and Lesbian Life

Costa Rica has a reputation of being more open towards gays and lesbians than its neighbouring countries. Some hotels and businesses now openly welcome a gay clientele. Thus, it is becoming much easier for gay and lesbian travellers to find establishments that cater specifically to them. The gay magazine **Gente 10** is available at select locations across the country.

Miscellaneous

Religion

Although Costa Rica is officially a Catholic country, freedom of religion exists. Ask hotel staff for a list of local places of worship, or check the newspaper for the times of the services. Of course, the farther you go from the Central Valley, the fewer non-Catholic religious establishments you will find. The Caribbean coast has a number of Protestant churches, though.

Electricity

Like in North America, wall sockets take plugs with two flat pins and work on an alternating current of 110 volts (60 cycles). Sockets do not always have the third hole that grounds the current, so bring along the appropriate adaptor.

Some Interesting Associations

The following is a short list of associations and special interest groups that have offices in Costa Rica:

Ornithological Club of Costa Rica
☎267-7191

Oenological Club of Costa Rica
☎228-9666

Canadian Club of Costa Rica
☎282-5580

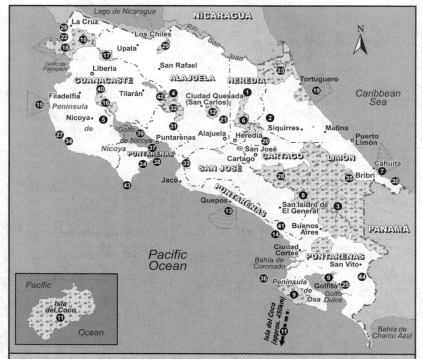

Parks and Nature Reserves

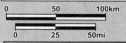

0	50	100km
0	25	50mi

©ULYSSES

1. Estación Biológica La Selva
2. Jardín Botánico Las Cusingas
3. Parque Internacional La Amistad
4. Parque Nacional Arenal
5. Parque Nacional Barra Honda
6. Parque Nacional Braulio Carrillo
7. Parque Nacional Cahuita
8. Parque Nacional Chirripó
9. Parque Nacional Corcovado
10. Parque Nacional Guanacaste
11. Parque Nacional Isla del Coco
12. Parque Nacional Juan Castro Blanco
13. Parque Nacional Manuel Antonio
14. Parque Nacional Marino Ballena
15. Parque Nacional Marino Las Baulas de Guanacaste
16. Parque Nacional Palo Verde
17. Parque Nacional Rincón de la Vieja
18. Parque Nacional Santa Rosa
19. Parque Nacional Tortuguero
20. Parque Nacional Volcán Irazú
21. Parque Nacional Volcán Poás
22. Refugio Nacional Bahía Junquillal
23. Refugio Nacional de Fauna Silvestre Barra del Colorado
24. Refugio Nacional de Fauna Silvestre Curú
25. Refugio Nacional de Fauna Silvestre Golfito
26. Refugio Nacional de Fauna Silvestre Isla Bolaños
27. Refugio Nacional de Fauna Silvestre Ostional
28. Refugio Nacional de Fauna Silvestre Tapantí
29. Refugio Nacional de Vida Silvestre Caño Negro
30. Refugio Nacional de Vida Silvestre Gandoca-Manzanillo
31. Refugio Silvestre Peñas Blancas
32. Reserva Biológica Bosque Nuboso Monteverde
33. Reserva Biológica Carara
34. Reserva Biológica de Nosara
35. Reserva Biológica Hitoy-Cerere
36. Reserva Biológica Isla del Caño
37. Reserva Biológica Isla Guayabo
38. Reserva Biológica Isla Negrito
39. Reserva Biológica Isla Pájaros
40. Reserva Biológica Lomas Barbudal
41. Reserva Biológica Oro Verde
42. Reserva del Bosque Nuboso del Colegio de Santa Elena
43. Reserva Natural Absoluta Cabo Blanco
44. Wilson Botanical Gardens

Outdoors

Costa Rica is
a nature-lover's paradise. Almost every kind of outdoor activity imaginable is available here.

The country has modern services to help you actively enjoy its vast open spaces, and most agencies are highly professional, punctual, safety-conscious, respectful of the environment and receptive to clients' questions and comments. Costa Ricans are proud, honest and courteous, and determined to make whichever outdoor activity you choose a highly enjoyable experience.

Suggested outdoor activities in each region, as well as names of agencies and places where "nature" and "adventure" invariably go together (mainly national parks) are listed in each chapter. What follows is an overview of the main outdoor activities available in this country, where the favourite local expression *Pura vide* (pure life) takes on a whole new meaning.

Parks

Costa Rica has 23 national parks, which make up 12% of the country's total area. In addition, there are nine ecological reserves, 30 national wildlife reserves, 12 forest reserves, 30 protected zones and 12 swamps. The total of all these protected areas covers 25% of the country. If you include the constantly growing number of private reserves, the percentage of the country's land found in conservation areas is the highest in the world.

The system of national parks has been completely restructured since 1995, in order to support decentralized regional planning. The parks are managed by the **SINAC** (Sistema Nacional de Areas de Conservación), a committee formed from the **MINAE** (Ministerio de Ambiante y Energía). The country is divided into 11 regions which correspond to the 11 conservation areas (*areas de conservación*) in which the parks are found.

There is usually an information centre in one of the larger cities in each region.

Guajira Morada

If you visit several of Costa Rica's national parks, you will notice that they are all quite different. Therefore don't expect the quality of services to be the same from one park to another, as you would in Canada or the United States, where park infrastructure is more consistent. The quality of park entrances, accommodations, camping facilities, picnic areas, maps and hiking trails vary considerably, as do the access roads leading to them, which are often unpaved and only passable with a four-wheel-drive vehicle.

Of course, each national park has its own unique features and natural splendours. However, because some of them really deserve a special mention, they have been star-rated like tourist attractions (★, ★★ or ★★★) to help you decide which ones to include in your itiner-

ary. **Rincón de la Vieja**, **Chirripó**, **Tortuguero**, **Corovado** and **Irazú** are absolute musts, and are sure to amaze you with their beauty and rich variety of flora and fauna.

Some parks are busier than others. In 1996, Parque Nacional Barra Honda received only 1,265 visitors (ranking 21st in popularity), while Parque Nacional Volcán Poás welcomed close to 175,000 (ranking no. 1). Together, the parks had a total of 658,657 visitors, of which 389,883 were Costa Ricans while 268,774 were foreigners. The parks of the Poás volcano, Manuel Antonio, and the Irazú volcano accounted for half of the visitors.

Admission to some parks and reserves is limited to protect these natural habitats from suffering too much damage. The parks of the Poás volcano, Manuel Antonio, the Irazú volcano, Tortuguero, and Carara all have visitor quotas.

Entrance fees to the parks is **$6** per person for foreign visitors, and $0.85 for Costa Ricans. Rights of access to these areas were vehemently contested in 1994, when park entry fees jumped from less than $2 per person to $15 per person! Travellers refused to pay this

price and avoided going to the parks, causing the number of visitors to decline drastically. In April 1996, the government lowered the rates to Also, the government is presently studying the possibility of varying a park's entry fees according to its relative importance. These new, more equitable fees might be in place at the start of 2001.

Here is a price list for the services found in the various parks:

● Overnight stay in one of the parks or at the park-keeper's house ($2/pers.);

● Overnight stay in dormitory-style accommodations in the Parque Nacional Santa Rosa ($14.60/pers./night);

● Camping ($1.25/pers./day)

● Booking a conference room ($14.60/day);

● Using a computer hook-up ($1.70/day);

● Using a laboratory ($1.70/day);

● Obtaining an underwater diving permit in protected zones ($4.20/pers./day);

● Parking (car $0.45, minivan $0.65, bus $1.05/day), when not included in the entrance fee;

• Hiring a guide from the national park service ($5/hr).

Please note: the telephone numbers for the visitor centres and park administration offices are listed in the chapters corresponding to the region in which the parks are found.

In Costa Rica, call ☎*192* (toll free) for general information about all national parks. You can also contact the offices of **SINAC** (☎*283-8004, ≈283-7343, Sistema Nacional de Areas de Conservación*) in San José.

Fundación de Parques Nacionales
Mon to Fri 8am to 5pm
Avenida 15 and Calle 23/25 near the Santa Terisita church
☎*257-2239*
≈*222-4732*
The Fundación de Parques Nacionales, or FPN, is an excellent source of information about visiting the various national parks. The staff is friendly and dedicated, and some speak English (ask for Alexia).

Outdoor Activities

Swimming

Costa Rica has dozens of idyllic beaches per-

Undertow

If you find yourself caught in strong undertow, remember that it doesn't do any good to struggle. The current is stronger than you. Instead, let yourself be carried towards the sea despite your reluctance. This way, you'll get out of the current without losing your strength. Once you're back in a calm spot, start heading for shore again, but swim diagonally towards it. If you go straight for it, you'll again be confronted by the force of the undertow. Swimming on the diagonal will make it easier for you to cross it.

fect for swimming. The salty waters of the Pacific Ocean and Caribbean Sea are warm—sometimes almost too warm! Some beaches are known around the world for their excellent surfing conditions: the waves are often high and very powerful. Keep in mind that these are not the best places for family swimming.

If you go to the beach with children, it is strongly recommended that you always accompany them into the water, or at least keep a close watch on them. In some places, the waves break almost on the beach itself, and children, as well as adults, can easily be knocked down by a sudden wave.

Rafting

If you've never gone rafting before, this is your perfect opportunity to try it, since Costa Rica's rivers are among the best in the world for this sport. Because some sections of the rivers are very calm while others are quite violent, you have plenty of choices—everything from a pleasant excursion through the surrounding scenery to a wild and unforgettable adventure that will get your adrenalin pumping.

The **Río Pacuare** is considered one of the most spectacular rivers in the tropics. Running through untamed forest, and comprising several waterfalls along the way, the river narrows as it enters a picturesque canyon that has some perfect spots for bathing. The trip is ranked moderately difficult (classes III and IV), but beginners in good physical shape and with a taste for adventure will enjoy it.

Outdoors

La Bandera Azul Ecologica

The Instituto Costarricense de Turismo (ICT) has set up an original program to control the condition of the country's beaches and avoid as many of the harmful effects of frantic development as possible. The distinction "Bandera Azul Ecologica" is awarded to coastal communities that work to safeguard the environment by maintaining necessary sanitary conditions. What's more, the presence of a blue flag indicates that local groups are working to sensitize the rest of the community, so that everyone will do their part in keeping the beaches clean and safe. In 1999, some 30 beaches proudly displayed this symbol of their award-winning efforts.

Unfortunately, the canyon is threatened by a huge hydro-electric dam that is scheduled to be built soon, which will definitely put an end to rafting in the area.

Another river that is renowned for its rafting possibilities is the **Río Reventazón**, which runs parallel to the Río Pacuare, slightly to the northwest. It has an easy stretch (classes II and III) that is perfect for beginners, as well as very difficult sections (classes IV and V) that will make even the most seasoned adventurers sweat a little.

In addition, the **Río Corobicí**, **Río Sarapiquí**, **Río Peñas Blancas** and **Río Chirripó** are also good for rafting. The **Río Corobicí**, located in Guanacaste, has a long, easy section that is a real boon for birdwatchers, since its leisurely pace gives them time to observe dozens of species of birds, as well as iguanas, monkeys and caimans.

Horseback Riding

You will be surprised by the number of horses in Costa Rica, especially in Guanacaste, which is sometimes called the "Far West" of Costa Rica. Because cars are relatively expensive, roads are rutted or in generally poor condition, and distances between villages are quite short, many Costa Ricans use horses to get around in the mountains and the countryside.

As a result, it is easy to find places that rent horses. However, caution is advised: while Costa Ricans are excellent riders, visitors are often novices. Look around (hotels are good places to start) for horses that are calm and used to being ridden.

Also, Costa Ricans do not usually use bits, a metal piece that is put in a horse's mouth to help direct it. Some tourists find that without it, they do not feel they have absolute control over the animal. Also, remember that it can get extremely hot (about 35°C or 41°F) on the beaches and along the coast, and that horses, like people, are susceptible to dehydration. If you plan to ride for several hours, ask the attendant about rules regarding rests, water, etc. and set the pace accordingly.

Golf

Like in North America and Europe, more and more people are discovering the pleasure of this sport in Costa Rica. While hardly any facilities existed several years ago, four new golf courses were built between 1996 and 1998, and there are plans for several more in the next few years. Some greens are located in the Central Valley near San José, while others, such as the **Playa Tambor**, **Playa Grande** and **Playa Conchal** courses are magnificently situated by the sea.

Costa Rica Golf Adventures
☎/≈*446-5547*
golf@centralamerica.com
To find out more about the various golf courses, and for the most up-to-date information about the newest additions, contact Costa Rica Golf Adventures.

Kayaking

Costa Rica's many rivers will set any kayak-lover's heart aflutter. The **Río Pacuare** and the **Río Reventazón** near the city of Siquirres (Limón province), the **Río Corobicí** near Cañas (Guanacaste), the **Río Sarapiquí** near Puerto Viejo (Heredia), the **Río Peñas Blancas** and the **Río Chirripó** near San Isidro de El General (Puntarenas) are all ideal places to practice this sport. However,

since these rivers are also popular with rafters, you will sometimes find whole groups of river enthusiasts sharing the waterway with you.

Sea kayaking is becoming increasingly popular in Costa Rica. Since the country is situated between two oceans (the Atlantic and Pacific) and has 1,228km (763mi) of shoreline, the potential growth for this sport is enormous. While few opportunities exist as of yet, the **Nicoya Peninsula** (north Pacific coast) and the **Osa Peninsula** (south Pacific coast) have calm waters where beginners can discover this wonderful sport that brings you close to the sea.

Wildlife Observation

The rules are simple: keep your eyes open, your ears alert and remain absolutely still! Costa Rica is the perfect place to observe wild animals, which will enchant you and give you a deeper appreciation for nature and the importance of preserving natural habitats. Monkeys, giant sea turtles, agoutis, sloths, white-tailed deer, iguanas, lizards, caimans, crocodiles, frogs and butterflies are among the most frequently seen animals in the

country, and are especially abundant in the national parks and reserves.

Although there are thousands of mammals, butterflies, reptiles, insects, fish and amphibians in Costa Rica, some visitors leave complaining that they didn't see any wildlife during their stay, even in the remote regions of the country. This is because many of these animals have developed highly effective forms of camouflage, stay well out of the way of humans, or only come out of hiding at night. Thus, we **strongly recommend that you go with a nature guide** who knows the best times and places to see dozens of animals and can answer your questions.

Bird-Watching

With 850 bird species, Costa Rica is undoubtedly one of the best places in the world for bird-watching. People come from around the world to see the famous **resplendent quetzal** *(Pharomachrus*

Outdoors

mocinno), which inhabits the **Monteverde** reserve, as well as the brilliantly coloured **scarlet macaw** *(Ara macao)*, which is found almost exclusively at the **Carara** reserve and on the **Osa Peninsula** (in the Parque Nacional Corcovado).

Hiring the services of a nature guide will allow you to see the largest number of bird species during your excursion—since the forest is very dense and the trees are covered in moss, creepers and all sorts of epiphytic plants, making it extremely difficult to see certain kinds of birds. Above all, don't forget your binoculars!

Fishing

With its numerous mountain rivers and lakes, including Lake Arenal, which is the largest in the country, Costa Rica provides many possibilities for freshwater fishing, including rainbow trout and rainbow perch.

With the Pacific Ocean on one side, and the Caribbean Sea on the other, Costa Rica has also made a name for itself in deep-sea fishing. You can catch swordfish, tarpon, pike, marlin, shark, sailfish, mackerel and tuna, among others. **Tarpon**, which is usually caught

between January and May on the Caribbean coast, is said to be best near Tortuguero. This enormous fish weighs over 35kg (77lbs) on average and is extremely ferocious, putting up a good fight that is as exhausting as it is memorable!

Windsurfing

Windsurfers from around the world come to experience the superb **Lake Arenal**, just west of the Arenal volcano (1,633m or 5,358ft), which is one of the planet's most active volcanoes. Measuring 39km (24mi) in length, and 5km (3mi) in width, the lake is the largest in Costa Rica. Favourable winds make Lake Arenal the best freshwater place to windsurf in Central America.

Scuba Diving and Snorkelling

With its 1, 016km (631mi) Pacific coast and its 212km (132mi) Atlantic coast, Costa Rica has many beaches and underwater escarpments from which you can go snorkelling and scuba diving. The southern section of the Atlantic coast, between Cahuita and Manzanillo, has superb

coral reefs. Certain islands in the Pacific, such as Isla del Caño, Isla del Coco, Isla Ballena and Isla Tortuga, as well as the countless bays of the Nicoya Peninsula (Guanacaste), are ideal places for snorkelling and scuba diving. Several agencies offer introductory courses and sea excursions.

Hiking

Hiking is one of the best ways to explore Costa Rica's parks, reserves and wildlife conservation areas. Since the country is small and mountainous, there are plenty of spectacular mountain hikes that pass by the major volcanoes (Rincón de la Vieja, Arenal, Irazú, Poás, etc.), as well as some mountains (Chiripó, Urán, etc.) with altitudes of over 3,000m (1,864ft). Some parks have scenic trails along the coast (Corcovado, Manuel Antonio, Cabo Blanco, Santa Rosa, Cahuita, Gandoca-Manzanillo, etc.). Though they are not very steep, these paths are strenuous because of the stifling heat and humidity. Luckily, there is almost always a beach where you can refresh yourself.

Many of the parks and reserves we visited have a small network of pathways, but few have extensive hiking trails. However, we found that **Chirripó, Rincón de la Vieja, Corcovado**, and **Monteverde** are some of the country's best places for hiking.

Bungee Jumping

Bungee jumping only caught on in Costa Rica several years ago. If you long to launch yourself from a bridge with your feet firmly attached to an elastic cord, call Tropical Bungee (☎233-6455), the only company offering this service. Jumps take place from the bridge spanning the **Río Colorado**, about an hour's drive from San José. It costs $45 for the first jump, and $25 for additional ones.

Surfing

Costa Rica has numerous beaches where you can go surfing, both on its Pacific and Caribbean coast. While some are well-suited for beginners, others attract die-hard surfers from around the world with their incredible waves.

Among the most popular beaches, where you can watch expert surfers in action, are **Salsa Brava, Naranjo** (Witch's Rock), **Tamarindo, Mal País, Hermosa, Dominical, Matapalo** and **Pavones**. The last beach has some of the longest waves in the world.

Cycling

Costa Rica's smaller roads are perfect for cycling. Paradoxically, the many potholes work in cyclists' favour, as they slow down traffic, making conditions safer. Many of these roads are unsurfaced, so mountain bikes are your best bet. However, once you leave the Central Valley, temperatures can get very high, preventing even the most determined cyclists from undertaking long excursions. If you really want to put yourself to the test, tackle the **Irazú volcano** (1,432m or 4,698ft), about 30km (19mi) north of the city of Cartago (Central Valley).

Canopy Tours

Tours of the forest canopy are very popular in Costa Rica. They involve climbing to solid platforms found at the top of one or several of the highest trees in a certain area. Some agencies have a pulley system rigged between the platforms, allowing you to travel from one to the next along cables. For the less adventurous, there are tours on networks of suspended bridges or motorized seats. You can also choose just to stay on one platform from which the surrounding flora and fauna (monkeys, parrots, toucans, orchids, etc.) can peacefully be observed. Canopy tours are available in almost all regions of Costa Rica.

San José

T he first thing that will strike you about the capital of Costa Rica is the feeling of being removed from nature—something you are not likely to experience elsewhere in the country.

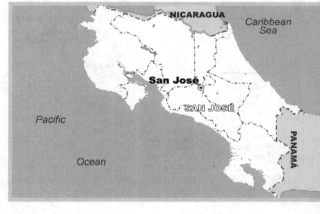

I ndeed, at first sight San José ★★ seems noisy, smoky and generally unremarkable. To discover its character, the city must be experienced over a certain period of time. Of course, it does not quite have the charm of old colonial cities, nor the sleek look of a North American megalopolis. But San José is a vibrant place with no shortage of people to mingle with in a safe environment. Here, you can go out every night, enjoy a delicious ice cream in the pedestrian zone with swarms of people streaming past, delve into the country's cultural scene, and succumb to the delights of its international cuisine.

S an José only became the nation's capital in the 19th century, when it supplanted the older and more historic city of Cartago following a short-lived civil war that led to the country's independence. Since the beginning of the 20th century, the city has grown steadily, and today its million inhabitants (suburbs included) constitute almost a third of the country's population. San José is still a constantly expanding city—the largest in the country—and has the

energy and restlessness that goes along with it.

I t seems appropriate that San José, the nation's capital, should lie in the middle of everything. Its urban sprawl is the point of convergence in the Central Valley, as it is centrally located amid the region's other major cities. This region, in turn, lies in the heart of the country as a whole. Furthermore, San José plays an integral role in the country's economy, transportation system and cultural life, all of which are centred around it.

In addition to all this, San José is only a short distance from the Central Valley's national parks. It is definitely worthwhile to visit this city, around which much of the country's life revolves.

Finding Your Way Around

Finding your way around San José is easy. Most of the city is laid out in a basic grid, with *calles* (streets) running north and south and *avenidas* (avenues) running east and west. Furthermore, almost all of the city streets and avenues are numbered, starting at the city centre where Avenida Central intersects Calle Central, and increasing as they extend outwards.

This orderly system is especially useful since houses are generally not numbered (see p 41). Instead, addresses are given in metres in relation to specific intersections of streets and avenues, and you will have to find your way according to these. Costa Ricans often use popular landmarks (for instance, "at Calle 5 and Avenida 7, behind the Holiday Inn") when giving directions.

Avenida Central, which becomes Paseo Colón, and Avenida 2 are the main roads leading into the capital from the west, via the highway from the airport.

The **Coca Cola** district that borders San José's central market is noisy and lively, but poor, and should be avoided after dark. Conversely, **Barrio Amón**, in north-central San José, is the city's charming historic district—it is even designated as such by the authorities—with some of the finest little hotels in the capital, as well as many cultural activities and night spots. You would be hard-pressed to find a completely quiet street, however. The calmer **Aranjurez** district is also close to the heart of the city, and some of its residences are being converted into hotels.

Escazú is one of San José's affluent suburbs where wealthy homeowners have taken up residence in the foothills just west of the city. This district boasts a certain number of high quality hotels and restaurants in a natural setting. **Pavas** (where the American embassy is located) has a few hotels and restaurants, but **Sabana** has many more and also contains La Sabana, a huge recreational park. **Rohrmoser** is another of the capital's posh tranquil neighbourhoods but has few hotels.

On the east side, **San Pedro** and **Los Yoses** are also quite fashionable San José districts. The former contains the University of Costa Rica and a few good, quiet hotels, while the latter boasts several embassies, restaurants and comfortable accommodations. Lastly, **Tournón**, just north of downtown, encompasses the popular little El Pueblo shopping centre and a few hotels.

The stretch of the General Cañas Highway leading to the international airport, located outside San José, is dotted with a whole series of large hotels that make use of the sizeable plots of land and their convenient location on the expressway. In this area, you will find the **Cariari** district.

Like in other major cities around the world, prostitution exists in San José. The south part of Morazán Park and the Coca Cola district are the so-called "red-light districts," as is the stretch of Calle 7 between Avenidas 1 and 3.

If you want to lose yourself in a crowd, stroll along the downtown stretch of **Avenida Central** that is closed off to traffic; it is often bustling with people and activities.

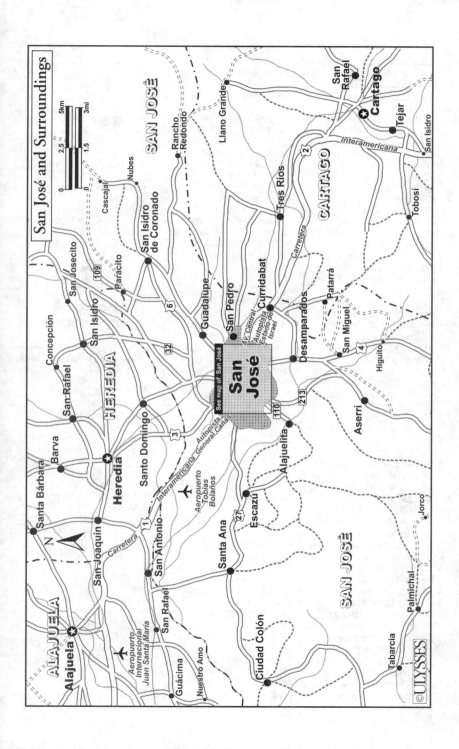

By Bus

San José is the hub where most of Costa Rica's inter-city, regional and international bus routes converge.

There are many departures from the Coca Cola district, located just west of the city centre and Mercado Central. The bus stops are scattered along main thoroughfares around the **Terminus Coca Cola**, located on Avenida 1 between Calles 16 and 18. For example, the coaches bound for the suburb of **Escazú** as well as **Nicoya** and Guanacaste-area beaches stop at the quadrilateral just west of the terminus. Those heading to **San Isidro de El General, San Ramón, Liberia** and **Playa del Coco** are found just east of the terminus. Buses for the **Volcán Poás, Alajuela** or **Heredia** are a little farther south, on Avenida 2, by the San Juan de Dios hospital. If you are not using the hotel shuttle, you can take the regular Alajuela-bound bus which also goes to the **international airport**. Along northbound Calle 12 are the coaches for **Tilarán, Monteverde, Puerto Jiménez, Guápiles, Puerto Viejo de Sarapiquí, San Vito, Playa Sámara, Playa Tamarindo, Playa Panamá** and **Playa Hermosa**. Departures for **Quepos, Manuel Antonio** and **Playa Jacó** as well as **Ciudad**

Quesada (San Carlos) leave from the Coca Cola terminal.

Departures for **Irazú** *(Avenida 2, near the Teatro Nacional)*, **Cahuita** *(Calle Central, Avenida 9/11)*, **Puerto Limón** *(Avenida 3, Calle 19, east of Parque Nacional)*, **Turrialba** *(Calle 13, Avenida 6)* and **Puntarenas** *(Calle 16, Avenida 10)* are at other locations around the city, but still downtown.

South of the Coca Cola bus terminal, the Tracopa company *(Avenida 18, Calle 4, ☎221-4214)* offers several daily departures for southern Costa Rica: **Ciudad Neily, Golfito, Palmar Norte** and **San Vito**.

The Sacsa company *(Calle 5, Avenida 18, ☎233-5350)* has daily departures for **Cartago**, in eastern Costa Rica. Travel within the valley only costs a few dollars, no matter how far away the destination.

For a list of addresses of the other main bus companies, see p 41.

To obtain an up-to-date list of the **city bus** routes (i.e. those to the suburbs), head to the ICT (see further below). Buses run frequently and make many stops, but you won't have to use them to visit the city centre, as everything is within walking distance.

By Taxi

There is no shortage of taxis in San José. There are many taxi stands (on Avenida 2, near the Ministerio de l'Economía, for example) and you can flag one down in the street any time of day or night. All taxis are red with a yellow sign on their front doors (see also p 41).

Practical Information

Tourist Information

As we mentioned earlier, the **Instituto Costarricense de Turismo** (ICT) customer service is not yet well set up to answer travellers' questions. A small information office sometimes opens its doors on the Plaza de la Cultura, but generally you have to go the institute's main office *(5/7 Avenida 4, Calle)* to get the information you want. However, hotels in the capital and several companies will also be able to help you out. Moreover, as we've also said, the government is constantly working to improve its services for foreign travellers.

San José

● ATTRACTIONS

1. Parque La Sabana
2. Museo de Arte Costarricense
3. University of Costa Rica Campus

○ ACCOMMODATIONS

1. Americano del Este
2. Aparthotel El Sesteo
3. Aparthotel La Sabana
4. Aparthotel Los Yoses
5. Aparthotel Maria Alexandra
6. Ara Macao
7. Bergerac
8. Casa Las Orquídeas
9. Colours
10. Corobici
11. Cristina
12. D'Galah
13. Don Fadrique
14. Don Paco Inn
15. Hampton Inn
16. Herradura
17. Irazu
18. Jacques et Helena
19. La Granja
20. Marriot
21. Melia Cariari
22. Palma Real
23. Parque del Lago
24. Pico Blanco Inn
25. Pine Tree Inn
26. Posada El Quijote
27. Radisson
28. Residencias de Golf
29. Rincón del Valle
30. San José
31. Tennis Club
32. Toruma
33. Villa Tournón

● RESTAURANTS

1. Angus Steak House
2. El Chicote
3. Il Bagatto
4. La Esquina de Los Mariscos
5. La Masia
6. Las Tunas
7. Lukas
8. Pastelaria Giacomin
9. Supermercado Yaohan

© ULYSSES

Banks and Foreign Exchange Offices

There are many banks in San José, especially downtown. Many of them have ATMs (automated teller machines), so you don't have to wait in the long lines for the tellers. Avoid making bank transactions on the street at night. Exchange rates and bank administrative fees are reasonable in Costa Rica, so it is not worth taking the risk of using money changers on the street.

Health

Hospital San Juan de Dios
Avenida 2, Calle 14
☎257-6282
The Hospital San Juan de Dios is a very large general hospital in downtown San José.

Hospital San José
Autopista Fernández, near Multi-Plaza.
☎231-0433
This hospital is located outside of the city.

Mail, Fax, Telegraph and Internet

San José's main post office is the Correo Central (*Calle 2, Avenida 1/ 3; Mon to Fri 8am to midnight, Sat 8am to noon*). The mail boxes for out-going letters and postcards are at the entrance, on the left.

Radiográfica
Avenida 5, Calle Central/1
You can dispatch telegrams and send or receive faxes at Radiográfica. Long-distance phone calls can also be made here, or from phone booths on the street.

As the Internet is widely used in Costa Rica (see p 50), the capital justifiably prides itself in having several cybercafés. Overall, their rates are pretty much the same, around $2 per hour, but some offer various deals. Their facilities can also vary a great deal: some just line up their computers without any ceremony, while others offer a real little café that is pleasant to visit even if you don't have a message to send! Among the latter variety, the **CyberCafe** (☎233-3310), located in the basement of the Centro Las Arcadas, just near the Plaza de la Cultura, has a convivial atmosphere.

Newspapers, Magazines and Books

The small magazine store next to the Supermercado Yaohan (*opposite the Corobici hotel*) sells many of the major Western newspapers and all kinds of periodicals: *El País, Le Monde, Le Figaro, The Wall Street Journal, USA Today*. It also has a good Costa Rican book section.

A few major hotels offer a selection of newspapers, as does Librería Lehmann (*Avenida Central, Calle 1/3*).

Exploring

We suggest you start your tour San José's west end, on the fringes of La Sabana Metropolitan Park. Proceed through the northern part of the city to the centre of town, and then continue east through Barrio Amón, and eventually return to downtown. The tour ends with a stroll through the Paseo de los Estudiantes district, on the south side.

Josefinos love their **Parque La Sabana** ★. Many recreational activities are possible in this vast green space, right in the capital. It has numerous sports facilities (an Olympic-size pool; footpaths and jogging tracks; tennis, volleyball and basketball courts; fúbol and baseball fields; a palaestra, stadium and more) and many tree-shaded picnic and rest areas and an artificial lake, all of which are unique to San José. Furthermore, the Museo de Arte Costarricense is located in the park, on Paseo Colón, which runs into the city. It is surprising to know that this extraordinary green space is located on the

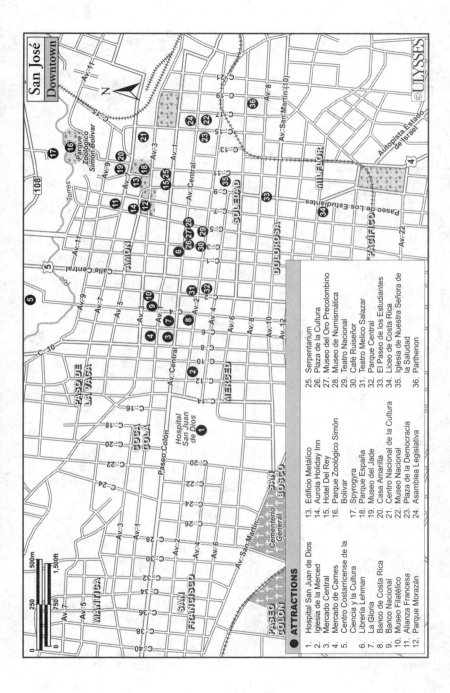

San José
Downtown

© ULYSSES

ATTRACTIONS

1. Hospital San Juan de Dios
2. Iglesia de la Merced
3. Mercado Central
4. Mercado de Carnes
5. Centro Costarricense de la Ciencia y la Cultura
6. Librería Lehman
7. La Gloria
8. Banco de Costa Rica
9. Banco Nacional
10. Museo Filatélico
11. Alianza Francesa
12. Parque Morazán

13. Edificio Metálico
14. Aurola Holiday Inn
15. Hotel Del Rey
16. Parque Zoológico Simón Bolívar
17. Spyrogyra
18. Parque España
19. Museo del Jade
20. Casa Amarilla
21. Centro Nacional de la Cultura
22. Museo Nacional
23. Plaza de la Democracia
24. Asamblea Legislativa

25. Serpentarium
26. Plaza de la Cultura
27. Museo del Oro Precolombino
28. Museo de Numismática
29. Teatro Nacional
30. Café Ruiseñor
31. Teatro Melico Salazar
32. Parque Central
33. El Paseo de los Estudiantes
34. Liceo de Costa Rica
35. Iglesia de Nuestra Señora de la Salúd
36. Parthenon

spot where the city's former airport used to be. In fact, the park has become such a central facet of life that the whole surrounding district has been named after it.

The **Museo de Arte Costarricense** ★★ *($2; Tue to Sun 10am to 5pm; Calle 42, opposite Paseo Colón in La Sabana Park,* ☎*257-5224)* exhibits works by the best artists in the country. Chamber music concerts are sometimes held in the museum's Salón Dorado.

Established in 1855, the large **Hospital San Juan de Dios** *(Calle 14, opposite Avenida 2)* is in the middle of San José, and marks off the west side of the city centre, an area which can easily be toured on foot. This neighbourhood's more recent development blends well with the older Manueline-style architecture.

A panel in front explains the history of the **Iglesia de la Merced** *(Avenida 2, Calle 10/12),* an eclectic Gothic-style church, which was built in 1894. Unfortunately, a wire fence bars access to the vast verdant grounds, which are very rare in the city centre.

The **Mercado Central** ★★ *(Avenida 1/Central, Calle 6/8)* is a fairly crowded indoor market where masses of people swarm through a war-

School Children

School, mandatory and free for all children, occupies an important place in the lives of Costa Ricans, who value it highly. Students go to school year-round, except during summer vacation between late December and early February, and on a few other holidays scattered throughout the year. To attend school, children must wear a uniform. In public schools (the colours are different in private schools), girls wear white blouses and blue skirts, while boys wear blue pants with white tops. If you're seated in a *soda* near a school when it lets out, you'll certainly chance on a stream of children coming to buy juice and candy in a happy tumult. You'll surely be graced with a few curious looks and many sincere smiles.

ren of narrow passages, closely hemmed in by *sodas* and other little stalls that sell everything from clothing and accessories to groceries and flowers, etc. This place is always busy, and provides an excellent opportunity to immerse yourself in everyday Costa Rican life. Plaques at the market's southeast entrance *(Avenida 1, Calle 6)* honour the memory of key political figures in Costa Rican history.

Opposite the Mercado Central is the **Mercado de Carnes** (meat market), which has a series of small delicatessen and butcher's stalls.

If you look north down Calle 4 from Avenida 5, there is a beautiful view of San José's former prison, which now houses the Costa Rican museum and cultural centre: the **Centro Costarricense de la Ciencia y la Cultura** ★★★. With its crenellated walls and towers flanking the entrance, this veritable fortress is a lovely scene at night, when the whole building is illuminated. The centre's children's museum, the **Museo de los Niños** *(Wed to Fri 10am to noon and 2pm to 5pm, Sat and Sun 10am to 1pm and 2pm to 5pm),* is unique in Central America, and is even worth the trip for adults. Its many vivid thematic hands-on exhibits that cover many different fields of knowledge make it a real learning experience!

Librería Lehmann *(Avenida Central, Calle 1/3)* is located in a Beaux Art-style building that could use some fixing up.

The downtown outlet of the **La Gloria** *(Avenida Central, Calle 4/6)* chain of department stores is worth a visit for its classic 1960s-style decor.

The main building of the **Banco de Costa Rica** *(Avenida 2, Calle 4/6)* is a fine example of the international monumental architecture of the 1960s and 1970s, whose domination of the urban landscape was meant to demonstrate the company's stature. The black marble facade makes the building all the more imposing. An elevator will take you to the eighth floor, from which there is a good view of San José, which is hard to come by since the city has few skyscrapers.

Art exhibitions are sometimes held at the tallest building in San José, the **Banco Nacional** *(Avenida 1, Calle 2/4)*.

Stamp collectors can visit the **Museo Filatélico** *(Mon to Fri 9am to 2pm; Calle 2, Avenida 1/3)*, on the second floor of the beautiful **Correo Central** (central post office) to admire Costa Rican commemorative stamps.

Correo Central

The building of the **Alianza Francesa** ★ *(Calle 7, Avenida 5)* is one of San José's beautiful and well-preserved colonial-style buildings. Its media library and exhibition halls are open to the public.

Surrounded by busy thoroughfares, the well-landscaped **Parque Morazán** *(Avenida 3, Calle 5/9)* is a quiet spot for locals and tourists to relax. Like many Costa Rican city parks, it has a concert bandstand.

The **Edificio Metálico** ★ *(Avenida 5, Calle 9)*, which now houses a school, stands opposite Parque Morazán. The building materials for this unique and interesting green steel structure were imported from France.

The **Aurola Holiday Inn** *(northwest corner of Parque Morazán)* is a popular landmark in San José's urban landscape. This huge building stands out from its neighbours with its mirrored exterior, and thus serves as a geographical reference point for anyone trying to find their way in the area. The same is true of the candy-pink **Hotel Del Rey**, located a stone's throw away, on the other side of Parque Morazán.

Though it is relatively small and doesn't house any particularly fascinating species, the **Parque Zoológico Nacional Simón Bolívar** *(Tue to Fri 8am to 4pm; Sat and Sun 9am to 5pm; Avenida 11, Calle 7, Parque Bolívar)* can make spot for a pleasant and instructive stroll.

San José

Parque Morazán

Also on the north side of Parque Bolívar, by the zoo, is **Spyrogyra** (*$5; every day 8am to 3pm; 100m or 328ft east and 150m or 492ft south of El Pueblo, just north of downtown, near the Guapiles hwy., 10 minutes' walking distance; take the "Calle Blancos" bus at Calle 3 and Avenida 5, get off at the El Pueblo shopping centre and follow directions from there or, if you're coming from Paseo Colón, take the downtown-bound "Periférica" bus to Centro Colón, or take the same bus from the Saprissa stop facing the Mönpik ice cream shop to the University of Costa Rica, ☎222-2937*), a butterfly garden where you can admire these beautiful creatures, as well as hummingbirds, in their natural surroundings.

There are other butterfly gardens in the country (in the Central Valley and in Monteverde), but this one is an excellent introduction to Costa Rica's natural history, and is conveniently located near downtown.

Parque España (*Avenida 3/7, Calle 9/11*) is another beautiful and peaceful park. The beautiful, fully-grown landscaping is inviting and is more natural than that found in most of the other parks in the city.

The **Museo del Jade** (*Mon to Sat 8am to 4:30pm; on the 3rd floor of the Instituto Nacional de Seguros, Calle 9, Avenida 7; ☎287-6034 or 223-5800*) has a lovely collection of artifacts made from the magnificent green stone, and also provides a beautiful view over the city. The museum closed its doors in 2000 to undertake important renovations, but should reopen again in 2001.

The **Casa Amarilla** ★ (*Avenida 7, Calle 11*) is one of the capital's most elegant buildings. Bequeathed to the nation by Andrew Carnegie, the rich and famous American philanthropist, the "Yellow House" now houses the Department of Foreign Affairs.

The **Centro Nacional de la Cultura** ★★ (*every day 10am to 5pm*) recently established itself in one of the city's oldest industrial facilities (the former National Liquor Factory, built in 1856). It is home to the national Ministry of Culture, Youth and Sports, the Museum of Contemporary Art and Design, the Hispano-American cultural centre, the Colegio de Costa Rica, the national dance company's rehearsal studios and performance spaces, etc. This beautifully renovated building no longer produces liquor since the state distillery has been relocated in Grecia.

The **Museo Nacional** ★★ (*Tue to Sat 8:30am to 4:30pm, Sun 9am to 4:30pm; Avenida 2, Calle 17, ☎257-1433*) is housed in the former Bellavista fortress (used in the Civil War of 1948), which has been renovated into a museum that exhibits a permanent collection of pre-Colombian gold and ceramic artifacts, as well as religious art works. The museum also has a display of the nation's history.

The **Plaza de la Democracia** *(Calle 15, Avenida Central/2)* adjoining the museum was laid out in the late 1980s to mark the occasion of a major international conference hosted by Costa Rica. It has many staircases that make it seem even bigger than it actually is. At the centre sits the statue of Don Pepe, José Figueres Ferrer, the president who most touched the hearts of Costa Ricans. Among other achievements, he abolished the army.

Museo Nacional

The **Asamblea Legislativa** ★, Costa Rica's legislative assembly, unites its whole administration in 11 buildings scattered around the area of the Museo Nacional. Don't be surprised, therefore, when you're visiting the area, to see large numbers of men and women in suits going from one building to the other with files

under their arms! The legislative council itself meets in a room in the **Edificio Central**. This room is not of great interest, unless you want to listen to the debates *(Mon to Thu, 4pm to 7pm)*. But in the room next to it, the **Salón de Expresidentes de la República**, you can see portraits of every president in office since 1833.

Moreover, on the main floor you can admire the **Rotonda de la Patria**, decorated with plaques commemorating the most important legislation, as well as an interior courtyard, **El jardín de la Madre Patria: España**. The latter, of *mudéjare* inspiration and decorated with mosaic tiles from Italy, is reminiscent of the Palacio de la Alambra

in Grenada, Spain—Costa Rica's mother country.

Another building that's worth a quick look is the **Castillo Azul**, dating from 1911. Blue in colour, it owes its name to the party colours of the first president, who used it as a *Casa presidential*. It is graced with a long gallery and a tower, just like a castle!

Next to it is the **Casa Rosada**, which has housed offices for deputies since 1991 and was built at the end of the 19th century. With its interior garden and wide corridors, it's reminiscent of the classical architecture of Valle Central colonial houses.

Opposite stands the **Antiguo Colegio de Nuestra Señora Sión**, built in 1888. It was first occupied by the nuns of this religious community, who opened a college here that was very well attended by the elite. You can arrange guided tours of these buildings by contacting the public relations department at ☎243-2547 or by fax ≠243-2551.

Behind the national assembly is the building that houses the Tribunal Supremo de Elecciones, the supreme election court. This is a large building covered with pink stucco and mirrors. In front is a little square christened the **Plaza de la Libertad Electoral**

San José

(Place of Electoral Liberty). It's surrounded by a vaguely neoclassical semi-circle of columns, probably to recall the country where democracy was born. Whatever the case may be, the whole set-up is a reminder that Costa Rica has been a proud democracy for more than a century.

Costa Rica's café and the Teatro Nacional's Café Ruiseñor and the Avenida Central pedestrian zone also border the square, so it is really not surprising that it is such a popular place to hang out at any time of day!

Plaza de la Libertad Electoral

The **Serpentarium** *(Mon to Fri 9am to 6pm, Sat and Sun 10am to 5pm; Avenida 1, Calle 9/11, ☎225-4210)* is the place to learn everything there is to know about Costa Rica's reptiles. There are live specimens from all over the world, including the deadly cobra and the famous piranha, which is fed every Monday, Wednesday and Friday at 5pm.

Plaza de la Cultura ★★ *(Avenida Central, Calle 3/5)* can be considered the most central of San José's downtown squares, if such a thing is possible! It is always bustling with young people, students, lovers and businesspeople—in short, with everyone! Numerous shops line the lovely terraced space. The Gran Hotel

Below the Plaza de la Cultura are a whole series of museums run by the Fundación Museos del Banco Central de Costa Rica *(☎243-4202)*. The **Museo del Oro Precolombino** ★★★ *(Tue to Sun 10am to 4:30pm)* houses a dazzling collection of precious gold objects from the pre-Colombian era to the time of the Spanish Conquest. The museum's doors have been closed since September 2000 to undergo considerable renovations. The museum will reopen for the 2001 season, when it will display its thousand gold pieces, placing more emphasis on their origin. The idea is to paint a picture of the people who created and used these pieces. To achieve this, the

museum even gained the participation of various indigenous peoples whose ancestors crafted and employed these precious objects as part of their daily life.

The **Museo de Numismática** ★ *(Tue to Sun 10am to 4:30pm)* relates the history of Costa Rican paper money. The complex also has spaces for temporary fine-arts and pottery exhibits.

The architecture of the **Teatro Nacional** ★★★ *(Mon to Sat 9am to 4:30pm; Plaza de la Cultura, Calle 3, Avenida 2)* is similar to that of the Paris Opera House. The national theatre was built when prima donna Andelina Patti refused to perform in Costa Rica, for want of an appropriate venue. It was inaugurated in 1897, and is now the headquarters of the **Orquesta Sinfónica Nacional y Juvenil** (National Symphony and Youth Orchestra). The building was classified as an historic monument in 1965, and it has undergone renovation and restoration work over the last few years to mark its centenary. If you go inside, you'll be struck by the decoration on the walls and ceilings with its gilt, marble and even mirrored trimmings.

The **Café Ruiseñor** *(inside the Teatro Nacional)* regularly presents temporary exhibitions.

Teatro Nacional

The **Teatro Melico Salazar** ★★ *(Avenida 2, Calle Central; opposite Parque Central,* ☎*222-2653)* is not only a theatre hall, but also the place where Costa Rica's independence came into being. Popular bands perform here on their Central American tours. The hall was named in honour of world-famous Costa Rican tenor Melico Salazar.

Parque Central *(Calle Central/2, Avenida 2/4)* is quite well-kept, but would be more accurately described as a square than a park, since much of its surface is paved.

This centrally located park has a lot of character with its lovely terraced design and large rotunda with voluted classical columns crowned with a cupola. If you want to stand beneath the cupola, be warned: neighbourhood pigeons like to roost on the inside edges.

Calle 9 is also known as **El Paseo de los Estudiantes** (the students' route), as it leads south to the **Liceo de Costa Rica**, one of the largest and oldest high schools in the country. During the school year, many students can be seen coming and going, clad in their school uniforms. Some of the Liceo's buildings are of architectural and historical interest.

The **Iglesia de Nuestra Señora de la Soledad** *(Calle 9, Avenida 6)*, on Paseo de los Estudiantes, is very well-kept and renovated. The church has beautifully made and very colourful lateral stained-glass windows. The white interior has a pleasant and almost magical feel to it, and its architecture as a whole makes it a worthwhile stop if you are passing through the neighbourhood.

Opposite the Iglesia de la Soledad, at Calle 9, north of Avenida 6, the small Paseo de los Estudiantes square is delightfully ornamented with plants. There are also commemorative plaques honouring Carlos Gardel, an ambassador of Argentinian culture who died under tragic circumstances.

A small, very lovely white classical parthenon stands on Calle 19, on the northwest corner of the grounds of the **Museo de Criminología**. Illuminated at night, it is the site where future president Oscar Arias Sanchéz gave the inaugural speech of the University of Costa Rica in 1941.

Farther east, in the San Pedro district, the very large campus of the **Universidad de Costa Rica** ★ is a lovely place for a quiet walk. The grounds include a beautiful tree-lined path almost 2km (1.8mi) long.

San José

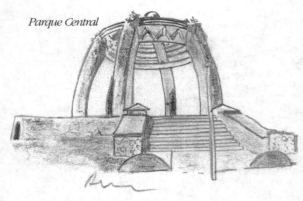

Parque Central

Accommodations

America
$
hw, sb
Avenida 7, Calle 4
☎221-4116
The rooms at the America hotel are clean, but offer minimal comfort. The windows do not open very wide.

Hotel Asia
$
sb/pb
Calle 11, Avenida Central/1
☎223-3893
⇄283-7957
Hotel Asia offers very basic rooms with single beds and a shared bathroom (only one room has a private bathroom). None of them have windows. However, the hotel is well-kept.

Boruca
$
hw, sb
Calle 14, Avenida 1/3
☎223-0016
The rooms at the Boruca are small (really small!), poorly decorated and have no windows. However, the place is clean. Beware: you might have to share your room with one of the people who live in the house! Conveniently located near numerous bus stops.

Centro Americano
$
hw, pb, ℜ
Avenida 2, Calle 6/8
☎221-3362
The reception desk at the Centro Americano hotel is down a corridor, at the back of the building. The rooms face small interior courtyards, providing a great deal of peace and quiet despite the fact that the hotel is situated on one of the busiest streets in San José; indeed, guests are asked to be extremely quiet after 9pm.

The decor is not particularly charming, but the hotel is clean and wheelchair accessible.

🏨 Hotel Johnson
$
hw, pb, ℜ
Calle 8, Avenida 2/Central
☎223-7633 or 223-7827
⇄222-3683
Hotel Johnson is extremely pleasant, clean and inexpensive if you want to stay in the popular neighbourhood around the central market. However, the establishment's style is somewhat outdated. Though it is always fairly busy, the hotel is nevertheless known for its tranquillity, which is rare in this area.

Hotel Marlyn
$
sb/pb
Calle 4, Avenida 7/9
☎233-3212
Hotel Marlyn has small and clean rooms that face an interior courtyard, but are furnished only with a bed. Very popular with budget-conscious travellers. Friendly staff.

Bienvenido
$-$$
pb, hw
Calle 10, Avenida 1/3
☎233-2161
⇄221-1872
The Bienvenido hotel is clean and friendly, and its inexpensive rooms are airy and fairly quiet. It also has a good location near the Mercado Central.

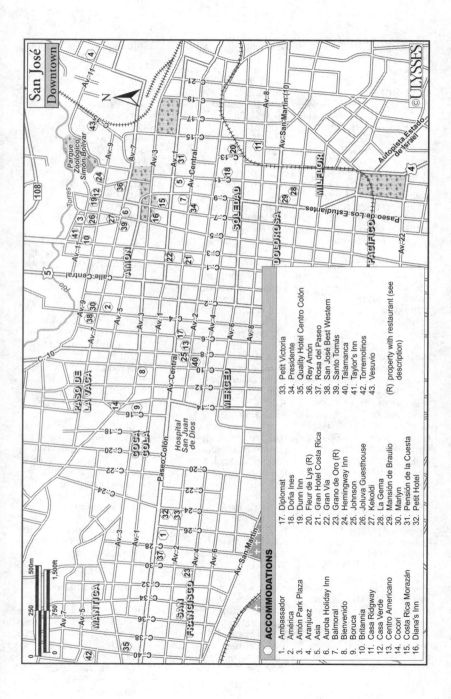

Casa Ridgway
$$
hw, sb
along Avenida 6, Calle 15
☎233-6168
The Casa Ridgway is
the quintessential youth
hostel. Located right
next to the Centro de
Amigos para la Paz, it is
a lively and sociable
place. Guests can stay
in dormitories or pri-
vate rooms, and have
access to the kitchen
and library. Special
rates for groups of
eight or more people.

Cocori
$$
hw, pb
Calle 16, Avenida 3
☎233-0081
⇌255-1058
The Cocori is a basic
but very decent hotel,
with clean and comfort-
able rooms. The build-
ing is simply yet taste-
fully designed, and
located in the vicinity
of the Coca Cola bus
terminal and the Hospi-
tal San Juan de Dios
(unfortunately, not the
most attractive of
neighbourhoods).

D'Galah
$$
K
opposite the gardens of the
Universidad de Costa Rica
campus, San Pedro
☎/⇌234-1743 or 253-7539
dagalah@rasca.co.cr
Peace and quiet prevail
at the D'Galah thanks
to its extensive verdant
grounds that shelter it
from the university
across the street.

La Granja
$$
*discounts for Hostelling
International cardholders*
hw, K, ℜ
Avenida Central, 50m (164ft)
south of Antiguo Higuerón, San
Pedro
☎/⇌225-1073 or 280-6239
Run by a friendly fam-
ily, the eight-room La
Granja hotel is a good
place to keep in mind.

Jacques et Helena
$$ bkfst incl.
hw
Urbanización Carmiol, Calle 8,
Casa 811, Sabanilla
☎224-6596
The very decent
Jacques et Helena bed
and breakfast is located
in a quiet neighbour-
hood some 10min from
the city centre.

Petit Hotel
$$ bkfst incl.
hw in a few rooms, sb/pb
Calle 24, Avenida Central/2
☎233-0766
⇌233-4794
Run by mother and
son, the Petit Hotel has
simple and clean
rooms, though the fur-
nishings are somewhat
old-fashioned.

🏷 **Toruma**
$$
sb
Avenida Ctl, Calle 31/33
☎224-4085
Toruma is the best-
known youth hostel in
San José. It is even
something of a centre
for the Costa Rican
network of youth hos-
tels. The hostel is a big
19th-century Victorian
home, which, although
stripped down, will
give you an idea of the
wealth of its former

inhabitants. The rooms
are distributed along
wide corridors and
contain bunk beds. It
goes without saying
that the atmosphere is
very friendly and the
large communal rooms,
as well as the little
courtyard, will certainly
enable you to make
interesting acquain-
tances. Kitchen and
laundry access.

Aparthotel El Sesteo
$$$
hw, pb, ctv, K, ℜ, ≈
in the continuation of the General Cañas Highway toward the
south side of La Sabana Park
☎296-1805
⇌296-1865
sesteo@rasca.co.cr
The main asset of the
Aparthotel El Sesteo is
its location, only a
short distance from La
Sabana Park and the
highway leading to the
international airport.
The building's ameni-
ties (common rooms
and guest rooms) are
very basic, but the inte-
rior courtyard, with a
swimming pool, whirl-
pool and garden, is
lovely and quite pri-
vate. However, the
apartments around this
courtyard are too close
together, which can be
a nuisance with noisy
neighbours and chil-
dren.

Aparthotel La Sabana
$$$ bkfst incl.
hw, pb, tv, ≈, ℜ, △, K
Sabana Norte, 50m (164ft) west
and 150 north of Burger King
☎220-2422
⇌231-7386
lasabana@rasca.co.cr
Like the El Sesteo, the
Aparthotel La Sabana is

only steps away from La Sabana Park and the highway to the international airport.

Ara Macao
$$$ bkfst incl.
K, pb
50m (164ft) south of Avenida Central, opposite Pizza Hut, in Barrio California
right before Los Yoses
☎*233-2742*
⇌*257-6228*
The apartment hotel Ara Macao has fine apartments with balconies. The common rooms are pleasant: a small dining room sheltered from the rain in a central atrium, and a patio where you can have barbecues while observing small turtles crawling in the fountain and frogs frolicking in the aquarium. A quiet place.

Aranjuez
$$$ bkfst incl.
hw, pb, ctv, ℜ
Calle 19, Avenida 11/13
☎*256-1825*
⇌*223-3528*
Located in the very quiet neighbourhood of the same name, Aranjuez is a lovely surprise: while its exterior is unassuming, the building's interior turns out to be very spacious. The rooms and bathrooms are large and clean, and the common living rooms are spacious, as are the gardens. Moreover, the owners are environmentally conscious (recycling, solar heating, etc.). Special weekly and monthly rates available.

Children under 10 years of age stay for free.

Diana's Inn
$$$
hw, pb, tv, ≡
Calle 5, Avenida 3
☎*223-6542*
⇌*233-0495*
Do not judge Diana's Inn by its entrance. The rooms upstairs are simply decorated but clean. The common rooms are quite lovely and bright. Moreover, it is right in the heart of the city, just opposite Morazán Park.

Diplomat
$$$
pb
Calle 6, Avenida Central/2
☎*221-8744 or 221-8133*
⇌*233-7474*
The Diplomat hotel has clean rooms offering basic comfort. Some windows open onto a shaft that allows air to circulate, making them cooler. The common areas are clean.

Doña Ines
$$$
hw, pb, tv
Calle 11, Avenida 2/6
☎*222-7443 or 222-7553*
⇌*223-5426*
The Doña Ines is Italian through and through: its ornately scrolled interior leaves no doubt as to the owner's country of origin. The place is spotless.

Dunn Inn
$$$ bkfst incl.
hw, pb, ctv, ⊗
Calle 5, Avenida 11
☎*222-3232 or 222-3426*
⇌*221-4596*
The very charming Dunn Inn has a peaceful interior decor, particularly in its "atrium restaurant."

La Gema
$$$
hw, pb, tv
Avenida 12, Calle 9/11
☎*257-2524*
⇌*222-1074*
La Gema is a simple little hotel with rather small rooms, some of which are stuffy. It has a pool table.

Gran Hotel Costa Rica
$$$
hw, pb, ctv, ℜ
Calle 3 and Avenida Central/2
☎*221-4000*
⇌*221-3501*
You would be hard-pressed to find a better hotel than the Gran Hotel Costa Rica in the centre of San José. Though its charm is somewhat faded, the place is clean and still very popular. There is a casino on the premises.

Gran Via
$$$
hw, pb
Avenida Central, Calle 1/3
☎*222-7737*
⇌*222-7205*
The Gran Via has been around for nearly 30 years and is one of the capital's oldest hotels. It shows its age, but the rooms are clean. Moreover, it is superbly located in the downtown pedestrian zone, and rooms with balconies cost only a little more.

San José

Joluva Guesthouse
$$$ bkfst incl.
hw, pb, ctv
along Calle 3, Avenida 9/11, No. 936
☎*223-7961*
⇌*257-7668*
joluva@racsa.co.cr
The small, comfortable Joluva Guesthouse welcomes a gay clientele. However, its hospitality is not always first-rate.

Kalexma
$$$ bkfst incl.
hw, sb/pb, K
50m (164ft) south of the Juan Pablo II Bridge
☎/⇌*232-0115*
The Kalexma is a rather humble, uncharming bed and breakfast in a quiet neighbourhood a fair distance from downtown, but close to the General Cañas Highway, which runs to the airport.

Hotel Kekoldi
$$$ bkfst incl.
hw, pb, ⊗
Calle 3 Bis, Avenida 9
☎*223-3244*
⇌*257-5476*
kekoldi@racsa.co.cr
The Hotel Kekoldi is decorated in striking pastels (the work of Helen Eltis), which is at once cheerful and relaxing. This charming, colourful little hotel offers large rooms with king-size beds and lovely little shared living rooms. Close to all the downtown attractions. Some rooms are noisier than others because of the traffic, so ask for a quiet room when you check in.

Pensión de la Cuesta
$$$ bkfst incl.
hw
Avenida 1, Calle 11/15
☎*256-7946*
⇌*255-2896*
The Pensión de la Cuesta is very decent for the price. Housed in a colonial-style building, its rooms are somewhat sombre, but the general liveliness of the place will cheer you up, particularly in the common living rooms where guests gather to chat. Guests have access to a kitchen.

Pico Blanco Inn
$$$
ℜ
San Antonio de Escazú
☎*228-1908*
⇌*289-5189*
The Pico Blanco Inn is a small, clean and pleasant mountain inn (rather hard to reach) where you can hear the parrots that live in the surrounding area. The view over the valley is breathtaking.

Pine Tree Inn
$$$ bkfst incl.
hw, pb, ctv, ≈
on a residential street opposite the Quiubo restaurant, in the Urbanización Trejos Montalegre district, Escazú, next to the Aparthotel María Alexandra
☎*289-7405*
⇌*228-2180*
The Pine Tree Inn has around fifteen comfortable rooms in a very quiet neighbourhood in Escazú. Gymnasium and racquetball nearby.

Rey Amón
$$$ bkfst incl.
hw, pb, ctv
Avenida 7, Calle 7/9
☎*233-3819*
⇌*233-1769*
The fairly quiet Rey Amón has small but clean rooms that are plainly furnished. A friendly welcome awaits you, as well as 0.5hr of free Internet access.

Talamanca
$$$ bkfst incl.
hw, pb, ctv, ⊗
Avenida 2, Calle 8/10
☎/⇌*233-5033 or 233-5420*
The Talamanca is a clean, modern hotel with a somewhat too predictable style. The bar on the top floor affords a splendid view of the city.

Taylor's Inn
$$$ bkfst incl.
hw, pb, ctv
Calle 3, Avenida 11
☎*257-4333*
⇌*221-1475*
Taylor's Inn, a decent little bed and breakfast, occupies a former residence with a dozen tidy rooms filled with wicker furniture. Non-smoking rooms are available.

Tennis Club
$$$
hw, pb, ≡*, ctv,* ≈*,* ℜ*,* ⌂
in the south end of La Sabana, next to the pyramidal Controlaría General de la República building
☎*232-1266*
⇌*232-3867*
hotel@crtennis.icr.co.cr
The main advantage of the Tennis Club hotel lies in the many activities guests can partici-

pate in at one of the oldest sports club in San José: tennis, bowling, sauna, gym, pool and recreation grounds are available to the clientele 24 hours a day. The rooms, however, are not very attractive and the beds are uncomfortable.

Hotel Vesuvio
$$$ bkfst incl.
hw, pb, ctv, ⊗, ℜ
Avenida 11, Calle 13/15, Barrio Otoya
☎/⇌*221-7586*
☎/⇌*221-8325*
☎/⇌*256-1616*
Hotel Vesuvio is clean and modern, but relatively small. The common spaces may be somewhat lacking in warmth, but the establishment is located right near the zoo, in a quiet neighbourhood with lovely architecture.

Sabana B&B
$$$-$$$$ bkfst incl.
pb, hw, tv, ⊗
☎*232-2876 or 296-3751*
⇌*232-2876*
sabanabb@racsa.co.cr
The Sabana B&B gets its name from the Sabana Norte district where it is located. Run by a Costa Rican family, it's a bed and breakfast with a friendly atmosphere.

Los Yoses City Inn
$$$$ bkfst incl.
pb, hw
100mts Sur y 100mts Oeste del Automercado Los
☎*283-0101*
⇌*225-3516*
www.costaricainn.com
Los Yoses City Inn is a bed and breakfast located in a suburban house with a real North American feel to it. It is owned by a couple who also own the Arenal Country Inn in La Fortuna (see p 209). This is an enjoyable place to stay and is located in a San José neighbourhood that is somewhat calmer than others. Comfortable rooms are available all throughout the house, from the basement to the top floor, as the owners do not live on the premises. Each room is named after a different region of the country, and decorated according to the style of the area. Breakfast is convivially served at a large table. The place is well kept and the welcome very friendly.

Aparthotel Los Yoses
$$$$
hw, pb, ⊗, ≡, *tv,* ≈
on the main street, 150m (492ft) west of Fuente de la Hispanidad, Los Yoses
☎*225-0033 or 225-0044*
⇌*225-5595*
The Aparthotel Los Yoses has large, clean, fully equipped and well furnished apartments, each of which has an adjacent washer and dryer outlet. Parking and babysitting available.

Aurola Holiday Inn
$$$$
hw, pb, ctv, ≈, ℜ, ○
Avenida 5, Calle 5, opposite Morazán Park
☎*222-2424*
⇌*222-2621*
aurola@racsa.co.cr
Aurola Holiday Inn is a San José institution, because it is one of the tallest skyscrapers in the downtown area, and the only one with mirrored windows. Other features include a sauna, gymnasium, casino, boutique and newsstand. You won't find another hotel of this scale with a better location in the heart of the city.

Hotel Balmoral
$$$$
hw, pb, ctv, ≡, ○
Avenida Central, Calle 7/9
☎*222-5022*
☎*800-961-4865*
⇌*221-1919*
www.balmoral.co.cr
Hotel Balmoral is one of those modern hotels that were popular in design a few years ago. However, the place is very clean and the service is gracious.

Hotel Le Bergerac
$$$$ bkfst incl.
hw, pb, ctv, ⊗, ⊛, ℜ
Calle 35, 50m (164ft) south of Avenida Central
☎*234-7850*
⇌*225-9103*
bergerac@racsa.co.cr
The rooms at the Hotel Le Bergerac are lovely and elegant, as is the rest of the hotel. The lavish gardens are perfect to relax in. The management is French, and the restaurant (see p 103) proves it.

Casa Las Orquideas
$$$$ bkfst incl.
hw, pb, tv, ⊗
Avenida Central, Calle 33/37,
75m (246ft) west of the
Automercado Los Yoses, Los
Yoses
☎*283-8203*
⇌*234-8203*
The pleasant, emer-
ald-green Casa Las
Orquideas is clean and
very charming, with
wood and ceramic ac-
cents in the decor,
lovely little rest areas
and skylights.

Costa Rica Morazán
$$$$
hw, pb, ≡, *tv,* ℜ
Calle 7, Avenida 1
☎*222-4622*
⇌*233-3329*
The design of the Costa
Rica Morazán dates
from the seventies.
Though its rooms are
rather small, they all
have air condition-
ers—a necessity in this
busy neighbourhood
where you will have to
sleep with the windows
closed. Discounts for
guests over 60 years of
age.

Aparthotel Cristina
$$$$
hw, pb, K, ctv, ≈
300m (984ft) north of ICE,
Sabana Norte
☎*231-1618 or 220-0453*
⇌*220-2096*
The Aparthotel Cristina
essentially caters to
businesspeople. The
apartments are clean
and have a simple de-
sign.

Hotel Don Fadrique
$$$$ bkfst incl.
hw, pb, ⊗, *ctv*
Calle 37, Avenida 8, Los Yoses
☎*225-8186*
⇌*224-9746*
Hotel Don Fadrique is
a remodelled
19th-century villa sur-
rounded by gardens
that insulate it from its
surroundings, and
make it a lovely spot
for intimate dinners.
Some rooms have di-
rect access to the gar-
dens. The hotel also
houses a collection of
Costa Rican art and the
portrait of a very
colourful national fig-
ure: Don Fadrique him-
self.

Don Paco Inn
$$$$ bkfst incl.
hw, pb, ctv
Calle 33, Avenida 11
☎/⇌*283-2012 or 283-2033*
The charming Don
Paco Inn is in a large
building that once
housed United Nations
offices. It has since
been renovated but has
preserved its colonial
style. The rooms are
stylish and very com-
fortable. The hotel is
located in an extremely
quiet residential neigh-
bourhood, and is a fair
distance from the
downtown core.

Fleur de Lys
$$$$ bkfst incl.
hw, pb, ℜ
Calle 13, Avenida 2/6
☎*222-4391 or 223-1206 or
257-2621*
⇌*257-3637*
florlys@racsa.co.cr
The Fleur de Lys is
housed in the former
home of a 20th-century
coffee baron. Needless

to say, the house has
plenty of style. The
combination of the
wooden staircases that
lead to the three floors,
the parquet floors, the
era paintings, the
French doors and all
the decorative elements
give it a luxurious at-
mosphere. The rooms,
named after flowers,
are situated in different
locations throughout
the house, making
them very private.
Some of them are very
large, while others are
on the small side, but
all are attractive. Al-
though located in the
centre of the city, the
establishment is in a
tranquil area, making
the charming front ter-
race very enjoyable.
The hotel's restaurant is
a must (see p ?). Also,
don't hesitate to use the
friendly services of the
hotel travel agent. The
Fleur de Lys, which
attracts a number of
satisfied customers ev-
ery season, has been
recently planning reno-
vations that will give it
additional rooms.

Hotel Grano de Oro
$$$$
hw, pb, ctv
Calle 30, Avenida 2/4
☎*255-3322*
⇌*221-2782*
granoro@racsa.co.cr
The Hotel Grano de
Oro, located in a quiet
neighbourhood close to
downtown, is a su-
perbly renovated
turn-of-the-century
manor that exudes
character and panache!
The rooms are inviting,
with elegant bathrooms

and fine wood furnishings. There is a delightful rooftop terrace with deckchairs and whirlpools, as well as a lovely garden with fountains. All rooms are non-smoking. The Hotel Grano de Oro is very popular, even in the off-peak season. Its restaurant (see p 102) is probably one of the best in the country.

Hampton Inn
$$$$ bkfst incl.
hw, pb, ≈
General Cañas Hwy. service road, 2min from the Juan Santamaría Airport
☎443-0043
⇌442-9532
The Hampton Inn offers North American standards of comfort, and is part of the chain of the same name. Its main asset is its location, just 2min from San José's international airport. Children as well as the third and fourth person sharing a room stay for free.

Hemingway Inn
$$$$ bkfst incl.
hw, pb, ctv, ⊛
Avenida 9, Calle 9
☎/⇌221-1804
The Hemingway Inn is owned by a Canadian who is involved with ecotourism, so feel free to ask him about the subject. The lovely little Spanish manor harbours fine rooms with all the modern conveniences. The rosewood decor blends harmoniously with the surrounding greenery.

Best Western Irazu
$$$$
hw, pb, ctv, ≈, ≡, ⌂
next door to the San José 2000 shopping centre, along the General Cañas Hwy.
☎232-4811
☎800-272-6654
⇌232-4549
Many rooms at the Best Western Irazu have a balcony overlooking the pool or the garden, and some are wheelchair accessible. Try not to get a room on the main floor near the common areas, as the commotion of the many tour groups coming and going may disturb you.

Mansión de Braulio
$$$$
hw, pb
Avenida 10, Calle 9
☎222-0423
⇌222-7947
The Mansión de Braulio is located on the top floor of a lovely building. Its rooms are clean, though their furnishings are a bit worn. The common living rooms are relatively well arranged, but the staff is not overly friendly.

Palma Real
$$$$
hw, pb, ⊛, ℜ
200m (656ft) north of ICE Sabana Norte
☎290-5060
⇌290-4160
www.hotelpalmareal.com
The Palma Real hotel essentially caters to a business clientele; facilities include meeting and conference rooms, as well as a business centre. The modern rooms have a standard

design, but are very comfortable. The restaurant serves international cuisine.

Petit Victoria
$$$$
hw, pb, ctv, ℜ
Calle 24, Avenida 2
☎233-1812 or 233-1813
⇌233-1938
The Petit Victoria offers stylish rooms in its very charming Victorian building. However, traffic around the hotel can sometimes get noisy.

Posada El Quijote
$$$$ bkfst incl.
hw, pb, ctv
take the first exit to Bello Horizonte and drive 1.3km (0.8mi) south, then 200m (656ft) west, 25m (82ft) south and finally 25m (82ft) east, Bello Horizonte de Escazú
☎289-8401
⇌289-8729
quijote@racsa.co.cr
The American owners of the Posada El Quijote purchased this magnificent residence from the United States embassy, which gives you a pretty good idea of what the place is like. It offers flawless comfort, and a superbly decorated interior. The rooms are spacious, and the bay windows in the living rooms afford a magnificent view over the Central Valley. The gardens are wonderfully relaxing. Shuttle service between the airport and San José is available. The road leading to the *posada* can be rather rough going.

San José

Hotel Presidente
$$$$
hw, pb, ctv, ≡, △, ⊛
Avenida Central, Calle 7
☎*222-3022*
≈*221-1205*
www.hotel-presidente.com
Hotel Presidente is very
well situated, in the
heart of the city. Its
modern layout guaran-
tees a good standard of
comfort, but makes for
standard rooms.

🌴 Rincón del Valle
$$$$ bkfst incl.
hw, pb, ctv, ≡
50m (164ft) east and 50m
(164ft) south of the Colegio de
Médicos, on the south side of La
Sabana Park
☎*231-4927 or 231-7881*
≈*231-5924*
palacio@racsa.co.cr
The Rincón del Valle
hotel is a member of
the Barceló chain. Its
dark reddish wood
gives it a tasteful, classical touch. The rooms
have a North American
level of comfort, and
the service is attentive.
Guests have access to a
pool, a gymnasium and
tennis courts next door.
Located in a quiet
neighbourhood, the
establishment is quite
far from the town cen-
tre. There are confer-
ence facilities in the
Quiubo restaurant in
Escazú.

Hotel Rosa del Paseo
$$$$ bkfst incl.
hw, pb, ctv, ⊗
Paseo Colón, opposite the Banco
Anglo, between Calles 28 and 30
☎*257-3225*
≈*223-2776*
Hotel Rosa del Paseo is
the former residence of
a *cafetaleras* (coffee
baron) that has been

painstakingly renovated
to preserve the unique
style of each of its
rooms (including the
guest rooms), while
adding touches of com-
fort. Baths.

Quality Hotel Centro Colón
$$$$
hw, pb, ≡, *ctv,* ℜ
Avenida 3, Calle 40
☎*257-2580*
☎*800-228-5151*
≈*257-2582*
The Quality Hotel
Centro Colón is primar-
ily a hotel for
businesspeople. Its
style and comfort con-
form to the norms of
international hotel
chains. However, its
location near La Sabana
Park, the Museo de
Arte Costarricense and
the airport-bound city
exit is quite far from
the centre of town.

Santo Tomás
$$$$ bkfst incl.
hw, pb, ctv, ⊗
Avenida 7, Calle 3/5
☎*255-0448*
≈*222-3950*
hotelst@racsa.co.cr
The Santo Tomás hotel
offers spacious and
elegant rooms, much
like the building as a
whole, for that matter.
It has been a sure value
for a certain number of
years now in San José,
especially since it is
located in one of the
best neighbourhoods in
the heart of the city,
namely Barrio Amón.

Best Western San José
$$$$ bkfst incl.
hw, pb, ctv, ≡, ℜ, ≈
Avenida 7, Calle 6
☎*255-4766*
≈*255-4613*
garden@racsa.co.cr
The Best Western San
José provides the type
of comfort typical of
this hotel chain. The
layout of the common
spaces, notably the
pool and garden area,
is rather lovely, and the
balconies overlooking
them are most pleasant.
The hotel is situated on
the fringes of a less
interesting neighbour-
hood than its neigh-
bour, Barrio Amón; the
building's architecture
looks out of place in
this environment. Free
shuttle service between
the airport and San
José, free parking and
complementary cock-
tail!

Torremolinos
$$$$
hw, pb, ctv, ≈, ⊛, ℜ
Calle 40, along Avenida 5,
near La Sabana
☎*229-9129*
≈*255-3167*
torremolinos@
centralamerica.com
Torremolinos is a mod-
ern establishment lo-
cated in a peaceful
neighbourhood quite
far from downtown. Its
classical streamlined
decor (rooms and
lobby alike) is attrac-
tive.

Villa Tournón
$$$$
hw, pb, ctv, ≈, ⊛, ℜ
☎*233-6622*
≈*222-5211*
The modern Villa
Tournón is located just

on the outskirts of downtown, to the north, in Barrio Tournón. The rooms are pleasantly furnished and comfortable. Children under 12 years of age stay in their parents' room for free.

Hotel Ambassador
$$$$-$$$$$
hw, pb, ctv, ℜ
Paseo Colón, Calle 26/28
☎ *221-8155*
⇋ *255-3396*
www.hotelambassador.co.cr
Though it has a good reputation, the Hotel Ambassador is showing its age. Everything from the narrow corridors to the colour scheme, carpets and furniture, obviously dates from the sixties. The ceilings are low, and the small rooms lack character. Moreover, the rooms are not necessarily made up each day. Some rooms overlook noisy Paseo Colón. Variety shows are held at the hotel.

Meliá Corobici
$$$$$
hw, pb, ctv, ≡*,* ≈*,* ⊛*,* ℜ*,* ⊘
the beginning of the General Cañas Hwy., past Avenida Sabana Norte
☎ *232-8122*
⇋ *231-5834*
corobici@racsa.co.cr
The Meliá Corobici hotel is a major hotel, even in terms of size. The main part is impressive, with a huge cathedral-like roof that crowns the common spaces in the middle of the complex (casino, restaurant, meeting rooms, conference rooms, etc.). The hotel

houses two good speciality restaurants: Japanese and Italian (see p 102).

Hotel Americano
$$$$$ bkfst incl.
hw, pb, tv, ≈
175m (574ft) north of the Subaru dealership, Los Yoses
☎ *253-0449*
⇋ *224-2166*
Hotel Americano is located at the end of a quiet street in the fashionable Los Yoses district. The standard design may be more suitable for people who are just passing through on business.

Alta Hotel
$$$$$
pb, hw, ≡*,* ℜ*,* ≈*,* ≡
Escazú
☎ *282-4160*
⇋ *282-4162*
The Hotel Alta offers an ideal atmosphere for those who seek luxury. The little road on which it's situated (the old road to Santa Ana) gives no inkling of the grandeur of this establishment. Designed in an architectural style that favours winding curves rather than straight angles, the building has stucco walls, wooden ceilings, doors and furniture and tiled roofs. The rooms, skilfully situated along cream-coloured corridors, offer blessed privacy. Each room has two large beds facing patio doors opening onto an isolated balcony, where you can enjoy the view and the tranquillity of the afternoon. Below, the swimming pool displays its

vivid colours— blue for the pool and yellow for the terrace, creating a charming oasis. The restaurant, La Luz, has a gourmet menu and very classy decor, with its stuffed armchairs covered with *fleur de lys* motifs. Take the Carretera Vieja toward Santa Ana from Escazú. You'll see the hotel on your right a little further on.

Amón Park Plaza
$$$$$
hw, pb, ctv
Avenida 11, along Calle 3
☎ *257-0191*
⇋ *257-0284*
amonpark@racsa.co.cr
The new Amón Park Plaza is classic and modern at the same time. Though it is designed to cater specifically to businesspeople, it may also appeal to tourists. The rooms are clean and well furnished. The hotel has a large restaurant that serves international cuisine in the evenings *(5pm to midnight)*, and light meals in its main lobby day and night. Casino.

Aparthotel María Alexandra
$$$$$
hw, pb, ctv, ℝ*, K,* ⌂
on a residential street across from the Quiubo restaurant, in the Urbanización Trejos Montalegre district, Escazú
☎ *228-1507*
⇋ *289-5192*
The Aparthotel María Alexandra is located in a very quiet, upscale residential district. Amenities include a laundromat, beauty

San José

salon, barbecue area and a video-rental counter (there are VCRs in the rooms). The overall design is luxurious, and the apartments are fully equipped. The hotel also has a very good restaurant (see p 101).

🏖 Britannia
$$$$$ bkfst incl.
hw, pb, ⊗, ctv, ℜ,
Calle 3, Avenida 9/11
☎223-6667
⇌223-6411
britannia@racsa.co.cr
The Britannia occupies an old Victorian home whose former charm has been preserved. As soon as you step over the threshold and into the entrance hall, you're engulfed in an atmosphere of luxury and opulence. The first sign of this is the enormous bouquet of tropical flowers that welcomes you. The rooms are large, the communal rooms inviting, and the decor is exquisite and exceptionally comfortable. The top floor has a particularly interesting feature: the outside wall of the corridor adjoining the rooms is entirely glass. The rooms themselves are graced with large windows that look out onto the corridor, so you can enjoy a view over the mountains in almost complete privacy! Moreover, the Britannia is located in the Amón district, one of the best areas to stay in the heart of the city. There is a shuttle bus to the airport.

Casa Verde
$$$$$ bkfst incl.
hw, pb, ctv, ⊗, △
Calle 7, Avenida 9
☎/⇌223-0969 or 257-1054
The Casa Verde was built in the Victorian era and has been so well restored that it has won several awards. The common areas are appealing, as are the guest rooms. It is worth a visit, even if you don't stay here.

🏖 Colours
$$$$$ bkfst incl.
hw, pb/sb, ⊗, ⊛,
≈, ℜ
Rohrmoser Blvd.,
El Triangulo
☎296-1880 or 232-3504,
⇌296-1597 or 305-534-0362
newcolours@aol.com
Colours is somewhere between a bed and breakfast and a small, intimate hotel. It is elegantly designed, and has a North American level of comfort. The establishment caters to a gay clientele, and is located in a tranquil neighbourhood that is quite far from downtown. The managers are very dynamic, and frequently organize activities for tourists and the local gay community. They are also very well informed about gay life in Costa Rica.

Herradura
$$$$$
hw, pb, ℜ, ctv, ≡, ⊛, △, ☺
Cariari hotel district, Cariari
☎239-0033
⇌239-2292
hherradu@racsa.co.cr
The Herradura is located halfway between San José and the inter-

national airport. A first-class complex with a wealth of services, including three restaurants (Japanese, Spanish and international, the latter open 24 hours a day), access to the neighbouring golf club and about ten tennis courts. Tennis lessons are also available. Sportfishing excursions can also be organized here. Some of the rooms have a private balcony and terrace. Free for children under 12 years of age sharing a room with their parents. There is a casino on the premises.

🏖 Marriott
$$$$$
hw, pb, ctv, ≈, △, ℜ
San Antonio de Belén
☎298-0000
⇌298-0011
The Marriott provides the luxury expected of this famous chain. Attention to detail is evident in the rooms and common areas, including the spacious lobbies and outdoor spaces. Elements of the 16th-century colonial style are evident in the design, which creates some interesting effects in such a huge modern complex. Free shuttle service to and from the airport and downtown. Amenities include a golf course (with driving range), a health club, saunas, whirlpools, jogging tracks, two swimming pools, a casino and conference reception facilities.

Meliá Cariari
$$$$$
hw, pb, ≡, ctv, ≈, ℜ, ☉
along the General Cañas Hwy.,
between the airport and San
José, at the San Antonio de
Belén intersection
☎*239-0022*
⇄*239-3007*
The Meliá Cariari is on
a vast 55ha (136 acres)
property. However, a
large part of it encom-
passes a golf club. This
superior-grade hotel is
part of the Sol Meliá
chain, and functions
both as a golf resort
and a conference cen-
tre. The decor is taste-
ful and conservative.

Parque del Lago
$$$$$ bkfst incl.
hw, pb, ctv, ≡, ℜ
Avenida 2, Calle 40/42
☎*257-8787*
⇄*223-1617*
parklago@racsa.co.cr
The classic Parque del
Lago caters primarily to
businesspeople, with
amenities such as work
and meeting rooms and
a business centre.

Radisson
$$$$$
hw, pb, ctv, ℝ, ≈, ☉, ℜ
Guapiles Highway, Barrio
Tournón
☎*257-3257*
⇄*257-8221*
The Radisson is another
of the capital's major
hotels, and is located in
Barrio Tournón, in
north-central San José,
just north of Barrio
Amón, near the El
Pueblo shopping cen-
tre. It is the kind of
place that is better
suited to the business
clientele (with confer-
ence rooms and
ejecutivos suites) or

tourists who are just
passing through.

Residencias de Golf
$$$$$
hw, pb, ≡, ctv, K, ⊛, ≈
between Residencial Los Arcos
and the Cariari hotel, in the
Cariari district
☎*239-2272*
⇄*239-2001*
residgo@racsa.co.cr
You wouldn't guess it
from the outside, but
the Residencias de Golf
has a large, peaceful
interior courtyard,
which is something to
keep in mind when
choosing your room.
All the rooms are at-
tractive and very com-
fortable. Guests have
access to the Cariari
Country Club. Free
airport shuttle.

San José Palacio
$$$$$
hw, pb, ≡, ctv, ≈, △, ☉, ⊛,
ℜ
on the General Cañas Hwy.,
between La Sabana and La
Uruca
☎*220-2034*
⇄*220-2036*
The San José Palacio is
a major hotel that be-
longs to the Spanish
Barcelo chain. Its de-
sign and decor conform
to North American
tastes. There are tennis
and racquetball courts
on the premises.

Restaurants

The restaurants of the
major hotels generally
offer good international
cuisine, and are your
best bet if you have

your heart set on an
American continen-
tal-style breakfast.

You can purchase all
kinds of food at the
numerous sidewalk
kiosks lining the streets
of San José: commercial
or freshly prepared
beverages, fruits, little
pastries—and more
daring types can try the
fried food, sandwiches
and meats cooked on
the spot.

Most of the major fast
food chains can be
found in the San José
area, so you should
have no difficulty find-
ing your favourite one.

To sample typical Costa
Rican fast food, try the
small **AS** restaurant
chain, which serves
quick regional meals in
an atmosphere similar
to McDonald's. There is
an outlet on Avenida 2,
between Calle 1 and
Calle Central.

Some restaurant chains
prepare more elaborate
meals. Among these is
Rosti Pollos, a favourite
among Costa Ricans.
This restaurant chain
serves very good
chicken—cooked just
about any way you
like. Take-out service is
also available.

Most restaurant menus
are in Spanish and Eng-
lish.

San José

Deceptive Names

To avoid unpleasant surprises at meals, here is a short list of terms that sometimes lead to confusion.

The "maple syrup" that often appears on menus, would never fool someone from eastern North America, not even someone with a heavy cold! It is actually corn syrup and has little to do with the tree that produces the incomparable genuine maple syrup.

On menus here, the term "lobster" means "spiny lobster," an entirely different species from its northern cousin.

Mantequilla is literally translated as butter. But since butter is scarce and very expensive in Costa Rica, what is usually served is a derivative that is somewhere between butter and margarine.

Jugos naturales are sometimes made with... powdered mix! Moreover, the term *fresco* is used for both freshly squeezed juice and a carbonized soft drink. Make sure you know what you're really being offered!

La Cañada
$
11am to 11:30pm
Calle 8, Calle 10/2
☎*222-1672*
La Cañada inexplicably won our hearts. Though its decor is not particularly remarkable, and the staff is not exceptionally friendly, the place is clean, popular (even among young people) and, above all, its *boca* dishes (with fries) are generous for the price, which means you can easily eat here for under $5! Moreover, the place is off the tourist circuit and really feels like a "neighbourhood restaurant."
A good opportunity to mingle with the city's local population.

La Cocina de Bordolino
$
Calle 21, Avenida 6
La Cocina de Bordolino is a cheap but decent little *soda* that serves Argentinian-style empanadas in a setting that includes the always noisy television set.

Chelles
$
Avenida Central, Calle 9
Chelles is a small and unpretentious *café-soda-bar* that has, among other things, a long counter for those in a hurry. Clean and inexpensive.

Soda Mauren
$
Avenida 4, Calle 3
Soda Mauren is a small *soda* where local workers gather to eat. Very clean and pleasant.

Mercado Central
$
Avenida Central/1, Calle 6/8
Mercado Central is another place that serves small, inexpensive meals.

Morazán
$
Morazán, located opposite the park of the same name, celebrated its 100th anniversary in 1997. Pleasant, unpretentious and very popular, it offers all kinds of different beverages, which are displayed along the walls, and serves very good *bocas*. The restaurant prides itself on serving the best "gourmet coffees."

Plants somehow manage to survive on the desolate rim of the Irazú Volcano.
- *Claude-Hervé Bazin*

A waterfall in verdant surroundings: typical of Costa Rican scenery.
- *Didier Raffin*

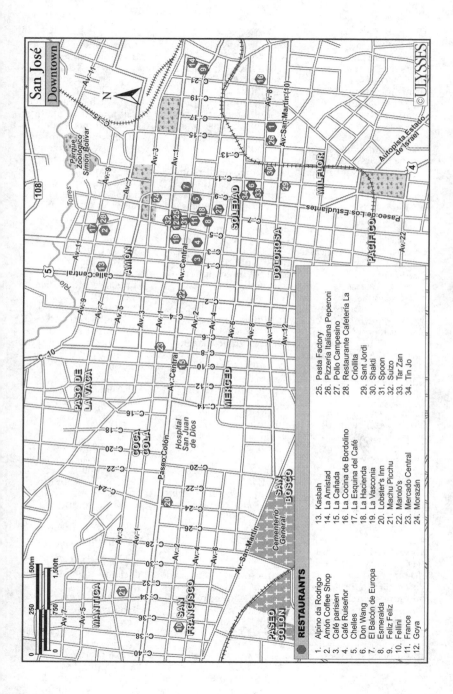

A great meeting place for Costa Ricans, students and foreigners alike. However, Morazán resounds with the sounds of a jukebox and two or three televisions. Alcoholic beverages are served from 10am to midnight. Cuban cigars and cigarillos are sold here, as well.

Papa Brava

$

every day until 2am
Carretera Prospero Fernández service road, opposite La Sabana Park
☎*220-7414*
Papa Brava *restaurant-soda* is a great find. The staff is young and friendly, and the place is ideal to go to after exploring La Sabana Park or playing a game of tennis at the sports club (whose young clientele often gets together here). The house speciality is *papa brava*, a delicious dish of potatoes stuffed with different ingredients. The restaurant also draws local businesspeople.

La Vasconia

$

Calle 3, Avenida 1
☎*223-4857*
Ill-assorted tables covered with waxed tablecloths make La Vasconia a simple, unpretentious *restaurant-soda* that draws a crowd from San José. The place offers all kinds of very reasonably priced *ceviches*.

Vishnu

$

Calle 1, Avenida 4; Avenida 1
Calle 1/3 or Calle 14
Avenida Central/2
You have to try the Vishnu vegetarian restaurants at least once. Tasty and original lunches are prepared with whole-grain flour and other healthy ingredients. There are many different dishes, whose presentation alone will rouse your tastebuds. The desserts are excellent. Moreover, the place is spotless. Note, however, that all three outlets are generally very busy; you may well have to wait a little while before finding a seat.

Supermercado Yaohan

$

opposite the Corobici hotel, Sabana Este
The cafeteria of the Supermercado Yaohan is also an excellent place for a good, fast meal served in very clean surroundings.

Il Bagatto

$$

Tue to Sat noon to 3pm and 7pm to 11pm, Sun noon to 3pm
Zapote, Curridabat, opposite the Registro Nacional
☎*224-5297*
Il Bagatto offers home-made Italian cuisine at inexpensive prices. A worthwhile choice.

El Balcón de Europa

$$

Calle 9, Avenida Central/1
☎*221-4841*
Right by the Hotel Del Rey, El Balcón de

Europa is a very pleasant restaurant whose walls are covered in old photographs. Open since 1909, the establishment has earned itself a solid reputation in the capital. Even Sunday nights can be packed with a lively crowd, and pleasant background music adds to the atmosphere. A delicious Italian cheese platter is served as a starter.

City Café

$$

Avenida 1, Calle 9
☎*221-7272*
The City Café is located in the Hotel Del Rey. The place is open day and night and serves good lunches in a fine ambiance, with photographs from the twenties on the walls.

El Farolito

$$

San Pedro
☎*234-9569*
Guadalupe
☎*234-2000*
At Farolito's two locations, you'll be served Mexican food that is prepared quickly yet well in a setting that is cross between a *taberna* and a fast-food restaurant.

La Esquina de Los Mariscos

$$

Mon to Fri 11am to 10:30pm, Sun 11am to 9pm
on the street along the west side of La Sabana Park
☎*443-8077*
La Esquina de Los Mariscos is a good, inexpensive seafood

restaurant that is very popular with Costa Ricans—always a good sign!

Feliz Feliz
$$
Calle 23, Avenida 1, next to the La Amistad restaurant
☎222-2320
Specializing in Chinese cuisine, Feliz Feliz has a varied menu that attracts families, particularly on Sundays. It has the simple, ordinary decor of a family restaurant. The *tacos chinos* (egg rolls) are very good, and the staff is fairly affable. One drawback is that the television set at the back of the room is always on.

Kasbah
$$
Mon to Fri 11am to 11pm, Sat and Sun 11am to midnight
Calle Central, Avenida 7/9
Kasbah serves good *ceviches*, among other things, in a somewhat Moorish interior with a pleasant, relaxed ambiance. The restaurant, which is popular with a gay clientele, is also a bar.

Mac's American Bar & Grill
$$
at the San Rafael and Escazú junction
Mac's American Bar & Grill is a small, unpretentious bar-restaurant with a decor to match. The place is always busy, with a crowd looking for a meal (North American fare) or a beer.

Machu Picchu
$$
Mon to Sat 11:30am to 3pm and 6pm to 10pm
Calle 32, Avenida 1
☎222-7384
The very simply decorated Machu Picchu serves Peruvian cuisine of excellent quality for the price. This place is worth checking out.

Pasta Factory
$$
Mon to Sat 11am to 10:30pm
Avenida 1, Calle 7
☎222-4642
The Pasta Factory offers fresh pasta as well as pizza in a congenial atmosphere.

Pollo Campesino
$$
every day 11am to midnight
Calle 1, Avenida 3/5
☎255-1438
Pollo Campesino is a rotisserie (take-out available) where you can see the chicken cooking on enormous rotating spits. The decor, however, is rather ordinary and somewhat cheesy, like that of 1970s fast food restaurants (plywood, booths, etc.).

The popular **Pollo Frito Pio-Pio** ($$; *Avenida 2, Calle 2*) serves fried chicken, as does **Campero** ($$), which has an outlet on Plaza de la Cultura.

Shakti
$$
Mon to Fri 7am to 4pm
Calle 13, Avenida 8, right near the Fleur de Lys hotel
☎222-9096
Shakti is a lovely little restaurant recommended for its macrobiotic cuisine. However, it closes very early.

Lamm's Steak House
$$
main street, Escazú
Lamm's Steak House has two simply decorated rooms, one of which is right on the street. Prices are reasonable, given the quality of the meals.

Tar Zan
$$
Calle 11, Avenida 6/8
☎223-1537
Tar Zan specializes in Americanized Chinese cooking. Its family atmosphere (with the television set always playing) means the food here is cheaper than in the neighbouring restaurants of the same kind. Clean.

Las Tunas
$$
open late at night
Sabana Norte
Las Tunas "restaurant-complex" *(complejo)* has a varied menu. The place is made up of several small dining rooms and a covered terrace, unified by an overall "cathedral" design. Of course, there is a television set in all four corners of the room. A convenient place for late-night victuals.

San José

Gran Italia

Escazú

$$-$$$

Set up outdoors at the entrance to a shopping mall on the noisy main street of Escazú, the Gran Italia celebrates Italy in a big way! Forget the traffic noises, and have a seat at lunchtime to savour the excellent homemade pasta garnished with delectable sauces. The prices are slightly high, but it is money well spent! The Gran Italia also doubles as a gourmet grocery store: you can stock up on grilled vegetables, pasta and all kinds of imported products from Italy. Don't forget the dessert counter, especially the selection of Italian ice cream.

Alpino da Rodrigo

$$$

11:30am to 2:30pm and 6:30pm to 10:30pm,
Avenida 8, opposite Calle 17
☎222-4950
Alpino da Rodrigo is a charming Italian restaurant that was the first in the country (1961) to offer pizza and Italian cuisine. The inviting interior has an Italian atmosphere, with blue-and-red tablecloths and wood decor. The wonderful aroma of tomatoes, spices and sauce fills the air. The establishment is composed of a restaurant (with television, unfortunately) and a dining room.

La Amistad

$$$

Calle 23, Avenida 1, right next to the El Cartel de la Boca del Monte bar
☎221-0559 or 223-8876
La Amistad specializes in Chinese cuisine. Its decor is simple and its service unpretentious.

Los Antojitos

$$$

several outlets, including one in the Rohrmoser district, on Route 104
☎231-5564
Los Antojitos serves very good Mexican cuisine and has a great holiday ambiance, with Mexican singers and musicians trying hard to outdo each other!

El Chicote

$$$

every day 11am to midnight
Avenida Las Américas, 400m west of the ICE building, Sabana Norte
☎232-0936 or 232-3777
El Chicote is a first-rate restaurant well-known for its grill dishes. It has a terrace and a bar. The *crema de pejiballe* and *pollo Chicote* are delicious.

Don Wang

$$$

Calle 11, Avenida 6/8
☎233-6484 or 223-5925
Don Wang serves authentic Cantonese and Szechwan cuisine in a stylish and tasteful decor. For a serious and distinguished clientele not necessarily willing to splurge.

Fellini

$$$

Calle 36, Avenida 4
☎222-3520
This Italian restaurant is recommended by the Italian diaspora living in San José. Enough said! You can savour the fine cuisine of the Italian peninsula surrounded by the warm decor. On some evenings the food is even accompanied by music played by guest musicians.

El Exotico Oriente

$$$

closed Sun
main street, Escazú, opposite the Mas X Menos supermarket
☎228-5980
El Exotico Oriente specializes in Thai food. The place has a lovely, very simple ambiance, and the staff is both friendly and attentive.

Goya

$$$

Mon to Sat 11am to 2:30pm and 5:30pm to 11pm
Avenida 1, Calle 5/7, next to the Suizo restaurant
☎221-3887
Named after the famous Spanish painter, Goya has a classy decor. *Paellas* and *tortillas* are the menu's highlights. Lunch specials are available.

La Hacienda

$$$

Calle 7, Avenida 2
La Hacienda is a steakhouse whose architecture (resembling a barn) distinguishes it from the surrounding buildings. It offers steaks, of course, but

also salads and chicken.

Lukas
$$$
El Pueblo shopping centre, in the Tournón district, north of downtown
☎*233-8145*
Lukas serves good, diverse cuisine. It is all the more appealing because it is open until 2am.

María Alexandra
$$$
Mon to Sat 11:30am to 2:30pm and 5:30pm to 11:30pm
in the apartment hotel of the same name, in Escazú, on the street opposite Quiubo, in the Urbanización Trejos Montalegre district
☎*228-4876*
The María Alexandra restaurant brings together a convivial clientele in an intimate setting.

Manolo's
$$$
24 hours a day
Avenida Central, Calle Central/2
☎*221-2041 or 222-2234*
Manolo's has a wonderful, lively atmosphere with its own musicians performing every night of the week (*from 7pm to 9pm*). Though the place is very popular, finding a table should not be too difficult as the restaurant has a huge upstairs dining room as well as a terrace.

Ponte Vecchio
$$$
every day 11am to 2:30pm and 6pm to 10:30pm
200m (656ft) west of the San Pedro church, and 25m (82ft) farther north
☎*225-9399*
Ponte Vecchio offers patrons warm and friendly service. The chef, a New Yorker, has gone to great lengths to ensure that his restaurant is recognized as one of the 100 best in Central America.

Quiubo
$$$
main street, Escazú
☎*228-4091*
Quiubo offers steaks and international cuisine (mainly Mexican and Costa Rican) in a pub-like atmosphere. The service is very friendly and attentive. Conference rooms are available. The restaurant pays the taxi fare of guests from the Rincón del Valle hotel.

Sant Jordi
$$$
Mon to Sat 11:30am to 3pm and 6pm to midnight, closed Sun
Avenida 10, Calle 9, beneath the La Mansión de Braulio hotel
Sant Jordi offers reasonably priced Spanish specialities.

Suizo
$$$
11:30am to 2:30pm and 6pm to 10pm, closed Sun
Avenida 1, Calle 5/7
Suizo is easy to recognize by its Swiss-chalet architecture, which makes it stand out from its surroundings. Inte-

rior decor to match. It has set the standard for Swiss cuisine for several years now.

Tiffany's
$$$
Herradura hotel, Ciudad Cariari
☎*239-0033 or 293-0136*
Tiffany's serves international fare in a classy environment. Open day and night.

Tinjo
$$$
Mon to Sat 11:30am to 3pm and 5:30pm to 11pm, Sun 11:30am to 10pm
Calle 11, Avenida 6/8
☎*221-7605*
Tinjo is a very good restaurant that serves Thai, Indian, Chinese and vegetarian cuisine. A stylish and tasteful establishment. Its decor is inspiring, as are the aromas greeting you as you enter.

Le Monastère
$$$-$$$$
San Rafael de Escazú
☎*289-4404 or 228-8515*
Tucked away at the top of a mountain that dominates the whole area, Le Monastère is no doubt frequented first and foremost for its view. But it has quite a few other attractions to offer. The building was probably a chapel constructed for a rich owner and was at one time used by monks. It radiates a medieval atmosphere, giving it a lot of charm. Upstairs, the restaurant serves delicious French cuisine. Prepared alongside international dishes, this cuisine

San José

honours the establishment's French name. Treat yourself while admiring the view. Even if the restaurant's prices prevent you from enjoying a meal, don't hesitate to come here because in the basement there's a pleasant bistro-tavern, **La Cava**, where you can get a drink and a bite to eat. Between Tuesday and Saturday, you can even enjoy *música en vivo* (live music) by candlelight. On both floors, the efficient service is provided by waiters in beautiful costumes. To get here, go first to San Rafael de Escazú, where you turn left after the Multicentro Paco; from there, follow the signs. Be careful though, as the signs are not always clear; the road is sometimes tricky and it's a steep climb!

Antonio's
$$$$
Mon to Fri noon to 11pm, Sat to Sun 5:30pm to 11pm
☎*239-1613 or 293-0622*
Right next door to the Herradura hotel, in Ciudad Cariari, Antonio's is an Italian restaurant that lives up to its country's romantic reputation. The classical atmosphere (with piano) that prevails here is perfect for fine dining.

Esmeralda
$$$$
11am to 5pm
Avenida 2, Calle 5/7
☎*233-7386*
Esmeralda is a huge restaurant with a lovely decor where a great variety of food is offered. The *mariachis* who perform here draw a good-sized crowd, particularly at night. Buffet and lunch menu are available.

France
$$$$
11:45am to 2pm and 6pm to 10:30pm, Sat 6pm to 10:30pm
closed Sun
Calle 7, north of Avenida 2
☎*222-4241*
The interior of France is plastered with posters of Toulouse-Lautrec, and the main language on the menu confirms this establishment's French allegiance. Scallop of seafood with Pernod, blanquettes of veal, rabbit pâté with green pepper and cognac as well as shrimp with lime are just some of the dishes offered by this stylish restaurant.

El Fuji
$$$$
Mon to Sat noon to 2:30pm and 6pm to 11pm
☎*232-8122*
El Fuji, at the Corobici hotel (see p 93) is an elegant restaurant that specializes in Japanese food.

Grano de Oro
$$$$
6am to 10pm
Calle 30, Avenida 2/4
☎*255-3322*
The cuisine at the Grano de Oro restaurant, in the hotel of the same name (see p 90), combines classic Costa Rican and European cuisine. The resident chef, Francis Canal, has done so well that the establishment is identified by some as one of the best restaurants in the country. The decor is both enchanting and soothing.

Fleur de Lys
$$$$
Calle 13, between Avenida 2 and Avenida 6
☎*223-1206 or 257-2621*
Located in the hotel of the same name, the Fleur de Lys is graced by the decor of this magnificent home that once belonged to a coffee baron. Its small dining room has only a few tables, and is adorned with drapes, wrought-iron chandeliers, a parquet floor and walls painted in a soothing yellow colour. Take a seat and immerse yourself in real French service. You'll be seduced... and will fall further under its charm when you see your plate! The French chef, Vincent Boutinaud, prepares fine French cuisine skillfully combined with local flavours. Having lived in the Carribean for a long time, he brought with him the taste for using tropical products to set

off his dishes. His menu also offers international cuisine, guaranteeing something to please everybody.

Île de France
$$$$
Los Yoses
☎ 283-5812

The Le Bergerac hotel, in the peaceful district of Los Yoses, houses a restaurant that is a real find. The French hoteliers were duty-bound to do justice to their country's cuisine by hiring a chef worthy of their establishment's name. Thus, Jean-Claude Fromont concocts dishes that could not be more French. The lamb *aux herbes provençales* is the star attraction on the menu! Moreover, the sumptuous Île de France's felt decor and its windows opening out on to the garden only add to the pleasure of dining here. Were it not for the view, you might think you were aboard a luxury liner!

🦐 Cerutti
$$$$
on the road from San Rafael to Escazú, past the junction

Hostario Cerutti is just the place to savour a real gastronomic experience—where Italian cuisine, seafood and steaks are the stars of the menu. It also has a streetfront terrace.

The Lobster's Inn
$$$$
Paseo Colón, Calle 24

The Lobster's Inn is, as its name suggests, a seafood restaurant, and

a very popular one at that. Its elegant decor is perfect for fine dining. Attentive service.

La Masia del Triquel
$$$$
Tue to Sat 11:30am to 2pm and 6:30pm to 10:30pm, Sun 11:30am to 3:30pm
100m (328ft) east of ICE and 175m (574ft) north, in the Casa España's building, Sabana Norte
☎ 296-3528

La Masia del Triquel is a high-class restaurant that specializes in Spanish cuisine, as you will note from its decor and service. It is also home to the Casa España, a Spanish social club that has been offering its members a host of activities for over 100 years. A great place for a stylish evening out.

Rias Bajas
$$$$
Mon to Sat noon to 3pm and 6:30pm to midnight
☎ 221-7123

Rias Bajas specializes in seafood. Though delicious, meals are expensive.

Sakura
$$$$
Mon to sat 11:30am to 3pm and 6pm to 11:15pm, Sun 12:30pm to 11pm
Ciudad Cariari
☎ 239-0033

Sakura, in the Herradura hotel (see p 94), is a very well-maintained Japanese restaurant with an Asian decor.

Sancho Panza Tasca
$$$$
Mon to Sat 11:30am to 3pm and 6pm to 11:15pm, Sun 12:30pm to 11pm
Herradura hotel, Ciudad Cariari
☎ 239-0033

Sancho Panza Tasca serves Spanish cuisine in an old-style Spanish ambiance, reminiscent of *Don Quijote* (hence the name). The place has received very favourable reviews.

Cafés, Bakeries, and Pastry and Ice-Cream Shops

There are a good number of cafés, bakeries, and pastry and ice cream shops in the region, providing you with ample opportunities to have a little snack or to take a break from your explorations!

Cafeterías Panaderías Deli City
$
Cafeterías Panaderías Deli City is a chain whose outlets have spread throughout San José and in certain other cities in the region. Light meals and pretty decent pastries are available. Ignore the late-1970s interior decor and colour scheme.

Cafetería Portofino
$
next to the Aparthotel María Alexandra, on the street facing Quiubo, in the Urbanización Trejos Montalegre district

In Escazú, the Cafetería Portofino offers excellent Italian ice cream. The style and decor are more refined than those of the Pop's chain, which has an outlet nearby.

Chocolatería San Simón

main street, Escazú
Also in Escazú is the Chocolatería San Simón, a chocoholic's dream come true.

 There are two cafés in Barrio Amón: **La Esquina del Café** and the **Amón Coffee Shop** (**$**; *along Calle 3, Avenida 9*), where you can savour this exalted beverage and its every conceivable accompaniment in the charming setting of a truly delightful little café.

Musmanni
$

There are many Musmanni *panderías* in San José. These bakeries and pastry shops are not excessively refined, but their substantial and rich treats will give you a taste of Costa Rican baking. Moreover, the names of each item (*quesadilla, pan de cebolla, strudel de manzana, enchillada, pan de ajo*) are enough to tempt you to sample every last one of them.

Panadería El Caballito
$

opposite the central market, on Avenida 1
Panadería El Caballito is a very good bakery and pastry shop that has been around since 1955. It sells all kinds of bread and pastries, as well as cheese, choc-

olate bars and refreshments. Prices are very reasonable and the staff is friendly.

Panadería Durand
$

Calle 4, Avenida 5
Open day and night, the bakeries of Panadería Durand offer a wide variety of pastries and breads. The place is both pleasant and clean. This is a popular spot, and gets quite lively at night.

Pastelaría Giacomín
$

Mon to Sat 8am to noon and 2pm to 7pm
near the Automercado de Los Yoses, on Avenida Central between Calles 39 and 41
☎*225-0356*
In the Los Yoses district, the Pastelaría Giacomín sells some of the best pastries, which are especially good with a coffee.

Clean and inexpensive, **Wall's** serves all kinds of ice cream. This chain has outlets on Avenida 3, between Calles 3 and 5, and on the corner of Avenida Central and Calle Central.

Pop's is another very popular Costa Rican ice cream shop. There are many locations throughout the country, and their cool treats are very refreshing after walking around in the sun. You should have no trouble finding one in San José (there is one on Avenida Central between Calles 3 and 5, for instance).

Spoon
$$

several locations: downtown, Avenida Central, Calle 5/7
Los Yoses, 100m (328ft) south and 100m (328ft) west of Cancún
Pavas, opposite the American embassy
western suburb, Multi-Plaza shopping centre, opposite the Camino Real hotel
Spoon's various outlets offer a rather extensive menu and have a much better reputation than Deli City (see p 103). The pastries here are absolutely delicious!

Café Ruiseñor
$$

Mon to Fri 10:30am to 6pm
Avenida 2, Calle 5, at the main entrance of the Teatro Nacional
Café Ruiseñor is a very lovely coffee shop with excellent food. It is just the place for late afternoon relaxation in the centre of town. Costa Rican art works are sometimes exhibited here.

Café Parisien
$$

Avenida 2, Calle 3, opposite the Teatro Nacional
☎*221-4000*
In the very heart of downtown, you can't miss the Café Parisien, located on the main floor of the Gran Hotel Costa Rica, on the square. This charmingly tranquil yet bustling café (it is located on the public square, after all!) has long drawn a large clientele. It is a fashionable place to go for 5 o'clock tea.

Delimundo

$$

in the basement of the Plaza
Colonial Escazú shopping
centre, on the main street
In Escazú, Delimundo
is a small restaurant
that serves bagels,
sandwiches, natural
juices, salads and a
selection of very good
breads (i.e. pumper-
nickel). Its interior,
however, is somewhat
cold and sterile.

Entertainment

Bars and Nightclubs

As you might expect,
San José is
hardly lacking
in nightspots.
The best way to
get anywhere at night
is by taxi. They are
affordable and you
won't have to walk
through unsafe
areas. You will
find lovely
places to have
a drink or
mingle with
the night
owls if
you stroll
around the
downtown
core. The
area north of
Avenida 2 and east
of Calle 4 is one of the
safest. The Amón dis-
trict (barrio) has an
especially interesting
nightlife.

The San Pedro shop-
ping mall houses the
largest nightclub in the
city, the **Planet Mall**, a
flashy place that attracts
a huge crowd.

El Pueblo is a shopping
mall with stores, restau-
rants and bars. Among
the latter, we should
mention the **Coco Loco**,
which exudes a pretty
crazy atmosphere; the
Plaza, a large nightclub
with quite a small
dance floor where peo-
ple dance in couples;
the **Infinito**, where the
dance floor vibrates to
a variety of romantic,
salsa and merengue or
more modern rhythms;
and finally, of quite
another order, the **Café
Arte Boruca**, a lovely
little bar whose pretty
decoration
adds to the
ambiance of
intimacy.

Most of the
friendly little bars
where you
can sit and
have a
drink are
in the
university
district,
San
Pedro.
Two of these are
Baco, a wine bar,
and the **Café Jazz**,
where you can
hear jazz.

El Balcón de Europa

Calle 9, Avenida Central/1
The popular El Balcón
de Europa restaurant is
a good place for a
drink, and its reputa-
tion is well deserved.

Café Plantter's

Escazú, on the main highway
Café Plantter's attracts
such a large crowd of
young people on Fri-
day nights that some
end up spilling out
onto the street, beer in
hand.

El Cuartel de la Boca del Monte

Mon to Fri noon to
2:30am, Sat and Sun
7pm to 2am
Avenida 1, Calle 21/23
☎221-0327
El Cuartel de la Boca
del Monte is well-know
for its good daytime
meals as well as for its
nighttime ambiance.
Even during the week,
you will often have to
make your way
through a tightly
packed crowd in the
evenings. Most of San
José's youth hang out
in this very pleasant
establishment. Meals
are served late into the
night, which is rare in
this city.

Esmeralda

11am to 5am
Avenida 2, Calle 5/7
☎233-7386
Go see (and especially
hear!) the mariachis at
the Esmeralda; they
literally sing at the top
of their lungs! The
songs (lyrics and mu-
sic) are sung in their
entirety; these mariachis
stay true to the origi-
nals! Indeed, they
gather on the sidewalk
in front of the restau-
rant at night, blocking
the flow of pedestrian
traffic somewhat.

San José

The Loft

at the San Rafael and Escazú junction
The Loft is a bar located above Mac's restaurant. A hip and friendly clientele shoots pool in its laid-back ambiance. The bar offers "2-for-1" specials.

Talamanca

Avenida 2, Calle 8/10
The top-floor bar of the Talamanca hotel provides its quiet clientele with an interesting view over the city.

Las Tunas

Sabana Norte
Las Tunas (see p 99) has a nightclub on weekends.

Gay Bars and Nightclubs

La Avispa

Tue to Sun
Calle 1, Avenida 8/10
La Avispa has been attracting a gay and lesbian crowd for 18 years now. A mix of Pop and the tropical rythms of Latin music is played here.

Café Mundo

Mon to Sat
Avenida 9, Calle 15, in the bend
Café Mundo is a rather quiet European-style restaurant that turns into a bar at night.

Deja Vu

Wed to Sun
Calle 2, Avenida 14/16
Featuring techno-pop mixed with Spanish hits, Deja Vu is described as the best club in Central America. Mixed crowd.

Kasbah

11am to 11pm, Fri and Sat until midnight
Calle Central, Avenida 7/9
The Moorish-style bar-restaurant Kasbah sometimes turns into a dance club at night.

Casinos

Casino Colonial

24 hours a day
Avenida 1, Calle 9/11, right near the Del Rey hotel
☎258-2807
If you want to try your luck at games of chance, there are many casinos in San José, most of which are open 24 hours a day. In addition to the many hotel gaming clubs, the Casino Colonial is an independent, high-class gambling house, as evidenced by its interior decor (vast spaces with high ceilings, ceramic-tiled floors, matching colours, and stately columns) and the doorperson in attendance. The building's façade is easily recognizable, with its columns, pediment and portico. The casino also houses a restaurant (*$$$*) with a North American atmosphere.

Cultural and Artistic Activities

Most of the nation's newspapers (the *Tico Times* and *La Nación* in particular) will provide you with information about the cultural and artistic activities being held in the capital.

Theatres

Teatro La Aduana, Teatro Fanal and Teatro 1987
Calle 25, Avenida 3/5
☎221-5205 or 257-0005

Teatro del Angel
Avenida Central, Calle 13/15
☎222-8258

Teatro Carpa
Moravia
☎234-2866

☎222-4376

Teatro Eugene O'Neill
Centro Cultural Costarricense Norteamericano
in the Dent district, Calle Los Negritos
☎253-5527

Teatro Laurence Olivier
Avenida 2, Calle 28
☎223-1969 or 222-1034

Teatro La Mascara
Calle 13, Avenida 2/4
☎255-4250

Teatro Melico Salazar
Avenida 2, Calle Central/2
☎221-4952

Teatro Nacional
☎233-6354

Teatro Vargas Calvo
Calle 5, Avenida Central/2
☎222-1875

An entirely new theatre **La Comedia** (☎255-3255) has just opened its doors on Avenida 2. This small theatre is dedicated to comedies that run for long periods of time—if they are popular, that is! At the entrance, there's a small café, which is just the ticket for pre- or post-show discussions.

Cinema

Sala Garbo
Avenida 2, Calle 28
Sala Garbo screens international films with Spanish subtitles.

Teatro Laurence Olivier
Avenida 2, Calle 28
Teatro Laurence Olivier presents plays and films. The complex also has an art gallery and a café.

The **Universidad de Costa Rica**, in San Pedro, presents modestly priced films in the auditorium of the **Estudios Generales** pavilion. Like at other North American universities, the films shown here are generally recent, often repertory, and intended primarily for the student population. However, screenings are also open to the general public.

Shopping

In addition to Costa Rican chain department stores, San José has the large, popular, Japanese-owned **Supermercado Yaohan** supermarket located opposite the Corobici hotel, in Sabana Este.

Librería Universal
Avenida 1, Calle Central/1
☎*222-5822*
≈*222-2992*
The Librería Universal is a very large bookshop and stationer's with one outlet in the heart of the city, and another on the Prospero Fernández Highway service road, which runs along the south side of La Sabana Park. A good place to pick up books about Costa Rica (photo and fact books) as well as popular books (business, etc.). Curios and other knick-knacks are also sold. You can sip an espresso on the second floor.

Librería Lehmann
Avenida Central, Calle 1/3
☎*223-1212*
The Librería Lehmann is another major bookshop located in the heart of the city.

Librería Internacional
300m (984ft) west of Taco Bell, in the Dent district, San Pedro
☎*283-6965, 253-9533*
≈*283-7857*
The Librería Internacional sells English, French, Spanish and German language books.

Chispas Books
9am to 6pm
Calle 7, Avenida Central/1
☎*256-8251*
There are several small bookshops, many of which sell used books, on or near Paseo de los Estudiantes. Chispas Books has a fine selection of English language books.

There are also numerous bookshops near the Universidad de Costa Rica campus, in San Pedro.

Mercado Central
Avenida Central/1, Calle 6/8
The bustling Mercado Central also merits a visit to pick up certain consumer goods (clothing, accessories, all kinds of food, flowers, etc.) while immersing yourselves in a pleasant and completely Costa Rican atmosphere.

Cigar Shoppe
Calle 5, Avenida 3
If you want to buy cigars, there are two places of interest around Parque Morazán. The first is the Cigar Shoppe, a small chic place on the main floor of Diana's Inn that offers Cuban, Honduran and Nicaraguan cigars. The second is the unpretentious **Morazán** restaurant, which stocks cigars and cigarillos near the cash register.

For arts and crafts, head to **El Pueblo** *(in the Tournón district, north of downtown,* ☎*222-5938)* shopping centre, which houses all kinds of galeries and stores carrying souvenirs, handicrafts and artwork, some by famous artists such as Bolívar García and Amighetti.

The **Mercado Central** also has kiosks selling handicrafts.

San José, of course, has several places where you can stock up on **coffee**: first and foremost, at the Mercado Central and in supermarkets, but also at souvenir and coffee shops scattered throughout the capital. **La Esquina del Café** as well as the **Amón Coffee Shop** *(near the corner of Calle 3 and Avenida 9, Barrio Amón)*, located almost next to each other, are also worth checking out. They have displays of coffee and its many uses; it's amazing what can be done with *granos de oro* these days! Both places feature all kinds of ideas for gifts to bring back. There are also a certain number of merchants that sell coffee, which they describe as *100% puro*, around Avenida 1 on the few blocks northwest of the Mercado Central.

The **shop at the Museos del Banco Central de Costa Rica** *(Calle 5, Avenida Central)* also offers visitors a golden opportunity (literally and figuratively) to do some great shopping.

The boutique is part of the underground museum complex located beneath Plaza de la Cultura that comprises, among other institutions, the Museum of Numismatics and the Museo del Oro Precolombino (Pre-Colombino Gold Museum). Sold here are gold reproductions of pre-Colombian and other art works, as well as beautifully crafted art and history books.

The **Mercado Nacional de Artesanía** *(Avenida 1, Calle 11)* sell handicrafts.

ANDA *(Avenida Central, Calle 5/7)* sells handicrafts made by Costa Rica's native people.

Atmósfera
Calle 5, Avenida 1/3
☎*222-4322*
For high-quality crafts, head to Atmósfera. They have everything from T-shirts to jewellery, not to mention knick-knacks and cigars, but their prices are quite high.

Mercado Nacional de Artesanía
Avenida 4 bis, Calle 11
☎*221-5012*
The Mercado Nacional de Artesanía offers a whole range of crafts for all tastes and budgets. The Arts and Crafts Gallery, which manages the store, also has a little outlet at the entrance to the Museo Nacional.

Galería Namu
Avenida 7, Calle 5/7
☎*256-3412*
Looking for something different and more authentic? Go to Galería Namu. This is a gallery whose goal is to promote the work of indigenous Costa Rican artists. The owners take particular care when they select works and above all, when they sell them, telling you in detail about the origins of the object, the history of the artist and the process of making it. The items are generally not too expensive and purchasing them is a way to encourage these emerging artists.

Finally, the region surrounding the capital is now crammed with American-style shopping malls. To mention only one, you'll find everything at the **Multi Plaza** on the Autopista Prospero Fernandez.

Motmot

The Central Valley

Cradled between mountains in the middle of the country, the Central Valley provided a fertile terrain for the country's economic development.

Thus, the country's first cities sprang up here, including the national capital, San José and three of the provincial capitals: Alajuela, Heredia and Cartago.

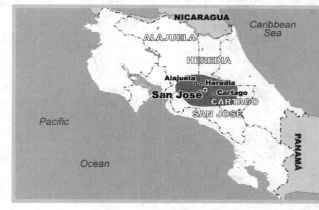

Today, the Valley attracts travellers for two different reasons. The larger, historic cities are home to many of the nation's cultural and artistic activities. Because these cities are more developed, they also have many of the country's best hotels and restaurants, as well as a thriving nightlife.

In addition to its cultural attractions, there is the extraordinary natural beauty of the Central Valley. The weather here is always temperate, and the fields, plantations and pastures in the countryside almost extrava-

gantly green. Lush forests and dense tropical jungle cover hillsides in tiers. And the entire valley is encircled by majestic volcanoes and mountain chains. Perhaps the best way to describe the Central Valley is to liken it to heaven on earth!

The fact that all this natural beauty is concentrated in a small area makes the Central Valley a great place to stay. The entire 50 by 20km (31 by 12mi) region can be travelled from one end to the other in a day. The

dramatic changes in elevation provide many striking views that combine all of the valley's most scenic elements: fields, forests, cliffs, volcanoes and cities.

While this chapter offers some suggested activities, feel free to venture off to do some random exploring on the roads in the area. Whichever direction you take, they lead to delightful surprises!

Finding Your Way Around

By Car

Western Central Valley

Alajuela: it's very easy to get to Alajuela from San José. Simply take the General Cañas highway, which starts at the Parque La Sabana, towards the international airport. Alajuela is close to the airport and the signs leading to it are quite clear.

Ojo de Agua: take the General Cañas highway west. Past the Cariari and Herradura hotels, turn left towards San Antonio de Belén. Stay on this road until Ojo de Agua.

Atenas: this town is off the General Cañas highway, a few kilometres past Alajuela if you're coming from San José. This is also an alternative route to Jacó, on the Pacific Coast (the other way is via Puntarenas). There's usually a fair amount of traffic, especially on weekends. On the other hand, it's a pretty drive through fabulous, hilly countryside.

The Butterfly Farm: take the General Cañas highway (west of the Hotel Cariari) towards San Antonio de Belén.

In San Antonio, turn right after the church, then left after the first block of houses. Stay on this road, which passes through the villages of San Rafael and La Guácima. Bear left at the fork in the road at Hacienda Los Reyes. Follow the signs to the nearby farm.

Madame Butterfly Garden: begin as if you were going to the Butterfly Farm. Take the General Cañas to San Antonio de Belén. Turn right after the church, then left after the first block of houses. Stay on this road through the villages of San Rafael and La Guácima. Then bear right at the fork in the road at Hacienda Los Reyes. Turn left at the Las Vueltas bridge after La Guácima.

Parque Nacional Volcán Poás: take the Interamericana Highway to Alajuela. Then take the secondary road through San Pedro de Poás and Fraijanes.

Northern Central Valley

Heredia: Heredia is very close to San José. Take the General Cañas highway; there is more than one exit to the city. Follow the signs.

Monte de la Cruz: take the road that goes north from San Rafael. (San Rafael is just a few kilometres northeast of Heredia).

Parque Nacional Braulio Carrillo and **Rainforest Aerial Tram**: from San José, take Calle 3 north. This road becomes the Autopista Braulio Carrillo (or Guápiles) *($0.85 toll)*. It takes about 20min to get to the park and 45min to get to the Aerial Tram.

Eastern Central Valley

Cartago: this city is found along the Interamericana Highway, which goes south to Cerro de la Muerte and the southern region of the country. This major highway has four lanes most of the way from San José to Cartago.

Parque Nacional Volcán Irazú: take the Interamericana to Cartago. Continue through the village of San Rafael and follow the signs to the park.

Refugio Nacional de Fauna Silvestre Tapantí: go to Cartago via the Interamericana. From there, take the secondary road through Paraíso, Orosi, Río Macho and Tapantí.

Monumento Nacional Guayabo: go to Cartago, then pass through Paraíso, Juan Viñas and Turrialba. Follow the signs for the Monumento Nacional Guayabo.

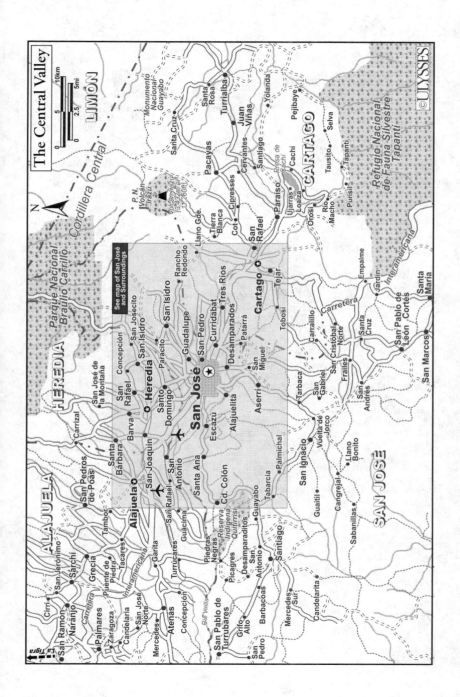

The Central Valley

By Bus

Western Central Valley

Alajuela: departures from San José are frequent. Buses leave from Avenida 2, between Calles 12 and 14. In Alajuela, the bus depot is to the west of the market and the central park.

Ojo de Agua: in San José, buses leave for Ojo de Agua every hour from the stop on Avenida 1, between Calles 18 and 20.

The Butterfly Farm: in Alajuela, the bus stop is 100m (328ft) south and 100m (328ft) west of the Tikal supermarket. Make sure the bus is marked "La Guácima abajo." There are four buses to the Butterfly Farm between 6am and 2pm. The trip takes about 40min. Ask the driver for "La Finca de Mariposas." From San José, there are two buses every day except Sunday. The buses leave at 11am and 2pm from the stop on Avenida 1 between Calles 20 and 22 that says "Ojo de Agua/San Antonio." Stay on the bus until the last stop of the 1hr trip. From the school, just follow the signs for 300m (984ft) to the farm. The bus returns to San José at 3:15pm. However, there are three direct buses to The Butterfly Farm every day. For information and reser-

vations, call the Farm at ☎*438-0400*.

Parque Nacional Volcán Poás: buses run only on Sundays and holidays at 8:30am (*$1.25; Calle 12, Avenida 2/4*).

Northern Central Valley

Heredia: buses leave San José for Heredia every 10min. The trip takes about 25min.

Barva: buses leave Heredia for Barva every 30min.

Parque Nacional Braulio Carrillo: buses leave from San José (*Calle 12, Avenida 7/9*) every 30min from 5:30am to 9:45pm. Ask the driver for the Quebrada González reception centre. To take the bus back to San Jose, wait for it near the road. Transport Empresarios Guapilenos (*$1.55,* ☎*223-1276*).

Rainforest Aerial Tram: the buses for Parque Nacional Braulio Carrillo continue on to here. Ask the driver for the Rainforest Aerial Tram.

Eastern Central Valley

Cartago: buses leave San José for Cartago every 10min.

Orosi: buses leave Cartago for Orosi about every 1.5hrs, between 6am and 10pm, Monday to Friday. The re-

turn trips depart between 4:30pm and 6:30pm.

Turrialba: buses leave San José for Turrialba and Guayabo every hour, between 5am and 10pm. The return buses follow the same schedule for the 50min trip.

Parque Nacional Volcán Irazú: there is bus service to the park on Saturdays and Sundays only. Departure time is 8am (*$4.20; Avenida 2, Calle 1/3,* ☎*272-0651*).

Refugio Nacional de Fauna Silvestre Tapantí: take the bus to Cartago, where you transfer to the bus for the Orosi Valley (☎*551-6810*). This bus takes you as far as the Río Macho (just past Orosi), about 9km (5.6mi) from the entrance to the park. From there, you can take a taxi (*about $6*) to the park.

Monumento Nacional Guayabo: take the bus to Turrialba and transfer to the bus that goes to the monument (☎*556-0583*).

Practical Information

The Central Valley is home to almost half of the population of Costa Rica and is thus highly urbanized. Also, because the three provincial capitals are only a few kilometres from the national capital, you shouldn't have any trouble finding the basic services anywhere in the region.

Western Central Valley

Alajuela: all the major national banks can be found in Alajuela. They are concentrated in the Parque Central area, and most have ATMs (automated teller machines).

The San Rafael hospital *(Calle Central, Avenida 9, ☎441-5011)* is north of the downtown area.

The departure area for most buses is two streets west of the Mercado Central, on Avenida 1.

Northern Central Valley

Heredia: there are several banks around the Parque Central and on Avenida 6.

The major bus stops are also around the Parque Central, on Calle Central.

San Vicente de Paul hospital *(☎261-0091)* is located west of the downtown area, at the end of Avenida 8, on Calle 14.

Eastern Central Valley

Cartago: most of the large national banks have branches in Cartago: Banco Popular

is located near the south side of the Parque de Las Ruinas.

The Max Peralta hospital *(☎551-0611)* is located to the south of Parque Central (and of Parque de Las Ruinas) on Avenida 5.

The bus stops are situated either on Calle 4 or nearby Avenida 3.

Exploring

Western Central Valley

West of the Mexico hospital, between San José and the Juan Santamaría airport, **Pueblo Antiguo** ★ *(☎296-2212 or 231-2001, ≈296-2212)* is a restoration of an historical village that shows what life in Costa Rica was like at the end of the 19th century.

Alajuela Cathedral

In addition to the village and old-fashioned countryside, there are performances by professionals *(music and dance: Fri to Sun 6:30pm; period craftsmanship: Sat and Sun 10am)*.

Ojo de Agua ★ *(5km or 3mi west of San Antonio, which is 3km or 1.9mi from the General Cañas highway, between Alajuela and San José)* is a recreational complex with underground springs that attracts people from all parts of the Valley. In addition to lakes, facilities include playgrounds, an amphitheatre and green spaces. A babysitting service is available. However, this public facility can get crowded, especially on weekends.

Coffee plantations and fields of decorative plants are fairly common sights in the Valley, particularly north of Alajuela (from Quebradas to San Isidro de Poás) and in the Atenas Valley.

The Alajuela Region

Alajuela ★, the capital of the province of the same name, is somewhat warmer than San José because of its lower altitude. Its main advantage is that it is only 5min away from the airport. However, thanks to the General Cañas highway, San José is also easy to reach from here. Alajuela is the province's transportation hub, but the modern highway makes it possible to bypass the town and visit most of the province's tourist attractions.

The architecture of the **Alajuela cathedral** *(Calle Central, Avenida Central/1)*, with its classical porch with pilasters and cupola in the centre of the transept, is vaguely Portuguese-Gothic. The **Iglesia La Agonia** *(Calle 9, Avenida Central/1)* is probably more attractive though and has a charming little park with a fountain and an enormous tree next to it.

The shady **Parque Central** in Alajuela is a very popular meeting place for the locals. Like most of Costa Rica's urban central parks, it has a pavilion for concerts, traditional festivals or neighbourhood theatrical productions.

The **Museo Juan Santamaría** *(free admission; Tue to Sun 10am to 6pm; one block north of Parque Central, inside a former prison)* retells the famous events of the mid-19th century when William Walker (see p 24) tried to invade Costa Rica and set up a pro-slavery political regime, but failed.

Los Chorros ★ *(a few kilometres north of Tacares, which is 15km or 9.3mi from Alajuela)* are two lovely falls, about 25m (82ft) high, which are protected by the national park service. Although this is officially private property and has a fence that no one seems to see, there are some amenities for visitors (parking, toilets and places for washing feet).

The view from the path going down to the falls, accompanied by the sound of the river, is enchanting. Walk down the slope, then follow the trail. Visiting Los Chorros is certainly a pleasant outing, and it's very popular with *Ticos* on weekends.

The Atenas Valley Region, between La Garita and San Mateo

In **La Garita**, **Zoo Ave** ★★ *($7; every day 9am to 5pm; 3km or 1.9mi from the Atenas exit off the Interamericana, ☎433-8989, ⇒433-9140)* is a zoo that was originally an ornithological garden *(ave means "bird" in Spanish)*. It now includes monkeys, reptiles and many varieties of plants. This zoo is unique because the animals were either abandoned, injured or confiscated by the authorities. Since 1995 it has been recognized by the Costa Rican government as an official animal shelter.

Monarch Butterfly

Further south in **La Guácime** is the largest and oldest enterprise of its kind in Costa Rica, **The Butterfly Farm** ★★★ *($15; every day 8:30am to 3:30pm; across from the Los Reyes Country Club, ☎438-0400, ⇒438-0300)*. The owners mainly raise butterflies for export, but add an educational aspect to it with an enlightening 2hr guided tour that explains the whole process of raising and selling butterflies, and includes a documentary presentation. Having a meal at the farm's restaurant or picnicking on the grounds is a nice way to round out your visit. There is a small shop on the premises.

Madame Butterfly Garden *(every day 8am to 4pm;* ☎*255-2031 or 255-2262)* is a greenhouse garden not far from The Butterfly Farm. One greenhouse is for raising butterflies and the other is for reproducing them. The owner has studied the subject for more than three years and can explain it in English.

For special entertainment that'll please horse lovers, head to **Rancho San Miguel** *(La Guácima,* ☎*220-4060 or 220-2828,* ✆*232-2048)*. This stable breeds Spanish horses and offers shows in which these incredible animals demonstrate all their grace and intelligence.

People say that the region of **Atenas** enjoys the best climate in the world. This, coupled with its geography, makes it is one of the most gorgeous places to visit in the entire country. Between La Garita and Atenas there are many incredible panoramas of the fairly steep mountains and the rivers that run between them. There is

only one real drawback to the area's lack of commercial development: there are no roadside restaurants where you can stop to eat while admiring the view.

Cooperativa Agropecuaria Industrial y de Servicios Multiples de Atenas *(*☎*446-5141)* is a coffee-producing co-op that offers a tour of its facilities if you make advance reservations, which is definitely worth it!

Between Atenas and San Mateo, the chain of mountains that separates the Central Valley from the Pacific Coast dominates the breathtakingly beautiful scenery. But pay attention, since the narrow and winding road demands the driver's full attention because it goes up one side of the mountain range and comes down the other, with some steep sections along the way. Unfortunately, there are few places to stop and take in the view, except for a rudimentary and not-too-clearly indicated lookout at Alto del Monte, not far past the Linda Vista bar near Atenas. This is an ideal trip—from a passenger's point of view!

The San Ramón and Zarcero Region

Bosque Nuboso Los Angeles ★★ *(between San Ramón and La Tigra, signs to it are fairly clear)* is a magnificent private

Fair-Trade Coffee

In recent years, diverse measures aimed at balancing North–South relations have been augmented. For example, we now hear more and more about "fair trade." Among other products, fair-trade coffee is increasingly available on markets in the North. Fair-trade coffee refers to coffee that is purchased on more equitable terms from small producers in the Southern Hemisphere—producers who, for a variety of reasons, are caught in the cycle of poverty and only rarely obtain a fair price for their coffee or labour from multinational companies. Certified fair-trade coffee guarantees the consumer that the small grower has been paid fairly for his crop. Nearly 300 cooperatives in 18 countries around the world now participate in this organization. Look for it in your neighbourhood at places that sell and roast their own coffee. What's more, it's usually delicious!

The Central Valley

reserve, literally nestled in the clouds, since you'll actually be walking through them at certain points during your visit! Former President Rodrigo Carazo owns this 800ha (1,977 acres) nature reserve. There are guided excursions on foot or on horseback and exploring the trails without a guide is also possible. Bosque Nuboso is easy to get to from San José and there are a growing number of services here, such as the Hotel Villablanca (see p 135).

The route to the reserve turns off the San Ramon-La Tigra road, and passes through picturesque valleys and pastures. About 5km (3mi) south of the dam between La Tigra and Los Angeles, there are some charming little waterfalls that make for interesting viewing—for your passengers, of course!

There are three outstanding places to visit in **San Ramón**, the "city of presidents and poets": the market, the San Ramón museum and the José Figueres historical and cultural centre. With a population of 50,000, San Ramón is a decent-sized town whose main attraction is its **market ★**. Saturday is market day and it's especially worth checking out because few tourists go. The market offers up a selection of the country's horticultural and agricultural

products. The farm produce is just as varied and abundant at the public indoor market in San Ramón, located between pedestrian-zoned streets that, lined with businesses, make for pleasant shopping. There are also a few interesting commercial streets near the church.

Museo de San Ramón *(free admission; Mon to Fri 1pm to 5pm; next to the former courthouse square, facing the park)* has displays explaining the region's history, including its important historical figures.

Zarcero's Church

The **Centro Cultural y Histórico José Figueres** *(Mon to Sat 9am to 11:30am and 1:30pm to 5:30pm, closed on holidays; on the same street as the church)* was built in honour of José Figueres, also known as "Don Pepe" (three-time President of Costa Rica), who was born in San Ramón in 1906. It is on the same street as the city's museum.
Mariposas y Orquideas de

San Ramón *(free admission; 1km or 0.6mi west of the San Ramón exit on the Interamericana, ☎445-4887)* is another, albeit less well-known, place to learn all about butterflies and perhaps buy a cocoon...

Coffee plantations give way to pine forests as the altitude increases on the way to **Zarcero ★★**. Driving through the region is highly enjoyable.

Zarcero is one of the prettiest little towns in Costa Rica and has a marvellous climate. Because the town is at an altitude of 1,700m (5,577ft), the weather is always slightly cool. The pastoral countryside is spectacular, as is the landscaping of the town. The central park is famous for its bushes, which are trimmed into various shapes. The brilliant white church that faces the park has an equally beautiful, colourful interior. Because the city is full of open spaces, every outing is a pleasure, whether on foot, by bike or by car. Zarcero's water is safe to drink and the place is so clean that there's no reason to fear eating in the local restaurants, especially those around the church and park squares. The people in Zarcero show their civic pride during their town's annual festival in February, which is the perfect time to pay a visit.

Bosque de Paz ★ *(between Zarcero and Bajos de Toro, ☎234-6676 or 225-0203)* is a private tropical rainforest reserve that forms a sort of natural corridor between the Poás and the Juan Castro Blanco national parks. It's becoming a highly acclaimed centre for ecotourism. There are 10 different nature interpretation trails with differing themes and degrees of difficulty. The reserve is extremely popular with amateur birders and ornithologists who keep tabs on the number of bird species. There is a restaurant here as well. The Britt coffee producers are associated with Bosque de Paz and offer passes to the reserve, but reservations are always required.

The Naranjo, Sarchí and Grecia Region

On the way back from Zarcero you can pass through **Naranjo ★**, a little town at an altitude of 1,000m (3,280ft). Its inter-esting Manueline-style church, with its many scrolled decorations, can be seen from a great distance.

Next to the church is a large archway of shrubbery which leads into a grotto devoted to the Virgin Mary. The overall effect is very aesthetically pleasing. The municipal building is also interesting, as is the central park, which has French gardens that surround a space used for ceremonies, concerts and theatrical productions. The city centre overlooks the residential areas in the valley around it, and affords splendid views of the coffee plantations, vegetable gardens and fields in the countryside.

Sarchí ★★, east of Naranjo, has a striking little church and town square. The general layout of the town is attractive, mostly because the buildings are well proportioned, clean and well maintained. The central park in Sarchí is part garden, part public square, and the site of the **Monumento a la Carreta**.

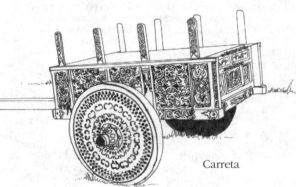

Carreta

This monument represents one of the typical carts that were used in the last century to transport coffee across mountains and valleys from the centre of the country to the Pacific Coast. The city's overall atmosphere is pleasant, especially in the late afternoon when the air is cooler and everything is calm.

Sarchí is known for its **woodworkers** and traditional carts, so it's not surprising that there are many shops and handicrafts studios all over town.

The Central Valley

Grecia, south of Sarchí, is an impeccably clean town. It's even been named as the cleanest town in Latin America and its residents are proud of this: they've even posted signs all over Grecia promoting respect for the environment. The town also has a lovely church with a handsome red metal roof.

Jewels of the Rainforest ★ *(admission fee; every day 9am to 5pm; municipal museum of Grecia,* ☎*244-5006)* is a fascinating museum, showcasing more than 50,000 species of insects from tropical rainforests all over the world. The collection was assembled by a couple from the U.S. over their lifetime.

In the region of Grecia, **El Bosque del Niño de la Reserva Forestal Grecia** ★ *(admission fee; closed Mon; follow the signs to it from Grecia, which are the same as those to Los Trapiches)* is a delightful forest where you can go for pleasant walks. Camping is permitted.

In the same area, **Los Trapiches** ★ *(between Santa Gertrudis Sur and Santa Gertrudis Norte,* ☎*444-6656)* will satisfy your sweet tooth. The *trapiche* (sugarcane press) on display here dates back to the 1860s and is probably the only one left in the country. Here, you can learn how sugar is produced (the cane extract

boiled and the cooked product moulded into shape). You can grab a bite at the restaurant or have a picnic on the grass. It is also nice to stroll on the lawns or go for a swim in one of the pools. Costa Ricans come here to enjoy the simple pleasures of life on weekends, so it can get a bit crowded.

El Mundo de las Serpientes *(every day 8am to 4pm; on the road leaving Grecia towards Alajuela, across from the Poró saw mill, Grecia;* ☎*494-3700)* is a serpentium (snake zoo). Indigenous snakes and species from other parts of the world, such as the rare albino Birman python, are displayed in large cages. Guided tours are available in English and Spanish. This establishment is located only 2min from downtown Grecia.

In the middle of Grecia, facing the park, the attractive pastel-coloured **church of San Isidro de Poás** adds a nice touch to the urban landscape. You can take in a splendid view of this ensemble from the top of the hill.

Parque Nacional Volcán Poás

The **Parque Nacional Volcán Poás** ★★★ *($6; every day 8am to 4pm;* ☎*290-1927 or 232-5324)* is the most popular park in Costa Rica. This is mainly because of its

proximity to San José (37km or 121mi) and the excellent paved road that goes all the way there (and even right up to the volcano). So don't expect to find solitude here. The drive is enjoyable in itself, passing through lovely countryside and the towns of Alajuela and San Pedro de Poás. Keep in mind that the park is swarming with tourists on Sundays.

Despite being crowded, there's a lot to see and do at the Poás Volcano: craters, lakes, short trails and an interpretation centre. There is a slide show about the volcano at the information centre, where there are also toilets, snack bar, a café, a souvenir shop and a small butterfly museum. There are also large signs and models explaining the formation of volcanoes. Several photos and models illustrate the history of the Poás Volcano, with its several significant periods of activity. The first well-documented eruption was in 1747. The most famous occurred in 1910, when the explosion sent lava 4,000m (13,123ft) into the air and volcanic ash as far away as Puntarenas, 70km (43mi) to the west. The park has been forced to close several times since 1989, when the volcano started spewing out cinders again.

This national park was created on January 25, 1971 to protect the 2,708m (8,884ft) high volcano and the dense forests around it. In 1993, the 6,506ha (16,076 acres) park has incorporated the Cerro Congo mountains in the south. The annual precipitation is rather heavy at 3.5m (11.5ft). Even during the dry period, which lasts from December to April, it's best to visit the park in the morning because clouds often obscure the view of the crater by afternoon. The average temperature is a cool 14°C (57°F) and can get as low as -6°C (21°F), and only goes up to 21°C (70°F), so always bring warm clothes and rain gear.

It is an easy 400m (1,300ft) walk to the star attraction of the park: the **main crater of the Poás Volcano**. One and a half kilometres (0.9mi) wide and 300m (984ft) deep, it is one of the largest craters in the world. The greenish water at the bottom of the crater is very acidic and sulfurous. As the water evaporates, it produces sulfur deposits and acid rain. This constant release of gasses probably reduces the volcano's internal pressure so that a devastating eruption is unlikely in the near future. Nevertheless, the state of the volcano is closely monitored and constantly analysed since this volcano has

more than one crater: nine have been counted so far.

Returning from the main crater, take the **Laguna Botos** (1km or 0.6mi round trip) trail, which leads to the pretty little lake that gave it its name. The trees along the trail are stunted and twisted because of the occasionally glacial temperatures, strong winds and acid rain. Lake Botos is actually one of the volcano's craters that has filled up with rainwater. It is 400m (1,300ft) wide and 14m (46ft) deep. The water temperature is always between 10°C (50°F) and 14°C (52°F). Although this trail is connected to the Escalonia trail on the park map, we had to turn around and backtrack. Returning to the information centre via the **Escalonia** (560m or 1,837ft) trail is interesting because of the interpretive signs that describe the native flora in this high volcanic region, specifically the *poás magnolia* and *escalonia* trees, as well as different varieties of oak.

Along this trail you can also observe some of the 79 species of birds that have been seen in the park, including hummingbirds and the famous quetzal.

Hummingbird

Northern Central Valley

The town of **Heredia**, called "Ciudad de las Flores," was founded in 1706. At a slightly higher elevation than San José, it has a somewhat cooler climate and is also less frenetic. It has the attractive urban landscape of a former colonial city and its proximity to San José makes it an ideal place to visit. Don't miss the beautiful **colonial church ★★** dating back to 1796 and flanked by two massive square towers. It is one of the three churches that can be toured in the centre of Heredia, the most modern of which is in the Art Deco style. The parks in front of these churches are ideal for relaxing. The covered central market is a great place to meet the owners of downtown businesses and locals, including students from the Universidad Nacional (east of town).

Built at the end of the last century, the **Gothic church at San Isidro de Heredia ★★** has a beautifully detailed carved wooden interior. It's worth the short detour to this village just east of Heredia.

The Central Valley

The immediate vicinity of San José has recently acquired a park that reconciles the capital somewhat with nature. **Inbioparque ★★** *($18; every day 7:30am to 4pm; Apartad. Postal 22-3100, Santo Domingo, Heredia, ☎244-4790, ≈244-4790),* nestled fairly close to the city centre, in Heredia, is intended as an introduction to nature, which is so much in evidence elsewhere in the country. Inbioparque, affiliated with a research centre, has the goal of teaching the population the "bio-ABCs." Thus, it prioritizes serving schoolchildren from the capital who come here for the advantages of instruction by professional guides, a library and all the services, which are available to both young and old. But visitors who stop over in San José before taking on the rest of the country, and who want to be thoroughly prepared, should make a detour to Inbioparque. Here, short interpretive trails covering the country's principal ecosystems can be explored alone or in the context of an interesting guided tour.

Also, there are interactive exhibits that tackle subjects like great scientists from Costa Rica and elsewhere, and scientific research using natural derivatives to make pharmaceuticals and cosmetics. Don't miss the creative multimedia show which introduces the country's parks and reserves, outlining their main characteristics. A 20min documentary on the evolution of life is also worth seeing. In short, this educational visit foreshadows the even richer nature into whose depths you are about to plunge! Restaurant and shop on site.

Coffee branch

North of Heredia

The area north of Heredia is extremely interesting to explore. An extraordinary alpine atmosphere extends all the way to the top of the highlands of **Monte de la Cruz ★★** with green pastures and enormous trees. Because it's close to the capital, the region of Monte Cruz includes excellent recreational parks, hotels, restaurants and a high-class residential area. The area is still under development.

The views from the **Paradero del Monte de la Cruz** are sensational, especially from its famous cross. You'll feel like you're on top of the world! The park is a great place for a stroll or a picnic. There is also a restaurant, but the menu is limited.

The charming church in **Barva ★** has an interesting vaulted interior. Despite laudable restoration efforts to preserve the 18th-century buildings downtown, the houses are rather basic. Overall, the town looks dreary.

Britt coffee production centre *(presentations: Mon to Sat 9am, 11am, 3pm; store: every day 8am to 5pm in high season; follow the signs on the road from Heredia to Barva, ☎260-2748, ≈238-1848, info@cafebritt.com)* produces excellent coffee for export, but that's not all that's produced here! The owner had the ingenious idea of offering guided tours of the facility *($20 for the 1.5hr tour),* complete with actors who present information about coffee production in an engaging manner. At the end of the tour, the coffee is sampled. A small shop on the premises sells coffee, and you can subscribe to Britt coffee here and receive it at home on a regular basis. Transportation from San José is available, and the visit can include an excursion to Bosque de Paz.

The **Butterfly Park** *($5; every day 8am to 4pm; beside the Autopista Braulio Carrillo,* ☎*382-3953)* is located 3km (1.9mi) past the Río Sucio bridge, just before the Rainforest Aerial Tram. There are 35 varieties of butterflies and five frog species displayed in large aviaries. The tour explains the life cycle of butterflies, their methods of reproduction and their role in the ecology of the forest. Behind the park, you can take a trail through the forest and a dip in the nearby river.

The **Rainforest Aerial Tram** ★★ *($47.50; every day 6am to 3:30pm;* ☎*257-5961,* ≈*257-6053)* is a cable car that travels above the rich and diverse tropical rainforest, giving you the chance to admire the plant and animal life of the canopy. Only a 1hr drive from San José, this is the ideal place to learn about the tropical rainforest in a short amount of time. If you're unable to visit the country's many parks, or have only one day to explore the forest, you should definitely come here—if you can afford the hefty admission fee.

The Rainforest Aerial Tram is part of a 450ha (1,112 acres) private nature reserve just a few minutes away from the Parque Nacional Braulio Carrello (see below). Donald Perry, a biologist from the

United States, came to Costa Rica in 1974 to study the extraordinary wealth of flora and fauna in the forest canopy. In order to spend hours comfortably observing plants, mosses, ants, insects, larva and reptiles in trees that are more than 30m (98ft) high, he devised various methods of installing himself in the canopy, including platforms. Then, he had the audacious idea of creating a cable-car ride that would allow visitors from all over the world to discover this hidden universe without disrupting the forest's ecosystem.

Donald Perry has written a book about his research, entitled *Life Above the Jungle Floor* (2nd edition, Don Perro Press, San José, 1991, 170 pages), which is available at the souvenir shop here and in most large bookstores in San José.

It took two years and 65 people to set up the 250,000kg (approx. 551,000lbs) of equipment for the project. Helicopters were used to install the 12 steel towers that support the cables. The tramway finally opened in 1994.

The best time of the day to visit is early in the morning, before the parking lot fills up. The park opens at 6am every morning except Monday, which is reserved for maintenance of the cable cars (6am

to 9am). First, there is a short walk or a gondola ride from the parking lot to the reception centre (large room, food, souvenir shop, toilets), where the tour is explained and a video about Donald Perry and his project is shown.

Next, small groups tour the forest on foot (1 to 1.5hrs) with a guide who explains the main features of the tropical rainforest's natural phenomena. Then, four or five people and a guide get into one of the ten cable cars for the 2.6km (1.6mi) ride through the canopy. With frequent stops for observing, asking questions and taking photographs, the tour takes about 1.5hrs. The cable car starts out at midtree level and then goes up to the canopy, which is teeming with life. It rains frequently here, so rain gear is a must.

Parque Nacional Braulio Carrillo

Just 20km (12mi) from San José, **Parque Nacional Braulio Carrillo** ★★ *($6; every day 8am to 4pm;* ☎*290-1027 or 232-5324)* encompasses lowland plains and high mountains. These mountains are the main source of water needed for agricultural and domestic purposes in the Central Valley, Costa Rica's most densely populated region. In spite of being so close to urban centres, the park is still very wild and largely unexplored. This is due to the height of the mountains, the density of the forest and the lack, until quite recently, of good roads leading to it.

With an area of 45,899ha (113,400 acres), this is the largest park in the Central Valley. It's named after the third president of Costa Rica, Braulio Carrillo, who governed from 1837 to 1842. Carrillo overthrew the elected president, and proclaimed himself "President for life." He was eventually deposed and exiled to El Salvador, where he was assassinated. Although this president was a merciless dictator, he is credited with conceiving the idea of building a road from the Central Valley to the Caribbean coast to make it easier to ship coffee to Europe. A small road to the coast was only completed in 1882. However, it was superceded by the railway between San José and Limón in 1891 and was subsequently abandoned after several bridges on it were destroyed.

It was only in 1977 that the project of building a road to the coast was revived. Because it was feared that building the road would lead to the destructive encroachment of settlements and massive deforestation, the Parque Nacional Braulio Carrillo was created to protect the area on April 15, 1978.

The road, **Autopista Braulio Carrillo ★ ★**, was finished in 1987. It is certainly one of the most spectacular in the country (note that it is sometimes called the Guápiles highway or the Siquirres highway), and provides easy access to protected virgin tropical rainforest just a few kilometres from San José. This park is important to Costa Rica because the country has lost two thirds of its forest since the 1950s. It's important to drive cautiously through the park: it rains every day in the mountains, so roads are very slippery and traffic is heavy.

Also, don't get too close to the edge of the road if you get out of your car to take pictures, because landslides have happened.

With an abundant 4.5m (15ft) of precipitation per year, plant life thrives in the park. There are seven different ecological life zones, ranging from tropical rainforest to high-altitude rainforest. The flora is exceptionally diverse because of this broad range of altitudes and climates. Some 6,000 species of plant life have already been counted. The lowest area of the park lies 36m (118ft) above sea level, while the highest altitude is 2,906m (9,534ft) at the top of the Barva Volcano. The average temperature varies between 25°C (77°F) and 30°C (86°F) in the low lying areas, and drops to an average of 15°C (59°F) in the mountains. Although it rains very often, there is less rain during the dry season, from January to April.

Howler monkey

Animal life in the park is also very diversified. There are over 100 species of reptiles and amphibians, and 135 species of mammals, including pumas, ocelots, jaguars, capuchin and howler monkeys, tapirs and sloths. Among the 350 birds species are toucans, aras, eagles and the famous quetzal.

Parque Nacional Braulio Carrillo is divided into five sectors of which the northernmost two are rarely visited (Ceibo and Magsasay). The Autopista Braulio Carillo runs to the other three sectors—Zurquí, Quebrada González and Barva—so they're easy to access. The Barva park district is hardest to reach of the three, but is the only one with campsites and a shelter. Note that the toll for cars that drive through the park is only $0.85 per vehicle. However, if you stop at the reception centre at one of the sectors, you must pay a $6 entrance fee to the hiking trails.

★
Zurquí Sector

This sector is only 20km (12mi) from San José, via the Autopista Braulio Carrillo. The reception centre is on the right, 1km (0.6mi) before the Zurquí tunnel. Behind the reception area there is a short 250m (820ft) trail through the surrounding forest. On the other

side of the road, a second trail climbs through primary forest and leads to the tunnel. On the way back, the trail follows the road. This 2.5km (1.6mi) loop takes less than 2hrs on foot and is said to be excellent for bird-watching.

★
Quebrada González Sector

This sector also borders on the Autopista Braulio Carrillo, but it's 43km (27mi) from San José. It has a reception centre and a parking area with a guard, as does Zurquí. The **Las Palmas** trail starts near the reception centre and makes a 1.6km (1mi) loop through dense tropical rainforest. The lush vegetation thrives on the approximately 6m (19.7ft) of rain that this part of the park receives annually! The trail is gorgeous, and there is a pamphlet that explains the flora at 12 interpretation points found along the way. The fifth interpretation point deals with the palm trees after which the trail is named. Another part of the trail goes along the González stream (for which the Quebrada González sector is named). It takes a little more than 1hr to do the whole trail. The **Botarama** trail (1.2km or 0.7mi) starts on the other side of the road and goes towards the Río Sucio. It is named after a species

of tree that grows in this region.

★★
Barva Sector

With its trails, lookouts, picnic area and campsites, this sector has the most to offer nature enthusiasts. It's lso the most difficult to get to by car. The 32km (20mi) trip from San José to the reception area should take about 1.5hrs—if everything goes well. However, because there are no signs pointing it out along the way, finding it can be difficult. The route goes through Heredia, Barva, San José de la Montaña, Porrosatí (or Paso Llano) and Sacramento. After Sacramento, there are only 4km (2.5mi) to go, but the road is so rocky that only a four-wheel drive vehicle can negotiate it. The park rangers at the reception centre (*$6*) are very welcoming and will answer any questions about the trails over a hot cup of tea or coffee. At this elevation of over 2,800m (9,186ft), the temperature goes down to 10°C (50°F) at night. The campsites (*$1.25/pers./night*), and the shelter that accommodates four (*$4.20/pers./night*), are next to the reception centre. You can make reservations for the campsites or the shelter from San José (☎283-5906).

The total distance of the trails in this park

district is 12.3km (7.6mi). Since there are very few hills, most hikers can easily cover all of them in one day. The highest point in the park (2,906m or 9,534ft) is at the top of the extinct **Barva Volcano**. This summit is completely different from the Irazú and Poás craters: trees have grown over it and there is no outward sign of its volcanic origin. The most stunning view in the Barva park district is at the **Mirador Varva Blanca**, 1.5km (0.9mi) farther along the trail. From this lookout (mirador) you can see fields of cultivated ferns stand out in startling black patches because of the canvases that cover them. The Poás Volcano (2,704m or 8,870ft) is the salient feature on the opposite side of the valley.

This sector's other star attraction is **Laguna Barva**, 3km (1.86mi) from the reception centre. The trail that climbs gradually up to Laguna Barva is a former service road. Plants with leaves that are 1m (3.3ft) wide *(Gunnera insignis)* grow alongside the path. They're more commonly known as *sombrilla de pobre*, which means "poor man's parasol." Tracks of Baird's tapir can often be seen in this region. This animal looks like a pig with a trunk-like snout, and can weigh up to 300kg (661lbs)! Laguna Brava

is only 70m (230ft) wide, but is located at an altitude of 2,840m (9,318ft). The water temperature hovers around 11°C (52°F). The trail continues 200m (656ft) past the lake to a lookout with a scenic view of the lake and the valley to the north.

There is a trail from Laguna Barva that ends at **Laguna Copey** 2km (1.2mi) away. Its one scenic view is of the eastern valley and the Irazú Volcano (3,432m or 11,260ft) with its distinctive transmission towers. The lake itself is something of a disappointment: it is only 40m (131ft) wide and 4m (13ft) deep. At 2,620m (8,596ft) above sea level, it is slightly lower than Laguna Barva. There is no cleared area or scenic lookout near the lake.

Many hikers just do Mirador Varva Blanca and Laguna Barva, a total distance of 8.3km (5.2mi), which takes less than half a day. When we were there, the park ranger informed us that the 40km (25mi) trail to the Magsasay park district was not officially open to the public. Rarely cleared and difficult to get to, the Magsasay takes three or four days to complete. Hikers who want to attempt it should find out ahead of time if it is open, by contacting either the park or the bureau of

national parks in San José (☎*192 or 283-8004, ⇌283-7343)*.

Eastern Central Valley

The little town of **Moravia** (or San Vicente de Moravia) is just 7km (4.3mi) east of San José. It's popular for its handicrafts, particularly leather-work (p 143).

Slightly farther east, there are some inviting areas for side trips to explore the natural beauty of this part of the Central Valley. **Rancho Redondo** and its lookout, **San Isidro de Coronado** and its festival on May 15, and **Las Nubes** and its pastures are especially worthwhile.

The Cartago and the Orosi Valley Region

Cartago ★ was the capital city of Costa Rica for several centuries, but its important historical buildings were destroyed by the numerous earthquakes over the centuries. Two buildings remain that are worth seeing. First, the **ruins** *(Calle 2/4, Avenida 1/2)* of the church in front of the central park. It was abandoned in mid-construction because of an earthquake. The ruins are in the centre of a charming little park that is an ideal place to relax and take in the modern urban scene.

Also, there is the **Basílica Nuestra Señora de los Angeles** ★★★ *(Calle 16, Avenida 2/4)*, to which thousands of pilgrims flock every year on August 2, some of them coming from San José, 22km (13.7mi) away, to pay homage to La Negrita (Our Lady of the Angels). The statue of La Negrita was found at the site of the present basilica. It is said to have mysteriously reappeared there after having been taken away, and many miracles have been attributed to it. Each year, people claiming to have been healed by the statue leave symbols of the part of them that was healed at the foot of the statue. Our Lady of the Angels has become the patron saint of Costa Rica. The basilica itself is lovely, built in a somewhat Byzantine style.

Between Cartago and Paraíso are the **Jardines Lankester** ★ *($2.50; every day 8:30am to 3:30pm; 6m or 20ft east of Cartago)*, gardens created by Charles Lankester, a British botanist. There are over 800 orchid species on display here (February, March and April are the best months to see them in bloom).

There is also an arboretum with plants and trees from the differing ecosystems found in Costa Rica. The gardens are now managed by the Universidad de Costa Rica and are open to the public.

The magnificent **Orosi Valley** ★★ starts at Paraíso and stretches out south of Cartago. It is a fertile valley, and well worth visiting. Four places are specifically recommended: Ujarras, Lago Cachi and its Charrarra tourist complex, and the city of Orosi.

Ujarras ★ *(7km or 4.5mi east of Paraíso)* is actually the ruins of a city that was abandoned after a flood at the beginning of the 19th century. The walls of the 17th-century church are still standing, but its roof has disintegrated. Landscaping surrounds the ruins. There are washroom facilities and a large parking area at the site.

Urjarras ruins

Lago Cachi is an artificial lake that is perfect for canoeing. It offers lovely views of the surrounding region.

Charrarra *($0.50; 8am to 5pm, closed Mon; a few km west of Ujarras)* is a tourist complex on the lake that is run by the Instituto Costarricense du Turismo. It has a swimming pool, basketball court and hiking trails. Boating is also available and there is a picnic area and a restaurant on the premises.

On the lake's south shore, on the road between the dam and Orosi, **Casa del Soñador** *(every day 8am to 6pm; 2km or 1.2mi from Represa Rumbo in Orosi; ☎533-3297)* is filled with wooden sculptures and even has some delightful scenes carved right into its wooden walls! The original artist Macedonio Quesada Valerín is now deceased, but others who were inspired by his work, including his sons, have transformed this residence into a studio for wood sculpting.

The Central Valley

Miguel, one of his sons, speaks a little English.

The city of **Orosi** ★ is named after an indigenous leader during the Spanish Conquest. This is the country's most intact colonial city, despite the frequent earthquakes that shake the region.

It's worthwhile to see the oldest surviving **colonial church ★**, which dates back to the 17th century.

Orosi's church

Beside it stands the **Convento de Orosi ★**, a Franciscan convent of the same period. The convent's tiled roof and long veranda are typical of colonial architecture. Inside there is a small museum of religious history which exhibits 100 objects related to religious life and art *(every day 9am to noon and 1pm to 5pm)*.

The Turrialba Region

Turrialba used to be a commercial link on the railway from San José to Limón. Now that the Guápiles highway has been built, Turrialba has transformed itself into a tourist town. Advantageously located near the tumultuous Pacuare and Reventazón rivers, the town itself attracts rafting enthusiasts from all over the world, especially during the winter months, when the town becomes a thriving community with plenty of activity (see p 131). Check out the central market across from the railroad station.

One of the most important centres for the study of tropical agriculture in the world is located in the Turrialba area. **Centro Agronómica Tropicao de Investigación y Enseñanzab**, or **CATIE ★★** *(☎556-6431)*, has a triple mission: to increase the productivity of food crops, to preserve the genetic diversity of tropical flora and to develop methods of agriculture that are consistent with sustainable development in the tropics. Ten thousand hectares (24,710 acres) of land are consecrated to the study centre, which also has one of the world's most complete library collections in the field of tropical agriculture. In addition to the greenhouses, a dairy processing plant, fields of experimental crops, an herb garden and a seed bank, there is housing for personnel and people who come to study at the centre. CATIE furnishes seeds for fruit trees and other tropical species, but special licenses are needed to export them. You can roam the paths of the complex at your leisure, but you must make arrangements with the centre for a guided tour of the facility.

Parque Nacional Volcán Irazú

Like the Poás Volcano, **Parque Nacional Volcán Irazú ★★★** *($6; every day 8am to 4pm; ☎290-1927 or 232-5324)* is very popular with visitors, and for many of the same reasons. Over 100,000 people come here every year, most from Cartago (31km or 19mi) and San José (53km or 33mi), which are relatively close by. Although there is no interpretation centre or real hiking trails, the road goes all the way to the top of the volcano whose spectacular beauty, impressive height and awe-inspiring craters make it a highlight of any trip to the Central Valley. Moreover, the little road (Route 8) that winds its way from Cartago to the park passes through vast plains serves up superb views of the Central Valley. There are attractive farms with green pastures and forests of oak trees that are comparable to English countryside. Drive carefully, because horses and cows share this road.

The Costa Rican conservation movement achieved one of its first successes on July 30, 1955 when 2,309ha (5,705 acres) of land around the Irazú Volcano became a protected area with the creation of Parque Nacional Volcán Irazú. The name is a variation on the Amerindian word *istarú*, which means "shaking and thundering mountain." As early as 1563, Spanish settlers noted that this high mountain (3,432m or 11,260ft) occasionally spewed out fire and ashes. Irazú's first recorded full-blown eruption of was in 1723.

The volcano's most famous eruption occurred on March 19, 1963. It coincided with U.S. president John F. Kennedy's official visit to Costa Rica. The eruption was so intense that tons of volcanic ash, up to 40cm (16in) deep, covered the entire valley, including the cities of San José and Cartago. People had difficulty removing it from the roofs and sweeping it up from the streets, and began carrying umbrellas, especially on windy days, to protect themselves from the ash.

This volcanic activity continued sporadically for two years. Since then, there have been only mild earthquakes and occasional emissions of gases and steam. The Irazú Volcano is not believed to be dangerous at the present time. The soil is enriched by deposits of volcanic ash so the earth in the Central Valley is exceptionally fertile.

The Craters

The parking area at the top of the volcano is over 3,400m (11,155ft) above sea level and the weather is much cooler than in the valley. The average temperature is only 11°C (52°F) and the wind can be blustery at times, so warm clothing is essential. Next to the parking area there are some picnic tables with roofs and a mobile *soda* that sells hot coffee to people who are trying to warm up.

The three largest craters are close to each other. The first, 100m (328ft) from the parking lot, is called **Diego de la Haya** in honour of one of the early 18th-century governors of Costa Rica. This crater is 690m (2,264ft) wide and 80m (26ft) deep, and has a small amount of water in its centre. The path around it consists of black volcanic earth, which makes the area resemble a lunar landscape.

Next to first crater is the immense **principal crater**, which is 1,050m (3,445ft) in diameter and 333m (1,093ft) deep. At the bottom of the crater is an emerald-green lake, which shows that the volcano has been dormant for quite a while. Prior to the eruption, the volcano had a forest-covered peak—just try to imagine the incalculable force it took to explode the top of the mountain and create such a deep crater! The ruins of a foundation are all that remain of the main building that scientists used to observe the volcano prior to the 1963 eruption. A sign at the end of the crater warns visitors not to proceed any further.

The third main crater is difficult to recognize. It consists of a large sandy area that begins south of the other two craters and extends west of the parking area and little reception building. It's called **Playa Hermosa**, or "beautiful beach." **La Laguna** and **Piroclastico** are east of the three main craters and are much smaller and less interesting. On a beautiful clear day, striking scenic views of the Valley can be had from the top of the nearby peak where the transmission towers are installed (2km or 1.2mi hike there and back). Incidentally, Parque Nacional Volcán Irazú is known as one of the

The Central Valley

few places in Costa Rica from which it is possible to see both the Pacific and the Atlantic Oceans. However, the sky is rarely clear enough to see that far, even in the morning. Nevertheless, under ideal conditions and using a telescope, it's possible to identify Lago de Nicaragua, northeast of Costa Rica's border.

Refugio Nacional de Fauna Silvestre Tapantí

Refugio Nacional de Fauna Silvestre Tapantí ★★ *($6; every day; ☎771-3297, ☎771-3155)* is not far from San José (50km or 31mi) and borders on the superb Orosi Valley (by way of Cartago and Paraíso). It is the perfect place to explore a peaceful, unspoiled wilderness. It is best to get here by car, as no overnight stays are permitted in the park and the closest bus stop is 9km (5.6m) away in Orosi. While you can take a taxi from the bus stop to the park, or to walk the distance, this time is better spent on the trails. There are roads that go through the park, with parking areas at the beginning of the trails.

The area was originally a national wildlife reserve covering some 6,080ha (15,023 acres) of dense tropical rainforest, until April 23, 1992, when it officially became the Refugio Nacional de Fauna Silvestre Tapantí. It receives an average annual rainfall of 6.5m (21ft), but sometimes gets as much as 8m (26ft). Four ecological life zones are found at different altitudes between 1,220m (12,208ft) and 2,560m (8,400ft). The best time to visit the refuge is between December and April. October has the heaviest rains. Rain gear, including rain boots or waterproof hiking boots, is necessary all year round, since the trails are always wet and muddy.

The area's heavy rainfall has helped the incredibly dense and varied flora grow: on a single hectare (2.5 acres) of land there are 160 different species of trees. The number of orchids, bromeliads, ferns and other epiphytic plants is simply amazing, and there are 72 different kinds of moss! The fauna is also exceptional, with 45 mammalian species, including some that are endangered, such as the ocelot and the *jaguarundi*.

There are 33 amphibian species and 28 species of reptiles. Because of the constant humidity, the park is crawling with snakes, salamanders and frogs. This is a famous area in the Central Valley for birdwatching, since it has over 250 listed species of birds including eagles, falcons and the magnificent quetzal.

Scenic Attractions

In response to requests from birders and other nature lovers, the Refugio Nacional de Fauna Silvestre Tapantí opens earlier, at 6am. Information about the trails and activities in the park is available at the reception centre at the park entrance near the administration buildings. A detailed plan of the trails costs $0.65. Both camping and fishing are prohibited.

A few kilometres from the reception centre is the park's first scenic attraction, the **Mirador**. A very short trail (100m or 328ft) climbs to this lookout from which you can see miles of vibrant green forest.

Ocelot

In the lowest valley, the Río Orosi makes its way through the dense vegetation. About 500m (1,640ft) in front of the lookout, an elegant waterfall, some 30m (98ft) long, cascades from midway down a mountain.

Heading back towards the main road, the short **La Pava** trail (800m or 2,625ft round trip) goes down to a spot on the Río Grande Orosi where you can have a picnic or go for a dip in the river. Once back on the main road, continue to the next parking area, about 2km (1.2mi) away. Here, there are two trails on opposite sides of the road. It is best to take **Natural Arboles Caído** (2km or 1.2mi loop) first, because it ascends and is the more difficult of the two. It starts on the southern side of the road (towards the Mirador), across from the parking area. It's a steep but relatively short climb that leads to tropical rainforest. Going down, the trail comes out on the road that leads back to the parking area.

Starting on the same side of the road as the parking area, the **Oropéndola** (1.2km or 0.75mi loop) leads to the Río Grande Orosi where former campsites have been turned into fairly secluded picnic areas. There are washrooms and drinking water here. At the end of the path beside the

river is a small beach, perfect for relaxing or swimming (the water is cool).

If you have a few hours to spare after visiting the Refugio Nacional de Fauna Silvestre Tapantí, we highly recommend stopping at **Agua Thermales de Orosi** (*$1.50*), next to Los Patios restaurant. There are two swimming pools filled with naturally-heated volcanic mineral water. The soothing water is a warm 41°C (106°F) in one and 51°C (124°F) in the other.

Monumento Nacional Guayabo

Monumento Nacional Guayabo ★ ★ (*$6; every day 8am to 4pm; ☎290-1927, ≈232-5324*) is the most important archeological site in Costa Rica, as well as a pleasant place to hike or relax. Nineteen kilometres (12mi) northeast of Turrialba, it is more than 80km (50mi) from San José (about a 2hr drive). There is a bus between Turrialba and Guayabo (see p 112). The site has a reception area, campsites, washrooms and drinking water. The site also varies in elevation from 960 to 1,300m (3,150 to 4,265ft), and the weather is warm and humid, with over 3.5m (11.5ft) of rainfall per year.

Statue found at the Monumento Nacional Guayabo

It was Don Anastasio Alfaro, a local naturalist, who first discovered the site at the end of the 18th century. However, real archeological research only began in 1968, under archeologist Carlos Aguilar Piedra. Digs uncovered a number of rooms as well as signs of urban development. The need to protect the area led to the creation of the *monumento nacional* on August 13, 1973. Today, it is part of the national park service. Of the 218ha (539 acres) consigned to the site, 20ha (49 acres) have been excavated so far.

Excavations and research have concluded that the site was inhabited for approximately 2,400 years, from

1000 BC until the 15th century. The structures and infrastructures that have been uncovered so far date back to the period between the fourth and eighth centuries AD. The reason for the demise of this well-structured and long-established community is still unknown. Some people believe that a large-scale war or a devastating disease put an end to this two-millennium-old social organization.

Some of the pottery and other items excavated from the site are on display at the Museo Nacional in San José (see p 80). You can also see the stone roads, mounds, bridges, foundations, support walls, aqueducts, water reservoirs, tombs and petroglyphs (pictograms) that have been uncovered. They were built with both round and large flat stones and level with the different elevations in the terrain.

The Sites

In order to help people understand the significance of these archeological excavations, the personnel of the Monumento Nacional Guayabo have set up a self-guided tour at the site. This tour is called **Los Montículos** and forms a 1.2km (0.75mi) loop with 15 interpretation points where signs refer to explanations in the pamphlet (in Spanish or English) distrib-

uted at the entrance. There are stops at a monolith, petroglyphs, tombs, a paved road, and a grass-covered mound. The social organization of the people of this period and its evolution are also explained. Beside the trail there is a little hill (with a lookout) that offers a good view of part of the excavations.

Another trail at the site, **Los Cantarillos**, makes for a pleasant stroll in the rainforest. An easy (1.1km or 0.68mi) loop, it goes through abundant vegetation that conceals diverse wildlife: armadillos, sloths, coatis, kinkajous, toucans, woodpeckers, hummingbirds and other animals. The trail leads to the bank of the Río Lajitas, a pretty river about 5m (16ft) wide, and returns to its starting point near the reception centre.

If you have a four-wheel drive vehicle, there is an unpaved road that you can take to get back to San José without retracing your route. It runs northwest of the national monument, through mountain scenery dotted with farms and houses. It ends, after 15km (9.3mi), at San Antonio. From there, continue northwest on the paved roads through Santa Cruz and Pacayas to Cartago.

Outdoor Activities

Hiking

The Central Valley contains many parks and other outdoor locations where the best way to explore the rich dense tropical forest is on foot. **Parque Nacional Braulio Carrillo** (see p 122) has very short trails in the Zurquí and Quebrada González sectors. The Barva sector offers longer (12km or 7.5mi), more interesting trails and camping is permitted.

Parque Nacional Volcán Poás (see p 118) has short trails to the craters and the lovely lake Botos, and through the spectacular forest where there are many bird species.

Refugio Nacional de Fauna Silvestre Tapantí (see p 128) is very wild and less crowded than the Poás or Irazú volcanoes. Four trails allow hikers to penetrate the tropical rainforest, admire a splendid panorama and picnic beside Río Grande Orosi.

Monumento Nacional Guayabo (see p 129) has two short trails; one is an educational tour of the archeological excavations, while the other goes through the surrounding forest.

Starting from the **Chalet Tirol** (see p 137) hotel, just a few kilometres before the **Monte de la Cruz** park, there are hiking and horseback riding trails, including some that lead into the park. This is also a good spot for birdwatching.

Rafting

Costa Rica's two most fabulous rivers, Río Reventazón and Río Pacuare, are internationally known for rafting and kayaking. The rivers start near Turrialba in the Central Valley and flow to Siquirres in Limón province.

Anyone, from beginner to expert, can spend an enjoyable day without too much excitement travelling down the **Río Reventazón ★★** (class III, 15km or 9.3mi) and through its scintillating green valleys. Other sections of the river are much wilder (class IV-V) and demand greater expertise.

Río Pacuare ★★★ (class III-IV) is a fabulous river that cut through wild tropical rainforest. It is among the ten most exciting rivers in the world for kayaking and rafting. However, this river is not just for experts: anyone in good physical condition can experience the thrill of this run with competent guides who know how to safely and skilfully navigate through the rapids. You can even take a dip in the river towards the end of the trip. The ride finishes with a slow glide down the river between high rocky cliffs.

Most rafting and kayaking excursions start in San José (or Turrialba) and last all day (*6am to 7pm*). The price (*about $85*) includes transportation (from your hotel), breakfast, lunch, all equipment, a certified guide and an introductory course. During the trip, the rafts are constantly surrounded by kayakers to rescue anyone who falls overboard. Often, photographers in kayaks take pictures of the rafters in action that cost only a few dollars and will be delivered to your hotel.

Some Agencies

Costa Rica Expeditions
(White Water)
☎257-0766
↔257-1665

Aventuras Naturales
☎225-3939
↔253-6934

Ríos Tropicales
☎233-6455
↔255-4354

Pioneer Raft
☎253-9132
↔253-4687

Aguas Bravas
☎292-2072
↔229-4837

Cycling

In the San José region, several agencies offer cycling tours in the Central Valley. Many of these excursions (road or mountain) last all day and include transportation, bicycle rentals and an accompanying guide. The most popular cycling trips are to the Irazú and Poás volcanoes, Monumento Nacional Guayabo, Refugio Nacional de Fauna Silvestre Tapantí and through the magnificent Orosi valley. Other bicycle rides, from 2 to 10hrs, allow you to peacefully explore the mountains and valleys inhabited by laid-back, friendly people.

Some Agencies

Aventuras Naturales
☎225-3939
↔253-6934

Río Tropicales
☎233-6455
↔255-4354
www.riostropicales.com

Costa Rica Tropical Cycling
☎255-2011
↔255-3529

Eco Treks Adventure
☎228-4029
↔289-8191

The Central Valley

Geoventuras
☎*221-2053*
⇌*282-3333*

Horizontes
☎*222-2022*
⇌*255-4513*

Golf

Cariari Country Club
☎*293-3211*
In San José, the Cariari Country Club has a superb 18-hole golf course.

Parque Valle del Sol
☎*282-9222*
Still farther west, in **Santa Ana**, Parque Valle del Sol has a golf course.

Accommodations

The Central Valley offers an excellent choice of places to stay outside the city. As mentioned at the beginning of the chapter, everything is relatively close by in the region and the highway system is excellent. While the capital is at the geographical centre of the area, there is no problem getting to other places in the region, even if you don't stay in San José.

It can be just as practical—and twice as nice—to stay amidst beautiful natural surroundings, such as a picturesque plantation or up on a hill with a breathtaking view of the town's lights twinkling below. Thus, staying in the western part of the Central Valley is often an superb alternative to staying in San José, especially on arrival or departure day, since in most cases you'll be quite near the airport, to which many hotels offer shuttle service. Moreover, it goes without saying that the surroundings are much more tranquil. The Central Valley is incredible. It features breathtaking landscapes that many hoteliers have used to good advantage. If you decide to spend your first night here, you'll probably wake up more rested, and you'll certainly enjoy the view!

Western Central Valley

The Alajuela Region

Mango Verde Hostel
$$
pb, hw in the shower, common tv room, access to the kitchen
Avenida 3, Calle2/4, 25m (82ft) west of the Juan Santamaría museum, Alajuela
☎*441-6330*
⇌*443-3814*
Mango Verde Hostel rents very clean, small rooms.

Pensión Alajuela
$$
sb/pb
Avenida 9, on the south side of the courthouse
Alajuela
☎*441-6251*
Pensión Alajuela is an economical option in the city centre.

Alberge El Marañon
$$$ bkfst incl.
pb/sb, hw
Barrio La Trinidad
☎/⇌*249-1761*
The El Marañon is a pretty bed and breakfast hidden away on a small road that makes its way through the villages of the Central Valley. You'll recognize the inn by the lovely yellow walls behind its gate. It offers six rooms: two on the main floor that are very small and each furnished with only a single bed; and four that are slightly larger, but low-ceilinged, one storey down. Rest assured, this doesn't mean you'll be sleeping in the basement; thanks to the declination of the land, the rear of the house is above ground. Indeed, you'll even have the benefit of a small terrace with an unbeatable view! The breakfast nook is convivial. The owners suggest all sorts of activities, from language courses to excursions.

Charly's Place
$$$
sb/pb
200m (656ft) north and 25m (82ft) east of the central park
Alajuela
☎*441-0115*
Charly's Place is a small urban hotel with clean rooms. The owner is very friendly.

La Guaria Inn
$$$ bkfst incl.
pb, hw, ℝ
225m (738ft)east of Juan Santamaría park
Alajuela
☎/≈*441-9573*
La Guaria Inn is clean, but plain. It is conveniently located right downtown.

Hotel 1915
$$$ bkfst incl.
three blocks from the central park
Alajuela
☎/≈*441-0495*
Also in downtown Alajuela, Hotel 1915 is one of the best places to stay. It's quiet, very clean, and the bedrooms and common areas have a certain charm. It is run by an dignified, older lady with a pleasant personality.

Islands B&B
$$$ bkfst incl.
Avenida 1, Calle 7/9, 50m (164ft) west of the Agonia church
Alajuela
☎*442-0573*
≈*442-2909*
Islands B&B rents very simply furnished but clean rooms. It is small but quiet, in spite of being right downtown. Student discounts are available. Communal tv

room and laundry service.

Michele's Hotel
$$$ bkfst incl.
between Alajuela and Grecia 200m (656ft) north on the road to Poás
☎/≈*433-9864*
Three kilometres (1.9mi) northwest of Alajuela, Michele's Hotel is a 14-room establishment on a large property with some great views of the surroundings. The rooms are spacious and handsomely decorated.

Paraíso Tropical Hotel
$$$ bkfst incl.
200m (656ft) north of the Punto Rojo factory on the road to Tuetal
☎*441-4882*
Paraíso Tropical Hotel has a real family atmosphere. The somewhat dark, but clean and modern rooms are in a separate building from the main house. The grounds are well laid out, and the owner will do anything to give her guests the best service possible.

🌿 B&B Pura Vida
$$$ bkfst incl.
hw, pb
1,500m (4,920ft) from the Punto Rojo factory, at the intersection of the Tuetal Norte and Sur roads
☎*441-1157*
B&B Pura Vida is extremely pleasant. The owner, originally from France, goes out of her way to make her customers' stay enjoyable. The house is clean and the rooms are cozy. There is also a little bungalow for rent on

the spacious grounds.

Villa Dolce
$$$
hw, pb, ☎, tv, ℝ,
on the road to Jacó, 7km (4.3mi) form the Alajuela airport
Alajuela
☎*433-9832*
Conveniently located on the way to the airport, Villa Dolce rents six clean rooms in a well-run establishment.

🌿 Posada Canal Grande
$$$$ bkfst incl.
pb, hw, ⊗, ≈
Piedades de Santa Ana
☎*282-4089 or 282-4101*
≈*282-5733*
Perched on a hill in the Central Valley, not too far from the highway or the airport, Posada Canal Grande nevertheless owes its name to the famous Venetian canal! The owner is indeed Italian. He is also, thankfully, a collector of antiques. You'll be surprised to see the beautiful old furniture housed under his roof, much of which comes from as far away as Asia. As for the rest of the hotel, it's fairly simply decorated with wicker furniture.

The rooms, most of them on the second storey, are large and airy. Fitted with large windows and, in some cases, balconies, they are certainly pleasant places to stay. In the middle of the patio, there is a swimming pool with a few tables around it where you can have breakfast or jot off a note during the day. Just below the road that goes to the *posada*, there's a good Italian restaurant with attractive decor. To get there, take Autopista Fernández, exit at Piedades de Santa Ana and follow the signs. There is also shuttle service to the airport.

Orquideas Inn
$$$$ bkfst incl.
sb/pb, ≈
no children
on the road to San Pedro de Poás, between Alajuela and Grecia
☎433-9346
↝433-9740
orchid@rasca.co.cr
The Orquideas Inn is charming in every way. The common rooms and the bedrooms are consistently stylish. The gardens surrounding the property set it back from the road, making it very relaxing. The popular Marilyn Monroe bar has an inviting atmosphere.

Hotel Alta
$$$$$
pb, hw, ℜ, ≈, ≡, ☉
☎282-4160
↝282-4162
For those seeking luxury, Hotel Alta provides the ideal atmosphere. The small road on which it's situated, the old road to Santa Ana, gives no idea of the lavishness of this establishment. Of rounded architecture, the building is ornamented with stucco walls, wooden ceilings, doors and furnishings, as well as a tiled roof. The rooms, cleverly dispersed

along cream-coloured corridors, provide welcome privacy. In each, two large beds face French doors that open onto a secluded balcony so that the view and the afternoon calm can be appreciated in tranquillity. Below, the gaily coloured swimming pool, with a blue basin and yellow terracing, creates a pleasant oasis. The La Luz restaurant is sophisticated in its decor, with upholstered armchairs decorated with the fleur de lys, and it offers a gourmet menu. Take Carretera Vieja towards Santa Ana, leaving from Escazú. You'll see the hotel on your right, a little farther on.

Xandari
$$$$$ bkfst incl.
ℝ, ≈, ⊛, ℜ, ☉
☎443-2020
↝442-4847
www.xandari.com
Six kilometres (3.7mi) north of Alajuela, Xandari is idyllically situated on a coffee plantation! Two sets of eight pretty, well-decorated villas are built on a hillside. Each villa has a private terrace and also shares the common terrace, which has a panoramic view and two swimming pools. Fruit, vegetables and herbs from the garden find their way into the restaurant's cuisine. The coffee is homegrown too, of course. There are 3km (1.9mi) of hiking trails and five natural waterfalls where you can swim. The shuttle to the airport is

free. Massage available.

The Atenas Valley and La Garita Region

Apartementos Atenas
$$$
≈, K, ☉
Atenas
☎446-5792
The Apartementos Atenas are attractive cottages in the forest, owned by a very welcoming German couple. Tennis court and laundry service.

Cafetal Inn
$$$$ bkfst incl.
≈
Santa Eulalia de Atenas
☎446-5785
↝446-7028
www.cafetal.com
Cafetal Inn is a little bed and breakfast in a modern house on a coffee plantation. In addition to charming rooms, it has a coffee bar where you can buy coffee products.

Chatelle
$$$$ bkfst incl.
≡, ctv, ℝ, ≈, K, ℜ
La Garita, 1km (0.6mi) from the Fiesta del Maíz restaurant on Bulevar de Las Flores
☎487-7781
☎487-7271 or 487-7050
↝487-7095
Chatelle is a tastefully decorated country resort complex with a subdued architectural style; the pink trim blends well with the brick walls and the wooden *casitas*. The rooms and *casitas* (with kitchenettes) are spacious and all open onto the pool area overlooking the La Garita countryside.

The San Ramón and Zarcero Region

Don Beto
$$$
sb/pb
on the north side of the Zarcero church
Zarcero
☎ *463-3137*
Don Beto is a charming little hotel right in the centre of the village. It's extremely clean and its rooms are attractively decorated in an old-fashioned, flowery style that's very relaxing.

La Posada
$$$ *bkfst incl.*
sb
50m (164ft) east of the Nueva Imagen vision centre
San Ramón
☎ *445-7359*
La Posada is a bed and breakfast in San Ramón. The bathrooms are shared, but everything is very clean and the hostess is friendly. Lunch and dinner are available.

Hotelera San Lorenzo at Valle Escondido Lodge
$$$$
hw, pb, bar, ℜ, ≈, ⊛
between San Ramón and Bajo Rodríguez
☎ *231-0906*
⇌ *232-9591*
Hotelera San Lorenzo at Valle Escondido Lodge is isolated from the rest of the world in its own hidden valley (hence *"valle escondido"*). There are a lot of interesting activities to take part in here, such as swimming in the river, horseback riding and cycling. The view is magnificent. The rooms are standard and clean.

Hotel Villablanca
$$$$ *bkfst incl.*
hw
next to Bosque Nuboso Los Angeles, between San Ramón de Alajuela and La Tigra
☎ *228-4603 or 289-6569*
⇌ *228-4004*
Hotel Villablanca is a hotel complex in the Bosque Nuboso Los Angeles reserve, and therefore seems far from civilization. It has a series of quaint *casitas* with fireplaces and bathtubs, situated on a large property with the main pavilion in the centre. The restaurant is in the main building, and the chefs can prepare special meals (vegetarian, salt-free and so on). The hotel can also accommodate large groups, and week-long retreats are also possible. The service is excellent.

The Naranjo, Sarchí and Grecia Region

Hotel Sarchí
$$
across from the ICE, between the central park and the church plaza, Sarchí
☎ *454-3309*
Hotel Sarchí rents out four quite plain motel rooms in downtown Sarchí.

Rancho Mirador
$$$
≈, ℜ, pb, hw, tv
San Miguel de Naranjo
☎ *451-1302*
⇌ *451-1301*
Rancho Mirador consists of clean, simple little cottages perched on a hill above the General Cañas highway, affording interesting views of the vast Naranjo region. You can't miss it: just look for the thatched-straw roof on the *rancho*'s restaurant.

Healthy Day Inn
$$$
⊛, ⊘, ⌂, ≈, ℜ
800m (2,625ft) northeast of the Grecia church on the road to Sarchí
☎ *444-5903*
The Tropical Spa in the Healthy Day Inn offers several kinds of natural therapies (massage, thalassotherapy, iridology, hydrotherapy, etc.). The hotel's concept is excellent and the rooms are quite comfortable, but could be better decorated. You can use the exercise room and equipment without being registered as a guest. There are even facilities for children to use while their parents exercise. The grounds are pleasantly landscaped, but the lot is rather small. There is a macrobiotic restaurant and a Turkish bath.

Villa Sarchí Lodge
$$$ bkfst incl.
fb or ½b also available,
≈, ℜ
500m (1,640ft) north of the
service station west of town
Sarchí Norte
☎454-4006
Villa Sarchí Lodge is a
clean little motel very
close to Sarchí. The
rooms are standard but
have great views of
Sarchí. The friendly
owners even offer
Spanish lessons. Free
shuttle service to the
airport is available. The
restaurant is inviting.

Parque Nacional Volcán Poás

Hotel Buena Vista
$$$$
ℜ, ≈
Las Pilas de San Isidro, 6km
(3.7mi) north of Alajuela
☎442-8595
≈442-8701
On the road to the
Poás Volcano Hotel
Buena Vista is a re-
cently built Spanish
colonial-style hotel but
with North American
standards of comfort.
It's on a coffee planta-
tion at an elevation of
1,300m (4,265ft), so the
views are magnificent,
especially from the
rooms with balconies.
Children under 12 can
share their parents'
room for free.

Northern Central Valley

The Heredia Region

America
$$$ bkfst incl.
hw, pb, ℜ
100m (328ft) south of the
central park, Heredia
☎260-9292 or 260-9293
≈260-7540
The hotel America is in
a former movie theatre
and the decor is inter-
esting, since certain
elements from the build-
ing's past have been
preserved. The hotel is
modern, with clean,
contemporary-style
rooms. The bar and
restaurant are open
night and day.

Apartotel Roma
$$$
100m (328ft) west of
Universidad Nacional
Heredia
☎260-0127 or 238-3705
≈260-6339
Apartotel Roma rents
very clean and practi-
cal, fully equipped
apartments right in
downtown Heredia.
What's more, its staff is
friendly and helpful.
Weekly or monthly
rates available.

Apartotel Vargas
$$$
ℜ, K, tv, P
750m (2,460ft) north of Colegio
Santa Cecilia
Heredia
☎237-8526 or 238-1810
≈260-4698
Apartotel Vargas rents
clean, fully equipped
apartments in a con-
crete building lacking

in style. Some of the
apartments have a
pretty view, which
helps; others are rather
dark, but all have small
balconies. Some single
rooms open onto the
outdoor walkway.

Debbie King's B&B Inn
$$$ bkfst incl.
pb, hw
San Rafael de Heredia
☎/≈268-8284
Debbie King's B&B Inn
belongs to a former
Hollywood restaurant
owner who can name
several celebrities
who've stayed at the
inn, attesting to its al-
lure. The inn is also
attractively located on a
small coffee plantation.
The establishment of-
fers warm, personalized
hospitality and appeal-
ing rooms. It might be
hard to find, so call
ahead for directions.

Casa Monticello
$$$$ bkfst incl.
sb/pb, hw, ℜ
3km (1.9mi) north of Heredia
☎237-8570
≈260-4618
monticello@cafebritt.com
Casa Monticello is
perched at an altitude
of 1,300m (4,265ft),
surrounded by coffee
plantations and fruit
trees. It comprises four
large, clean and com-
fortable rooms, as well
as a spacious dining
room. The Belgian
managers, Dominique
Manet and Daniel
Beissel, cook wonder-
ful traditional European
dishes and can tell you
all about the country.

Posada de La Montaña
$$$$ bkfst incl.
sb/pb, hw, ≈
1.5km (0.9mi) north of San
Isidro de Heredia
☎/⇌268-8096
Posada de La Montaña
has bright, attractive,
clean rooms, as well as
cottages with kitchens
and fireplaces. There's
a common living room
with a television, a
fireplace, and a cov-
ered veranda from
which you can enjoy
the scenery. The exten-
sive grounds are nicely
landscaped and include
a covered barbecue
area. Weekly or
monthly rates available.

Rosa Blanca
$$$$$ bkfst incl.
pb, hw ℜ
near Santa Bárbara de Heredia
☎269-9392
⇌269-9555
www.finca-rblanca.co.cr
Rosa Blanca is a classy
hotel. The owners have
added their personal
touch to the decor of
the rooms. Drive care-
fully: the road to the
hotel becomes increas-
ingly difficult to negotiate as it slowly narrows
into a dirt road.

Valladolid
$$$$$
pb, hw, ≈, ≡, ctv, K
Calle 7, Avenida 7
Heredia
☎260-2905
⇌260-2912
Valladolid offers all the
comforts of a large
hotel, but on a reduced
scale proportionate to
the small city of
Heredia. Nevertheless,
it is probably the high-
est building in this city.
Each of the 12 rooms

has a kitchenette. There
are a whirlpool, a
sauna, a solarium and a
bar on the upper floors
of the hotel, providing
excellent views of the
Central Valley.

**The Region North of
Heredia**

Chalet Tirol
$$$$
pb, hw, ℜ
in the residential neighbourhood of Del Monte
Monte de la Cruz
☎267-7371 or 267-6222
⇌267-6229
tirolcr@sol.racsa.co.cr
Chalet Tirol is a five-
star hotel complex. All
the buildings are in a
uniform Tyrolean style
appropriate to the
area's alpine climate.
The landscaping is as
stylish as the building.
The hotel is in a chic
residential neighbour-
hood, which is in the
middle of protected
rainforest next to
Parque Nacional
Braulio Carrillo. The
service is high class.
The French restaurant
is strongly recom-
mended (see p 141).
There is also a Salzburg
concert-café, which
presents classical music
concerts during Costa
Rica's international
music festival, which
draws famous Costa
Rican and inter-
national guests.

**Hotel Occidental La
Condesa**
$$$$$
pb, ≈, ℜ
☎267-6000
⇌267-6200
condesam@sol.racsa.co.cr
Just before the fork in
the road where one
branches off to the Del
Monte residential park
and the other to the
Mirador del Monte de
la Cruz is the Hotel
Occidental La Condesa.
It is part of a classy
chain, Groupe Occi-
dental Hotels. There
are 100 rooms and
suites, three conference
rooms and two restau-
rants. All sorts of out-
door activities are of-
fered on its splendid
site.

**Eastern Central
Valley**

**The Cartago and the
Orosi Valley Region**

Montaña Linda
$
hw, K, sb
☎533-3640
⇌533-3132
In the village of Orosi,
Montaña Linda is a little
place that rents inex-
pensive rooms. It's very
near the town's hot-
springs swimming pool
(*$1 for clients of Montaña
Linda*). The owner will
gladly suggest various
activities for your en-
joyment.

The Central Valley

Los Angeles Lodge
$$$ bkfst incl.
hw, pb
on the north side of Plaza de la
Basílica
Cartago
☎551-0957
In Cartago itself, Los
Angeles Lodge is the
best place to stay in
terms of location.

Albergue y Cabinas Mirador de Quetzales
$$$
hw, ℜ
at Km 70 on the
Interamericana, after Empalme
☎381-8456
Albergue y Cabinas
Mirador de Quetzales
claims to be the best
place to observe that
most famous of
birds—the quetzal.
There are rooms in the
main house and two
cabinas that can each
accommodate six. On
the whole, it's pretty
rustic.

Albergue Tapantí
$$$$
pb, hw, ℜ
at Km 62 on the
Interamericana, south of Cahén
☎/≈232-0436
Albergue Tapantí is on
a little private reserve at
the far edge of the Cen-
tral Valley. There are
two-bedroom cottages
(not very attractive)
dispersed on the
grounds, each with a
private terrace. Rooms
with single beds are
also available in the
inn. A heater for your
room is available on
request. The restaurant
is worth checking out
(see p 141).

The Turrialba Region

Hotel Interamericano
$
sb/pb
near the railroad station
Turrialba
☎556-0142
Hotel Interamericano is
an economical place to
stay in downtown
Turrialba.

Turrialtico
$$
pb, hw, ℜ
8km (5mi) east of Turrialba, on
top of a hill
☎556-1111
If you have to stay in
Turrialba, Turrialtico
offers decent accommo-
dations. The rooms are
clean, comfortable and
inexpensive. The res-
taurant is fabulous
(see p 142).

Albergue de Montaña Pochotel
$$$
pb, hw
11km (6.8mi) from Turrialba
towards Limón
☎556-0111 or 284-7292
≈556-6222
Albergue de Montaña
Pochotel is above the
village of Paves. A
lookout tower (the
view is extraordinary)
and a playground for
children round out the
facilities of this highly
recommended little
hotel. Campsites are
available.

Hotel Wagelia
$$$ bkfst incl.
hw, tv, ℜ, ≈
150m (492ft) west of the central
park, Turrialba
☎556-1566
≈556-1596
Right in downtown
Turrialba, Hotel
Wagelia has clean,
pretty little rooms.

🦎 Casa Turire
$$$$$
pb, ℜ, ctv, ≈, ℜ
20km (12mi) southwest of
Turrialba
☎531-7111 or 531-1111
≈531-1075
Casa Turire is a luxury
hotel that is associated
with five others in
Costa Rica (including
Grano de Oro, in San
José, see p 90). All are
small-scale, high-class
hotels with character.
Casa Turire is built in
the style of a plantation
manor. The fields of
coffee, macadamia nuts
and sugar cane that
surround it have be-
longed to the same
farming family for 50
years. The hotel has
meeting rooms and is
close to Río
Reventazón. They also
offer many excursions
in the area including
kayaking trips and ar-
cheological tours.

Refugio Nacional de Fauna Silvestre Tapantí

Kiri Lodge
$$ bkfst incl.
fb also available, pb, hw
≈533-3040
In the Orosi region, but
on the road to Tapantí
park, Kiri Lodge rents

large, simple rooms
with comfortable beds.

Monumento Naciona Guayabo

La Calzada
$$$
sb/pb, hw, ℜ
400m (1,312ft) before the entrance to the national monument
☎556-0465
≈556-0427
Near the Monumento
Nacional Guayabo, La
Calzada is a highly recommended hotel (comfortable, bright rooms)
and the owners are
very helpful in planning activities in the
region.

Restaurants

Western Central Valley

The Alajuela Region

There are some fast-food chains in Alajuela.

Trigo Miel
$
Calle 3, Avenida Central/1
Alajuela
☎221-8995
Trigo Miel is a popular,
friendly *panadería-soda-pastelaría*. Great for a
small, quick bite to eat.

Italiana
$$
100m (328ft) north of the Agoya
church, Alajuela
The pizzeria Italiana
serves good pizzas in a
simple little dining
area.

La Jarra
$$$
200m (656ft) west of Plaza
Feria, Alajuela
☎441-6708 or 441-5913
La Jarra is a bar-restaurant that serves a variety of Costa Rican
dishes. The outdoor
bar, in a small hut,
contributes to the atmosphere and general
layout of the place.

El Cencerro
$$$$
every day 11am to 10pm
on the south side of the central
park, above McDonald's
Alajuela
El Cencerro is the most
popular steak house
and grill in Alajuela. It
has an attractive dining
room.

The Atenas Valley

La Fiesta del Maís
$$
Fri to Sun
on the road to La Garita, on the
corner of the road to Bosque
Encantado
Alajuela
La Fiesta del Maís is a
great place to try all
sorts of homemade
corn-based Costa Rican
dishes. The large dining
room is noisy.

La Lora Verde
$$$$
no credit cards
on the road between La Garita
and the Interamericana
☎487-7846
La Lora Verde serves
international cuisine in
pleasant surroundings
and is ideal for more
formal occasions.

The San Ramón and Zarcero Region

There are few "real"
restaurants in San
Ramón de Alajuela.
There are three decent
and inexpensive *sodas*
upstairs in the public
market, just next to the
church: **Bella Visa**, **Piri**
and **Julia**.

The Naranjo, Sarchí and Grecia Region

Super Pan
$
☎454-4121
In Sarchí, the Super
Pan bakery (*panadería*)
is a super spot to buy
bread or pastries, or to
have a coffee or sandwich. The premises are
very clean. It is the
perfect place to relax,
people-watch, admire
the surroundings and
enjoy the slow pace of
life of this charming
little town.

On the road running
along the east side of
the recreational park in
Sarchí is another little
soda called **Donald** that
is worth trying. It's extremely popular with
the locals and is busy
until late at night.

La Chimenea
$$
8am to midnight
☎*494-1988 or 444-6656*
In Los Trapiches, take advantage of the convenient hours kept by La Chimenea. The menu varies, but it features *tico* dishes.

El Río
$$
at the end of Sarchí, on the road to Naranjo
☎*454-4980*
Inside the El Río tourist centre is an outdoor restaurant with the same name. It has a round hut-style roof and a simple, modern set up. The menu has *tico* and Italian selections in all price ranges.

⚲ Restaurante El Mirador
$$
Tue to Sun 6am to 8pm
☎*451-1959*
Restaurante El Mirador is a great place to stop between Naranjo and Zarcero. It's a pleasure to eat in the attractive wooden building (with terrace) and customers can also buy jellies and snacks for the road. The view from the lookout is fantastic. There is even a telescope to get a closer look at the surroundings.

Parque Nacional Volcán Poás

Hotel Buena Vista
$$$
Las Pilas de San Isidro, on the road to the Poás Volcano, 6km (3.7mi) north of Alajuela
☎*442-8595*
The restaurant in the Hotel Buena Vista is a convenient breakfast stop on the way to the volcano. The view is also terrific, since the restaurant is located at an altitude of 1,300m (4,265ft). The restaurant serves good, energizing Costa Rican food.

Northern Central Valley

The Heredia Region

El Rancho del Fofo
$$
Avenida Central, Heredia
El Rancho del Fofo is a little restaurant that has live *mariachi* music on some nights.

La Choza and **El Bulevar** *(Avenida Central, Calle 7, Heredia)* are small, friendly bar-restaurants that are very popular with students.

⚲ Le Petit Paris
$$$
Tue to Sun 11am to 10pm
Calle 5, Avenida 2/Central
Heredia
☎*238-1721*
Le Petit Paris serves wonderful French cuisine. There are also a library and paintings by

different Central American artists every month. There are two dining rooms: one is indoors and decorated with posters, while the other is in a covered tropical garden that is even frequented by some hummingbirds. Situated in the heart of Heredia, right on the university campus, this is a great starting point for a walking tour of the town!

North of Heredia

Las Fresas
$$
between Sabana Redonda de Poás and Fraijanes, north of San Pedro de Poás
☎*448-5567*
Las Fresas is recommended for Italian food, especially the pizza, which is cooked in a wood-burning brick oven. There are also well-prepared Costa Rican specialties on the menu.

⚲ Country Club El Castillo
$$$
Monte de la Cruz, San Rafael de Heredia
☎*267-7111 or 267-7112*
The restaurant at the Country Club El Castillo is open to the public and provides first-class service and a splendid view of the club grounds and the Central Valley. The El Castillo Country Club was created for the well-to-do of Costa Rica. Everything has been done here to induce recreation, relaxation and contemplation (the site is ideal

because of its location overlooking the Central Valley). After 25 years, it's still the largest and chicest recreational centre in the country (5,000 members). Permission to use the facilities of this private club must be requested at the manager's office. The name, El Castillo, comes from the small castle (*castillo*, in Spanish) on the grounds that now houses a museum exhibiting objects from earlier Costa Rican cultures. (If you want to see the museum or go to the restaurant, you must specify this at the entrance to the club).

Le Barbizon
$$$$
Mon to Sat 11:30am to 10:30pm
Monte de la Cruz
☎267-7449
Le Barbizon is a high-class French restaurant on top of a hill. The beautifully constructed building is surrounded by pastures that contain a little lake to attract waterfowl.

Chalet Tirol
$$$$
every day 8am to 10pm, Sun 8am to 6am
Monte de la Cruz
☎267-7371
The restaurant at the Chalet Tirol hotel serves exquisite food. It belongs to the prestigious French gourmet association, "La chaîne des rôtisseurs." The restaurant's distinguished tone, welcoming personnel, tasteful decor and gorgeous

natural surroundings will completely seduce you before you've even tasted the culinary delights!

Eastern Central Valley

Rancho Redondo

Le Cabernet
$$$$
Rancho Redondo
☎229-1113
Le Cabernet is located in the eastern part of the Central Valley at a considerable distance from San José. This is its chief disadvantage since, if you're staying in the city centre, you'll have to make a special effort to dine here. But if you have a designated driver who is willing to abstain from the pleasures of alcohol, why not venture this far? Note that the driver will be making a real sacrifice: Le Cabernet is named in reference to the fact that it has one of the best wine cellars in the country! Added to that, the French chef creates cuisine worthy of Paris. So have a good trip and above all, enjoy your meal!

The Cartago and the Orosi Valley Region

Coto
$
Parque central, Orosi
Coto is an attractive little *soda* that belongs to the owners of Albergue Montaña Orosi.

Albergue Tapantí
$$
at Km 62 on the Interamericana, south of Cahén
☎232-0436
The restaurant in the Albergue Tapantí radiates warmth with its inviting alpine charm. The menu lists a variety of dishes, but trout is the specialty.

Kiri Lodge
$$
between Orosi and the Refugio Nacional de Fauna Silvestre Tapantí
☎533-3040
The restaurant at Kiri Lodge also specializes in trout.

Posada de la Luna
$$$
west of the Cervantes church halfway between Turrialba and Cartago
For an original meal, try Posada de la Luna. This restaurant serves excellent *tico* specialties and is a veritable museum with all sorts of items on display: old swords and rifles, archeological and pre-Columbian objects, among others. This place is very popular with outdoor enthusiasts on their way to go rafting or kayaking on the nearby rivers.

The Turrialba Region

There are very few good restaurants in Turrialba proper, except for **Kingston** (*$$; leaving Turrialba for Limón,* ☎556-1613) where the chef prepares *tico* dishes with a Jamaican accent, and the great restaurant at

Hotel Wagelia *($$$; 150m or 492ft west of the central park, Turrialba,* ☎*556-1566 or 556-1596).*

Turrialtico
$$$
8km (5mi) east of Turrialba towards Limón
☎*556-1111*
The restaurant at Turrialtico also serves good *tico* dishes in tasteful decor with a stunning view of the surroundings.

Albergue de Montaña Pochotel
$$$
11km (6.8mi) east of Turrialba towards Limón
☎*556-0111*
The restaurant at Albergue de Montaña Pochotel serves Costa Rican cuisine from its elevated location with a panoramic view of this striking region. There is also an observation tower on the premises.

Parque Nacional Volcán Irazú

Linda Vista
$$
On the road to the Irazú Volcano, Linda Vista has a pretty view of the valley from the dining room, though the inexpensive food is rather ordinary.

Monumento Nacional Guayabo

Hotel La Calzada
$$$
400m (1,312ft) before the entrance to Monumento Nacional Guayabo
☎*556-0465*
⇌*556-0427*
The restaurant at the Hotel La Calzada serves Costa Rican country-style food.

Entertainment

Western Central Valley

The Alajuela Region

Marilyn Monroe
on the road to San Pedro de Poás, between Alajuela and Grecia
☎*443-9346*
Marilyn Monroe is a popular and friendly bar at the Orquideas Inn.

La Jarra
200m (656ft) west of Plaza Feria Alajuela
☎*441-6708*
La Jarra is a lively outdoor bar under a hut-style roof.

Northern Central Valley

The Heredia Region

America
100m (328ft) south of the central park, Heredia
☎*260-9292 or 260-9293*
The hotel bar at the America is open 24hrs a day.

Shopping

Western Central Valley

The Alajuela Region

Alajuela has an indoor central market not far from the central park. All sorts of things, from meat to clothing, are for sale here. Also, a shop that sells religious articles is open during the day in the Alajuela cathedral annex.

The Naranjo, Sarchí and Grecia Region

Sarchí is known for its handicrafts and typical Costa Rican carts. There are little shops and artisans' workshops just about everywhere in town, both in Sarchí Norte and in Sarchí Sur. Take a shopping tour of them on foot. Among others, there is the **Fabrica de Carretas Chaverri**, which has been making *carretas* in Sarchí since 1903. Next to the Muebleria El Sueño, there is a large store selling locally made handicrafts. **La Plaza de la Artesanía**, in the heart of downtown, is a huge shopping mall with a unique and appealing architecture, inside and out. It has numerous stores and shops that sell crafts, furniture and souvenirs. **Valle de Mariposa**, a little farther along, is also an interesting crafts and souvenir shop.

On the road to Naranjo, just outside of Sarchí, the **El Río** tourist centre consists of a large store that sells of handcrafted furniture and wooden souvenirs.

Tierra Linda
on the road between Grecia and Sarchí
☎454-4934
Tierra Linda is another handicrafts centre with a small jewellery store.

Northern Central Valley

The Heredia Region

Heredia has a covered central market not far from the central park. It sells almost everything.

Eastern Central Valley

In **San Vicente de Moravia** (or simply, Moravia, as the *Ticos* call it), there are some good leather items for sale at **Caballo Blanco** *(opposite the central park, Moravia, ☎235-6797)*. Moravia is good for last-minute shopping before you leave Costa Rica, because it is located only a few kilometres east of the national capital. **Artesanía Bribrí**, in the same area, sells hand-crafted items made by the Bribrí on the Atlantic coast. There is also the **Mercado de Artesanías Las Garzas** *(every day 8:30am to 6pm; 100m or 328ft south, and 75m or 246ft east of the town hall, ☎236-0037)*, a small shopping centre which, like the one in Sarchí, sells local handcrafted articles.

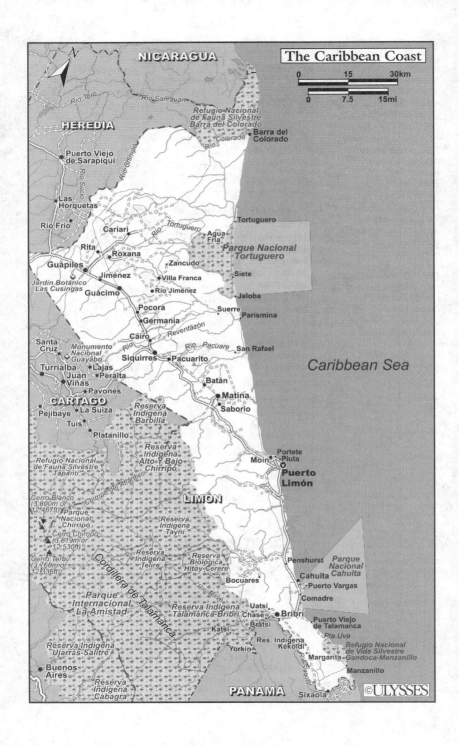

The Caribbean Coast

The Caribbean coast encompasses the whole province of Limón; the port city of Puerto Limón is the region's capital and its largest town.

Washed by the waters of the Caribbean sea, the coast stretches 212km (132mi) between Nicaragua in the north and Panamá in the south, while the Pacific coast is almost five times longer (1,016km or 631mi). The Caribbean coast is unique because of its more humid climate, the flatter and swampy terrain, and the cultural and linguistic differences.

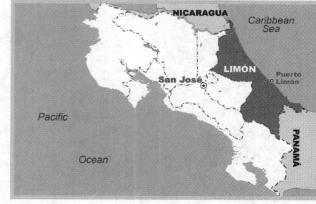

This region is home to a proud and fascinating people, many of whom originate from the West Indies (more specifically Jamaica), but also from China, Europe and North America. Even *Joséfinos* (residents of San José) will admit to feeling out of place when they visit this part of Costa Rica. This is mostly due the coast's distinctive language—a mix of Creole and English.

In general, it's cheaper to stay on the Caribbean coast than elsewhere in Costa Rica. In addition, the regional cuisine is delicious and refined, with excellent fish and seafood dishes. Many foods are of African-Caribbean origin, and prepared with coconut milk. Rundown (a fish and vegetable stew) and Pan Bon (a fruit and spice bread) are not only delicious, but nutritious as well.

The warm ambiance in the southern part of this region is reflected in the reggae and calypso music that plays in the restaurants, bars and hotels. It's not uncommon to be greeted with a laid-back "Hi, brother" or "Hi, sister" by a dreadlocked Rasta calmly strolling down the street in Cahuita or Puerto Viejo, or on the beach, singing to himself. Hats, bracelets, belts, and other items with the African colours are readily available from a street vendor or in one of the local shops.

Be Careful!

Visitors travelling in the area should be careful, especially after sunset. The cool and relaxed atmosphere of the coast sometimes seduces unwary tourists into forgetting to keep an eye on such things as their money, passport and jewellery. Drug smuggling is widespread here. A little bit of caution should go a long way into making your trip to the beautiful Caribbean coast enjoyable.

M ost people visit the Caribbean coast for its magnificent black- and white-sand beaches lined with palm trees, where the word "vacation" takes on its full meaning. The beaches of this region are considered among the most paradisiacal in all of Costa Rica and some of them are among the most beautiful in the world.

I n addition to its Fantasy-Island-like beaches, the Caribbean coast also has huge tracts of wilderness teeming with flora and fauna. In the south, the coral reefs in Parque Nacional Cahuita and Refugio Nacional de Vida Silvestre Gandoca-Manzanillo are natural wonders. The Reserva Biológica Hitoy Cerere and the various indigenous reserves are fascinating places, and off the beaten track. Parque Nacional Tortuguero in the north is only accessible by plane or boat and is one of the country's small hidden treasures that should not be missed.

T he Caribbean coast is synonymous with abundance. Nature is as diversified as it is omnipresent. There are 450 families of plants, with some 2,500 species. Birds abound, with about 500 species belonging to 58 distinct families, accounting for more than half of all the species found in the country. The Tortuguero region alone is home to toucans, egrets, trogons, parakeets, herons and other water birds. You can also see a variety of other animals including howler and white-faced capuchin monkeys, sloths, sea turtles (four species), freshwater turtles, crocodiles, iguanas, lizards and poison-arrow frogs.

Indigenous Reserves

The first indigenous reserves (Cocles, Bribrí, Cabécar, Telire, Teyni) were established in the Talamanca region between 1976 and 1977. The **KéköLdi** reserve, which extends into the mountains south of Puerto Viejo de Talamanca, was created in 1976 to protect this part of the country, home to about 200 Bribrí and Cabécar descendants. The reserve was first named Cocles after the river which runs through its territory. It was renamed KéköLdi (*KéköL* means tree essence; *di* means water or river) in 1989, and refers to a sacred tree growing on the banks of the Río Cocles, whose wood was used to make sacred ceremonial lances for shamen. It is said that the first indigenous peoples were created by the god Sibö from grains of corn. Sibö came to the Talamanca region to explain how he created the earth, sea, plants, and animals, and to instruct the people in how to live their lives. This fundamental knowledge has been passed down by oral tradition to the present day.

One April 22...

On April 22, 1991, at around 4pm, a violent earthquake that measured 7.4 on the Richter scale shook the country, especially Limón province. The epicentre was in the small community of Pandora, not far from Cahuita. Fortunately, this natural disaster claimed few lives, probably between 30 and 50 if you include those who died of ensuing heart attacks. Although the capital, San José, suffered little damage, more than 3,000 buildings were destroyed in the province of Limón, lea-ving more than 12,000 homeless.

Many buildings, roads and bridges completely collapsed, bringing things to a standstill in certain areas. The popular railway between San José and Puerto Limón, dubbed the "jungle train" by Costa Ricans and tourists, was so badly damaged that authorities decided to shut it down.

A Costa Rican friend told us that he travelled to the area several days after the earthquake and was horri-fied to see that the sea level had gone down 1.5m (4.9ft)! He later learned that this was not the case, but rather that the shoreline itself had been thrust up 1.5m (4.9ft)! This massive upheaval also damaged a large part of the coral reefs by exposing them to the air, thereby weakening their structure. The elevated coral reef made the canals between Moín and Barra del Cororado (100km or 62mi) shallower and totally impassable at certain points.

For tourists passing through the region, it's relatively difficult to visit these reserves and encounter the people who live in them. Most of the reserves are located deep in the forest and are difficult to access, even with a four-wheel-drive vehicle. Often, the only way to get there is on foot or horseback. Also, since these people live in isolation, communication can be difficult. Thus, it is better to contact a guide who knows how to get there, make contact with the indigenous people and teach you about their lifestyle. **ATEC** (see p 156) and **Terra Aventuras** (see p 158) in Puerto Viejo de Talamanca, as well as **Cahuita Tours** (see p 154) in Cahuita, offer guided tours of KéköLdi and several of the region's other reserves.

You can find out more about the past and present of the ecologically-minded indigenous people of the KéköLdi reserve by reading *Taking Care of*

Sibo's Gifts (*Paula Palmer, Juanita Sánchez and Gloria Mayorga, Editorama, Costa Rica*), a wonderful little book available at ATEC, among other places.

Finding Your Way Around

By Plane

The isolated regions of Tortuguero or Barra del Colorado are reachable either by boat or by plane with **Travelair** (☎220-3054, =220-0413) and **Sansa** (☎221-9414, =255-2176) airlines in San José. It costs $90 for a return ticket. Many hotels in the region include the flight in their packages.

By Bus

Puerto Limón: buses leave every 30min from the Parque Nacional in San José *(Avenida 3, Calle 19/21)* between 5am and 7pm. The trip takes approximately 2.5hrs. Companies such as Coopelimón *(regular: $2.20, express: $2.70; ☎223-7811)* and Transportes Caribeños *(regular: $2.60, express: $3.20; ☎257-0895)* go to this popular destination. The schedule is similar for the return trip *(Puerto Limón, Calle 2, Avenida 1/2)*.

Cahuita and **Sixaola:** buses leave daily from San José *(Calle Central/1, Avenida 11)* at 6am, 1:30pm and 3:30pm for regular service, and 10am and 4pm for express service. The trip to Cahuita takes about 3hrs *($4.60)* and 1hr *($6.25)* to Sixaola with Transportes Mepe *(☎257-8129)*.

Puerto Viejo de Talamanca and **Manzanillo:** daily departures from San José *(Calle Central/1, Avenida 11)* at 10am and 4pm. The trip to Manzanillo takes about 4.5hrs *($6)* with

Transportes Mepe *(☎257-8129)*.

Puerto Limón–Cahuita–Puerto Viejo de Talamanca: buses leave from Puerto Limón *(Avenida 4, Calle 3)* at 5am, 10am, 1pm and 4pm. It takes 1hr to get to Cahuita *($1)* and about another 30min to Puerto Viejo de Talamanca *($1.25)* with Transportes Mepe *(☎758-1572 or 258-3522)*.

By Car

The quickest way to get to the Caribbean coast is through the extraordinary Parque Nacional Braulio Carrillo *(toll: $0.85)*. From San José, take Calle 3 north to the Guápiles Highway, built in 1987. The road through the park goes up a very steep hill, then winds downward and can become congested with traffic. Be careful because roads may be slippery: it rains almost every day in the high mountains of the park and there may be fog. But don't worry, it becomes hot and sunny again toward the Atlantic plain. The road to **Puerto Limón** is well maintained, so you can drive at a steady speed, but don't go too fast—there are police radar stations, especially active on Sundays! After Siquirres, the villages make way for fields of banana plantations, which are the main source of eco-

nomic activity in the region. The trip between San José and Puerto Limón (162km or 101mi) takes 2 to 3hrs.

If you have more time (at least 4hrs) on your hands to travel between San José and Puerto Limón, you can take the absolutely charming country road past Cartago, Paraíso, Cervantes, Juan Viñas, Turrialba and Pavones, and then on to Siquirres, where there are magnificent valleys of coffee plants and macadamia trees, mountainside villages and lovely rivers, including the famous Río Reventazón, a rafter's paradise.

You can get to **Moín**, 7km (4.3mi) northwest of Puerto Limón, by passing Puerto Limón. On the road to Puerto Limón, there'll be a sign indicating which road to take (the one to the left) to reach Moín and its port.

From Puerto Limón, the road heads directly south to **Cahuita**. This road is 43km (27mi), in pretty good condition, and runs along the Caribbean Sea and its beaches. It takes about 45min to get to Cahuita.

Puerto Viejo de Talamanca is about 20min, or 18km (11mi), south of Cahuita. After 12km (7.5mi), you'll come to a fork in the road: go straight on the unpaved road (and not to the right on the paved road which will take you to Bribrí and Sixaola) to get to Puerto Viejo de Talamanca. There's a police station on the road to discourage smuggling between Costa Rica and Panamá. You'll be signalled either to stop and be searched, or to continue on your way, depending on the officer's mood. From Puerto Viejo de Talamanca to **Manzanillo**, the 13km (8mi) road is unpaved, but in fairly good condition.

By Boat

Most vacationers who want to visit Tortuguero or Barra del Colorado either go through an agency in San José or reserve a room in one of the region's hotels, whose packages include a return trip from San José by minibus and boat. If you go on your own, you'll have to go to **Moín** and take a boat to Tortuguero. Note that this type of boat transportation is not regulated and you'll have to arrange the terms and conditions of your passage. At the Moín Quay, ask which boats go to Tortuguero, when they leave (varies according to the water level in the canal) and how much it costs. It takes anywhere between 2.5 and 4hrs for the trip, depending on the speed of the boat

and how many stops are made to admire the vegetation along the canals. Prices are negotiable, especially for groups.

The guided package offered by tour agencies in **Cahuita** or **Puerto Viejo de Talamanca** is a good deal. It costs around $55 (two days/one night) or $65 (three days/two nights) and includes a guide and the return boat trip.

Practical Information

Puerto Limón

The **Tony Facio Hospital** (*north of Puerto Limón, near the sea*, ☎758-2222) is the only hospital on the Caribbean coast.

In Puerto Limón, there is also the **Clínica Santa Lucía** (*Calle 2, Avenida 4/5*, ☎758-1286). You'll find a few **pharmacies** in downtown Puerto Limón, between Calle 2, Calle 4, Avenida 2 and Avenida 4.

South of Puerto Limón, there is a medical clinic in the small village of **Bribrí**.

For **emergencies**, call ☎758-0580 or **911**.

The **Banco de Costa Rica** (*Avenida 2, Calle 1*) and **Banco Nacional de Costa**

Rica (*Avenida 2, Calle 3*) are located in downtown Puerto Limón.

There are no banks south of Puerto Limón and you'll have to go to **Bribrí**, where there's a **Banco Nacional de Costa Rica**.

Many hotels can convert traveller's cheques or U.S. currency into *colones*. In Cahuita, the **Cahuita Tours** agency (see p 154) also offers this service.

Exploring

The Guápiles Region

The plain resurfaces after the mountains of Parque Nacional Braulio Carillo. The small town of **Guápiles**, about 60km (37mi) from San José, is an important banana shipping centre. East of the town, towards Guácimo, is the **Jardín Botánico Las Cusingas** (*$5; 4km or 2.5mi south of the main road*, ☎382-5805), owned by Jane Segleau and Ulyses Blanco. It contains a variety of medicinal plants (80 species), ornamental plants (80 species of orchids and 30 species of bromeliad) and fruit trees. The 20ha (49 acres) site protects a portion of the humid tropical forest and ensures reforestation. There are guided tours that describe the plants and their medicinal uses, as well as general nature tours. Small paths crisscross the surrounding forest; one of them leads to the Río Santa Clara. A hundred or so bird species have already been identified. A small rustic *cabina* with two rooms and a kitchenette for four people can be rented (see p 168). During the rainy season, the road leading to the botanical gardens is more easily accessible with a four-wheel drive vehicle.

Banana tree flower

Twelve kilometres (7.5mi) east of Guápiles, in the village of **Guácimo**, is the Escuela de Agricultura de la Región Tropical Húmida, or simply **EARTH** *(east of Guácimo,* ☎*255-2000)*. The school offers specialized university-level courses on tropical agriculture that attract students from all over Latin America. Guided tours are also offered to the public. The site includes an experimental banana plantation, which uses environmentally friendly methods of cultivation, and a 400ha (988 acres) rainforest reserve with hiking trails; the school also runs a hotel on the premises (see p 168).

North of Guácimo, the 120ha (297 acres) **Finca Costa Flores** *(*☎*716-6457,* ⇌*716-6439)* grows over 600 species of heliconias and tropical plants, some of which are exported. Guided tours *($15)* explain this type of crop. The farm also includes lovely landscaped gardens with footpaths and marshes, as well as a restaurant.

The small town of **Siquirres** used to be a major railway centre. But ever since the arrival of the Guápiles Highway in 1987, which goes through Parque Nacional Braulio Carrillo, and the abandonment of the San José-Limón railway following the 1991 earthquake, Siquirres has become a quiet little town where few visitors linger. The charming road that passes through Cartago, Paraíso, Cervantes, Juan Vinas and Turrialba eventually arrives at Siquirres.

The exhilarating rafting descent on the very popular **Río Pacuare** (see p 166) ends on the outskirts of Siquirres, underneath the bridge of the main road. Another well-known rafting paradise, the **Río Reventazón**, runs just north of Siquirres.

Between Siquirres and Puerto Limón (58km or 36mi), you'll come across a number of

small villages with names like Bristol, Boston, Stratford, Venecia, Buffalo and Liverpool—names that have nothing to do with banana plantations!

The Puerto Limón Region

Puerto Limón ★, or simply Limón, is the capital of the province of the same name. When Christopher Columbus set foot here on September 18, 1502, the town was an indigenous village called Cariari. Columbus spent several days here to have his boats repaired.

According to popular legend, the town and its surroundings were once prey to numerous epidemics of yellow fever and other tropical diseases. The only lemon tree in the region, located where city hall now stands, apparently possessed miraculous healing powers. The inhabitants would come to pick the ripe fruit, as well as the green ones whose leaves were used to make therapeutic infusions for curing yellow fever. Because of the tree's increasing popularity (it even served as a town landmark), the name El Limón gradually replaced that of Cariari. However, it was only in October 1852 that the town officially adopted the name Puerto Limón. The canton of Limón was created in 1892 and became a province on August 6, 1902.

Today, Puerto Limón is the country's largest port, but its level of activity has diminished considerably over the past few years. At the beginning of the 17th century, the town was one of the prettiest in Costa Rica, with attractive architecture, spacious docking facilities, a spectacular park and the country's first paved

roads. However, unemployment, partly due to the withdrawal of United Fruit Company in the 1940s, and the earthquake in 1991 have left the town in a state of neglect.

Puerto Limón's only real tourist attraction is its **Carnaval ★★**, attended by 100,000 people annually from all over Costa Rica. The carnival officially starts on October 12, the day Christopher Colombus

landed in the Americas, and continues for several days. Music of all kinds, parades, dancing and flamboyant costumes liven up the town. Make your hotel reservations long in advance, or you'll have great difficulty finding a decent place to stay.

The popular **Mercado Central** (*Avenida 2, Calle 3/4*), which is surrounded by *sodas*, restaurants and inexpensive hotels, is the busi-

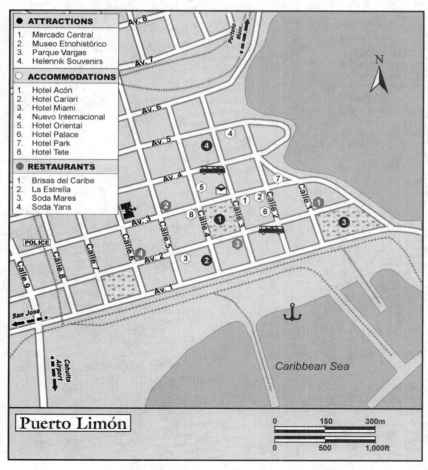

● ATTRACTIONS
1. Mercado Central
2. Museo Etnohistórico
3. Parque Vargas
4. Helennik Souvenirs

○ ACCOMMODATIONS
1. Hotel Acón
2. Hotel Cariari
3. Hotel Miami
4. Nuevo Internacional
5. Hotel Oriental
6. Hotel Palace
7. Hotel Park
8. Hotel Tete

● RESTAURANTS
1. Brisas del Caribe
2. La Estrella
3. Soda Mares
4. Soda Yans

Puerto Limón

Caribbean Sea

0   150   300m
0   500   1,000ft

est place in town. The population has a mixed Spanish, Chinese and West Indian ancestry. The central market and the downtown area are also favourite hangouts of pickpockets and thieves, so be on your guard at all times.

You can learn more about the history and culture of the region's people at the **Museo Etno-Histórico** *(Tue to Sat 9am to 5pm; Calle 4, Avenida 2,* ☎ *758-3903),* near the Mercado Central.

There is a pretty park on the outskirts of town. **Parque Vargas ★** *(Calle 1, Avenida 1/2)* is named after the Governor of Limón, Don Balvanero Vargas, whose bust is located in the centre of the park. The busts of Christopher Columbus and his son Fernando face the ocean, commemorating their arrival in Puerto Limón. Large palm trees and lush greenery were planted here at the beginning of this century to beautify the city. Vargas also put up a **sea wall ★**, by filling a section of sea with earth. The powerful waves apparently used to reach all the way to the central market! A stroll along the sea wall is truly refreshing.

Isla Uvita, where Christopher Columbus landed in 1502, is located approximately 1km (0.6mi) from town. This small island can be

visited by boat: inquire at your hotel or at one of the hotels that organize tours.

The closest swimming beach to Puerto Limón is **Playa Bonita ★★**, 4km (2.5mi) northeast of town, towards Moín. It's surrounded by lush vegetation and is very popular with tourists for relaxing, swimming and picnicking. Playa Bonita is also considered a good beach for surfing.

Reserva Biológica Hitoy Cerere

Sixty kilometres (37mi) south of Puerto Limón, the Reserva Biológica Hitoy Cerere *($6; every day;* ☎ *283-8004 or 758-3996)* was established in April 1978. It is the least visited park in the region and has only the most basic tourist facilities. However, nature-lovers will enjoy its wild countryside, with its abundant rivers, flora and fauna, including 115 species of birds. Terra Aventuras (see p 158) in Puerto Viejo de Talamanca organizes safe guided tours of the reserve.

The name of the reserve, which comes from indigenous words meaning 'bed of moss' *(Hitoy)* and 'clear water' *(Cerere)*, perfectly describes this humid region with its incredibly dense vegetation. The

9,155ha (22,622 acres) reserve covers entire valleys and mountains, with the highest peak at Mount Bitarkara (1,025m or 3,363ft), in the western part of the park. With annual rainfalls exceeding 3.5m (11.5ft), there are many rivers and waterfalls formed by the runoff from the mountains. The Río Hitoy and Río Cerere join together in the valley.

Hiking is without a doubt the most popular activity in the reserve. Wilderness abounds, to the delight of ornithologists and botanists alike. It's best to go on a guided hiking excursion, because the network of trails is poorly indicated and thus confusing. Most of the trails run along the rivers.

To get to the reserve, go through the Valle de la Estrella via Penshurst (20km or 12.4mi). The many small roads make it difficult to access, and four-wheel drive vehicles are essential. This area of the mountains receives a lot of rain year-round, so there really is no ideal time to visit. Migratory birds pass through the reserve between September and December.

The Cahuita Region

The small village of **Cahuita ★**, located 43km (27mi) south of Puerto Limón, is picture-perfect, with its

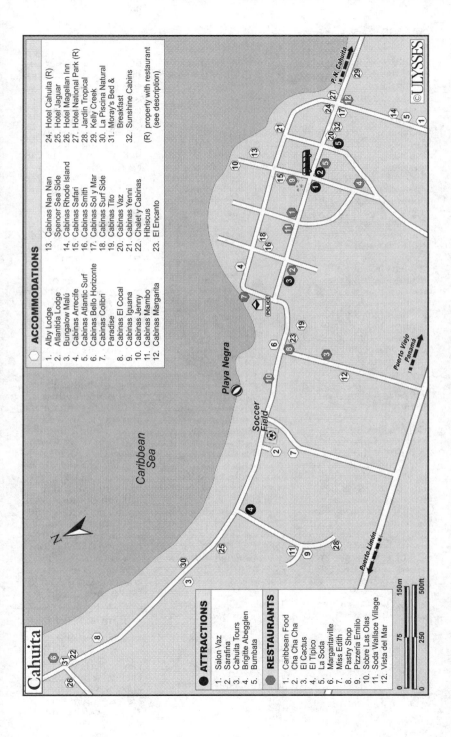

Cahuita

◯ ACCOMMODATIONS

1. Alby Lodge
2. Atlantida Lodge
3. Bungalow Malú
4. Cabinas Arrecife
5. Cabinas Atlantic Surf
6. Cabinas Bello Horizonte
7. Cabinas Colibri Paradise
8. Cabinas El Cocal
9. Cabinas Iguana
10. Cabinas Jenny
11. Cabinas Mambo
12. Cabinas Margarita
13. Cabinas Nan Nan Spencer Sea Side
14. Cabinas Rhode Island
15. Cabinas Safari
16. Cabinas Smith
17. Cabinas Sol y Mar
18. Cabinas Surf Side
19. Cabinas Tito
20. Cabinas Vaz
21. Cabinas Yenni
22. Chalet y Cabinas Hibiscus
23. El Encanto
24. Hotel Cahuita (R)
25. Hotel Jaguar
26. Hotel Magellan Inn
27. Hotel National Park (R)
28. Jardin Tropical
29. Kelly Creek
30. La Piscina Natural
31. Moray's Bed & Breakfast
32. Sunshine Cabins

(R) property with restaurant (see description)

● ATTRACTIONS

1. Salon Vaz
2. Sarafina
3. Cahuita Tours
4. Brigitte Abegglen
5. Bumbata

⬣ RESTAURANTS

1. Caribbean Food
2. Cha Cha Cha
3. El Cactus
4. El Tipico
5. La Soda
6. Margaritaville
7. Miss Edith
8. Pastry Shop
9. Pizzeria Emilio
10. Sobre Las Olas
11. Soda Wallace Village
12. Vista del Mar

Caribbean Sea

Playa Negra

Soccer Field

Puerto Viejo
Panamá

Puerto Limón

P. N. Cahuita

N

© ULYSSES

sand-covered streets, small hospitable hotels and restaurants, and the Caribbean Sea as a backdrop. The atmosphere is relaxed and tourists wander around and socialize with each other.

Most of these tourists are young people who come to relax and have a good time, since Cahuita and Puerto Viejo are two of the least expensive places to stay in Costa Rica. It's easy to find a double-occupancy room for under $25 a night and prices can be negotiated for groups and longer stays. For dinner, several small restaurants serve excellent local, Caribbean-style cuisine, where fish and coconut milk are featured prominently.

Originally settled by Jamaicans in mid-19th century, Cahuita was a small, quiet village for many decades. The name Cahuita is derived from two indigenous words, *kawe* (mahogany) and *ta* (point), and refers to the point in the Parque Nacional Cahuita. Until the mid-1980s, when the Guápiles highway was built, getting to this region was an adventure in itself. First, you would have to take a narrow road to get from San José to Puerto Limón. The second part of the trip between Puerto Limón and Cahuita required a good half-day, because

there were neither roads nor bridges linking the towns. You had to take the train to Penshurst, cross the Río Estrella in a canoe and complete the last leg of the trip in an old bus along an unpaved road. Nowadays, it takes less than 45min to get from Cahuita to Puerto Limón, and under 4hrs from San José.

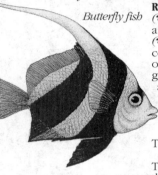

Butterfly fish

There is nothing much to see in Cahuita. The beaches are located at either end of the village. **Playa Negra** is a black-sand beach, good for swimming, which runs several kilometres northwest of the village. Two other white-sand beaches are located to the east of the village in the **Parque Nacional Cahuita ★★★** (see further below). The first beach is at the Cahuita National Park Hotel. Access to this part of the park is free.

Cahuita Tours (*7am to 8pm, north of the main road,* ☎ *755-0232 or 221-9029,* ✆ *755-0082*) is a good place to go for general information on the region, including

hotels, restaurants, indigenous culture, and so on. There are a currency exchange counter, taxi, telephone and fax services; bus tickets for San José are sold and cycling and snorkelling equipment can be rented. This tour operator also offers guided tours of the region.

Roberto Tours (☎ *755-0117,* ✆ *755-0092*) and **Turística Cahuita** (☎ *755-0071*), in the centre of town, also offer a number of guided tours of the area and rent cycling and snorkelling equipment at approximately the same prices as Cahuita Tours.

To know more about the fascinating history of Cahuita's inhabitants and the Talamanca coast, Paula Palmer's excellent book **What Happens** (*Publications in English: San José, Costa Rica, 1993, 264 pages*) gives an interesting account of these descendants of the original Caribbean island settlers and of their traditions. This book can be purchased in several places along the coast and in the large bookstores of San José.

Parque Nacional Cahuita

Parque Nacional Cahuita ★★★ (*free entry or $6 depending on the sector; camping;* ☎ *755-0060*) became a national monument in 1970 and then a national park in April 1978. The park was created primarily to protect the magnificent coral reef surrounding Punta Cahuita. With a total surface area of 1,067ha (2,637 acres) on land, and more than 600ha (1,483 acres) of ocean, the park encompasses a superb tropical rainforest as well as two wonderful white-sand beaches.

This coral reef is one of the largest and most fully grown in the country. There are approximately 35 coral species (some of which are about 2m (6.6ft) in diameter), 123 species of fish, 44 species of crustaceans, 140 species of molluscs and 128 species of seaweed.

However, this unique habitat is threatened with extinction by the deforestation of the surrounding areas and the waste being dumped into the rivers that flow through the banana plantations. The coral was severely damaged by the 1991 earthquake, when the shoreline was raised by as much as 1m (3.3ft) in certain places, exposing and killing much of the reef. Some coral still sticks out of the water. Despite everything, the reef is still one of the best snorkelling spots in Costa Rica.

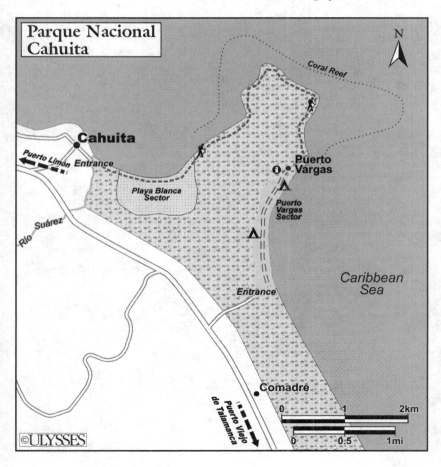

Parque Nacional Cahuita

©ULYSSES

Parque Nacional Cahuita is bordered by the Río Suarez to the north, Río Carbon to the south, and the road between Cahuita and Puerto Viejo runs along its west side. There park has two sectors. The first is called **Playa Blanca** and encompasses the actual village of Cahuita and its superb white-sand beach. Access to the beach is now free, thanks to the efforts of the residents of the village who not only saw the beach as theirs, but considered the admission fee harmful to their town's tourist industry. The second sector, **Puerto Vargas** *($6)*, is 5km (3.1mi) south of the village, and includes the administrative buildings, as well as magnificent beach-side campsites (see p 170).

Since the park receives almost 3m (9.8ft) of rain a year, it is better to visit during the drier seasons from February to May or from August to October, when the average temperature is a balmy 25°C (77°F).

In addition to swimming, snorkelling, beach sports and nature observation, hiking is an excellent way of getting from one sector of the park to the other.

The Puerto Viejo de Talamanca Region

Puerto Viejo de Talamanca ★ is a small, lively village where tourists, primarily young North Americans and Europeans, stay longer than planned to fully enjoy the marvellous white-sand beaches, the small inexpensive hotels and restaurants, and especially the "cool" reggae music-playing atmosphere.

Just a few years ago, Cahuita was the place to stay for its tourist amenities. However, Puerto Viejo has rapidly been gaining ground in recent years. An added attraction is the beach, which literally borders the village and is within walking distance. In addition to the white-sand one, a black-sand beach stretches for several kilometres to the west of the village. It's even possible, albeit strenuous, to walk the entire 18km (11.2mi) along the beach to Cahuita.

The village of Puerto Viejo, also known as Puerto Viejo de Talamanca (so as not to confuse it with Puerto Viejo de Sarapiquí in the north) is the gateway to the Talamanca Coast, which extends all the way to the Panamanian border to the south (via Cocles, Playa Chiquita, Punta Uva, Manzanillo and Gandoca). For more information about the region, consult the little newspaper *Talamanca's Voice* (☎ 750-0062, ≈223-7479, *wolfbiss@racsa.co.cr*), which is chock-full of cultural, historical and other information of interest to tourists. The quarterly newspaper was founded by Wanda Bissinger and Robin Short in 1996, and provides a contemporary perspective on this rich southern part of the Caribbean coast.

At the centre of the village, in front of the Tamara *soda*, the Associación Talamanqueña de Ecoturismo y Conservación, or **ATEC** *(every day 7am to 7pm; on the main street, ☎/≈ 750-0188, atecmail@racsa.co.cr, www.greencoast.com/atec.htm)*, is a good place for information about environmental protection and regional culture. This nonprofit grassroots organization was established in 1990 to encourage local guides, businesses,

Miniature frog

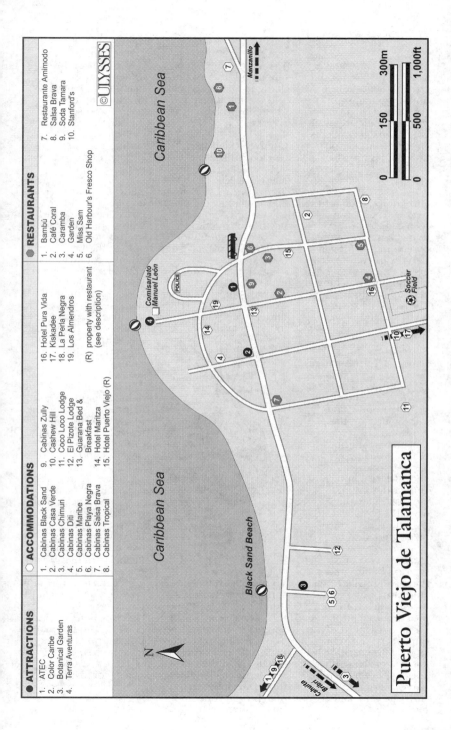

Puerto Viejo de Talamanca

● ATTRACTIONS

1. ATEC
2. Color Caribe
3. Botanical Garden
4. Terra Aventuras

○ ACCOMMODATIONS

1. Cabinas Black Sand
2. Cabinas Casa Verde
3. Cabinas Chimuri
4. Cabinas Diti
5. Cabinas Maribe
6. Cabinas Playa Negra
7. Cabinas Salsa Brava
8. Cabinas Tropical
9. Cabinas Zully
10. Cashew Hill
11. Coco Loco Lodge
12. El Pizote Lodge
13. Guarana Bed & Breakfast
14. Hotel Maritza
15. Hotel Puerto Viejo (R)
16. Hotel Pura Vida
17. Kiskadee
18. La Perla Negra
19. Los Almendros

(R) property with restaurant (see description)

● RESTAURANTS

1. Bambú
2. Café Coral
3. Caramba
4. Garden
5. Miss Sam
6. Old Harbour's Fresco Shop
7. Restaurante Animodo
8. Salsa Brava
9. Soda Tamara
10. Stanford's

© ULYSSES

Caribbean Sea

Black Sand Beach

Comisariato Manuel León

POLICE

Soccer Field

Manzanillo

0   150   300m
0   500   1,000ft

restaurants and hotels to do their part for the environment. Educational programs and courses on environmental issues are available for local residents. Groups from various universities are also welcome.

ATEC offers excursions and guided tours of the region. These tours focus, among other things, on indigenous communities, African-Caribbean culture, the environment, history, hiking, bird-watching, snorkelling and fishing. The guides are very qualified and professional.

The likeable Juan Carlos at **Terra Aventuras** *(beside the Comisariato Manuel Leon, near the beach, ☎750-0004)* will be able to give you information on the region's hotels, restaurants, bars and boutiques. Inside you'll also find Indigenous and African-Caribbean crafts from the region of Talamanca for sale. Terra Aventuras also organizes guided tours

Here are two of the region's better guides: **Harry** (originally from Germany, but a long-time resident of Costa Rica and owner of Cabinas Tropical), who offers several excursions in the region and the rest of the country, and **Juppy** (whose real name is Roberto Hansel) who knows the mountains of

Talamanca, the region's fauna and flora (particularly medicinal plants) and the traditional life of the Bribrí better than anyone.

On the side of the black-sand beach (Black Beach), the **Botanical Gardens** ★ *($3; Thu to Sun 10am to 4pm)*, whose entrance is located 200m (656ft) north of Pizote Lodge, has a wide variety of ornamental plants, fruit trees and spices. The location is excellent for observing the tiny, colourful poison-arrow frogs, sloths and many bird species. Guided tours are available.

Sloth

To see experienced surfers bravely riding the waves, go to **Playa Salsa Brava** ★★, just southeast of the village. The waves of this internationally renowned beach are at their best and most challenging from December to March or in June and July. The main danger

lies in the coral reef underneath, where many surfers have smashed up their boards and severely injured themselves. Outside of these peak surfing months, the sea is quite calm and swimming is good.

Between Puerto Viejo and Manzanillo, the coast is interspersed with gorgeous white-sand beaches that are among the best in the country for swimming and relaxing. However, you should inquire about swimming conditions before you go, because at certain times of the year the waves and currents are too strong for safe swimming.

The little unpaved road linking Puerto Viejo to Manzanillo is pleasant to cycle along, not only to soak up the beauty of the scenery, the beaches and the sea, but also to stop at a *pulpería,* café, or restaurant to chat with the locals, particularly the older crowd, who always have interesting tales to tell! A small detour to **Punta Uva** ★, via a small road branching to the left, leads to a pleasant resting place beneath the coconuts or on the beach, where you can contemplate the magnificent point jutting into the sea. This is one of the coast's best places for swimming.

The Manzanillo Region

Manzanillo has not yet been invaded by tourists, but the number of hotels along the road from Puerto Viejo de Talamanca to Manzanillo is growing, which means that within a few years this small coastal village will become a prime tourist destination. For now, there is little tourist infrastructure. This peaceful village, with its happy children playing on the road or beach, is only rivalled by the wild beauty of the scenery. **Aquamor Adventures** (☎391-3417, *aquamor@racsa.co.cr*) offers guided tours, boat tours (dolphins) and scuba diving courses and excursions. They also rent kayaks and snorkelling equipment.

Willy Burton, a friendly, experienced guide, lives in a small house at the end of the village, close to the entrance of the **Refugio Nacional de Vida Silvestre Gandoca-Manzanillo ★★** (see below). Willy can take you fishing or snorkelling in the park's coral reefs by boat. You can also park your car at his house before walking down the path to Punta Una.

Refugio Nacional de Vida Silvestre Gandoca-Manzanillo

The **Refugio Nacional de Vida Silvestre Gandoca-Manzanillo ★★** was established in October 1985 to protect one of the most beautiful areas of Costa Rica from harmful tourist development. The park encompasses 5,013ha (12,387 acres) of land and 4,436ha (10,961 acres) of sea, and runs south of Puerto Viejo de Talamanca, up to the Río Sixaola, near the border of Panamá.

Rarely visited by tourists, probably due to the lack of facilities, the park is still an exceptional site that protects threatened flora and fauna. It's home to immense coral reefs (Punta Uva, Manzanillo and Punta Mona), an oyster bed, a mangrove swamp, fields, a rich, dense tropical rainforest and breathtakingly beautiful white-sand beaches bordered by coconut trees.

Caiman

There are some 360 species of birds, including pelicans, toucans, parakeets and eagles, as well as howling monkeys, capuchins, sloths, tapirs, caimans and crocodiles. The park also has four species of turtles, including the impressive leatherback turtle, the largest turtle in the world, which lays its eggs between March and July.

The park was named after the tiny villages of Manzanillo and Gandoca, which are located in the southern part of the park and existed before this region became a protected territory. If you decide to explore this park on your own, stop first at the small information office (*oficina de información*) in Manzanillo. Camping is allowed in the park, but there are no facilities (no parking or washrooms). Furthermore, with the heat, the mosquitoes and the snakes, you may prefer the accommodations at the beach or in the village.

Since there is so much to discover here, we strongly recommend that you join a tour group or hire an experienced guide who knows all the secrets of this natural reserve (see above, under "Manzanillo" and "Puerto Viejo").

The main park activities are hiking and snorkelling, and you can do both on the same day. Or you can try reeling in a feisty tarpon near

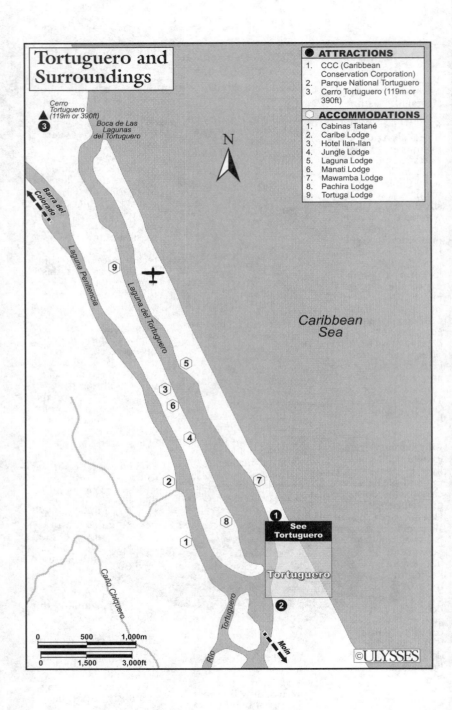

Tortuguero and Surroundings

Cerro
Tortuguero
(119m or 390ft)

Boca de Las
Lagunas
del Tortuguero

N

Barra del
Colorado

Laguna Penitencia

Laguna del Tortuguero

Caribbean
Sea

⑨

⑤

③
⑥

④

②

⑦

⑧

①

Caño Chiquero

Río Tortuguero

❶ See
Tortuguero

Tortuguero

❷

Moín

See Tortuguero

● **ATTRACTIONS**

1. CCC (Caribbean Conservation Corporation)
2. Parque National Tortuguero
3. Cerro Tortuguero (119m or 390ft)

⬡ **ACCOMMODATIONS**

1. Cabinas Tatané
2. Caribe Lodge
3. Hotel Ilan-Ilan
4. Jungle Lodge
5. Laguna Lodge
6. Manati Lodge
7. Mawamba Lodge
8. Pachira Lodge
9. Tortuga Lodge

0   500   1,000m
0   1,500   3,000ft

©ULYSSES

Costa Rica's exceptional flora. The country contains 5% of the earth's plant and animal species.
- *Didier Raffin*

Frogs are among the most commonly seen animals in Costa Rica.
- *Didier Raffin*

The pretty church in Sarchí's central park. The town is also known for its woodcrafts.
- *Didier Raffin*

Taking a break from herding the cattle in Guanacaste.
- *Roger Michel*

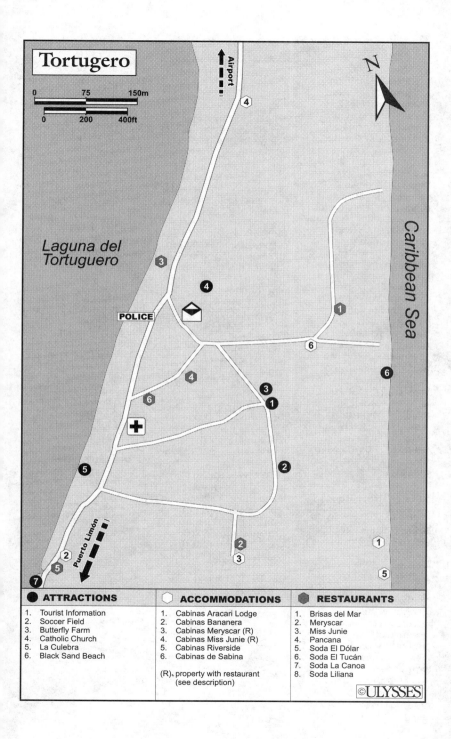

Tortugero

0   75   150m

0   200   400ft

Laguna del Tortuguero

Caribbean Sea

Airport

Puerto Limón

POLICE

N

©ULYSSES

the Río Sixaola! The main trail runs from Manzanillo to Punta Mona, and is 5.5km (3.4mi) one way. Remember to bring enough water and insecticide. This trail runs through the forest to several small isolated and idyllic beaches where you can snorkel to an incredibly beautiful coral reef. The coral here abounds with captivating marine life and is apparently in better shape than in Cahuita, since there's less pollution. However, the waves and currents are rather strong. But thanks to these geographical conditions, many gorgeous seashells can be found along the beach. Back in the forest, it's very easy to spot the toucans and small, brightly-coloured poisonous frogs. The trail ends at Punta Mona (Monkey Point), where there is a lovely beach and a view of Panamá.

The Bribrí Region

Bribrí, located about 12km (7.5mi) from Puerto Viejo de Talamanca, has few tourist attractions because it serves primarily as the administrative centre of this region of green valleys. There are a bank, offices, a clinic and a few businesses. A 34km (21mi) road winds south of here, through the banana plantations to the little border village of **Sixaola** and into Panamá.

The Tortuguero Region

This region includes the village of Tortuguero, an extensive network of canals, and Parque Nacional Tortuguero. It has some of the most spectacular flora and fauna in the country. Because it's not very easily accessible (only by boat or plane), the area is virtually unspoilt and nature still dictates the inhabitants' way of life. Things might change soon because this destination, just 250km (155mi) from San José and 80km (50mi) from Puerto Limón, is becoming more popular and already has a number of hotels.

A minimum stay of three days (and two nights) is needed to navigate along the canals, wander through the village, relax on the beach, visit the seaturtle museum and leave time to sit back in a hammock and contemplate the lush green surroundings. Also keep in mind that the boat trip (from Moín, or by bus and boat from San José) takes at least half a day.

The canals of the Tortuguero region were built so that the local inhabitants wouldn't have to sail out on the rough sea in their small boats. The 100km (62mi) canal network runs from **Moín**, near Puerto Limón, to Barra del Colorado, and was completed in 1974. Since the 1991 earthquake, however, the shoreline has risen in numerous places, which sometimes makes navigation difficult.

The Tortuguero region has an especially abundant flora and fauna due to its favourable climate. It receives over 5,000mm (16ft) of rain annually—one of the highest rates of precipitation in the world! There is no dry season per se, although less rain does fall in February, March and September. It's therefore extremely important to bring along boots (hiking or rubber), as well as a raincoat. Many of the region's hotels provide ponchos for their guests.

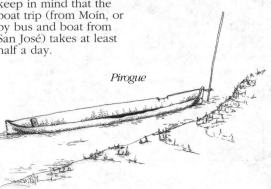

Pirogue

An umbrella is also very useful, not only for the rain, but also against the sun, which shines more intensely after a sudden rainfall. The region also has high humidity, but it rarely gets hot enough to be stifling. The average annual temperature is 26°C (79°F) and the nights are cool. If you plan on walking in the forest, remember to bring along your insect repellent or you'll be too busy swatting at these pesky creatures to get any really great photos of the many brightly coloured frogs!

Swimming in the Tortuguero region is somewhat risky. The ocean waves and currents are often very powerful and sharks have occasionally been sighted. The brown water in the canals is not at all inviting and is inhabited by crocodiles. However, close to Tortuguero village, there are often children splashing about in the canal's murky waters or in the waters of the Caribbean Sea, but it's not advisable to imitate them.

The little village of **Tortuguero** ★★ was founded in the 1920s, but had no electricity until the beginning of the 1980s. It's bordered on one side by the Río Tortuguero and on the other by the Caribbean

Sea. The 500 or so inhabitants lead a peaceful, tranquil life and the majority make their living from tourism. The village has a few picturesque, unpaved streets, which are less than 1m (3.3ft) wide. The small yellow **Catholic church** stands in the centre of town. There are also some friendly neighbourhood restaurants and two souvenir shops.

Tortuguero's church

The most popular attraction in the area is the canal, which you can venture along to explore the surroundings in a dugout canoe rented (with or without a guide) from the village (available at La Culebra, the *pulpería*, at the entrance of Parque Nacional Tortuguero, or at most of the hotels).

North of the village, near the Río Tortuguero, the Caribbean Conservation Corporation, or **CCC** ★★ *(voluntary donation; Mon to Sat 10am to 5:30pm, Sun 2pm to 5pm; ☎224-9215)* has a natural history museum highlighting sea turtles. The

CCC has been involved in sea turtle conservation projects since 1959. Four species are found in the region (green, leatherback, Hawksbill, and loggerhead turtles). The museum presents information on the various species of turtle and educates visitors on how to protect their natural habitats. An 18min video also explores the region's flora and fauna. A small on-site souvenir shop selling books, videos, T-shirts and more finances the museum.

A **black-sand beach** starts at the village and stretches 5km (3.1mi) north along the lagoon, all the way to the mouth of the Tortuguero River. Strolling next to its lush forest is extremely pleasant. Along the way, you'll be able to see Tortuguero's small airport, busy each morning between seven and eight o'clock. At the end, at the mouth of the lagoon, there are often fishers in the water up to their knees, trying to catch enormous fish. On the western side of the lagoon is Cerro Tortuguero, the region's highest peak.

Cerro Tortuguero ★★ stands 119m (390ft) tall and is located 5km (3.1mi) from the village. It's accessible only by boat, from the mouth of the lagoon. Then, a short but steep path leads to its summit. It takes about 30min to make it to the top, which will give you plenty of time to stop and admire the monkeys, small, colourful poison-arrow frogs and great variety of plants and trees in the forest. At the top, there's a view of the canals, the forest and the vast ocean; and if you look straight down, you can clearly see the mouth of the Laguna Tortuguero at the bottom of the hill.

Parque Nacional Tortuguero

The **Parque Nacional Tortuguero** ★★★ *($6; the Cuatro Esquinas entrance, south of Tortuguero; or the Jalova entrance, south of the canal, near Parismina)* is one of the most popular sites on the Caribbean coast. It's not that crowded because visitors are spread out along different canals and over the many places of interest (river, beach, trails, and so on). The quality and quantity of flora and fauna is incredible and the sloths hanging from branches, howler monkeys or capuchins, freshwater turtles, iguanas, lizards, venomous frogs and even camouflaged caimans can be safely observed from the narrow canal.

Tortuguero's turtles have been hunted for their eggs (tortuguero means "turtle hunter" in Spanish), which are a delicacy, ever since people first lived in the region. Their over-hunting for overseas markets in the 20th century has threatened the survival of this species. This led Dr. Archie Carr, a marine biologist and founding member of the CCC (see p 163), to wage a global public-awareness campaign against hunting these turtles, which still goes on. The organization has managed to turn many turtle hunters into excellent tour guides, who have given up poaching to work for the park or for the region's hotels.

To see turtles lay their eggs on the beach, you'll have to go with a guide and respect certain rules (no talking, disturbing the turtle, flash photography, etc.) so as not to disrupt the process.

Green turtle

A female turtle will lay between one and six sets of eggs, 10 to 14 days apart, every two to four years at sundown, when the tide is high. Green turtles lay eggs between July and October and leatherback turtles lay theirs between February and June.

In addition to the four species of turtle found in the Tortuguero region, there are 107 other reptile species, 57 species of amphibians, 55 species of freshwater fish, 60 species of mammals and over 300 species of birds, including toucans, trogons, parakeets, herons and other egrets, which can easily be observed up close, provided you have the proper equipment. In fact, walking along the canals of Tortuguero without binoculars is a bit like fishing without a rod! There are also great hiking trails near the Cuatro Esquinas entrance, by Tortuguero, and around Jalova, south of the park (see p 166).

Barra del Colorado

North of Tortuguero, the wild Barra del Colorado region has many canals, lagoons and rivers, and has remained relatively untouched by tourists. It's renowned for its excellent sport fishing; many lodges have been set up for this purpose and all sorts of packages are available. Although this region is one of the most remote in Costa Rica, about 2,000 people live here.

This region has been protected since 1985 when it was incorporated into the **Refugio Nacional de Fauna Silvestre Barra del Colorado** ★. With an area of 92,000ha (227,329 acres), it's the largest national wildlife reserve in the country. This reserve is primarily made up of swamps and tropical rainforest, and runs north to Río San Juan, the natural border between Costa Rica and Nicaragua. The Río Colorado runs west to east through the park and empties into the Caribbean Sea, north of the small airport in the village of Barra del Colorado and south of Machuca Island.

If you want to stay in the area, you should make reservations, since there's little tourist infrastructure and hotels are far and few between. Also, accommodations are expensive and organized activities mainly involve fishing. The region is internationally renowned for its tarpon fishing. If you want to travel along the canals with a guide to explain the flora and fauna, we recommend that you specify this when you reserve because some hotels don't offer this or, if they do, they usually hire external guides for sports fishing excursions.

Outdoor Activities

Cycling

One of the loveliest rides in the region is along the small, unpaved road between Puerto Viejo de Talamanca and Manzanillo (13km or 8mi), past incredible white-sand beaches where you can stop to rest and swim. There are also small restaurants, *sodas* and *pulperías* along the road. In Cahuita, **Cahuita Tours** *(7am to 8pm; north of the main street,* ☎ *755-0232,* ⚏ *755-0082)* rents out bicycles.

Hiking

The **Reserva Biológica Hitoy Cerere** (see p 152) has three hiking trails that'll take you through the rainforest in the area around the administrative building, which is also used as a reception centre. The **Tepescuintle** trail involves approximately 1hr of hiking, and passes by the Río Cerere; the **Espavel** trail requires just over 2hrs and takes you through a dense, rich forest

with 50m-tall (164ft) trees; and the **Bobócara** trail, which takes 2.5hrs and winds through the tropical rainforest's abundant epiphytic plants, such as ferns, orchids and bromeliads.

The 7km or 4.3mi (one-way) trail in the **Parque Nacional Cahuita** (see p 154) starts in the village of Cahuita (free entry) and finishes at the beach at Puerto Vargas. The trail is wide, well maintained and practically flat. It runs along a beautiful forested white-sand beach, where you'll be able to see splendid flora and fauna. The park is home to many species, including howler monkeys and capuchins, *pizotes* (badgers), coatis, raccoons and sloths, which you can see as long as you don't do anything to scare them off.

Halfway there, the trail runs along the Punta Cahuita, where one of the largest coral reefs in the country is located. The fine sand is composed of millions of tiny pieces of coral. The trail ends by the park's administrative offices and campsites, near an incredible beach which runs further south. If you don't have transportation back to Cahuita, you can either return via the trail or leave the park at the Puerto Vargas exit and wait for the bus (or a taxi), or walk along the main road to the village (7.5km or 4.7mi). **Warning:** the main road attracts many thieves who hide in the forest waiting to rob hikers of their cameras, jewellery and money. Therefore, we recommend that you leave any valuables behind and undertake this excursion in groups. Most of the region's hotels, as well as Cahuita Tours, can help you form a group.

The main trails of **Refugio Nacional de Vida Silvestre Gandoca-Manzanillo** (see p 159) runs 5.5km or 3.4mi (one way) from Manzanillo to Punta Mona.

The **Cerro Tortuguero** (see p 163), 5km (3.1mi) from the village of Tortugeuro, overlooks the region from a height of 119m (390ft). It can only be accessed by boat. The trail that goes to the summit is short but steep. It'll take you approximately 30min to get to the top.

The main activity in the **Parque Nacional Tortuguero** (see p 164) is a boat tours of the flora and fauna, but there are also some hiking trails. Near the Cuatro Esquinas entrance and the village of Tortuguero, the **Gavilán Trail** (2km or 1.2mi, 30min) will take you through the tropical rain forest and the beach where turtles come to lay eggs at nightfall (from July to October). **La Ceiba**

(500m or 1,640ft, approx. 2hrs) is a nice trail over land and water: you have to cross the small Chiquero canal by canoe to get to the entrance of this short trail, from which you'll see many different kinds of tropical plants and maybe even monkeys (howler and capuchin), butterflies, bats, venomous frogs and jaguar tracks. Near Jalova, further south, the **El Tucán Trail** (1.5km or 0.9mi, 30min) runs through the outstanding vegetation in this part of the park where more than 50 species of freshwater fish thrive.

For guided hikes in the regional parks, contact **Cahuita Tours** (☎755-0232, *Cahuita*), **ATEC** (☎750-0188, *Puerto Viejo*) or **Terra Aventuras** (☎750-0004, *Puerto Viejo*) for information about the different tours they offer.

Rafting

Two rivers in the Siquirres Region, the **Río Pacuare** and **Río Reventazón**, are great for rafting. Although most whitewater-rafting companies are located in San José, this sport is also offered on the Caribbean coast. In Cahuita, **Cahuita Tours** (*7am to 8pm; north of the main road,* ☎755-0232, ≈755-0082) offers day-long trips on the Río

Reventazón or the Río Pacuare. In Puerto Viejo, **Terra Aventuras** (*beside the Comisariato Manuel León, on the beach,* ☎750-0004) also organizes excursions on the Río Pacuare.

Kayaking

Whitewater kayaking can be done on the Río Pacuare and Río Reventazón. In Manzanillo, **Aquamor Adventures** (☎391-3417) offers guided tours and kayak rentals.

Surfing

Four kilometres (2.5mi) northwest of Puerto Limón, towards Moín, **Playa Bonita** is known as one of the best surfing beaches on the coast.

In Cahuita, **Black Beach** has become a favourite with surfers.

But by far the most famous surfing beach on the Caribbean coast is **Playa Salsa Brava**, just southeast of Puerto Viejo de Talamanca. This internationally renowned beach has foaming, challenging waves between December and March, as well as in June and July.

Fishing

Most hotels in the **Tortuguero** region and even more around **Barra del Colorado**, offer fishing packages. These regions have an excellent reputation for ocean and river sports fishing, especially when it comes to tarpon.

In Puerto Viejo, **ATEC** (*☎/≈ 750-0188*) organizes fishing trips.

In Manzanillo, **Willy Burton** can take you deep-sea fishing on his boat. Just stop by his house, the last one in the village near the trail to Punta Mona, if you're interested.

Scuba Diving and Snorkelling

In Cahuita, **Cahuita Tours** (*7am to 8pm; north of the main street, ☎755-0232, ≈755-0082*) rents snorkelling equipment.

In Puerto Viejo, **ATEC** (*☎/≈ 750-0188*) organizes snorkelling excursions. **Terra Aventuras** (*beside the Comisariato Manuel León, by the beach, ☎750-0004*) rents out snorkelling equipment.

In Manzanillo, **Aquamor Adventures** (*☎391-3417*) offers excursions and courses in scuba diving and rents snorkelling equipment. **Willy Burton,** also in Manzanillo, will take you out to the coral reefs by boat so that you can go snorkelling. To contact him, go directly to his house, the last one in the village, near the trail to Punta Mona.

Swimming

The closest beach to Puerto Limón is at **Playa Bonita**, 4km (2.5mi) northwest of the city.

The southern part of the coast, especially between Cahuita and Manzanillo, has many black-sand and white-sand beaches that are perfect for swimming. These beaches are some of the country's most beautiful. However, you have to be careful in some area, since there are coral reefs.

Horseback Riding

In Cahuita, **Brigitte Abegglen** (*50m or 164ft west of the Ancla Restaurant, Playa Negra, ☎755-0053*) rents out horses and offers two guided tours: one in the mountains to 10m (33ft) waterfalls where you can swim and the other along a trail on the beach and the forest.

In Puerto Viejo, **Terra Aventuras** (*next to the Comisariato Manuel León, beside the beach, ☎750-0004*) offers horseback riding on the beach or in the mountains.

Accommodations

The Guápiles Region

Guápiles

Happy Rana Lodge
$$$ bkfst incl.
pb, hw
8km (5mi) west of Guápiles
☎710-6794 or 385-1167
≈710-2301
The Happy Rana Lodge is a bed and breakfast focussing on nature and relaxation in the forest. The *cabinas* are rustic, very large and comfortable. On the terrace there are hammocks shaded by the tropical rainforest. The owners, Heidi and Alvaro Monge, offer

different activities like guided hiking tours, horseback riding and rafting.

Jardín Botánico Las Cusingas
$$$
pb, K
☎382-5805
At the Jardín Botánico Las Cusingas (see p 149), you can stay in a rustic but comfortable two-bedroom *cabina* complete with kitchenette, livingroom and wood stove. Perfect for families.

Casa Río Blanco
$$$$ bkfst incl.
pb, hw
6km (3.7mi) west of Guápiles, take the short road to the right, past La Ponderosa Restaurant
☎/≈382-0957
crblanco@racsa.co.cr
The pleasant bed and breakfast Casa Río Blanco is owned by Thea Gaudette and Ron Deletetsky, who'll show you the wonders of this region. The rooms are clean and comfortable. There are trails throughout the forest and the river is perfect for swimming. Guided tours, including morning hikes, are offered.

Hotel Country Club Suerre
$$$$$
pb, hw, ≡, ⊛, ctv, ℜ
Guápiles
☎710-7551
≈710-6376
The Hotel Country Club Suerre is a big North American-style hotel with air-conditioning in the rooms and an elaborate sports complex. There are an Olympic swimming pool, a wad-

ing pool for children, water slides, a children's play area, tennis and basketball courts, and a sauna, as well as several hiking trails in the neighbouring reserves and gardens. The 30 rooms are spacious and comfortable.

Guácimo

EARTH
$$
pb, hw, ☽, ⊗, ≈
☎255-2000
EARTH (see p 150) has its own hotel with simple, but clean rooms. There is also a pool and exercise equipment.

Hotel Río Palmas
$$$
pb, hw, ⊗, tv, ≈, ℜ
☎760-0305
≈760-0296
Hotel Río Palmas is located just over 0.5km (0.3mi) past EARTH, east of Guácimo. Although it is on Limón's busy road, it is an excellent choice for anyone who does not want to go directly to the Caribbean coast or San José. Rooms are spacious, clean, comfortable and tastefully decorated. Its restaurant has an excellent reputation. There are also a pool and short hiking trails.

The Puerto Limón Region

Unfortunately, Puerto Limón is not the safest city around, nor the most pleasant. Most vacationers who visit

this city tend to stay in Cahuita or Puerto Viejo, to which they return in the evening. However, Puerto Limón has many places to stay, for all tastes and budgets. Surfers and anyone else wishing to visit Tortuguero by boat should stay around the Playa Bonita, Portete and Moín, less than 7km (4.3mi) from Puerto Limón.

Hotel Cariari
$
sb
Avenida 3, Calle 2, Puerto Limón
☎758-1395
Hotel Cariari is one of the cheapest hotels in town, but the rooms have neither airconditioning, nor fans.

Hotel Palace
$-$$
sb/pb, ⊗
Calle 2, Avenida 2/3, Puerto Limón
☎758-0419
Hotel Palace has different types of rooms that are of good value for the price.

Hotel Oriental
$$
sb, ⊗
Calle 4, Avenida 3/4, north of the market, Puerto Limón
☎758-0117
Hotel Oriental is inexpensive and relatively clean.

Hotel Acón
$$
pb, hw, ≡, ℜ
Avenida 3, Calle 3, near the
market, Puerto Limón
☎*758-1010*
⇋*758-2924*
Hotel Acón has 39
rooms, a restaurant and
a nightclub, so it gets
noisy on weekends.

Hotel Miami
$$
pp, ≡, ⊗, tv
Avenida 2, Calle 4/5, west of the
market, Puerto Limón
☎*758-0490*
⇋*758-1978*
Hotel Miami has 30
well-maintained, air-
conditioned rooms, but
no hot water.

Hotel Moín Caribe
$$
pb, hw, ⊗, ≈, ℜ
Moín
☎/⇋*758-1112*
In Moín, the Hotel
Moín Caribe has 15
simple rooms. Its night-
club is very popular on
weekends.

Hotel Tete
$$
pb, hw, ≡, ⊗
Avenida 3, Calle 4, Puerto
Limón
☎*758-1122*
⇋*758-0707*
The Hotel Tete is lo-
cated near the market
and has 14 clean
rooms. Rooms with a
balcony facing the
street are noisier than
those without.

Nuevo Internacional
$$
pb, hw, ⊗, ≡
Avenida 5, Calle 2/3, Puerto
Limón
☎*758-0662*
The Nuevo
Internacional, north of
the village, has very
clean rooms, available
with or without air
conditioning.

Hotel Park
$$-$$$
pb, hw, ≡, tv, ℜ
Avenida 3, Calle 1, north of
Parque Vargas, Puerto Limón
☎*758-3476*
⇋*758-4364*
The old-fashioned Ho-
tel Park is one of the
most popular places to
stay in Puerto Limón.
Right on the beach near
Vargas Park, it has dif-
ferent types of rooms,
the cheapest of which
do not have hot water.
Obviously, the rooms
with an ocean view,
hot water and televi-
sion are the best and
most expensive. Hotel
Park also has a good
restaurant.

Apartotel Cocori
$$-$$$
pb, ≡, ⊗, K, ≈
Playa Bonita
☎/⇋*758-2930*
Northwest of Puerto
Limón, towards the
Playa Bonita, Apartotel
Cocori has 21 clean
rooms with kitchen-
ettes, available with or
without air condition-
ing. The view of the
sea from the restaurant
is spectacular.

Hotel Matama
$$$$
pb, hw, ≡, ≈, ℜ
Playa Bonita
☎*758-1123*
⇋*223-6378*
Opposite the Apartotel
Cocori, the 16 rooms of
Hotel Matama are at-
tractive and very clean.
The location is beauti-
ful with its tropical
gardens and magnifi-
cent view.

Hotel Maribú Caribe
$$$$-$$$$$
pb, hw, ≡, ≈, ℜ
Playa Bonita
☎*758-4543*
⇋*758-3541*
The hillside Hotel
Maribú Caribe, 3km
(1.9mi) from Puerto
Limón, near Playa
Bonita, definitely has
the best view in the
region. The 17 circular
cabinas are extremely
pretty and clean. There
is also a casino, an
open-air restaurant with
a great view, two pools
and the opportunity to
take part in one of the
many organized
excursions offered.

South of Puerto Limón

Los Aviarios del Caribe
$$$$/day
pb, hw, ⊗
☎/⇋*382-1335*
Ten kilometres (6.2mi)
north of Cahuita, and
1km (0.6mi) from Río
Estrella, Los Aviarios
del Caribe is a private
wildlife sanctuary (75ha
or 185 acres), home to
over 250 species of
birds, monkeys, sloths,
caimans, river turtles
and venomous frogs,

among others. Small hiking trails lead to a rich, dense forest. Guided tours, usually in canoes, are available for bird-watching and nature study. The rooms are modern, clean and tastefully decorated. The site managers, Judy and Luis Arroyo, will be pleased to share their knowledge with you.

Hotel Selva Mar Club Campestre
$$$$ bkfst incl.
pb, hw, ≡, ⊗, ≈, ℜ, *tv*
☎/≈*758-2861*
Halfway (22km or 13.7mi) between Puerto Limón and Cahuita, the Hotel Selva Mar Club Campestre has 51 rooms and a wide range of activities (fishing, kayaking, hiking and volleyball for example), all less than 200m (656ft) from an incredible beach.

Selva Bananito Lodge
$$$$/day
pb, hw
☎*253-8118*
≈*224-2640*
costari@netins.net
The Selva Bananito Lodge is in the middle of the forest, at the foot of the Talamanca mountain range. To get to this private reserve (850ha or 2,100 acres), take the small trail west towards the Río Bananito. This trail is in very poor condition, so it's best to phone ahead to have someone come and pick you up. The *cabinas* are lovely and have solar-powered water heaters. The terraces have hammocks

and a spectacular view of the tropical forest. Activities include walking in the forest and along the river to the waterfalls, horseback riding and a forest canopy tour.

Cahuita

You should have no trouble finding a room to fit your budget in the tiny town of Cahuita. Many hotels and *cabinas* outside of the village will pick you up at the village bus stop. Just tell them when you make your reservations when you'll be arriving.

Parque Nacional Cahuita
$1.25/pers./day
At the Parque Nacional Cahuita, there are 50 very good campsites next to the fine-sand beach; some have fire pits for cooking and sheltered picnic tables. There are showers and washrooms behind the sites, near the building.

The **Cabinas Atlantic Surf** (**$**; ⊗; ☎*755-0086*) and **Cabinas Rhode Island** (**$**; ⊗; ☎*755-0264*), behind the Sol y Mar Restaurant, have six and eight plain, inexpensive rooms respectively.

Cabinas Bello Horizonte
$
sb/pb, hw
☎*755-0206*
Opposite the El Encanto bed and breakfast, the Cabinas Bello Horizonte has inexpensive rooms and *cabinas*, as well as a "café-soda."

Cabinas Smith
$
sb, hw, ⊗
☎*755-0068*
Near the school, the Cabinas Smith has six clean rooms that won't break the bank.

Cabinas Sol y Mar
$
sb, hw, ⊗
☎*755-0237*
The Cabinas Sol y Mar, opposite Hotel Cahuita, rents out 11 reasonably priced rooms. There's also a *soda* that serves breakfast.

Cabinas Surf Side
$
pb, hw
☎*755-0246*
The Cabinas Surf Side are directly opposite the school. There are 23 clean rooms, plus a private parking lot with a guard. It's definitely the cheapest place to stay in Cahuita.

Cabinas Vaz
$
hw, ⊗, ℜ
☎*755-0218*
The Cabinas Vaz are located in the heart of the village. The establishment has 14 adequate, inexpensive rooms, but gets noisy when the restaurant blares its music.

Hotel Cahuita
$
ℜ, ≈
☎*755-0233*
The Hotel Cahuita has nine simple, cheap rooms next to the main building, lined up motel-style on one floor. There are also a bar and restaurant.

Cabinas Jenny
$-$$
pb, hw, ⊗
☎*755-0256*
⇌*755-0082*
This is one of the best budget establishments in Cahuita. Literally right on the sea, with a view of the headland and the magnificent beach of Parque Nacional Cahuita, Cabinas Jenny has eight rooms with private washrooms, hot water and hammocks, among other amenities. It's worth spending a few more dollars for one of the four upper rooms with balconies overlooking the ocean.

🛏 Cabinas Nan Nan Spencer Sea Side
$-$$
pb, ⊗, ℜ
☎/⇌*755-0027*
Cabinas Nan Nan Spencer Sea Side, right beside Cabinas Jenny, is a great place to stay in the village, since it's close to the sea. The rooms are airy, comfortable and perfect for relaxing. Some of the higher priced ones have kitchenettes.

Cabinas Margarita
$-$$
pb, hw, ℜ
☎*755-0205*
The Cabinas Margarita, just off the road near the El Cactus pizzeria, has 10 simple and inexpensive *cabinas*.

La Piscina Natural
$-$$
pb, ec, ⊗
La Piscina Natural is named for the natural cavity on its beach

where water gets trapped when the tide goes out. Located 1.5km (0.9mi) from the village, on Playa Negra, it has five rooms, a garden and hammocks.

🛏 Cabinas Arrecife
$$
pb, hw, ⊗, ℜ
☎/⇌*755-0081*
The reasonably priced Cabinas Arrecife has 10 rooms and a lovely view of the sea. Brand new, the rooms are clean and well kept. A refreshing sea breeze sometimes blows in the area.

Cabinas El Cocal
$$
pb, ⊗, K
☎*755-0034*
The Cabinas El Cocal is near Playa Negra, 2km (1.2mi) from the village. The two *cabinas* have fully equipped kitchens, including utensils.

Cabinas Mambo
$$
pb, hw, ⊗, ℜ
The Cabinas Mambo has four charming rooms with balconies.

Cabinas Safari
$$
⊗, K
☎*755-0078*
Some of Cabinas Safari's seven rooms have a kitchenette.

Cabinas Yenni
$$
pb, hw, ⊗
☎*755-0256*
The Cabinas Yenni are 200m (656ft) west of the park, facing the sea. There are seven rooms

with private bathrooms, hot water, balconies and hammocks.

Jardín Tropical
$$
pb, hw, ⊗, K
☎/⇌*755-0033*
The Jardín Tropical, located outside the village, south of the Cabinas Iguana, has three *cabinas* that can accommodate a handful of people. All have kitchen facilities. Jimi and Arlene run the place, as well as the small *soda* and a popular bar.

National Park Hotel
$$
pb, hw, ⊗, ℜ
☎*755-0244*
The National Park hotel has one of the best locations in Cahuita. A hop, skip and a jump from Cahuita national park and its outstanding beach, this hotel has 13 rooms, some with a view of the sea. There are also a restaurant and bar.

🛏 Moray's Bed & Breakfast
$$ bkfst incl.
pb, ⊗, ℜ
☎*755-0038*
Moray's Bed & Breakfast, on Playa Negra, approximately 2km (1.2mi) from the village, has four rooms and a natural coral pool. The restaurant, Margaritaville (see p 181), is excellent. This is a good place to stay if you don't mind walking to the village.

Cabinas Iguana
$$-$$$
pb/sb, ≈, ℝ, K
☎755-0005
⇌755-0054
The Cabinas Iguana, owned by a Swiss couple, Christina and Martin, has small cottages with kitchenettes for five people, *cabinas* with private bathrooms and refrigerators, as well as three rooms with a shared bathroom. There are also an organic garden, a small library and a nice pool, all along a 200m (656ft) stretch of the beach.

La Rocalla
$$-$$$
pb, ⊗, K
☎755-0291
La Rocalla has two small houses with terraces and hammocks.

Bungalow Malú
$$$
pb, hw, ⊗
☎755-0006
Bungalow Malú has seven round wooden bungalows.

Cabinas Colibri Paradise
$$$
pb, hw
☎755-0055
Cabinas Colibri Paradise is just outside the village, behind the *fútbol* field. To get there by car take the main road and not the road along Playa Negra. There are four attractive *cabinas*. The owner, Mario, from Quebec, has opened two campsites *($4/day)*, each with a terrace and kitchen.

Cabinas Tito
$$$
pb, ⊗
☎755-0286
Outside Cahuita near Playa Negra are the Cabinas Tito, four clean and well-maintained *cabinas*.

Kelly Creek
$$$
pb, hw, ℜ
☎755-0007
Kelly Creek is just a few metres from the entrance of Parque Nacional Cahuita. The attractive wooden *cabinas* are very clean and cosy. Kelly Creek also has a Spanish restaurant.

Sunshine Cabins
$$$
pb, hw, ⊗, K
☎755-0368
The Sunshine Cabins, near Sol y Mar, has four *cabinas* with kitchenettes.

Alby Lodge
$$$
pb, hw, ⊗, ♯
☎/⇌755-0031
The Alby Lodge rents out beautiful wooden *cabinas* with thatched roofs, which can accommodate four people. Since they are located only 200m (656ft) from Cahuita national park, the *cabinas* are surrounded by trees and tropical gardens.

El Encanto
$$$-$$$$ bkfst incl.
pb, hw, ⊗
☎755-0113
El Encanto is a bed and breakfast with three wooden, clean and extremely comfortable *cabinas*, run by Michael and Karen Russell. They also offer three rooms in a house, two of which have balconies. It's far enough away (300m or 984ft) from the village to relax, but still close to the action.

Chalet y Cabinas Hibiscus
$$$-$$$$
pb, hw, ℝ, K, ≈
☎755-0021
⇌755-0015
As its name indicates, Chalet y Cabinas Hibiscus rents lovely wood *cabinas*, as well as two fully equipped cottages. Located over 2km (1.2mi) from Cahuita, on Playa Negra, this establishment also has a pool, a volleyball court, a pool table, a parking lot and a bar.

Hotel Jaguar
$$$-$$$$ bkfst incl.
pb, hw, ≈, ℜ
☎755-0238
jaguar@racsa.co.cr
The Hotel Jaguar, with 45 rooms, is the largest hotel in Cahuita. Located just over 1km (0.6mi) from the village, on Playa Negra, it has clean, airy rooms, half of which are luxury suites. There are also a restaurant, a bar, a pool, a few short hiking trails and a floral garden.

Atlantida Lodge
$$$$ bkfst incl.
pb, hw, ⊗, ≈, ℜ
☎/⇌755-0213
atlantis@racsa.co.cr
The Atlantida Lodge, beside the soccer field, is a mini-hotel complex containing 30 rooms,

managed by French Canadian Lucas Généreux. The rooms are attractive and comfortable and are surrounded by a tropical garden. There is also a restaurant, which serves local and international cuisine, as well as a bar, a gym, a pool and a medical clinic. The Atlantida Lodge offers different guided tours of the region.

🦎 Magellan Inn
$$$$ bkfst incl.
pb, hw, ⊗, ≈, ℜ
☎/≈*755-0035*
Over 2km (1.2mi) from Cahuita, near the Playa Negra, Magellan Inn has a calm, relaxing and warm environment. There are six pleasant, large, very clean and airy rooms with private terraces and deckchairs. Breakfast is served on the poolside terrace, which is surrounded by trees and exotic plants. The landscaping has been so thoughtfully laid out that it even attracts various species of birds!

The Puerto Viejo de Talamanca Region

Like Cahuita, the village of Puerto Viejo de Talamanca has plenty of hotels and restaurants. For the past few years, the number of establishments has been on the rise, especially along the road to Manzanillo.

Contact the **Terra Aventuras Tourist Information Centre** (☎*750-0004*) or the **ATEC** (☎/≈*750-0188*) for a list of hotels in the area. Before this hotel boom, it was difficult to find a vacancy without a reservation.

Puerto Viejo de Talamanca

In the village of Puerto Viejo de Talamanca, you can camp right beside the **Cabinas Salsa Brava**. Hotel Puerto Viejo may have campsites available, but it's best to inquire ahead of time.

Two of the cheapest places to stay in Puerto Viejo are the **Hotel Kiskadee** (*$; sb*), just a few minutes' walk from the soccer field, and **Cashew Hill** (*$-$$; sb*), right next to the field. They're like youth hostels, with dormitory-style rooms, access to the kitchen and a friendly atmosphere.

Cabinas Diti
$
pb
The Cabinas Diti, near the Hotel Maritza, has four *cabinas* with private bathrooms that are among the cheapest in the area.

Cabinas Zully
$
sb
The Cabinas Zully are located near the Black Sand Beach, approximately 2km (1.2mi) west of Puerto Viejo de Talamanca. The area is

quiet, the rooms relatively plain and there's a stove available for cooking.

Los Almendros
$
pb
☎*750-0099*
Los Almendros is located behind the Terra Aventuras tourist information centre. Rooms are plain, but clean and comfortable.

Cabinas Salsa Brava
$-$$
pb, ⊗
The Cabinas Salsa Brava are among the only affordable *cabinas* with private bathrooms and ocean views. There is also a café, open all day.

Hotel Puerto Viejo
$-$$
pb/sb
In the middle of the village, Hotel Puerto Viejo has 30 inexpensive rooms, some with private bathrooms. Since the hotel is popular with surfers, it can get rather noisy at times. The upstairs rooms are better.

🦎 Cabinas Black Sand
$$
sb, ℜ, K, ⚡
☎*750-0124*
Cabinas Black Sand is an inexpensive place, about 2km (1.2mi) west of the village, on the beach. The small *bribri*-style house has four rustic rooms and a shared kitchen where you can prepare your own meals. Whether you're in a group (better deal) or on your

own, the Californian owners Darcy and Victor will do everything to make your stay an enjoyable one.

Cabinas Chimuri
$$
sb, K
☎750-0119
The Cabinas Chimuri is in the mountains, over 2km (1.2mi) from Puerto Viejo de Talamanca, and quite well-known. There are rustic *bribrí*-style *cabinas* made out of bamboo with thatched roofs and a shared kitchen.

West of the village, on a small, quiet road leading to the Botanical Gardens, there are the **Cabinas Maribe** *($$; ⊗; ☎750-0182)*, with simple but decent rooms, and **Cabinas Playa Negra** *($-$$; pb, K; ☎750-0063)*, with small two- or three-room houses with kitchens. Prices are more than reasonable for groups of four to six.

Coco Loco Lodge
$$
pb, hw, ⊗, ♯
☎750-0188
atecmail@racsa.co.cr
The Coco Loco Lodge is located just outside the village. The two friendly Austrian owners, Sabine and Helmut, tastefully decorated the three attractive *cabinas*, which are surrounded by luxuriant greenery.

Hotel Maritza
$$
pb, hw, ⊗, ℝ
☎750-0003
⇄750-0313
The Hotel Maritza is in the centre of Puerto Viejo de Talamanca, but faces the sea. It has plain but comfortable rooms.

Hotel Pura Vida
$$
sb/pb, hw, ⊗, K
☎750-0002
⇄750-0296
The Hotel Pura Vida has 10 lovely, clean rooms. You can also make use of their kitchen. The hotel's large terrace and garden make it an excellent choice in downtown Puerto Viejo de Talamanca.

Cabinas Casa Verde
$$-$$$
sb/pb, hw, ⊗, ♯
☎750-0015
⇄750-0047
www.greenarrow.com/x/ casaverd.htm
The Cabinas Casa Verde is one of the area's best-priced hotels in terms of quality. Very clean and soberly decorated, its rooms have a balcony where you can relax in a hammock. A small, affordable house with a kitchen is also for rent. To complete the picture, there's a tropical garden with tiny venomous frogs.

Guarana Bed & Breakfast
$$-$$$ every day
pb, hw, ♯
☎750-0034
⇄750-0188
In the centre of Puerto Viejo de Talamanca, near Mr. Pratt's Bakery, the Guarana Bed & Breakfast has 12 very clean and comfortable rooms with balconies. The owners speak French, English and Italian, as well as Spanish.

Hotel La Perla Negra
$$$
pb, hw, ⊗, ℜ, ≈
☎750-0111
⇄750-0114
The Hotel La Perla Negra is located 2km (1.2mi) west of the village, along a black-sand beach. It comprises three attractive, wooden buildings, each housing spacious, clean rooms with balconies. With a pool facing the sea, a restaurant and a bar, all in a tranquil setting, this hotel is a great choice outside of the village.

Cabinas Tropical
$$$
pb, ⊗
Cabinas Tropical has five clean and well-kept rooms. The buffet-style breakfast *($)* will help you start your day off right. Rates go down for longer stays. The owner, Harry, is a well-known guide throughout the region and organizes several outings in the area, the country and even to the magnificent islands in

Parque Nacional Bastimentos Marine in Panamá.

El Pizote Lodge
$$$-$$$$
pb/sb, ⊗, ℜ
☎*221-0986 or 750-0088*
⇄*223-8838*
El Pizote Lodge is 1km (0.6mi) west of the village, amidst tropical gardens and wilderness. There are eight rooms, six *cabinas* and a house. A bar and restaurant complete the picture.

Between Puerto Viejo de Talamanca and Playa Salsa Brava

Cabinas Calalú
$$-$$$
pb, K, ℜ
☎*750-0042*
The Cabinas Calalú come with kitchenettes. All are clean and comfortable and surrounded by luscious tropical vegetation.

Cabinas David
$$-$$$
With the large sign on its fence, you can't miss Cabinas David, which offers eight clean and attractive attached *cabinas*.

Cabinas Yucca
$$-$$$
pb
Across the street from Cabinas David, Cabinas Yucca has four bungalows with king-size beds and a veranda facing the beach.

Costa de Papito
$$$
pb, ⊗
☎/⇄*750-0080*
www.greenarrow.com/ x/papito.htm
The Costa de Papito rents four charming *cabinas* in lush greenery.

Escape Caribeño Bungalows
$$$
pb, hw, ⊗, ♯
☎*750-0103*
The Escape Caribeño Bungalows has pretty little *cabinas* with a ceramic-tiled terrace, mosquito net and hammock.

Cariblue Bungalows
$$$$ bkfst incl.
pb, hw
☎/⇄*750-0057*
Cariblue Bungalows are run by an Italian couple, Sandra and Leonardo. The *cabinas* are simple but comfortable and set in a garden with fruit trees.

Playa Salsa Brava and Playa Cocles

Cabinas Surf Point
$-$$
sb/pb, ⊗
☎*750-0123*
The Cabinas Surf Point are owned by Nelida, a local woman. Half of the six *cabinas* have private washrooms. All look out onto the world-famous surf beach, Salsa Brava, and are therefore popular with surfers.

Cabinas Eltesoro
$$$
pb, hw
☎*750-0128*
The three brand-new Cabinas Eltesoro sleep two to five people each and are huge and clean. Homemade bread is served for breakfast (not included). Carmen, one of the owners, also sells jewellery that she makes herself.

Playa Chiquita

Near Playa Chiquita, you can go **camping** beside the dirt-cheap **Irie Cabinas** (*$*).

Cabinas Villa Paraíso
$$$
pb, hw
Cabinas Villa Paraíso has eight bungalows surrounded by a garden, all beside the La Paloma Café Restaurant.

Hotel Kashá
$$$
pb, hw
☎*288-2563 or 750-0127*
⇄*222-2213*
Surrounded by a lovely garden, Hotel Kashá has six rooms and two houses for rent. The rooms are large and clean, with hammocks on the terrace. The Reef Café serves breakfast and drinks.

Yaré
$$$
pb, hw, ⊗, ℜ
☎/⇄*750-0106*
The hotel-restaurant Yaré rents 21 *cabinas* and a big house. The brightly coloured *cabinas* are clean and

The Caribbean Coast

well maintained. The *cabinas* are connected by raised wooden walkways that cut through dense, peaceful vegetation.

Playa Chiquita Lodge
$$$ bkfst incl.
pb, ⊗
☎/⇔*750-0062*
wolfbiss@racsa.co.cr
The Playa Chiquita Lodge rents wooden *cabinas* that blend in perfectly with their natural surroundings, only 50m (164ft) from the sea and a spectacular white-sand beach. Each *cabina* is very clean and has a private bathroom plus a veranda with hammocks and rocking chairs for relaxation. There are also three well-equipped houses for rent. They plan to open a "jungle health spa." The manager, Wanda Bissinger, is also the founding editor of a very interesting little newspaper, *Talamanca's Voice* (see p 156).

Cabinas La Caracola
$$$$
pb, hw, ⊗, K
☎*750-0135*
Cabinas La Caracola, facing the sea, has colourful double rooms with kitchens.

Casa Camarona
$$$$
pb, hw, ℜ
☎*750-0151*
⇔*750-0210*
camarona@ticonet.co.cr
The Casa Camarona has 18 lovely rooms with an ocean view.

Best Western Hotel Punta Cocles
$$$$
pb, hw, ≡, ⊗, ≈ ℜ, ctv
☎*234-8055*
⇔*234-8033*
The Best Western Hotel Punta Cocles has 60 air-conditioned rooms, a pool, whirlpool, children's play area and a private section of the beach just 500m (1,640ft) from the hotel, where there are also showers, a bar and a restaurant. Your typical large chain hotel.

Miraflores Lodge
$$$$ bkfst incl.
pb/sb, ⊗
☎*750-0038*
www.mirafloreslodge.com
The Miraflores Lodge has eight rooms, some quite large with private bathrooms. This bed and breakfast is tastefully decorated, even on the outside with exotic plants and countless heliconias. Pamela Carpenter, the owner, is very interested in the environment, agriculture and culture of the region. She organizes outings to the Kéköldi reserve.

Villas del Caribe
$$$$
pb, hw, ⊗
☎*750-0203*
⇔*221-2801*
Villas del Caribe has 12 apartments with a spectacular view of the beach from their balconies.

Hotel Shawandha
$$$$$ bkfst incl.
pb, hw, ℜ
☎*750-0018*
⇔*750-0037*
The 12 enormous palm-roofed *cabinas* at the Hotel Shawandha are perfect for rest and relaxation. Each is tastefully decorated in its own particular style and has a bright bathroom designed by French ceramist Filou Pascal. A short 200m (656ft) trail leads to a beautiful white-sand beach.

Punta Uva

Selvin's Restaurant & Cabinas
$
sb, ℜ
Although Selvin's Restaurant & Cabinas has modest rooms, the restaurant is said to be one of the best in the region (see p 183).

Cabinas Casa Angela
$$-$$$ bkfst incl.
pb, hw
⇔*750-0144*
Not far from Punta Uva, the Cabinas Casa Angela are owned by Angela, a very friendly Swiss woman who makes sure that everything runs smoothly.

The Manzanillo Region

Camping is permitted at the Refugio Nacional de Vida Silvestre Gandoca-Manzanillo, but since there are neither designated sites nor services, most people prefer to sleep in the village of Manzanillo or in Puerto Viejo de Talamanca.

Maxi's Cabinas
$
sb, ℜ
near the bus stop
Maxi's Cabinas, located in the small village of Manzanillo, rents out rooms and has a restaurant, bar and nightclub (open on weekends). This place is definitely not one of the quietest on the Caribbean coast!

Almonds and Corals Lodge Tent Camp
$$$$
pb, ⊗, ℜ
8km (5mi) south of Puerto Viejo
☎272-2024
↩272-2220
www.geoexpediciones.com
Almonas@racsa.co.cr
The Almonds and Corals Lodge Tent Camp, 300m (984ft) off the road to the beach, deserves a four-star rating for camping. The 20 *cabinas* are nothing more than a roof covered by a giant mosquito net, under which there are a tent, table, washroom and hammock. Each *cabina* is connected to the others by a wooden walkway, which also leads to the restaurant and superb white-sand beach. This establishment belongs to **Geo Expediciones**, a tour operator that organizes outdoor excursions on land and water.

The Tortuguero Region

There are sites for camping near the entrance to the **Parque Nacional Tortuguero**. Because it rains a lot in this region, you might want to rent one of the reasonably priced *cabinas* near the park instead.

Since the Tortuguero region, which includes Parismina and Barra del Colorado, is difficult to access (airplane or boat only), you should reserve a place to stay ahead of time. Most of the local hotels offer two- or three-day all-inclusive packages (transportation, accommodation, food, guided activities, etc.).

If you want to go to Tortuguero on your own and stay in one of the village's low-budget hotels, you can take the boat from Moín (near Puerto Limón).

Cabinas Tatané
$
sb
☎223-2240
On the second canal, on the Penitencia Lagoon, a few minutes from the village by boat, the Cabinas Tatané are nothing fancy, but are cheap.

Caribe Lodge
$$
sb, ℜ
☎224-3348
The Caribe Lodge, on the Penitencia Lagoon, has nine very rustic

cabinas with a shared bathroom for up to 30 people. Transportation to the village is free and excursions along the different canals can be organized.

Manati Lodge
$$$ *bkfst incl.*
pb, ⊗, ℜ
☎383-0330
The small Manati Lodge was built in 1980. Its six rooms are plain but pleasant and very affordable for a hotel right on the Tortuguero canal. The owner, Fernando Figuls, offers excursions along the canals and in Parque Nacional Tortuguero. This lodge also has a games room for the whole family and a small bar.

Hotel Ilan-Ilan
$$$$ *fb*
pb, ⊗, ℜ
Agencia Mitur
☎255-2262 or 255-2031
↩255-1946
mitour@racsa.co.cr
Hotel Ilan-Ilan is located about 3km (1.9mi) from the village in the middle of lush tropical vegetation. The hotel was built in 1989 and named for a tree, the *Cananga odorata*, which is almost exclusive to the area and produces pretty yellow flowers. There are 24 clean and comfortable *cabinas* in a row.

Jungle Lodge
$$$$
pb, hw, ⊗, ℜ
☎ *233-0133 or 233-0155*
⇌ *233-0778*
cotour@racsa.co.cr
The Jungle Lodge is a bit outdated, but charming nonetheless. Its 50 rooms are clean and comfortable. There are also several activities, such as hiking on the 400m (1,312ft) trail near the hotel.

Laguna Lodge
$$$$
pb, ⊗, ℜ
☎ *225-3740 or 280-7843*
⇌ *283-8031*
The Laguna Lodge is one of the only two lodges near the village and has direct access to the beach. There are 27 attractive and very clean rooms, divided into seven sections of four rooms. This lodge is peaceful and well kept.

🛶 Mawamba Lodge
$$$$
pb, hw, ⊗, ≈, ℜ
☎ *223-7490 or 710-7282*
⇌ *222-5463*
mawamba@racsa.co.cr
The Mawamba Lodge is the only lodge within walking distance of the village (approx. 1km or 0.6mi). There is a short trail to the beach. The 36 wooden rooms are extremely pleasant and clean. Mawamba also has a restaurant, a bar, a souvenir shop and a conference room, where slide shows of the regional flora and fauna are presented. The centrepiece of this lodge is its fanciful pool with a small bridge, where you can relax between excursions organized by the hotel.

🛶 Pachira Lodge
$$$$
pb, hw, ⊗, ℜ
☎ *256-7080*
⇌ *223-1119*
The Pachira Lodge is just outside the village of Tortuguero. It's one of the most attractive and charming hotels in the region, with 34 clean rooms, tastefully decorated in pastels. The hotel was mainly built of wood and still smells like freshly chopped timber (built in 1995). It also has a superb restaurant, a bar, a small souvenir shop, a games room and two short hiking trails.

🛶 Tortuga Lodge
$$$$$
pb, hw, ⊗, ℜ
☎ *257-0766 or 222-0333*
⇌ *257-1665*
costaric@expeditions.co.cr
The Tortuga Lodge is owned by the famous Costa Rica Expeditions. The tour agency lives up to its reputation by offering a hotel with unparalleled ambiance, rooms, food and service. Here, they pull out all the stops to insure a pleasant and memorable stay. In 1996, the rooms and landscaping were redone to blend in better with the natural surroundings. The impeccable rooms, four per building, are luxurious and spacious and have huge windows on three walls. The bathrooms are large, practical and elegant. Rooms on the upper floors share a large covered terrace spanning the entire exterior, where you can take in the serene view of the canals and the forest. A small trail behind the hotel (remember to bring your insect repellent!) leads through the dense, enchanting forest. Some of the many species you may encounter include the magnificent small, brightly coloured, venomous frogs.

The stylish restaurant, with its long terrace, is located on the waterfront, and serves some of the best meals in the country. The large tables are close together, making it easy to meet fellow travellers. The Tortuga Lodge also has some of the best guides in the region, from whom you'll certainly learn a lot about the region's impressive flora and fauna. There are many organized activities available, from sea turtle watching to tarpon fishing, to nature watching along the canals and climbing the Cerro Tortuguero.

Tortuguero Village

Cabinas Aracari Lodge
$
pb
☎ *798-3059*
The Cabinas Aracari Lodge, behind the soccer field, has rooms with private bathrooms for as little as $10.

Cabinas de Sabina
$
sb/pb, ℜ
The Cabinas de Sabina has several rooms, three with private bathroom.

Cabinas Meryscar
$
sb
Cabinas Meryscar has very simple rooms that cost next to nothing.

The **Cabinas Riverside** (*$$; pb*) and **Bananera** (*$; sb*) also have modest rooms at decent prices.

Cabinas Miss Junie
$$$
pb, ⊗, ℜ
☎710-0523
At the northern end of the village, the Cabinas Miss Junie have very clean rooms with private bathrooms, as well as an excellent restaurant (see p 183).

Parismina

Chito's Lodge
$$$$
pb, hw, ≈, ℜ
☎768-8195
A stay at Chito's Lodge includes transportation, as well as room and board. The rooms are clean and the gardens around the pool are striking. You can also take a day-long nature excursion that focuses on local flora and fauna.

Río Parismina Lodge
$$$$$
pb, hw, ≡, ℜ, ≈
☎257-3553
The Río Parismina Lodge offers good fishing packages. A three-day stay including transportation, room, and fishing excursions costs approximately $1,500 per person. The 12 rooms are very clean and comfortable. The lodge also has stunning tropical gardens and a few short hiking trails through the forest.

Barra del Colorado

Río Colorado Fishing Lodge
$$$$
pb, hw, ≡, ⊗, ℜ
☎232-8610
⇌231-5987
tarpon4u@cyperspy.com
The Río Colorado Fishing Lodge, on the south side of the river of the same name, is the most famous hotel in the region. Founded by Archie Fields, but now managed by Dan Wise, it's one of the best places to relax, eat well and, in particular, go on guided fishing expeditions to catch one of the famous gigantic tarpons for which the area is known. The non-fishing "nature" package includes meals, accommodation and boat transportation from Puerto Viejo de Sarapiquí to Barra del Colorado on the first day, then on to the hotel in Moín (near Puerto Limón) after visiting the Parque Nacional de Tortuguero on the second day.

Casa Mar Fishing Lodge
$$$$$
pb, hw, ⊗, ℜ
☎433-8834
⇌433-9287
The Casa Mar Fishing Lodge, north of Barra del Colorado, on the Agua Dulce Lagoon, has clean, comfortable *cabinas*. This hotel offers one-week fishing trips, but also has a number of shorter packages. The hotel is only open during the fishing seasons (Jan to mid-Mar and Sep to Oct).

Isla de Pesca
$$$$$
pb, hw, ⊗, ℜ
☎223-4560
⇌221-5148
Just south of the Casa Mar Fishing Lodge, Isla de Pesca has 20 A-frame *cabinas* with thatched roofs. Packages are available from three to seven days for both fishing and nature observation, which will take you mostly around the Parque Nacional de Tortuguero.

Rain Goddess
$$$$$
sb, hw, ≡, ℜ
☎231-4299
⇌231-3816
The *Rain Goddess* is a luxurious 20m-long (66ft) houseboat belonging to Dr. Alfredo López. There are six spacious, comfortable *cabinas* and a well-equipped "restaurant-" kitchen that serves refined cuisine. There are fishing and nature excursions.

Silver King Lodge
$$$$$
pb, hw, ⊗, ≈, ℜ
☎/≈381-1403
The Silver King Lodge, south of the Río Colorado Fishing Lodge, has a great reputation in the area for fishing and for its comfortable hotel. The rooms are very clean and large. The restaurant serves high-quality food, and the hotel adds some extra touches (free soft drinks, beer and coffee, coffee makers in the rooms and so on) to make your stay all the more enjoyable. The hotel rents out guides and boats for fishing excursions, mostly for tarpon, which the area is known for. Canoes, with or without guides, can be rented to explore the natural surroundings.

Restaurants

Puerto Limón

In Puerto Limón, there are many quaint restaurants and *sodas*, which mostly serve Caribbean cuisine and cheap fish dishes. Several hotels have restaurants, that are open to everyone.

Three of the most popular *sodas* with residents and travellers alike are **La Estrella** (*$-$$; Calle 5, Avenida 3*), where the atmosphere, service, food and prices are excellent; the very pretty **Soda Mares** (*$; Avenida 2, Calle 3/4*) with a varied, low-priced menu and the exciting atmosphere of the nearby *mercado*; and the inexpensive **Soda Yans** (*$; Avenida 2, Calle 5/6*), a local hangout.

Brisas del Caribe
$-$$
Calle 1, Avenida 2
Brisas del Caribe, beside Vargas Park, is the place to go for a reasonably priced sandwich or a *casado*, or just a coffee. At the end of the day, music takes you into the evening.

Arrecife
$$
☎758-4030
Arrecife is a good seafood restaurant on the way to Playa Bonita.

Springfield
$$
☎758-1203
A bit further along the road to Playa Bonita is Springfield, popular for its savoury Caribbean, fish and seafood dishes.

Kimbambú
$$-$$$
Kimbambú, facing Playa Bonita, is a good place to try Caribbean specialties, including fish, soup, chicken and *ceviche* dishes.

Cahuita

The small village of Cahuita has restaurants for all tastes and budgets. Most of these serve local Caribbean-style cuisine with lots of fish and coconut. Some also have international cuisine, such as Chinese, French, Italian, Swiss, Spanish and German dishes.

In addition to the restaurants below, many hotels also have a restaurant or *soda*.

Pastry Shop
$
9am to 6pm
☎755-0275
If you have a craving for a good cake or pastry, stop by the Pastry Shop, near Playa Negra, approximately 350m (1,148ft) from the village.

Wallace Village
$
7am to 7pm
Wallace Village, a *soda* in front of the Turística Cahuita, serves Creole cuisine.

El Cactus
$-$$
5pm to 10pm
☎755-0276
El Cactus is a pizzeria that serves good pasta, just outside the village.

Delle Alpi
$-$$
every day noon to 10pm
☎755-0230
You can enjoy good pizza, pasta and other Italian dishes for little money at the Delle Alpi at the Cahuita Hotel.

Hotel National Park
$-$$
7am to 10pm
☎755-0244
The restaurant at the Hotel National Park serves Costa Rican and

international dishes at reasonable prices. People mostly come here for a drink during happy hour while taking in the incredible vista of the sea.

Miss Edith
$-$$
7am to 9pm, closed Sun
☎*755-0248*
Miss Edith, near the post office and police station, is quite well-known and somewhat busy—and with good reason. It serves excellent, cheap local dishes. The decor is pretty basic, with a few closely placed wooden tables, but the place is clean and painted orange.

Pizzería Emilio
$-$$
4pm to 11pm
☎*755-0063*
Pizzería Emilio, beside the municipal park, serves pizzas and other fast food.

Caribbean Food
$-$$
7:30am to 7pm
Also near the municipal park, but right on the main street, Caribbean Food serves delicious low-priced local cuisine.

La Soda
$-$$
every day 7am to 8pm
☎*755-0055*
The tiny downtown restaurant La Soda has terrific breakfasts with fresh fruit, prepared by Quebecer Mario, who lives right beside it.

From lunch until closing, two chefs, one an amusing Italian, the other a Costa Rican from the area, prepare good and inexpensive local specialties. They sing and joke with their guests while preparing tasty piña coladas.

Sobre Las Olas
$-$$
Sobre Las Olas, 600m (1,969ft) from the village, serves international continental cuisine. With windows everywhere, you can enjoy a superb view of the sea, making this place very popular at happy hour.

El Típico
$-$$
5pm to 10pm
☎*755-0118*
Southwest of the village, El Típico serves affordable Caribbean and international cuisine.

Vishnú
$-$$
7am to 10pm
☎*755-0263*
Vishnú specializes in Italian food. It doesn't, therefore, belong to the San José restaurant chain of the same name, but it does serve great vegetarian breakfasts with homemade bread.

Vista del Mar
$-$$
7:30am to 10pm
☎*755-0008*
At the Vista del Mar, near the entrance to Cahuita national park, you can eat a gigantic plate of Chinese food for next to nothing. However, the service is often very slow.

Cha Cha Cha
$$-$$$
evenings only
Cha Cha Cha, next to Cahuita Tours, is owned by a Quebecer. It specializes in *del mundo* cuisine, including pasta, seafood and steak. Although the place is tastefully decorated in blue and white, the chairs (made of tree trunks) are quite uncomfortable.

Margaritaville Restaurant
$$-$$$
evenings only, closed Wed
2km (1.2mi) west of the village, Playa Negra
☎*755-0038*
The Margaritaville Restaurant, in Moray's Bed & Breakfast (see p 171), is undeniably charming. It's located on the second floor, completely finished in wood, has an open-air kitchen and a friendly, family atmosphere. Run by Canadian Sandra Simla, the restaurant makes typical Caribbean and Canadian dishes from home-grown produce.

The Puerto Viejo de Talamanca Region

Puerto Viejo de Talamanca

Bambu Restaurant
$
as you leave the village towards Manzanillo, next to Stanford's Restaurant
At the Bambu Restaurant, fresh food is always available, but people come here especially to spend a few hours listening to the reggae music.

Café Coral
$
one street west of the ATEC, then south
The Café Coral serves the best breakfast in town. You can savour the delicious homemade bread, yogurt, muesli and crepes. Their chocolate cake is supposedly divine.

Monchies
$
The Monchies is a pastry shop that opens at 6am and serves excellent whole-wheat bread and breakfasts.

Miss Sam
$
one street east and two streets south of the ATEC
At Miss Sam, you can enjoy reasonably priced Caribbean specialties such as fish, rice and beans. Good value for the money.

Old Harbour's Fresco Shop
$
opposite the bus stop
The Old Harbour's Fresco Shop serves tasty breakfasts with homemade whole-wheat bread. You can also order cheap, tasty fish dishes.

Salsa Brava
$
Next to the Bambu Restaurant, the restaurant-café **Salsa Brava** now serves breakfast.

MexiTico
$-$$
MexiTico at the Hotel Puerto Viejo (see p 173) prepares great Mexican and vegetarian cuisine.

Stanford's Restaurant
$-$$
as you exit the village towards Manzanillo, near the sea
This restaurant serves reasonably-priced seafood and Caribbean cuisine. It has a popular nightclub that is open on weekends.

Tamara
$-$$
in front of the ATEC
Tamara is a *soda* that serves breakfasts and local dishes, like the Rundown, a seafood soup. You can also eat good lobster dishes without spending too much.

Caramba
$$
one street east of the ATEC, on the right
Caramba serves gigantic pizzas and good desserts.

Garden Restaurant
$$
near the soccer field
The Garden Restaurant, is a favourite with tourists and locals. It serves Caribbean, Asian and vegetarian dishes, as well as tasty desserts and fresh fruit.

Restaurante Amimodo
$$
near the western end of the village
The Restaurante Amimodo specializes in Italian cuisine, as well as fish and seafood. The owner is in the process of opening up a new restaurant in town, so he left his son in charge of the restaurant in Puerto Viejo.

Playa Salsa Brava and Playa Cocles

Beach Creak
$-$$
Playa Salsa Brava
Beside the Cabinas Surf Point, opposite the world-class Salsa Brava surfing beach, Beach Creak serves breakfast and sandwiches.

Extravaganzia Art Café
$-$$
Playa Cocles
Extravaganzia Art Café prepares excellent Italian food at a good price, all in a relaxed ambiance and decor. Creations of local artists are also on display.

Lapalapa
$$-$$$
Playa Cocles
☎ *750-0151 or 224-3050*
The incredible restaurant Lapalapa is located

next to La Casa Camarona Hotel. The large terrace is decorated in matte, subdued tones. On the menu are fresh fish and seafood as well as typically Caribbean and Jamaican dishes.

Playa Chiquita

Elena's Restaurante
$-$$
Elena's Restaurante, owned by Elena Brown, is recommended for its tasty fish and local dishes.

Paloma Café
$-$$
next to the Cabinas Villa Paraiso
Also on the Playa Chiquita, the Paloma Café has Caribbean and international cuisine as well as seafood.

Soda Aquarius
$-$$
Nearby, the Soda Aquarius is open for breakfast and dinner, but with reservations only.

Punta Uva

Soda y Restaurant Naturales
$-$$
right before Punta Uva, coming from Puerto Viejo de Talamanca
Soda y Restaurant Naturales is just off the main road and has an incredible view of the sea. You can eat breakfasts complete with homemade bread, as well as other dishes, and admire the local crafts that decorate the restaurant.

Selvin's Restaurant
$-$$
Wed to Sun
Selvin's Restaurant is one of the best in the region. It's good and cheap, serving the most delicious Caribbean and fish dishes. This open-air restaurant is rather small, but a pleasant atmosphere prevails.

El Duende Feliz
$$-$$$
Across from the Punta Uva *pulpería*, just before the small trail leading to the magnificent summit, El Duende Feliz is good value for Italian dishes. Moreno and Fabrizio assure a great atmosphere and service.

The Tortuguero Region

For a village as small as Tortuguero, it's surprising to find so many *sodas*, or small restaurants, in addition to the restaurants, hotels and lodges located in the surrounding area. *Sodas* such as **El Dólar** *($-$$; near Tienda de Artesanía)*, **El Tucán** *($-$$; north of the medical clinic)*, **Liliana** *($-$$; near the medical clinic)* and **La Canoa** *($-$$; near the Parque Nacional Tortuguero information centre)*, and restaurants like **Brisas del Mar** *($-$$; behind the school)* and **Meryscar** *($-$$; southwest of the soccer field)* serve excellent homemade Caribbean food, as well as North American dishes like sandwiches.

Miss Junie *($-$$; north of the village)* prepares great chicken, fish and steak, whereas **Pancana** *($-$$; southwest of the soccer field)* offers sandwiches and other dishes, such as excellent homemade brioches.

Entertainment

Cahuita

The most popular spot in Cahuita, especially on a Saturday night, is the **Vaz**, where you can listen to reggae music as well as salsa and merengue.

Jimmy is a very popular spot to play pool. You can also play chess or checkers while listening to rock 'n roll and blues.

The other hip place in town is the **Sarafina**, which plays international music and serves reasonably-priced food, including pizza.

Puerto Viejo de Talamanca

Bambú
as you leave the village towards Manzanillo
The Bambú is a bar that plays reggae music.

Stanford's
as you leave the village, past the
football field, near the sea
The locals hang out at
Stanford's, a nightclub
mixing reggae, calypso
and salsa.

Jonny's Place
near the police station
The most popular
nightclub among tour-
ists in the region is
Jonny's Place, which
plays international mu-
sic. It gets packed after
10pm.

Manzanillo

Maxi
near the bus stop
The Maxi bar becomes
a dance club on week-
ends.

Shopping

Puerto Limón

Helennik Souvenirs
Calle 3, Avenida 4/5
Helennik Souvenirs
sells local crafts and
clothing.

Cahuita

T-shirts, original cloth-
ing, jewellery and many
reggae-style items can
be found at **Bumbata**,
Cahuita Soul and **Coco
Miko**.

Puerto Viejo de
Talamanca

Color Caribe *(main street,*
☎ *750-0075)* sells original T-shirts, jewellery,
hammocks and crafts.

ATEC *(main street,*
☎ *750-0188)* sells some
books, maps and other
documentation on the
area. **Terra Aventuras**
*(beside the Comisariato
Manuel León, by the
beach,* ☎ *750-0004)* also
sells local crafts.

Tortuguero

Paraíso Tropical, **Jungle
Shop** and **Tienda de
Artesanía**, all down-
town, sell regional sou-
venirs.

CCC
just outside the village
The natural history mu-
seum CCC (see p 163)
has a small souvenir
shop inside where you
can find documenta-
tion, videos, books,
among other items.

Northern Costa Rica

is an often overlooked part of the country. It wasn't on the most popular tourist routes for many years, but this is in the process of changing.

Though there are no beaches in the region, the north boasts the largest lake in the country, known for the best windsurfing in Central America! And where else can you see a volcano in the process of erupting? It's also in the north that visitors will find some of the most beautiful reserves of virgin forest in all of Costa Rica!

The area described in this chapter is made up of four large regions, northwest of the Valle Central. The regions of Puerto Viejo de Sarapiquí, Monteverde and Caño Negro (in the far north, bordering on Nicaragua) are known for their vast protected green spaces. The region of Arenal, in the middle, is interesting to visit because of its still-active volcano and immense artificial lake. This last area is part of the huge San Carlos *llanura* (lowland plains), a dairy farming and crop-raising region with Ciudad Quesada (see p 191) as its main town.

The vast region of the north, beyond the Cordillera Central and the Cordillera de Tilarán, has several distinct climates. There is something for everyone: hot, rainy Sarapiquí, the humid San Carlos *llanura*, the cooler Monteverde and the drier, more windy extreme northwest, in the Arenal region. The entire region was once an immense forest. The vast area of the San Carlos *llanura* was transformed into fields and pastures (or banana plantations in Sarapiquí). Although the conversion of the forest to agricultural land certainly has had consequences on the region's environment, the patchwork quilt pattern of pastures and fields under cultivation is charming to travel through.

Mostly thanks to a few ecologists and dedicated nature lovers, the other regions of the Costa Rican north have retained large expanses of dense tropical rainforest that shelter innumerable unidentified birds, plants and animals.

Though it's little known, this region has certain advantages. After all, it's much less crowded for anyone who ventures here!

Finding Your Way Around

By Car

The Puerto Viejo de Sarapiquí Region

Puerto Viejo de Sarapiquí: there are two roads to Puerto Viejo de Sarapiquí from the Central Valley. One starts north of Heredia and Alajuela, runs between the Barva and Poás Volcanoes, and then heads east to Puerto Viejo after passing through San Miguel and La Virgen. This is a striking route with some scenic stops along the way, such as the Poás Volcano and some magnificent waterfalls, including those at La Paz. The trip takes approximately 2.5hrs, non-stop.

The second and faster way is to take the Guapiles Highway towards the Caribbean Coast and go through the spectacular Parque Nacional Braulio Carrillo. Then, turn left near Santa Clara and head almost due north. This route passes within 2km (1.2km) of the La Selva ecological reserve, which is about 4km (2.5mi) south of Puerto Viejo.

If you're coming from Guanacaste, La Fortuna, or Ciudad Quesada (all on the same route), simply go northeast to Puerto Viejo de Sarapiquí in the Central Valley, passing by Ajuas Zarcas and San Miguel (north of the Poás Volcano) and La Virgen.

Rara Avis

Rara Avis is some 15km (9.3mi) southwest of Las Horquetas, which is southeast of Puerto Viejo de Sarapiquí. Arrange transportation to Rara Avis well ahead of time because the road going there is extremely rough and hilly and parts of it must be navigated by tractor or on rented horses. Four-wheel drive vehicles can travel 12 (7.5mi) of the 15km (9.3mi) to the reserve, but no more. It takes at least 2hrs to get there from Las Horquetas.

The Ciudad Quesada Region

To get to **Ciudad Quesada** (San Carlos), take the General Cañas Highway to the Naranjo exit, which is about 25km (15.5mi) west of Alajuela, and drive due north through Naranjo and Zarcero.

The Arenal Region

La Fortuna: the road to La Fortuna goes through Zarcero and San Carlos (Ciudad Quesada), then heads directly north to Muelle. Once at Muelle, turn left and go due west. The scenery is attractive with the Arenal Volcano rising above the lowland plains of the San Carlos *llanura*.

There is a small road between **Monteverde** and **La Fortuna**. Starting from Monteverde, head to Santa Elena. From there, take the unpaved road north to Tilarán. This road zigzags between high valleys with splendid panoramic views of the region, and is sometimes impassable—check its condition before you go. Shortly before Tilarán, the road becomes paved. At Tilarán, go north to Lake Arenal and follow the road along the northern shore of the lake. Past the village of Nuevo Arenal, the road is in bad shape for some 10km (6mi), then it suddenly becomes excellent again.

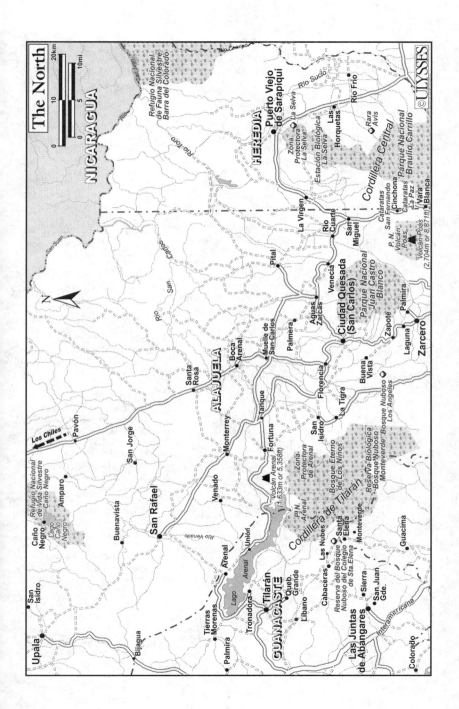

The North

NICARAGUA

ULYSSES

The 117km (73mi) trip will take 4 to 5hrs.

Nuevo Arenal: you can get to Nuevo Arenal from Guanacaste (west of Lake Arenal) or from La Fortuna (east of the lake). From Guanacaste, the road goes through Tilarán and follows the west side of the lake, which is windier and is good for water sports. The eastern route follows the shore for almost the whole length of the lake. The road is in pretty good condition until the last few kilometres before Nuevo Arenal. From there on, it's unpaved and barely passable. Travelling it at night is to be avoided.

Parque Nacional Arenal

The entrance to the Parque Nacional Arenal is located on the south side of the Arenal volcano, 15km or 9.3mi (about 30min) from the village of La Fortuna, on the east side. Take the road around the volcano, close to the Tabacón hot springs. Then, near the lake, take the small, unpaved, poorly maintained road to the park and the Arenal Observatory Lodge.

The Monteverde Region

From San José, take the Inter-American Highway north towards Puntarenas. At the intersection near Puntarenas, stay on the highway and head towards Cañas, rather than turning off towards Puntarenas. Less than 20km (12mi) further, at Rancho Grande, there's a sign on the right indicating the road to Monteverde. It is 32km (20mi) long and usually in terrible condition, with many steep pitches and heavy traffic. The long climb ends at the village of Santa Elena. From there, the road descends for about 5km (3mi) to Monteverde and the reserve of the same name. The drive takes about 4hrs, depending on the season, the state of the road and the vehicle (a four-wheel-drive is ideal).

Monteverde is not built like a typical village with a grid-like pattern of streets and central square. Instead, its houses, hotels, restaurants and stores line the 5km (3mi) stretch of unpaved road that runs from the village of Santa Elena to the Monteverde reserve.

Refugio Nacional de Vida Silvestre Caño Negro

This reserve is located 165km (103mi) from San José and 21km (13mi) from Los Chiles. From San José, the highway passes through Naranjo, Zarcero, Ciudad Quesada (San Carlos), Floriencia, Muelle de San Carlos and Los Chiles. From the province of Guanacaste, you can get to the park via the small town of Upala, which is 36km (6.2mi) west of Caño Negro. From Upala, take the road going to San Rafael and after about 10km (6.2mi), at Colonia Puntarenas, take the small road indicated by the sign to Caño Negro.

By Bus

The Puerto Viejo de Sarapiquí Region

Puerto Viejo de Sarapiquí: At least six buses per day go from San José to Puerto Viejo de Sarapiquí. They leave from Avenida 11 between Calles Central and 1. Some buses take the road to Heredia, others take the Guapiles Highway. The trip lasts about 4hrs. Some of the buses that travel along the highway stop in Río Frío, making the trip longer.

There are three departures daily from **Heredia**. Buses leave almost every 2hrs from **San Carlos** for **Puerto Viejo de Sarapiquí**. The trip takes at least 1hr.

The Ciudad Quesada Region

Ciudad Quesada: there is excellent bus service to this destination from San José (Coca Cola bus terminal). In fact, there are hourly depar-

tures from 5am to 7pm.
The trip takes 3hrs.

The Arenal Region

La Fortuna: There are
three departures every
morning from San José
to La Fortuna, leaving
from the Coca Cola bus
terminal. There is a
mid-afternoon return
trip to San José. The
trip takes at least
4.5hrs. Buses leave
Ciudad Quesada for La
Fortuna practically ev-
ery 2hrs. The trip takes
about 1hr.

Nuevo Arenal: Two buses
per day leave Ciudad
Quesada for Arenal-
Tilarán: one in the
morning and one in the
afternoon.

The Monteverde Region

There are two buses
daily from San José
(*Calle 14, and Avenidas
9/11*), at 6:30am and
2:30pm. The trip takes
about 4hrs (*$5.30;
Transportes Tilarán,
☎222-3854*).

Refugio Nacional de Vida Silvestre Caño Negro

There are two buses
daily from San José
(*Calle 12, and Avenida
9*), at 5:30am and
3:30pm. The trip from
San José to Los Chiles
takes about 2.5hrs
(*$2.20; Autotransportes,
☎460-5032*).

Practical Information

Monteverde

Although difficult to get
to (one wonders how
trucks delivering bottles
make it without break-
age!), Monteverde of-
fers ample services of
all kinds. It has a bank
(lacking an ATM how-
ever), a service station,
a pharmacy and a gro-
cery store, as well as
Internet and taxi ser-
vices.

Travel Agencies

Aventuras Arenal (*☎479-
9133, ≈479-9295*), on
the main street of
La Fortuna, organizes
all sorts of excursions
in the region: by car,
by bicycle, on foot or
on horseback. You can
also visit the Caño Ne-
gro Park or go fishing
on Lake Arenal with
them.

AveRica (*☎479-9076,
≈479-9456*) in La
Fortuna organizes bird-
watching expeditions
around Lake Arenal,
Refugio Nacional de
Vida Silvestre Caño
Negro, the Río Frío and
Parque Nacional Juan
Castro Blanco.

Albergue Tío Henry (*San
Rafael de Guatusi, north
of Nuevo Arenal;
☎464-0211*) offers
guided tours of the
Refugio Nacional de

Vida Silvestre Caño
Negro, the Río Celeste
waterfalls (on horse-
back) and the 3.2km
(2mi) long Cavernas de
Venado—and even
visits a caiman and
Ujuminican crocodile
farm!

Eco Tours (*Playa
Hermosa, on the corner of
Guanacaste, ☎/≈672-
0175*) organizes guided
bird-watching in the
**Refugio Nacional de Vida
Silvestre Caño Negro**
where there are many
different bird species.

Stable (*3km or 1.9mi west
of Nuevo Arenal; ≈694-
4092*) offers horseback
riding excursions for all
levels.

Exploring

The Puerto Viejo de Sarapiquí Region

A visit to the Puerto
Viejo region will help
you better understand
oour planet's fragile
ecology. The region's
reserves, parks and
other undeveloped
areas help preserve
entire ecosystems that
shelter thousands of
species of flora and
fauna. But don't expect
sunny, cool weather:
most of this area lies in
the hot and humid Ca-
ribbean zone of the
country. However, it's
this tropical climate that
fosters the luxuriant
growth of the rain-
forest.

From the looks of it, **Puerto Viejo de Sarapiquí** doesn't seem very interesting, but it was once the country's most important port. In the era before modern transportation links were constructed, boats used to sail north on Río Sarapiquí to get to Río San Juan (the natural border between Costa Rica and Nicaragua) and the Atlantic Ocean.

A few kilometres southwest of Puerto Viejo is **MUSA ★** (*El Tigre, on the road to Horquetas*), a local women's co-operative farm where herbs are grown for medicinal, cosmetic and other commercial purposes. A small donation is requested from visitors. The place is both pleasant and educational to visit. Everyday products containing these herbs are sold here.

There are three noteworthy waterfalls in the region. The first is the spectacular **Catarata San Rafael ★** in La Cinchona, a little spot about halfway between San José and Puerto Viejo.

Cataratas La Paz ★, on the river of the same name, is located on the road from Poás to Puerto Viejo de Sarapiquí. By crossing the river via the bridge, you can get a beautiful view of what looks like one waterfall but is actually two superimposed. The mist produced by the waterfall

is a refreshing break from the heat. The falls are lit up at night and look magnificent, with the surrounding greenery also illuminated. It's not safe to go behind the waterfalls because the path is extremely slippery.

Cataratas San Fernando ★, a little farther north along the road going from Poás to Puerto Viejo de Sarapiquí, is also worth seeing. The falls can be admired from **El Parador**, a private house that is open to the public. The owners feed a bevy of hummingbirds that are interesting to watch, especially when they drink energy-giving sugar-water from feeders outside the house.

Rara Avis

Rara Avis ★ (☎/≠253-0844, *www.rara-avis.com*) is a private nature reserve established by Amos Bien from the U.S., who first visited Costa Rica in 1977. Fascinated by the rich ecosystems in this part of the world, he soon realized that they

were threatened by clear-cutting and the excessive burning of the rainforest to make pasturage, as seen in Guanacaste and along the Río Sarapiquí. Therefore, in 1983, he created the Rara Avis reserve next to the La Selva reserve and the Braulio Carrillo national park. The 1,300ha (3,212 acres) terrain was meant to demonstrate that it was possible to use Costa Rica's ecological resources in an economically viable way without destroying them.

As a functioning centre for research and nature preservation, this reserve is relatively far from the tourist-beaten path and therefore ideal for adventurous types with a passion for nature. There are several reasons we say this: firstly, because the road leading into the reserve is really pretty terrible and requires considerable patience and endurance (see p 186). Secondly, it rains nonstop. Lastly, the standards of the accommodations provided are nowhere near those of a large hotel. However, if you decide to make the trip, you'll be rewarded with a fascinating variety of animals and plants. There is also a magnificent 55m (180ft) high waterfall in the reserve's jungle. The trails can be explored alone or with a guide.

La Selva

La Selva ★ *(3km or 1.9mi south of Puerto Viejo de Sarapiquí, ☎ 740-1515, ⇌740-1414, or via OTS ☎240-6696, ⇌240-6783)* is a 1,600ha (3,954 acres) ecological reserve managed by the Organisation for Tropical Studies (OTS), which is dedicated to the study of tropical and subtropical green spaces. Its members hail from universities and research centres across the United States, Puerto Rico and Costa Rica. The reserve is essentially a research and study centre that attracts specialists and students from all over the world and facilities have been set up to do fieldwork on site. It is, however, possible to visit, or even stay at the reserve, if reservations are made in advance.

It should be kept in mind that, while it is more accessible than Rara Avis, La Selva's climate is just as hot and rainy and thus requires special clothing. The number of plant and animal species that have been identified here is impressive. In fact, the reserve is home to more than 400 species of birds—not bad for 1,600ha (3,954 acres)! To explore the reserve, you must be accompanied by one of their guides *($20)*. This is done so as not to disturb the scientific research going on. The trails are, however, in excellent condition and wheelchair-accessible most of the way.

Overnight stays are possible with advance reservations (see p 207). By staying here, you'll come to appreciate the admirable, ecological ideals of the people running the station.

The Ciudad Quesada Region

The region of **Cuidad Quesada** (called **San Carlos** by its residents) is located in the San Carlos *llanura* (lowland plains), which run all the way to the Nicaraguan border in the north. It's one of the most productive agricultural regions in Costa Rica and you'll certainly notice this if you're coming from San Ramón and Zarcero.

The **region between Zarcero and Ciudad Quesada ★★** has some extraordinary landscapes with valleys and rivers, fields of crops and cows grazing in pastures, making it hard to concentrate on the road. There are too few places to stop and admire the scenery!

Though Ciudad Quesada is a fair-sized town with a population of 35,000, people mostly come here for the surrounding countryside and tourist resorts.

Ciudad Quesada is also a good place to stop midway between San José and the Arenal region. You have to pass through it if you want to get to the region of Puerto Viejo de Sarapiquí without taking the road to the Poás Volcano.

The region of **Zarcero** is described in the chapter on the Central Valley (see p 116).

The Awakening!

Note that the still–active Arenal Volcano produced some substantial eruptions during the summer of 2000, even claiming some lives. Remember that it is important to respect safety regulations to the letter, and stay out of unauthorized areas.

The Arenal Region

The region of Arenal is characterized by two geographical formations: its active volcano and its lake, the largest in the country. Both contribute to the imposing landscape of the flatlands in the east and the gentle valleys in the west. In addition, the roads to the region are being improved every year.

The North

The Reawakening of Arenal

The Arenal Volcano wasn't always a fire-and-stone-spitting monster. In fact, until the end of the 1960s, the mountain was quiet, and people living around it believed it to be extinct. Then, on July 29, 1968, the mountain suddenly awoke. A very violent explosion blew the top off its cone, and sent tons of rock flying into the air, followed by lava flowing down its sides. The impact of the eruption was so powerful that it destroyed the villages of Pueblo Nuevo and Tabacón, and a large part of the surrounding forest. Seventy-eight people were killed, and hundreds of others had to evacuate the area. The explosion was so violent that the tremors from it could be felt as far as Boulder, Colorado, in the United States!

If the weather permits (the volcano often has its head in the clouds), on the way you'll see the **Arenal Volcano ★★** rising up in the distance. With a height of 1,633m (5,358ft) and a perfectly conical shape, often topped by a plume of white smoke, the volcano certainly dominates the plains. It is the perfect image of a stereotypical volcano, with rumbling subterranean explosions sending a halo of smoke and fire to the surface. With a little luck (if the weather is good and the volcano is in an active period), the nighttime spectacle is breathtaking. Sometimes you can even see lava flowing down the crater. A better volcano would be hard to find! See "**Parque Nacional Arenal**," p 195.

The Arenal Volcano has only been active since the late 1960s. The last time it erupted there were 68 deaths and the towns of Pueblo Nuevo and Tabacón were destroyed. The giant awoke with earthquakes, rockslides, smoke and noxious gases, and covered the lush vegetation on the mountainside with a thick layer of volcanic ash. Since then, the volcano rumbles and spits periodically during the year.

People have capitalized on the volcano's reawakening and the new lake nearby has a whole slew of interesting activities and facilities for visitors. All this makes it more pleasant to stay longer in this region.

The La Fortuna Region

La Fortuna is the closest town to the volcano. It was originally an agricultural centre, but thanks to the popularity of the nearby volcano, it quickly became a tourist town with more and more businesses opening up in the city and on the road leading to the volcano. Therefore, you should have no problem finding comfortable and reasonably priced accommodations. The many new hotels and *cabinas* must keep prices down to remain competitive. There are almost too many places from which to choose in every price category. One thing that might make your decision a little easier is to pick one with a pool right beside your *cabina*, because La Fortuna is relatively hot, since it is only 250m (820ft) above sea level. Outings in the surrounding area are easy to arrange through several organizations and hotels. All kinds of sports equipment can be rented around here as well.

Five and a half kilometres (3.4mi) south of

La Fortuna is the **Catarata La Fortuna** ★ *(take the first street west of the church, which crosses the Río Burío)*, accessible by car, on horseback or even on foot. Pay attention to the road, as it can get difficult in places (especially during the rainy season).

Also, the way to the falls is not clearly marked. The waterfall is gorgeous, cascading down the rock face in tiers. It can be seen from the parking lot, but you can get closer to it by taking a steep path to the foot of the falls. Some people swim here, but the strong current can be dangerous.

The **Tabacón Resort** ★★★ *($17/day; every day 10am to 10pm; 13km or 8mi west of La Fortuna en route to the Arenal Volcano,* ☎*256-1500,* ≈*221-3075, www.tabacon.com)* hot springs are superbly designed: 10 swimming pools with thermally heated water from the Río Tabacón, waterfalls, two restaurants (see p 218) and two bars (one actually in a swimming pool) provide true relaxation! Each swimming pool is set at a specific temperature, from 23° (73°F) to 40°C (104°F). It's a fun little place surrounded by vegetation and with a view of the volcano. Try the waters or the restaurant at

night when it's dark, or even foggy outside.

Note that it also features an attractive health spa, Iskandria, where a wide range of men's and women's heath and beauty options will add to your enjoyment. It's usually crowded, even during the low season.

A new hot springs establishment has opened on the same road as the Tabacón, slightly closer to La Fortuna. **Baldi Termae** *($7; 10am to 10pm;* ☎*479-9651 or 479-9652)* is not on the same scale as its competitor, but the pools are certified and it's much more affordable. It offers four pools with water at temperatures

The North

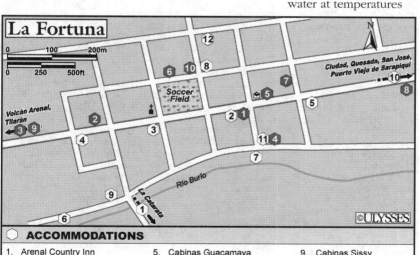

⬡ ACCOMMODATIONS

1. Arenal Country Inn	5. Cabinas Guacamaya	9. Cabinas Sissy
2. Burío Inn	6. Cabinas Jerry	10. Cabinas Villa Fortuna
3. Cabinas Carmela	7. Cabinas Mayol	11. La Fortuna
4. Cabinas Grijalba	8. Cabinas Oriuma	12. San Bosco

⬣ RESTAURANTS

1. El Jardín	5. Los Antojitos	9. Pizzería/Spaghettaría
2. La Choza de Laurel	6. Wall's	Vagabondo
3. La Pradera	7. Nene's	10. Rancho La Cascada
4. La Tía Ara	8. Pizzería Luygi's	

of between 37°C (99°F) and 63°C (145°F). The no-frills facilities seem a little bare. Bringing food onto the premises is not allowed; a restaurant and bar on site will meet your needs.

Formerly, most of the lava spewed out by the Arenal Volcano coursed down the mountain on the same slope as the Arenal Observatory Lodge (see p 195). Today, after another of the volcano's whims, the path of the lava has changed slightly, and it runs down the side where the Los Lagos estate is instead. So **Los Lagos** *($7;* ☎*479-8000 or 479-9126)*, a huge property, now devotes itself to tourists. You can stay overnight (see p 219) or spend the day enjoying some of the many activities available here. Among the possibilities are fishing for *tilapia* in one of the two lakes for which it is named, swimming in a pool with slides for children, relaxing in a hot springs or observing crocodiles in an artificial pond. Of course, don't forget to take the trail to have a closer look at the famous lava, which is still, understandably, a respectable distance away.

Around Lake Arenal

Head west from Tabacón Resort and the park road to get to the dike that retains the newer part of **Lake Arenal ★**. Originally smaller, the lake is in fact a large reservoir that provides water for irrigation systems in the area and electricity for the country. The water is clean, *guapotes* (rainbow perch) are plentiful and there is constant wind, particularly in the western part of the lake. It is not surprising that swimmers, fishers, boaters and windsurfers are often seen on the lake. The road runs parallel to the shore and offers glimpses of the superb view of the lake with the volcano rising above it. Because the scenery is so beautiful and there are so many possibilities for recreational activities in the area, some hotels have been built in recent years on the beach and on hills overlooking the lake.

Cavernas de Venado *($15; the road starts a few kilometres east of Nuevo Arenal)*, 1hr from Lake Arenal, form a grotto some 2km (1.2mi) in length. During the guided tour of the caves, all the expected geological forms like stalactites and stalagmites can be seen—as well as bats!

Lake Coter is also to the north of Lake Arenal (4km or 2.5mi), and only accessible via a road a few kilometres west of Nuevo Arenal. All sorts of water sports are practiced here, especially swimming (see "Lago Coter Eco-Lodge," p 212).

Jardín Botánico Arenal ★ *($4; every day 9am to 5pm; on the road between La Fortuna and Tilarán, 5km or 3.1mi east of Nuevo Arenal and 25km or 15.5mi west of the Lake Arena dike,* ☎*694-4273,* ⇌*694-4086)* is a lovely little botanical garden. Its paths wind through more than 1,200 plants from all over the world. Several species of birds and butterflies are regular visitors here. There is even a small butterfly farm on the premises. It can be toured without a guide.

The area around **Nuevo Arenal** *(midway between La Fortun and Tilarán)*, on the northwest shore of the lake, enjoys a better climate than La Fortuna, where it's almost always oppressively hot and humid. This village, which is also referred to simply as Arenal, was built when the original site was submerged due to the artificial expansion of the lake: hence "Nuevo." The town has grown somewhat, but it's still quiet. To date, there aren't many establishments that can accommodate tourists. It is a pleasant place to take a stroll.

The closer you go to the western end of Lake Arenal, the windier it gets. Because of this, the nights are cool. From the south shore to the western end of the lake there are many **windmills**, putting this constant and economical source of energy to a good use. The Arenal-Tilarán road, which runs along the northwest side of the lake, provides a good vantage point from which to admire the arresting landscape created by these dynamic, silent giants cresting the hills. This part of Lake Arenal is the most popular for windsurfing. There are a few places where the public can access the lake, such as at the government-owned wharf *(just past the Rock and Surf hotel, about 4km or 2.5mi towards Tilarán)*.

Parque Nacional Arenal

The Arenal Volcano is the archetypical erupting volcano: its elegant, conical form makes it stand out from the neighbouring mountains, and it's not part of the mountain range. With an altitude of 1,633m (5,358ft), it can be spotted easily from all directions, most particularly from the west, with Lake Arenal in the foreground. It's also the image of a "real" volcano because it's one of the most active in the world. People come from all over the planet to admire its boiling crater. They hope for a clear night so that they can see glowing lava flow down its sides.

In 1994, 12,016ha (29,691 acres) were added to the Area de Conservación Arenal, which was then renamed **Parque Nacional Arenal ★ ★** *($6; every day, 8am to 10pm;* ☎*460-1412 or 695-5908,* ≈*460-0644)*. The park was created to protect the region and inform the public about this very active volcano. The park tries to dissuade overly adventurous people from climbing up to the crater of the volcano: over the years, there have been dozens of accidents here, some of them fatal. Hikers who were a little too curious probably got too close to the volcano and fell in.

At the entrance to the park there is a reception area with a parking lot, toilets, telephones, drinking water, maps of the park, and so on. The park authorities have a learning centre and other tourist facilities in mind for the future.

Most visitors to the park go to the **Mirador** observation point, about 1.3km (0.8mi) from the entrance. It's accessible via a footpath or by car and there's parking available. Since this observation point is at the foot of the volcano, it's probably the best place to see, hear and feel the volcano's power. From here, you can see the lava that runs to the base of the mountain, destroying everything in its path. On some days, ash explodes from the top of the volcano. And don't be startled if you feel the earth shaking and hear a loud rumbling, as though the Arenal wants to demonstrate its power and destructive force.

Park employees have cleared trails to the base of the volcano and the lava flows. The **Las Heliconias** trail (1km or 0.6mi) goes to the Mirador observation point. Different species of plants that have managed to grow after the 1968 eruption can be found along this path. This trail also branches off onto the **Las Coladas** trail (2km or 1.2mi), which leads to the area where only lava flows. Along the trail at different points are scenic views of the Chato Volcano to the east, the Lake Arenal dike to the west, and the Arenal Volcano itself. Another trail, **Los Tucanes** (2km or 1.2mi), winds its way through exotic flora and fauna including toucans, monkeys, and armadillos. The last trail, **Los Miradores** (1.2km or 0.75mi), next to Lake Arenal, used to be a service road to the hydroelectric dam.

Located at the edge of Parque Nacional Arenal, the **Arenal Observatory Lodge ★ ★** *($2.75; bar-restaurant,* ☎*257-9489,* ≈*257-4220; past the park, follow the signs, www.arenal-observatory.co.cr)* is a fantastic spot for volcano-watching (see also p 209). For the first

25 years after it exploded, the hotel was exclusively used by researchers from the Institute of Seismology at the national university of Costa Rica. Now, anyone can spend a memorable day, or an even more extraordinary evening here, enjoying the best possible vantage point for observing the volcano. On clear nights, if the volcano is spitting fire, visitors go out on the terrace of the hotel to better admire the spectacle put on by the roaring monster. Most of the excellent nighttime photographs of the volcano emitting huge amounts of glowing, orange lava were taken from this terrace. A network of five trails has been set up from the hotel so visitors can explore the rich, dense vegetation in this part of the rainforest. This is a great place to spend a day, or more. The road to the hotel is very bumpy. If your vehicle does not have four-wheel drive, call ahead to ask about road conditions.

The Monteverde Region

The region of Monteverde is made up of vast forests that cover large valleys and mountains that are between 800 and 1,800m high (2,625 and 5,906ft). Just getting there by car or by bus is an experience in itself and will give you

The Quetzal

The best time to spot the quetzal (*Pharomachrus moccinno*) at the Monteverde reserve is between March and May. This is mating season, when the birds make their nests high in the trees, some 10m (32.8ft) above the ground. At other times of the year, the bird is harder to spot. However, an experienced guide can show you the most frequented areas. This is how, in early December, we were able to observe both a male and a female quetzal. The quetzal is a member of the trogon family and is remarkably large. They are 35cm (13.8in) tall on average and have an extraordinary emerald green train, or extension to the tail, that can be up to 60cm (23.6in) long! The quetzal makes its home in the tropical rainforest from southern Mexico to Panama, at elevations between 1,200 and 3,000m (3,937 and 9,843ft).

the impression of going to the end of the earth. But after 2hrs of snaking along the little ribbon of a road, you actually arrive in a region with a whole gamut of hotels and nature-related activities. This is a popular destination for people from all over Costa Rica and the world. A veritable botanical and ornithological paradise, the region of Monteverde is a year-round attraction for nature lovers, some of whom are scientists while others are ordinary tourists, hoping to see the rare **quetzal**, a superb, large, emerald, red and blue bird that lives at high altitudes in the tropical rainforest.

For centuries, the Monteverde region was an extremely wild and remote area with only a few isolated family farms. Then, in 1951, 44 settlers arrived, determined to live in harmony with nature. They were a group of 11 **Quaker** families who fled the United States during the early 1950s to escape imprisonment in their native Alabama for refusing military service. These pacifists

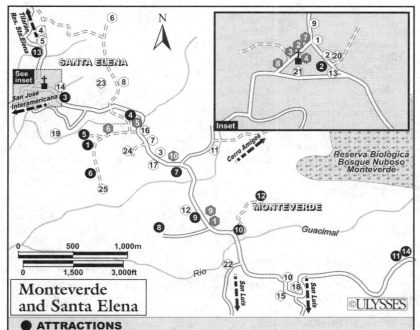

Monteverde and Santa Elena

0   500   1,000m

0   1,500   3,000ft

©ULYSSES

chose to live in Costa Rica because the country has no standing army and is politically stable. To secure their freedom and live out their convictions, they bought land in Monteverde, which, at that time, was accessible only by horse and buggy.

It is easy to understand why the residents refuse to pave their road: the village receives enough tourists on foot or horseback, by bicycle and car. If the road that connects them to

Quakers

Quakers are a Protestant sect founded by an English cobbler, George Fox (1624-1691), who believed he had been called by the Holy Spirit and began preaching in 1647. His followers called themselves the "Religious Society of Friends," but became known as Quakers with reference to Fox's expression to "quake before the word of God." Because the central facet of the Quaker faith is the presence of the Holy Spirit in the individual, they have no clergy or liturgy.

the Inter-American Highway were to be paved, even more tourists would come—by the busload—disturbing the tranquil way of life.

Today, what is called Monteverde consists of a small village, **Santa Elena**; Monteverde itself, a region near the reserve that still belongs mainly to the Quakers; as well as the area between the two, called Cerro Plano because the landscape is just slightly flatter than elsewhere! Don't expect to find an actual village outside that of Santa Elena. Instead, a main road and a few secondary roads with hotels, restaurants and other services alongside them go through the region. The main road terminates at the Santa Elena reserve at one end, and at the Monteverde reserve at the other.

The area between the regions of Arenal and Monteverde is simply magnificent. You'll travel through bucolic landscapes of lush countryside, tranquil pastures, fields clinging to the mountainsides, not to mention picturesque little villages. The road from Santa Elena to Tilarán is generally in good condition (see p 186) and will allow you to see everything. Note too, that while this route takes 8hrs by bus and 5hrs by car, it takes 3hrs on horseback. Several businesses at both ends

of the road offer this ride, which you certainly won't regret.

The private 80ha (198 acres) **Reserva Sendero Tranquilo** (*$20, including a 3.5hr guided tour; information at the El Sapo Dorado hotel, ☎645-5010*) lives up to the meaning of its name in Spanish (quiet trail), providing a peaceful part of the forest for visitors to explore. A mandatory guide leads each group of two to six people on silent, but enriching excursions.

Monteverde has tackled Canopy Tours' wave of popularity head on and there are local businesses offering a variety of activities that allow you to have a closer look at the tropical forest. Refer to the "Outdoor Activities" section for the most acrobatic of them. One of the easiest to do is **Sky Walk** (*$12; every day, 6am to 5pm; ☎/≈645-5238*). This is a system of elevated walkways and suspended bridges that rises above the treetops of the tropical rainforest. Open since March of 1997, the trail was designed for visitors to take quiet walks into the lush forest where every tree is covered with lianas, mosses and flowering epiphyte plants. Along the 2km (1.2mi) loop, there are five suspended bridges, which are approximately 1m (3.3ft) wide, 100m (328ft) long and 40m

(131ft) above the ground. To get there, go north on Santa Elena's main street to the Colegio Santa Elena and follow the signs from there.

As for **Aventuras Aéreas** (*$12; 7am to 6pm;* ☎*645-5960*), it features a really interesting chair-lift ride. The electricity-driven chairs take you to different heights in the tropical forest found, among other places, on the border of the Finca Ecológica and above the Monteverde country-side. Spectacular! The tour takes about 1hr and best of all, each individually controlled chair can be stopped by its passengers if they want to examine a multicoloured butterfly or a rare bird more closely. The cruising speed of 1.6km/hr (1mph) allows plenty of time to spot these gems!

On the outskirts of the village, near the Finca Valverde hotel, the **Serpentario** (*$3; every day 9am to 5pm;* ☎*645-5238*) exhibits Costa Rican snakes, but focusses on those found in the Monte-verde region. The aim is not to frighten, but rather to teach people how to recognize the most dangerous spe-cies, which include poisonous vipers like formidable Central American fer-de-lance (*Bothrops asper*). Now you'll know how to

react if you happen to encounter one of these dangerous reptiles in the wild!

A small garden on the Monteverde road should catch your eye. **Proyecto de Investigación Orquídeas de Monteverde** ★★ (*$5; 8am to 5pm;* ☎*645-5510*) is open to visitors who want to learn more about that fascinating flower, the orchid. The botanist in charge, a true enthusiast, has personally discovered six orchid species. This is a prolific family with many members that are indigenous to Costa Rica! In this Monteverde garden alone, more than 400 species grow year in and year out. The gar-den's beauty is en-hanced by the fact that different species are at their peak each month. Don't be surprised when you're given a magnifying glass at the entrance. Many of these flowers are very small, though no less lovely! Touring the different sections of the garden on paths takes about 1hr.

Orchid

The **Finca Ecológica** (*$6; every day 7am to 5pm;* ☎*645-5222*) is a private, 17ha (42 acres) ecologi-cal reserve that gives you the chance to ob-serve a large variety of birds (a list is provided) and butterflies. Many wild animals can also be seen, such as coatis, agoutis, sloths and ca-puchin monkeys. Be-cause the place is lo-cated at a lower alti-tude, it receives less rain than the tropical rainforest, and the veg-etation is consequently less dense. There are even a few small ba-nana trees and coffee plants. Four pedestrian paths cover the area of the reserve and lead to different scenic views, including a waterfall. There is a 10min path from the very elegant Monteverde Lodge (see p 216) to the farm.

The **Jardín de mariposas** ★★ (*$7 in-cluding guided tour; every day 9:30am to 4pm; pic-nic area, souvenir shop;* ☎*645-5512*) is the ideal place to see the unique and stunning butterflies of the tropical forest. The guides are very friendly and explain the complicated and in-triguing stages in the life of a butterfly. Inside the interpretation cen-tre is a large collection of butterflies and each is identified by its shape and colours. Some have distinc-tive markings re-ferred to as "eyes" on their wings to frighten predators. Others are camouflaged like leaves, so that their enemies will overlook them. In one of the showcases, you can actually see caterpillars weaving themselves into chrysalides and you might even be lucky enough to see a new butterfly emerge from its cocoon and take its first flight!

After the visit to the interpretation centre there is a tour of the aviary, which houses four distinct gardens. Each garden has climatic conditions and plant varieties similar to those found in the natural habitat of several species of butterflies. The gardens are home to hundreds of butterflies from the 40 or more local species. This is a great place to take photographs! One of the most spectacular butterflies is the "blue morpho." Measuring about 10cm (3.9in) in length, its wings are pure blue, bordered with brown and white speckles on one side, and with "eyes" on the other. Though the tour takes only 1hr, we recommend that you bring a lunch and stay half a day: you can stroll through the gardens again, picnic next to the interpretation centre, or relax in the sunshine and observe the many different birds that share the premises. You'll be amazed by the grace and beauty of the vividly coloured butterflies that create a captivating spectacle.

Bosque Eterno de los Niños *(every day 8am to 5pm; across from the service station,* ☎*645-5003,* ⇒*645-5104),* or the Children's Eternal Forest, is a brilliant conservation project that protects the environment by purchasing the forests around the Reserva Biológica Monteverde. The League for the Conservation of Monteverde was formed in 1986. Thanks to a donation from Swedish children, it began buying land around the reserve in 1987—and the forest has not stopped growing since! Today, it covers more than 18,500ha (45,713 acres). The organization's goal is to create a natural corridor so that the exceptional fauna and flora in the region of Monteverde can survive.

Since the project's beginning, children and adults from 44 countries have collected funds to safeguard a part of the tropical rainforest for future generations. Working in concert with local communities, the League for the Conservation of Monteverde is also involved in research and education. It has two education centres deep in the forest: Poco Sol and San Gerardo. These have facilities for housing, classrooms and laboratories, as well as networks of well-maintained hiking trails. Both centres are on the Atlantic side of

the Cordillero de Tilarán Divide. The line runs just east of Monteverde and Santa Elena.

Easier to access, **Bajo del Tigre** ★ *($5; every day 8am to 4:30pm; near the CASEM)* is also associated with the League for the Conservation of Monteverde. This network of short trails (3.3km or 2mi) goes through forest that is less dense than the Bosque Eterno, but just as teeming with plant and animal life. Part of the Pacific Divide of the Cordillera de Tilarán, it affords lovely views of the Gulf of Nicoya. A visit here starts at the nature interpretation centre with an explanation of what there is to see and do in the surroundings. Educational games for children introduce them to the ecology of the tropical forest. Among other things, the area is considered an superb place for ornithology. More than 200 bird species have been listed. Before setting out on the trails, which lead to the Río Máquina canyon, visitors are given an excellent booklet about the 22 interpretation points that explain the flora and fauna that you'll see along the way.

Several women in the region of Monteverde have united to form a local handicrafts cooperative called **CASEM** *(every day 8am to 5pm;* ☎*645-5190,* ⇒*645-5262).*

They create handmade items, including clothing, decorated with motifs of the region's flora and fauna. Profits from the sale of these handicrafts foster the artisan tradition in the Monteverde community.

Halfway between Santa Elena and the reserve is a cheese factory, **La Lechería** *(every day 7:30am to 4pm, except Sun until 12:30pm;* ☎*645-5136)*, founded by Quakers in 1953. Visitors can see the manufacturing process for many different kinds of cheese (edam, gouda, emmenthal, cheddar and so on), including the very famous and popular *monterico*. The factory's output, which started at 10kg (22lbs) per day in the 1950s, has grown to 1,000kg (2,205lbs) per day. The cheese is distributed to all parts of the country, and more than 100 people are employed by the factory.

There is a hummingbird gallery just at the entrance to the reserve. **Galería Colibrí** ★ *(every day 10am to 4:30pm,* ☎*645-5030)* displays the work of the famous English photographers Michael and Patricia Fogden, who used to live in the area. In addition to slides and photographs, the shop sells all sorts of art objects, articles of clothing and jewellery, mostly inspired by plant and animal themes. At

4:30pm there is a slide show presentation by a local biologist *($3)*. Feeders hung outside the gallery attract dozens of hummingbirds, representing the nine indigenous species. It's a unique experience to see these tiny birds darting around, buzzing like bees. This may be the only chance you'll ever have to take photographs of these charming little birds.

La Reserva del Bosque Nuboso de Colegio de Santa Elena

If the Monteverde Reserve is too large for you, visit the rainforest at the smaller **Reserva del Bosque Nuboso del Colegio de Santa Elena** ★★ *($7; every day 7am to 4pm;* ☎*645-5390,* ≈*645-5014)*. This 310ha (766 acres) reserve is located 6.5km (4mi) from the village of Santa Elena. At an altitude of 1,670m (5,479ft), the reserve receives a lot of precipitation, so dress accordingly (rain boots can be rented at the reserve).

Originally, this area was supposed to be turned into an experimental farm for research and educational purposes, but the plans didn't work out. Then, in 1989, with the support of Youth Challenge International, a Canadian non-profit organization, it was turned into a tropical

rainforest reserve. It's now administered by the college in Santa Elena, with profits (from entrance fees, boot rentals, guide services, souvenirs, transportation, etc.) going to preserve this precious territory and to improve the environmental education of the region's students. Moreover, many groups of students from several countries, as well as volunteers from Canada and the United States, come to help maintain the trails and the visitor reception centre.

To get to the reserve, go north on Santa Elena's main road to the Colegio Santa Elena, and follow the signs from there. The reserve is 6.5km (4mi) north of the village, which has an information bureau that provides transportation to the reserve *($1.70; departure every day at 7am)*. At the reserve, there are a reception and information centre, a snack bar, a souvenir shop and toilets. Documentation about the reserve is also available.

The reserve has four hiking trails that total 12km (7.5mi). Each trail makes a loop that takes between 45min and 4hrs to complete, and has some scenic lookouts *(miradores)* along the way. Among others, there is a view of the famous Arenal Volcano (1,633m or 5,358ft), one of the most active volcanoes in the world, though the views from the lookouts are often obstructed by clouds or fog. It's said that on a clear day you can see not only Lake Arenal and its volcano, but also the Tenorio (1,916m or 6,286ft), Miravalles (2,028m or 6,654ft) and Rincón de la Vieja (1,895m or 6,217ft) volcanoes in the northwest, and the Gulf of Nicoya to the south!

One of the trails, called **The Youth Challenge** (0.8km or 0.5mi), is very educational. There is a guide booklet that explains what there is to see at the 15 interpretation points along the path, which goes through primary and secondary forests, displaying a wealth of fauna and flora. Eighty percent of the Santa Elena reserve is primary forest. The other 20% is secondary forest, with smaller and shorter trees that let in more sunlight. It takes approximately 80 years for the younger trees of the secondary forest to mature and be classified as primary forest.

Though it's unlikely that you'll spot an animal, it's quite common to see tracks left by peccary, kinkajou, ocelot and puma. Birds are also numerous. Because this reserve is smaller than that of Monteverde, some ornithologists argue that this makes it quieter and thus better for ob-

servations. And, like at Monteverde, you might chance on one of the fabulous quetzals that live in the region.

Reserva Biológica Bosque Nuboso Monteverde

The **Reserva Biológica Bosque Nuboso Monteverde** ★★★ *($9; every day 7am to 4pm; reception centre, restaurant, souvenir shop, guides, explanatory material, rain boot rentals; ☎645-5122, ⌐645-5034, montever@rasca.co.cr)* is deservedly the main tourist attraction in the region for its outstanding natural features. The Monteverde reserve is actually a private ecological reserve, owned by the Centro Científico Tropical de San José. This nonprofit organization carries out scientific research and ecological education. Through the reserve, the organization manages to raise visitors' awareness about the need to preserve the national treasure that is the tropical rainforest which, in addition to protecting flora and fauna, is a source of water for many of the surrounding valleys.

The concept of preserving this tropical rainforest entered the minds of scientists George and Harriet Powell in 1972, when they visited the region. With the help of a local resident, Wilford

Guindon, they publicized the urgency of setting aside land to create a reserve to protect the rainforest. The Centro Científico Tropical de San José finally bought the land and created protected zones. The reserve began with 328ha (810 acres). Then, in 1975, they received another 554ha (1,369 acres) from the Quaker community. Today, the reserve covers over 10,500ha (25,945 acres) of the tropical rainforest and, along with the Bosque Eterno de los Niños (see p 200) around the reserve, and the other nearby reserves and protected forests, the region of Monteverde can be seen as a model for environmental protection.

The Continental Divide runs through the park: rivers to the west of it flow toward the Pacific Ocean, while those to the east empty into the Caribbean. The Continental Divide is about 2km (1.2mi) east of the reception and information centre. Because of this line, there is great geographical and climatic diversity in different parts of the park, which can be experienced without having to travel long distances. While hiking along the trails in the reserve, be prepared for changeable weather conditions (rain, sun, wind, more rain, extreme humidity and so on). Bring a change of clothing, rain boots, a raincoat, or other rain gear, as well as a camera and insecticide—and don't forget your binoculars! The reserve is in the mountains (the reception centre is at an elevation of 1,530m or 5,020ft), so mornings can be quite cool and humid. The average temperature is around 17°C (63°F), and the annual precipitation exceeds 3m (9.8ft).

The landscapes change according to altitude. The lowest section, at 600m (1,969ft), is near the Río Peñas Blancas. The highest point is at the summit of Cerro Tres Amigos (1,842m or 6,043ft), in the northwest part of the reserve. Between these two extremes, the vegetation consists of rich forests with sometimes enormous trees covered in mosses, lianas and thousands of epiphytes that prevent the sun from reaching the ground. Among the approximately 2,500 plant species, there are no fewer than 420 kinds of orchids. The reserve is divided into six different horticultural zones, and the biodiversity of each is so complex that new scientific discoveries are constantly being made.

The reserve is also home to 100 mammal species, including the jaguar, the ocelot and Baird's tapir. Though they're hard to spot, they sometimes leave their paw marks in the ground. On the other hand, mischievous howling and capuchin monkeys make themselves visible, or at least heard! And let's not forget amphibians and reptiles. Finally, over 400 bird species make the reserve a birdwatcher's paradise!

The Trails

The Monteverde reserve has seven hiking trails with a total length of 12.4km (7.7mi, not including the trails where access is limited). Only 120 visitors are allowed on the trails at one time. It's best to reserve your admission ticket a night in advance (most hotels can do this and hire a guide for you) so you can arrive early the next morning and get in a few hours of birdwatching. You can also spend the night in one of the three shelters off the trails, or in the shelter right at the entrance to the reserve (priority is given to groups and researchers). It is highly recommended to take the reserve's guided nature tour to learn more about the flora and fauna here. The **guided tour** *(day or evening at 7:30pm, reservations recommended, $15/pers., plus entrance fee)* lasts about 3hrs. It begins at the Galería Colibrí (Hummingbird Gallery) with a short (10min) slide presentation. It continues along a series of very short trails on which the guide explains the diversity of the plant and animal life. After the tour, you can either attend another longer slide presentation (30min) at the Galería Colibrí, or roam freely on designated trails through the reserve.

The very well-signed and maintained hiking trails in the reserve make it easy to explore the tropical rainforest (a map of the trails is included in the entrance fee). The most popular trails form a triangle (El Triangulo) to the east. The **Río** trail leads to Río Cuecha and its little waterfalls. The **Chomogo** trail climbs to an altitude of 1,680m (5,512ft) and accesses the scenic lookout on the **Roble** trail. Finally, the nature interpretation trail, **Bosque Nuboso** (booklet available at the reception centre) consists of 28 numbered interpretation points that explain the reserve's flora and fauna. This trail ends at the scenic lookout, **La Ventana**, where the view extends for miles in all directions.

It's a 2 to 6hr hike to the **three shelters** *($3.50/pers./night, by reservation only)* that can accommodate up to ten hikers each and are equipped with a stove, cooking utensils, drinking water and a shower, but not electricity.

The North

Refugio Nacional de Vida Silvestre Caño Negro

Refugio Nacional de Vida Silvestre Caño Negro ★ *($6; every day 8am to 4pm;* ☎*460-1412,* ⇨*460-0644)* is in the extreme north of the country, near Nicaragua. The 9,969ha (24,633 acres) reserve is popular mostly for its 800ha (1,977 acres) lake. Actually, the size of the lake varies: during the rainy season it expands and sometime swells the Río Frío, whereas during the dry season, between January and April, it gradually shrinks and sometimes even disappears!

Ornithologists, biologists and other naturalists are the most frequent visitors to this reserve, but more and more organized groups are coming to spend the day observing the exceptionally large number of animals in the reserve.

Most visitors enjoy exploring the reserve by boat or canoe along the Río Frío, starting from Los Chiles. During the excursion, caimans, turtles, iguanas, monkeys and other animals can be spotted. Among the abundant avian species you might see are American anhingas *(Anhinga anhinga)*, roseate spoonbills *(Ajaia ajaja)*, white ibises *(Eudocimus albus)*, American jacanas *(Jacana spinosa)*, Amer-ican wood storks *(Mycteria Americana)*, whistling ducks *(Dendrocygna autunmalis)* and American jabirus *(Jabiru mycteria)*. The reserve is also home to the largest colony of olive cormorants *(Phalacrocorax olivaceus)* in Costa Rica, and the only colony of Nicaraguan grackles *(Quiscalus Nicaraguensis)*.

Apart from boat rides and observing the fauna, there is little to do in the way of outdoor activities at the reserve. When the lake dries up during the first half of the year, it can be explored on foot. Camping is permitted. The small park rangers' house is also the reception and information centre. We strongly recommend visiting the reserve through a tourist agency (in San José or in La Fortuna), or with a guide from Los Chiles.

Outdoor Activities

Hiking

Parque Nacional Arenal (see p 195) has short, but extremely interesting trails that lead to excellent viewpoints of the volcano and lava flows.

Right next to the park, **Arenal Observatory Lodge** (see p 195) also has a network of hiking trails and an incredible view of the volcano.

The region of **Monteverde** has everything an experienced hiker could desire. The flora and fauna of the tropical rainforest attract people from all over the world. The trails in the Santa Elena reserve, the Finca Ecológica, the Children's Eternal Forest and the Sendero Tranquilo reserve are also accessible to visitors.

Water Sports

Tilawa Windsurf Spots & Boat Rental and **Tico Winds Windsurf Spot & Equipment Rental**, both at the western end of Lake Arenal, provide services and equipment for various water sports.

Bird-Watching

The region of **Monteverde** has over 400 bird species, including the rare quetzal (see p 67).

Ornithologists consider the **Refugio Nacional de Vida Silvestre Caño Negro** (see p 204) one of the best-kept secrets of

Costa Rica. Avian fauna here is abundant and diverse. There are several species of water birds.

Rafting

Aguas Bravas
☎*229-4837 in La Fortuna*
☎*292-2072 in San José*
Aguas Bravas offers white-water rafting on Río Sarapiquí (class III) or on the Haut Sarapiquí (class IV and V) in the area of Puerto Viejo, as well as on Río Peñas Blancas (class II and IV) near the Arenal Volcano.

Horseback Riding

In the region of Arenal and Monteverde you can go horseback riding with or without a guide. Renting a horse costs between $8 and $12/hr. Just ask at the hotel. In Monteverde, **Meg's Stables** (☎*645-5560*) and **Caballeriza El Palomino** (☎*645-5479*) give guided horseback rides that are very popular.

Canopy Tours

Canopy Tour
☎*645-5243 or 257-5149*
On the Canopy Tour you can pretend you're

Tarzan swinging from treetop to treetop in the forest, only you will be wearing a harness attached to a pulley system. The activity consists of hoisting yourself onto a platform at the top of an enormous tree, then sliding along cables from one treetop to another. This is a unique way to observe the dense vegetation from 30m (98ft) up in the air! The tour lasts about 2.5hrs, including the short walk through the forest to the starting point. The organizers are busy constructing a longer course that should be even more thrilling.

At the most recently opened tour, **Monteverde Canopy Tour** (*$35*; ☎*645-5929*), you'll really get an eyeful! Survey the tropical forest in close proximity to the Reserva Santa Elena along 14 platforms perched at dizzying heights and connected by cables up to several metres in length! The facilities, among the largest in the country, are safe and the personnel is skilful and competent, which is somewhat reassuring! In any case, even those afraid of heights will soon forget their troubles as they become absorbed by the beauty of the surroundings.

You can also try this activity at the **Original Canopy Tour** (*$45*; ☎*645-5243*) or at **Sky Trek** (*$12*; ☎*645-5238*),

which is associated with Sky Walk (see p 198). Both offer the same sort of circuit, but over shorter distances.

Accommodations

The Puerto Viejo de Sarapiquí Region

Puerto Viejo de Sarapiquí

Cabinas Monteverde
$
pb, ⊗
☎*766-7236*
Cabinas Monteverde offers the basic comforts to travellers on a tight budget and is located near a popular restaurant.

Mi Lindo Sarapiquí
$$
hw, pb, ⊗, ℜ
on the south side of the soccer field
☎*766-6281 or 766-6074*
Mi Lindo Sarapiquí is another reasonably-priced hotel in Sarapiquí. The rooms are bright and clean, but simply decorated. It also has a good little restaurant (see p 216).

El Bambu
$$$$ bkfst incl.
pb, hw, ⊗, *tv*
on the west side of the soccer field
☎*766-6005*
⇌*766-6132*
El Bambu is the best hotel in the city of Puerto Viejo de

Sarapiquí as far as appearance and layout are concerned. Free for children under 12 if they stay in their parents' room.

West of Puerto Viejo de Sarapiquí

Islas del Río
$$$$ bkfst incl.
hw, sb/pb, ⊗, ℜ
6km (3.7mi) west of Puerto Viejo, Bajos del Chilamate
☎766-6898
Islas del Río has 30 very comfortable rooms and offers discounts for Youth Hostelling International members. They offer white-water rafting on the river, and there are hiking and horseback riding trails in the vicinity. Some rooms have bathtubs.

La Quinta de Sarapiquí
$$$$
pb, hw, ⊗, ℜ
5km (3.1mi) north of La Virgen on the main road between Puerto Viejo and La Virgen, then 1km (0.6mi) west
☎761-1052
www.laquintasarapiqui.com
La Quinta de Sarapiquí is a country house with about 10 rooms, set in a beautiful garden on the banks of the Río Sardinal. This is a fun place to stay because of the many activities suggested by its friendly hosts, such as swimming in the river, mountain biking, bird-watching, horseback riding and sailing.

La Selva Verde
$$$$$
in Chilamate, a few kilometres west of Puerto Viejo
☎766-6800
⇌766-6011
La Selva Verde is a rustic hotel, set in its own 200ha (494 acres) reserve. Its lovely verandas, little library, restaurant, well-tended flowerbeds and trails in the reserve add to its charm. Whether you explore the trails alone or with a guide, you'll come across birds, butterflies, mammals, reptiles and all their friends. There are also outings on the Río Sarapiquí. Free for children under 12 if they stay in their parents' room.

South of Sarapiquí

Ecolodge Sarapiquí
$$$/pers. fb
sb, ⊗
just west of La Selva
☎766-6122 or 253-2533
⇌253-8645
Ecolodge Sarapiquí is a family-run affair on an 80ha (1,977 acres) dairy farm. The rooms are on the second floor of the main building and the bathrooms are on the ground floor. The place is as clean as can be and the home-cooked meals are good. You can go swimming in the Río Puerto Viejo, which runs through the property.

El Plastico
$$$/pers. fb
hw, sb
12km (7.5mi) from Horqueta Rara Avis
El Plastico in the Rara Avis ecological reserve was once a jungle penal colony. It's rustic (shared rooms and showers) but comfortable. Meals are vegetarian. Discounts for students and researchers.

Waterfall Lodge
$$$$/pers. fb
guided tours and transportation from Horquetas
hw, pb
Waterfall Lodge 3km (1.9mi) from El Plastico, Rara Avis is next to a pretty waterfall, hence the name. Slightly less rustic than El Plastico, with a private bathroom and a balcony in each room, but no electricity.

North of Sarapiquí

El Gavilán Lodge
$$$$ bkfst incl.
hw, sb/pb, ⊛
4km (2.5mi) northeast of Puerto Viejo
☎234-9507
⇌253-6556
El Gavilán Lodge is tucked away in a 100ha (247 acres) tropical rainforest reserve. It has fairly spacious rooms and *cabinas* with large, private bathrooms (a few of the rooms have shared baths). They organize horseback riding and excursions in the reserve and the surrounding area. You can bird-watch while enjoying meals made with freshly picked fruits from the jungle.

Oro Verde Station
$$$$ bkfst incl.
sb/pb
40km (25mi) north of Puerto
Viejo
☎/≈*233-7479*
Much farther north, Oro
Verde Station is a
2,500ha (6,177 acres)
reserve located on the
Río Sarapiquí, not far
from the Nicaraguan
border. It offers rustic
cabinas with shared or
private baths, but with-
out hot water. There is
also a dormitory *($)* for
travellers on tight bud-
gets. Few of the staff in
this remote place speak
English, but if you un-
derstand Spanish they
can tell you a lot about
the surrounding envi-
ronment.

La Laguna del Lagarto Lodge
$$$$
pb/sb, hw, ⊗, ℜ
Apartado Postal 995-1007
Centro Colon, San José
☎*289-8163*
☎/≈*289-5295*
lagarto@racsa.co.cr
Nestled in northern-
most Costa Rica, just a
stone's throw away
from the Nicaraguan
border, in a region as
unspoiled as can be
where forests and rivers
serve as a backdrop for
an incredible wealth of
wildlife and plants, La
Laguna del Lagarto
Lodge is a paradise for
novice ecologists. The
owner, of German ori-
gin, hand-built the
large building in which
he lodges, feeds and
lavishes attention on
his visitors. For nearly
10 years he has been
busy creating a conviv-
ial atmosphere that

welcomes nature lov-
ers. His 500ha (1,236
acres) domain is criss-
crossed with marked
trails along which are
signs identifying the
trees. What's more,
over 350 bird species,
including the great
green macaw, have
been listed here. There
are myriad suggested
activities for enjoying
all this! When you
make you reservation,
ask which roads you
should take to get here.

La Selva

La Selva
$$$$$ fb
sb
3km (1.9mi) south of Puerto
Viejo de Sarapiquí
☎*740-1515*
≈*740-1414*
via OTS
☎*240-6696*
≈*240-6783*
You can stay at the
ecological reserve, La
Selva, by making reser-
vations in advance. The
bedrooms are in bun-
galows, with four beds
per room. Everything is
very clean. Meals are
served in the dining
hall where researchers
and students also eat.

Ciudad Quesada and Surroundings

Hotel del Valle
$
pb, hw
200m (656ft) north and 50m
(164ft) west of the central park,
Calle 3 Avenida 0, Ciudad
Quesada
☎*460-0718*
Hotel del Valle is a
typical small-city hotel,

ideal for people on a
tight budget who want
to spend the night in
Cuidad Quesada.

La Central
$$
hw, pb, tv
on the west side of the central
park, Cuidad Quesada
☎*460-0766 or 460-0301*
≈*460-0391*
La Central may be one
of the best places to
stay in town. With 48
clean rooms, it has the
feel of a large hotel. It
also houses a casino.

DonGoyo
$$
pb, ℜ, hw
100m (328ft) south of the
central park
Ciudad Quesada
☎*460-1780*
DonGoyo is newer
than La Central, and
has a more modern
design. The 13 rooms
are clean, and there is a
small restaurant on the
main floor.

La Garza
$$$
pb, hw, ⊗, ≈
Platanar, between Florencia and
La Muelle, northwest of Ciudad
Quesada
☎*475-5222*
≈*475-5051*
If you stay here, the
herons that nest around
La Garza can be seen
from your hotel win-
dow in the evenings.
The hotel was named
after them: *garza* is
Spanish for "heron."
The hotel complex is
near a ranch, a dairy
farm and a 300ha (741
acres) forest where
guests can participate
in many activities. The
wooden decor of the

The North

rooms is charming. The majestic Arenal Volcano is part of the landscape. Laundry service available.

Tilajari Resort
$$$$
hw, pb, △*,* ≡*,* ☎*,* ≈*,* ℜ
Muelle de San Carlos, 22km (13.2mi) north of Ciudad Quesada
☎*469-9091*
469-9095
www.tilajari.com
Tilajari Resort is a large hotel in the heart of the San Carlos Valley, 40min from the Arenal Volcano. The 12ha (30 acres) property nurtures more than 150 species of tropical plants and trees that grow around the Río San Carlos. Hiking, horseback riding and butterfly "hunting" are some of the activities offered. The housekeeping meets high standards. The large hotel complex includes a pool, a whirlpool, a sauna; tennis, racquetball and basketball courts; games and conference rooms; a bar, a nightclub and a souvenir shop.

Meliá El Tucano
$$$$
hw, pb, ≈*,* ⊛*,* △*,* ℜ
8km (5mi) northeast of San Carlos on the road to Aguas Zarcas
☎*460-6000*
460-1692
meliatuc@racsa.co.cr
Meliá El Tucano is really a spa in the middle of a 182ha (450 acres) forest. It offers physiotherapy and therapeutic baths with water from the area's hot springs.

This modern and attractively decorated hotel complex includes tennis courts and even minigolf. An Italian restaurant and a vegetarian restaurant complete the facilities.

The Arenal Region

La Fortuna and Surroundings

La Fortuna hotel establishments often offer horseback-riding excursions to the volcano and elsewhere. There are also so many little *cabinas* for rent that you should have no problem finding one, even during high season. However, not all of them have swimming pools, a real disadvantage given how hot it can get in this part of the country.

Cabinas Sissy
$
hw, pb
100m (328ft) south and 100m (328ft) west of the church, La Fortuna
☎*479-9256*
The Cabinas Sissy is a good choice for anyone on a limited budget.

Hotel La Fortuna
$ bkfst incl.
hw, pb, ⊛*,* ℜ
☎*479-9197*
Right in the city of La Fortuna, on the road along the Río Burío, is Hotel La Fortuna, a well-maintained, basic establishment whose outgoing owner organizes all kinds of excursions in the area. The restaurant serves simple

tica and North American dishes in a friendly and sedate atmosphere.

Cabinas Mayol
$$
pb, ⊗*,* ≈
☎*479-9110*
The Cabinas Mayol have eight sparsely furnished rooms (true of most of the cabinas in the area).

Cabinas Carmela
$$
hw, pb
one street past the La Central hotel, near Avenida 0 and Calle 0, next to the church, La Fortuna
☎*479-9010*
Cabinas Carmela offer the same type of accommodations as the other *cabinas* in the region (small bedrooms in small detached units on the property).

Burio Inn
$$
hw, pb, ⊗
on Principale, between the El Jardin restaurant and the soccer field, La Fortuna
☎*/479-9076*
Burio Inn offers attractively decorated rooms in the owners' home. The place is often full, even in the low season.

Cabinas Guacamaya
$$$
hw, pb, ≡*,* ℝ
at the eastern edge of La Fortuna
☎*/479-9393*
Cabinas Guacamaya are two clean, modern *cabinas* set out in the owners' family garden. The little shaded porches are perfect for relaxing and admiring the volcano in hot

weather. The friendly owner has gone even further to beat the heat: he personally installed air-conditioning and refrigerators in the *cabinas.*

Cabinas Villa Fortuna
$$$
≈, *pb, hw,* ℝ, ≡
500m (1,640ft) east of the Colegio Agropecuario, La Fortuna
☎479-9139
Cabinas Villa Fortuna is immaculate. The layout of the rooms (in the small motel) or apartments makes it all the more pleasant to stay here, which is not the case for all the cabinas in the area. The owners are hospitable, even to animals—they lovingly care for all the injured birds in the neighbourhood.

San Bosco
$$$
hw, pb, ≡
Calle 2, Avenida 1, 200m (656ft) north of the service station, La Fortuna
☎479-9050
≈479-9109
San Bosco is a 29-room hotel with two *casitas* that are clean and comfortable, but simply decorated. There is even an observation tower. This is probably the one place among the town's establishments that deserves to call itself a hotel.

Las Cabañitas
$$$$
hw, ⊗, *pb,* ≈, ℜ
☎479-9400 or 479-9343
≈479-9408
gasguis@racsa.co.cr
Between La Fortuna and El Tanque, Las Cabañitas offers very stylish wooden *cabinas* with pretty little verandas. There is a swimming pool on the fair-sized grounds.

🦎 Arenal Country Inn
$$$$ bkfst incl.
pb, hw, ≡, ≈, ◙
☎479-9670 or 479-9669
≈479-9433
www.costaricainn.com
Located a short distance away from the village of La Fortuna (1km or 0.6mi before it from the direction of San Ramón), but still at the foot of the ever-present volcano, the property of the Arenal Country Inn exudes country peacefulness. This is exactly the effect the friendly owners had in mind. The reception area and breakfast (delicious!) tables are set up in a corral; horses graze in the nearby meadows and the landscaping has been done with great care. Thus, the 20 small two-room bungalows are scattered around the property. Each room is set up with two beds and a small round table and is bright with several tulle-curtained windows. There is even a skylight in the ceiling! Newly built, these facilities are modern and practical. Each has a wooden bench in front, from which you can

admire the volcano when it is revealed through the clouds. A restaurant is planned for the near future; meanwhile, those in the village are only 5min away by car.

Around the Arenal Volcano

La Catarata Lodge
$$$ bkfst incl.
hw, pb, ℜ
1.5km (0.9mi) south of the main road to the volcano from La Fortuna
☎479-9522
The ecotourism inn La Catarata Lodge has a butterfly garden, a little restaurant and very decent rooms. The main reason for staying here is to support the Associación Para el Ambiente y el Desarollo Sustenable, a local association that promotes sustainable development.

Cabinas Rossi
$$$ bkfst incl.
hw, pb, ⊗, ℝ
1km (0.6mi) outside La Fortuna towards the volcano, next to the La Vaca Muca restaurant
☎479-9023
≈479-9414
Cabinas Rossi are a cut above the rest.

Arenal Observatory Lodge
$$$$
hw, pb, ℜ
Lake Arenal
☎257-9489
≈257-4220
arenalob@racsa.co.cr
There is nothing fancy about the accommodations at the Arenal Observatory Lodge, but it's the best place to observe the volcano.

The North

There are three bunk beds to a room, and meals are served in a communal dining hall. This establishment functions as a research centre for seismologists from the Smithsonian Institute and the Universidad Nacional de Costa Rica. There are organized visits to nearby points of interest.

Jungla y Senderos Los Lagos
$$$$$
pb, ≈, ℜ
between La Fortuna and the Tabacón Resort
☎*479-8000 or 479-9126*
⇌*479-8009*
Very close to the volcano, Jungla y Senderos Los Lagos has very comfortable rooms and little *cabinas* in a complex that includes swimming pools with water slides, a lake for swimming and another for fishing. The hiking trails lead to the volcano's restricted zone, where you can touch hardened lava from the 1968 eruption. On the premises you will also find a camping area, a restaurant, tennis courts and hot springs.

Hotel Arenal Paraíso
$$$$
ctv, ℜ, ≈, hw, pb, ⊗, ℝ
7km (4.3mi) west of La Fortuna, very close to the Tabacon Resort
☎*460-5333*
⇌*460-5343*
www.arenaparaiso.decostarica.co.cr
Hotel Arenal Paraiso rents clean, simply decorated little *cabinas* that have private closed-in verandas with picture windows from which you can admire the volcano up close. There are hiking trails through the 60ha (148 acres) property.

Arenal Lodge
$$$$
hw, sb, ℜ, ⊗
2.5km (1.6mi) from the Lake Arenal dike, between La Fortuna and Nuevo Arenal
☎*228-3189 or 383-3957*
⇌*289-6798*
arenal@racsa.co.cr
The Arenal Lodge has a "woodsy" decor and so do its rooms in the main building and its little cottages. The library doubles as a billiards room, so you won't be bored! The view of the lake and of the volcano is wonderful. Guided fishing trips on the lake are organized.

La Pradera
$$$$
pb, hw, ⊗/≡, ⊗, ℜ
on the road between La Fortuna and the Arenal Volcano
☎*/⇌479-9167*
The hotel La Pradera offers modern, comfortable and very clean rooms in a motel-style building.

Montaña de Fuego
$$$$$ bkfst incl.
pb, hw, ⊗
8km (5mi) west of La Fortuna towards the Arenal Volcano
☎*460-1220 or 460-6760*
⇌*460-1455*
monfuego@racsa.co.cr
Montaña de Fuego has little wooden cottages with adorable solariums that look out to the volcano. The tropical landscaping is already pretty and is sure to improve as it fills out.

Around Lake Arenal

Los Héroes
$$$$ bkfst incl.
pb, hw, ≈, ℜ, ⊗
☎*/⇌441-4193*
Some 30km (18.6mi) from La Fortuna, Los Héroes is a Swiss chalet-style hotel on a little hill. The hotel's common areas are decorated with Swiss memorabilia, and the restaurant menu includes some Swiss dishes (see p 218). This is a fairly comfortable place to stay, with simple, sedate rooms.

Villa Decary
$$$$ bkfst incl.
pb, hw, K
2km (1.2mi) east of Nuevo Arenal, on Lake Arenal
☎*383-3012*
⇌*694-4330*
Villa Decary is outstanding. The clean rooms offer the utmost in comfort and are beautifully decorated with wooden furnishings. They also have lovely little verandas with a view of the lake. The property also includes a separate cottage with kitchenette and a large porch. Tranquillity prevails here. The owners are eminently charming and their breakfasts are divine. Don't hesitate to ask them anything about the region. Credit cards are not accepted.

Tabacón Lodge
$$$$$ bkfst incl.
pb, ≈, ℜ, ≡, hw, ◐ *ctv*
Apartado Postal 181-1007
Centro Colón, San José
☎**256-1500**
⇄**221-3075**
www.tabacon.com
For ages, hotels have been built near hot springs. This tradition lives on in Costa Rica! Tabacón Resort now has a luxury hotel that is still in the process of expansion. For the 2001 season, there are plans to open two new buildings, one of which will have bridal suites. For now, the hotel has three buildings that overlook the springs. All have identical rooms that meet North-American standards. That the decor of the rooms lacks warmth goes without saying, but a little balcony with French windows and a view of the volcano compensates for this. Especially since, with unlimited access to the baths (even on arrival and departure days), you probably won't be spending much time in your room!

What's more, the health spa offers every imaginable beauty, relaxation and health amenity. If you don't feel like going down the hill to the "resort," there are hot springs, a restaurant, a swimming pool with a literally "wet" bar and a whirlpool near the buildings.

Nuevo Arenal

Cabinas Rodríguez
$
sh/pb, hw
across from the soccer field
☎**694-4237**
Cabinas Rodríguez has inexpensive rooms without much furnishing, besides the bed. Breakfast isn't available here, but the owner is very friendly.

Aurora Inn B&B
$$$ bkfst incl.
hw, ⊗
☎**694-4245**
⇄**694-4262**
Aurora Inn B&B in downtown Nuevo Arenal is more like a hotel in terms of cleanliness and comfort. There is no restaurant, but there is a bar open at night, with a view of the lake.

Joya Sureña
$$$
hw, pb, ℜ, △, ☉, ≈
☎**694-4057**
⇄**694-4059**
joysur@racsa.co.cr
Joya Sureña is a small hotel complex on a coffee plantation with a splendid view of Lake Arenal. The rooms are soberly arranged. The main building is more Canadian in design, with sloping roofs and dormer windows (relatively rare in Costa Rica).

Between Nuevo Arenal and Tilarán

Rala de Arenal
$$
hw, pb, ℜ
close to the main road between Nuevo Arenal and Tilarán, the road that goes to Lago Coter Eco-Lodge and Telarán
Rala de Arenal is a simple little hotel recommended for its small but clean rooms. The rooms are on the first floor; on the second is a restaurant with little tables and a cozy, quiet bar. The building is set back from the road in the lush tropical vegetation that acts as a noise buffer. There are a small river and a fountain. The access road is in pretty good condition.

Chalet Nicholas
$$$-$$$$ bkfst incl.
pb, hw
2km (1.2mi) west of Nuevo Arenal
☎**694-4041**
nicholas@racsa.co.cr
Located on a hill, Chalet Nicholas is a very attractive bed and breakfast where guests are encouraged to feel at home. The owners are friendly, with a strong interest in ecology (organic gardening, reforestation and so on), which has won them several awards. They'll be more than happy to tell you what there is to see and do in the area. You will be greeted by the "babies" of the house, three enormous Great Danes! Note that credit cards are not accepted. Non-smokers only.

The North

Villas Alpino
$$$
hw, pb, K
12km (7.5mi) west of Nuevo
Arenal going towards Tilarán
☎284-3841
Villas Alpino consist of
large *cabinas* with lots
of rustic charm. They
have bar-kitchenettes
and large balconies
with a view of the lake
and the volcano in the
distance. Even the little
road to the hotel is in
good condition (which
is unusual for this
area).

Mystica Resort
$$$ bkfst incl.
pb, hw, ℜ
Apartado Postal 29-5710
Tilaran
Guanacaste
☎382-1499
≈695-5387
Don't be fooled by the
use of the term "resort."
This is actually a small
property with no more
than six rooms in a
row, motel-style. It's
nonetheless a great
place to stay. The
rooms are simple but
tastefully decorated by
the artist-owner. Good-
sized, they contain sev-
eral beds and feature
colourful walls and
original paintings.
There's a front terrace
where you can enjoy
the view… and what a
view it is! Well-tended
gardens in full bloom
descend sharply to-
wards the turquoise
waters of the lake—you
could spend hours with
your eyes glued to the
scene! You can also
enjoy the excellent
food served in the res-
taurant (see p 219).

To get here, follow the
signs that begin a few
kilometres before
Tilarán. It is located off
the main road.

Cabinas Vista Lago Inn
$$$
pb, hw
17km (10.6mi) from Tilarán,
towards Nuevo Arenal, near the
municipality of Guadalajara
☎661-1363
Cabinas Vista Lago Inn
has a few clean *cabinas*
near the lake.

Xiloe Lodge
$$$
pb, hw
☎259-9806
≈259-9882
A little bit past the popular windsurfing spot,
on the western side of
Lake Arenal, Xiloe
Lodge has comfortable
little *cabinas* and is
sheltered from the
noise of the road by
some large trees. The
management suggests
places for going out, as
well as horseback rid-
ing and boat rides.

Lago Coter Eco-Lodge
$$$$
hw, pb, ℜ
near Lake Coter, northwest of
Nuevo Arenal
☎257-5075
≈257-7065
Lago Coter Eco-Lodge
is a real lodge for na-
ture lovers with an
attractive rustic decor
that's very inviting,
especially after making
the arduous journey up
the road to get here!
You can participate in
the many outdoor activ-
ities (hiking, horseback
riding, mountain bik-
ing, bird-watching,
water sports, excur-

sions to different points
of interest in the area,
and so on), or just stay
indoors and just relax
in front of the fireplace
in the living room of
the main building, play
billiards, or watch tele-
vision or videos in the
game room. Some of
the rooms have balco-
nies. The lodge has
private access to 260ha
(642 acres) on Lake
Coter and to the private
biological reserve near
the lake.

Rock River Lodge
$$$$
pb, hw, ℜ
between Nuevo Arenal and
Tilarán, on Lake Arenal, near
the town of Guadalajara
☎695-5644
Rock River Lodge is
owned by a dedicated
sports lover. It reflects
the great outdoors, with
its wooden construction
and all the outdoor
activities it offers. The
rooms are quaint and
the cottages are charm-
ingly rustic. The bar
and restaurant (see
p 219) are also very
attractive. The view of
Lake Arenal is breath-
taking! Windsurf boards
and mountain bikes
can be rented here.

Tilawa
$$$$
hw, pb, ≈, ℜ
between Nuevo Arenal and
Tilarán, at the eastern end of
Lake Arenal
☎695-5050
Tilawa is an extraordi-
nary little hotel com-
plex, thanks to the
owner's wife who dec-
orated it like the palace
of Cnossos, on the is-

land of Crete. The rooms are modern and comfortable and have excellent views of this very windy section of Lake Arenal. There is a tennis court and guided horseback and sailboat rides are offered. Mountain bikes can also be rented. The wind makes the evenings quite chilly, and the fireplace in the hotel's living room provides welcome warmth.

The Monteverde Region

The village of **Santa Elena** is full of inexpensive little inns and *pensións*. Some of the roads leading to the hotels can be in bad condition due to the heavy rains. Because the region of Monteverde is one of the most popular tourist destinations in the country, it's best to make reservations in advance, particularly during the high season, from mid-December to April.

In Santa Elena, the Albergue Santa Elena (see below) offers places for **camping** (*$3/pers.; ☎645-5051*).

Hospedaje El Banco
$
sb, hw
Located behind the Banco Nacional de Santa Elena, Hospedaje El Banco rents single rooms, ideal if you're on a limited budget.

Cabinas Marín
$
sb, hw
Cabinas Marín is located some 300m (984ft) north of Santa Elena. The rooms are small, but decent enough for the price.

Pension Colibrí
$
sb, hw
Pension Colibrí is somewhat far from the village. It has reasonably priced rooms and organizes horseback rides.

Albergue Santa Elena
$
pb/sb, hw, ℜ
☎645-5051
⇆645-5147
In the heart of Santa Elena, Albergue Santa Elena offers small reasonably priced rooms in a youth-hostel atmosphere. Students receive a discount. The restaurant serves varied but tasty cuisine: the menu includes everything from traditional cooking to vegetarian dishes.

Hotel El Tucán
$-$$
sb/pb, hw, ℜ
☎645-5017
⇆645-5462
Hotel El Tucán is run by Señora Rosa Jiménez Venegas and her family. It is located 100m (328ft) east of the Banco Nacional, in Santa Elena, and offers basic, clean rooms. The restaurant serves delicious home-style Costa Rican cooking that is sure to please tourists on tight budgets.

Pensión El Sueño
$-$$
sb/pb, hw
☎645-3656 or 645-5021
Pensión El Sueño offers very simple and inexpensive rooms in a family atmosphere.

Pensión La Flor de Monteverde
$-$$
sb/pb, hw, ℜ
☎/⇆645-5236
At the northern end of Santa Elena, near the Reserva Bosque Nuboso Santa Elena, Pensión La Flor de Monteverde provides immaculate rooms in a peaceful, family environment. The owner, Eduardo Venegas, is also an administrator at the *Reserva*. They offer transportation to the reserve and different guided activities.

Albergue Marbella
$$
pb, hw
☎645-5153
⇆645-5159
Near the bank, Albergue Marbella has large, clean rooms and a relaxed atmosphere.

Cabinas Gulf View B&B
$$$ bkfst incl.
pb, hw
☎645-5263
Cabinas Gulf View B&B also rents simple rooms at a reasonable price. From here, you can see all the way to the Gulf of Nicoya.

El Gran Mirador Lodge
$$$
sb/pb, hw, ℜ
☎/⇆645-5087
El Gran Mirador Lodge is over 8km (5mi) from

The North

Santa Elena, in San Gerardo. Guests can rent *cabinas* with private bath, or stay in a dorm with shared bath. This establishment is peaceful and isolated, and has a superb view of the region with the imposing Arenal Volcano in the background.

Sunset Hotel
$$$ bkfst incl.
pb, hw, ℜ
☎*645-5048*
About 1km (0.6mi) from Santa Elena, Sunset Hotel has attractive and very clean rooms. You can also see the Gulf of Nicoya from here. The likable owner, of German origin, has lived in the region for ages and will tell you what there is to see.

Cloud Forest Lodge
$$$-$$$$
pb, hw, ℜ
☎*645-5058*
≈*645-5168*
Cloud Forest Lodge is located northeast of Santa Elena, in a lush tropical forest. The wooden *cabinas* are comfortable and spacious. You can hike through the forest and even explore it from the canopy (see p 205). There is an attractive view of the Gulf of Nicoya from the terrace in the garden and from the bar-restaurant.

Santa Elena to the Reserva Biológica Bosque Nuboso Monteverde

Pensión Manakin
$$
sb/pb, hw
☎/≈*645-5080*
About 4km (2.5mi) from the Monteverde reserve, Pensión Manakin offers modest rooms with or without private bath.

Pensión Monteverde Inn
$$
pb, hw
☎*645-5156*
Near the Butterfly Garden (see p 199), Pensión Monteverde Inn has a friendly family atmosphere in a private, tranquil and striking setting. A trail descends to the canyon in the valley, offering a magnificent view. The rooms are modest and inexpensive (*$10/pers.*), while breakfast (*$3.50*) is reputedly excellent.

Pensión Flor Mar
$$-$$$
sb/pb, hw, ℜ
☎/≈*645-5009*
Near La Lechería cheese factory (see p 201), Pensión Flor Mar has ordinary rooms in a warm family atmosphere. The meals are excellent.

Cabañas Los Pinos
$$$
pb, hw, K
☎*645-5252*
≈*645-5005*
Cabañas Los Pinos are comfortable *cabinas* with kitchenettes. The owner, Señor Jovinos

Arguedas, also runs a 140ha (346 acres) farm where he raises Brahma bulls.

El Establo
$$$
ℜ, pb, hw
☎*645-5033*
≈*645-5041*
Ruth Campbell and Arnoldo Beeche are the owners of El Establo. They provide simple rooms in a relaxed atmosphere. Behind the establishment are 60ha (148 acres) of tropical rainforest just waiting to be explored. There is also a dining room that is only open to hotel guests.

Hotel El Bosque
$$$
pb, hw
☎*645-5221*
≈*645-5129*
Hotel El Bosque offers modest, but extremely clean rooms. The hotel also provides green spaces for campers. You can walk to the nearby Bajo del Tigre reserve, which is great for hiking and bird-watching.

Hotel Finca Valverde
$$$
pb, hw, ℜ
☎*645-5157*
≈*645-5216*
Just at the end of the village of Santa Elena, near the road going to Monteverde, Hotel Finca Valverde rents wooden *cabinas* near the family farmhouse which has a balcony on the second floor.

Hospedaje Mariposa
$$$ bkfst incl.
pb, hw
☎*645-5013*
Hospedaje Mariposa offers three clean, simple rooms. The owners, Luzmery Mata and Rafael Vargas, serve meals exclusively to their guests.

San Luis Ecolodge and Biological Station
$$$-$$$$ fb
sb/pb, hw, ℜ
☎*/≈645-5277*
smithdp@ctrvax.
vanderbilt.edu
Staying at the San Luis Ecolodge and Biological Station is a whole different kind of vacation experience thanks to the many activities offered by its owners, ecologists Diana and Milton Lieberman. The 70ha (173 acres) biological research station is geared towards ecotourism and education. There are two types of accommodations: dormitory with shared bath, or room with private bath.

🐾 Hotel Belmar
$$$$
pb, hw, ℜ
☎*645-5201*
≈*645-5135*
High on a hilltop, Hotel Belmar looks out over the Gulf of Nicoya. To get there, take the little road next to the service station. The spacious, comfortable bedrooms are in two charming mountain cottages, with very pleasant surroundings. The restaurant serves tasty international cuisine.

Hotel Heliconia
$$$$
pb, hw, ℜ
Apartado Postal 10921-1000
San José
☎*645-5109 or 223-3869*
≈*645-5007*
heliconia@racsa.co.cr
The Heleconia is one of the oldest hotels in Monteverde. The main wooden structure stands alongside the road to the reserve. The first additions, behind it and higher on the hill, were two buildings that offer comfortable rooms with double beds. Higher still, and therefore possessing an outstanding view, is a new two-storey building with very pleasant rooms and suites. What makes them even more enjoyable is the long porch where you can relax and watch the sunset. All the rooms have been designed to offer occupants the best possible view of the surrounding countryside. They all have large windows, admittedly their best decorative feature! Unless you're travelling in a group, avoid the rooms in the main building since they're noisy and starting to show their age.

Hotel Montaña
$$$$
pb, hw, ℜ
☎*645-5046*
≈*645-5320*
monteverde@racsa.co.cr
Right on the main road, Hotel Montaña is one of the oldest hotel establishments in the area. Its 32 rooms and suites offer comfort and

luxury. Guests have access to the mineral baths, whirlpool, sauna, restaurant, bar, conference room, hiking trails, evening slide presentation, among other things.

Hotel Fonda Vela
$$$$-$$$$$
pb, hw, ℜ, ⊗, ℝ
☎*645-5125 or 257-1413*
≈*645-5119*
fondavel@racsa.co.cr
Hotel Fonda Vela, near the Monteverde reserve, is an elegant hotel. Its owners, the Smiths, have created a relaxing, country atmosphere. There are 28 spacious rooms and suites. You can explore the surrounding tropical rainforest on hiking trails. Wheelchair accessible.

Hotel Villa Verde
$$$$-$$$$$ bkfst incl.
pb, hw, K, ℜ
☎*645-5025*
≈*645-5115*
estefany@racsa.co.cr
Off the main road, about 2km (1.2mi) from the Monteverde reserve, Hotel Villa Verde offers total relaxation in standard, comfortable rooms or suites with kitchenettes and fireplaces. The restaurant serves Costa Rican dishes and international cuisine. There is a free slide presentation in the evenings about the region's wealth of flora and fauna.

El Sapo Dorado

$$$$$
pb, hw, ℜ, ℝ
☎*645-5010*
⇌*645-5180*
elsapo@racsa.co.cr

North of the main road to the Monteverde reserve, El Sapo Dorado offers 30 luxurious mountain *cabinas* in two categories. The "Sunset Hill" *cabinas* have refrigerators and a spectacular view of the Gulf of Nicoya, while the "Classic" ones have fireplaces and are more romantic. The restaurant (see p 220) is one of the best in the region.

Monteverde Lodge

$$$$$
pb, hw, ℜ, ⊛
non-smoking
☎*257-0766 or 645-5057*
⇌*257-1665*
costaric@expeditions.co.cr

The well-respected Monteverde Lodge is owned and operated by Costa Rica Expeditions and blends harmoniously with the tropical rainforest. This luxury hotel has been redesigned to emphasize the beauty of the natural treasures surrounding it. The Monteverde Lodge is particularly proud of its gardens: little paths run through them, along which you can discover plants indigenous to the region and many different bird species.

The 27 tasteful and elegantly decorated rooms are also very charming. A table for two in front of a large window looking out onto the forest is the perfect place to relax after a day of exploring in the Monteverde reserve. The spacious bathroom is fully functional. The meals in the restaurant are superb (see p 220).

In the evening, guests gather around the circular fireplace in the bar next door to exchange stories about the day's adventures. The 15-person hot-tub is also relaxing. Most of the activities take place in the Monteverde and Santa Elena reserves. The guided night tour is especially interesting because it gives you the chance to observe nocturnal animals and plants. There is a 10min-long path from the hotel to the Finca Ecológica, where there are more trails and scenic views. In the evening, there is a slide presentation in the conference room about the region's flora and fauna. Note that smoking is strictly forbidden inside the hotel.

Quetzal

Restaurants

The Puerto Viejo de Sarapiquí Region

El Bambu
$$
7am to 10pm
on the east side of the soccer field, Puerto Viejo
☎*766-6005*
⇌*766-6132*

El Bambu is one of the most modern and well-maintained restaurants in the city. It serves mainly Costa Rican food and a few international dishes.

Mi Lindo Sarapiquí
$$
9am to 10pm
south side of the soccer field
Puerto Viejo
☎*766-6281 or 766-6074*

We recommend the hotel restaurant at the Mi Lindo Sarapiquí (see p 205) not only for the quality of the food, but also for the service.

Ciudad Quesada and Surroundings

El Parque
$
Avenida 0, Calle 0

Cuidad Quesada has a whole series of little restaurants that are more like *sodas* than real restaurants, particularly around the central park. El Parque is one of them.

Pizzería y Pollo Frito Pin Pollo
$

Avenida 1, Calle 0, Cuidad Quesada
☎460-1801

As its name implies, Pizzería y Pollo Frito Pin Pollo serves pizza and fried chicken at reasonable prices.

La Jarra
$$

south side of the cathedral in Ciudad Quesada
☎460-0985

La Jarra serves local cuisine and fast food (hamburgers). It's clean and one of the few restaurants in the downtown area that isn't better described as a hole in the wall.

Tonjibe
$$

on the avenue alongside the park, between Calle Central and Calle 1, Cuidad Quesada
Tonjibe serves a variety of dishes and is cleaner than most of the other restaurants in the city. A dance club in the back gets going at night.

The Arenal Region

Near La Fortuna

Los Musmanni
$

For pastry, go to the *panadería-repostería*-coffee shop Los Musmanni, next to the La Fortuna post office.

Wall's
$

For ice cream, there is a Wall's in La Fortuna.

Pizzería Luygi's
$
☎479-9636

Just before leaving La Fortuna, towards El Tanque, Pizzería Luygi's serves good pizza.

🦞 Casa de La Tía Ara
$

every day 6am to 10pm
diagonally across from the La Fortuna Hotel
☎479-9172

This tiny *soda* is a great find! Aunt Ara serves wonderful little hamburgers and other fast-food dishes with a smile.

El Jardín
$$

on Principale, one block from the soccer field, in La Fortuna
El Jardín is a large restaurant with an outdoor terrace. Its *tica* dishes are good quality for the price.

Rancho La Cascada
$$

Calle 2, Avenida 1, La Fortuna
On the opposite side of the park, Rancho La Cascada is in a huge hut with a thatched-palm roof. The food is good and provided by the San Bosco hotel (see p 209).

La Pradera
$$
☎479-9167

Also at the limit of La Fortuna, towards the volcano, is La Pradera, which serves *tico* dishes, as well as steaks and seafood in an enormous, open-air hut. Service is courteous.

Pizzería-Spaghettaría Vagabondo
$$

Mon to Fri 5pm to 11pm, Sat and Sun noon to midnight
1.5km (0.9mi) west of the church in La Fortuna, towards the Arenal Volcano
☎479-9565

Pizzería-Spaghettaría Vagabondo is run by Italians. Excellent pizzas are served in an open, airy dining room. Relaxed atmosphere.

Nene's
$$-$$$
☎479-9192

On a small cross street off the main road, the bright lights of Nene's large dining room contrast sharply with the dimly lit street. The flourescent lighting and ever-blaring television add little to the warmth of the surroundings. Nonetheless, the extensive menu features meat, fish, poultry, pasta, rice and other dishes. Many come for the steak, which is served in a generous portion at a reasonable price. This restaurant is recommended by local residents.

Choza de Laurel
$$-$$$

At the entrance to the village, under a high roof, a platter overflowing with fruit crowns an arrangement of picnic tables. Servers wearing traditional costume will bring you regional dishes like *casados* and *gallo pinto*. Although served on plastic plates, the food is certainly wholesome and tasty.

The North

Note that no one in the place is deprived of the "luxury" of television.

Near the Arenal Volcano

El Novillo
$$
between La Fortuna and Arenal not far from Tabacón Resort
International cuisine is served under the roof of a large hut at El Novillo. This is *the* place for outdoor dining.

Tabacón Resort
$$
every day 10am to 10pm
13km (8mi) west of La Fortuna, on the road to the Arenal Volcano
☎*222-1072 or 233-0780*
≈221-3075
The restaurant at the Tabacón Resort really lights up at night. It's nicely set up next to the hot spring swimming pools. It serves international, *tica* and even vegetarian dishes, often spread out buffet-style.

Vaca Muca
$$
closed Mon
3km (1.9mi) west of La Fortuna on the road to the Arenal Volcano
☎*479-9186*
Vaca Muca, which means "cow without horns," serves Costa Rican cuisine on a terrace surrounded by gardens, or in a large indoor dining room with big wooden chairs. This is a very popular restaurant.

Around Lake Arenal

Sabor Italiano
$$
A few kilometres before the village of Nuevo Arenal, Sabor Italiano serves home-cooked Italian food and also has a lovely handicrafts shop.

Los Héroes
$$$
about 30km (18.6mi) from La Fortuna on Lake Arenal
☎*/≈441-4193*
The hotel-restaurant at Los Héroes serves *tica*, international and Swiss specialties, like fondues. The interior decor is very Swiss.

Nuevo Arenal

Tom's Pan
$
☎*694-4547*
On the road that runs around the lake, on the hill that leads down from the village, a German baker has found a new home. Every day, Tom's Pan produces a delicious mixed batch of brioches, croissants and muffins and a variety of breads such as rye, linseed and wholewheat.

On the second-largest street in the village of Nuevo Arenal, across from the park and very near the social welfare building, there are two little restaurants worth mentioning: the *panadería-cafetería* **La Sabrosa** *($)* and **Pipo's Fast Foods** *($; every day 6am to 10pm)*. All serve Costa Rican food and simple international

fare. You can get some good tourist information (mostly verbal) and even take Spanish lessons here.

Mirador Típico Arenal
$$
Nuevo Arenal
☎*694-4159*
The bar-restaurant Mirador Típico Arenal has a terrace facing the lake. The owners are friendly and serve simple, mostly *tica* food.

Pizzería Tramonti
$$
11:30am to 3pm, and 5pm to 10pm, closed Mon
Nuevo Arenal
☎*694-4282*
Right in the middle of the village of Nuevo Arenal, Pizzería Tramonti is known for its excellent pizza cooked in a wood-burning oven.

Concha del Mar
$$$
every day 10am to 9pm closed Tue
Nuevo Arenal
☎*694-4169*
Quebecer Luc and his wife Soledad own the Concha del Mar, a seafood restaurant with a lovely decor. They can also give you some good tourist information.

Between Nuevo Arenal and Tilarán

Equus BBQ
$$
11am to midnight
At the base of the Xiloe Lodge there's a very popular little barbecue restaurant, Equus BBQ. Its outdoorsy, western

ranch-style decor suits the setting. It's pleasantly surrounded by trees and faces the lake—the perfect place to relax outside in the evening with friends and discuss the day's events. The food is prepared on an outdoor grill.

Los Lagos
$$
6am to 10pm
8km (5mi) west of Nuevo Arenal on the road to Tilarán
☎ 694-4271

The American owner and chef of the hotel-restaurant Los Lagos is always cooking up something new. The view of the lake is worthwhile in itself. The restaurant also has complete bar service and a fireplace.

Rock River Lodge
$$
between Nuevo Arenal and Tilarán, on Lake Arenal
☎ 695-5644

The restaurant and bar of the Rock River Lodge are very attractive with their stylish wooden decor, magnificent fireplace and splendid view of Lake Arenal. The menu is varied, and the owners claim that their breakfasts are the best in the area. The bar is open from 5pm until midnight.

🔥 Mystica
$$$
☎ 382-1499

The restaurant at the Mystica hotel (see p 212) certainly merits a detour. No matter when you're in the

region, plan to treat yourself to a meal at Mystica... you won't regret it! The view alone is worth a visit, whether from the terrace (with half-windows for protection from gusting wind) or from the attractive dining room. The decor, the layout on several levels and the use of warm colours make this a place where you'll want to enjoy a long, leisurely meal. With fresh ingredients atop sublimely tender crust, the delicious pizzas here are cooked in a wood-fired oven. You can also treat yourself to fresh pasta, meat dishes or a salad that would be perfect for lunch. It's an absolute must to save room to for dessert though, so you can taste the banana cream pie. Positively exquisite! All this will be served with a smile in a very professional manner. There is also a small shop that sells a few hand-crafted objects.

The Monteverde Region

The little village of **Santa Elena** has a few reasonably priced restaurants and *sodas*. There are also some restaurants and cafés on the road to the Monteverde reserve. Most hotels have restaurants for their clientele and some of them are open to the public.

The **Panadería Jiménez** *($-$$; ☎ 645-5035)*, in the village of Santa Elena, is a bakery that serves light snacks as well as homemade bread and pastries. Upstairs, the **Rocky Road Soda** *($-$$)* serves sandwiches and gigantic hamburgers.

El Daiquiri *($-$$; ☎ 645-5133)* and **Soda Central** *($-$$)* are two *sodas* across the street from the *panadería* in Santa Elena that serve very simple local dishes.

Stella's Bakery
$-$$
Monteverde
☎ 645-5560

Across from the CASEM cooperative, Stella's Bakery makes excellent homemade breads, doughnuts, cookies and other little treats to take out or eat in while sipping a good cup of coffee.

Bromelias
$$
until 5pm only
☎ 645-6093

Perched high on a hill at the end of a short, tree-lined road, behind blooming flowerbeds, Bromelias exudes tranquillity and originality. This small café doubles as an art gallery. Not surprisingly, the decor is attractive, with lovely wooden tables, batik lampshades and some of the gallery's original artworks on display (the others are upstairs), including an amusing piano. Regular coffee is available as well as excellent espresso, fresh fruit

The North

juices, cakes and both sweet and savoury crepes that are well worth sampling. All this takes place behind large windows that, since this is Monteverde, provide wonderful views of the exuberant natural surroundings.

Morphos
$$
☎645-5607
Set in the heart of the village of Santa Elena, Morphos, with large storefront windows, attracts a clientele of travellers who, like the butterfly after which it is named, alight here for coffee, breakfast or a more substantial meal. The restaurant serves *tica* cuisine, including a good *gallo pinto* vegetarian dishes and desserts like a memorable fruit salad and ice cream. The decor is simple, and the atmosphere is quite warm.

Among the hotel-restaurants that are open to the public, two of the best are at **Hotel Fonda Vela** *($$-$$$; ☎257-1413)* and **Hotel Belmar** *($$-$$$; ☎645-5201)*. Their excellent meals are very popular with tourists.

Pizzería de Johnny
$$$
☎645-5066
Open all day, Pizzería de Johnny is always full. And for good reason! Most of the dishes served here are simply delicious. What's more, this new location is

stylishly designed with a tile floor, a wooden ceiling and furniture, and flower-print tablecloths. Outside, the terrace is set up next to the forest where a little brook adds to the ambiance. Besides pizza, you can sample pasta, chicken and other dishes. But the selection of toppings and a perfect crust will convince you to opt for one of the originally named pizzas. The selection of Spanish wines and soft music in the background will also contribute to a pleasant time. The place also has a small shop and bar.

El Sapo Dorado
$$-$$$$
☎645-5010
El Sapo Dorado is in the luxury hotel of the same name (see p 216). There are international and Costa Rican dishes on the menu, including some that are vegetarian. The terrace looks out over the Gulf of Nicoya. With subdued lighting and candles on the tables, the ambiance is meant to be romantic and relaxing. As for the service, it strives for efficiency, but is overly insistent at times.

Monteverde Lodge
$$$-$$$$
☎645-5057
The non-smoking, airy restaurant at the Monteverde Lodge (see p 216) is unquestionably one of the best in the region. The mainly wooden decor and the

many windows create a very attractive setting. The atmosphere and service are matched only by the quality and freshness of the food. International and regional dishes are served, and the portions are generous and tasty. The salads and the fish are particularly delectable.

Tingo's
$$$$
☎645-6034
The newest restaurant in Monteverde is easy to find thanks to the enormous signs at its entrance! The small dining room, done completely in wood, is surrounded by large windows embellished with friezes. The upholstered armchairs are covered with flower-printed fabric. All three meals are served here, so the menu covers everything from classic and *casados* breakfasts to items as varied as hamburgers, pizza, pasta, meat and fish dishes, rice and salads.

Restaurante de Lucía
$$$$
☎645-5337
Restaurante de Lucía is one of Monteverde's favourites. Set up on a small street, it opens its large, low-ceilinged dining room to customers who are eager to eat. Once inside, make yourself comfortable at your table and wait for the server to bring you the menu. Don't be surprised when it arrives on a wooden plank! The cuts of beef

and filets of fish and chicken are presented for your scrutiny before being prepared according to taste. The results are savoury and the meat is as juicy as can be. A quiet place with attentive service.

Entertainment

The Arenal Region

La Fortuna

Located about 4km (2.5mi) from La Fortuna, **Discoteca Look** gets the region dancing on Thursday and Saturday nights. A view of the volcano is a plus here.

The Monteverde Region

Monteverde has various fun places for an evening out. Among them, **Taberna Valverde**, in the village of Santa Elena, not far from the youth hostel, raises its banner: "Full party all night!"

Farther away, on the road to the reserve near the waterfall to which it owes its name, **Discoteca La Cascada** drowns out the sound of the water with rhythms that make dancing a must!

Shopping

The Puerto Viejo de Sarapiquí Region

MUSA
El Tigre, on the Horquetas road
While in the region of Puerto Viejo de Sarapiquí, stop at the MUSA cooperative (see p 190), where natural products (shampoo, for example) made from the herbs grown on this farm are for sale. Authenticity is guaranteed!

The Arenal Region

Around Lake Arenal

La Unión de Nuevo Arenal, between Nuevo Arenal and La Fortuna, sells prints, ceramics

and hand-crafted wooden items at **Sabor Italiano**, a restaurant that serves homemade Italian cuisine (see p 218).

The Monteverde Region

In the Monteverde area, the local handicrafts co-op **CASEM** (see p 200), **Galería Colibrí** (see p 201) and **Galería Sarah Dowell** (near the cheese factory) are good places to pick up some souvenirs to bring home. The Monteverde and Santa Elena parks, and the Butterfly Garden (see p 199) also have interesting little souvenir shops.

Chunches
Santa Elena
☎/≈*645-5147*
A visit to Chunches can be very convenient. It is a café and laundromat that sells new and second-hand books as well as stationary. The friendly owners, Wendy and Jim Standley, know all about the activities, hotels and restaurants in the region.

Arbol de Guanacaste

The Province of Guanacaste

Guanacaste is one big province! Thanks to the international airport in Liberia, its 300km (186mi) of shoreline and 70 beaches have become more accessible to travellers.

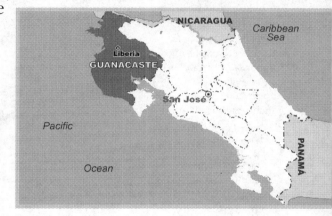

A whole slew of activities awaits visitors to this coastal region: fishing, swimming, windsurfing, surfing, scuba diving and turtle- and bird-watching.

Guanacaste isn't all sand and surf, however; it also has many parks and wildlife reserves protecting lakes, volcanoes, forests and caves. In fact, more than a third of the country's parks are located in this province. Guanacaste also lays claim to the world's largest protected expanse of tropical dry forest, which once covered some 550,000km^2 from the southern Pacific coast of Mexico to Costa Rica. Only 2% of this huge forest has survived; the rest has been cut down for timber or cleared for farming and livestock breeding.

Once part of Nicaragua, Guanacaste first allied itself with Costa Rica so that country would have a large enough population to elect a representative in Spain. Then, in 1825, the residents of Guanacaste chose to become part of Costa Rica. Guanacaste is a very lively place during the week of July 25, when locals commemorate the day the province joined Costa Rica. Though Guanacaste is the largest province in the country, it is home to less than 10% of the population.

Away from the coast, which is undergoing massive development, livestock breeding has traditionally been the main activity in Guanacaste. It is not uncommon to see locals on horseback following their cattle through the fields; you might even encounter people riding their horses in town! Horses can be seen grazing right next to the Interamericana or roaming freely along secondary roads. It should be noted that you won't see a lot of luxuriant tropical vegetation while exploring Guanacaste, but rather vast stretches of steppes and prairies, which might look very dry during the busy tourist season.

A country within a country, Guanacaste enjoys a hot but dry climate that helps to make it one of Costa Rica's most popular tourist destinations.

Finding Your Way Around

By Plane

Though Liberia's **Aeropuerto Daniel Oduber Quiros** *(open every day 6am to 9pm;* ☎*667-0199 or 667-0032,* ≠*667-0000)* (see p 37) is technically an international airport, most of its traffic consists of charter flights for tourists arriving from North America. Car rental agencies are located nearby.

Sansa *(*☎*221-9414)* and **Travelair** *(*☎*220-3054)* both offer daily flights from San José to **Tamarindo**, usually very early in the morning. Both airlines' schedules vary, so be sure to inquire beforehand. A return ticket costs between $110 and $140.

Sansa and Travelair both offer daily service from San José to **Nosara**; Sansa leaves early in the morning, Travelair around noon. A return ticket costs between $110 and $140.

Sansa and Travelair also offer daily flights from San José to the little airport at Playa Carillo, which serves the entire **Playa Sámara** region. The planes usually leave in the morning. Reservations are recommended during the tourist season.

By Car

Around Tilarán - Cañas - Bagaces

Tilarán lies at the edge of the province, near Lake Arenal. To get there from the village of Nuevo Arenal, follow the west shore of the lake, then head inland toward Guanacaste for about 10km (6.2mi). The road is clearly indicated. If you are coming from

Guanacaste, take the Interamericana to Cañas, where a lovely road leads 25km (15.5mi) northeast to Tilarán.

Cañas and **Bagaces** are both located on the Interamericana, about 25km (15.5mi) apart, and are thus easy to reach from either San José or Liberia.

Parque Nacional Palo Verde and Reserva Biológica Lomas Barbudal

From the town of Bagaces, located on the Interamericana, take the small, unpaved road leading southwest (on the left if you are coming from San José). The road is across from a gas station, and there is a small sign for the park. Turn right at the first intersection, left at the second, then follow the signs to the park, located 28km (17.3mi) from the Interamericana. At one point, you'll come to a T-shaped intersection. Parque Nacional Palo Verde lies to the left, the Reserva Biológica Lomas Barbudal to the right.

Parque Nacional Rincón de la Vieja

To get to the **Las Pailas sector**, located 25km (15.5mi) from Liberia, take the Interamericana northwards for 5km (3.1mi), then turn right on a small, unpaved road (there will be a

A veritable paradise for birds and plants, the Monteverde region attracts ornithologists as well as tourists for its rare quetzals.
- *Roger Michel*

The small village of Montezuma on the Nicoya Peninsula boasts magnificent, seemingly endless beaches.
- *Roger Michel*

The stork, one of the country's many winged species.
- *Didier Raffin*

Sugar cane fields dance in the wind as far as the eye can see.
- *Stéphane G. Marceau*

sign). After about 200m (656ft), head to the left and continue to the village of Curubandé (15km or 9.3mi). A few kilometres past the town, you'll have to stop at a gate and pay an entrance fee (*$2/pers.*), since the road runs over private property (the Hacienda Lodge Guachipelín). The last 1.5km (0.9mi) of the road leading to the park entrance is rough going; if you don't have four-wheel drive, you should leave your car by the side of the road and walk.

To get to the **Santa María sector**, also located 25km (15.5mi) from Liberia, take Avenida 6 from the Barrio La Victoria, in the east part of town and follow the little road that leads to the park entrance by way of San Jorge (18km or 11mi). Depending on the season, the road might be impassable by car (call the park before setting out).

Parque Nacional Guanacaste

To reach the **Maritza biological station**, located 60km (37mi) from Liberia, take the Interamericana north for 43km (27mi), then turn right on the small, unpaved road that begins across from the road leading to the little town of Cuajiniquil. From there, it's a pretty bumpy 17km (10.6mi) to the station, so you'll need a four-wheel

drive vehicle.

To get to the **Cacao biological station**, about 40km (25mi) from Liberia, take the Interamericana north for 23km (14.3mi), then turn right on the little road leading to the village of Quebrada Grande (7km or 4.3mi). From there, a small, unpaved road on the left leads north to the station. A four-wheel drive vehicle is a must for this last stretch of the trip (approx. 10km or 6.2mi).

North of Liberia

La Cruz is located on the Interamericana, about 60km or 37mi (a 1hr drive) from Liberia.

Parque Nacional Santa Rosa

La Casona, the park headquarters, the research station and the campsites are all located at the **main entrance of the park**, located 42km (26mi) from Liberia. To get there, take the Interamericana north for 35km (22mi). The little road leading to the park entrance and facilities (7km or 4.3mi) will be on your left; look for the sign.

To reach the **Murciélago sector**, 62km (39mi) from Liberia, drive north on the Interamericana for 43km (27mi), then turn left on the road leading to the little town of Cuajiniquil (8km or 5mi). From there, a

small road leads west to the administrative office for this sector of the park (9km or 5.6mi).

Refugio Nacional Bahía Junquillal

This park lies 57km (35mi) from Liberia. Take the Interamericana north for 43km (27mi), then turn left on the road leading to the little town of Cuajiniquil (8km or 5mi). Continue for 2km (1.2mi) then turn right on the little road leading to the park entrance (4km or 2.5mi).

Around Liberia

Liberia, the capital of Guanacaste, lies in the heart of the province. It is the gateway to the northern part of the region and the beaches on the Nicoya Peninsula. It is located on the Interamericana, about 50km (31mi) north of Cañas (45min).

There are three gas stations at the intersection of the Interamericana and the main road to Liberia, all of which are open on holidays.

Playa del Coco, **Playa Hermosa** and **Playa Panamá** are all located about a 30min drive from Liberia. For the last two, follow the signs for Condovac La Costa from the intersection right before Playa del Coco. The first road to Playa Panamá is

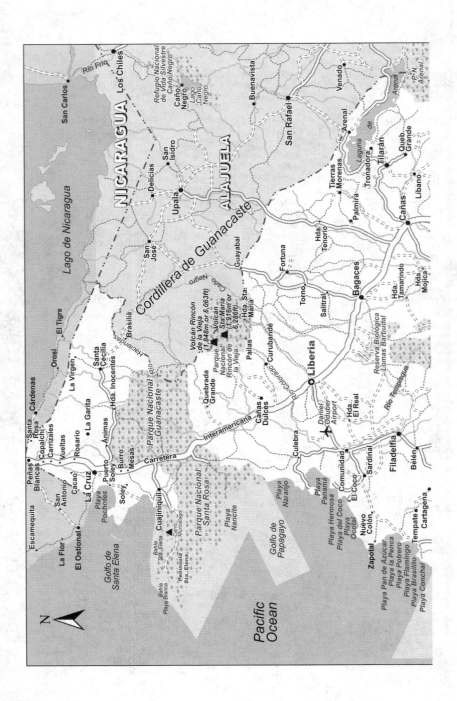

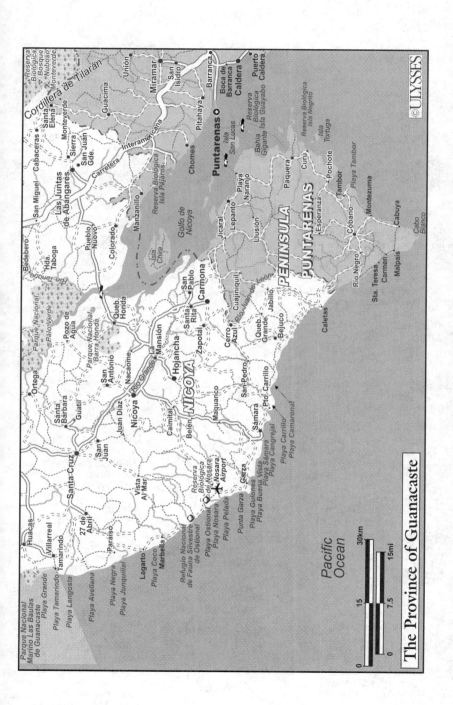

The Province of Guanacaste

paved. After that, a dirt road leads to the hotels like the Sula Sula and the Blue Bay.

There is a gas station on the road to Playa del Coco, after the turn-off for Sardinal.

Around Filadelfia

About 10km (6.2mi) south of Filadelfia (just south of Belén), on the road to Nicoya, there is a road leading to a string of beaches (**Playa Conchal**, **Playa Brasilito**, **Playa Flamingo**, **Playa Potrero**, **Playa Penca** and **Playa Pan de Azúcar**). When you get to Huacas, turn right; the first beach, Playa Brasilito, is less than 10km (6.2mi) away. The last few kilometres to Playa Pan de Azúcar make for a pretty bumpy ride.

There are no real gas stations in this area. If you're running low on fuel, head to the *abastecedor* **Villamar** (at the corner of the road to Playa Brasilito and the road to the other beaches farther north), where an employee will pour a few litres into your tank from a can. A lifesaver in a pinch!

Tamarindo: To get to **Playa Grande** from Belén, you have to pass through Huacas and drive west, toward Matapalo. Playa Tamarindo lies nearly 15km (9.3mi) south of the village of Huacas.

Parque Nacional Marino Las Baulas

From Liberia, take Highway 21 southwest to the little town of Filadelfia (31km or 19.2mi). Continue 6km to the village of Belén, then turn right toward famous Playa Tamarindo. Stay on this road until you reach Huacas (24km or 15mi), then take the unpaved road leading to Salinas, Playa Grande and the park entrance (8km or 5mi). The total distance is 69km (43mi), about a 1.5hr drive.

Around Santa Cruz

Santa Cruz lies on the big road between Liberia and Nicoya, about 60km (37mi) southwest of Liberia. The road is paved and generally in very good condition.

An alternative route is to take the ferry (see further below) across the Río Tempisque to the town of Nicoya, south of Santa Cruz. To do so, follow the paved road that branches off the Interamericana just north of the exit for Las Juntas (there's a sign for the ferry).

Playa Junquillal: If you are coming from Liberia on the road to Nicoya, you'll see the road to the beach just before Santa Cruz; there is a sign showing the way. When you get to the village of Veintisiete de Abril, turn left and continue to Paraíso. Playa

Junquillal lies 12km (7.5mi) farther. The road could really use some repairs, especially near Santa Cruz.

You'll have a hard time finding a gas station in the Playa Junquillal area, but the first little village on the beach sells gas from a can.

Playa Avellanas lies about 5km (3.1mi) north of Playa Junquillal. From Santa Cruz, go to the village of 27 de Abril, then follow the signs. It's likely to be a bumpy ride, especially during the rainy season. Inquire about the road conditions before setting out.

Around Nicoya

Nicoya: As in the case of Santa Cruz, there are two routes to Nicoya. If you are coming from Liberia, simply take the Liberia-Nicoya highway (approx. 80km or 50mi). If you are coming from San José, join the road to the Río Tempisque from the Interamericana (a few kilometres north of the exit for Las Juntas; look for the sign), take the ferry (see further below) across the river then continue to Nicoya.

Playa Nosara and **Playa Guiones**: From Nicoya, take the road that leads southwest out of town, toward Sámara. After 30km (18.6mi), you'll come to a fork in the road; Nosara is on the right. From that point on, the journey becomes a bit more of an adventure, as the dirt road is not always in the best condition; you'll even have to ford a few rivers! The Ostional beach and the Reserva Biológica de Nosara are at the end of the road, which, after Nosara, becomes impassable if you don't have four-wheel drive.

Playa Sámara, **Playa Buena Vista**, **Playa Carrillo** and **Playa Camaronal**: Like Nosara, the beaches in the Sámara area are accessible via the road that leads southwest out of the town of Nicoya. When you reach the fork in the road 30km (18.6mi) farther, turn left and head to Sámara. The road is in very good condition.

To reach Playa Buena Vista from the village of Sámara, head north on the street where the Isla Chora hotel is located. You'll know you're going the right way if you pass the Mágica Cantarana hotel. The beach is at the end of this stretch of road (which can be hard to negotiate during the rainy season), after a small lagoon that can fill up at high tide.

Just as you are entering the village of Sámara, you'll see a road on your left. This leads to Playa Carillo, located a few kilometres to the south. The road is pretty bad in places but gets much better near

the beach. Playa Camaronal lies farther south on the same road.

Parque Nacional Barra Honda

If you are coming from the Interamericana, you'll have to take the ferry across the Río Tempisque then follow the little highway about 15km (9.3mi) until you reach a small road (on the right) leading to the village of Nacaome and the park entrance. If you are arriving from Nicoya (23km or 14.2mi from the park entrance), take the main road south and turn left on the road to the Río Tempisque ferry. Not far from the intersection, a small road on the left leads to the village of Nacaome and the park entrance.

By Boat

To get to Nicoya peninsula from the mainland, you must cross the Río Tempisque. Ferries run around the clock between Puerto Vispero on the mainland and Puerto Moreno on the the peninsula *(every hour from 5am to 8pm, every 2hrs from 8pm to 5pm)*.

By Bus

Around Tilarán-Cañas-Bagaces

Tilarán: The bus from Ciudad Quesada to

Arenal passes through Tilarán. There are two daily departures, one at 6am and the other at 3pm. The buses heading in the opposite direction leave Tilarán at 7am and 1pm. The trip takes 4hrs. There is also daily bus service from Monteverde to Tilarán. The bus leaves Monteverde at 7am, with return service at 1pm.

Parque Nacional Rincón de la Vieja

The youth hostel in Liberia (Hotel Guanacaste) offers a shuttle service to and from the park. During the high season, there are up to three departures, beginning at 7am.

North of Liberia

La Cruz: There are four daily departures from San José to La Cruz; the buses continue on to Peñas Blancas, at the Nicaraguan border. The trip from San José to La Cruz takes about 6hrs; the bus stop in San José is on Calle 14, between Avenidas 3 and 5. There are five buses per day to Liberia, departing between 5:30am and 6pm, and nine buses in the opposite direction, leaving between 6am and 6pm. The bus stop is right in the centre of La Cruz; for more information, call ☎224-1960.

Nicaragua: The buses to La Cruz continue on to the Nicaraguan border,

14km (8.7mi) farther north. At the border, you have to walk about 800m, then wait for a minibus to take you to customs, 4km (2.5mi) farther.

Around Liberia

Liberia: There is frequent bus service between San José and Liberia—nearly every 2hrs from 7am to 8pm for the trip to Liberia, and from 4:30am to 8pm for the trip back to San José. The ride takes 4hrs. There is bus service to Liberia from Santa Cruz and Puntarenas as well, once a day at around 5:30pm for the trip there, and around 8:30am for the trip back. It takes 2 to 2.5hrs to travel from Puntarenas to Liberia. Buses to and from San José depart from and arrive at the Palmitán bus station (*Avenida 3, Calle 12*). There is another station for local buses on Avenida 7, just east of the Interamericana.

Playa del Coco: There is daily bus service from San José to Playa del Coco at 8am and 2pm. The trip takes 5hrs. There are also four buses per day from Liberia to Playa del Coco between 5am and 5pm. You can catch a bus back to Liberia between 7am and 6pm.

Playa Hermosa and **Playa Panamá**: There is only one bus per day from San José to Playa

Hermosa and Playa Panamá. It sets out at 3:20pm (*Calle 12, Avenida 5/7*), while the bus back leaves each morning at 5am. There is bus service between Liberia and these two beaches as well.

Around Filadelfia

Playa Conchal, **Playa Brasilito**, **Playa Flamingo**, **Playa Potrero**: There is daily bus service from Santa Cruz to these beaches at 6:30am and 3pm. You can catch a bus back to Santa Cruz at 9am or 5pm. There are also two daily departures for Playa Brasilito and Playa Flamingo from San José at 6:30am and 3pm. The buses back leave at 9am and 5pm.

Playa Tamarindo: A bus sets out for Playa Tamarindo from San José every day at around 4pm. The trip takes a good 6hrs. The bus from Santa Cruz to Playa Tamarindo leaves every night at 8:30pm; the bus back, every morning at 6:45am.

Around Santa Cruz

Santa Cruz: There are four buses per day from San José to Santa Cruz between 7:30am and 6pm; the trip takes over 5hrs. The main bus station is about 400m (1,312ft) east of downtown. There is a stop on the north side of Plaza de Los Mangos for buses to Nicoya and Liberia.

Playa Junquillal: A bus sets out from San José for Playa Junquillal every day at 2pm (*Avenida 3, Calle 20*). The trip takes 6hrs. The bus back leaves at 5am. The bus from Santa Cruz to Playa Junquillal leaves at 6:30pm and heads back at 5am.

Around Nicoya

Nicoya: There is frequent bus service from San José (*Calle 14, Avenida 5*) between 6am and 5pm, with no fewer than eight departures (approximately one every 2hrs). The trip takes at least 4hrs. Buses set out for Nicoya from Liberia every hour from 5am to 7pm. The bus station is near the Río Chipanzo, on Calle 5, south of downtown.

Nosara: The bus to Nicoya leaves Nosara every day at 1pm and starts back at 6am. The trip takes 2.5hrs. There is direct bus service from San José to Nosara, with a daily 6am departure. There is also direct bus service from Nosara to Liberia (4am).

Playa Sámara, **Playa Buena Vista**, **Playa Carrillo** and **Playa Camaronal**: The Alfaro bus company offers direct service to Sámara from San José. The bus leaves every day at noon (*Avenida 5, Calle 14/16, ☎222-2750, 223-8227 or 223-8361*), with an estimated travel time of 6hrs. There are also daily departures from Nicoya at 8am, 3pm and 4pm, with return service at 5:30am and 6:30am. The buses from Nicoya stop at Playa Carrillo.

Practical Information

Around Tilarán-Cañas-Bagaces

Cañas: You'll find a Banco de Costa Rica near the south side of the central park and a Banco Nacional on the north side. There is a pharmacy (Farmacía Cañas) on the road that runs alongside the central park then continues northward. The bus stop is near Avenida 11 and Calle 1, north of downtown.

North of Liberia

La Cruz: There is a tourist information office in La Cafetería, a pleasant little restaurant on the street that heads out of town to Playa Pochote. A bank can be found on the Interamericana on the way into town.

Around Liberia

Liberia: There is a hospital in Liberia (*Avenida 9, Calle 13*).

You can find branches of all the main banks in this regional capital.

There is a Banco Popular with an automated teller machine on Avenida Central, near Calle 8, and a Banco de Costa Rica immediately northeast of Parque Central.

The staff at the **Info-Cen-Tur** tourist information centre, in the Centro Commercial Bambú (*Calle 1, Avenida 3*), will be glad to help you in any way they can. A few English-language papers are usually available here during the high season.

Playa del Coco: There is a Banco Nacional on the road to the village, just past the road leading to Playa Ocotal. You'll also find a supermarket on the road that runs alongside the beach and heads west after the soccer field.

Around Filadelfia

Playa Flamingo: Since Playa Flamingo is a high-class resort town, you'll find many tourist services such as banks and supermarkets here.

Playa Tamarindo: A few kilometres before Tamarindo, you'll pass a tourist information centre. Although it is only open during the high season, there is a sign outside indicating the local points of interest year-round. There is another tourist information centre in the village (at the edge of town, opposite the El Milagro hotel), as

well as a shopping centre (a little farther into town, across from the Tamarindo Diriá hotel) with a small grocery store and a gift shop. A larger grocery store, the Super Mercado El Pelicano, can be found on the road that runs around the traffic circle in the centre of the village. The local Banco Nacional is at the edge of town, on the beach side of the road. It should be noted, however, that there are no pharmacies or automated teller machines in Tamarindo.

Around Nicoya

Nicoya: Nicoya has a hospital with all the basic facilities and services. It is located north of the downtown area, on Calle 3, the main street off the Nicoya-Liberia road. On the same street, just south of the hospital, you'll find a Banco Popular with an automated teller machine, right across from the local branch of the Banco Nacional. You'll also find gas stations.

Playa Nosara: The Supermercado Nosara is a big grocery store for this area—it even sells film. Outside of town, you'll find a community centre and a tourist information office on the road to the beaches (south of Nosara, near the restaurant La Dolce Vita), but there's no gas station.

The Province of Guanacaste

Playa Sámara: There is a grocery store (Super Sámara) in the centre of the village, on the road that runs along the beach. There is also a garage on the outskirts of the village.

Guided Tours

At **Eco Tours** *(Playa Hermosa,* ☎*672-017;* ⇌*672-0146)* Marc, the Quebecois owner (soon to be naturalized as Tico), offers excursions to almost anywhere in Guanacaste. He knows the region like the back of his hand and obviously loves Costa Rican nature. It is well worth finding out about the activities available and the rooms he rents.

Exploring

Around Tilarán-Cañas-Bagaces

A cathedral town, **Tilarán** lies in a part of Guanacaste that is fairly windy, because of its altitude, but nonetheless enjoys a pleasant temperature year-round. The area is also quite sunny, since it lies west of Lake Arenal, where it is much drier than east of the lake, which has more clouds and capricious temperatures. Tilarán itself is hilly but has little charm. Its **ca-thedral** is relatively

modern, with an interior decorated with marquetry, lending it a distinctive character. All in all, Tilarán is a quiet place with few tourist attractions to speak of.

The town does have two points of interest, however. First, the area is home to the **largest tree in the country ★** —according to local residents, at least. It is indeed a very impressive specimen: the base alone has a girth of more than 30m (98.4ft)! However, it happens to stand on private property, about 5km (3.1mi) southeast of town. After a good meal at La Carreta (see p 276) in downtown Tilarán, ask the owner, who knows everyone, if he can take you to see it.

The other attraction around Tilarán is the **waterfalls ★**, located near the little town of **Libano**. To get there from Tilarán, go through Libano, cross the river, pass the church and the school, then follow the signs for the *cascadas*.

Located 80m (262ft) above sea level, **Bagaces** is hot and doesn't qualify as a top-notch tourist resort. Like **Cañas**, however, it can be a practical place to stop during your tour of the province's hinterland, most notably to visit **Parque Nacional Palo Verde ★** or the **Reserva Biológica Lomas Barbudal** (see further on).

While in Cañas take a look at the church across from the central park, which has recently been redecorated using a colorful marquetry technique that creates a most pleasing and original effect.

Parque Nacional Palo Verde

Avid bird-watchers won't want to miss **Parque Nacional Palo Verde ★** *($6; every day 8am to 4pm;* ☎*659-9039 or 284-6116,* ⇌*659-9039)*, where 279 avian species have been spotted. The diversity of the birds found here can be attributed to the fact that the park contains a large variety of natural habitats: a low-altitude, tropical dry forest made up of wooded hills, salt- and freshwater lagoons, mangrove swamps, marshes and grasslands. Furthermore, a large part of the territory is flooded by heavy rains and overflow from the Tempisque and Bebedero rivers, which run along the edge of the park. Because the water drains slowly, the grasslands turn into swamps for months at a time, transforming the landscape of the park. Because these damp coastal areas are quite rare in Guanacaste and elsewhere in Costa Rica, Parque Nacional Palo Verde was included in the Ramsar Convention in 1992.

There is more in the park than wetlands and flood zones, however. Over 150 species of trees have been identified to date, including the *palo verde* (green wood), whose trunk, branches and leaves remain green year-round. Of course, the *palo verde* happens to be found mainly in the swampy parts of the park...

Parque Nacional Palo Verde, which covers an area of 16,804ha (41,522 acres), was founded as an ecological reserve in April 1978 and became a national park in June 1980. It lies about 30km (18.6mi) southwest of the little town of Bagaces, where the Río Tempisque starts widening its way to the Gulfo de Nicoya. It takes about 1hr to drive from Bagaces to the middle of the park (see p 224), where the welcome centre and administrative offices are located. The OTS *(Organization of Tropical Studies,* ☎*240-6696)* research centre, located a little farther (7.5km or 24.6mi), has accommodations for visitors wishing to stay in the park for a few days, and gives guided tours *($17, lunch included)* that focus on the area's natural history. Camping is also permitted (see p 259) in the park.

It is generally best to visit the park during the dry season (December to March), and more specifically in January and February. During these months, most of the water has receded from the fields and the rivers are at their lowest point, so most of the animals are grouped in well-defined areas, making it easier to observe them. In the evening, scores of animals flock to the few watering places in the region. You're likely to spot some white-faced capuchin monkeys, as well as howler monkeys, coatis, iguanas and white-tailed deer. The **Río Tempisque** is home to many crocodiles, some of which are up to 5m (16.4ft) long!

During the wet season, on the other hand, Parque Nacional Palo Verde is more interesting for its birdlife; its watering places, swamps and wetlands attract some 300 species of land and water birds, including toucans, parrots, wigeons, egrets, herons and white ibises. The scarlet macaw, now very rare in Costa Rica, has been spotted here as well. Furthermore, **Isla Pájaros** (2.3ha or 5.7 acres), located in the Río Tempisque, has one of the largest colonies of black-crowned night herons (*Nycticorax nycticorax*) in the country. Parque Nacional Palo Verde also boasts the largest concentration of water and wading birds in Central America.

Finally, the park is the only Costa Rican breeding ground of the endangered jabiru, a huge wading bird with a large beak, that is a close relative of the stork.

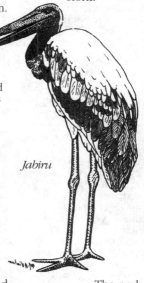

Jabiru

The park has a small network of hiking trails (6km or 3.7mi total), as well as a few forest roads. The heat can be truly suffocating during the dry season, so don't forget to bring along a large supply of fresh water. **Las Calizas** (300m or 984ft), **El Manigordo** (1.5km or 0.9mi), **El Mapache** (2km or 1.2mi) and **La Venada** (2km or 1.2mi) are short trails, but still give visitors a chance to see the many types of natural habitats that make up this region, as well as view the magnificent surrounding hills and the plains that flood during the wet season.

However, before you head down one of these trails or pitch your tent, ask for the latest information about the ferocious African bees *(Abejas africanizadas)* that have taken up residence in the park.

Reserva Biológica Lomas Barbudal

The Reserva Biológica Lomas Barbudal *($6; every day)* covers 2,279ha (5,631 acres) just northwest of Parque Nacional Palo Verde. Here, too, the climate is oppressively hot during the dry season (December to March). Visitors to the reserve can go hiking, camping *($1.25/pers./day; near the welcome centre)*, observe the local plant and animal life or cool down by a river that flows year-round. Depending on the season, there might not be anyone on duty at the welcome station, which means that you'll have to explore the park without first obtaining all the necessary information and advice to ensure that your visit is as safe and enjoyable as possible.

Before setting out to explore this stretch of tropical dry forest, take note that some 240 species of bees, includ-

ing the aggressive African bee, are found in the reserve. Make sure that you understand all posted safety precautions (usually in Spanish only) and steer clear of the places that the bees have claimed as their territory.

Bees!

If you have the misfortune of being pursued by these winged psychopaths, run in a zigzag and cover your head with your arms. Of course, this is easier said than done, since the terrain or path you're on might not be well-suited to this unusual exercise!

Aside from bees, the reserve is home to 60 species of butterflies and over 200 species of birds, including scarlet macaws and jabirus. Mammals commonly spotted here include monkeys such as howlers and white-faced capuchins, as well as coatis, raccoons and coyotes.

The Reserva Biológica Lomas Barbudal contains seven natural habitats, though about 70% of its territory is covered by deciduous forests. During the dry season, these trees lose

their leaves, just like broad-leaved trees in North America do each autumn. Furthermore, in March, a beautiful but fleeting phenomenon occurs: the blossoming of the *Tabebuia ochracea*, referred to by Costa Ricans as the *corteza amarilla* (yellow bark). All at once and for only a few days, these trees are literally covered with thousands of yellow flowers, lending the landscape a surreal appearance.

In addition to this spectacular tree, the reserve contains magnificent rosewoods, which are a purplish hue mixed with black and yellow, and mahoganies, an American tree whose hard, reddish wood is still much coveted throughout the world. Of course, these trees are becoming rarer and rarer in Costa Rica and elsewhere in the Americas, and the parks and reserves deserve a great deal of credit for their tremendous efforts to preserve them.

Deforested regions like eastern Guanacaste can suffer greatly during the kind of drought caused by El Niño in 1997, which turned the landscape into vast, desolate yellow stretches. Canada and other countries are helping Costa Rica reforest this area. The results so far can be seen a few kilometres east of the Interamericana, between Bagaces and Cañas.

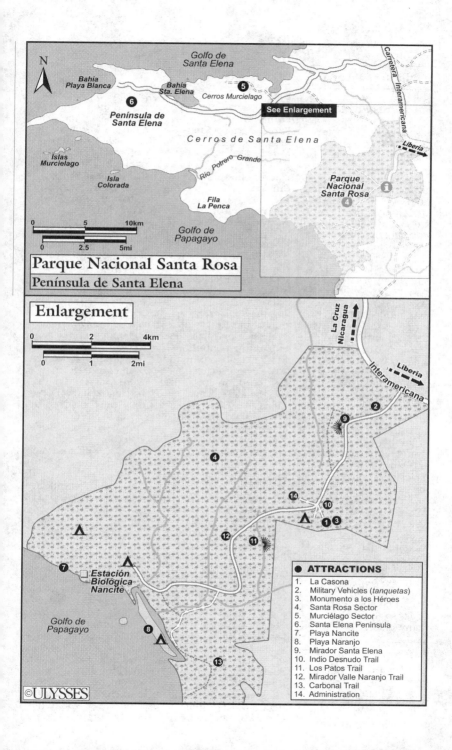

N

Golfo de
Santa Elena

Bahía
Playa Blanca

Bahía
Sta. Elena

Cerros Murcielago

6

Península de
Santa Elena

See Enlargement

Carretera Interamericana

Islas
Murcielago

Cerros de Santa Elena

Liberia

Isla
Colorada

Río Potrero Grande

Parque
Nacional
Santa Rosa

1

Fila
La Penca

4

| 0 | 5 | 10km |
| 0 | 2.5 | 5mi |

Golfo de
Papagayo

Parque Nacional Santa Rosa
Península de Santa Elena

Enlargement

| 0 | 2 | 4km |
| 0 | 1 | 2mi |

La Cruz
Nicaragua

Liberia

Interamericana

2

9

4

14

10

12

11

1 **3**

7

Estación
Biológica
Nancite

Golfo de
Papagayo

8

13

© ULYSSES

● ATTRACTIONS

1. La Casona
2. Military Vehicles (*tanquetas*)
3. Monumento a los Héroes
4. Santa Rosa Sector
5. Murciélago Sector
6. Santa Elena Peninsula
7. Playa Nancite
8. Playa Naranjo
9. Mirador Santa Elena
10. Indio Desnudo Trail
11. Los Patos Trail
12. Mirador Valle Naranjo Trail
13. Carbonal Trail
14. Administration

North of Liberia

The area north of Liberia mainly consists of vast stretches of protected wilderness. The only sizeable town is **La Cruz** (not to be confused with Santa Cruz, on the Nicoya Peninsula), which has a population of a few thousand and is the last stop on the Interamericana before the Nicaraguan border. There is little to do in La Cruz, other than going to **Playa Pochote**, where Costa Ricans like to go swimming, and which is one of the last beaches in the country before Nicaragua. The other beaches in the area that are worth visiting are located in the parks.

In this region, you can also see the Guanacaste of the big *rancheros* (cattle and horse ranchers), and admire the majestic silhouettes of the volcanoes in the Cordillera de Guanacaste, such as Rincón de la Vieja and Orosí, rising up amidst the rather flat surroundings.

It should be noted that few people live between Liberia and La Cruz, so there aren't many places to eat.

Parque Nacional Santa Rosa

It isn't often that you find sand, surf, plains, mountains, tourist facilities and a well-preserved historic site in one park. And yet that's exactly what awaits you at the impressive **Parque Nacional Santa Rosa** ★ ★ *($6; every day 8am to 4:30pm; ☎/≈695-5598 or 695-5577)*, located in the northwestern most part of the province, just a few kilometres from the Nicaraguan border.

Covering an area of 37,117ha (91,714 acres), the park was designated a national site in 1966, then became a national park in 1971. It occupies a large portion of the Santa Elena Peninsula and has been expanding continuously for years, absorbing the Murciélago sector, farther north, in 1980, and the Hacienda Santa Elena in 1987. It has not finished growing either: negotiations with area landowners are still underway.

Parque Nacional Santa Rosa is not only one of the largest parks in Costa Rica, but also the fourth most popular with tourists. There are a number of reasons for this. First, the park is located right near the Interamericana, at the end of a 7km (4.3mi) long paved road, making it easy to get to. Furthermore, **La Casona** ★ *(free admission; near the park headquarters)*, a large and fascinating historic site, lies within its boundaries. La Casona is the main house of the Hacienda Santa Rosa, one of the largest ranches in Costa Rica, which has played an important role in the country's history since the 18th century. A symbol of Costa Rican independence and national pride, La Casona was the scene of three decisive battles, whose outcome helped preserve democracy in the country.

The first of these conflicts took place on March 20, 1856, when an American named William Walker (see p 24) came here from Nicaragua with a band of 200 mercenaries to stir up a revolution in Central America. Late one afternoon, while Walker and his men were quartered at the Hacienda Santa Rosa, they were attacked by Costa Rican troops. Supposedly, the battle lasted only 14min, with the Costa Ricans emerging victorious.

The second conflict, known as the Sapoá Revolución, occurred on May 8, 1919, when a group of 800 men tried to overthrow the government of President Federico Tinoco. While camped at the hacienda, these revolutionaries were defeated and forced to flee back to Nicaragua, where they had come from.

The third battle began in 1955, during the presidency of José Figueres, known as Don Pepe. Apparently, a large group of former

Costa Rican president Dr. Rafael Ángel Calderón Guardia's supporters invaded the country from Nicaragua. Though Costa Rica had eliminated its army in 1948, the population rose up to defend their country's freedom. There was violent fighting around La Casona, and Figueres's troops managed to fight off the invaders. Two military vehicles *(tanquetas)* abandoned during the battle can be seen 3km (1.9mi) from the park entrance.

Nowadays, La Casona is a quiet, peaceful place, invaded only by the blazing sun and the bats who rest here during the day. Constructed with big wooden planks and topped with ceramic tiles, La Casona has numerous rooms, a large veranda stretching the entire length of its main façade, and balconies on the second floor. At the back, a number of buildings have been joined together, forming a large courtyard. The house is open to the public. Some of the rooms are decorated with period furnishings, complete with mannequins decked out in vintage clothing. An assortment of riding equipment is also on display. One of the buildings contains a small souvenir shop that sells statuettes, handicrafts and various other objects related to La Casona and the park. Outside, near

some stately trees, is a long, low stone wall that was built over 300 years ago.

The **Monumento a los Héroes** was erected near La Casona in memory of the courageous men and women who fought in the battles of 1856 and 1955. Consisting of a large beam supported by two brick columns, the monument sits on a hill, and can only be reached by climbing a long flight of stairs. The view from the hill extends all the way to the Cacao and Orosí volcanoes, in Parque Nacional Guanacaste, and to Volcán Rincón de la Vieja.

Parque Nacional Santa Rosa is divided into two sectors: the **Santa Rosa sector**, which is most popular with visitors, and the smaller **Murciélago sector** farther north. Between them lie the Santa Elena Peninsula and the mountains of the same name. The park contains one of the last remnants of the tropical dry forest that once extended along the Pacific coast from Mexico to Panamá. It thus serves the dual purpose of protecting these woodlands and providing the proper environment for the surrounding pastures to be reforested. The process of regeneration occurs in a variety of ways: some seeds are scattered by the wind, while others are consumed by animals,

then excreted in various parts of the park.

Many scientists are studying this process and making sure that the forest reestablishes itself in the area. To ensure the project's success, it has been necessary to educate local residents, who have been clearing the land continuously since the 16th century, to sell the wood and create huge pastures; after all, Guanacaste is known as the Far West of Costa Rica. Fortunately, the park still has some majestic trees, which lose their leaves during the dry season (November to May). Some magnificent specimens of the impressive *guanacaste* (*Enterolobium cyclocarpum*), the tree after which the province is named, can be found near La Casona.

This vast park contains a variety of natural habitats (sea, beaches, mangrove swamps, plains, mountains, etc.) and is thus home to a remarkable assortment of animals. To date, 115 species of mammals, 250 species of birds, 100 species of amphibians and reptiles—and over 30,000 species of insects have been counted! With a bit of luck, you can see white-faced capuchin monkeys, howler monkeys, white-tailed deer, coatis and large iguanas (*Ctenousaura similis*). Pumas, coyotes and boa constrictors are

The Province of Guanacaste

among the less commonly spotted denizens of the park.

Playa Nancite is considered one of the two most important breeding grounds of olive ridley turtles (*Lepidochelys olivacea*, known to Costa Ricans as the *tortuga lora*) in the world, the other being Playa Ostional in the Refugio Nacional de Vida Silvestre de Ostional (see p 256). These turtles are not very big, weighing only 40kg on average, but thousands of them come to the beach to lay their eggs. This spectacular phenomenon, which local residents refer to as *arribadas* (massive influxes), occurs frequently between the months of July and November and most often in August and September.

Of all the parks in Guanacaste, Parque Nacional Santa Rosa is best equipped to welcome visitors. An eight-room facility that accommodates 64 people is available, as are campsites (see p 261) and a cafeteria that serves excellent food.

The Santa Rosa sector has a number of hiking trails, which lead past various natural attractions. Near the park entrance, a lookout known as the **Mirador Santa Elena** offers a view of the Santa Elena Mountains, which are about 85 million years

old. Near La Casona, you can go on a 30min hike along the **Indio Desnudo trail** (*0.8km or 0.5mi*), from which you can observe the various plant and animal species that coexist harmoniously in the tropical dry forest. Near a small natural bridge, are some petroglyphs carved into the stone.

A small, unpaved road leads from the park headquarters to **Playa Naranjo**, 12km (7.5mi) away. It is only passable during the dry season (November to May), and even then a four-wheel drive vehicle is required. In fact, the road is in such poor condition that motorists often run into problems, so be sure to ask for authorization before setting out.

If you want to camp at Playa Naranjo and decide to go by foot, it will take you between 3 and 4hrs to get there. Don't forget to bring along a good supply of food and drinking water, enough to last you the duration of your stay. The other campground is located near Playa Nancite, 5km (3.1mi) farther north. There are two small, pleasant secondary trails along the road from the park headquarters to Playa Naranjo. On the left, **Los Patos** (1.5km or 0.9mi, each way) leads into the wooded valley of the Río Poza Salada.

A little farther and on the right, the **Mirador Valle Naranjo** (1km or 0.6mi, each way) leads to a lovely lookout from which you can admire the dry forest, the valley and part of Playa Naranjo and the Real estuary. South of the beach, the **Carbonal** trail (3km or 1.9mi, each way) runs along the Limbo lagoon, where howlers, white-faced capuchins and even spider monkeys can often be spotted.

To get to the **Murciélago sector**, leave the park and head north on the Interamericana (see p 225). This part of the park has campsites (*$1.25/pers./day, drinking water, showers, bathrooms*), picnic areas and a network of hiking trails, as well as several small, unpaved roads (four-wheel drive required) leading to the bays of **El Hachal**, **Santa Elena** and **Playa Blanca**. The Murciélago sector has a lengthy history. A farm named El Murciélago (The Bat) was built here in 1663 and served its original function until the 1970s, when it was purchased by the family of Nicaraguan dictator Anastasio Somoza and converted into a military base. The Costa Rican government expropriated the Somozas in 1979 and made the farm part of the Área de Conservación Guanacaste (ACG) in November 1980.

Refugio Nacional Bahía Junquillal

The Refugio Nacional Bahía Junquillal (*$1.50; every day 8am to 5pm; ☎/≈695-5598 or 695-5577*) lies about 20km (12.5mi) south of La Cruz (by way of Puerto Soley), which is the last sizeable town before the Nicaraguan border. This small nature reserve, which covers an area of just over 500ha (1,235 acres) and is also part of the Área de

Conservación

Parque Nacional Guanacaste is part of the **Área de Conservación Guanacaste** (ACG), whose headquarters are in Parque Nacional Santa Rosa. Located in the northwest part of the province of Guanacaste, the ACG includes three national parks, Guanacaste, Santa Rosa and Rincón de la Vieja, as well as the Refugio Nacional Bahía Junquillal and the Horizontes forestry station. It protects a total of over 120,000ha (296,516 acres) of land and 75,000ha (185,322 acres) of shoreline.

Conservación Guanacaste (ACG). It has a magnificent beach that stretches about 2km (1.2mi) and occasionally serves as a nesting ground for ridley, leatherback and green turtles.

In addition to lounging on the beach and observing the wide variety of aquatic birds, you can also go swimming and snorkelling here. A small trail known as **El Carao** leads about 600m (1,968ft) through the dry coastal forest, where you can observe the process of regeneration. Twenty-five campsites (*$1.25/pers./day*) have been laid out here, and visitors have access to picnic tables, grills, drinking water, restrooms and showers.

Parque Nacional Guanacaste

Parque Nacional Guanacaste ★ (*$6; every day 8am to 5pm; ☎/≈695-5598 or 695-5577*) was created on July 25, 1989, the provincial holiday. Covering an area of 32,512ha (80,336 acres), it is actually an extension of Parque Nacional Santa Rosa, which lies on the other (west) side of the Interamericana. This stretch of parkland forms a natural corridor that is crucial to the survival of all sorts of animals. Many of these species require vast hunting grounds; depending on the season,

they stalk their prey in the mountains, on the plains or along the shore. This park protects an assortment of natural habitats, all the way from the Pacific coast to the top of Cacao volcano, 1,659m (5,443ft) above sea level. Efforts are being made to create a similar natural corridor by joining Parque Nacional Guanacaste and Parque Nacional Rincón de la Vieja, just a few kilometres to the southeast. The project is going well, and only a small strip of land on either side of the highway remains to be protected between the two parks. However, as these pieces of land are privately owned, an agreement will probably require lengthy negotiations.

Authorities naturally want to keep Parque Nacional Guanacaste as pristine as possible, while still allowing visitors to admire the natural treasures contained within its boundaries. An emphasis has been placed on research, so that all the plant and animal species in the area can be identified. Scientists come here from all over the world to work, to help conduct research or to teach various techniques of biological cataloguing. Given that the park is home to 3,800 species of geometrids (large moths) alone, the project is quite complicated and

labourious—not to mention time-consuming!

Three research stations, **Maritza**, **Cacao** and **Pitilla**, were built so that scientists would not have to leave the park every evening after roaming the valleys and the mountains. Maritza stands at the foot of **Orosí Volcano** (1,487m or 4,879ft), while Cacao is at an altitude of 1,100m (3,609ft), near the volcano of the same name (1,659m or 5,443ft). Pitilla sits on the east side of Orosí, which receives more precipitation and is thus damper than the Pacific side of the volcano. The rivers on the volcano's east side flow eastward to the Caribbean Sea, just under 200km (124mi) away.

When these three stations are not occupied by researchers, visitors and tourists passing through the area are welcome to stay in them. The accommodations are rustic—dormitory-style rooms with shared bathrooms and no hot water. Reservations are required, and visitors must bring their own food. Though there are no actual campsites, you can pitch your tent near the stations *($1.25/pers./ day)* if you ask permission beforehand.

There are several hiking trails around the stations. **El Pedregal** (3km or 1.9mi total), near Maritza, runs through pastures and a transitional forest (tropical dry to tropical rain). It leads to the foot of Orosí, where you can admire some of the 800 pre-Columbian petroglyphs carved onto boulders made of volcanic rock. The **Cacao-Maritza trail** (6km or 3.7mi, each way) takes about 2hrs and links the two stations after which it is named, passing Casa Fran, a house used occasionally by park employees,along the way. If you want to climb to the **top of Cacao** (1,659m or 5,443ft), you are better off setting out from the Cacao station (2km or 1.2mi total) than the Maritza station (14km or 8.7mi total). From the Cacao station (1,100m or 3,609ft), the trail climbs continuously, winding its way through the tropical rain forest to the top of the volcano. It's a short (1km or 0.6mi each way) but steep hike (change in altitude: 559m or 1,834ft), requiring considerable effort. The top of the volcano is wooded, but there is a lookout that offers a sweeping view of the surrounding valleys.

Parque Nacional Rincón de la Vieja

Quite simply one of the most beautiful parks in Costa Rica, **Parque Nacional Rincón de la Vieja** ★★★ *($6; every day 7am to 5pm; ☎/=659-5598 or 659-5577)* has everything a nature lover and hiking enthusiast could hope to find. Oddly enough, it is only the ninth most popular park in the country. So get out there and enjoy it while it's still a well-kept secret! The park boasts magnificent scenery, breathtaking views, a distinctive volcano, soothing rivers, spectacular waterfalls, relaxing hot springs, places to swim, picnic areas, campgrounds and well-marked trails, not to mention detailed documentation (brochures and maps)—something of a rarity in Costa Rica.

Parque Nacional Rincón de la Vieja covers an area of 14,084ha 934,801 acres), and lies about 25km (15.5mi) northeast of Liberia, the capital of the province of Guanacaste. It is divided into two sectors, **Las Pailas** and **Santa María**, which are about 8km (5mi) apart. For directions to these sectors, see p 224. The park was created in 1973 to protect the region's rich plant and animal life and the many water sources that supply some parts of the province.

Anyone who has been to the arid regions of Guanacaste will be amazed by all the rivers in the park! Because the watershed runs along the Cordillera de Guanacaste and the Continental Divide, past

Rincón de la Vieja

The name Rincón de la Vieja (Old Woman's Place) comes from a Native American legend. Long ago, the great chief Curubandé's daughter, Princess Curubanda, fell in love with Prince Mixcoac, the chief of a neighbouring enemy tribe. When Curubandé learned of this dangerous liaison, he had the prince captured and taken to the top of the volcano. With no further ado, poor Mixcoac was thrown into the crater. Curubanda was so distraught that she lost her mind. It is said that she went to live at the top of the fear-some volcano to be near her deceased lover. A baby was later born of this tragic union. Wanting the child to live with his father, the grief-stricken princess threw him into the mouth of the crater as a final offering to her beloved. According to the legend, after years of isolation, Curubanda became a great healer, using plants, mud and volcanic ash. When people climbed the volcano to consult the *curendera* (healer), they would say *"voy para el rincón de la Vieja"* (I'm going to the old woman's place).

dating from 1851, describing eruptions, ash and smoke, are more plausible. Numerous minor eruptions were reported over the following years. Then, around 1967, when the volcano started spewing out large stones (up to 2kg or 4.4lbs), local residents began to fear the worst. Several forests and meadows were destroyed, and a number of rivers were polluted by toxic gases.

Further activity in 1983, 1984, 1991 and again in 1995 confirmed that the volcano was erupting regularly, as if to show that it could unleash its fury at any moment. The most recent eruption took place in the spring of 1998, mainly affecting the nearly uninhabited north side of the volcano, which faces Nicaragua. Fortunately, this side of the volcano has borne the brunt of the eruptions so far, while the south and west sides, where most of the villages, hotels, park facilities, trails and tourist attractions are located, have been spared. Vulcanologists believe that the numerous geysers and mudpots, which emit sulfurous fumes, allow for a constant release of internal pressure, reducing the risk of a major eruption.

The park's varied elevation, which ranges from 600 to nearly 2,000m (1,969 to 6,562ft), allows for a very wide

Rincón de la Vieja (1,895m or 6,217ft) and Santa María (1,916m or 6,286ft), the rivers flowing north and east empty into the Caribbean Sea, while those flowing south and west empty into the Pacific, watering Liberia and various villages along the way. No fewer than 32 rivers originate in the park, and 16 additional streams form during the rainy season. Many of these rivers link up with the Río Tempisque, the largest waterway in the province and one of the most impressive in all of Costa Rica.

Volcán Rincón de la Vieja, which has nine craters, has always attracted lots of attention. It is said that in the past, the volcano erupted so often that sailors making their way along the Pacific coast would use it as a sort of lighthouse. However, the first observation reports

The Province of Guanacaste

range of vegetation to grow here, a phenomenon which is enhanced by the frequent rainfall and fertile volcanic ash to which the region is exposed. A dry forest made up of species like the *guanacaste* (*Enterolobium cyclocarpum*), the laurel (*Cedrela odorata*) and the *cedro amargo* (*Cedrela odonta*) flourishes between 600m (1,969ft) and 1,200m (3,937ft) above sea level. Between 1,200m and 1,400m (3,937 and 4,593ft), where the rainfall is heaviest, is a rainforest characterized by the presence of numerous *copey* (*Clusia rosea*) trees, which thrive in this environment. Above 1,400m (4,593ft), the trees be-

come stunted before giving way to shrubs and moss. Lilac-coloured cattleya orchids, which are the national flower of Costa Rica and known as the *guaria morada*, also abound in the park.

The park's animal life is as fascinating as it is varied. With a little luck, and if you're very quiet, you'll see iguanas, agoutis, coatis, howlers, white-faced capuchins and spider monkeys. Less commonly seen creatures include armadillos, Baird's tapirs, peccaries, ocelots, pumas and jaguars. Some 300 avian species make their home here as well, most notably parrots, toucans, trogons (in-

cluding the odd quetzal), hummingbirds, doves, woodpeckers, owls and eagles. You'll also come across some magnificent butterflies.

Las Pailas Sector

This sector, located at the foot of Rincón de la Vieja, is named after the numerous "cauldrons" (*pailas*)—hot springs, geysers and mudpots—found here. At the information and welcome centre at the entrance to the sector, you can pick up documentation on the park (brochures and maps). A large model of the park is also on display. Nearby, on the Río Colorado, there are well-shaded campsites equipped with picnic

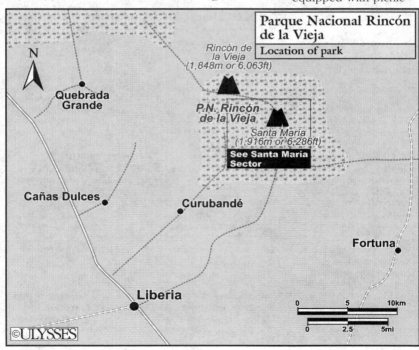

Parque Nacional Rincón de la Vieja

Location of park

N

Rincón de la Vieja
(1,848m or 6,063ft)

Quebrada Grande

P.N. Rincón de la Vieja

Santa María
(1,916m or 6,286ft)

See Santa María Sector

Cañas Dulces

Curubandé

Fortuna

Liberia

0   5   10km

0   2.5   5mi

©ULYSSES

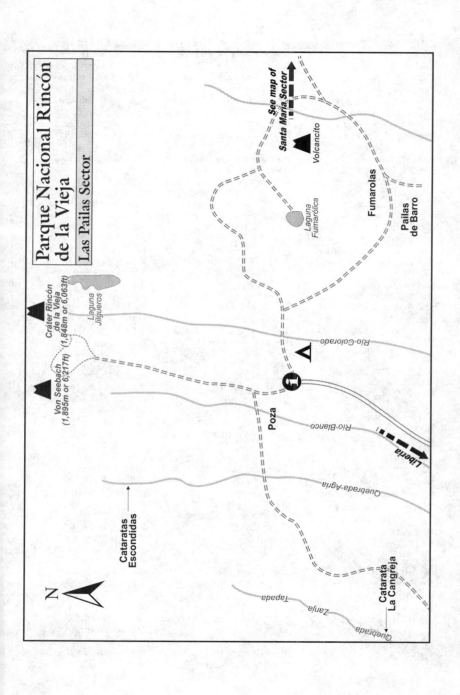

tables (*$1.25/pers./day, drinking water, showers, restrooms*).

If you only have a few hours, we strongly recommend taking the easy and fascinating **Pailas trail** (3km or 1.9mi), a loop that leads past a lovely waterfall, fumaroles, boiling mudpots and a miniature, newly formed volcano known as *volcancito*. You'll walk through fields and a luxuriant forest echoing with the cries of howler monkeys.

If you want to go to the **Santa María sector**, take the Pailas trail to the halfway point, where you'll see a sign for the

Be Careful!

Many visitors have suffered serious burns by applying masks of volcanic mud. If you're interested in trying out this beauty treatment, ask an experienced guide from the park or a local hotel for advice.

Also, be aware that very serious accidents have occured with tourists who have carelessly gone too close to the edge of a crater, so keep your distance!

path to follow. The welcome centres of the two sectors are about 8km (5mi) apart.

About 800m (2,625ft) from the Las Pailas welcome centre, you can take an invigorating dip in the cold waters of the **Río Blanco**. A short but steep little trail leads down to a swimming hole where hikers often come to cool off in the water or lounge about on the rocks.

In the same direction, but 4.3km (2.6mi, each way) from the welcome centre is a trail leading to the **Cataratas Escondidas** (Hidden Falls), three waterfalls located west of the Escondida and Agria streams. Two of the falls are visible from the canyon, but you have to walk a bit farther to see the third, where you'll also find a good spot to go swimming.

Even farther west and more to the south, you'll come to a magnificent waterfall known as **La Cangreja** (The Crab). At the foot of the falls, which plunge about 25m (82ft), a lovely pool with turquoise waters beckons visitors to go for a dip. La Cangreja is 5.1km (3.2mi each way) from the welcome centre.

If you want to climb to the **top of Rincón de la Vieja** (1,895m or 6,217ft), it is best to set

out around 7am or 8am, since the trail is about 16km (9.9mi, return) and takes 6 to 8hrs to hike (plus stops, picture taking, lunch, etc.). Furthermore, since there is a 900m (2,952ft) change in altitude and the trail climbs continuously, only those in reasonably good physical condition will be able to fully enjoy this memorable outing. By leaving early (allow at least 1hr for the drive from Liberia to the park), you will also avoid arriving at the top of the volcano in the late afternoon, when the clouds are more menacing, and finishing the hike in the dark (night falls at around 5:30pm), with matches or flashlight in hand. Don't forget to bring along warm, waterproof clothing, a sufficient supply of food and lots of water.

The first part of the trail leads through a dense forest where spider monkeys and woodpeckers thrive.

After 4km (2.5mi), the trees give way to shrubs and moss. The trail becomes more difficult, and you have to climb some big mud steps. From that point on, there is lots of wind, rain and fog. On the positive side, the trail is well marked with little flags, cairns and signs. At the top, it runs along the edge of the volcano and becomes very narrow—about 1m (3.3ft) wide! If the wind is blowing hard, which is often the case, it is wise to rope yourselves together to avoid any disastrous falls. You can relax and enjoy the 360 degree view until you get a lungful of sulfur fumes, at which point you'll probably feel like heading back. Because the trail is so steep, the trip down takes almost as long as the climb up.

Santa María Sector

This sector lies about 8km (5mi) east of Las Pailas, but you'll have to take a different road from Liberia (see p 224) if you want to drive there. One of the largest haciendas in this mountainous region was in operation here until 1973. Cattle and dairy cows were kept on the farm, which also produced coffee and sugarcane. Visitors can tour the main house, known as La Casona, which has been converted into a welcome centre (see p 242). One of the rooms contains an exhibition of photographs of the volcano and an assortment of tools that were once used at the hacienda.

There are picnic areas and campsites (*$1.25/pers./day, drinking water, showers, restrooms*) near La Casona. Next to the campsites, the **Colibrí trail** (500m or 1,640ft) leads through a secondary forest and to the place where the sugarcane used to be pressed.

On the east side of La Casona, is a short trail (about 500m or 1,640ft each way) which leads to a ***mirador*** that offers a magnificent view of the park, the surrounding plains, the town of Liberia and Volcán Miravalles (2,028m or 6,653ft). On the west side, another trail leads to the **Pailas de Agua Fría** (1.6km or 0.9mi, each way), or cold-water springs. Even closer to La Casona (1.1km or 0.7mi, each way), on the Río Zopitote, you'll find the lovely waterfall known as the **Bosque Encantado** (Enchanted Forest). One of the sector's main attractions,

Parque Nacional Rincón de la Vieja

Santa María Sector

N

Santa María
(1,916m or 6,286ft)

See Las Pailas Sector

Pailas de Agua Fría

Aguas Termales

Sendero El Colibrí

Mirador

Catarata

Bosque Encantado

Casona

Liberia

©ULYSSES

however, are the **Aguas Termales** (hot springs), located 2.8km (1.7mi, each way) from La Casona. Produced by volcanic activity, these hot, sulfurous springs are believed to have medicinal powers. Whether or not that's true, it is wonderfully relaxing to soak in them, and that's got to be good for you! Be careful not to get the sulfurous water in your eyes, though, and take a few short dips (about 5min at a time) rather than soaking for a long time.

Around Liberia

Liberia and Surroundings

The capital of the province of Guanacaste, **Liberia** ★ has a population of about 40,000. All in all, it is quite a pleasant town and has lots of shops and services, which can be helpful when you're heading off to the beaches or the local attractions. Liberia is bustling with activity during the day and remains lively at night.

If it doesn't seem that way to you, go to the big **Parque Central**. Shaded by lovely old trees during the day, the park fills with people after dinner. Calle Central, which runs between the park and the church of the Immaculate Conception has been turned into a pedestrian street, making the park that much more popular. The shrubbery around the Parque Central is home to scores of birds, who make quite a racket.

Playa del Coco and Surroundings

This is the first of the string of beaches that makes Guanacaste one of the country's major seaside resort areas. The three beaches in this region each offer a different atmosphere: Playa de Coco is a fishing port and mainly frequented by Ticos; by contrast, Playa Panamá comprises a series of huge, hotel complexes for tourists. Playa Hermosa is somewhere in between (geographically as well), as it attracts both Ticos and tourists.

Zebu

Playa del Coco ★ lies about 35km (22mi) from Liberia. One of the closest beaches to the capital, it was also one of the first in Guanacaste to attract tourists.

Playa del Coco is actually two beaches separated by a small stream, which is why it is sometimes referred to as Playas del Coco. Though they are right next to each other, each section has its own access road. Both are very popular, though the one to the south is more residential. People use all sorts of small boats to get around the little bay in which the beach is located, and these vessels are moored offshore. Playa del Coco has a pier and a small central park by the edge of the beach, and is surrounded by bars and inexpensive restaurants, many over 20 years old. All these factors make it a pleasant spot for visitors looking for an authentic Costa Rican experience. The farther you get from the centre of town, the newer the hotels become, as more are going up all the time. The area has been quite densely developed, and has a distinctly Costa Rican feel about it. Playa del Coco is also a bustling fishing port. The beach is fairly wide at low tide, but almost disappears at high tide.

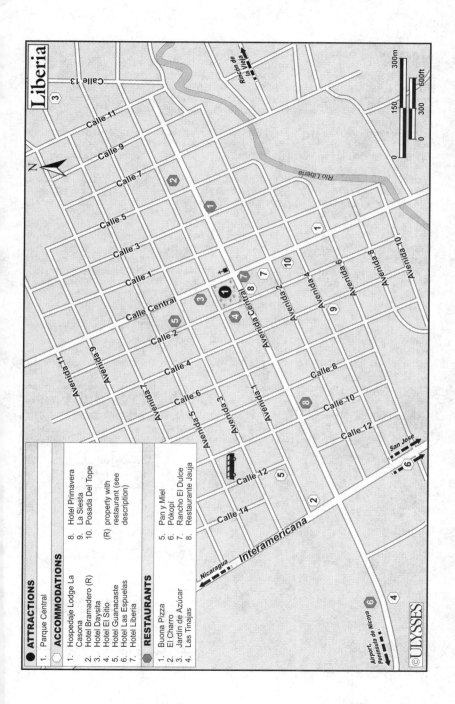

Liberia

ATTRACTIONS

● 1. Parque Central

ACCOMMODATIONS

1. Hospedaje Lodge La Casona
2. Hotel Bramadero (R)
3. Hotel Daysita
4. Hotel El Sitio
5. Hotel Guanacaste
6. Hotel Las Espuelas
7. Hotel Liberia

8. Hotel Primavera
9. La Siesta
10. Posada Del Tope

(R) property with restaurant (see description)

RESTAURANTS

1. Buona Pizza
2. El Charro
3. Jardín de Azúcar
4. Las Tinajas

5. Pan y Miel
6. Pókopí
7. Rancho El Dulce
8. Restaurante Jauja

© ULYSSES

Playa Ocotal lies a few kilometres farther south. If you're looking for peace and quiet but don't want to stray too far from town, you might want to try this magnificent little beach, which is nestled in a cove and flanked by steep slopes. For safety's sake, you should stick to the middle part of the beach if you want to go swimming.

Located to the north, **Playa Hermosa ★** ("Beautiful Beach" in Spanish) is also quieter (and cleaner) than Playa del Coco. It stretches 1.5km (0.9mi), and is nice and wide. Partly sheltered by a bay, the water here is relatively calm and

clear, and the sand is on the grey side. One of the best things about this beach is that it is fairly well shaded by the vegetation growing alongside it. It is also flanked by rocks, making it a good place to go surfing.

Playa Panamá, just north of Playa Hermosa, lies practically in the middle of the bay formed by the Punta Culebra, a spit of land a few kilometres farther north, so the water here is fairly calm. This beach has only been developed quite recently, because it is hidden away in a magnificent wooded area. Still, large-scale residential and resort developments, complete with an 18-hole golf course, have al-

ready been built. All these projects are supposedly "ecological", meaning sizeable portions of the land is supposed to be kept in its natural state. Nevertheless, the presence of humans is evident throughout.

Around Filadelfia

You have to go through **Filadelfia** and **Belén** to get to the beaches south of the Liberia area. The road from Belén leads to two groups of beaches (those around Flamingo and those around Tamarindo) that have been undergoing residential and tourist development for several years now.

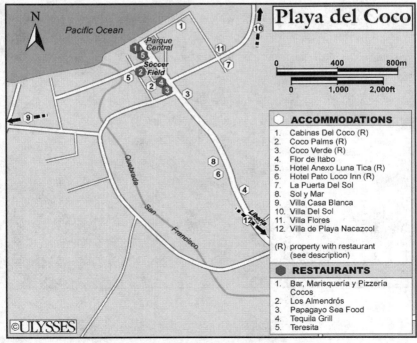

Playa del Coco

N

Pacific Ocean

Parque Central

Soccer Field

Quebrada

San Francisco

Liberia

0   400   800m

0   1,000   2,000ft

⬤ ACCOMMODATIONS

1. Cabinas Del Coco (R)
2. Coco Palms (R)
3. Coco Verde (R)
4. Flor de Itabo
5. Hotel Anexo Luna Tica (R)
6. Hotel Pato Loco Inn (R)
7. La Puerta Del Sol
8. Sol y Mar
9. Villa Casa Blanca
10. Villa Del Sol
11. Villa Flores
12. Villa de Playa Nacazcol

(R) property with restaurant (see description)

⬤ RESTAURANTS

1. Bar, Marisquería y Pizzería Cocos
2. Los Almendrós
3. Papagayo Sea Food
4. Tequila Grill
5. Teresita

©ULYSSES

Playa Flamingo and Surroundings

There are actually six beaches along this part of the coast, but we have lumped them all together under the name of the swankiest of the group, Playa Flamingo, which is this area's hub.

Playa Flamingo ★ is both a point that extends into a bay and a strip of white sand (it used to be called Playa Blanca, meaning "White Beach"). The only full-service marina on the northwest coast is located here. Playa Flamingo is a mecca for sport fishing and hosts an annual tournament. Many affluent people have a secondary residence on the shore here. There are a few restaurants and stores selling consumer goods (including a supermarket) at the base of the point, the rest of which is occupied by big hotels and upscale residential complexes. It is fashionable (and quite expensive) to stay at Playa Flamingo.

Not far to the south, **Playa Brasilito** is the exact opposite of Playa Flamingo. A little village made up mainly of middle-class homes (permanent and vacation), it doesn't have much appeal except for its authenticity and the fact that it is still relatively undeveloped. The sand in this area is quite grey.

Immediately south of Playa Brasilito, gorgeous **Playa Conchal** ★★ is aptly named (*concha* is the Castilian word for shell), since a large part of it is covered with shells. In fact, you'll even find shells in the strip of vegetation growing alongside it and in the water as well, blanketing the ocean floor immediately offshore. The beach is dominated by the famous Melia Playa Conchal hotel complex (see p 266).

North of Flamingo, the shore is interspersed with several other beaches, which are nearly undeveloped and thus feel more private.

The first of these, **Playa Potrero**, attracts few beach-goers. A 4km (2.5mi) long, curving strip of brownish-grey sand, it is nonetheless perfect for swimming. A little farther, you'll come to **Playa Penca**, a white sandy beach. Still farther north lies another white-sand beach, **Playa Pan de Azúcar**.

Playa Tamarindo and Surroundings

We have named this part of the province after Tamarindo simply because the town is a populous centre. The road out of the village actually leads to a vast region encompassing **Parque Nacional Marino Las Baulas** ★★ (see p 250) and the two beaches at its edges (Playa Grande and Playa Tamarindo).

Primarily a surfer's hangout, **Playa Grande** ★★★ is a magnificent, uncrowded beach right near Parque Nacional Marino Las Baulas. Sheltered by the park, it is very clean and has lovely, light-coloured sand. The beach is accessed by a bumpy road that leads through the park. Developers are presently negotiating with park authorities so that they can start building hotels in this heavenly spot. Sites have already been cleared for residential development some distance from the beach, outside the park's boundaries. Since the roads still need some work, the few local inhabitants are living pretty much in the wild. At the same time, roads have been cleared through the forest and are simply waiting to be paved. A few houses and hotels have sprung up here and there. Nevertheless, there are barely a dozen oceanfront homes on the 3km (1.8mi) long beach.

Though **Playa Tamarindo** ★ is under continuous development, most of the hotels built here are smaller than those at Playa Flamingo. Still, the place is attracting more and more people, particularly surfers, and several surf shops have

The Province of Guanacaste

opened up in town. The beach itself is a long strip of white sand with little vegetation growing along it, so the village is somewhat dusty. **Warning**: The surf can be quite heavy and there are lots of rocks jutting out of the water offshore. Keep your distance from the estuaries or you might find yourself carried out to sea by the currents.

Playa Langosta lies at the far end of Playa Tamarindo, nestled in a bend in the shoreline. In recent years, this beach has started to see some of the development that has been going on in Tamarindo. This is a great spot for surfing, especially near the little river that empties into the ocean.

Parque Nacional Marino Las Baulas

If you're looking for a fascinating, moving and enriching experience, head to **Parque Nacional Marino Las Baulas ★★** (*$6, guided tour included; open year-round,* ☎/≈680-0779) to watch **leatherback turtles** (*Demochelys coriacea*) lay their eggs on **Playa Grande**. This spectacle can be observed nearly every night from October to March, particularly in December and January.

Parque Nacional Marino Las Baulas has a total area of 22,500ha (55,596 acres), only 500 (1,235 acres) of which

are on land. It was created in 1991 to protect this breeding site, one of the largest in the world. Over the years, the area had become overrun with tourists, some of whom were so careless that they would ride around on the turtles' backs!

Nowadays, park officials keep a close watch over the beach during the laying season and visitors are only welcome in groups and must be accompanied by a guide. Unfortunately, the guides usually speak in Spanish and might not be able to explain the egg-laying process in English. If you aren't fluent in Spanish, stop by the El mundo de la tortuga museum (see below) before your outing to get a better understanding of what you are about to see.

Turtle Observation

A number of rules should be followed. One of the most important is to keep quiet and stay behind the turtle so you don't frighten it. The use of cameras with flashes and video cameras with lighting is also strictly forbidden.

The **El Mundo de la Tortuga museum ★★** (*$5, children admitted free of charge; every day after 4pm, early Oct to mid-Mar; just before the park entrance,* ☎/≈653-0471) is a must if you want to learn more about sea turtles in general and leatherbacks in particular. Furthermore, if you're planning a trip to Parque Nacional Marino Las Baulas to watch the leatherbacks lay their eggs, this is the perfect place to wait for the tide to go down, since it has a small outdoor café and a souvenir shop where you can while away the time (sometimes several hours).

When you enter the museum, you will be given a headset. The 30min recorded tour (available, in English, French, Spanish and German) takes you to 27 stops, where you'll see stunning photographs of these impressive but vulnerable creatures and gain insight into their reproductive cycle, how they live, the threats they face and the efforts being made to protect them. The tour ends at the souvenir shop, where the staff will gladly answer any questions you might have. This museum is sure to touch your heart and fill you with wonder. Those who know nothing about leatherback turtles will emerge 30min later feeling that they understand the captivating world of the biggest sea turtles on Earth. For this reason, we strongly recommend visiting the museum before going to the park, not after.

The museum opened in 1996, thanks to the efforts of three French-men and a Spaniard with a passion for marine turtles. In 1994, Corina Esteban, one of the museum's founders, came to the region and worked as a volunteer at Parque Nacional Marino Las Baulas. Shortly thereafter, she had the idea of open-ing a small museum so that tourists could learn about the turtles they would be observing. Park officials are thrilled with the museum. Furthermore, the park guides and museum staff talk to each other by walkie-talkie while waiting for the

The Leatherback

Las Baulas is the plural of the Costa Rican name for the leather-back *(la baula)*. This giant turtle, which grows to a length of 1.5 to 2m (6.6ft) and weighs around 500kg or 1,184lbs (the record is about 900kg or 1,984lbs), can dive to depths of over 1,300m (4,265ft). Researchers Karen and Scott Eckert calculated that it takes a leatherback turtle an average of 37min to reach a depth of over 1,200m (3,937ft). Its size and diving feats aren't the only things that distinguish the leatherback from your average turtle, howe-ver; it also has an elongated shape and seven clearly visible ridges along the length of its shell. Further-more, the shell is not made of the same hard substance as that of other marine turtles, but rather of thick, leathery skin; hence the turtle's name.

Leatherbacks feed almost exclusively on jellyfish. Sadly, many choke to death each year after ingesting plastic bags that litter the sea and can easily be mistaken for jelly-fish. The leatherback makes one of the longest migratory voyages of any animal in the world. One tagged turtle was found nearly 6,000km (3,728mi) from its usual breeding site! Female leatherbacks supposedly return to the same beach every two or three years to lay their eggs. On the Pacific coast, the laying season falls between October and March; on the Atlantic, between April and August.

During the egg-laying season, each female returns to the same beach four to 10 times to lay eggs. Using her front flippers, she digs a hole about 70cm (27.6in) deep, in which she lays nearly 100 soft-shelled eggs, each about the size of a tennis ball. Once she has finished, she care-fully covers the hole with sand and heads back into the water. The incubation period lasts about 68 days, after which the hat-chlings make their way to the sea, guided by the moonlight reflected on the water. Unfortunately, they sometimes get confu-sed by the lights of the houses and hotels along the beach and head inland, where they succumb to dehy-dration or exhaustion.

The Province of Guanacaste

Important Notice

The turtles only lay their eggs on the beach at night, during low tide. To avoid a long wait, we strongly recommend calling the El Mundo de la Tortuga museum a few hours beforehand to get an update on the tides and find out the best time to go.

turtles to arrive at night, so that everyone knows when a turtle has made it to the beach and the tourists can be divided up into groups.

The museum offers a package rate to visitors staying in the Playa Grande and Tamarindo areas.

Around Santa Cruz

Santa Cruz and Surroundings

Its *fiestas* (particularly those in January) and distinctive regional cuisine make **Santa Cruz** the national folklore capital of Costa Rica. There is nothing really special about the town itself, though it does have a lovely central park, an attractive modern church, an historic bell tower and a pretty little public square. On the east side of the square, is a small covered market that is open at night and sells good produce, among other things.

The little village of **Guaitil ★** is about 12km (7.5mi) east of Santa Cruz and known for its magnificent pottery (vases, plates, bowls, etc.). Most of the pieces are made according to Amerindian designs, using traditional Chorotega (the pre-Columbian inhabitants of this region) decorations and natural colours. The artisans sell their pottery themselves, and it is fun to go from one house to the next and chat with them. You will likely hear that some families of craftsmen are descendants of the Chorotegas. Though Guaitil attracts plenty of tourists (therefore try to go in the late afternoon), the prices are still very affordable. You'll find all sorts of small items that can easily fit in your suitcase. The small paved road leading to the village is absolutely lovely and makes for a delightful trip. You'll pass by tall trees, pastures and herds of zebus. If you don't have a car, you can take the bus from Santa Cruz.

Playa Junquillal and Surroundings

The town of Santa Cruz is the gateway to the Playa Junquillal area, which is relatively undeveloped in comparison to Playa Tamarindo and Playa Flamingo farther north. To get to this part of the coast, you have to take a bumpy road, which is particularly bad right near Santa Cruz. Four-wheel drive vehicles are recommended.

Playa Avellanas is fully exposed to the sea: unlike Sámara, farther south, it is not protected by coral reefs, which curb the power of the surf. It is thus perfect for surfing but unsuitable for swimming, particularly its central portion, where rocks can be seen jutting out of the water. Located some 5km (3.1mi) from Playa Junquillal, Playa Avellanas is also relatively isolated.

Playa Junquillal is bounded by tall grass, which distinguishes it from most of the other beaches in the country. This place truly feels like the middle of nowhere, and what little activity there is centres entirely around the hotels. There are only a few little hotels scattered about in the forest and on the waterfront, which comprises 1km (0.6mi) long stretch of clean, dark sand. The water is not very deep and the surf is quite heavy.

Playa Negra is a nearly undeveloped, dark-sand beach just north of Playa Junquillal, and is perfect for surfing.

Around Nicoya

Nicoya and Surroundings

The city of **Nicoya** ★ (named after an early 16th-century Native American chief) is the peninsula's commercial hub. It is also the centre of activity for the local cattle industry and hosts a rodeo every July. Nicoya lays claim to the **second oldest colonial church in the country** ★, which stands at the northeast corner of its central park.

Nicoya's church

The town serves mainly as a gateway for people exploring the region, particularly **Parque Nacional Barra Honda** ★ (see p 254) and the beaches around Sámara. Many Chinese people immigrated to Nicoya in the past, and their descendants own a good number of the local businesses.

Nosara, Sámara and Carrillo are the seaside

resorts in this part of the province. Sámara lies between the two others and is the most populous of the three. There are also two stretches of protected wilderness in the area, both immediately north of Nosara: the **Refugio Nacional de Fauna Silvestre de Ostional** ★ (see p 256) and the **Reserva Biológica de Nosara** (see below).

Playa Nosara and Surroundings

The **Reserva Biológica de Nosara**, which lies along the coast north of Nosara, is a private wildlife reserve with Swiss owners.

Located along the **Río Nosara**, it contains mangrove swamps and a rainforest which are home to over 170 species of birds, as well as monkeys, *jaguarundis*, crabs, reptiles and amphibians. If you want to visit the reserve, your best option is to stay at the owners' nearby hotel, the Lagarta Lodge (see p 273).

The village of **Nosara** is in the middle of the area immediately south of the reserve (5km or 3.1mi inland), but has no attractions per se. However, the regional airport, the **Aeropuerto de Nosara**, is located here, along with various services, including a gas station and a fairly well-stocked supermarket.

The **countryside around Playa Nosara** ★ (between Nosara and the beach) is scattered with a small number of restaurants and places to stay. The area is being developed but the process is still in its early stages, so visiting here will still give you a good feel for life in the Costa Rican jungle. Nosara's **Playa Pelada** is not suitable for swimming, particularly the section with the public entrance. Though pretty, the beach is pounded by heavy surf and hemmed in by large rocks on either side.

Nosara's **Playa Guiones** lies south of Playa Pelada, on the other side of the Punta Garza.

Playa Sámara and Surroundings

The area immediately surrounding **Playa Sámara** ★★ can be divided into three sections. First, there is **Buena Vista**, a large, uninhabited (and thus quiet) beach a short distance north of crowded Sámara. To get there, take Isla Chora street north from the village of Sámara. Next is **Playa Congrejal**, which is more or less the northern extension of Playa Sámara and has a few hotels and restaurants. Finally, there is **Playa Sámara** itself, a pretty beach that is protected by coral reefs and thus has calm waters perfect for swimming. The village of Sámara, located alongside the beach, offers a fairly broad range of services for the region—it even has a few bars and night-clubs worth checking out (see p 286).

Samara Beach is one of the finest in the country. But if you're even more adventurous, be sure to visit Carillo, only 5km (3mi) from Samara. The crescent-shaped **Playa Carillo ★★**, with its shimmering white sand, is breathtaking. Nestled against a grove of coco-nut trees that resembles an emerald necklace, with the waves of the sea gently lapping the shore, this almost de-serted oasis is pure paradise. There are no services at Playa Carillo, but the village of Punta Carillo is a little to the south. Please respect the regu-lations here to protect this haven from pollu-tion.

The road to Playa Carrillo also leads to the other beaches south of Sámara, including **Playa Camaronal**.

Parque Nacional Barra Honda

Parque Nacional Barra Honda ★ *($6; every day 7am to 4pm; ☎/≠659-9039 or 659-9194)* lies 23km (14.3mi) north-east of the little town of Nicoya. It was created in 1974 to protect the numerous caves, some very deep, that had just been found. Most local residents didn't know this network of caves existed before it was discovered by members of Costa Rica's speology association in the early 1970s. They believed that these holes in the mountain

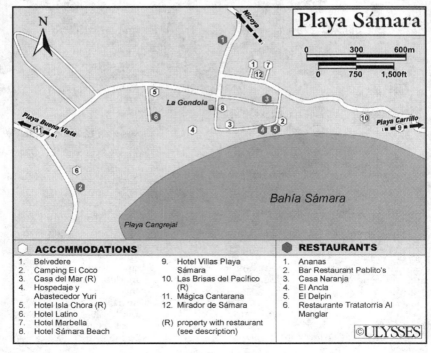

Playa Sámara

La Gondola

Playa Buena Vista

Playa Carrillo

Bahía Sámara

Playa Cangrejal

ACCOMMODATIONS		
1.	Belvedere	
2.	Camping El Coco	
3.	Casa del Mar (R)	
4.	Hospedaje y Abastecedor Yuri	
5.	Hotel Isla Chora (R)	
6.	Hotel Latino	
7.	Hotel Marbella	
8.	Hotel Sámara Beach	
9.	Hotel Villas Playa Sámara	
10.	Las Brisas del Pacífico (R)	
11.	Mágica Cantarana	
12.	Mirador de Sámara	

(R) property with restaurant (see description)

RESTAURANTS	
1.	Ananas
2.	Bar Restaurant Pablito's
3.	Casa Naranja
4.	El Ancla
5.	El Delpin
6.	Restaurante Tratatorria Al Manglar

©ULYSSES

Matapalo

Matapalo, literally "tree killer," is the name commonly applied to certain tree species, like the *ficus*, that grow at the expense of another species. Large, strong, erect trees are invaded by the tentacles of the plant that grows by strangling it. The process starts when the seed of a *matapalo* falls on the crown of a healthy tree. The *matapalo* then starts extracting the latter's sap and sends down long shoots resembling lianas, attached to the trunk. Once these reach the ground, they bury themselves in the earth and develop roots. The process takes time of course, tens sometimes even hundreds of years, but the shoots multiply, grow larger and finally fuse together, creating a new truck wrapped completely around the first. The worst thing about this easy-to-observe phenomenon is that it occurs frequently and is very beautiful! On your walks, you'll soon spot these wooden lianas sculpting lovely curves along a condemned trunk.

were of volcanic origin. However, the rumblings they heard and attributed to the volcano actually came from huge cavities inside the mountain.

Barra Honda is the name of the mountain that towers over the plain from an altitude of 423m (1,388ft). It is about 60 million years old and was forced from the depths of the sea by tectonic pressure. The mountain is composed mainly of limestone and, due to the effects of rain and carbon dioxide, has become riddled with caves where stalactites and stalagmites have formed over the centuries.

Since the 1970s, 42 caves have been discovered. To date, scientists have explored 19 of them, the longest being Santa Ana, which is 240m (787ft) deep. Tourists can safely explore **Terciopelo**, a 62m (203ft) deep cave which got its name because a dead fer-de-lance, one of the most poisonous and dangerous snakes in the world, was found here when the cave was first being explored. Fortunately, no others, either alive or dead, have been seen here since. For now, Terciopelo is the only cave open to the public, and **visitors must be accompanied by a local guide** (*about $25/pers., and much less for a group; a maximum of eight people may visit* *the cave at once; reservations required;* ☎*685-5580 or 685-5667).* Using safety cords, you will be lowered to a depth of 20m (66ft), where you can admire some stalagmites (projecting upward from the ground) and stalactites (hanging down from the roof of the cave) whose distinctive shapes (columns, pearls, flowers, mushrooms, etc.) have earned them evocative names. One is called **El Organo** (The Organ) because it makes all sorts of sounds when you tap on the stalagmites and stalactites.

Among the other caves in the park, **La Trampa** has the longest continuous descent (52m or 170ft) and the largest galleries discovered so far. **Pozo Hediondo** is home to the largest concentration of bats in the park. From an historical point of view, however, **Nicoa** is the most interesting, since human skeletal remains were discovered inside it along with pre-Columbian objects, which would indicate that it was a burial place. Supposedly, explorers even found a stalagmite that had formed on a human skull!

Though Parque Nacional Barra Honda is not very big, visitors only have access to its southwestern part, where the welcome centre, park headquarters, picnic areas and campsites (*$1.25/ pers./day*) are located. Campfires are not permitted due to the risk of forest fires. If you don't have food or a portable stove, you can eat at the park's facilities if you reserve your meal a day ahead.

The lovely hiking trail called **Los Laureles** is a 9.3km(5.8mi) loop that leads past the park's most interesting sites. The outing takes 3 to 5hrs. Though the trail leads all the way to the top of the **Cerro Barra Honda** (423m or 1,388ft), 70% of it is flat, so it makes for an easy hike. The view from the hilltop is stunning, encompassing a large part of the Gulfo de Nicoya, Chira Island

and a vast plain covered with forests and little villages.

The trail also goes past the famous cave known as Terciopelo and offers hikers a chance to observe the local plant and animal life, which are perfectly adapted to the mountain rising up in the midst of the plains. The park is home to numerous species of trees, including the *matapalo*, the *javillo*, the laurel and the *tempisque*. Some of these bear fruit, providing a feast for many of the animals who inhabit the area (bats, parrots, macaws, agoutis, white-tailed deer, monkeys, etc.).

Agouti

Since it can get incredibly hot in the park (over 35°C) in the afternoon, it is very important to bring along plenty of fresh water on your outings. Furthermore, the fact that two German tourists disappeared in 1992 after venturing onto a part of the mountain that was supposed to be off-limits to visitors should be enough to convince you to stick to the trails. This unfortu-

nate incident, which made news all over the country and found its way into most travel guides, has unfortunately led to a drop in the number of tourists visiting the park.

Refugio Nacional de Fauna Silvestre de Ostional

The **Refugio Nacional de Fauna Silvestre de Ostional ★** (*$6; open year-round;* ☎/≈659-9039 *or 659-9194*) lies about 50km (31mi) southwest of the town of Nicoya, by Playa Nosara and Playa Ostional. It is 8km (5mi) long but only a few hundred metres wide, covering a total area of 162ha (400 acres) of land and an additional 587ha (1,450 acres) of sea. The sanctuary was created in order to protect an area where thousands of marine turtles come to lay their eggs each year.

Playa Ostional and Playa Nancite, both in Parque Nacional Santa Rosa (see p 238), are considered the most important breeding sites in the world for the **olive ridley turtle** (*Lepidochelys olivacea*), which Costa Ricans refer to as the *tortuga lora*. These turtles are relatively small (40kg or 88lbs on average) compared to leatherbacks (360kg or 793lbs), but they come to this beach by the thousands to lay their eggs. This remarkable nocturnal phenomenon, known as *arribadas* (massive influxes), takes place frequently between July and November and most often in August and September. The touching and unique spectacle can thus be observed nearly every month, usually when the moon is in its third quarter. Even if there are no *arribadas* during your visit, you'll probably still see a few lone turtles.

In addition to the ridley, certain other kinds of turtles, including the **leatherback** (*Dermochelys coriacea*) and the **green turtle** (*Chelonia mydas*) sometimes lay their eggs at the Refugio Nacional de Fauna Silvestre de Ostional as well. Even if there are no turtles to be seen during your visit, you'll certainly have a chance to observe some capuchin monkeys and hear the loud calls of howler monkeys in the forest bordering the beach. You're also likely to see iguanas, coatis, crabs and some of the 100 species of birds that live in the area. There is a mangrove swamp southeast of the sanctuary, at the mouth of the Río Nosara, while Punta India, a rocky point strewn with numerous pools of water teeming with marine life, lies to the northwest.

Outdoor Activities

Cycling

Small, unpaved trails (not the hiking paths) in **Guanacaste** and **Santa Rosa parks** are wonderful for mountain-biking. The trail from La Casona to Playa Naranjo (12km or 7.5mi) and Playa Nancite (5km or 3.1mi north of Naranjo) in Parque Nacional Santa Rosa is especially worth mentioning. To rent a bicycle, ask at your hotel reception or Liberia's tourist information office. At press time, the bicycle shop at the centre of town had closed down.

Hiking

Parque Nacional Rincón de la Vieja (see p 240) has by far the best network of hiking trails in Guanacaste, and one of the best in the country in general. The climb to the top of the Volcán Rincón de la Vieja is very challenging, but is one of the most superb mountain hikes in Costa Rica, along with that of Cerro Chirripó.

Parque Nacional Barra Honda (see p 254) also has an enjoyable 10km (6.2mi) long trail. If you are looking for a shorter trek, go to **Parque Nacional Santa Rosa** (see p 236), which is easy to get to and has an interesting history.

Rafting

Safaris Corobicí
Cañas
☎/≈*669-1091*
The Safaris Corobicí agency specializes in rafting, particularly on the Río Corobicí, as its name indicates.

Fishing

Guanacaste is one of the best places in Costa Rica for deep-sea fishing. Many hotels offer excursions during the fishing season, or can refer you to a local agency. If not, contact the **Americana Fishing Services** (☎*223-4331*, ≈*221-0096*) to get the name of the nearest agency that offers such excursions.

The owner of the French bakery and restaurant **El Cocodrilo** (*Tamarindo*, ☎*653-0661*, ≈*653-0255*), located at the entrance of Tamarindo (next to the lagoon of the same name), also has two fishing boats available for the excursion of your choice *(around $300/half day)*. Drop by the restaurant near the end of the day to discuss the next day's trip. He can also take you to some interesting places for snorkelling.

Surfing

Most beaches in Guanacaste are known for their good surfing conditions. The Protero Grande, Naranjo (Witch's Rock), Grande, Tamarindo, Langosta, Avellanas, Negra and Nosara beaches are considered excellent. **Basoa Surf Expeditions** *(☎257-1138)* and **Papagayo Surf Trips** *(☎670-0354)* organize surfing expeditions.

Scuba Diving and Snorkelling

Scuba Diving and snorkelling are possible all along Guanacaste's coast, especially in the province's northwest. The Hermosa, Del Coco, Ocotal and Flamingo beaches are reputed to be excellent places to practice these sports. **Bill Beard's Diving Safari** *(☎/≈670-0012)*, **Rich Coast Diving Company** *(☎/≈670-0176)*, **El Ocotal Diving Safari** *(☎222-4259)* and **Resort Divers de Costa Rica** *(☎/≈670-*

0421) offer diving lessons and excursions.

Horseback Riding

Los Inocentes
☎679-9190
≈265-6431
East of Santa Cruz, the Los Inocentes farm is the best place for horseback riding in this part of Guanacaste. The horses are properly trained and well-treated. Various outings into the mountains and through the countryside are organized.

Bird-Watching

Parque Nacional Palo Verde (see p 232) is well-known for the diversity and abundance of its bird species. Close to 300 types of birds have been spotted here.

Parque Nacional Santa Rosa (see p 236) is home to nearly 250 species of birds in its many different natural habitats (sea, beach, pastures, mountains, etc.).

Golf

The **Ranchos Las Colinas** *(☎/≈654-4089)* golf club at **Playa Grande** has an

18-hole course.

The **Melia Beach and Golf Resort** *(☎654-4123)* at **Playa Conchal** has an 18-hole course along the Pacific Ocean.

Canopy Tours

North of Liberia

Close to Hacienda Guachipelin near Parque Nacional Ricón de la Vieja, the **Original Canopy Tour Company** *($45; ☎257-5149; ≈256-7626; www.canopytour.com)* offers a canopy tour that is a little different from the others since it takes you down into a canyon. Discover the magnificent beauty of the Kazm Canyon as you descend on pulleys and cables between connecting platforms, hanging safely from a harness! Scale the canyon walls! The ultimate experience!

Situated on the road that climbs to the national park of the same name, the **Rincón de la Vieja Volcano Mountain Lodge** *(☎/≈695-5553)* offers **canopy tours** *($50 for 4hrs, or $77 for the day)*, which allow you to view the forest from 16 solid platforms high in the treetops.

Water Sports

Aquasport
on the road along the beach
☎*670-0450*
Aquasport rents sports equipment on Playa Hermosa.

Flamingo has a **Marina** (☎/≈*654-4203)* offering all kinds of services.

Accommodations

In addition to the hotels listed here, it's also possible to rent houses or condos in Costa Rica, particularly in Guanacaste, for longer stays, or if you come with a family or large group.

Around Tilarán-Cañas-Bagaces

For the region north of Tilarán, around Lake Arenal, see "The North" chapter.

Tilarán

Cabinas El Sueño
$
hw, pb, ⊗, tv
next to the cathedral
☎*695-5347*
Cabinas El Sueño rents basic clean rooms with a large balcony from which you can see what's happening on the street. You can also rent a television.

Hotel Tilarán
$-$$
sb/pb, hw, ℜ, tv
west side of the cathedral park
☎*695-5043*
Hotel Tilarán is behind the restaurant of the same name. The rooms are small and lacking in charm, but clean.

Hotel Naralit
$$
hw, pb, ctv, ⊗, ℝ
on the south side of the cathedral
☎*695-5393*
≈*695-6767*
Hotel Naralit is by far the best deal in Tilarán in terms of quality/price ratio. The lobby is nothing special, but the place is well-kept, and the rooms are comfortably furnished—they even have desks. The hotel has been laid out with green spaces. You can ask for a refrigerator for your room.

Cañas

Hotel Guillen and **Hotel El Parque** (*$; sb/pb, ⊗; south side of the central park;* ☎*669-0070 for Guillen,* ☎*669-2213 for El Parque)* are perfect for travellers on a low budget who aren't fussy about room size and amenities.

La Pacífica
$$$$
hw, pb, ⊗, ≡, ≈, ℜ
5km north of Cañas, on the Interamericana
☎*669-0050 or 220-4047*
≈*669-0555*
pacifica@racsa.co.cr
One of the best places to stay in the area is the *hacienda* La Pacífica.

Horseback rides, mountain bike excursions and hikes are organized along the property's trails, most notably along Río Corobicí. Hacienda La Pacífica is more than a hotel—it is an example of sustainable development, combining cattle-raising, cultural tourism, reforestation and forest conservation. Guests stay in charming little well-ventilated *cabinas* with big windows that let in a lot of light. Each has a patio that leads onto the rest of the vast premises (most *cabinas* have two units). Unfortunately, it seems that Pacífica is exclusively reserved for use by Costa Rican companies.

Bagaces

Albergue Bagaces
$$
pb, ⊗, ℜ
on the Interamericana, east side of the gas station
☎*671-1267*
Albergue Bagaces is the best place to stay in town. The rooms are simple, but the bathrooms are impeccable. The owners are British. Breakfast is served in the restaurant (see p 277).

Parque Nacional Palo Verde

The Organization for Tropical Studies, which protects the park's natural environment, has dormitories *(45 beds)* for researchers, students and anyone interested in staying here (*40$/person, meals incl.; sb; ☎240-3671, ⇋240-6783, pverde@ns.ots.ac.cr*). This place is very popular, so reservations should be made one month in advance. It takes 45min to get to the park from Bagaces on a relatively well-maintained dirt road. Camping is also permitted (*$1.25/pers./day, bathrooms, showers and running water*) next to the park warden's residence.

North of Liberia

Cabinas Santa Rita
$
pb
opposite the Tribunales de Justicia, La Cruz
☎*697-9062*
Cabinas Santa Rita are worth keeping in mind for their good price.

Amalia's Inn
$$$
hw, pb, ≈, ⊗
main street, La Cruz
☎*697-9181*
Amalia's Inn is a family-style inn (more like a bed and breakfast) run by a friendly elderly lady. The rooms are tastefully decorated and large—they even have a sofa to relax on! There is a magnificent view of Bahía Salinas from here.

Colinas del Norte
$$$
pb, hw, ≈, ℜ
6km (3.7mi) north of La Cruz, on the Interamericana
☎/⇋*679-9132 or 284-3972*
Colinas del Norte is an interesting hotel north of La Cruz. Its guest rooms and common areas are tastefully decorated with wood furnishings. There is a beautiful view of the surrounding area from the rooms. The hotel has a weekend nightclub and an Italian restaurant called Marco Polo (see p 277), which also serves Costa Rican dishes.

Hacienda Guachipelin
$$$ bkfst incl.
sb/pb, hw
5km (3.1mi) from the Parque Nacional Rincón de la Vieja "Las Pailas" entrance via the road to Curubande
☎*442-2818 or 284-2049*
⇋*442-1910*
www.guachipelin.com
Hacienda Guachipelin is on a 100-year-old ranch. Though the rooms in the lodge are simple, the whole pleasure of staying here is in the experience of farm life. The hacienda is involved in a reforestation project on 40% of its 1,300ha (3,212 acres). Various excursions to Parque Rincón de la Vieja and the surrounding area—are organized: the Azufrales hot springs, the Las Pailas sands, the volcano, the Jilgueros lagoon, the falls, etc. Live like a cowboy and take all

your meals communally on site in the heart of Guanacaste country!

⛵ Los Inocentes
$$$$
hw, pb, ≈, ℜ
14km (8.7mi) off the Interamericana on the road that leads to Upala and Santa Cecilia, several km before La Cruz
☎/⇋*265-5484 or 679-9190*
It's home on the range at Los Inocentes, a horse and cattle ranch. The place is off the beaten tourist track and has a relaxed atmosphere with its wooden lodge, spacious common rooms, hammocks and rocking chairs. The owners have become increasingly dedicated to conservation and sustainable development since they began their cattle-raising enterprise. People come from all over to participate in Los Inocentes' hiking and horseback riding excursions, which are just some of the goodies in store for you here. The hacienda borders Parque Nacional Guanacaste to the north. The rooms are simple and comfortable, and the service is attentive. There is also a good view of the Volcán Orosí from here.

Rincón de la Vieja Volcano Mountain Lodge
$$$$
pb, ≈, ℜ
Apartado Postal 114-5000 Liberia
☎*666-0473 or 661-8156*
⇋*666-1887*
This pleasant hotel is situated at the foot of the Rincón de la Vieja

Volcano, at the entrance to the park a few kilometres past Hacienda Guachipelin. The hotel exudes a warm atmosphere even if the comfortable rooms are rather bare. The outdoor amenities—a pool, and hammocks, the horses grazing in the field—all contribute to this homey feeling, even if at the end of such a long trip you feel like you've reached the end of the world. The restaurant, with its pretty decor, serves all three meals. You can fill your days with activities such as horseback riding, trips in the park, and don't forget the Canopy Tour (see p 258)! The lodge even has a scientific library and a collection of insects, butterflies and snakes.

Posada El Encuentro
$$$$$ bkfst incl.
hw, pb, ≡, ≈
mailing address:
apartado 5000-367 Liberia
off the road to Parque Nacional Rincón de la Vieja, near Curubande
☎/≈382-0815
encuentro@arweb.com
Located on a 200ha (494 acres) property that includes tropical dry forest, Posada El Encuentro offers rooms of the highest comfort and cleanliness. The family atmosphere makes the service personalized. Plenty of indoor games, such as ping-pong, to entertain its guests. A swimming pool and a telescope grace the terrace, from

which you can take in a view of the surrounding area. Like the rest of the property, the terrace has no shade, and the heat is intense under the beating sun. Breakfast and other delicious meals prepared by the mother of the family are served in the establishment's charming little dining room.

Parque Nacional Santa Rosa

The Parque Nacional Santa Rosa has the best accommodation setup with 8 rooms for 64 people, including students, researchers and tourists (if there's room). Lodging here costs $15 per person, and a little less if you stay at the Nancite beach biological station. A **campsite** (*$1.25/pers./day*) with running water, bathrooms, showers, picnic tables, garbage cans, etc. has been set up between the administrative offices and La Casona. There are two more campgrounds north and south of Playa Naranjo (bring your own food and drinking water), about 12km (7.5mi) from the administrative offices. There is a cafeteria (*bkfst. $3.50, lunch $5, supper $4.25*), but if you camp near the administration and want to eat there, you have to give them 3hrs notice.

Around Liberia

Liberia and Surroundings

There is **camping** on the grounds of Liberia's youth hostel (Hotel Guanacaste see below).

Hospedaje Lodge la Casona (*$; pb/sb, tv, ⊗; 300m or 984ft south of the central park, ☎/≈666-2971*) is hospitable, but like **Posada del Tope** (*$; sb; 150m or 492ft south of the central park, ☎385-2383 or 666-3876*), is more like a youth hostel in terms of comfort.

Hotel Guanacaste
$
discounts for Hostelling International card holders
pb, ⊗, ≡
25m (82ft) west and 100m (328ft) south of Pulmitan's bus station
☎666-0085
≈666-2287
www.hostelling-costarica.com
Hotel Guanacaste is a youth hostel with simply furnished rooms. Like most establishments of its type, Hotel Guanacaste is appealing for its warm reception and personalized service. There is a friendly neighbourhood restaurant inside. The hotel is often full. Laundry service.

Hotel Liberia
$$
pb, ⊗
75m (246ft) south of the plaza on Calle 1
☎/≈666-0161
Hotel Liberia has clean rooms which are usu-

ally booked. The staff is friendly and the place is furnished like a youth hostel. The hotel can do your laundry and serves breakfast. Souvenir shop.

Hotel Daysita
$$
hw, pb, ⊗, ≡, ≈, ℜ
south side of the stadium
☎ *666-0197*
⇆ *666-0927*
Hotel Daysita, in the centre of Liberia, provides clean rooms and free airport pick-up. There is a nightclub on the premises.

Hotel Primavera
$$
pb, ⊗, tv, ≡
south side of the central park
☎ *666-0464*
⇆ *666-2271*
The very tidy Hotel Primavera offers great value for your money, and therefore is often full to capacity, even in low season. The hotel is located at the end of a courtyard.

Hotel Bramadero
$$$
hw, pb, ≡, ≈, ℜ
on the Interamericana, near Liberia's main thoroughfare
☎ *666-0371*
⇆ *666-0203*
One of the oldest hotels in the area, the Hotel Bramadero, whose name has something to do with bullfighting, offers motel-style rooms with a non-descript decor. Try to get a room as far away as possible from the noisy restaurant-bar and Interamericana.

La Siesta
$$$
hw, pb, ≡, ℜ
5 streets into Liberia, 250m (820ft) right of Farmacia Lux
☎ *666-0678*
⇆ *666-2532*
La Siesta, in the middle of Liberia, is more of a motel: it's long shape encloses a small garden and a swimming pool. Overall, a clean and friendly place.

Hotel El Sitio
$$$$ bkfst incl.
hw, pb, ctv, ⊗, ≡, ≈, ☉
off the road to Santa Cruz, near Liberia
☎ *257-0744 or 666-1211*
⇆ *666-2059*
Hotel El Sitio looks like Hotel Las Espuelas with its large property, but is lower in quality and price. There is a pool, *rancho*-style restaurant, children's games and a whirlpool onsite, and a travel agency and souvenir shop in the hotel itself. The common rooms open out onto a spacious outdoor patio with elegant floor tiles. We found the service could have been a bit more refined, and the same can be said for the rooms, despite their being air conditioned and renovated (the bedding was worn, for example).

Hotel Las Espuelas
$$$$$
pb, hw, ctv, ≡, ≈, ℜ
2km (1.2mi) south of Liberia on the Interamericana
☎ *666-0144*
⇆ *666-2441*
Modern and classy, Hotel Las Espuelas is one of the better hotels in town. The one-floor

establishment is surrounded by wide-open green spaces in the countryside, away from the highway. The rooms are fairly attractive and clean, as is the restaurant. The place has a very definite cowboy-style: *Espuelas* is Spanish for "spurs." This is Guanacaste, after all!

Playa del Coco and Surroundings

Playa Panamá

Blue Bay
$$$$$ all inc.
hw, pb, ctv, ≈, ⊗, ≡, ℝ, ≈, ⊗, ℜ, ☉
near Giardini di Papagayo, at the end of the road
☎ *672-0130 or 233-8566*
⇆ *672-0139*
www.bluebayresorts.com
The Blue Bay is a huge luxury hotel complex on a vast stretch of land sloping toward the ocean. There is plenty to do here (water and land sports). Souvenir shop. Treat your body and mind to a relaxing massage—a service you'll find in most high-end hotels.

Costa Smeralda
$$$$$
hw, pb, ≡, ≈
Bahía Culebra, on the Golfo Papagayo, north of Panamá
☎ *672-0191*
⇆ *672-0041*
smeralda@racsa.co.cr
Costa Smeralda is a large resort with lots of activities for its guests; everything from scuba diving to Spanish and dance lessons. The hotel is located on an inlet.

Sula Sula Beach Resort
$$$$$
hw, pb, ctv, ≡, ≈, ℜ, ℝ
☎*672-0116*
Sula Sula Beach Resort was one of the first hotel complexes built in Playa Panamá. Everything has been done to make the place wheelchair accessible, and the resort is located on flat ground. Each double-occupancy two-room unit is tastefully decorated in subdued tones, and comes with a refrigerator and shared patio.

Playa Hermosa

Villa del Sueño
$$$
pb, hw, ⊗, ≈, ℜ, ≡
☎*/≈672-0026*
www.arweb.com/
villadelsueno
Email:
delsueno@racsa.co.cr
Villa del Sueño is a place to check out. Owned by six friendly Quebeckers, this hotel offers first-class comfort and service. The guest rooms and common areas are at once sunny and subdued, and tastefully decorated with wood and ceramics. Sit back and relax, read a magazine, chat with other guests, or linger over a coffee or fresh fruit juice on the shaded terrace in front of the hotel. In the evenings, the restaurant is set up on the same terrace (see p 279). The hotel is about 100m (328ft) from the beach, providing total peace and tranquillity. The pool and bar are popular afternoon meeting places, especially when the owners decide to break out their musical instruments to liven up the scene.

Villa Huetares
$$$$
pb, ≈, ≡
150m (492ft) from the beach, off the public road to Playa Hermosa
☎*/≈460-6592*
Villa Huetares rents neat little villas with kitchens and dining rooms. There is a volleyball court on the property, and the landscaping complements the surrounding countryside.

El Oasis
$$$$
pb, hw, K, ℝ, ℜ, ≈, ≡
☎*672-0026*
www.villadelsueno.com
The owners of Villa del Sueño (see above) manage several housing projects in the region, and have recently opened El Oasis, a condominium complex. The condos are rented out when their owners are not there. The one-room apartments and studios are quite comfortable if you plan to stay for a while. The studios don't have full kitchens, but are equipped with toaster ovens, mini-refrigerators and coffee makers, which might be all you really need. All the apartments have the same pleasant decor. There are also magnificent outdoor facilities, with a stunning swimming pool surrounded by lush vegetation.

El Velero
$$$$-$$$$$
hw, pb, ⊗, ≡, ≈, ℜ
☎*672-0036*
☎*/≈672-0016*
Email:
elvelerocr@yahoo.com
El Velero is a small, stylish beach-side hotel and a refreshing change from the surrounding mega-resorts. The second-floor rooms are a little simpler than those on the ground floor. Souvenir shop, water sports equipment rental.

Cacique del Mar
$$$$$
hw, pb, ≡, ≈
☎*670-0345*
Cacique del Mar is actually two resort villages: **Los Altos del Cacique** is a residential complex currently under construction on the point that separates Playa Hermosa and Playa del Coco, and **La Costa del Cacique** is a hotel and villas just north of Playa Hermosa. It is part of a huge hotel development project in the area. Definitely worth looking into.

Condovac la Costa
$$$$$
hw, pb, ctv, ℜ, K
north end of the beach, next to the Sol Playa Hermosa hotel
☎*221-2264 or 233-1562*
≈*222-5637*
Condovac la Costa is located on a coastal inlet. This resort-style hotel offers its guests a number of services and activities, the latter including fishing, surfboarding, waterskiing, jet-skiing, scuba

diving and tennis. The villas are spread over the property; there is a shuttle service to the beach. Nightclub.

Sol Playa Hermosa
$$$$$
pb, hw, ≡, ctv, ≈, ℜ, K
☎*290-0565*
⇌*290-0566*
hermosol@racsa.co.cr
Sol Playa Hermosa is a huge resort complex that is part of the Sol chain. Surprisingly, the rooms are simply furnished for such an up-scale hotel. However, the magnificent view of the ocean from the balcony makes up for the lack of decor. The villas come fully equipped—some even have their own pool! A souvenir and sports equipment rental shop, tennis courts, ping-pong tables and conference rooms are just some of the facilities you'll find here.

Playa del Coco

Cabinas Sol y Mar
$$
pb
150m (492ft) north of the club Astilleros, off the road to Playa del Coco
☎*670-0368 or 551-3706*
The large *cabinas* have a bedroom, living room, small kitchen and veranda. Everything is very clean.

Hotel Anexo Luna Tica
$$$
pb, ⊗
☎*670-0127*
⇌*670-0459*
Hotel Anexo Luna Tica is a small Tico hotel.

The rooms are gloomily furnished but clean.

Cabinas del Coco
$$$
pb, ⊗, ℜ
right on the beach facing the public pier
☎*670-0110 or 670-0276*
⇌*670-0167*
Cabinas del Coco was built in the 1950s. The rooms are minimally furnished but clean. This hotel is right in the middle of Playa del Coco, and is the closest one to the beach. However, its central location means more noise, especially from the nightclub next door. Restaurant availalble (see p 278).

Hotel Pato Loco Inn
$$$
pb, ℜ
800m (2,625ft) from the beach, off the road to Playa del Coco
☎/⇌*670-0145*
Hotel Pato Loco Inn has simply furnished rooms with a small back yard. Very clean, but the only facility on its small grounds is a restaurant (see p 278).

Villa del Sol
$$$ bkfst incl.
hw, pb/sb, ≈, ⊗
1km (0.6mi) east of Playa del Coco's main street, on a perpendicular road that passes by San Francisco Treats
☎/⇌*670-0085*
A few metres from the beach, Villa del Sol is more like a Bed & Breakfast, but its owners from Québec also rent out two fully equipped houses for stays of several days or longer.

Puerta del Sol
$$$$
hw, pb, ≈, ☉, ℜ
150m (492ft) from the beach, one street east of Playa del Coco's main street
☎/⇌*670-0195*
The Puerta del Sol will catch your eye with its attractive yellow exterior. The modern rooms with comfortable sofas are kept very clean. However, because the plants are still quite young, the outdoor common areas could be better shaded. The restaurant, El Sol y la Luna, is appealing (see p 279).

Flor de Itabo
$$$$
hw, pb, ≈, ≡, ctv, ℜ
1km (0.6mi) from the beach, on the way into Playa del Coco
☎*670-0011 or 670-0292*
⇌*670-0003*
Flor de Itabo is a pretty little hotel. Its rooms are very well decorated and clean. It is a bit far from the beach—but from the noise of the town, as well. The restaurant serves Italian cuisine. Bungalows and apartments for rent.

Villa Casa Blanca
$$$$ bkfst incl.
hw, pb, ≡
on the way to El Ocotal
☎/⇌*670-0448*
vcblanca@racsa.co.cr
Villa Casa Blanca is a pretty little Bed & Breakfast a few minutes away from the beach. Its natural surroundings and romantic decor make it an enchanting place. The common areas are calm and cozy. The breakfast served is a combination

of Costa Rican and North American, something other hotels in the area don't do. The Western Canadian owners know how to treat their guests well.

Villa Flores
$$$$ bkfst incl.
hw, pb, ≈, ≡, ☉
200m (656ft) east of Playa del Coco's main street
☎670-0269
Villa Flores is well maintained and decorated, with elegant and relaxing gardens surrounding it. Since it is almost opposite Puerto del Sol, it's a few minutes walk to the beach. Friendly owners.

Coco Verde
$$$$ bkfst incl.
hw, pb, ≡, ≈, ℜ
200m (656ft) from the beach, on the Playa del Coco's main street
☎/≈670-0494
Coco Verde is a modern ensemble of lodgings in a large building that is stylish on the outside. Once inside, however, the rooms are clean but lack the charm of other hotels in the area. They are minimally equipped, and strung out in a row along a shared balcony.

Playa Ocotal

Ocotal Inn B&B
$$$ bkfst incl.
pb, ≡
☎670-0835
Just 0.5km (.31mi) before Playa Ocotal, the Ocotal Inn B&B has five rooms with two single beds or one double bed. The rooms are built around a small

interior courtyard, where you can cool off in the very tiny pool. Breakfast is served next to the pool on round tables covered with pretty blue tablecloths.

El Ocotal Beach Resort
$$$$$
hw, pb, ctv, ℝ, ⊗, ≡, ≈, ⊛
☎670-0321 or 670-0323
≈670-0083
El Ocotal Beach Resort is a classy hotel perched on a hill overlooking Playa Ocotal—and what a view! The rooms come with a kitchen table, desk and coffee machine. If you are not staying at the hotel, you can still dine in its restaurant (see p 279) just to see the place. Tennis court.

Around Filadelfia

Playa Flamingo and Surroundings

Playa Pan de Azúcar

Hotel Sugar Beach
$$$$$
hw, pb, ⊗, ≡, ≈, ℜ
15km (9.3mi) from the turnoff to Huscas
☎654-4242
≈654-4239
www.sugarbeach.com
At Hotel Sugar Beach you can get away from it all. It is the only hotel on the beach, at the end of the road leading there. There is a beautiful view of the ocean from the restaurant on the hillside. Monkeys, iguanas, toucans and parrots can all be spotted here. The decor, however, is nothing out

of the ordinary. The hotel rents all kinds of equipment for watersports and land excursions.

Playa Penca

El Sitio Cielomar
$$$$ bkfst incl.
hw, pb, ⊗, ≡
☎654-4194
≈666-2059
El Sitio Cielomar has the same owners as El Sitio de Liberia. It has no pool, which is surprising for a chain hotel. The rooms are standard in terms of decor and comfort. The lawn in front of the hotel sprawls out to the ocean. Water sports equipment rental.

Playa Potrero

Bahía Potrero Beach Resort
$$$$$ bkfst incl.
hw, pb, ⊗, ≡
☎654-4183
≈654-4093
Bahía Potrero Beach Resort is a small, comfortable hotel, featuring decent-sized rooms with a table set in the corner. The front lawn sprawls out to the ocean. All in all, a very good place for rest and relaxation, the elements of a perfect vacation.

Playa Flamingo

Mariner Inn
$$$$
hw, pb, ctv, ≡, ≈, ℜ
☎654-4081
≈654-4024
It's not hard to find your way around the Mariner Inn, next to the marina. Everything, including the rooms, is

located in the one building of this small hotel complex (the swimming pool is on the second floor, for example). The place is laid back, as you can tell by its restaurant (see p 280) and guests. Good view of the marina. The beach is 300m (984ft) away.

Fantasias Flamingo
$$$$$
hw, pb, ≡, ≈, ℜ
☎654-4350 or 654-4347
flamingo@racsa.co.cr
Fantasias Flamingo is very North American indeed. The architecture's shape and colour is a bit cold, however. Some rooms access the pool directly, and all have a beautiful view of the ocean. The hotel has recently changed ownership and there are plans for considerable change.

Flamingo Beach Resort
$$$$$$
hw, pb, ctv, ⊗, ≡, ≈, ☺, ℜ
☎233-9233 or 654-4010
⇌654-4060
Flamingo Beach Resort is a huge luxury hotel complex. The very comfortable rooms and suites all have balconies, and all buildings face the ocean. A classic in the area along with the Flamingo Marina Resorts.
Game room for kids.
Casino.

Flamingo Marina Resorts
$$$$$$ bkfst incl.
hw, pb, ⊗, ≡, ℝ, ≈, ℜ, ⊛, ctv, K
☎290-1858 or 654-4141
⇌231-1858
www.flamingo.com
Flamingo Marina Resorts practically take up all of Flamingo Bay! There are actually three hotels in one: the **Flamingo Marina Hotel**, with rooms facing the marina; the **Flamingo All-Suites**, which has suites with kitchenettes (some even have jacuzzis!); and finally, **Club Playa Flamingo**, which has fully-equipped apartments. There is a tennis court and souvenir shop on the premises. All sorts of activities are offered at this huge complex.

Presidential Suites
$$$$$$
hw, pb, ctv, K, ≈
☎654-4485
⇌654-4486
The residents of the Presidential Suites rent their condos when they're away. Therefore, what you get is a fully equipped apartment that can have a somewhat lived-in feel. The magnificent view of the beach, only 10min away, makes up for this, though. The place is enormous, but lacks the charm of smaller complexes. Maid service. The longer you stay, the more you save.

Playa Brasilito

Cabinas Nany
$$ bkfst incl.
pb, ⊗, ≈, shared kitchen
200m (656ft) south of and 75m (246ft) east of the village soccer field
☎654-4320
Cabinas Nany are clean, but basic and a bit overpriced. Friendly owners.

Ojos Azulejos
$$ bkfst incl.
hw, pb, ⊗
on Playa Brasilito's main street
☎654-4346
Ojos Azulejos has friendly Swiss owners. The rooms are simply furnished, clean and big enough for a family.

Hotel Brasilito
$$
pb, ⊗, ℜ
☎654-4237
⇌654-4247
Hotel Brasilito is somewhat outdated, but right near the ocean in the centre of Brasilito. It can get noisy because of its location. Basic, clean rooms.

Playa Conchal

Meliá Playa Conchal
$$$$$$
hw, pb, ⊗, ≡, ≈, ℜ, ctv
☎654-4123
⇌654-4181
Meliá Playa Conchal is a beach and golf resort on Playa Conchal, south of Brasilito. Each suite comes with a balcony, bedroom and big living room. Kids under 12 can stay for free in their parent's room. Tennis courts, health and aqua club, casino, bar, nightclub, and of

Cattle egret

course—golf! Impeccable service. The place has an original setup—just go to the rental office overlooking the hotel to see for yourself.

Playa Real

Bahía de los Piratas
$$$$
pb, hw, K, ≈, ℜ, ≡
Apartado
postal 1055-1007, Centro Colón
San José
☎*222-7010 or 654-4654*
⇌*654-4650*
The setting of Hotel Bahía de los Piratas, in the middle of a small bay on one of the prettiest beaches in the region, is captivating. The two- or three-bedroom, fully equipped bungalows are on a hill facing the ocean and offer first-rate comfort, especially if you like to make the most of your vacation by settling in somewhere. It is possible to spend one night here, but why not stay longer and take advantage of the kitchenette, living room with sound system and bedrooms with private bathrooms? The hotel offers a host of activities, and the restaurant serves delicious food, including hearth-baked pizzas that will make you forget about cooking for yourself! The sheer uphill walk (or drive) to your bungalow may be off-putting, but once you're there, the view makes up for it. The road is not one of the easiest. Ask to be sent a map of the region before you leave so that

you can familiarize yourself with the area. Remember that after Belén you have to drive as far as the village of Matapalo, 3km (1.8mi) past Huacas. From there, the route is signposted, but you are still better off with a map.

Playa Tamarindo and Surroundings

Playa Grande

Centro Vacacional Playa Grande
$$$
pb, ⊗, K, ℜ
1.5km (0.9mi) from Playa Grande, at the entrance to Parque Nacional Marino Las Baulas
☎*237-2552 or 260-3991*
☎/⇌*653-0467*
Centro Vacacional Playa Grande is almost like a vacation campground with its bungalows with bunk-beds and kitchenettes.

El Bucanero
$$$ bkfst incl.
hw, pb, ℜ
☎/⇌*653-0480*
El Bucanero is a small hotel with large, basic, clean rooms. There is a superb view of the beach from its ground-floor restaurant. The whole place has a pleasant, summery atmosphere.

Lotus Surf Lodge
$$$
pb, hw, ⊗, ℜ
☎*653-0490*
www.lotussurflodge.com
Probably the first thing you'll notice upon arrival at Lotus Surf Lodge is, keeping true

to its name, the smell of incense wafting out. Apart from being a truly fragrant place, this hotel primarily attracts surfers and other young people lingering in the area. There are eight rooms, which occupy two floors running the length of a wooden gallery. The hotel also offers yoga classes and has a vegetarian restaurant, and its generally mystical atmosphere is all the rage.

Cantarana
$$$$ bkfst incl.
½b also available
hw, pb, ⊗, ≡, ≈
☎*653-0486*
⇌*653-0491*
The Cantarana rents clean rooms with a table, chairs and a comfortable bed. The outside is tastefully set up near the river. The beach is 5min away, at the end of the property.

Villa Baula
$$$$
hw, pb, ⊗, ≈, ℜ
☎*653-0493*
⇌*653-0459*
www.villabaula.com
Villa Baula is peacefully isolated, as it is the last hotel on the beach strip before the river that separates Playa Grande from Playa Tamarindo. The rooms are large with wood furnishings. Bungalows on stilts with kitchens and large balconies can also be rented. A charming place! Everything is set up in close contact with nature: the hotel is right next to the beach—ideal for turtle-watching.

Casa Linda Vista
$$$$-$$$$$
hw, pb, tv, ⊗, K
☎*653-0474*
www.tamarindo.com/kai
Chalet-style Casa Linda Vista is on a hill and has a beautiful view of its surroundings. It comes with a kitchenette and sleeps six. Peace and tranquillity assured, as this place is 500m (1,640ft) from the beach. Very good value for your money.

Hotel las Tortugas
$$$$$
hw, pb, ≡, ≈, ⊛
☎/≈*653-0458*
Located on Playa Grande, Hotel las Tortugas was carefully set up to prevent light from reaching the beach and disrupting the egg-laying process of the many turtles who frequent it. The rooms have stone floors that have a cooling effect if you don't want to use air-conditioning. The owners have done everything they can to protect the turtles and natural surroundings. You will appreciate the view from the hotel restaurant.

Playa Tamarindo

In addition to the hotels mentioned below, you can pitch your tent right beside the beach at **Tito's Camping**, opposite Cabinas 14 de Febrero, and at **Paniugua Camping**.

Cabinas Coral Reef
$$
hw, pb
☎*653-0291*
Cabinas Coral Reef are simple but clean and ideal for surfers. The beach is not far away.

Cabinas Dolly
$$
sb
Cabinas Dolly seems like a youth hostel with its young clientele and basic rooms. The bathrooms are clean, however. Directly on the beach. The grounds are small and simple, but the beach is like a front yard.

Cabinas 14 de Febrero
$$
hw, pb, K
☎*653-0238*
Cabinas 14 de Febrero are clean and charming. The place forms a square around a simply laid-out tropical garden. Since it was recently built, the rooms were made mostly out of plaster and wood. There is a laundry space behind the main building and you can cook meals in the communal kitchen. You can have breakfast on the outdoor terrace.

Cabinas Marielos
$$$
pb, ⊗, K
☎*653-0141*
Cabinas Marielos are small, basic, clean, and fairly bright. The owners are friendly and the gardens are lovely. Guests can use the kitchen.

Cabinas Arco Iris
$$$
pb, hw, ℜ
Cabinas Arco Iris are small, colourful cottages next to the vegetarian restaurant of the same name (see p 281).

Cabinas Pozo Azul
$$$
pb, ≡, K, ≈
just after entering the village
☎*653-0280*
The owners of Cabinas Pozo Azul rent standard comfort rooms equipped with a small stove and refrigerator.

Vila Alegre
$$$-$$$$ bkfst incl.
pb, hw, ≡, ⊗, ≈, K
☎653-0270
≈653-0287
vialegre@racsa.co.cr
Quite close to the Hotel Capitan Suizo in the village of Tamarindo, a friendly Californian couple has opened a pleasant bed and breakfast. Vila Alegre offers quality accommodations in four rooms in the main residence and two cottages. Each room is named for a country (Mexico, Japan, and so on) and is tastefully decorated in the called-for style. This lovely house has an agreeable, peaceful atmosphere.

Cabinas Zully Mar
$$$-$$$$
hw, pb, ⊗, ≡
near the loop of the first road along the beach
☎*653-0140*
Cabinas Zully Mar are ideal for travellers on tight budgets. There are

two kinds of rooms, built at different times: the oldest are smaller, whereas the newer ones have a better layout, but both are clean. Located in the middle of the village, right near the beach.

Pueblo Dorado
$$$$
hw, pb, ≈
☎*653-0008*
⇌*653-0013*
The rooms at Pueblo Dorado are simply and modernly furnished with a table and chairs.

Hotel El Milagro
$$$$ *bkfst incl.*
hw, pb, ⊗, ≡, ≈, ℜ
on your left once in the village
☎*653-0042*
⇌*653-0050*
flokiro@racsa.co.cr
Hotel El Milagro has two types of rooms: the first has fans and cold water only, while the other has air-conditioning and hot water. The hotel's natural surroundings are well kept, and the *cabinas* have an original layout: the shaded terraces with big patio doors almost seem like an extra room. The *cabinas* face each other, with lots of vegetation between them. The beach is across the street and the restaurant has a good reputation (see p 281).

Hotel Pasatiempo
$$$$
pb, hw, ≈
☎*653-0096*
⇌*653-0275*
Located in Tamarindo, not far from the beach, Hotel Pasatiempo is

shaded by lush vegetation. The small bungalows have two rooms with terraces. There is a pool in the middle of the grounds.

Tropicana del Pacífico
$$$$
hw, pb, ⊗, ≡, ≈
☎/⇌*653-0261*
Tropicana del Pacífico is set back from the road across from the beach, and is built around its swimming pool. The rooms are large, clean and decently furnished. Italian owners.

Casa Banyan
$$$$$ *bkfst incl.*
hw, pb, ≈
☎*653-0072*
Casa Banyan is a bed and breakfast in a huge modern house right on the beach.

Hotel Capitán Suizo
$$$$$ *bkfst incl.*
hw, pb, ⊗, ≡, ℝ, ≈
south end of the village
☎*653-0075*
⇌*653-0292*
Hotel Capitán Suizo is a small luxury hotel that belongs to the same chain that owns Grano de Oro in San José and four other hotels in the country, so you can expect the utmost in comfort. The place is built on different levels, creating a lovely architectural effect. The rooms are in duplexes; those on the ground floor have a terrace and are air-conditioned, while those on the second floor have a balcony and are cooled by breezes. The rooms are also spacious and fur-

nished with a sofa bed, pretty chairs, a writing desk and a small refrigerator. The hotel has wonderful gardens, a swimming pool, and even a *rancho.* There are also bungalows for rent and obviously lots of organized activities and excursions.

Residence Luna Llena
$$$$$
hw, pb, K, ≈
200m (656ft) east of Iguana Surf
☎*653-0082*
⇌*653-0120*
lunallena@yellowweb.co.cr
Residence Luna Llena is an intimate place with a pretty interior decor (wood and ceramics) and a unique spiral staircase that leads to the rooms upstairs. It is just as lovely from the outside, and the beach is only 200m (656ft) away.

Sueño del Mar
$$$$$ *bkfst incl.*
hw, pb, ⊗, ≡, ℜ
☎/⇌*653-0284*
The Sueño del Mar reigns at the south end of the second beach road, where it forms a loop in the village of Tamarindo. The small rooms have an eclectic but tasteful decor. *Casita* rentals available.

Tamarindo Vista Villas Hotel
$$$$
hw, pb, ≡, ℜ, *ctv,* ≈, K
☎*653-0114*
⇌*653-0115*
Tamarindo Vista Villas Hotel rents modern apartments with a kitchen, dining and living room, and a pa-

tio or balcony with a splendid view of the ocean. The hotel is now a member of the Best Western chain.

Tamarindo Diriá
$$$$$ bkfst incl.
pb, hw, ctv, ⊗, ≡, ≈, ℜ
☎*653-0031 or 258-4224*
⇔*653-0208*
tnodiria@racsa.co.cr
Tamarindo Diriá looks pleasant but shows its age—it was one of the first hotels built in the area, over a decade ago. The rooms are charming in an out-dated way, but rather confining, and all share a balcony. The hotel is tucked in tropical vege-tation and its gorgeous gardens greatly en-hance the look of the place, especially the restaurant. It's worth coming here just to see the natural surround-ings or to have a drink looking at the sun set on the sea. Souvenir shop and tennis court. There is a little shop-ping complex next to the hotel, as well as the beach.

Casa Cook
$$$$$$
hw, pb, ⊗, ≈, K
☎/⇔*653-0125*
Casa Cook is a private property with two lovely fully equipped *cabinas* (with living rooms) and a suite on the second floor of the main house. The suite has a large patio, two bedrooms and two bathrooms. You will find peace of mind and all the comforts at this modern and luxurious property by the ocean.

El Jardin del Edén
$$$$$$ bkfst incl.
hw, pb, ≡, ≈, ⊛, tv, ℜ
200m (656ft) from the beach
☎*653-0137*
☎/⇔*653-0111*
www.jardin-eden.com
The Mediterranean style of El Jardin del Edén is expressed in its white stucco walls, russet-tiled roof and light flag-stone floors. However, it still has the same neon lighting that it has had for years, and this is definitely not an as-set. Nevertheless, the rooms offer a superb view of the sea from their large terraces and balconies. What's more, there is a garden that does full justice to the name of the place. Lux-uriant and obviously lovingly tended, it adds enormously to the ho-tel's charm. In the mid-dle of this garden of Eden, there is a swim-ming pool and an open-air restaurant (see p 281) that serves ex-cellent breakfasts.

Around Santa Cruz

Santa Cruz and Surroundings

Santa Cruz

El Diriá
$$$
pb, hw, tv, ≡, ≈
☎*650-0442*
Motel-style El Diriá is nestled in lush tropical vegetation. Bungalows are clean, share a big shaded terrace, and surround the garden. Friendly staff.

Playa Negra

Finca Los Pargos de Playa Negra
$$$
pb, ℜ
The Finca Los Pargos de Playa Negra is made up of a series of two-room *cabinas* on stilts with palm-thatched roofs, in the middle of an open grasslands area. There are even some goats that live on the grounds! This natu-ral and "grungy" estab-lishment is found at the end of the road that leads to Playa Negra. There is an Italian res-taurant on the pre-mises.

Mono Congo Lodge
$$$
sb, hw, ℜ
Apartado Postal 177-5150
Santa Cruz
☎*382-6926*
Playa Negra is develop-ing fast and promises to soon become a lively tourist attraction. For now, it is quite authen-tic, and its few facilities are scattered along little dirt roads that cut through dense vegeta-tion. One of these is Mono Congo Lodge, striking for its landscap-ing that seems to blend in with the austere sur-roundings. The large dark brown wooden house has only four rooms, including a small one on the top floor. The bathrooms are large and attrac-tively decorated with ceramic tiles. The com-munal spaces open out onto the natural sur-roundings, giving the place a peaceful,

friendly atmosphere. The lodge offers several activities, including horseback riding on their own horses.

Pablo Picasso
$$$
pb, ℜ, ≡, K
☎*382-0411*
The Pablo Picasso Restaurant also rents cabins *(cabinas)*, mostly to surfers who are attracted by the waves in the area. There are currently three rooms, two of which are air conditioned and sleep up to six people. If you don't want to have all your meals at the restaurant that has earned the place its reputation, the rooms all have kitchenettes.

Hotel Playa Negra
$$$$
hw, pb, ≈, ℜ
☎*382-1301*
⇄*382-1302*
playanegra@paradise.co.cr
Located on Playa Negra, the Hotel Playa Negra is somewhat secluded, but it is definitely a pleasant hideaway! The round *cabinas* with palm-thatched roofs are pretty, bright and airy, with comfortable furnishings consisting of a table, chairs, sofa and a bed. If you come here during the rainy season, ask about the condition of the road leading to the hotel, since you often need a four-wheel drive vehicle to reach it. The restaurant (see p 282) serves French cuisine, in addition to other types of food.

Playa Junquillal and Surroundings

Playa Avellanas

Cabinas Las Olas
$$$
hw, pb, ⊗, ℜ
☎*233-4455*
⇄*222-8685*
Cabinas Las Olas has 10 comfortably furnished rooms. It is surrounded by nature, including a mangrove swamp which you can visit via a raised path. The owners go to great lengths to protect the flora and fauna. Playa Avellanas is also a beautiful surfer's beach.

Playa Junquillal

Camping Los Malinches
$
☎*653-0429*
Camping Los Malinches has extremely friendly owners, lots of trees, and faces the ocean.

Hotel Junquillal
$$
hw, ℜ
next to the public beach on Playa Junquillal
☎*653-0432*
Hotel Junquillal is a 30-year-old establishment whose small wooden *cabinas* are simply furnished. There are hammocks strung about everywhere. Very popular with travellers on a tight budget. You can camp on the grounds, as well.

Hibiscus
$$-$$$
pb
right near the public entrance to Playa Junquillal
☎*653-0437*
The small, family-style Hibiscus is charming with its simply decorated but inviting *cabinas* in the middle of a garden; however, they are a little too close to each other.

El Castillo Divertido
$$$
pb, hw
no phone number
El Castillo Divertido, across the street from the beach, looks like a chateau with its rotundas and castellated border along the roof. The rooms of this German-owned establishment are not very large, but those upstairs have a balcony.

Guacamaya Lodge
$$$
pb, hw, ≈, ℜ
☎/⇄*653-0431*
alibern@raacsa.co.cr
Perched atop a hill, Guacamaya Lodge is very clean and pretty. Each bungalow has two large rooms and a front terrace. There is also a large, fully-equipped *casita (*$$$$$*)* with a marvellous view from its balcony. The owners' parrot is amusing!

Villa Serena
$$$$ fb
hw, pb, ⊗, ≈
☎*653-0430*
Villa Serena rents two-person *cabinas* spread over its large property. Their decor is slightly outdated, and their

The Province of Guanacaste

furnishings rather minimal, but they are clean nonetheless. Directly on the beach. Tennis court.

Hotel Antumalal
$$$$$ bkfst incl.
hw, pb, ⊗, ℜ, ≈
at the end of the beach-side road
☎/⇌653-0425
Even though Playa Junquillal has only been recently developed for tourism, Hotel Anumalal has been around the longest, about 20 years. The bungalows are spaced well apart and have two rooms that share a terrace. The rooms are very bright, simply but tastefully decorated, and have comfortable beds. Directly on the beach. There is a nightclub on weekends.

Iguana Azul
$$$$$ bkfst incl.
hw, pb, ≈, ℜ
1km (0.6mi) north of Playa Junquillal
☎/⇌653-0121
iguanazul@ticonet.co.cr
The Canadian-owned Iguana Azul would be greatly improved by making its grounds more lush, especially around the terrace's bungalows. The rooms, however, are prettily decorated with pastel colours and ornaments. The hotel's real draw is its two beaches: one is rocky, and the other is sandy. All kinds of sports equipment rentals and outdoor excursions are offered. The outdoor restaurant brings you even closer to the beach.

Around Nicoya

Nicoya and Surroundings

Jenny
$$
pb, tv, ≡
100m (328ft) south of the southwest corner of the square
☎685-5050
Jenny is a small, simple urban hotel right in the centre of town.

Cabinas Nicoya
$$-$$$
hw, pb, ≈, ≡
500m (1,640ft) east of the Banco Nacional
☎686-6331
The Cabinas Nicoya are also located right in downtown Nicoya. The owner is friendly and very attentive to his clients' needs. The small rooms have a certain charm, thanks to such details as the pretty bedspreads. The grounds could be better-kept, especially since they are not that large.

Complejo Turístico Curime
$$$
hw, pb, ≈, ≡, ℜ, ℝ
south of Nicoya, on the road to Playa Sémara
☎685-5238
⇌685-5530
The Complejo Turístico Curime's 1970s furniture is a little outdated and drab. The grounds, however, are pleasant and give the impression of being isolated from the nearby road. The hotel has pool tables and tennis courts.

Playa Nosara and its Surroundings

Playa Nosara and Playa Pelada

Almost Paradise
$$$ bkfst incl.
hw, pb, ℜ
Playa Pelada de Nosara
⇌685-5004
Almost Paradise is a "Swiss Family Robinson"-style establishment on a hillside. A little restaurant with a scenic view is also on the premises. The charming *cabinas* are made of wood, and each have their own terrace with a hammock. Very friendly owners at this laid-back hotel.

Estancia Nosara
$$$-$$$$
≡, hw, pb, K, ≈, ℜ
5min from the beach, 4km (2.5mi) south of Nosara
☎/⇌680-0378
The Estancia Nosara feels like a secluded place as it is situated in the middle of a tropical 10ha (24.7 acre) property. Its rooms, restaurants, and gardens are all impeccable and tranquil. Swiss owners. Tennis court.

Hotel Rancho Suizo
$$$$ bkfst incl.
hw, pb, ⊗, ℜ
Nosara's Playa Pelada
☎/⇌284-9669
aratur@racsa.co.cr
Right beside the Playa Pelada, the Hotel Rancho Suizo is in a relaxed setting surrounded by luxurious vegetation. The rooms are very clean and comfortable. Most peo-

ple come here for birdwatching. Grilled dishes are featured on the menu of the hotel's Pirata's Bar (see p 286), which also has a dance floor at night.

Lagarta Lodge
$$$$ bkfst incl.
hw, pb, ⊗, ≈, ℜ
Playa Nosara
☎680-0763
The Lagarta Lodge is located near Nosara's private ecological reserve, and belongs to the same Swiss owners. Perched on a hilltop, it affords magnificent views of the surrounding region. The rooms are comfortable, very clean, and have a certain charm. People come here to visit the reserve, which harbours Ostional turtles, or simply to feast their eyes on the natural surroundings. The hotel is also not far from the beach. Because of its loction, the establishment offers its guests some interesting excursions (watching the turtles on the beach, a trip up the Río Nosara, etc.).

Playa Guiones

Rancho Congo
$$ bkfst incl.
pb, hw, ⊗
Apartado Postal 72
Bocas de Nosara
☎682-0078
Rancho Congo has only two rooms and the rates are reasonable. The rooms are in a building with a very high palm roof, which makes it well ventilated. It is in the middle

of a huge property only 700m (2,296ft) from the beach. The rooms do not have much in the way of decor, but they do have fairly large bathrooms. The road that passes nearby should not bother you, nor should the owner and her two dogs!

Café de Paris
$$-$$$
hw, pb, K, ⊗, ≈, ℜ
500m (1,640ft) from Playa Guiones
☎682-0087 or 682-0207
⇝682-0089
The Café de Paris hotel has Swiss-French owners and five bungalows for rent, each consisting of a large room with a kitchenette, including a refrigerator and a smaller room that can be rented separately. Numerous excursions into the surrounding countryside are possible, and you can rent sports equipment from the hotel. The place has some pretty gardens.

Casa Romántica
$$$ bkfst incl.
pb, hw, ⊗, ℜ, ≈
☎682-0019
casaroma@racsa.co.cr
The setting of the aptly named Casa Romántica is so romantic that you'll be tempted to both stay and dine here. The restaurant's small tables are set up next to the pool in a charming decor. The four hotel rooms, lined up motel style, are large and have several beds. They are not very elaborately decorated but they do face a gar-

den overlooking the beach, adding another romantic touch. The entrance hall is nicely adorned.

Hotel Villa Taype
$$$ bkfst incl.
hw, pb, ≡, ≈, ℜ
between Punta Pelada and Playa Guiones
☎382-7715
The Hotel Villa Taype is one of the largest establishments in the area. The place is made up of a motel-style row of little houses, each containing two simple, clean rooms. There are lovely tropical gardens and large common areas, some of which are covered to shelter guests from the sun as well as the rain. There are tennis courts and ping-pong tables, and the beach is only a short distance away.

Olas Grandes Gringo Grill & Surf Shack
$$$
sb, ℜ
Olas Grandes Gringo Grill & Surf Shack is perfect for people who love to surf and party! Each little cabin has two large rooms with ordinary furnishings. The staff is quite "alternative."

Harbour Reef Lodge
$$$$
pb, hw, ≡, K, ℜ, ≈, ⊗
☎682-0059
⇝682-0060
www.harborreef.com
Harbour Reef Lodge has only recently opened. After the American owners cleared the undergrowth on what was a

vacant lot, they turned it into a peaceful haven completely surrounded by greenery. The rooms are actually small apartments with kitchenettes and enclosed, air-conditioned rooms. Built in teak from floor to ceiling, all the rooms have several windows and are well ventilated. Some of the balconies have a little table. Landscaped gardens snake their way around a small pool in which stands a stone sculpture of a serpent!

El Villaggio
$$$$$ bkfst incl.
hw, pb, ≈
near Punta Garza
☎ *680-0784 or 233-2476*
⇄ *222-4073*
Along with the Hotel Villa Taype (see above), El Villaggio is the largest hotel of its kind in this area, which is better known for its smaller establishments. The rooms are in spacious, airy huts, and have private terraces. The large French doors let in a lot of light and open onto the magnificent scenery outside. Because the hotel is situated on a little bay, guests have almost exclusive access to the beach. A souvenir shop is available.

Hotel Playa de Nosara
$$$$$
hw, pb, ⊗, ≈, ℜ
on Punta Pelada
☎ *680-0495*
Standing on Punta Pelada's headland, the Hotel Playa de Nosara is easy to spot because of its whitewashed,

somewhat kitschy, turret in which the reception and restaurant are found. The rooms are well-ventilated and pleasantly shaded, but the price is a bit too high for their decor and level of comfort. Because the hotel is slightly elevated, it has a great view of the surrounding scenery. Direct access to Guiones beach.

Playa Sámara and its Surroundings

Camping El Coco
$3 per person
electricity
Camping El Coco is a small "urban" campground in the middle of Sámara, right by the beach. The sites are on sand and very shady, which is a blessing given how hot it can get here. The grounds are clean, if somewhat crowded, since lots of people come here in the summer. The owners are very friendly.

Hospedaje y Abastecedor Yuri
$
northern section of the beach
The Hospedaje y Abastecedor Yuri has amazingly clean and tidy rooms. The furnishings are minimal, but the beds are comfortable. Though the building's exterior is not exactly pretty, the quality/price ratio of the rooms is very good, and the owners are friendly.

Hotel Marbella
$$
pb, ≈, ℜ
☎/⇄ *656-0122*
The exterior and common areas of the Hotel Marbella are interesting, but the rooms are small and uncomfortable.

Belvedere
$$$ bkfst incl.
hw, pb, ⊛
across from Hotel Marbell
☎ *656-0213*
The A-frame *cabinas* at the Belvedere have a certain charm, even though the rooms are small. They have large and attractive private balconies.

Casa del Mar
$$$ bkfst incl.
hw, pb/sb, ⊛, ℜ
on the main street
☎ *656-0264*
⇄ *656-1029*
In the middle of Sámara and just 75m (246ft) from the beach is the Casa del Mar. Owned by Quebecers, this place has bright rooms situated around a small, landscaped courtyard in the centre of which is a whirlpool. The white walls and floor (painted or tiled) make the rooms seem more spacious, but the sparse furnishings have a jarring effect. The rooms are, however, impeccably clean. Very friendly staff.

Giada
$$$ bkfst incl.
pb, hw, ⊗, ≈
☎ *656-1032*
⇄ *656-0131*
The Giada is an attractive hotel. Although the rooms are small, they

each have a small desk and a balcony or patio. Most open onto a charming inner courtyard that is beautifully landscaped with tropical vegetation. Try to get one of these rooms, rather than one facing the street. The beach is only 150m (164ft) away.

Hotel Latino
$$$ bkfst incl.
pb, hw, ⊗, ℜ
northern section of the Playa Cangrejal
☎/≈656-0043
Like the Mágica Cantarana (see below), the Hotel Latino has comfortable rooms in a long, two-storey building. The grounds could be in better condition. The balconies are quite large and private. The beach is only 200m (656ft) away.

Mágica Cantarana
$$$ bkfst incl.
pb, hw, ⊗, ≈
Playa Buena Vista, several km north of Playa Sámara
☎656-0071
≈656-0260
The Mágica Cantarana hotel is situated near the road from Sámara to Playa Buena Vista. It has clean and comfortable rooms in a two-storey building that faces the swimming pool. A balcony runs along the rooms in the front, while another at the back has a view of the green pastures surrounding the hotel. You can also rent a fully equipped apartment and take diving courses here.

Las Brisas del Pacifico
$$$$
hw, pb, ⊗, ≡, ≈
southern section of the beach
☎656-0250
≈656-0067
labrisa@racsa.co.cr
Las Brisas del Pacifico is an attractive hotel complex amidst tropical greenery. The rooms are very clean and situated on beach level or on the hill. The latter have a magnificent view of the surroundings. Each room has a private terrace. Direct access to the beach.

🌊 Hotel Isla Chora
$$$$ bkfst incl.
hw, pb, ≡, ⊗, ≈, ℜ
☎656-0174
≈656-0173
The Hotel Isla Chora is one of Sámara's premier little hotel complexes. Its delicious Italian restaurant (see p 284) even has an ice cream parlour that serves wonderful gelato! The buildings' attractive modern design and the scenic landscaping add to the tasteful colours, furniture and general comfort of the rooms. The service is also first class: in high season, international newspapers are available to guests, and useful information about local attractions is always on hand. The hotel offers all sorts of excursions. There is also a nightclub.

Hotel Sámara Beach
$$$$-$$$$$
≡, hw, pb, ≈, ℜ
on the road to the beach's public entrance
☎656-0218
≈656-0326
The area surrounding the buildings of the Hotel Sámara Beach is covered with dense vegetation. The rooms are pleasantly subdued, with French windows that open out onto individual terraces.

Mirador de Sámara
$$$$$
≈, ⊗, hw, pb, K
☎650-0044
≈656-0046
www.miradordesamara.com
Thanks to the design of its buildings and its hilltop location, the Mirador de Sámara hotel has a splendid view of Sámara's surroundings. The panorama can be enjoyed from hotel's attractive apartments, which are quite comfortable despite the thin foam mattresses on the beds, and are fully equipped and quite large. In 2000, the owners built a welcome addition: a swimming pool surrounded by a lovely multi-level wooden terrace and mature gardens.

Hotel Villas Playa Sámara
$$$$$
hw, pb, ≈, ⊗, ℜ
☎256-8228
≈221-7222
btlvilla@racsa.co.cr
The Hotel Villas Playa Sámara is a huge hotel and residential complex on the edge of Sámara, on the beach. The units

consist of one-, two- or three-bedroom villas with sunny rooms and red-tiled floors. The buildings blend harmoniously with the landscape and a small, pretty pathway winds through the grounds. There are tennis, volleyball and badminton courts on the premises, as well as a wading pool.

Playa Carillo

El Sueño Tropical
$$$$
≡, hw, pb, ≈, ℜ
just south of Playa Carillo
☎*656-0151*
≈*656-0152*
El Sueño Tropical is set back from the bustle of the Sámara and Carillo beaches. The rooms are fitted out with tasteful, tropical furniture and open onto a patio and the gardens of the vast property.

Guanamar
$$$$$
hw, pb, ctv, ≡, ≈, ℜ
☎*656-0054*
≈*656-0001*
Guanamar hotel is a well-laid-out and shady hotel complex on a hillside overlooking Carillo beach. The large, airy, charming rooms have their own bathrooms and private terraces, with French windows that seem to bring the outdoors inside.

Restaurants

Around Tilarán-Cañas-Bagaces

Tilarán

If you're headed for Lake Arenal, see p 216 for other restaurants around Tilarán.

A series of small, inexpensive eateries can be found in the street northwest of the cathedral. The *soda* **Stefani** cooks up country-style food, **Nuevo Fortuna** (*11am to midnight*) serves Chinese food, and **Mac Pato** sells hamburgers, fries and other fast food in a friendly setting.

Restaurant Tilarán
$$
☎*695-5043*
The Restaurant Tilarán serves seafood and Costa Rican meals. The linen table cloths lend this dining room a touch of elegance. Clean and well kept.

La Carreta
$$-$$$
every day from 7am to 9pm
on the road behind the church
☎*695-6654*
≈*695-6593*
La Carreta prepares excellent Italian and other dishes such as hamburgers. This family-owned establishment is the best place to eat in Tilarán—just

look at the enthusiastic comments in its guest book! Meals are served indoors or on the veranda. Furthermore, the friendly owners will be more than happy to recommend local attractions.

Cañas

Although Cañas is not reputed for its restaurants, a stroll through its centre lets you choose from fried chicken at **Pollo Frito Mimi** (*north east corner of the central park*), Chinese food at **Tai Va Alicia Lo Ho** (*north side of park*) or at **El Primero** (*west side of the park*, ☎*669-0219*), or a light snack at the town's **Musmanni**, close to the central park.

Hotel El Corral
$-$$
☎*669-0367*
On the Interamericana, the restaurant at Hotel El Corral serves hearty country-style meals.

Restaurant Rincón Corobicí
$$
8am to 10pm
on the Interamericana, 4km (2.5mi) north of Cañas
☎*669-1234*
Stop at the Restaurant Rincón Corobicí near Cañas for its international and Costa Rican cuisine (fish, steak, sandwiches and so on). The restaurant's unique vantage point over the Río Corobicí will delight your senses as you take a seat on its terrace in this enjoyable setting. A great place to

stop if you're on your way to Liberia and best appreciated in daylight.

Bagaces

Albergue Bagaces
$-$$
on the Interamericana, east of the gas station
☎**671-1267**
The restaurant at the Albergue Bagaces serves tasty seafood dishes in a large airy dining room. Breakfast is also served.

North of Liberia

La Cruz

Dariri
$
every day 7am to 10pm
on the main street, near the Cabinas Santa Rita, La Cruz
Dariri is a clean and friendly restaurant that prepares Costa Rican meals and tasty seafood platters, including delicious garlic shrimps.

La Cafetería
$-$$
50m (164ft) east of the central park, La Cruz
☎**679-9276**
In La Cruz, La Cafetería is a good spot for *bocadillos*, hamburgers, *emparedados* and, of course, excellent coffee. The English-speaking owner, Ricardo Bolaños, is also an excellent tour guide, and his restaurant doubles as a tourist information centre.

Marco Polo
$$
6km (3.7mi) north of La Cruz on the Inter-American
☎/≈**679-9132**
The restaurant of the Colinas del Norte Hotel (see p 260), Marco Polo has an inexpensive Costa Rican and Italian menu. The restaurant occupies the second floor of the hotel, so you have a lovely view of the scenery. Local bands perform at the hotel on weekends.

Ehecatl
$$-$$$
10am to 10pm
150m (492ft) east of the central park, La Cruz
☎**679-9104**
With a name that means "god of winds" in the language of the Chorotegas, Ehecatl is perched high above the lowlands surrounding Salinas bay, and thus provides a panoramic view of the bay and ocean, best enjoyed at sunset. The restaurant itself unfortunately does not live up to its spectacular view: the ordinary service and standard Latin American food are not exactly what you call "fine dining." The second floor is a little more stylish, however, and serves a selection of seafood dishes.

Around Liberia

Liberia and Surroundings

Jardín de Azúcar
$
one street north of the main square, Calle Central, Avenida 3
The Jardín de Azúcar has an eclectic, affordable menu.

Pan y Miel
$
Calle 2, Avenida 3
Sit down and enjoy delicious cakes and scrumptious enchiladas at the Pan y Miel bakery and pastry shop.

Rancho El Dulce
$
Avenida Central, Calle Central
Rancho El Dulce is a small fast-food establishment that also sells an array of candies and chocolates. Just try to control you sweet tooth!

Las Tinajas
$
on the north side of the central park
Las Tinajas is a busy "soda-restaurant" that serves popular food like hamburgers and fries.

Pókopí
$-$$
every day 11am to 10pm
just outside Liberia, on the road to Santa Cruz, facing the El Sitio Hotel
☎**666-1036 or 666-0769**
Despite its modest exterior, the Pókopí has an elegant dining room and, unlike other restaurants outside of town, features a variety

of tasty dishes (fish, steak, pizza, chicken, etc.). For a quiet meal, be sure to eat before 9pm as the dance club next door can get noisy!

Buona Pizza
$$
☎*666-3535*
Buona Pizza serves—you guessed it—good pizza! This small fast-food counter also delivers almost anywhere in town. The choice of toppings could not be more extensive and the thick crust is fantastic. With its plastic furniture and television, it's a typical little *soda*.

Bramadero Hotel
$$
on the Interamericana, near the main boulevard in Liberia
☎*666-0371*
≈*666-0203*
Red meat from the Guanacaste region is the specialty at the restaurant of the Bramadero Hotel. Although very popular, it's not a top-notch steak house.

El Charro
$$
275m (902ft) east of the Banco de Costa Rica
☎*666-2239*
The El Charro *marisquería* and bar serves decent seafood dishes.

Restaurante Jauja
$$
every day, restaurant 9am to 10pm, bar 10am to 2:30am
on the main boulevard in Liberia, just off the Interamericana
☎*666-0917*
Restaurante Jauja serves pizza and pasta. The place becomes a popular bar at night.

Playa del Coco and Surroundings

Playa del Coco

Teresita
$
This small *soda* is located on the corner across from the main park. It has a large menu of filling *tica* food: *casados* (black beans, rice and meat), sandwiches and *gallo pinto* (black or red beans and fried rice served with meat or eggs). The place is clean and tidy.

Cabinas del Coco
$-$$
on the beach, in front of the public pier
☎*670-0110 or 670-0276*
Popular Costa Rican dishes are on menu at the restaurant of the Cabinas del Coco.

Bar, Marisquería y Pizzería Cocos
$$
on the other side of the square that is right by the beach
☎*670-0113*
The Bar, Marisquería y Pizzería Cocos is a nice place for a meal or a drink. The restaurant is quite busy, as people

come here for a light snack as well as an evening out. It becomes lively at night.

Pato Loco Inn
$$
Fri to Wed, 6am to 9pm
800m (2,625ft) from the beach on Playa del Coco road
☎*670-0145*
The spaghettería located in the Pato Loco Inn serves authentic Italian food at very good prices.

Pura Vida
$$$
in front of the central park where the beach meets the main road leading downtown
☎*670-0272*
The Pura Vida stands out from most restaurants in the region because of its open setting and varied menu.

Coco Verde
$$-$$$
200m (656ft) from the beach, on Playa del Coco's main road
☎*670-0494*
The restaurant located in the hotel Coco Verde offers a varied menu.

Tequila Grill
$$$
As you might have guessed, the Tequila Grill is a Mexican restaurant! The generous portions of fajitas, enchiladas and guacamole, not to mention the grilled meats, are spicy enough to give your tastebuds a jolt!

Papagayo Sea Food
$$$
The Papagayo Sea Food restaurant serves fresh fish and seafood for all tastes. The

owner hails from New Orleans, as is evident in the Cajun accent of some of the dishes. The setting is not the warmest since the restaurant's open room faces the main road and is decorated with white tiles, but after all, it's the food that counts!

El Sol y La Luna
$$$
every day 7am to 10am, 11am to 1pm and 6pm to 11pm
150m (492) from the beach, one street east of the main road in Playa del Coco
☎*670-0195*
El Sol y La Luna is a handsome trattoria whose modern Mediterranean design matches that of Puerta del Sol, the hotel in which it is situated (see p 264). The young and friendly owner specializes in Italian cuisine and can also make all kinds of coffee. Breakfast is served.

Flor de Itabo Hotel
$$$
approx. 1km (0.6mi) from the beach, at the entrance to Playa del Coco
☎*670-0011 or 670-0292*
The Flor de Itabo Hotel has an excellent Italian restaurant with a good reputation.

Playa Ocotal

Father Rooster Bar
$$
The Father Rooster Bar is in a renovated ranch house that faces the El Ocotal Beach Resort, with which it is affiliated. This laid-back restaurant and bar is

the perfect place to go for a bite to eat if you're on the beach—you can walk in simply wearing your bathing suit! Dancing in the evenings.

El Ocotal Beach Resort
$$$-$$$$
☎*670-0321 or 670-0323*
The restaurants of the El Ocotal Beach Resort propose an international menu that features seafood dishes. The food is wonderful, but the magnificent view of Papagayo Gulf steals the show!

Playa Hermosa

Puesta del sol
$$$
☎*672-0103*
Among the increasing number of beachside restaurants available to tourists, a Spanish restaurant stands out. The Puesta del Sol, run by salt-of-the-earth Spaniards, offers a menu that leans to the spicy. The fare offered here, including paella, tapas and sangria, blends in perfectly with the decor. What's more, there is a stunning view of the ocean and the sunset. The restaurant, furnished in wood with a palm roof, is situated in front of a garden that descends in stages to the sand.

Aquasport centre
$$$
every day 9am to 9pm
☎*670-0450*
Next to a small supermarket and a sports equipment rental service, the restaurant of the Aquasport centre cooks up a variety of dishes, with a special emphasis on seafood. Relaxed ambiance and good food.

🦞 Villa del Sueño
$$$
☎*672-0026*
The restaurant of the Villa del Sueño (see p 263) is undoubtedly one of the better restaurants in the region. Situated on the spectacular terrace in front of the hotel, it has a cozy decor and soft, pleasant music. Every evening, the menu features fixed-price menu offering four main courses, including fish, pasta and meat dishes. Everything is meticulously prepared by an obvious lover of the culinary arts. A place not to be missed!

Playa Panamá

Costa Cangrejo
$
Tue to Sat 10am to 10pm, Sun 10am to 6pm
south of the Sano Sano centre beside the public access to the beach
☎*670-0050*
Costa Cangrejo features Costa Rican dishes and fast food.

Around Filadelfia

Playa Flamingo and Surroundings

Playa Pan de Azúcar

Hotel Sugar Beach
$$-$$$
every day 6am to 11pm
15km (9.3mi) from the turnoff to Huscas
☎654-4242
The Hotel Sugar Beach has a circular open-air restaurant. Enjoy the marvellous view as you watch monkeys, iguanas, toucans and parrots carousing on the hotel grounds. International menu and lunchtime specials.

Playa Potrero

Bahía Potrero Beach Resort
$$-$$$
☎654-4183
Seafood, steak and a nice ocean view are what you'll find at the restaurant of the Bahía Potrero Beach Resort.

El Grillo
$$$
Thu to Tue 5pm "'til you drop!"
El Grillo is a brand new restaurant and bar that specializes in French cuisine. Happy hour from 5pm to 9pm.

Playa Flamingo

Mariner Inn
$$-$$$
☎654-4081
Next to the marina, the restaurant at the Mariner Inn serves seafood in a relaxing setting.

Marie's Restaurant
$$-$$$
near the Flamingo Marina Hotel
☎654-4136
Marie's Restaurant is a pleasant place with an alluring decor and lovely landscaping. The spacious, airy interior combines lush greenery with wooden trim. This is very popular restaurant ideal for breakfast, lunch or a simple evening meal. Mostly Mexican cuisine.

Amberes
$$$-$$$$
every day 6:30am to 10pm
near the Flamingo Marina Hotel
☎654-4001
Amberes is a restaurant, night club and casino that's very popular because it isn't attached to a hotel. It specializes in seafood, but many other dishes are available.

Playa Brasilito

There may be several *sodas* in Brasilito like tiny **El Mirto**, but not many are as cute. **La Casita del pescado** is a bit bigger and has tables in the shade. **Heladería Super Mercado** offers refreshing treats like ice cream.

Las Playas
$$
☎654-4237
Las Playas is the restaurant of the large beachfront Hotel Brasilito. It offers basic and affordable food, mostly salads, fish and seafood, in an outdoor setting.

Restaurante Chulamate
$$
☎675-0246
As you travel from Filadelfia to beaches such as Brasilito or Conchal, stop at the roadside Restaurante Chulamate for a quick and inexpensive meal. The owners are friendly and the dining room is spacious.

Playa Tamarindo and Surroundings

Playa Tamarindo

Panadería Francesa
$
On entering the city, you'll certainly notice this French corner bakery, especially if you're a food lover. They make real croissants, baguettes and various pastries that all do credit to their country of origin. Not to be missed for breakfast, a snack or picnic.

Galería Pelicano
$
☎653-0318
As its name indicates, the Galería Pelicano is primarily an art gallery showcasing regional artists' work. But it also doubles as a deli where you can sample small dishes that are perfect for a snack or lunch in an agreeable atmosphere on the little terrace. Bagels with cream cheese, muffins, cheese cake, coffee— all the classics are served to be savoured. You can even do your shopping here. A must!

Cocodrilo
$-$$
☎653-0255
Just behind the French bakery on the route into town, the same family has opened a charming little restaurant. On the edge of the lagoon that gives the restaurant its name, this establishment consists of just a few tables nestled under the coconut trees. There is even a little path that leads in a few steps to the beach. Cocodrilo serves only lunch—sandwiches, salads, grilled meats and the perennial hearth-baked pizza, all to be washed down with a good cold beer!

Zully Mar Restaurant
$-$$
every day 7am to 11pm
at the end of the first street that borders the beach, in the bend
☎653-0140
The popular Zully Mar Restaurant offers savoury Costa Rican dishes (the *ceviche* is excellent!) along with a nice view.

Iguana Surf
$$
☎653-0148
The Iguana Surf is an institution in the midst of bustling Tamarindo. With a surfing boutique, tour company and equipment rental centre, it's definitely well known to the fun-loving surfing crowd that comes here. It's also striking because of its location, in a large wooden building with a facade sporting big wooden sculptures, just

behind a giant *matapalo* tree. Hidden in the heart of this cavernous building is a *trattoria* that serves a vast menu to sustain athletic types, but that is nevertheless quite original. You can also enjoy an espresso in a tropical setting while pondering the purchase of your next item of surfing gear!

Stella
$$
☎653-0127
The tables and well-stuffed armchairs in the Stella Restaurant are arranged under a high palm roof, on a round concrete slab that resembles a dance floor. The lack of decor and rather deafening music might seem uninviting at first, but let yourself be tempted by one of the dishes on their enormous menu. Moreover, the menu gets bigger every evening as various specials are offered—chicken curry or *chicken à l'orange*, veal, seafood, hearth-baked pizzas and pasta are just some of the choices that might lure you back to eat at Stella's. This restaurant probably has one of the best price/quality ratios in the region. Credit cards are not accepted.

Arco Iris
$$
Tue to Sun
Arco Iris serves inventive vegetarian cuisine.

Fiesta del Mar
$$-$$$
at the end of the first street that borders the beach, in the bend
Fiesta del Mar serves steak and seafood cooked in a wood-fired oven. Open 24hrs!

El Milagro
$$-$$$
every day 7am to 11pm
on the left as you enter the village of Tamarindo
☎653-0042
Nestled in lush gardens and surrounded by wonderfully carved sculptures reminiscent of pre-Colombian times, El Milagro is an attractive place to dine on *tica* and continental cuisine.

Tamarindo Diriá
$$-$$$
☎290-4340
The Tamarindo Diriá is definitively worth a stop, if only to admire its picturesque landscape. The kitchen prepares tasty international dishes that vary from day to day.

El Jardín del Edén
$$$-$$$$
☎654-4111
Ensconced under a palm roof by the pool, the restaurant at El Jardín del Edén hotel (see p 270) is enhanced considerably by the garden, its namesake, with its ravishing colours and scents. Wicker furniture with comfortable cream-coloured cushions and small lamps lend the place a soothing atmosphere. Lobster is the house speciality, but they also offer dishes

from Italy, where the friendly owners come from. Pasta, fish (such as *tilapia*) and desserts are prepared according to the high standards of "the boot." It has all the ingredients of a delightful evening, even if you're not staying at the hotel.

🛳 Mama Mia
$$$-$$$$
☎654-4111
Mama Mia probably ranks among the best restaurants in the region, even in the country. The chef, Andrea Rossi, recently arrived from Italy and can't stop himself from importing many of his ingredients directly from the old continent. These include prosciuto and other tender, tasty cold cuts, fine cheeses and even truffles, which he adds to a pasta sauce that reaches the heights of culinary excellence. Besides pasta, he prepares divine veal scallops and other meats smothered in the most succulent sauces. Not to be outdone, the simpler items like hearth-baked pizzas are also mouthwatering. Do save room for dessert—among other little treats, they serve flambéed mangoes! The restaurant is tastefully decorated and opens out onto the great outdoors. The service is outstanding and overall, Mama Mia has all the elements of an unforgettable evening.

Coconut
$$$$
☎653-0086
On the main route from Tamarindo, a restaurant perched on a raised platform under a palm roof will surely catch your eye. You may be attracted by the white lights, but most striking is the beautiful and classic decor, with its white tablecloths, wooden furniture and charming atmosphere. The French owners of the Coconut draw on French traditions both in the preparation of the dishes as well as in all other aspects of serving a good meal. The art of the table put into practice! Here you can savour fish and seafood dishes that are delectable, if a bit expensive.

Around Santa Cruz

Playa Junquillal and Surroundings

Playa Negra

Las Hermanas
$
closed Mon
On the road to Playa Negra, just before you get to the sea, you'll come to a gorgeous yellow house at the bottom of a garden, behind a wooden fence. This is the home of the Las Hermanas sisters, who together opened a surfing boutique and the most charming little bakery. It has a few tables outside and inside and is the perfect place to

stop. On the menu are sandwiches, fresh bread, muffins, granola and other delicious breakfast fare. Don't miss the homemade cakes and cookies, which are a real treat.

Pablo Picasso Restaurant and Bar
$$
Easy St.
Surfing fanatics flock to the Pablo Picasso Restaurant and Bar. Owned by an American who also adores the sport, this inexpensive, laid-back eatery serves up large portions of popular food like hamburgers.

Playa Negra Hotel
$$-$$$
☎382-1301
The restaurant at the secluded Playa Negra Hotel is worth the extra mile (see p 271). Its Basque chef prepares French culinary treats and hotel employees speak French. During the rainy season, enquire about road conditions before you head out. Most clients use four-wheel drive vehicles.

Playa Junquillal

Junquillal Hotel
$$
beside the public access to Playa Junquillal beach
☎653-0432
The restaurant at the Junquillal Hotel is a simple but friendly establishment that serves Costa Rican and North American food.

Guacamaya Lodge
$$-$$$
☎653-0431
The restaurant at the Guacamaya Lodge specializes in Swiss and international cuisine. It has lunchtime specials and a more elaborate dinner menu.

Around Nicoya

Nicoya and Surroundings

Café Daniela
$
☎686-6148
Stop at Café Daniela on Nicoya's main street for a light snack (pizza, chicken) or a rich desert.

Restaurante Nicoya
$$$
Restaurante Nicoya is an unassuming Chinese restaurant located on the main street.

Playa Nosara and Surroundings

Playa Nosara and Playa Pelada

The village of Nosara offers several choices of *sodas* if you don't want to go right to the sea for a bite to eat. The **Rancho Campesino** serves down home *tica* food as well as good pasta and pizza under a high palm roof. The **Soda Vanessa**, hidden behind the vegetation, has a pleasant atmosphere.

Olga's Bar
$-$$
every day 6:30am to 10pm
beside the public access to Pelada de Nosara beach
Next to the beach, Olga's Bar serves light meals (sandwiches, *casados*) and cool drinks.

Luna Bar and Grill
$$-$$$
Playa Pelada de Nosara, next to the public beach access
The Luna Bar and Grill has a unique design with its tasteful interior opening onto a stunning terrace facing the sea. Owned by the Playas de Nosara Hotel, this beachfront bar and grill is ideal for a meal or drinks. The kitchen prepares roast chicken, seafood, salads and traditional Costa Rican dishes.

Estancia Nosara
$$$
4km (2.5mi) south of Nosara
☎680-0378
The charming and spacious restaurant at the hotel Estancia Nosara is surrounded by 10ha (25 acres) of tropical gardens. International menu.

Villa Taype Hotel
$$$
between Punta Pelada and Playa Guiones
☎382-7715
The restaurant of the Villa Taype Hotel proposes an international menu in a most relaxing environment.

Playa Sámara and Surroundings

Playa Guiones

Boulangerie Café de Paris
$
At the reception of the Café de Paris hotel, there is a bakery/pâtisserie where they concoct sweets reminiscent of those in France. The baguettes, croissants, chocolate eclairs and other treats will satisfy even the pickiest tastes! Be sure to arrive early for the best choice. Not surprisingly, the reception also houses a souvenir shop.

Café de Paris
$$
The name of this restaurant, taken from the hotel, may at first glance appear to be a misnomer since the menu, which is not very elaborate, doesn't really offer French dishes. However, the dishes are created with the attention to detail that is synonymous with French cuisine. The baguette sandwiches and the large mixed grills are especially tasty.

Olas Grandes Gringo Grill
$$
Olas Grandes Gringo Grill serves Costa Rican and North American dishes, as well as grill specialities, in a relaxed setting. At sundown, young surfers liven up the bar.

The Province of Guanacaste

La Dolce Vita
$$-$$$
Tue to Sun 5pm to 11pm
The menu at La Dolce Vita is Italian, and Italian only. The place lives up to its name: life does seem to be at its sweetest as you quietly sup beneath the canopy of a hut nestled in the jungle.

Giardino Tropicale
$$$
Giardino Tropicale cooks Italian dishes in a wood-burning oven.

Playa Sámara

Ananas
$
The small Ananas *rancho* has a long semi-circular bar and a few tables. To get here, you have to cross over a pretty little wooden bridge. As you may have guessed, fruit is the main attraction: fruit salads and freshly squeezed juices abound in colours and flavours. You can also have a good breakfast or just stop to devour a piece of cake in the middle of the day.

Casa del Mar
$-$$
☎656-0264
The restaurant at the Casa del Mar Hotel is run by a young Quebecois couple. Since they don't have much experience in restaurants, their menu is limited. Breakfasts of bacon or sausages will appeal to North American palates!

Casa Naranja
$$
☎656-0220
Set inside a charming house in the middle of the village of Sámara, the Casa Naranja's menu is completely oriented toward metropolitan France, from where its owners hail. It's highly recommended by the locals. So settle down on the little terrace in back and savour the crepes, a house speciality, *vol-au-vent*, duck *à l'orange* or any other delicacy that comes out of their ovens. On your way out, don't forget to stock up on Provence-style jams!

Hotel Isla Chora
$$-$$$
☎656-0174
When it comes to Italian food, the pizzeria of the Hotel Isla Chora deserves high praise. It serves a variety of delicious pizzas and fantastic Italian ice cream in a lovely decor that opens to the outdoors.

The **Delfín** (*$$$*) and **El Ancla** (*$$$*) are right next to each other at the edge of the village. They are so close to the beach that their tables are almost in the sand. Their extensive menus feature classic seaside fare like fish and seafood. The El Ancla extends an especially warm welcome.

Hotel Las Brisas del Pacifico
$$$
southern section of Playa Sámara
☎656-0250
The restaurant at the Hotel Las Brisas del Pacifico serves international, *tico* and German dishes in a beautiful natural setting.

Playa Carillo

El Mirador
$$
☎656-0307
Hearty food like steaks and hamburgers are found on the menu of the seaside El Mirador. A good place to quell midday hunger pangs.

El Yate de Marisco
$$
☎656-0179
El Yate de Marisco is a seafood restaurant perched high on the cliffs towering over Carillo beach. The view of the coastline and the sea is spectacular.

Fuego Latino
$$
every day 7am to 11pm
☎656-0450
Owned by cool young Italians, the Fuego Latino restaurant and bar has a tropical atmosphere with its thatched-roof dining area that opens on three sides. It specializes in Italian and Costa Rican flavours. Located near the El Sueño Tropical restaurant.

Playa Laguna Beach Resort
$$
☎*656-0005*

The restaurant of the Playa Laguna Beach Resort serves Spanish cuisine in a very charming decor. This establishment's eye-catching design is quite extraordinary in the surrounding wilderness, not to mention in Costa Rica. Decorative details like ceramic-topped tables, fashionably modern chairs, walls painted in warm south ern colours, and a lovely green-stained wooden counter make it an aesthetic master piece. And the excel lent food is no less exceptional— especially the Andalusian gaspacho.

Guanamar Hotel
$$-$$$
☎*656-0054*

An international menu is available at the res taurant and bar at the Guanamar Hotel, which also has an attractive setting and a superb view.

El Sueño Tropical
$$$
every day 7am to 9:30pm
south of Playa Carillo
☎*656-0151*

In a large hut on a hill, the brightly decorated El Sueño Tropical ca ters to lovers of Italian food in the hotel of the same name (see p 276).

Entertainment

Bars and Nightclubs

Around Liberia

Liberia and Surroundings

Kurú
at the edge of Liberia on the road to Santa Cruz, in front of the El Sitio Hotel, Liberia
☎*666-1036 or 666-0769*
There is lively dance music at Kurú every Wednesday through Sunday. A giant screen TV also provides enter tainment. The club opens at 9pm and is situated next door to the Pókopí restaurant (see p 277).

Daysita Hotel
on the south side of the sta dium, Liberia
☎*666-0197*
A congenial dance club and bar oc cupies the base ment of the Daysita Hotel.

Playa del Coco

The Playa del Coco is without a doubt *the* nocturnal gath ering place in the area. It has several bars and nightclubs that come to steamy life after 10pm! Among the most popu lar clubs are the **Jungla**, the **Banano Bar** and the new **Lizard Lounge**, which share a clientele

that is thirsty for excite ment.

Coco Mar
in front of the central park behind the Cabinas del Coco
For several years now, the Coco Mar has been a lively dance club.

Astillero Disco Club
☎*670-0120*
The Astillero Disco Club is located on the road leading to Playa del Coco.

Playa Hermosa

Monkey Bar
☎*672-0267*
Just outside Playa Hermosa, on the Playa Panamá road, there is a *rancho* that is a little out of the ordinary. This huge structure of palm trees and wood is the home of the Monkey Bar, which usually abounds with atmosphere. In the middle of the room there is a large circular bar where you can have cocktails mixed for you. They also serve very fill ing Mexican food, and on evenings when the bar isn't rock ing with live musi cians, you can play pool or table soccer. And if you are wonder ing what monkeys have to do with the bar, it's located right next to a

magnificent, enormous *matapalo* tree that is often home to a colony of screaming monkeys!

Around Filadelfia

Playa Tamarindo

Playa Tamarindo is renowned for its lively nightlife. The bars and nightclubs throb with the young and the not-so-young—tourists and locals alike—as they get together to down a beer or dance. For dancing, the **Noai** club is the first choice. For chatting with friends, there is **Cantina Las Olas**, which is completely devoted to the art of surfing, or **Mambo**, at the end of the village road, which attracts a large enough crowd every evening to create a good atmosphere.

Around Nicoya

Playa Nosara and Surroundings

Olga's Bar
beside the public access to Pelada de Nosara beach
Olga's Bar is popular with Costa Ricans on Saturday nights and opens out onto a spacious open-air dance floor.

Pirata's Bar
Nosara
☎*284-9669*
At Pirata's Bar, which is part of the Rancho Suizo Hotel, you can slow dance in tropical surroundings next to the beach.

Playa Sámara and Surroundings

La Gondola
on the road leading to the public access to Sámara beach in front of the Sámara Beach Hotel
Jamaican rhythms and intimate corners create the warm atmosphere of the bar La Gondola. You can also enjoy a game of ping-pong, pool or darts here.

Isla Chora Hotel
☎*656-0174*
Young people dance the night away in the chic decor of the nightclub in the Isla Chora Hotel.

Shopping

Around Liberia

Liberia and Surroundings

Tiffany
Mon to Sat
100m (328ft) south of, and 50m (164ft) west of Coopeconpro Plaza 25 de Julio, Liberia
☎*666-0440*
In Liberia, Tiffany offers a wide choice of souvenirs and handcrafted items such as stained-glass windows, jewellery and leather goods.

Info-Cen-Tur
Calle 1, Avenida 3, Liberia
☎*666-1833*
Located in Liberia's Bambú shopping centre, Info-Cen-Tur sells North American newspapers (during high season) and has a wealth of information on regional tourist attractions.

Kaltak
4.5km (2.8mi) west on the road to the airport
☎/≈*667-0076*
Kaltak is a reputable handicraft and souvenir shop located on the road from Liberia to Santa Cruz.

Playa del Coco and Surroundings

Playa Hermosa

Aquasport
☎*670-0450*
In the vicinity of Playa Hermosa, Aquasport has a small supermarket that sells *The Miami Herald*.

Playa del Coco

You can buy your souvenirs at the Playa del Coco, where a host of boutiques and open-air markets carry large quantities of T-shirts, hats and trinkets, among other things.

Comercial Porto Fino
southeast corner of the playground, Playa del Coco
The handsome boutique Comercial Porto Fino sells basic medications and cosmetics, as well as souvenirs and gift ideas.

Around Filadelfia

Playa Tamarindo and Surroundings

Playa Grande

The **El Mundo de la Tortuga** museum (see p 250), located at the entrance to the Parque Nacional Marino Las Baulas near Playa Tamarindo, has a pleasant souvenir shop whose products focus on the region's giant turtles (clothes, jewellery, books, photos and so on).

Around Santa Cruz

Santa Cruz and Surroundings

Guaitil Artesanía
☎ *686-6608*
on the road between Santa Cruz and Nicoya
Handcrafted terracotta pieces are available at the Guaitil Artesanía.

Guaitil, a small village near Santa Cruz, produces the lovely ceramics that decorate many hotels and restaurants in the Guanacaste region.

La Casona, Parque Nacional Santa Rosa

Sunset over magnificent Playa Panamá, a tropical forest hideaway.
- *Roger Michel*

A church in the Central Valley surrounded by lovely magenta bougainvillea.
- *Didier Raffin*

Ox carts are still used in some parts of the country.
- *Didier Raffin*

The Central Pacific Coast

Costa Rica's central Pacific coast is its most popular tourist destination, and is a favourite with Costa Ricans and foreigners alike.

Countless hotels have sprung up along this stretch of the coast, which benefits from its proximity to the national capital and the country's international airport.

While the opening of the Liberia airport has brought an increasing number of tourists north to the province of Guanacaste, the central Pacific coast remains the destination of choice for many package tours and independent vacationers. The area's attractions include the relatively untouched wilderness to be experienced in the southern part of the Nicoya Peninsula, reached via Puntarenas, and the combination of stylish development and exquisite natural settings which makes the re-

gion between Quepos and Manuel Antonio ideal for vacations. Meanwhile, the Jacó region has all the facilities of a great resort area, and is less than two hours from the nation's capital!

Hidden pieces of unspoiled nature can be found in the less developed regions between these fashionable hot-spots, providing tranquil settings for leisurely strolls that

leave you with a greater appreciation of Costa Rica's magnificent natural surroundings.

The climate is pleasantly temperate, in contrast to the exceptionally dry conditions in Guanacaste and the extreme humidity in the southern part pf the country. Vacationers, especially those escaping cold climates, bask in the sun during dry season, while during the wet season the annual rains restore the lush plant life to its opulent splendour.

With all these natural marvels, the allure of the central Pacific coast of Costa Rica is hard to resist!

Finding Your Way Around

By Plane

The Nicoya Peninsula

Tambor: **Sansa** (☎221-9414) and **Travelair** (☎220-3054) offer daily flights from San José to Tambor. The flight takes about 30min and the round-trip costs about $100.

South of Puntarenas

Quepos: has a small airfield that receives domestic flights. The airlines Sansa and Travelair (see above) both offer regular daily flights from San José. The trip takes about 20min and costs approximately $75 for a round-trip. Once in the country, enquire about the flight schedule, as it is liable to change. The airport is about 5km north of Quepos.

By Boat

The Nicoya Peninsula

Puntarenas–Paquera Ferry: visitors travelling by car should take the car ferry to Paquera rather than Playa Naranjo (see below), because the road between Playa Naranjo and Paquera is winding and poorly maintained. There are five departures every day in each direction (from both Puntarenas and Paquera, from 6am to 8:30pm). The fare is $1.25 for adults (*$3.35 in first class*) and $8.75 per car. The crossing takes about 1.5hrs (☎661-2084 or 661-3452). During the high season you should arrive 1hr in advance to be sure to make the next departure. There is also a passenger ferry (*3 departures daily, between 6am and 5pm; $1.25;* ☎661-2830).

Puntarenas–Playa Naranjo Ferry: this car ferry is the best way to reach Carmona and Nicoya. There are five departures daily between 3:15am and 7pm. The crossing takes about an hour and the fares are comparable to those of the Puntarenas–Paquera ferry (*Ferry Conatramar,* ☎661-1069).

Isla del Coco: there is no regular boat or ferry service to Isla del Coco. Most cruises depart from the city of Puntarenas and last one

or two weeks. The crossing alone takes about 36hrs. The agencies **Okeanos Aggressor** (☎290-6203, ≈290-6205) and **Undersea Hunter** (☎228-6535, ≈289-7334) offer excursions of about 10 days.

You can take a boat directly from Puntarenas to **Montezuma**, which is a wonderful cruise that eliminates the bus trip between Paqueras and Montezuma. Also, you get to see Montezuma at its best if you arrive by sea. Ask around at the Puntarenas docks to find a reliable carrier who is setting out at a time that suits your schedule.

By Car

The Puntarenas Region

Puntarenas can be reached from the Central Valley by taking the Interamericana Highway west to the Pacific coast. The Puntarenas exit is clearly indicated, about two hours into the trip.

The Nicoya Peninsula

The Southern Nicoya Peninsula: go to **Puntarenas** and take the ferry from there (see above). The road is unpaved between **Paquera** and **Cóbano** (35km or 21.7mi), except for a short section near Tambor. However, the

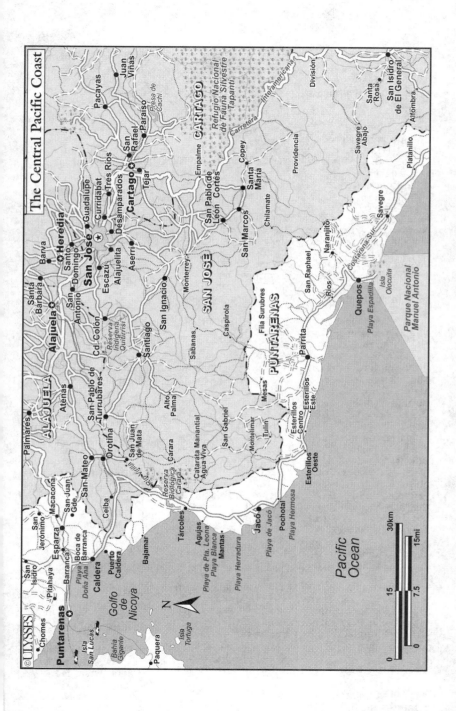

The Central Pacific Coast

road is regularly maintained and in good condition between Cóbano and **Montezuma** (7km or 4.3mi). Depending on the season, the road between Cóbano and **Malpaís** (about 12km or 7.5mi) can be difficult for cars without four-wheel drive to negotiate.

If you arrive on the Puntarenas–Playa Naranjo ferry, be aware that the road that links Playa Naranjo and Paquera is very rough and poorly maintained. It can take over an hour to complete the 26km trip.

Nicoya–Montezuma: from Nicoya, in the province of Guanacaste, you can drive south to Tambor, Montezuma and Malpaís, instead of returning to the Interamericana Highway, driving to Puntarenas and taking the ferry. Head in the direction of the little town of **Carmona**, and about 5km (3.1mi) before reaching it, take the little road on the left that leads to **Jicaral**, **Lepanto** and **Playa Naranjo**. The road is in good condition up to Playa Naranjo, but deteriorates between Playa Naranjo and Paquera. The trip from Nicoya to Montezuma is approximately 135km (83.4mi) long and takes about 5hrs by car.

South of Puntarenas

Playa Doña Ana: the off-ramp that leads to this beach is found just before the highway bridge that is visible as you leave Puntarenas. The sign indicating the road is difficult to spot so be attentive.

Reserva Biológica Carara, Playa Herradura and Playa Jacó: a 2hr drive from San José. Leave the Puntarenas Highway at the Atenas exit. About 20min before reaching Jacó, you will come to the entrance of Reserva Biológica Carara. The car entrance to Esterillos Oeste is 22km (13.7mi) south of Jacó, and the entrance to Esterillos Este is about 5km (3.1mi) further south.

A new section of highway now permits travellers coming from Puntarenas to reach these beaches in one hour. This road continues on to Quepos (70km or 43.5mi further), Dominical and San Isidro de El General.

Quepos and **Manuel Antonio**: it takes 3.5hrs to get from San José to Manuel Antonio via the Atenas exit and the little, winding road that crosses the Aguacate mountains. In addition to beautiful panoramic views, this road provides glimpses of rural Costa Rican life. If you prefer highways, you can continue in the direction of Puntarenas, follow the directions for Jacó and continue on to Quepos. Although the latter route looks much longer on the map, it takes only a half hour longer to cover the distance.

By Bus

The Puntarenas Region

San José–Puntarenas: departures every day, every half hour between 6am and 9pm. The trip takes two hours ($2.30; Calle 16, Avenida 10/12; Empresarios Unidos, ☎221-5749).

The Nicoya Peninsula

Paquera–Montezuma: a bus waits for the ferry from Puntarenas at the dock in Paquera, and shuttles travellers to Cóbano and Montezuma. There are departures from Montezuma every day at 5:30am, 10am and 2pm.

South of Puntarenas

Jacó: there are three departures daily from San José. Plan for a two-and-a-half-hour trip.

Quepos and **Manuel Antonio**: three buses per day make the four-hour trip from San José. Buses travelling the **Puntarenas–Quepos** route leave three times a day, but this trip is only slightly shorter, taking 3.5hrs. There is frequent service on the short **Quepos–Manuel Antonio** hop, especially during the high season, for a minimal fare *($1)*. This bus stops at hotels on request.

Practical Information

The Nicoya Peninsula

The southern Nicoya Peninsula is well supplied with services of all kinds. Since Tambor is a resort for well-to-do tourists, many services lost no time in opening their doors for business in the region. Thus, you should have no problem finding gas or health care. In Montezuma, the most popular destination, services are not as plentiful in the village itself—except of course for Internet services, which go hand in hand with young, "with-it" travellers.

The Puntarenas Region

Puntarenas is the capital of the Costa Rican province of the same name, and offers all the basic services, which is very convenient for travellers headed to the sparsely populated tip of the Nicoya peninsula. The town's Mercado Central is on the north side of the spit *(Calle 2, Avenida 3)*, right near where the

ferry and fishing boats dock. Buses leave from the beach on the south side of Puntarenas, near Calle 2. The Banco Nacional and Banco de Costa Rica (with ATM's) are located between the Museo Histórico Marino and the Mercado Central. Puntarenas also has a hospital at the corner of Paseo de los Turistas and Calle 9.

South of Puntarenas

Jacó is the largest town on the Pacific coast between Parrita and Puntarenas. It boasts *supermercados* (supermarkets), *farmacías* (pharmacies), a post office, banks with automated teller machines, laundromats, Internet access, bus stations, car rental offices and even a number of little shops that sell all sorts of merchandise. All of these services can be found on the main street that runs parallel to the beach. Jacó has a shopping mall, Centro Commercial Jacó Plaza, located north of the town on the main street, which also serves as a bus stop. There is a gas station at the edge of Jacó, on the road to Quepos.

Quepos

Quepos provides all the basic services. In addition to an airport and a recently built hospital a few kilometres north of the town, there is a *mercado central* in the

heart of Quepos, as well as a bus station and a nearby taxi stand. There is a post office across from the soccer field, and the Banco Nacional, Banco Popular and Banco de Costa Rica, all equipped with automated teller machines are located on the quadrant of streets that make up the downtown, right near the entrance road into town (coming from San José and Jacó). Farmacía Quepos is a little south of downtown on this same street, near the park. There is a gas station on the road to the airport.

In small, but recently enlarged premises, the cybercafé **Internet Tropical** provides a pleasant background for a bit of surfing. Their fresh juices make it tempting to stay in front of the screen a little longer!

Exploring

The Puntarenas Region

People come to Puntarenas for two main reasons. The port of **Puntarenas** links the coast and the tip of the Nicoya Peninsula, so it is a convenient stopover for travellers on their way to the peninsula. But Puntarenas also has its own merits because of the histori-

Ecotourism

For some years, a wave of ecotourism has been spreading across the travel world. More and more conscious of the importance of preserving our natural resources, tourists are increasingly choosing trips that are in harmony with the environment. However, even the term "ecotourism" is still the subject of debate, and meanwhile, many are trying to cash in on the bonanza. In the course of your journey to Costa Rica and in advertizing brochures, you'll see many businesses claiming to offer ecology–conscious excursions or services. Before setting off with one, ask a few questions to find out if the managers and employees demonstrate a true concern for the environment. Sometimes by digging a little deeper, you'll discover that their techniques are not all that sound.

cal role it played in the country's development.

For a long time, most of Costa Rica's export commodities were shipped to Europe from the coast of Puntarenas on the Pacific, because it was geographically the easiest to reach by mule or wagon, especially for the *cafeteros* of the Central Valley. Thus, Puntarenas was the gateway to Costa Rica's major markets in Europe during the 19th century. With foreign trade flourishing, Puntarenas grew continuously throughout this period.

The Pacific coast nonetheless had one major disadvantage as the centre of foreign trade: the European markets were across the Atlantic, so exporters had to send their merchandise on quite a trip to reach the "old world:" goods were shipped down the entire coast of South America, around Cape Horn at the southern end of Chile, and then back up north to the European trade centres. Quite a journey! Going via Asia was even longer. (The Panama Canal was only inaugurated in the early 20th century.)

Though it was obvious that a port on the Caribbean could only facilitate trade, the hostile climate, geography and nature of the Atlantic side of the country hindered such a project for a long time. The Central Valley was finally linked to the Caribbean coast by railroad in 1890.

This much more direct route to the European market took a little wind out of the sails in Puntarenas' port. The very recent inauguration of Puerto Caldera, a little to the south, put an end to the city's vocation as a commercial port once and for all.

Despite its decline, Puntarenas remains one of the largest cities in Costa Rica with its 100,000 residents. An important centre in the Costa Rican fishing industry, it is also the capital of the province of the same name, which extends to the southernmost part of the country along the coast.

The city's most interesting feature by far is the narrow spit of land that juts into the Gulf of Nicoya and gives the city its name, a corruption of "*punta de arena*," which means "point of sand" in Spanish. The downtown and historic sections of the city are both located on this spit and draw a lot of visitors in the dry season. Meanwhile, the district is very quiet and peaceful during the rainy season.

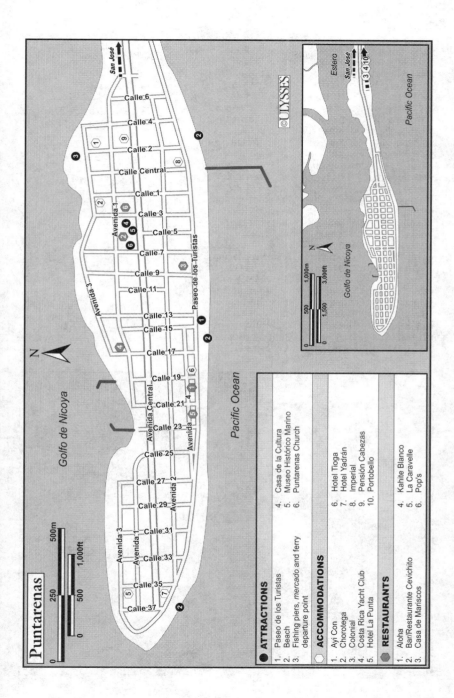

Puntarenas

ATTRACTIONS

1. Paseo de los Turistas
2. Beach
3. Fishing piers, *mercado* and ferry departure point
4. Casa de la Cultura
5. Museo Histórico Marino
6. Puntarenas Church

ACCOMMODATIONS

1. Ayi Con
2. Chorotega
3. Colonial
4. Costa Rica Yacht Club
5. Hotel La Punta
6. Hotel Tioga
7. Hotel Yadrán
8. Imperial
9. Pensión Cabezas
10. Portobello

RESTAURANTS

1. Aloha
2. Bar/Restaurante Cevichito
3. Casa de Mariscos
4. Kahite Blanco
5. La Caravelle
6. Pop's

© ULYSSES

Golfo de Nicoya

Pacific Ocean

San José

Estero

San José

Pacific Ocean

Golfo de Nicoya

Paseo de los Turistas (tourist road) runs alongside the town's beach on the southern shore of the spit. It can be very crowded with tourists who roam among the food stands and the various little shops. However, the Paseo is not completely without charm. Efforts have been made to clean up the beach, though the water is still not the most pristine in the country and is not ideal for swimming. Camping on the beach should also be avoided.

It is easy to get around Puntarenas because, although the city is a few kilometres long, it is only four streets (a few hundred metres at most) wide at most parts. The fishing docks, the **mercado** and the ferry landings overlook the shore opposite the beach (north side). A stroll through this area will give you a taste of daily life in this city.

The **Casa de la Cultura** *(Avenida 1, Calle 3, Puntarenas, ☎661-1394)*, in the city centre, houses an art gallery and hosts concerts and plays. The **Museo Histórico Marino** *($1; Tue to Sun 9am to 5pm; Avenida Central, Calle 3/5, Puntarenas)* presents the history of the city in a multimedia exhibition. The **Puntarenas church**, on Avenida Central west of the Museo Histórico Marino, is probably the most beautiful building in the city.

The Southern Nicoya Peninsula

Unlike the rest of the peninsula, the southern Nicoya Peninsula is not part of Guanacaste province but rather belongs to the province of Puntarenas, which extends southward along the coast to Dominical. Because there was no well-maintained road to the area from Nicoya, and the ferry crossing takes an hour and a half, it was decided that this part of the peninsula would be annexed to

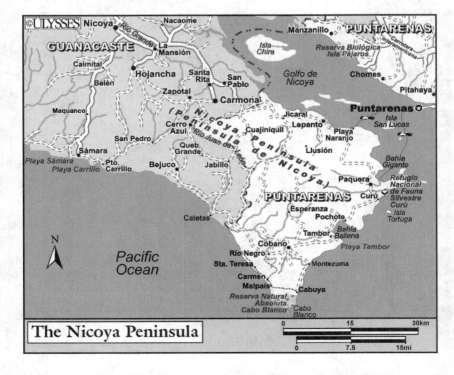

The Nicoya Peninsula

the province of Puntarenas. The vast majority of tourists and residents still take the Puntarenas–Paquera ferry to reach this magnificent corner of the country.

Paquera

The little village of Paquera is situated 4km (2.4mi) from the ferry landing. It has a grocery store, a bank, and a campground, as well as a few places to stay and some small, moderately priced restaurants. Most tourists only stop in Paquera overnight if they want to make the first ferry the next day. Thus, the place has retained the peaceful atmosphere of a little out-of-the-way village, despite the heavy traffic that runs through it because of the ferry.

North of Paquera

To the north, the **Playa Naranjo** area is seldom visited by tourists. Although there are a few hotels, useful for people planning to take the early morning ferry, this region has no pretty beaches or special attractions. Moreover, the road between Playa Naranjo and Paquera is in a deplorable state, ensuring an unpleasant start to any excursion you might want to make from here.

Further south, **Bahía Gigante** is an attractive bay in the Gulf of

Nicoya, where visitors can discover **Isla Gitana** and its native burial ground. Once called Isla de los Muertos ("the island of the dead"), this island welcomes visitors for a day trip or a longer stay, as it has accommodations, campsites, a restaurant and a bar. There are trails, a pretty beach and many opportunities for water sports, as well as boat transportation to the island (**☎**661-2994, ≈661-2833).

Paquera to Montezuma

South of the **Refugio Nacional de Fauna Silvestre Curú** ★(see p 300), the road leads to the magnificent **Bahía Ballena** near the small village of **Pochote**. Pochote has preserved its picturesque quality and seems to be resisting the ongoing tourist development that is being undertaken in the surrounding area. Bahía Ballena is an immense bay, the largest in the southern Nicoya Peninsula, which stretches between Punta Tambor and Punta Piedra Amarilla. In the crux of the bay is a beautiful beach that is suitable for swimming and stretches over 8km (5mi) between the villages of Pochote and Tambor. The bay got its name because whales can sometimes be seen here (ballena means "whale" in Spanish), though it is more likely to be dotted with sail-

boats that come here for shelter from the great winds of the open sea.

Tambor is a tiny village with reasonably priced places to stay and small, inexpensive restaurants. However, the region has its share of well-off tourists who stay in the large hotel complexes that have been built nearby. These resorts offer all-inclusive packages: prearranged vacations that include accommodation, meals, travel and numerous activities.

Past Tambor, the road veers back into the undulating farmland of the interior. Herds of zebus, large Indian bovines that have successfully adapted to the Costa Rican climate, can be spotted here— they are easily recognizable by their (most often) whitish colour, very long hanging ears and distinctive bump on the back near the head.

The village of **Cóbano** is 11km (6.8mi) from Tambor, and has many services, such as a bank, post office, medical clinic, public telephones and a service station, as well as a few grocery stores, shops and little sodas. To reach Montezuma from here, take another little road on the left, heading south, from the village centre.

The Central
Pacific Coast

★
Montezuma

Just 7km (4.3mi) from Cóbano, Montezuma is a pretty little seaside village with superb beaches and a vast selection of hotels, many of which are very affordable, as well as quite a few restaurants. It is reached via a small road that descends a very long, steep hill just before the village. Montezuma is small and has only a few streets, but many hotels are located at the edge of the village, on the roads to Cabuya and Cóbano.

Montezuma is overrun with young, free-spirited people from various countries (including Canada, Germany and the United States): hipsters, hippies, freaks and "granolas" stay here for weeks on end, and for very little money. Unfortunately, Montezuma was literally invaded by hordes of unscrupulous campers a few years ago. They polluted the area, and some didn't think twice about cutting down trees to fashion shelters, drink coconut milk or make bonfires on the beach. Because of these incidents, the village got a bad reputation as a haven for penniless drug users, youths and squatters who had been coming here since the early 1980s, making themselves unpopular with the region's locals by sunbathing nude.

Surprising Crabs

On the Pacific Coast, at the start of the rainy season, there's a good possibility that you'll witness a strange phenomenon: just after the first rainfall, the seashore is the site of mass migration by a small crab called *tajalín*. This is the period when the *tajalín* leaves the sea to lay its eggs on dry land, sometimes at a considerable distance from the beach and in numbers that are simply stupefying. Dark–coloured when in the water, this crab takes on vivid colours as its shell dries out. You can't fail to notice these little mauve and orange creatures (travelling in groups and moving sideways) as they flee from your approach or pretend to attack you with their claws!

Finally, the residents got together to improve the situation and protect Montezuma's natural beauty. Together with hotel-owners, they formed groups such as CATUMA (Cámara de Turismo de Montezuma), which organized cleanup and reforestation crews and led a campaign to sensitize other residents to the importance of preserving the region's environment. They also determined to keep Montezuma from becoming an overly developed tourist destination made up only of hotels or immense resort complexes like those around Quepos, Jacó and Tambor.

Their efforts were successful, and Montezuma has remained on a manageable scale where residents and tourists recognize and greet each other in passing. Of course, Montezuma is still a very popular tourist destination, so visitors looking for perfect tranquillity are better off near Malpaís or Cabuya. But if your budget is limited and you do not have a car, Montezuma is still an inviting, multifaceted region that abounds with all sorts of activities for all budgets.

You'll find tourist agencies that promote the regions many activities and attractions at the **Parque Central**. Among

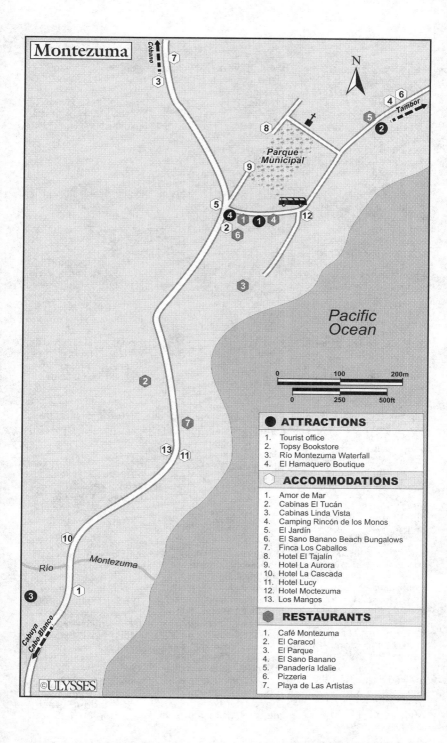

Montezuma

N

Pacific Ocean

Río Montezuma

Cabuya Cabo Blanco

Cóbano

Tambor

Parque Municipal

| 0 | | 100 | | 200m |
| 0 | 250 | | 500ft | |

● ATTRACTIONS

1. Tourist office
2. Topsy Bookstore
3. Río Montezuma Waterfall
4. El Hamaquero Boutique

⬡ ACCOMMODATIONS

1. Amor de Mar
2. Cabinas El Tucán
3. Cabinas Linda Vista
4. Camping Rincón de los Monos
5. El Jardín
6. El Sano Banano Beach Bungalows
7. Finca Los Caballos
8. Hotel El Tajalín
9. Hotel La Aurora
10. Hotel La Cascada
11. Hotel Lucy
12. Hotel Moctezuma
13. Los Mangos

⬡ RESTAURANTS

1. Café Montezuma
2. El Caracol
3. El Parque
4. El Sano Banano
5. Panadería Idalie
6. Pizzeria
7. Playa de Las Artistas

©ULYSSES

the most popular tours, we recommend those of the superb **Reserva Natural Absoluta Cabo Blanco** ★★(see p 302) and the spellbinding **Isla Tortuga** ★. The excursion to Isla Tortuga *($35)* takes all day *(9am to 4pm)* and includes round-trip transportation by speedboat, breakfast, snorkelling equipment and a variety of fun activities. It is an unforgettable day on an idyllic island covered with white sand washed by turquoise water...

Montezuma can be visited on foot, and if you come by a car, parking can be difficult. Opt for public parking lots, especially if you want to leave luggage in your car. To pick up reading material for a day on the beach, head to **Topsy** bookstore, where used books are bought and sold. In the evenings, **El Sano Banano** restaurant shows popular films, and visitors can enjoy the entertainment or just chat over one of their fabulous milkshakes.

A lovely stroll, as pleasant as it is refreshing, leads to the **Cascada Río Montezuma** ★★. Take the road to Cabuya for about 700m (2,297ft), until you reach hotel La Cascada on the north bank of Río Montezuma. Past the little bridge is a sign that indicates the path that climbs through the forest to the waterfall. After about 15min of walking, you will arrive at the waterfall and its relaxing basin that is wonderful for swimming. Although many tourists dive in from the top of the falls, this is quite dangerous. In fact, in 1990 one tourist lost his footing while attempting just such a plunge and died. This should be enough of a warning to discourage any would-be Tarzans.

South of Montezuma

Cabuya is a tiny village located about 8km (5mi) south of Montezuma, and constitutes the entrance to Reserva Natural Absoluta Cabo Blanco, 2km (1.2mi) to the south. It is quieter than Montezuma, and has a good selection of hotels, *cabinas*, and campsites nearby. The cemetery is unique in that it is located on an island, Isla Cabuya. The island can be reached on foot when the tide is at its lowest point.

Northwest of Cabo Blanco

Situated northwest of the **Reserva Natural Absoluta Cabo Blanco** ★★ (see p 302), the region of **Malpaís** ★ and **Santa Teresa** ★ is one of the best-kept secrets of the southern Nicoya Peninsula. First discovered by surfers attracted by its excellent waves, this region offers idyllic, semi-deserted (depending on the season) beaches as well as a good selection of hotels and restaurants in every price range. There is no commercial hub, but rather a small road lined with houses, hotels and restaurants that skirts the ocean for about 6km (3.7mi).

If you are looking for a quiet, peaceful spot and are not sure that Montezuma fits the bill, opt for this area—you will not be disappointed! Mountain biking and horseback riding, surfing classes, and full days of sunbathing or hours of swimming in the sea are among the activities to enjoy. Here, the days end with spectacular sunsets that are best appreciated from a hammock, drink in hand!

Refugio Nacional Fauna Silvestre Curú

Refugio Nacional de Fauna Silvestre Curú ★ *($5; every day; reservations required;* ☎*661-2392,* ⚏*641-0060)* is located 7km (4.3mi) south of Paquera. This private 84ha (208 acres) park is part of the Curú hacienda (1,496ha or 3,697 acres), owned by the Schutt family since 1933. Its name comes from the *guanacaste* tree, which area natives called *curú*. Part of the hacienda was declared a national wildlife preserve in 1983 in order to protect the fragile marine habitat on the coast and the beach that borders it. The reserve also shelters a tropical dry forest, a tropical rainforest, mangroves, pastures and fruit-tree orchards.

The Schutt family worked hard to gain recognition for this area, whose bio-diversity is representative of the region as it was several decades ago. The place is now recognized at once as a site for scientific research, agriculture. Its great variety tourism and attracts different groups of visitors who come to discover or study this complex environment, whose abundant fauna and flora are remarkably concentrated on only a few hectares of land.

Coati

Refugio Nacional de Fauna Silvestre Curú is relatively unknown and rarely visited by tourists passing through the area. This is unfortunate, because they miss out on a fascinating new experience—the reserve is a wild, enchanting place that holds many surprises! The entrance to the wardens' house is at the edge of the main road from Paquera to Tambor. A few hundred metres further, a barrier marks the park

gate, which visitors must open themselves. One of the functions of this barrier is to keep the livestock away from the main road.

Past the barrier, a small 2.5km (1.6mi) long road leads to the main buildings, the administrative offices and the visitor's centre. These building are set near the pretty beach nestled in the bend of the bay's shoreline. The Río Curú flows south of the beach, and empties into the waters of the Gulf of Nicoya.

Northeast of the bay, Punta Quesera juts into the Gulf, while to the south, Isla Tortuga, a veritable paradise for snorkellers, kayakers and swimmers, protrudes from the sea.

The park shelters truly exceptional flora and fauna. There are 500 species of plants, and part of the hacienda (200ha or 494 acres) has been reforested with about 10 types of indigenous trees. There are also 232 bird spe-

cies, 78 mammal species, 87 reptiles species and 26 amphibian species. Depending on the day, you can observe sea turtles (Hawksbill and Ridley), iguanas, crocodiles, boa constrictors, peccaries, armadillos, agoutis, pumas, monkeys, etc., whether you are accompanied by a guide or not. The park is home to three species of monkeys: howler monkeys, capuchins and spider monkeys. The spider monkey, which is now extremely rare in Costa Rica, was completely exterminated in the region of Curú between 1960 and 1965. It was reintroduced to the reserve about 10 years ago and in 1993 "Francisco" became the first spider monkey to be born in the region since the species' near extinction 30 years earlier.

You can snorkel, swim and walk in the park, which also has a picnic area. The network of walking trails includes 17 short paths whose lengths vary from a few hundred metres to 4km (2.5mi). The trails run through tropical forest, mangroves, pastures and orchards and lead to Punta Georgia in the south and Punta Quesera north of the park. Some trails reach the shore of the Gulf of Nicoya, while others climb to lookouts over the region.

The Central
Pacific Coast

An Exemplary Endeavour

The reserve's short history dates back to 1955, when the Swedish couple Nils Olof Wessberg and Karen Morgenson settled on a farm in the area. Witnessing the rapid deforestation caused by the lumber industry, and realizing that the virgin forest of Cabo Blanco would disappear in a few years if logging continued to proceed at this rate, they went to great lengths to protect this wild region, which was home to jaguars, ocelots, coyotes, and other animals. After taking three years to convince skeptics, they succeeded in amassing enough money (about $30,000) to buy the 1,250ha (3,089 acres) of forest that make up the point of Cabo Blanco. Thus, the point became a nature reserve, and since then Nils Olof Wessberg is recognized as the father of national parks in Costa Rica. Continuing his work as a naturalist and forest protector, Wessberg travelled to the Osa Peninsula in the southwest of the country, in the summer of 1975 to promote the creation of a new park. Unfortunately, he was assassinated there and thus did not live to see the creation of Parque Nacional Corcovado in October of that same year. There is a commemorative plaque in his honour near the reserve's visitor's centre.

Reserva Natural Absoluta Cabo Blanco

Reserva Natural Absoluta Cabo Blanco ★★ *($6; Wed to Sun 8am to 4pm;* ☎/≈642-0093*)* is a haven of natural riches only 11km (6.8mi) from Montezuma. The small road that leads to the reserve runs through Cabuya, is in good condition and passable for most cars. If you come from Malpaís by four-wheel-drive vehicle, on horseback, or by mountain bike, you can take the small 7km (4.3mi) long forest road that links Malpaís and Cabuya. Its entrance is well marked by a small sign and the road itself passes the Star Mountain Eco Resort after 2km (1.2mi). If you take this route, the trip to the reserve is only 9km (5.6mi) long, instead of the 30km (18.6mi) if you go via Cóbano, Montezuma and Cabuya.

The reserve was created October 21, 1963 for the sole purpose of protecting the wildlife and vegetation of this spectacular point situated at the southern tip of the Nicoya Peninsula. It got its name because, until the end of the 1980s, it was *absoluta*, meaning access was restricted to authorized researchers and visitors were not permitted at all. Since then, two hiking trails have been laid out and visitors are welcome to use them. However, a large proportion of the reserve is still off-limits to visitors, who must stay on the paths.

The visitor's centre is about 400m (1,312ft) from the parking lot by foot. The staff is very friendly and many volunteers work here. The visitor's centre is right by the sea and is an excellent spot for picnicking; tables have even been set up for this very purpose.

There are also washrooms, potable water, a shower and a little *soda* run by locals.

The rules of the reserve, the paths and attractions are explained at the visitor's centre. Lists of the various mammals and birds, with a map of the reserve on the back and a flier describing a dozen of these mammals can be obtained here. Rain boots and ponchos can be rented, as can binoculars for watching some of the 133 bird species that come to the reserve.

The reserve is crisscrossed by many trails, but only two of these are open to the public, the others are reserved for researchers. The **Danés** trail forms a 2.3km (1.4mi) loop and runs through a replanted forest that shows the different stages of the flora's regeneration. The reserve is made up of 85% secondary forest and 15% primary forest that has not been cut by area residents before or after the creation of the reserve. The trail also crosses Río Cabo Blanco, with its trickle of crystalline water. It takes about 1.5hrs to complete the loop.

The other path is called **Sueco** and is 4.2km (2.6mi) long (8.4km or 5.2mi round trip). It leads to the beach south of the reserve where there are potable water, picnic tables and

showers. It's a pleasant spot for swimming, which is permitted. In addition to the 1,250ha (3,089 acres) of forest, the reserve comprises 1,700ha (4,200 acres) of protected waters, extending about 1km (0.6mi) offshore. Three kilometres (1.9mi) from the visitor's centre, the trail comes to a lookout (*mirador*) over the point, the sea and Cabo Blanco island, 1km (0.6mi) from shore. The interpretive panels about the plant and animal life in the reserve were created by Colombian students. The round trip takes about 4.5hrs to complete.

Parque Nacional Isla del Coco

Parque Nacional Isla del Coco (*$6; every day;* ☎256-0365 *or* 233-4533, ⚏256-0365) is a true national treasure because of its rich vegetation and, above all, the clear, lively waters of the Pacific Ocean that surround it. Because the park is an island situated about 540km (336mi) off Cabo Blanco (Nicoya Peninsula), it remains much less frequented than the other national parks in Costa Rica.

Its offshore location has had the positive effect of preserving the place's natural beauty and wealth. With an area of 2,400ha (5,930 acres), Isla del Coco is situated at 5°30'34"

latitude North and 87°18'6" longitude West. The marine section of the park alone covers about 73,000ha (180,380 acres). The island is named for the many coconut trees that were found here originally, though over the years they have given way to low altitude tropical rainforest, which receives an average of close to 7m (23ft) of rain annually. The vegetation here is very dense and three plant species that are unique to the island have been discovered. Because the island is made up of many mountains, the tallest of which is the 634m (2,080ft) mount **Iglesias**, there are dozens of impressive waterfalls, some of which cascade directly into the sea.

According to Mario A. Boza, author of the book *Parques Nacionales de Costa Rica*, Isla del Coco was discovered by the Spaniard Joan Cabezas, who navigated along the island's shores in 1526. Over the centuries, sailors would stop here to stock up on potable water. Some even left livestock (pigs, goats, dogs) on the island to be picked up on a later voyage or if they ran out of food. Over the years, the pigs adapted to the island particularly well and became numerous enough to damage the environment, since hoofed animals cause excessive erosion by digging in

The Central Pacific Coast

the ground, especially during periods of heavy rain. Some even say that their presence here affected the coral reefs!

Even more fascinating is the legend that the island shelters three well-hidden treasure-troves. Between the end of the 17th century and the beginning of the 19th, pirates William Davies, Benito Bonito and William Thompson visited the island successively to hide money and valuables, including a life-size solid gold statue of the Virgin Mary! However, close to 500 expeditions undertaken so far have not found anything. The only treasure to have been discovered to date is the island itself!

Isla del Coco is renowned for its interesting ornithological site where 87 species of birds have been counted, including three that are specific to the island: its cuckoo (*Coccyzus ferrugineus*), flycatcher (*Nesotriccus ridgwayi*) and passerine (*Pinaroloxias inornata*). This last one is actually a descendant of those found in the Galápagos Islands.

However, the main attraction on Isla del Coco is unquestionably the marine setting that surrounds it. Several years ago, the island acquired an international scuba diving reputation. Most of the 2,800 visitors who

come here each year are experienced divers who stay for about 10 days to discover a fabulous world of 18 coral species and over 300 fish species. They encounter various species of sharks, including hammerheads (*Sphyrna Lewin*) and white sharks (*Triaenodon obesus*). Reports even say that it's not uncommon to observe up to 500 sharks in the course of a single dive!

Since there are no services on the island and camping is prohibited, visitors must sleep on boats. Most of the cruises leave from the town of Puntarenas and last for one to two weeks. The crossing alone requires about 36hrs. The agencies **Okeanos Aggressor** (☎290-6203, ≈290-6205) and **Undersea Hunter** (☎228-6535, ≈289-7334) offer 10-day, all-inclusive (transportation, cabin, meals, diving gear, guide, and so on) scuba-diving excursions *(about $2,500/pers.)*.

South of Puntarenas

Puntarenas to Jacó

Playa Doña Ana and **Boca Barranca** are two little beaches situated a little over 10km (6.2mi) southeast of Puntarenas.

Because they're the first clean beaches in the area, they can get very busy on weekends and during any Costa Rican holiday. Picnic tables, small food stands and a changing area are found on the edge of Playa Doña Ana. Surfing is pretty good at both of these beaches. There are relatively few places to stay around here, given the area's proximity to the Central Valley, which is where most of the visitors are from.

Two kilometres (1.2mi) south of **Reserva Biológica Carara** ★(see p 310) is a little road that climbs up into the hills surrounding the **Catarata Manantial Agua Viva** ★, apparently the tallest waterfall in the country. The road winds around hairpin turns for several kilometres before it reaches the hills' summit, providing a magnificent, beautiful view. (Be especially careful when descending this road as you head back; in addition to being very steep, it's covered with gravel that is like little marbles under the tires and can easily make the car slip.) The waterfall can be reached from the first entrance, run by a private entrepreneur (a little cabin on the right), but we recommend continuing 4km (2.3mi) to the "official" entrance run by the La Catarata Manantial Agua Viva (☎661-1787) ecological complex, which offers guided walks. There's a picnic area adjoining this entrance. Bring along lots of drinking water for this hike, which can be pleasant if you're well-prepared, since it passes rivers suitable for swimming.

Across from the road to the waterfall (on the national highway San José–Jacó), there is an access road to the little village of **Tárcoles**. Tárcoles is of interest only because it has a nearby river that is inhabited by crocodiles (they sometimes carry birds as "accessories"!). Mario Fernando offers trips on the river to see this sight (*$30; Jungle Crocodile Safari;* ☎292-2316 or 383-4612, ⇉292-3808).

Playa de Punta Leona is a pretty little gray-sand beach nestled in a small, calm bay. **Playa Blanca** is situated a few hundred metres south of Punta Leona and has larger waves. The Ridley Scott movie *1492—Conquest of Paradise*, starring Gérard Depardieu, was filmed

here. Although all Costa Rica's beaches are public, the edges of Punta Leona and Playa Blanca are owned by the Punta Leona resort. Buses travel to Playa Blanca from the centre of the Punta Leona resort every 30min from 8am to 5pm daily.

Herradura is the largest public beach closest to San José. Situated 7km (4.3mi) north of Jacó, it's shaded by vegetation, which is a blessing in the region's heat, and partly covered by rocks. It's not particularly charming, but it is clean and the water is calm.

Crocodile

This beach is divided into two sections: the one to the north is more public, while the one to the south is more residential and next to the old village. The beach is completely overrun on the weekend. Like Playa Doña Ana, this area has few hotels.

The Jacó Region

Playa Jacó ★★ is a beautiful, wide, dark-sand beach with giant waves that attracts surf-

ers and sunbathers alike. Jacó's developement began long before Tamarindo in Guanacaste and is therefore larger. Hotels are abundant and almost all the amenities of urban life are available. City officials decided to make the beach look like a vacation resort with a large access boulevard from the national highway and a main street parallel to the beach. The latter is broad and well landscaped with sidewalks separated from the road by decorative shrubbery. The street is lined by shops and restaurants of all sorts.

With the cross streets that branch off from this main strip, there's enough room here for a whole armada of tourists! Many foreign travel agencies offer all sorts of package deals for vacations in Jacó.

Jacó is also an ideal place to "see and be seen." The spot attracts very trendy surfers, which has led to the development of a series

The Central Pacific Coast

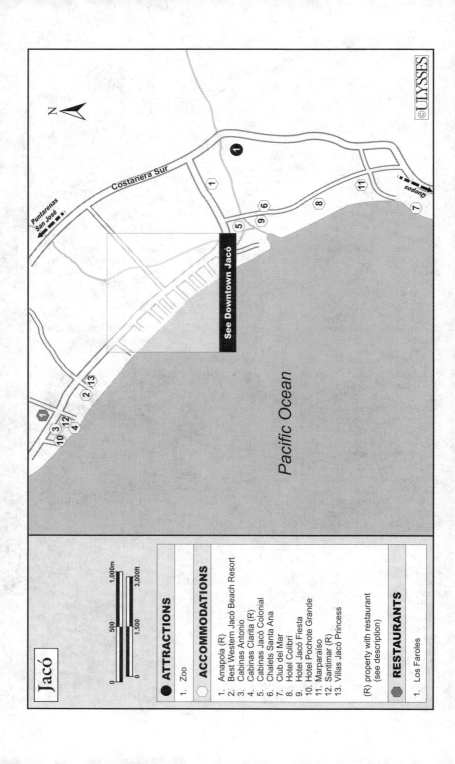

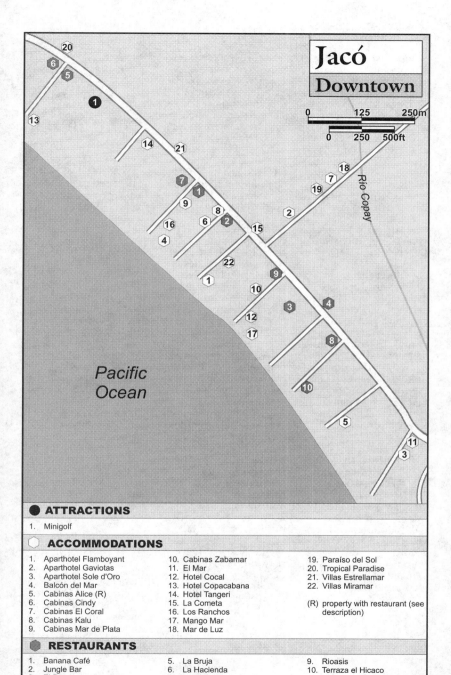

Jacó
Downtown

0   125   250m
0   250   500ft

Rio Copay

Pacific
Ocean

● **ATTRACTIONS**

1. Minigolf

○ **ACCOMMODATIONS**

1. Aparthotel Flamboyant
2. Aparthotel Gaviotas
3. Aparthotel Sole d'Oro
4. Balcón del Mar
5. Cabinas Alice (R)
6. Cabinas Cindy
7. Cabinas El Coral
8. Cabinas Kalu
9. Cabinas Mar de Plata
10. Cabinas Zabamar
11. El Mar
12. Hotel Cocal
13. Hotel Copacabana
14. Hotel Tangeri
15. La Cometa
16. Los Ranchos
17. Mango Mar
18. Mar de Luz
19. Paraíso del Sol
20. Tropical Paradise
21. Villas Estrellamar
22. Villas Miramar

(R) property with restaurant (see description)

⬡ **RESTAURANTS**

1. Banana Café
2. Jungle Bar
3. El Recreo
4. El Riconcito Peruano
5. La Bruja
6. La Hacienda
7. La Ostra
8. Poncho Villa
9. Rioasis
10. Terraza el Hicaco

©ULYSSES

of hip businesses. Jacó is a popular and happening place, even more so because it is so easily accessible for a weekend or even for a day trip for most Costa Ricans who live in the Central Valley. The streets that lead to the beach in the centre of town are especially lively, both during the day and at night.

Jacó has a **zoo** (*$6; just south of Jacó, on the Jacó-Quepos national highway*) where visitors can have their pictures taken with small animals indigenous to the country (monkeys, toucans and parrots, among others). In addition to the admission fee, donations are welcomed for the animals' upkeep. The zoo is at the foot of a mountain that can be explored on marked trails of various levels of difficulty.

In the same vein, **Butterfly Fantasy** (*Tue to Sun 8am to 5pm; across from Best Western, ☎643-3231*) is a botanical garden where you can see butterflies in aviaries. Call beforehand, since visits are organized according to reservations. There is also a **miniature golf course** in Jacó, on the main street along the river.

Jacó to Quepos

Because there are still only a few hotels around **Playa Hermosa**, it's a quiet spot, although it's popular with surfers.

Driving on the national highway toward Quepos provides some excellent opportunities for admiring the sea since the road often runs quite high above the ocean, especially between Playa Hermosa and Jacó. Some lookouts have been laid out along the way specifically for this purpose.

A little over 20km (12.4mi) south of Jacó, **Esterillos Este**, **Esterillos Centro** and **Esterillos Oeste** are little neighbouring communities separated by small rivers. Their beaches have some pretty heavy surf (the waves can even be violent at times) and are covered with dark sand that is even finer than at the beach in Jacó. Laid out side by side, the Esterillos beaches are very long—several kilometres in fact—and are mostly bordered by residential areas. The few hotels that have opened here thus offer their guests a very tranquil setting, especially compared to the urban bustle of nearby Jacó.

The only sizeable town between Jacó and Quepos is **Parrita**. The city itself is of little interest, but the nearby beaches are attracting an increasing number of hotels and, therefore, vacationers.

The Quepos Region

Quepos ★ is quite pretty overall. Many

Palm Oil

In the area of Quepos and pretty much everywhere on the southern Pacific coast, you'll be surprised to see trucks transporting a strange-looking fruit. You'll also go through immense plantations that are the source of this harvest, which will no doubt intrigue you. Ask no further, these are plantations of the trees used in the making of palm oil!

different bars, restaurants and other businesses are concentrated in the centre of town. It's the last large town in the area. However, visitors should avoid swimming in Quepos because the water is polluted.

Quepos to Manuel Antonio

Playa Espadilla is the main beach between Quepos and **Parque Nacional Manuel Antonio** ★★ (p 312). It's a very beautiful and is popular with surfers for its waves: swimmers should be prudent, however. Hotels are spread along the long strip of forested coastal

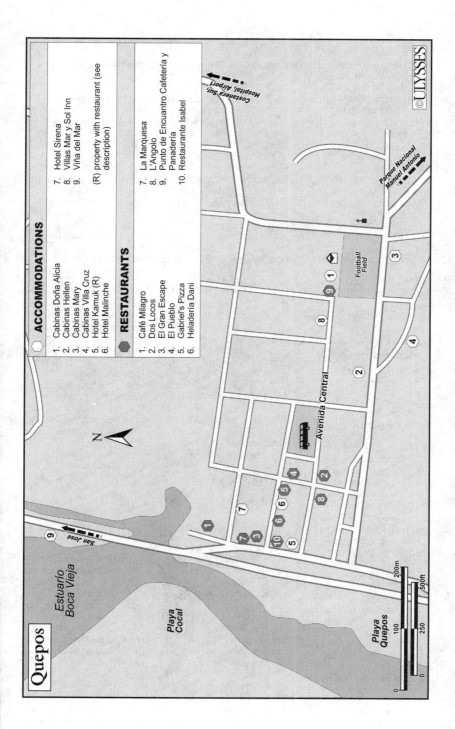

Quepos

ACCOMMODATIONS

1. Cabinas Doña Alicia
2. Cabinas Hellen
3. Cabinas Mary
4. Cabinas Villa Cruz
5. Hotel Kamuk (R)
6. Hotel Malinche
7. Hotel Sirena
8. Villas Mar y Sol Inn
9. Viña del Mar

(R) property with restaurant (see description)

RESTAURANTS

1. Café Milagro
2. Dos Locos
3. El Gran Escape
4. El Pueblo
5. Gabriel's Pizza
6. Heladería Dani
7. La Marquesa
8. L'Angolo
9. Punto de Encuantro Cafetería y Panadería
10. Restaurante Isabel

Estuario Boca Vieja

San José

Playa Cocal

Playa Quepos

Avenida Central

Football Field

Costanera Sur Hospital, Airport

Parque Nacional Manuel Antonio

© ULYSSES

N

0   100   200m

0   250   500ft

land above the beach. The landscape is hilly and thus provides extraordinary views of the ocean. Hotels have taken advantage of this topography and are built in such a way as to give guests fabulous views of the beautiful blue and green expanses of the surrounding ocean and countryside.

A series of small *sodas* and little shops line the last kilometre (0.6mi) of Espadilla beach before Manuel Antonio park, which was established to preserve at least a part of this superb natural setting.

Reserva Biológica Carara

A bird-watcher's paradise, the **Reserva Biológica Carara** ★ *($6; every day 7am to 5pm; ☎416-6576, ≈416-7402)* was created in April 1978 to protect this part of the province of Puntarenas. Situated only 17km (10.6mi) from Jacó, one of the country's tourist hot spots, the reserve encompasses some 4,700ha (11,614 acres) of forest, the preservation of which remains a priority especially since many animal species depend on it. The Carara reserve, which is part of the national parks system, ranks fifth among the most frequented parks in the country.

The reserve comprises two types of forest: tropical rainforest, which predominates in the southwest of the country, and tropical dry forest, which is found in the northwest of Costa Rica, mainly in the province of Guanacaste. The reserve is situated in the transition zone between these forests. With altitudes varying from around sea-level to just over 1,000m (3,281ft), it contains five different Holdridge Life Zones, or natural habitats.

Carara's lush forest is made up of 750 species of plants and trees, which sometimes reach gigantic heights of over 50m (164ft). Among the plants most characteristic of the region are the *espavel (Anacardium exelsum), ceiba, higuerón, gallinazo, javillo (Hura crepitans)* and *guácimo colorado (Guazuma ulmifolia).*

Scarlet Macaw

It is a happy realization that the reserve's varied fauna have adapted and thrived within the limits of this wild territory surrounded by farms and pastureland. The most commonly

seen animals are monkeys (white-faced capuchins, howler and spider monkeys), sloths, agoutis, coatis and Virginia white-tailed deer. Mammals such as coyotes, anteaters and big cats (jaguars, pumas, ocelots) are very rarely spotted, though you might occasionally see tracks. Going around a bend in a path may result in a surprise encounter with an iguana, a lizard, a toad or a little black-and-green venomous frog. However, the reserve also has several species of snakes, including the fearsome "fer-de-lance" (spearhead), which Costa Ricans call *terciopelo.*

Despite all these attractions, it's the winged fauna that attracts most visitors. In fact, with its high number of bird species per square kilometre, Reserva Biológica Carara is classed as one of the best birding spots in Costa Rica. Aside from the overwhelming quantity—the total number of species has yet to be determined—Carara has some truly unique kinds of birds. Visitors can see the superb and impressive **scarlet macaw** *(Ara macao),* which Costa Ricans call *lapa roja.* These huge multicoloured parrots are now very rare outside of Parque Nacional de Corcovado, in the southwest, and Reserva Biológica Carara. One

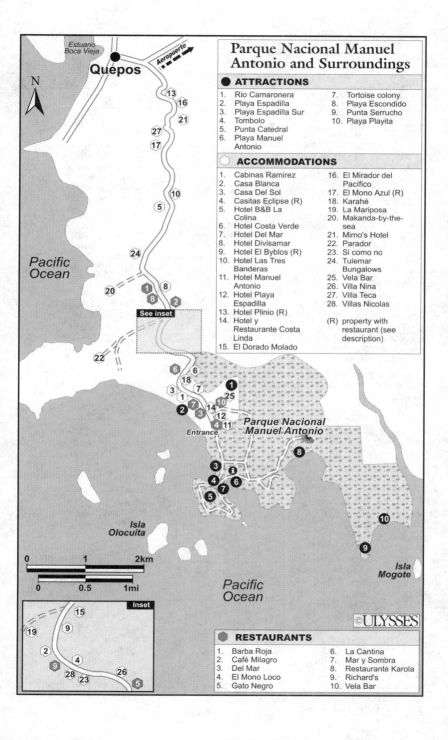

Parque Nacional Manuel Antonio and Surroundings

● ATTRACTIONS

1. Río Camaronera
2. Playa Espadilla
3. Playa Espadilla Sur
4. Tombolo
5. Punta Catedral
6. Playa Manuel Antonio
7. Tortoise colony
8. Playa Escondido
9. Punta Serrucho
10. Playa Playita

◯ ACCOMMODATIONS

1. Cabinas Ramirez
2. Casa Blanca
3. Casa Del Sol
4. Casitas Eclipse (R)
5. Hotel B&B La Colina
6. Hotel Costa Verde
7. Hotel Del Mar
8. Hotel Divisamar
9. Hotel El Byblos (R)
10. Hotel Las Tres Banderas
11. Hotel Manuel Antonio
12. Hotel Playa Espadilla
13. Hotel Plinio (R)
14. Hotel y Restaurante Costa Linda
15. El Dorado Molado
16. El Mirador del Pacífico
17. El Mono Azul (R)
18. Karahé
19. La Mariposa
20. Makanda-by-the-sea
21. Mimo's Hotel
22. Parador
23. Si como no
24. Tulemar Bungalows
25. Vela Bar
26. Villa Nina
27. Villa Teca
28. Villas Nicolas

(R) property with restaurant (see description)

⬡ RESTAURANTS

1. Barba Roja
2. Café Milagro
3. Del Mar
4. El Mono Loco
5. Gato Negro
6. La Cantina
7. Mar y Sombra
8. Restaurante Karola
9. Richard's
10. Vela Bar

Quepos

Estuario Boca Vieja

Aeropuerto

N

Pacific Ocean

See inset

Parque Nacional Manuel Antonio

Entrance

Isla Olocuita

Isla Mogote

Pacific Ocean

0   1   2km
0   0.5   1mi

Inset

©ULYSSES

of the best spots for observing scarlet macaws is the Río Tárcoles bridge where they make their nocturnal migration at about 5pm, flying from the reserve's tropical forest to the mangroves at the mouth of the river. The number of scarlet macaws in the region is estimated at around 300. Among the other birds likely to be spotted are toucans, trogons, hawks and hummingbirds.

Reserva Biológica Carara also has 15 archeological sites, dating back to the area's two main eras of settlement; the Pavas era (from 300 BC to the 4th century AD), and the Cartago period (from the 9th century to the 16th century AD). These sites mainly attract archeology students, though visitors can reach them with the help of a guide.

The reserve has two official hiking trails. The **Las Aráceas** (1km or 0.6mi) trail forms a loop that can be walked in under 1hr. It penetrates the primary forest and runs through four Life Zones where many species of flora and birds can be seen. The **Laguna Meándrica** trail (4km or 2.3mi each way) winds through a secondary forest to a spot near Río Tárcoles. Monkeys and brown coatis, called *pizotes* in Costa Rica, are frequently encountered along this path. Leave

yourself about 3hrs to make the 8km (5mi) round trip with enough time to appreciate the reserve's wildlife and vegetation.

To see a large variety of animals and identify the many plants and trees in the reserve, we strongly recommend that you go with a naturalist guide who knows the area. Most hotels around Jacó and Quepos, and in San José, offer guided tours of the Carara reserve. As well, many agencies that specialize in outdoor activities, such as **Geotour** (☎534-1867, ⇝227-4029), **Costa Rica Expeditions** (☎257-0766, ⇝257-1665) and **Expediciones Tropicales** (☎257-4171, ⇝257-4124) (all three of which are based in San José) organize guided tours of the reserve. These tours cost about $70 per person, including round-trip transportation from San José, breakfast, lunch, admission and a naturalist guide. Sometimes the day is topped off by a trip to the beach in Jacó, for a relaxing swim before returning to the hotel.

Parque Nacional Manuel Antonio

The Quepos region has quickly become one of Costa Rica's most developed tourist destinations. Within just a few years, hotels have sprouted up like mushrooms, considerably reducing the amount of

lush vegetation found in the area. Fortunately, it was decided early on to protect a portion of this territory by creating the Manuel Antonio national recreational park on November 15, 1972, which became **Parque Nacional Manuel Antonio** ★★ *($6; Tue to Sun 7am to 5pm;* ☎777-0644, ⇝777-0654) in August 1982.

Situated only 7km (4.3mi) from the village of Quepos, and 157km (97.6mi) from San José, Parque Nacional Manuel Antonio is one of the smallest parks in Costa Rica, with an area of 682.7ha (1,687 acres). However, it's also the second most visited park in the country, after Parque Nacional Volcán Poás. Since its inception, the popularity of this park has skyrocketed, as evidenced by the number of visitors surveyed over the years.

Park authorities were forced to limit the number of visitors to better manage the area and protect the fauna and flora before it could be subjected to irreparable damage. Today, the number of tourists is limited to 600 during the week and 800 on weekends. As well, the number of people on the hiking trails is restricted to 400 at any given time, and no more than 300 people are allowed on the beaches at one time. The number of hikers per group is also limited and the departures of these groups are spaced out so that there are not too many visitors in one area at once. Camping in the park is strictly prohibited. On Mondays, the park is closed to the public.

Parque Nacional Manuel Antonio is overflowing with natural beauty that will enrapture any visitor. Tropical dry forest meets rainforest in this transitional forest where primary and secondary forests stand side by side and lagoons can be found along with vegetation that grows only along the beaches. However, the park's old-growth forest was hard-hit by Hurricane Gert on September 14, 1993. Many thousands of trees were knocked down and flora that had taken decades to grow to maturity were destroyed in one fell swoop. Fortunately, the hurricane didn't hit the seaside and the beach regions with as much ferocity, leaving these paradisiac settings relatively intact, compared to the wooded hills.

One of the most deplorable consequences of this hurricane was the disappearance of about half the population of **marmosets** (*Saimiri oerstedii*), which Costa Ricans call *mono tití*. The marmoset is the smallest of the four monkey species found

in Costa Rica, but, more importantly, it's the rarest of the four. The Parque Nacional Manuel Antonio shelters a few families, as does the Parque Nacional Corcovado in the southwest of the country. Incidentally, although it is quite rare to spot a marmoset, visitors are almost guaranteed a sighting of a white-faced **capuchin** or to hear the powerful cries of the **howler monkeys**, which are much smaller than one would expect (they are 50 to 60cm or 19.7in to 23.6in tall, and usually weigh between five and 8kg or 11lbs to 17.6lbs).

Toucan

Other animals that populate the park include coatis, agoutis, iguanas, sloths, racoons, lizards and many species of snakes. Of these last, a few are venomous, so visitors must be constantly alert on the trails or when taking breaks. **Always** look down when you walk, and carefully examine leaves, plants

and trees before touching any of them. These simple safety rules apply to every region of Costa Rica. Other species that live in the park include 109 mammals and 184 birds.

Parque Nacional Manuel Antonio also has a pleasant climate with an average temperature of 27°C (80.6°F). The annual precipitation is 3.8m (12.4ft) of rain, and the dry season extends from December to April. The park is crisscrossed by a small network of hiking trails that total about 5km (3.1mi), and permit visitors to admire all of its natural attractions, including four magnificent beaches, as well as pretty points that jut into the ocean and a lush forest bustling with life.

To reach the park, cross the mouth of the Camaronera stream, south of the village of Manuel Antonio. Now, you're near **Playa Espadilla**, which most locals call "first beach." The path then runs along the second beach, **Playa Espadilla Sur**, which leads to a small bay. This 800m (2,625ft) long beach is not recommended for swimming because the waves are especially powerful here.

At the end of the beach stands a geomorphological formation that is unique in the world, the **tombolo of Punta Catedral**. The tombolo is a strip of land that formed over the millennia between what was once Catedral island and the mainland. This spectacular formation was created by a sand bar on which vegetation flourished until it finally became a natural path of grasses and trees. Researchers estimate that it took 100,000 years to create this geomorphological phenomena, which is one of the most beautiful of its kind on the planet. It takes about 1hr to hike around Punta Catedral, a distance of 1.5km (0.9mi). Along the way are majestic trees, among the oldest in the park, and a superb lookout over the Pacific Ocean.

The third beach, called **Playa Manuel Antonio**, lies near Punta Catedral. This is the most popular beach in the park because it consists of beautiful white sand and is safe for swimming. The spot is also renowned for snorkelling, especially during the dry season from December to April when the water is incredibly clear. There are 19 species of coral, 17 species of algae, 10 species of sponge, 24 species of crustaceans, and 78 species of fish that live in the area, many of them extremely colourful.

Manuel Antonio beach also served as a sea turtle hunting ground

about 1,000 years ago. The indigenous people who lived in the area lined up a series of stones in a semi-circle, creating a natural dam to prevent the turtles from returning to sea when the tide went out. When the tide is at its lowest, it is possible to see these turtle traps at the western end of the beach.

Further east is **Playa Escondido** (the fourth beach), which is less frequented and quieter because it is partly covered by water at high tide. Not far from here, a trail climbs to a lookout from which there is a view of **Punta Serrucho**, which jauntily juts into the sea. The fifth and last beach, **Playita**, is hidden on the other side of this point.

Outdoor Activities

Cycling

The area around the villages of **Montezuma**, **Cabuya** and **Malpaís** is perfect for cycling trips since the unpaved roads are not very busy. Many hotels in the area rent bicycles, as does the **Surf & Sport Camp** (*$10/day, ☎642-0047*) in Malpaís.

Hiking

The **Refugio Nacional de Fauna Silvestre Curú** (see p 300) has a pleasant network of trails from which you can observe the abundant and diverse wildlife.

In the **Reserva Natural Absoluta Cabo Blanco** (see p 302), you can meander through the secondary forest to a superb beach along the two trails open to visitors.

Walking is the best way to discover the **Reserva Biológica Carara** (see p 310), where you can admire scarlet macaws and crocodiles, among other animals.

The hiking trails in **Parque Nacional Manuel Antonio** (see p 312) lead to superb beaches, to points of land that jut into the ocean and to lookouts over the surrounding area.

Surfing

The villages of **Malpaís** and **Santa Teresa** are increasingly recognized as good surfing destinations. To take an introductory course, rent a board, watch videos or get tips from the surfing fanatics, head to the **Surf & Sport Camp** in Malpaís (see p 321).

You can rent or buy surfboards in Jacó. Around Jacó, the best beaches for surfing are **Playa Doña Ana** and its neighbour **Boca Barranca**; **Playa Hermosa**, the **Esterillos** beaches as well as **Espadilla** beach, between Punta Quepos and Manuel Antonio park.

David Klostermann (**☎**643-1569) gives surfing lessons (*$25/hr*) in the **Jacó** area.

Scuba Diving and Snorkelling

Located over 500km (311mi) offshore in the Pacific, **Parque Nacional Isla del Coco** (see p 303) is unquestionably the most spectacular destination for scuba diving. The distance, however, doesn't make it a day-trip option.

Isla Tortuga is a natural paradise of beaches and crystalline waters off the coast of Curú and the Nicoya Peninsula. Snorkelling here is easy, pleasant and safe. The vast majority of hotels around Montezuma and Tambor organize daytrips with snorkelling equipment included. From San José, **Calypso Tours** (**☎**256-2727, ≈256-6767) and **Bay Island Cruises** (**☎**258-3536, ≈258-1189) also offer unforgettable day trips to Isla Tortuga. Budget about $100 per person for the

day, which includes transportation by bus, the ferry crossing, activities, food, snorkelling equipment, and so on.

At **Parque Nacional Manuel Antonio** (see p 312), snorkelling is reportedly excellent near Playa Manuel Antonio, which can only be reached by foot.

Horseback Riding

The southern section of the Nicoya Peninsula is marvellous for horseback riding and the long beaches and hills around **Montezuma**, **Cabuya** and **Malpaís** offer breathtaking scenery. While you can rent horses and hire a guide almost anywhere (ask at your hotel), the excursions organized by Barbara MacGregor, a Canadian, at the "ranch-hotel" **Finca Los Caballos** (see p 320) near Montezuma, have a superb reputation in the area.

David Klostermann (**☎**643-1569) leads very worthwhile outings on horseback in the area surrounding **Jacó**. The horses are well-treated and gentle, and David, who used to own horses in California, is very friendly. He also gives riding lessons.

Playa Hermosa Stables (**☎**643-3808) organizes horseback riding excursions (*$35/pers. for*

4hrs.); inquire at the David hotel in Playa Hermosa.

Bird-Watching

If you're a birding buff, you'll certainly want to see the superb **scarlet macaws** that brighten the skies of **Reserva Biológica Carara** (see p 310).

Golf

Golfers can indulge in their favourite sport at the **La Roca Beach Resort and Country Club** in **Caldera**, south of the town of Puntarenas.

The new hotel complex Los Sueños (see p324) has a somewhat bland golf course.

A very pretty nine-hole course awaits golfers at the **Tango Mar Resort and Country Club** (**☎**289-9328 or 683-0001) in **Playa Tambor**.

Water Sports

Punta Leona has an organization that specializes in all sorts of water activities at sea and on the nearby Río Tárcoles: **J.D.'s Watersports** (**☎**257-3857, 256-8268 or

669-0511 ext. 34, ≈256-6391, jdwater@racsa.co.cr).
Deep-sea fishing, sea kayaking, snorkelling, windsurfing and river cruises are offered—and more!

Kayaking

In Jacó, **Kayak Jaco** (*☎/≈643-1233, www.kayakjaco.com*) offers a series of ocean or river-kayak rides. Their package deals will please everyone in the family.

Accommodations

The Puntarenas Region

For some strange reason, all the hotels in Puntarenas are exorbitantly priced. In general, their standards are based on the requirements of Costa Ricans travelling within the country, yet their prices are disproportionately high.

Be sure that your room is at least equipped with a fan, since the city is hot, especially in the dry season.

Pensión Cabezas
$
sb, ⊗
Avenida 1, Calle 2/4
Puntarenas
☎661-1045
Pensión Cabezas is friendly, clean and very reasonable. The rooms are rather small.

Ayi Con
$-$$
sb/pb, ⊗, ≡
Calle 2, Avenida 1/3,
Puntarenas
☎661-0164 or 661-1477
Located near the market, Ayi Con is clean, but has some rather dark rooms.

Chorotega
$$
sb/pb
Calle 1, Avenida 3, Puntarenas
☎661-0998
The cleanliness of the rooms at Chorotega makes this hotel an excellent value for travellers with limited budgets. Also, it is located near the downtown bus terminal.

Costa Rica Yacht Club
$$$
hw, ≈
Puntarenas
☎661-0784
≈661-2518
About 3km (1.9mi) east of downtown, but still on the peninsula, the Costa Rica Yacht Club offers plain, but comfortable rooms. However, it's mainly reserved for club members. Free mooring for sailboats.

Imperial
$$$
sb/pb, ⊗
near Calle Central and Paseo de los Turistas, Puntarenas
☎661-0579
The old wooden building of the Imperial charms almost anyone who lays eyes on it. It has a good location, right by the beach and near the bus stops. The upper rooms have balconies and a view of the ocean. The ground-floor rooms, however, are darker.

Hotel La Punta
$$$
hw, ⊗/≡, ≈, ℜ
Calle 35, Avenida 1, Puntarenas
☎661-1900
≈661-0690
West of the city and near the ferries, the little Hotel La Punta is clean and quiet. The rooms have balconies.

Hotel Tioga
$$$-$$$$ bkfst incl.
hw, pb, ≡, ≈, ℜ
Paseo de los Turistas
Calle 17/19, Puntarenas
☎661-0271
≈661-0127
After 35 years, Hotel Tioga is still popular. The clean rooms have views of the ocean or the pool. The upstairs dining room has a gorgeous view of the open sea.

Las Brisas
$$$$
hw, pb, ≡, ≈
Paseo de los Turistas, Calle 31
Puntarenas
☎661-4040
≈661-2120
Las Brisas has large, clean rooms.

Colonial
$$$$$ bkfst incl.
hw, ≈, ℜ
Puntarenas
☎*661-1833*
⇌*661-2969*
and
Portobello
$$$$
hw, ≈, ≡, ℜ
Puntarenas
☎*661-2122 or 661-1322*
⇌*661-0036*
These two hotels have
pleasant rooms and
good restaurants. The
grounds of the latter
are ravishing. Free
yacht mooring.

Hotel Yadrán
$$$$$
hw, pb, tv, ≡, ≈
Paseo de los Turistas, Calle 35
Puntarenas
☎*661-2662*
⇌*661-1944*
Hotel Yadrán is a large,
beautiful hotel complex
(bar, casino, nightclub),
nicely located near the
end of the sand spit on
which the city is built.

The Southern Nicoya Peninsula

Paquera

There are rudimentary
campsites *($2/pers.)* on
the road that leads to
the ferry landing. In-
quire with the shop-
keeper at the little gro-
cery store next to the
sites.

**Cabinas y Restaurante
Ginana**
$
pb, ⊗, ℜ
☎*641-0119*
The little village of
Paquera also has a few
modestly priced lodg-

ings. Cabinas y
Restaurante Ginana is
one of the most popu-
lar in the area. It has
about 20 clean, simple
rooms.

North of Paquera

Playa Naranjo

Oasis del Pacífico
$$$ bkfst incl.
pb, hw, ⊗, ≈, ℜ
☎/⇌*661-1555*
Near the dock for the
ferry from Puntarenas,
the **Oasis del Pacífico**
hotel has 39 rooms
with private washrooms
and hot water. The ho-
tel's advertisement
promises free lodgings
for one night if the sun
doesn't shine during
the day! It has a pool, a
tennis court, a volley-
ball court, a restaurant
and a bar.

Bahía Gigante

Bahía el Gigante
$$$-$$$$
pb, hw, ⊗, ≈, ℜ
☎/⇌*661-2442*
Activities centre around
sport fishing at the
Bahía el Gigante hotel.
There are rooms or
condos for rent, both of
which are very comfort-
able. The restaurant
serves Costa Rican and
international cuisine.

Isla Gitana

Isla Gitana
$$-$$$ fb
pb/sb
☎*661-2994*
⇌*661-2833*
Right in the middle of
Bahía Gigante, a few
minutes by boat from
the shore, Isla Gitana

was once called "Isla
de los Muertos" be-
cause an indigenous
burial ground was dis-
covered on the island.
Three types of accom-
modation are offered:
basic rooms with pri-
vate washrooms and
cold water, rooms with
shared bathrooms and
camping. The island
has hiking trails that
lead through the forest,
as well as a white-sand
beach. You can partici-
pate in various water
sports including
kayaking, windsurfing
and scuba diving.

Paquera to Montezuma

Pochote

🏨 **Hotel y Restaurante
La Paillote**
$$$
pb, hw, ℜ
☎/⇌*683-0190*
Nestled in the magnifi-
cent hills near the little
village of Vainilla, 3km
(1.9mi) from the beach
of Pochote, is the Hotel
y Restaurante La
Paillote. Franck, Aline,
Alain and Christine, all
from France, run the
hotel and are very wel-
coming and friendly.
Six pretty, comfortable
rooms are found in
three small *cabinas* with
terraces. Perched a little
higher, the restaurant
(see p 336) has a pan-
oramic view of the
valley. Many excursions
are organized, espe-
cially the spectacular
horseback riding out-
ings in the back coun-
try.

Tambor

If you prefer **camping**, head to the restaurant-bar **Los Gitanos** or to **Camping y Soda Albergue Río Mar**.

Cabinas y Restaurante Cristina
$-$$
sb/pb, ⊗, ℜ
Cabinas y Restaurante Cristina has six modestly priced rooms, three of which have private bathrooms. The restaurant serves excellent food at reasonable prices.

Hotel Dos Lagartos
$$
sb/pb, ⊗, ℜ
☎*683-0236*
Next door to Tambor Tropical (see further below) is Hotel Dos Lagartos, which faces the ocean and rents out very simple, clean rooms with private or shared bathrooms. Ideal if you're travelling on a limited budget in this part of the Peninsula, where hotel rates are often exorbitant.

Cabinas y Restaurante Tambor Beach
$$
pb, ℜ
Located near the river, Cabinas y Restaurante Tambor Beach has simple rooms at affordable rates.

Barceló Playa Tambor
$$$$$ all incl.
pb, hw, ≡, ⊗, ctv, ≈, ℝ, ℜ
☎*683-0303*
⇝*683-0304*
tambor@racsa.co.cr
The huge Barceló Playa Tambor hotel complex offers an all-inclusive package with a multitude of activities. In addition to its 402 rooms, the hotel has restaurants, pools, three bars and a disco, among other amenities. However, it's been accused of violating environmental laws to build the resort.

🐚 Tango Mar
$$$$$$ bkfst incl.
pb, hw, ⊗, ≡, ⊗, ≈, ctv, ℜ
☎*289-9328 or 683-0001*
⇝*289-8218*
Pleasantly located next to a beautiful white-sand beach, Tango Mar is a luxurious vacation resort. It offers different types of lodging including large, comfortable rooms with views of the ocean, spacious palm-thatched *cabinas* on stilts and sumptuous villas that can house up to six people. There are a nine-hole golf course, a pool, trails, a 12m (39.4ft) waterfall, tennis courts, a volleyball court and more on the grounds. Among the organized activities are horseback riding, sport fishing, sailing and sea outings.

Tambor Tropical
$$$$$$ bkfst incl.
pb, hw, ⊗, K, ≈, ℜ
☎*683-0011*
⇝*683-0013*
tambort@aol.com
Facing the ocean on a property enhanced by lush vegetation are the 10 spacious, attractively designed *cabinas* of Tambor Tropical. Each *cabina* is comprised of two rooms on two storeys, both equipped with kitchenettes. The upper rooms have a better view. The rates are the same year round. This spot is a true oasis of tranquillity and relaxation if you want to escape from the pressures of work, which is why the owners from the United States decided not to put televisions, fax machines or telephones in the rooms. As well, children are not encouraged as guests. In addition to the swimming pool with whirlpool right next to the beach, various activities are organized in the area.

Montezuma

Montezuma has suffered from the effects of careless campers who have installed themselves haphazardly on the beach and around the village for some time now. It's recommended, and safer, to set up camp at **Rincón de los Monos** *($3)*, near the beach, 400m (1,312ft) north of the village. There are toilets, showers, a *soda* and various equipment for rent like tents, hammocks, windsurfers and bicycles.

Cabinas el Tucán
$
sb, ⊗
☎*642-0284*
Cabinas el Tucán, which has been owned by a very friendly local woman, Marta Rodríguez, since 1990, comprises nine small, tidy rooms that are

rented at affordable rates. However, the owner's dogs are quite noisy.

Hotel Lucy
$
sb, hw, ℜ
☎*642-0273*
Across from Hotel Los Mangos, Hotel Lucy has very simple rooms at modest rates. This small, rustic wooden hotel was built on the seaside. The restaurant serves typical Costa Rican cuisine. There's also a souvenir shop on the premises.

Hotel Montezuma
$-$$
sb/pb, ⊗, ℜ
☎*642-0258*
⇌*642-0058*
Hotel Montezuma is located in the centre of the village, near the beach. It rents out 32 reasonably priced rooms, some with private bath. The site is noisy, however. The restaurant and bar offer a beautiful view of the ocean and are very busy.

Hotel La Aurora
$$
pb/sb, ⊗, ≡, ℝ
☎/⇌*642-0051*
On the main street, adjacent to the municipal park, Hotel La Aurora rents out 10 rooms, including an apartment that can accommodate up to five people and has a private terrace. This wooden building exudes an antiquated charm with its many hammocks and its library. Breakfast is

served from 7am to 11am, while coffee, tea and purified water are available free of charge throughout the day.

Cabinas Linda Vista
$$-$$$
pb, hw, ⊗, ℝ
☎*642-0274*
⇌*642-0104*
The Cabinas Linda Vista, less than 2km (1.2mi) from Montezuma, are seven *cabinas* that can accommodate up to seven people each. Each *cabina* has its own refrigerator, terrace and hammocks, and an incredible view of the ocean below. The owner, Arnoldo Rojas, lives in a house near the *cabinas.*

Hotel La Cascada
$$$
pb, ⊗, ℜ
☎/⇌*642-0057*
Hotel La Cascada got its name because of its proximity to the trail leading to the imposing Río Montezuma waterfall. The 14 rooms are simple and clean. The owners, William and Viky Sánchez, also run the restaurant next door to the hotel, which serves a regional cuisine that often includes fresh seafood.

El Jardín
$$$
pb, hw, ⊗, ℜ, ℝ, ≡
☎/⇌*642-0074*
The superb wood-panelled rooms at El Jardín provide perfect comfort and relaxation. Every room has its own terrace with a view of the sea. The hotel is

slightly set back and is surrounded by exquisite, lush gardens. The restaurant serves Italian cuisine. There are also an information booth and a small souvenir shop on the premises.

Amor de Mar
$$$-$$$$
sb/pb, hw, ⊗, ℜ
☎/⇌*642-0262,*
shoebox@racsa.co.cr
Amor de Mar, owned by Richard and Ori Stocker, is just across the Río Montezuma bridge. The hotel was built on a magnificent plot along the Río Montezuma that faces the sea. The ground floor and upstairs rooms are prettily decorated and comfortable. Some of them have private terraces and ocean views. The site is dotted with palm trees between which many hammocks are suspended. Homemade bread and yogurt are served at breakfast and lunch, among other treats.

Los Mangos
$$$-$$$$
sb/pb, hw, ⊗, ≈, ℜ
☎*642-0076 or 642-0259*
⇌*642-0050*
About 400m (1,312ft) from the village, toward Cabuya, Los Mangos comprises 10 rooms and 10 bungalows, in addition to a charming pool. Some rooms in the main building have private bathrooms. The attractively decorated wooden bungalows have private washrooms with hot water, terraces and hammocks. The restaurant

serves tasty Italian cuisine.

Hotel El Tajalín
$$$$
pb, hw, ≡, ⊗, ℜ
☎642-0061
⇌642-0527
Next door, the Hotel El Tajalín, run by Italians, comprises 12 clean, comfortable rooms, some of which are air-conditioned. A cafeteria on the top floor provides a view of the ocean.

Finca Los Caballos
$$$$
pb, hw, ⊗, ≈, ℜ
☎/⇌642-0124
naturelc@racsa.co.cr
Up in the mountains, 3km (1.9mi) from Montezuma, Finca Los Caballos has a stunning view of the forest and the sea. Conceived and built by a Canadian, Barbara MacGregor, this small farm resembles a Spanish ranch and includes eight pretty, comfortable rooms with terraces. It is the perfect place for relaxation, especially around the blue-tiled pool surrounded by a tropical garden. The open-air restaurant serves high-quality international cuisine. Mrs. MacGregor is passionate about horseback riding and organizes various excursions in the area.

El Sano Banano Beach Bungalows
$$$$
pb, ⊗, ℜ, ≈
☎642-0638 or 642-0636
⇌642-0068
elbanano@racsa.co.cr
Magnificently located between the edge of the beach and the hillside, and only a 15min walk from the village, the *cabinas* at El Sano Banano Beach Bungalows are owned by Lenny and Patricia Iacono, who also own the restaurant of the same name in the village. If you don't have a reservation, ask at the restaurant counter, since the hotel is slightly out of the way and you can't get there by yourself. In fact, to reach it, you must leave your car in the village (safe parking) and entrust both yourself and your worldly goods to an aging four-wheel-drive vehicle that will take you to the bungalows by way of the beach, when the tide permits (check beforehand to avoid a long wait).

The bungalows are actually small round rooms with domed roofs. Beside the sea or amidst vegetation on the hillside, they're connected by a path that lights up at dusk, creating a beautiful effect. Though not very far apart, they are nevertheless peaceful retreats that mainly attract people seeking rest. With whitewashed walls, louvred wooden shutters and colourful bedspreads, these cozy little houses don't shut out the sounds of nature, especially once night has fallen. Each bungalow has large front doors opening onto a balcony and a hammock hung beneath palm trees. To the side, a built-in shower is installed... outside! A six-room building is also available. A delightful new feature here is a marvellous swimming pool with waterfall. While the hotel has no restaurant, the rooms provide a refrigerator. For a complete meal, you have to walk down the beach to the village. The return trip by moonlight only adds to the romantic flavour of it all...

South of Montezuma

Cabinas El Yugo
$$
pb, ⊗, K
☎642-0303
In Cabuya, the seaside Cabinas El Yugo include five pretty *cabinas* that can accommodate up to eight people each. They're equipped with kitchenettes and private bathrooms and are very affordable. Guests have free use of a washing machine.

Cabinas Las Rocas
$$-$$$
sb/pb, ⊗, K, ℜ
☎/⇌642-0393
Facing the sea, and 2.5km (1.6mi) from Montezuma, Cabinas Las Rocas offer several

types of accommodation. These include four simple, clean rooms with a shared bathroom in the family home of Reto Müller and Gisella Di Falco. In a nearby building there are two rooms with private bathrooms and fully equipped kitchens. The room on the ground floor can house two people and the upstairs room is large enough for three guests. The small open-air restaurant serves healthy cuisine made with fresh ingredients.

🏡 El Ancla de Oro
$$$
sb/pb, ⊗, K, ℜ
☎/≈642-0369
ancladeoro@multicr.com
Located 7km (4.3mi) from Montezuma and 2km (1.2mi) from Cabo Blanco, the restaurant (see p 337) and *rancho* El Ancla de Oro offers vacationers a real wilderness experience in traditional *cabinas,* some of which have kitchenettes. Three small rooms can be rented in the main building. Various activities are organized, including horseback riding and sea excursions.

🏡 Hotel Celaje
$$$
pb, hw, ⊗, ≈, ⊛, ℜ
☎/≈642-0374
Hotel Celaje has seven superb two-storey thatch-roofed *cabinas,* wonderfully located at the edge of the white-sand beach. The pool, surrounded by palm trees, is one of the prettiest in the area. The

open-air restaurant-bar serves international cuisine. Many water sports and other activities are organized.

Northwest of Cabo Blanco

Malpaís

Cabinas Mar Azul
$-$$
pb, ⊗, ℜ
☎/≈640-0098
With its splendid seaside location, Cabinas Mar Azul also serves as a meeting place for locals to play pool and chat at the bar. The *cabinas* are somewhat neglected but are modestly priced. You can also pitch a tent here; you'll have access to the showers and toilets.

Cabinas Bosque Mar
$$
pb, hw, ⊗, ℝ
☎226-0475
Cabinas Bosque Mar rents clean, comfortable *cabinas* that can accommodate up to four people each. Gas stoves may be rented.

🏡 Surf & Sport Camp
$-$$$
sb/pb, hw, ⊗, ≈, ℜ
≈642-0047
As its name indicates, the Surf & Sport Camp caters to people who come to the area to ride its famous waves. You can stay in simple but pretty shelters, in *cabinas* or in a superb, spacious, comfortable house. The landscaping is extremely attractive and the large pool is inviting. Introductory surfing lessons are

available and surfboards and mountain bikes can be rented by the day. The establishment also includes a restaurant (see p 337), a bar and pool tables.

🏡 Star Mountain Eco Resort
$$$$ bkfst incl.
pb, hw, ⊗, ≈, ℜ
☎296-2626, ext. 125080
info@starmountaineco.com
Located 2km (1.2mi) from Malpaís, on the little road that links Malpaís and Cabuya, the Star Mountain Eco Resort provides rest and relaxation in the mountains on a vast 87ha (215 acres) estate. The long, covered terrace furnished with rocking chairs is the perfect place to unwind. Next door, an old wooden house is available to families and groups. The open-air restaurant-bar (see p 337) serves delicious food. The pool has a whirlpool and is surrounded by rich, dense forest teeming with life.

🏡 Sunset Reef Marine Lodge
$$$$$
pb, hw, ≡, ⊗, ≈, ℜ, ⊛
☎/≈640-0012
sunreef@racsa.co.cr
At the southern tip of Malpaís, almost at the border of the Cabo Blanco reserve, the Sunset Reef Marine Lodge is magnificently situated on a rocky point of land in the sea. This point is embellished by marvellous gardens, from which fantastic sunsets can be seen. Enjoy the sight

from a hammock for the most idyllic experience! There is a pool with a whirlpool and a small waterfall, surrounded by greenery and tropical plants.

The 14 wood-panelled rooms are large, comfortable and very clean. The meals are excellent. A friendly Belgian couple, Nathalie and Eric, make sure that guests have a pleasant, relaxing stay. Among the many activities offered (fishing, scuba diving, kayaking, horseback riding, and so on), there's one that is as educational as it is pleasant: early in the morning, the hotel manager, William Granados, leads a short nature walk in the surrounding area. A true bird lover, William can tell you all about the 83 bird species spotted here to date and about the flora and various animal species that inhabit the area.

Santa Teresa

Cabinas Camping Zeneida's
$
sb, ℜ
Cabinas Camping Zeneida's has simple, rustic, inexpensive rooms overlooking the beach. You can also camp here for a small fee. The manager, Zeneida, prepares succulent meals if you ask in advance. You can even negociate the prices for the rooms, campsites and meals with this friendly woman.

Cabinas Santa Teresa
$-$$
pb, ⊗, K
Managed by a very laid-back man, the Cabinas Santa Teresa are located across from the Saloon Laura Amarilla, about 200m (656ft) from the ocean. Of the eight *cabinas*, two come with kitchenettes. The rooms are large, clean and inexpensive.

Cabinas El Bosque
$$
pb, K
Set in the forest, about a 100m (328ft) from the road, the three Cabinas El Bosque can accommodate up to four guests each. The A-frame *cabinas* are simple but clean, with the bedrooms upstairs. The friendly Costa Rican owner, Gladio Montoza Villagas, lives in the pretty house on the edge of the road.

Frank's Place
$$
pb
Located between Malpaís and Santa Teresa, where the road climbs toward Cóbano, Frank's Place is a popular restaurant (see p 337) that also rents out four rooms and three clean, comfortable *cabinas*.

🦎 Casa Cecilia
$$$ bkfst incl.
pb
in Québec:
☎*(418) 775-2898*
☎*(418) 775-3209*
⇌*(418) 775-9793*
Casa Cecilia is a pretty, comfortable bed and

breakfast owned by friendly Quebecers, Cécile Wedge and Jean-Pierre Pineault. From June to October, they manage another bed and breakfast in Sainte-Flavie, Québec, called La Québécoise. Built at the edge of a superb white sand beach, Casa Cecilia has four impeccable rooms with ocean views. Breakfast and lunch are served in an open-air dining room. Transportation and company (optional) are provided for guests to the restaurants in the area. Cécile and Jean-Pierre have created a package that is very popular with vacationers, including shuttle service from the airport in San José, ferry crossings, 14 nights accommodation, breakfast and transportation to restaurants for supper.

🦎 Tropico Latino Lodge
$$$$
pb, hw, ⊗, #, ≈, ℜ
☎*/⇌640-0062*
tropico@centralamerica.com
The Tropico Latino Lodge directly overlooks the spectacular white-sand beach and consists of six charming, comfortable Italian-style bungalows. Spacious and nicely decorated, they have a large terrace that is perfect for unwinding in a hammock. The managers, Steve and Florencia, strive to maintain the place's natural peace and tranquillity. The pool is worth the trip in itself: it has a whirlpool and a fabulous setting, almost

right on the beach!. There is also a restaurant (see p 338) on the premises.

South of Puntarenas

Puntarenas to Jacó

Cabinas Paradise
$$$
hw, ≈
on the San José-Jacó road
☎*267-0157 or 228-9430*
A little north of Punta Leona, Cabinas Paradise is slightly set back from the road in a small residential neighbourhood between the road and the ocean. The A-frame *cabinas* are too close to each other. Some of them have two storeys, with bedrooms upstairs. The site as a whole is not very attractive, but the cottages offer an acceptable level of comfort.

Villa Lapas
$$$$
hw, pb, ≈, ℜ
at the beginning of the road to Catarata Manantial Agua Viva from the San José-Jacó road
☎*663-0811*
⇋*663-1516*
If staying on the beach is not a priority, Villa Lapas is an enticing option. The hotel is actually set on the banks of a river in the forest, and is thus surrounded by pleasant background sounds. Dinner in the attractive restaurant is an excellent opportunity to enjoy this natural music to its fullest (see p 339). The rooms, all in a row in one build-

ing, have a standard modern, wooden decor, but are very clean. There is a miniature golf course on the premises.

Hotel Fiesta
$$$$$
pb, hw, ctv, ≡, ≈, ☺, ℜ
11km (6.8mi) southeast of Puntarenas
☎*663-0808*
⇋*663-1516*
Near Playa Doña Ana, Hotel Fiesta is a luxurious establishment. In fact, it's really more of a resort: in addition to its hundreds of rooms, the Fiesta also has suites and condominiums. Guests have direct access to the beach and many restaurants. There are several pools, as well as tennis and volleyball courts. A casino, conference rooms and a gym complete the facilities. Sea outings are possible.

Leona Mar
$$$$$
hw, pb, ≈, ℜ, bar
near Punta Leona Mar, on Playa Blanca
☎*231-3131*
⇋*232-0791*
The Leona Mar is an extremely pretty condominium complex hidden away in the wilderness on a hill overlooking Playa Blanca, not far from the Punta Leona Resort, with which it is affiliated. The condos are fully equipped: microwave ovens, dishwashers, washers and dryers, and so on. The buildings are painted in bright pastel colours that reflect the region's

eternal summer. There is a minimum stay of three nights. Guests have access to the services of the Punta Leona Resort.

Punta Leona Beach Hotel
$$$$$
hw, pb, ctv, ≡, ≈, ℝ, K, ℜ
a few km north of Herradura
☎*231-3131 or 661-1414*
⇋*232-0791*
puntaleo@racsa.co.cr
The Punta Leona Beach Hotel is set on the edge of the beaches of Punta Leona and Blanca. This large resort deserves its reputation: it covers a huge area of land, parts of which have been left untouched, and provides all sorts of services and facilities (soccer, basketball, volleyball, conference rooms, nightclub, wading pool, souvenir shop, etc.) and many styles of lodging (standard rooms, one- or two-bedroom cottages with living rooms and kitchenettes or apartments). The general layout is very pleasing, and is an ideal setting for a family vacation. Hotel guests have exclusive access to Punta Leona beach. There is a shuttle to neighbouring Playa Blanca.

🐟 Villa Caletas
$$$$$$
pb, hw, ⊗, ≡, ≈, ℜ
☎*257-3653*
⇋*222-2059*
caletas@racsa.co.cr
Ah, the Villa Caletas! This place is nothing short of dream, far away from its neighbours, perched on a huge rocky peak that

dominates the surrounding landscape. This airy Victorian building blends perfectly with its natural surroundings. The attractive design of its rooms and its first-class service combine to make it one of the best establishments in the area.

To give you an idea of how much care went into its design, the hotel pool is built on one of the mountain's cliffs, so it has a view that extends to the ocean, making it seem like one continuous expanse! Also, the hotel's magnificent open-air amphitheatre is one of the stages of the Festival Internacional de Música de Costa Rica. Just imagine listening to a concert with a breathtaking view over the gulf of Nicoya as the backdrop! This refinement is carried through to your room, of course, no matter which one you chose. Some go as far as to provide private gardens with swimming pools, but all are decorated in exquisite taste. For the illusion of being on a boat, rent room no. 30, which is built entirely of teakwood and where an entire wall, even in the bathroom, is open to the ocean in the distance below… Bon voyage! The only possible drawback is the restaurant—the food is not up to the high standards of an establishment such as this.

Los Sueños Marriott Beach & Golf Resort
$$$$$$
pb, hw, ≡, ℜ, ℝ, =
Playa Herradura
Apartado Postal 502-4005, San Antonio de Belén
☎ *630-9000 or 298-0000*
⇄ *630-9090*
costaric@marriott.co.cr
The newest of the region's large hotel complexes opened in autumn 1999. A member of the international Marriott chain, it certainly lives up to its name. The Los Sueños is truly a dream spot! Its large buildings facing the sea have an intentionally rustic style. The lobby greets you with a vaulted brick ceiling, supported by a series of arches creating a lovely effect. Its roof and those of the other buildings around it are covered with red tiles that blend well with the ochre colour of the exterior walls. Artwork in various styles is scattered throughout the numerous common areas. Some of it is simply astonishing, like the old wooden fishing boat hung with bottles containing messages… Adding to the rustic charm of the place are objects like large urns and wrought-iron lighting fixtures.

Most common areas lead towards the rear of building and to the superb swimming pool of cascades and canals that parallels the beach. Though not the most inviting in the area, the beach is divided by a

long wharf that attracts cruise ships and thus offers many nautical activities. Also, an equipment stand supplies guests with all they need for broad range of activities. The hotel's bars and restaurants, such as the Vista where you can eat poolside, or the Nuevo Latino where new culinary discoveries await, are also found in the rear… After all this, what can be said about the rooms? Distributed over four storeys, along rather anonymous hallways, the approximately 200 rooms prove to be simply ravishing. With their wood and ceramic floors, new furniture, completely successful decoration, large and exquisite bathrooms, they represent the epitome of luxury and comfort. Some have views of the ocean, others look out onto the golf course that fills the expanse in front of the hotel and which, no doubt for want of mature vegetation, looks slightly forlorn. In short, one resort among many, but one with splendid panache!

The Jacó Region

Cabinas Antonio
$
pb, hw
300m (984ft) north of Hotel Jacó Beach, at the corner of the street that runs along the beach at the northern end of Playa Jacó
☎*643-3043*
Cabinas Antonio is a small family establishment that offers rather plain, but clean rooms.

Cabinas Clarita
$
pb, ⊗
50m (164ft) west of the restaurant Santimar, Playa Jacó
☎*643-3013*
Cabinas Clarita has simple rooms that provide minimal comfort and is right on the beach, though it has no outdoor facilities. Ideal for surfers who just want the beach, the sun and the sea. Renovations have been made and a second floor has been added.

Santimar
$
pb, ⊗
200m (656ft) north and 200m (656ft) west of Hotel Jacó Beach
☎*643-3605*
The Santimar restaurant has a few tiny rooms for rent. They have no particular charm, but are clean.

La Cometa
$-$$
⊗, sb/pb
on the main street, Playa Jacó
☎*643-3615*
The Canadian-owned La Cometa has clean, simple rooms for rent.

On the streets that run from Jacó's main boulevard to the beach, you can find a whole series of small hotels set up on this neighbourhood's long, narrow lots that run down to the sea. The unpretentious little *cabinas* at **Cabinas Sol y Palmeras (*$$*)** and **Cabinas Cindy (*$$; pb,* ☎*450-0532)*** are found on one of the liveliest streets in the heart of the town.

Aparthotel Gaviotas
$$
hw, pb, ctv, ⊗, K, ≈
25m (82ft) north and 50m (164ft) east of Banco Nacional de Costa Rica
Playa Jacó
☎*643-3092*
⇄*643-3054*
Aparthotel Gaviotas rents 12 apartments with fully equipped kitchenettes, small living rooms, separate bedrooms and terraces by the pool—all this at relatively modest rates! Unfortunately, the buildings look like concrete boxes and are somewhat too crowded around the pool.

Cabinas Alice
$$
≈, ℜ
100m (328ft) south of the Red Cross, on one of the streets to the beach
Jacó
☎/⇄*643-3061*
The Cabinas Alice are attractively decorated and have an almost-private terrace. The grounds are right next to the beach. An apartment with a fully equipped kitchenette can also be rented.

Cabinas Jacó Colonial
$$
hw, pb, ≈
diagonally across from Cabinas Naranjas, on the road to the hotel Club del Mar, Playa Jacó
☎*643-3359*
Cabinas Jacó Colonial is similar to most of the motels on Jacó's little side streets and has about 10 rooms laid out on two storeys of a building on a small lot. The surrounding foliage separates it from its neighbours. Also, the building is well designed and blends in quite well with its surroundings.

Cabinas Kalu
$$
☎*643-1107*
Next door to Cabinas Cindy, the rooms at the Canadian-owned Cabinas Kalu are slightly cleaner and more modern than those at the neighbouring establishment. However, all of the rooms share one terrace.

Cabinas Mar de Plata
$$
Jacó
☎*643-3580*
Cabinas Mar de Plata is a good place for people on a tight budget and is popular with surfers.

Cabinas Roble Mar
$$
on one of the streets to the beach, Jacó
☎*643-3173*
Cabinas Roble Mar is a series of small *cabinas* housed in a building that sits on one of the long, narrow plots of

land typical in this area. Relatively clean and very popular with surfers because of its proximity to the beach.

Chalets Santa Ana
$$-$$$
hw, pb, ⊗
Playa Jacó
☎*643-3233*
The Chalets Santa Ana have a rather simple decor, but are clean and comfortable. They are not on the beach and are also quite far from the centre of the town. Rooms and *cabinas* are available. The latter of which can accommodate up to five people.

Apartamentos El Mar
$$$
hw, pb, ⊗, *K,* ≈
Playa Jacó
☎*643-3165*
The Apartamentos El Mar are clean and quiet, with pretty landscaping. The apartments are in a building that surrounds the beautiful large pool and have fully equipped kitchens and private terraces.

Aparthotel Flamboyant
$$$
hw, pb, ⊗, *K*
Playa Jacó
☎*643-3146*
⇌*643-1068*
Aparthotel Flamboyant is pleasantly calm. The *villas-cabinas* are very well designed with gorgeous, large and very private terraces in the front and small but pretty kitchens and bathrooms, both completely decorated in clean white ceramic

tiles. The beautiful tropical garden isolates the establishment from its noisy surroundings in the centre of town. There is direct access to the beach.

Apartamentos Nicole
$$$
hw, pb, K
on the main street, Jacó
☎/⇌*643-3384*
The Apartamentos Nicole are found behind the stores of the same name. They offer rooms with fully equipped kitchens in a relatively large but rather dark space. The buildings are on a small, unadorned lot.

Balcón del Mar
$$$
hw, pb, ≡, ℝ, ≈
next to the police station on the beach, Playa Jacó
☎/⇌*229-2222 or 643-3251*
The hotel Balcón del Mar lives up to its name. Its rooms are spread over three storeys and each has a little balcony with a view of the establishment's pool and the nearby beach. The balconies are slightly recessed to increase their privacy.

Hotel Arenal Sol
$$$
hw, ⊗
on the beach, Playa Jacó
☎*643-3419 or 643-3770*
⇌*643-3730*
A small stream runs through he grounds of the Hotel Arenal Sol, adding to the establishment's special charm. The rooms are simple and attractive, but don't have outdoor terraces.

Hotel Mango Mar
$$$
hw, pb, ≡, *K,* ≈
Playa Jacó
☎*643-3670*
Despite its name, Hotel Mango Mar rents out small apartments rather than hotel rooms. The exterior is quite appealing, given the site's limited space. The pool and the beach are just next to the hotel— and very inviting!

Marparaíso
$$$
pb, ⊗, ⊛, ≈, ℜ
near the southern end of the beach, Playa Jacó
☎*221-6544*
⇌*221-6601*
The Marparaíso is essentially geared toward groups. The patios are quite spacious, but the service and decor is rather indifferent. Especially popular with Costa Ricans.

Mar de Luz
$$$
hw, pb, ≡, *K,* ≈
on one of the streets that runs from the main street toward the interior, Jacó
☎*643-3259*
Mar de Luz belongs to a very friendly man from the Netherlands. The hotel is very clean and is elegantly decorated with the beautiful use of wood and stone, pleasant kitchenette-dining areas in the rooms and tasteful furniture on the rooms' private patios. It is a bit of a walk to the beach.

Paraíso del Sol
$$$
pb, hw, ⊗, ≡, K, ≈
100m (328ft) from the ice
factory, Playa Jacó
☎*643-3250*
⇒*643-3137*
Paraíso del Sol is a
small complex whose
buildings are tightly
clustered around a
pool. It can get noisy
when the pool area is
busy, especially since
the rooms' terraces are
quite close together
and all surround the
pool. The slightly
crowded grounds leave
little room for greenery.
The hotel offer a laun-
dry service.

Hotel Pochote Grande
$$$
hw, pb, ≈
Playa Jacó
☎*643-3236*
⇒*220-4979*
pochote@racsa.co.cr
You'll easily recognize
the Hotel Pochote
Grande by the
immense tree (*pochote*)
that towers over its
grounds. The rooms are
clean, simple and quite
spacious, with large
terraces and windows.
The setting is very
pretty, covered with
striking tropical vegeta-
tion, right next to the
beach. Ideal for relax-
ation.

Villas Estrellamar
$$$
hw, pb, ⊗, ≡, ≈, K
Jacó
☎*643-3102*
⇒*643-3453*
brunot@racsa.co.cr
Villas Estrellamar are
beautiful large villas
that can accommodate
up to five people each.

They are well spaced
out in attractively land-
scaped surroundings
and have good-sized
terraces as well as all
the necessary amenities
to make for a pleasant
stay of more than one
night. The Estrellamar
is very popular, so res-
ervations are a good
idea. A short walk from
the beach.

Cabinas Zabamar
$$$-$$$$
≡, ⊗, *hw, pb, ≈, ℝ, ℜ*
Playa Jacó
☎/⇒*643-3174*
Squeezed onto a tiny
lot, the cabinas
Zabamar are clean and
simply but adequately
furnished.

Hotel Copacabana
$$$$-$$$$$
≡, *K, pb, hw*
Playa Jacó
☎/⇒*643-3131*
Hotel Copacabana is
the place for active—
and passive—sports
enthusiasts. Various
equipment for athletic
activities (kayaks, for
example), or for relax-
ation (lounge chairs
and so on) can be
rented, or you can sim-
ply watch sports on the
hotel's satellite televi-
sion. Apartments with
kitchenettes and living
rooms are also avail-
able. The hotel is aging
a bit and its rooms are
a little worn. The
owner is friendly and
strives to make the
place welcoming for
surfers.

Tropical Paradise
$$$$
hw, pb, ≡, ctv, K, ≈
Playa Jacó
☎*256-0091*
⇒*256-0027*
The condominiums at
Tropical Paradise make
up a semi-autonomous
little village in the town
of Jacó, with streets
and a "business" centre
in the heart of the
agglomeration! They're
for sale (fully
equipped), but it's also
possible to rent them.

Barceló Amapola
$$$$
hw, pb, ≡, ctv, ⊗, ≈, ℜ
near the southern exit of the
town, Jacó
☎/⇒*643-3668 or 643-3337*
Barceló Amapola rents
out rooms as well as
three beautifully deco-
rated, uncompromis-
ingly comfortable cot-
tages. The establish-
ment was carefully
designed, both inside
(common day rooms,
restaurant, etc.) and
out. The room's ter-
races are well isolated.
Amapola has an Italian
restaurant (see p 339),
but is somewhat far
from the beach (500m
or 1,640ft) and from the
centre of the town
(2km or 1.2mi).

Aparthotel Sole d'Oro
$$$$
pb, hw, ≡, ≈
Playa Jacó
☎/⇒*643-3172*
Aparthotel Sole d'Oro
shares a very cramped
lot with its small swim-
ming pool, so its layout
leaves something to be
desired. The interior is
simple and clean.

Cabinas El Coral
$$$$
pb, ≈, K, ctv, ≈
100m (328ft) north and 75m
(246ft) east of Supermercado
Rayo Azul, Playa Jacó
☎643-3133
The Cabinas El Coral
are pretty and spacious,
with kitchenettes and
living rooms. The estab-
lishment's overall decor
is rather plain, but
clean. It can get a bit
noisy since the con-
crete units are set quite
closely around the
pool.

Hotel Jacó Fiesta
$$$$
pb, hw, ≈, ctv, K, ℝ, ≈, ℜ
Playa Jacó
☎643-3147
≈643-3148
jacofiesta@racsa.co.cr
People come to the
Hotel Jacó Fiesta
because of its—in our
opinion overrated—
reputation. The rooms
are rather ordinary and
it's hard to believe that
this hotel has won
prizes for ecological
distinction, as adver-
tized in its brochures.
The outdoor layout is
certainly pleasant
enough, but doesn't
reveal any particular
preoccupation with
integrating the estab-
lishment into its natural
surroundings.

Hotel Tangeri
$$$$
hw, pb, ≈
on the main street, Playa Jacó
☎643-3001
Hotel Tangeri is
extremely well
designed. About 10
small, clean, pretty
villas can accommodate
up to eight people

each. Located along a
beautiful little path that
leads to the pool, they
are idyllic little summer
cottages with large
terraces. There are even
a volleyball court and a
children's wading pool
on the premisses.

Villas Miramar
$$$$ bkfst incl.
hw, pb, ⊗, K, ≈
Playa Jacó
☎643-3003
The Villas Miramar are
clean, tastefully deco-
rated and provide
plenty of privacy on
their relatively small lot
in the centre of the
town. The landscaping
is exquisite and the
area as a whole is very
quiet, although it is just
two steps from the
beach. Good value.

Best Western Jacó Beach Resort
$$$$$
hw, pb, ≈
Playa Jacó
☎220-1772 or 220-1725
≈232-3159
jacohotel@racsa.co.cr
As a large hotel com-
plex that is part of a
chain, the Best Western
Jacó Beach Resort is
very popular with tour-
ists, especially Cana-
dians. This hotel is
often included in vaca-
tion packages, so it's
very busy. The clientele
consists mostly of fami-
lies, which the hotel's
services cater to, with
facilities that include
ping-pong tables, pin-
ball, tennis and volley-
ball courts nad bicycles.
Disco music is played
in the reception area.
The hotel grounds, vast
and well-landscaped,

are directly on the
beach. The hotel is a
short walk from the
centre of the town. The
hotel also has confer-
ence rooms and a
dance club.

🦎 Club del Mar
$$$-$$$$$
hw, pb, ≈, ℜ, ≈, K
Playa Jacó
☎/≈643-3194
Club del Mar is a very
attractive resort in a
stunning setting, set
back from the bustle of
the town at the very
southern end of Jacó's
beach. The owners
have perfectly inte-
grated their establish-
ment with the natural
environment on a large
property right on the
beach. The four types
of rooms are tastefully
decorated and most
have private balconies.
There is a beautiful,
large common reading
area for guests. Its main
attraction, however, is
the friendly and atten-
tive owners who take
pleasure in organizing
outings in the area for
guests. The restaurant
specializes in seafood
and Chateaubriand.

Hotel Cocal
$$$$ bkfst incl.
hw, pb, ≈, ≈
Playa Jacó
☎643-3067
≈643-3082
The rooms at Hotel
Cocal are arranged
single file along a
shared terrace. Those
facing the ocean are
not air-conditioned.
The layout of the exte-
rior is quite polished,
despite the fact that it is
somewhat crowded

around the pool.

Villas Jacó Princess
$$$$$
hw, pb, ctv, K, ≡, ≈
Playa Jacó
☎*220-1441*
⇆*232-3159*
The condominiums at
Villas Jacó Princess can
accommodate five
guests each. In addition
to kitchenettes, they
come with living rooms
and private patios.
Guests have free use of
bicycles and the facili-
ties at the Best Western
Jacó Beach Resort (see
further above).

Jacó to Quepos

🛏 **Auberge du Pélican**
$$$
sb/pb, hw, ⊗, ≈, ℜ
Playa Esterillos Este
⇆*779-9236*
Run by friendly
Quebecers Mariette
Daignault and Pierre
Perron, the Auberge du
Pélican offers excellent
value. The grounds are
pretty and the patios
and balconies are rela-
tively private. The
rooms are clean and
comfortable, and guests
are lulled to sleep by
the sound of the ocean
waves. The inn is situ-
ated directly on the
magnificent and very
calm Playa Esterillos
Este, one of the most
beautiful beaches on
the Pacific, where the
sunsets are absolutely
heavenly! The owners
have made two rooms
wheelchair accessible.
The grounds include a
nice pool, a hopscotch
game that is lit up at
night, lounge chairs,
parasols and plenty of

hammocks that are
perfect for relaxing!
The hosts can organize
deep-sea fishing excur-
sions, horseback rides
or outings into the
mountains of the back
country in an all-terrain
vehicle. The only draw-
back of this place is
that the charming restau-
rant's delicious food is
only available for
guests.

Beso del Viento
$$$ bkfst incl.
pb, hw, ≈
⇆*779-9108*
There are still very few
hotels around Parrita.
However, 5km (3.1mi)
from the town on Playa
Palo Seco is the
Québec-owned bed
and breakfast Beso del
Viento where you can
stay in a family atmo-
sphere near a gor-
geous, little-known
beach. You can also
rent an apartment and
have lunch and dinner
at the inn.

Cabinas Vista Hermosa
$$$
pb, K
Playa Hermosa
☎*643-3422*
⇆*224-3687*
Cabinas Vista Hermosa
are similar to Cabinas
Las Olas (see below).
There's a small pool
table used by local
young people and
guests.

La Felicidad
$$$
hw, pb/sb, ⊗, ≈, ℜ, K
Esterillos Centro
☎/⇆*779-9003*
Québec-owned La
Felicidad is set in a
perfectly tranquil loca-

tion. Some of its rooms
have kitchenettes and
two have been adapted
for wheelchair access.
The restaurant serves
local and international
dishes. Weekly and
monthly packages are
available. Direct access
to the beach.

Las Olas
$$$
pb, hw, K
Playa Hermosa
☎/⇆*643-3687*
Las Olas has several
bunk beds or single
beds on the upper
floors of A-frame
cabinas. This establish-
ment is perfect for surf-
ers. Rates are negotia-
ble, especially for stays
of more than one
week.

Villa Ballena
$$$
hw, pb, ≈, K
Playa Hermosa
☎*643-3373*
⇆*643-3506*
Villa Ballena has a
lovely exterior and
offers *cabinas* with fully
equipped kitchens sur-
rounded by beautiful
tropical vegetation.
Directly on the beach.
Guests have free access
to the gym at the Plaza
Jacó (see p 343).

Cabinas Flor de Esterillos
$$$-$$$$
pb, hw, K, ≈, ℜ
a bit east of Auberge du Pélican
Esterillos Este
⇆*779-9141 or 779-9108*
Like the Pélican and La
Felicidad, Cabinas Flor
de Esterillos are also
Québec-managed. The
cabinas are fully
equipped with kitchen-
ettes. The entire site is

surrounded by greenery and there is direct access to the beach. The owners offer reduced rates to guests who stay for several nights.

Terraza del Pacífico
$$$$
hw, pb, ctv, ≡, ≈, ℜ
on the national highway
Playa Hermosa
**☎*643-3222*
≈*643-3424*
www.terraza-del-pacifico.com
Terraza del Pacífico has about 50 rooms spread over a two-storey complex surrounded by rather charming landscaping. Each room has a patio or a balcony. A band plays here on a regular basis and special events are often organized. Every year, the Terraza del Pacífico also hosts an international surfing event. There is direct access to the beach, but swimming is prohibited.

The Quepos Region

Apart from a few moderately-priced hotels near the entrance to Parque Nacional Manuel Antonio or in the town of Quepos itself, the region between Quepos and Manuel Antonio is generally frequented by a relatively well-off clientele. This is reflected in the quality of the hotels in the area, many of which have breathtaking settings in the hills overlooking the sea.

Bus service between Quepos and Manuel Antonio is frequent, making travel easy for tourists without cars.

The **Cabinas Cali** *($$)* are set at the end of a small street that leads into a hilly region north of downtown Quepos. It offers minimal comfort, but has very good rates. At the corner of the street, the **Las Palmas** *($$)* restaurant rents *cabinas* of similar quality.

Cabinas Doña Alicia
$$
pb
near the northeast corner of the soccer field
☎777-0419
Cabinas Doña Alicia are absolutely utilitarian and nothing more. For tight budgets.

Cabinas Hellen
$$
hw, pb
one street south of the Sansa offices
☎777-0504
The rooms at Cabinas Hellen provide a decent level of comfort and lead directly out onto the small, plain property. Guests have access to the parking lot.

Cabinas Mary
$$
pb
across from the soccer field
☎777-0128
The Cabinas Mary have very clean *cabinas* for the price. Travellers with limited budgets know this and flock here in great numbers.

Cabinas Ramace
$$
hw, pb, ⊗, ℝ
☎777-0590
The Cabinas Ramace are very clean. The friendly owners rent out three rooms on their small, simple but pleasantly arranged property.

Cabinas Villa Cruz
$$
pb
☎777-0271
≈*777-1081*
The Cabinas Villa Cruz are also very clean. The *cabinas* are lined up in one building and share a terrace that looks out over a small, cramped, but tranquil courtyard.

Hotel Malinche
$$$
≡, ⊗, pb
75m (246ft) west of the bus terminal
☎777-0093
Hotel Malinche has two types of rooms: the older rooms are equipped with fans and are rather antiquated, while the newer, prettier rooms have air-conditioning.

Viña del mar
$$$
pb, ≈, ≡
☎777-0070
Viña del mar has some rather rundown rooms, but is an interesting place to stay because of its location slightly outside of the town on the lagoon.

Hotel Kamuk
$$$$
hw, pb, ≡, ≈, ℜ
on the main street facing the ocean
☎ *777-0379*
⇄ *777-0258*
Hotel Kamuk is a very urban little hotel that has recently been bought up by Best Western. Its rooms are spread over three storeys of a building right in the middle of town, are clean and comfortable and have the decor you would expect of this type of establishment. Some have balconies overlooking the ocean. The pool is refreshing, especially after spending a day walking around in the heat.

Hotel Sirena
$$$$ bkfst incl.
pb, hw, ≡, ≈
50m (164ft) east of Costa Rican Sportsfishing, one block from the bridge, at the centre of Quepos
☎ *777-0528*
The Hotel Sirena can get noisy when people are using the pool in the middle of the building. The rooms are nothing special, but they're clean and their windows open onto the pool.

Hotel Rancho Casa Grande
$$$$
pb, hw, ≡, ⊗
Apartado Postal 618-2010 Zapote
☎ *777-0330 or 777-1646*
⇄ *777-1575*
hotelrcg@racsa.co.cr
On the road that continues south towards the airport, there is a pleasant place to stay.

The Rancho Casa Grande features prettily coloured *cabañas*, the largest of which have living rooms and fully enclosed bedrooms. Hammocks slung in front of some of the rooms will give you a healthy taste of the vacation atmosphere that reigns here. The grounds are crossed by paths, several of them long enough for an interesting stroll. There's restaurant under a *rancho* surrounded by vegetation in the centre of the *cabañas*, as well as a tiny swimming pool that is sadly bare. The reception is extremely welcoming and even includes flowers placed in your room before your arrival.

Hotel Villa Romántica
$$$$ bkfst incl.
pb, hw, ≈
at the exit from the town Quepos
☎/⇄ *777-0037*
Hotel Villa Romántica has beautiful rooms and is tucked away in natural surroundings that create welcome shade in this hot region.

Quepos to Manuel Antonio

Hotel y Restaurante Costa Linda
$
sb/pb, K
on the last cross street before the park
☎ *777-0304*
Hotel y Restaurante Costa Linda is a small, plain youth hostel with no particular charm.

The establishment is perfectly suitable for young backpackers.

El Mono Azul
$$
pb, hw, ⊗, ≡, ≈, ℜ
☎/⇄ *777-1954*
monoazul@racsa.co.cr
El Mono Azul (Blue Monkey) features an ambiance so festive it can lead you to folly! The owner Jennifer, her children and staff will welcome you warmly to this little, meticulously run hotel. The children have opened an original shop (see p 344) and the restaurant serves worthy fare (see p 342). The eight rooms face a very small pool. They're simply but thoughtfully decorated using an assortment of fabrics. Their rear windows look out onto still-virgin territory where the vegetation is gorgeous. If you're interested in the environment, don't hesitate to discuss it with Jennifer, who always has more than one project in mind! Among others, in the summer of 2000 she was working on expanding the number of her rooms by buying the hotel next door.

Cabinas Ramírez
$$
⊗, pb
near the entrance to the park on the beach side, Manuel Antonio
☎ *777-0003*
Cabinas Ramírez are owned by a friendly Quebecer-Costa Rican couple. This clean establishment is especially recommended to

young backpackers. The *cabinas* have a minimal level of comfort, but are very close to Manuel Antonio park!

Hotel Del Mar
$$$
hw, pb, ≡
on the Quepos-Manuel Antonio road, on the inland side 1km (0.6mi) before the park
☎777-0543
Hotel Del Mar is made up of two buildings. The small, colourful rooms are very bright and comfortable, with large windows in the front. The patios are shared, however. Very clean.

Hotel B&B La Colina
$$$ bkfst incl.
hw, pb, ≡, ℝ
about 3km (1.9mi) from Quepos toward Manuel Antonio
☎/≈777-0231
Hotel B&B La Colina is extremely warm and friendly and comprises two buildings perched on a steep slope. The establishment as a whole is very compact, but the hill and the vegetation makes it seem more private. The breakfast has a lot of variety and includes pancakes with syrup!

Hotel Manuel Antonio
$$$
pb, ⊗, ℝ
next to the park
Manuel Antonio
☎777-1237
Hotel Manuel Antonio is a small, fairly clean hotel with small rooms on the building's upper floor. Its main advantage is its proximity to the park, the beach and

the surrounding natural environment. Obviously, these assets attract young travellers. There is a restaurant on the ground floor.

Hotel California
$$$$
hw, pb, ⊗, tv, ≈
slightly set back from a road that intersects the Quepos–Manuel Antonio route
☎777-1234
☎/≈777-1062
Until quite recently, the Hotel California was owned by a painter from Québec whose extremely original decorations included colourful murals. It was just purchased by a Californian whose daughter is also an artist and who seems to have many plans for refurbishing the place, which has lost a bit of its gloss. To be watched!

Karahé
$$$$
hw, pb, ≡, ≈, ℝ, ⊗, ℝ
on the Quepos-Manuel Antonio road
☎777-0170
≈777-1075
Karahé has three types of *cabinas*. The oldest are also the least expensive. Set on a hill, they have beautiful views—but guests must climb quite a slope to reach them! More cottages are located across the road and the most expensive are near the beach. In addition to the upstairs restaurant, lunch is served downstairs, near the pool.

Vela Bar
$$$
hw, pb, ⊗, K, ℝ
on the Quepos-Manuel Antonio road, near the park entrance 100m (328ft) from the main road
☎777-0413
≈777-1071
Vela Bar rents out small, worn and not very comfortable rooms whose charm is somewhat faded. However, the owner is very friendly.

El Dorado Molado
$$$ bkfst incl.
hw, pb, ≡, K
on the Quepos-Manuel Antonio road
☎777-0368
≈777-1248
El Dorado Molado has rooms decorated in subdued tones, with large windows that open onto the surrounding scenery.

🦋 Casa Del Sol
$$$$
hw, pb, K
on the Quepos-Manuel Antonio road, near Cabinas Ramírez
☎777-1805
≈777-1311
verdemar@racsa.co.cr
The Canadian-owned Casa Del Sol offers spacious rooms that are decorated with warm shades of ochre in Mexican-Californian style and that easily meet North-American standards of comfort. Also, the owner is ecologically minded—the beach is accessed via a raised boardwalk to protect the marshy vegetation between the hotel from the seaside.

Casitas Eclipse
$$$$
pb, hw, ⊗, ≈, K
on the Quepos-Manuel Antonio road
☎*777-0408*
⇌*777-1738*
eclipseh@racsa.co.cr
Casitas Eclipse has standard rooms, as well as very bright, clean, airy cottages whose beautiful, multi-pane windows and living rooms (equipped with full kitchens) add to their appeal. The establishment is situated on a huge property with a gorgeous view.

Mimo's Hotel
$$$$
hw, pb, K, ≡, ≈
on the Quepos-Manuel Antonio road, 4km (2.5mi) from the park
☎/⇌*777-0054*
Mimo's Hotel is proudly Italian. Its rooms and suites are tastefully decorated and very spacious. The grounds abound with lovely greenery. The hotel also has rooms that are wheelchair-accessible.

El Mirador del Pacífico
$$$$
hw, pb, ≈, ℜ, ≡
on the Quepos-Manuel Antonio road, Quepos
☎/⇌*777-0119*
El Mirador del Pacífico is largely made of wood. The rooms are very pleasant, with attractive furnishings and white walls. They are also large and bright. However, they all share one terrace. Guests can have their meals on the *mirador* (hence the name), while enjoying a

superb view of the surroundings.

Hotel Playa Espadilla
$$$$ bkfst incl.
K, ℜ, pb, hw, ≡, ≈
Playa Espadilla
☎/⇌*777-0903*
Hotel Playa Espadilla has small, very clean apartments with fully equipped kitchens. Their decor is simple but pleasant. The landscaping will improve when the vegetation matures.

Hotel Las Tres Banderas
$$$$
pb, hw, ≡, ≈, ⊗, ℜ, bar
on the Quepos-Manuel Antonio road
☎*777-1284 or 777-1871*
⇌*777-1478*
www.hotel-tres-banderas.com
Hotel Las Tres Banderas rents about 10 rooms in one villa with a shared patio. The rooms are tastefully decorated with wood and ceramic tiles.

Hotel Villabosque
$$$$
hw, pb, ⊗, ≡, ≈, ℜ
on the Quepos-Manuel Antonio road, a few hundred metres before the park entrance and 125m (410ft) from the beach
☎*777-0463*
⇌*777-0401*
Hotel Villabosque is very charming. The building itself is beautiful, the ornamental landscaping is accomplished and the well-proportioned rooms have a Spanish flavour. The rooftop pool is rather original.

Villa Nina
$$$$ bkfst incl.
hw, pb, ≡, ℝ, ≈, ℜ
on the road that branches off on the Quepos-Manuel Antonio road near Casitas Eclipse
☎*777-1628*
⇌*777-1497*
Villa Nina has appealing rooms in a Florida Art Deco-style building with lots of character.

Villa Teca
$$$$ bkfst incl.
pb, hw, ≡, ≈, ℜ
on the Quepos-Manuel Antonio road
☎*777-1117*
⇌*777-1578*
Villa Teca has two simple, pleasant rooms per building or villa, each of which has a small patio. It's very clean, and the large property that surrounds it is natural.

Casa Blanca
$$$$-$$$$$
pb, hw, ≡, ℝ, ≈, ℜ
on the Quepos-Manuel Antonio road
☎/⇌*777-0253*
cblanca@racsa.co.cr
Casa Blanca is restricted to a gay and lesbian clientele and their friends. The rooms, suites and apartments are very nicely decorated and the grounds are thoroughly relaxing and enjoyable. There's also a fully equipped cottage that is perfect for honeymoons. The beach is a 20min walk from the hotel.

The Central Pacific Coast

Hotel Costa Verde
$$$$-$$$$$
hw, pb, ≈, ℜ
on the Quepos-Manuel Antonio road
☎*777-0584*
⇌*777-0560*
costaver@racsa.co.cr
Hotel Costa Verde has a magnificent view of the ocean. It's difficult to find airier lodgings than those at Costa Verde—fair-sized sections of the rooms are actually open to the outdoors, thanks to large screened windows and glass doors. In front, there's a relatively private terrace furnished with leather rocking chairs. Also, the place is visited regularly by a colony of squirrel monkeys, absolutely fascinating to watch!

Hotel Plinio
$$$$-$$$$$ bkfst incl.
hw, pb
set back about 100m (328ft) from the road, 1km (0.6mi) from Quepos
☎*777-0055*
⇌*777-0558*
plinio@racsa.co.cr
Hotel Plinio is truly charming with its wooden building that creates a tastefully rustic atmosphere. It's managed to preserve its idyllic character for decades now. The dark wood-panelled rooms are very stylish and are located on two floors, with large terraces along the front. Very clean.

Villas Nicolas
$$$$-$$$$$
hw, pb, ⊗, K, ≈
next to Si Como No, on the Quepos-Manuel Antonio road
☎*777-0481*
☎/⇌*777-0451*
Villas Nicolas is a 10-year-old condominium complex whose units are rented out by the owners when they're not there. Some of the living quarters are rather faded, though the general design of these condos is far from lacking in charm. They have extraordinary views of the jungle and the sea below from the private veranda. The most expensive condos have two storeys, two balconies with hammocks, two bedrooms and two bathrooms, as well as fully equipped kitchens.

Hotel El Byblos
$$$$$
hw, pb, ℝ, ctv, ≡, ≈
on the Quepos-Manuel Antonio road
☎*777-0411*
⇌*777-0009*
Hotel El Byblos is French owned. Bungalows and suites are available; all of them have balconies, are spacious and are decorated in a refreshing style with tile, rattan and pastel tones. The hotel restaurant is worth a stop (see p 342).

Hotel Divisamar
$$$$$
hw, pb, ≈, ≡, ℜ
on the Quepos-Manuel Antonio road, Quepos
☎*777-0371*
⇌*777-0525*
Hotel Divisamar is owned by a Costa Rican family. The rooms share the veranda in the middle of the multi-storey buildings. The rooms are clean and have large windows. The light colours of their decor make them even brighter.

Villas de La Selva
$$$$$
hw, pb, ≈, ⊛, K
on the Quepos-Manuel Antonio road
☎/⇌*777-1137*
San José
☎*253-4890*
Villas de La Selva are apartments and *cabinas* with private terraces and fully equipped kitchens. They are somewhat rustic, but quite pleasant. The whole the complex is very attractive overall and has a breathtaking view of the bay of Manuel Antonio. The villas are a bit of a walk from the beach, which is reached by a path. The villas are on a road that branches off the main road. A childcare service is available. Groups can rent a villa and an adjoining apartment.

La Mariposa
$$$$$
hw, pb, ≡, ⊛, ≈, ℜ
at the intersection of a marked road that also leads to the El Parador hotel and the Quepos-Manuel Antonio road
☎ *777-0355 or 777-0456*
⇄ *777-0050*
www.lamariposa.com
La Mariposa has beautiful two-storey villas with a magnificent view that can be appreciated from the rooms' whirlpools! The bamboo, tile and wood interiors are also truly charming. A gay pride flag flutters over the entrance.

Makanda-by-the-Sea
$$$$$$ bkfst incl.
hw, pb, K, ≈
1km (0.6mi) down a road that branches off from the Quepos-Manuel Antonio road toward the sea, near the restaurant Barba Roja
☎ *777-0442*
⇄ *777-1032*
makanda@racsa.co.cr
Makanda-by-the-Sea definitely knows how to make a good first impression and extends an absolutely perfect welcome to guests when they arrive. The emphasis is on attentive service—with a smile! The fully equipped villas have to be seen to be believed: they overlook the sea, providing natural ventilation and contact with the outdoors that are hard to beat. The "cathedral ceilings" and the combination of wood and tile in the decor add to their charm. They're scattered on a hillside in such a way as to guarantee privacy. At low-

tide guests have access to a beach where the receding waters reveal well renowned pre-Columbian turtle traps.

El Parador
$$$$$$
pb, hw, ctv, ≡, ≈
at the end of the marked road that also leads to La Mariposa and the Quepos-Manuel Antonio road
☎ *777-1414*
⇄ *777-1437*
parador@racsa.co.cr
El Parador is luxury itself! On top of a rocky peak, it offers first-class accommodations in a natural environment. Its rooms and villas are extremely comfortable and each has its own terrace. The common living areas are elegantly furnished and, very pleasant. There's an absolutely breathtaking view of the surroundings from the dining room! The impeccable service is extremely courteous and attentive.

Si Como No
$$$$$$
hw, pb, ⊛, ≡, ≈, ⊛, ℜ
4km (2.5mi) from Quepos, on the Quepos-Manuel Antonio road
☎ *777-0777*
⇄ *777-1093*
www.sicomono.com
With its terraced architectural design on a mountainside, the Si Como No hotel complex is absolutely gorgeous! Its views are striking, and the ecologically minded owner uses solar energy, recycled water, and cultivated wood (instead of the country's rare natu-

ral wood) to run his hotel. This takes absolutely nothing away from the establishment's uncompromising beauty and comfort. A shuttle takes guests to the beach. Films can be screened in a small private movie theatre!

Tulemar Bungalows
$$$$$$ bkfst incl.
hw, pb, ≡, ≈
on the Quepos-Manuel Antonio road
☎ *777-0580*
⇄ *777-1759*
www.tulemar.com
Tulemar Bungalows are located on a large property, most of which has been left in its natural state, so you can go on instructive forest hikes. The bungalows' octagonal form gives them multiple points of access to the outdoors. They're comfortable and pleasantly decorated. Guests can use sea kayaks for no additional charge. Children under 12 stay for free. The hotel has its own access to Tulemar beach, below the complex, where you can see the pre-Columbian turtle traps at low tide.

Restaurants

The Puntarenas Region

There are many little restaurants in the city of Puntarenas, including those found in most of the better hotels.

You can enjoy good seafood for prices that are more than reasonable at **Casa de Mariscos** (*$-$$; Puntarenas*) and **Bar-Restaurante Cevichito** (*$-$$; Puntarenas*).

Kahite Blanco
$-$$
Avenida 1, Calle 15/17, Puntarenas
☎*661-2093*
Kahite Blanco is very popular, especially with Costa Ricans, as it serves generous portions of seafood and hearty *bocas*.

Aloha
$$-$$$
west of the Tioga hotel
Puntarenas
☎*661-0773*
Aloha is considered one of the better restaurants in the city, especially for seafood.

La Caravelle
$$$
Tue to Sun
on the ocean side, Puntarenas
Finally, the French restaurant La Caravelle is renowned for its entrées. It can be very busy, especially during high season.

The Southern Nicoya Peninsula

Paquera to Montezuma

Tambor

Bahía Ballena Yacht Club
$$-$$$
10am to midnight
Located next to the dock, the restaurant-bar Bahía Ballena Yacht Club has a varied menu

of dishes with Mexican, Cajun and Caribbean flavours.

🦞 **La Paillote**
$$-$$$
☎*683-0190*
Located in the mountains near Tambor and Pochote, La Paillote serves succulent food. This French restaurant is perched just high enough to offer a panoramic view of the lush, green valley and the hills. The menu is made up of excellent and affordable French cuisine, made with fresh ingredients. The kitchen can cook up your very own "catch of the day" on request. This establishment also provides accommodations (see p 317).

Perla Tambor
$$-$$$
A Swiss flag hangs at the seaside location of the restaurant-bar Perla Tambor, which prepares international cuisine.

Ristorante Italiano
$$-$$$
11am to 11pm
☎*683-0148*
Ristorante Italiano has a view of the ocean and serves pizza, pasta and seafood.

Montezuma

Many of the hotels in Montezuma have restaurants that are open to the public.

Across from Topsy bookstore is **Panadería Idalie**, a bakery that makes fresh bread and

pastries and has a tiny terrace.

Café Montezuma
$-$$
Café Montezuma serves superb breakfasts and lunches, as well as tasty fruit juices, at modest prices. A small **pizzeria** next door is open in the evening.

El Carcol
$$
Tucked into a curve in the road, the *soda* El Caracol's colourful sign is in keeping with its decor. A few tables are set up outdoors for guests to sample breakfast, or later meals, consisting of typical *soda* fare with a slight North American accent. The homemade cookies are delicious!

El Parque
$$-$$$
On the beach near Hotel Montezuma, the menu at El Parque features fresh fish.

🌴 **El Sano Banano**
$$-$$$
☎*642-0068*
For more than a decade, El Sano Banano served as meeting place, rallying point and landmark in the centre of the village of Montezuma. This open-air restaurant serves vegetarian cuisine made from the finest ingredients. Patricia, the owner, puts a lot of effort into choosing the elements that make up her recipes. And look at the results! The dishes you'll taste here will delight you. Simple

but flavourful, the sandwiches (try the veggie-burger), pastas, soups and salads are all mouthwatering. Not to mention sweets, such as muffins, cakes and fruit salad! The freshly squeezed juices and milkshakes will add the final touch to your enjoyment. The restaurant was renovated in the summer of 2000, but has kept its festive format, showing a film on the big screen every night.

Playa de las Artistas
$$$-$$$$

At the end of a courtyard near the beach, the Playa de las Artistas restaurant seems hidden away in the vegetation. It is nestled under a low roof that augments the feeling of envelopment. Each of the tables has its own originality: one is set up under the stars, another, on a lower level, but all of them are on a floor made of... sand! To add to the unique character of the place, the decor is filled with lovely pieces that are often made of natural materials, such as lampshades made from coconuts and tables made from tree trunks. The owners of the place are real artists and their talent is evident. They're better versed in artistic creation than in waiting tables, however, and it shows in the service. But this hardly detracts from an evening spent in such enchanting surroundings. You'll certainly enjoy the fish, grilled on a barbecue that is set up off to one side and served whole on a large board covered with an almond tree leaf. Delicious!

South of Montezuma

Cabuya

El Ancla De Oro
$$-$$$
☎642-0369

El Ancla De Oro is still one of the best restaurants in Cabuya. The owner, Alex Villalobos, is a first-class chef who has an excellent reputation in the region. The menu features simple, original cuisine that emphasizes seafood, fish and vegetarian dishes at reasonable prices. The establishment also rents out *cabinas* (see p 321).

Northwest of Cabo Blanco

The vast majority of the hotels in this area have restaurants that are open to the public.

Break Point
$-$$
Santa Teresa

Across from the *cabinas* at Zaneida's campground is the *soda* Break Point, which serves French-style fast food.

Frank's Place
$-$$
between Malpaís and Santa Teresa
☎642-0296

Certainly the best value in the region, Frank's Place is a very friendly meeting place where people flock after a day of outdoor adventures. A variety of local and international dishes can be sampled, including excellent and inexpensive scampi.

Surf & Sport Camp
$-$$
Malpaís
☎642-0047

The Surf & Sport Camp (see p 321) has a restaurant that serves affordable international cuisine. People come here to play pool or sip a beer at the bar while watching surfing videos or satellite television.

Albimat Dulce Magia
$$-$$$
Malpaís

For tasty pasta, pizza and seafood, or simply to sip a rich espresso, the open-air restaurant Albimat Dulce Magia is the place to go. The Neapolitan owners are especially proud of their fish fondue and *ceviche*. The restaurant also has a very busy bar that is popular with tourists and Costa Ricans alike.

Star Mountain Eco Resort
$$$
Malpaís
☎296-2626, ext. 125080

The Star Mountain Eco Resort is located in the mountains, 2km (1.2mi) from the sea. The open-air restaurant-bar serves excellent international cuisine in a friendly atmosphere. Restaurant guests can also spend the afternoon at the hotel's splendid pool (see p 321).

Sunset Reef Marine lodge
$$$
Malpaís
☎640-0012
The restaurant at the Sunset Reef Marine lodge (see p 321) serves excellent food. The Belgian chef, Nathalie, prepares tasty international, European and local dishes. Since fishers dock at the village just a few metres from the hotel, the fish here is always remarkably fresh.

Tropico Latino Lodge
$$$
☎640-0062
The Tropico Latino Lodge in Santa Teresa has an open-air restaurant that serves Italian and local cuisine. The curried chicken is especially scrumptious.

South of Puntarenas

The Jacó region

Cabinas Alice
$
100m (328ft) south of the Red Cross, Playa Jacó
☎643-3061
The restaurant at Cabinas Alice serves Costa Rican dishes in a shady area.

El Recreo
$
Jacó
☎643-3012
El Recreo serves wonderful, inexpensive food (the price of the shrimp is unbeatable). The restaurant is quiet and the Latin American background music is trully pleasant.

Restaurante Clarita
$
50m (164ft) west of the Santimar restaurant, Playa Jacó
☎643-3013
Restaurante Clarita, adjoining the *cabinas* of the same name, is clean and serves mainly Costa Rican cuisine in a very simple dining room. Its main advantage is its location right on the beach.

Sunrise Grill
$
Thu to Tue 7am to noon
on the main street, Jacó
The Sunrise Grill is known as "the breakfast place" because of its reasonably priced American-style morning repast: waffles, pancakes, toast and eggs.

Los Faroles
$$
every day
at the corner of the main street and the northern entrance to Jacó from the San José-Jacó highway
Los Faroles is a seafood restaurant and bar with reasonable prices.

La Fiesta del Marisco and Tico Tico
$$
just south of Steve & Lisa's restaurant on the San José-Jacó road, Punta Leona, on the seaside
The *pescadería* La Fiesta del Marisco and Tico Tico both specialize in seafood served in a generally attractive decor.

La Hacienda
$$
on the main street, Jacó
The restaurant-bar *marisquería* La Hacienda is where Jacó's young people go to see and be seen, especially on the front terrace.

El Riconcito Peruano
$$
Jacó
On the main street, across from the road to Discoteca La Central and next to the Rayo Azul supermarket, El Riconcito Peruano serves tasty Peruvian dishes.

Santimar
$$
Fri to Tue 11am to 9pm
200m (656ft) north and 200m (656ft) west of the Jacó Beach hotel, next to the Clarita, Playa Jacó
☎643-3605
Santimar is a pretty, good little restaurant with a refined decor that serves Costa Rican cuisine.

Steve & Lisa's
$$
on the seaside on the San José-Jacó road, Punta Leona
Steve & Lisa's serves Costa Rican specialties. You'll recognize this

attractive restaurant by its small *mirador* (look-out) near the ocean where you can dine *a fresco*.

Banana Café
$$-$$$

Playa Jacó

The Banana Café is a North American-style restaurant that serves seafood, sandwiches, breakfasts, Chinese food and, according to some, the best steaks in town.

Riosasis
$$-$$$

☎*643-3354*

One of the most recent of Jaco's many restaurants, Riosasis has great ambiance. Whether inside in the cozy dining room with small-paned windows, or outside on the terrace dotted with *heliconias,* you'll receive attentive service from smiling personnel. The extensive menu is very tempting—*focaccia* with creative fillings, thin-crust pizza cooked in a wood-fired oven, Mexican food—and the dishes placed before you are equally so.

Terraza El Hicaco
$$-$$$

Wed to Mon

☎*643-3226*

The *hicaco* is a beautiful tree and this restaurant is named for the fine specimen standing in front of its open-air dining room. Quite close to the beach, it serves fish and seafood of all kinds. Friendly service and a pleasant atmosphere.

Barceló Amapola
$$$

near the southern exit from town, Jacó

☎/≈*643-3668 or 643-3337*

The restaurant at the hotel Barceló Amapola prepares pizza from a wood-burning oven. Like the rest of the building, the dining room has a refined decor.

La Bruja
$$$

Three houses south of La Hacienda, the very clean Swiss-run restaurant-bar La Bruja comes highly recommended. Swiss and international specialties are served.

La Ostra
$$$

at the corner of Jacó's main street and the road to Los Ranchos, Jacó

La Ostra serves very good meals of various types (seafood, steaks, hamburgers). The decor and service are quite pleasant.

Pancho Villa
$$$

on the main street at the corner of the road to Discoteca Los Tucanes, Jacó

The Pancho Villa has an attractive decor and good food.

Villa Lapas
$$$

at the beginning of the road to Catarata Manantial Agua Viva where it branches off the San José-Jacó road

☎*663-0811*

≈*663-1516*

Looking for a special atmosphere and a good meal? The restaurant at

Villa Lapas fits the bill. The hotel's location (see p 323) in a very sonorous forest next to a river lets you take in all the seductive sounds of Costa Rica's wilderness while dining in its very pretty restaurant. The natural surroundings and pleasant decor add to the enjoyment of the restaurant's international cuisine.

Jacó to Quepos

Parrita

Los Tucanes
$

across from Supermercado La Julieta, on the main street Parrita

☎*779-9129*

Parrita is the place to stop for a bite to eat between Jacó and Quepos. Los Tucanes is an unpretentious restaurant that serves simple Costa Rican dishes.

Café Yoli
$$

every day 7am to 11pm

near the exit from the town toward Jacó, on the main street Parrita

Café Yoli is the best place for a meal. Although its Québécoise owner has put together a menu of mainly pizza, you can also have good hamburgers, breakfasts and Costa Rican meals in its inviting, stunning surroundings.

The Quepos Region

Heladería Dani

$

every day 10am to 11pm
An irresistible urge for ice cream? In that case, you won't miss the large papier mâché ice cream cone on the sidewalk in front of Dani's ice cream parlour. A large variety of flavours await the aficionado who'll put aside gourmet tastes to enjoy this unassuming and refreshing treat!

The market adjacent to the bus station is a good spot for a light lunch.

☕ Café Milagro

$

along the road parallel to the estuary
☎777-1707
Café Milagro is everything you could ask for in a café. The desserts are excellent (chocolate and cheese brownies... what a treat!) and there is an extensive selection of coffees, jams, syrups, coffee cups and cigars. The atmosphere is pleasant and friendly, with the enticing aroma of coffee wafting through the air. Some popular North American magazines, such as *Mademoiselle*, *The Enquirer* and *Billboard*, as well as dailies like *USA Today*, are available.

Punto de Encuentro Cafetería y Panadería

$

Avenida Central, next to Cabinas Doña Alicia
Punto de Encuentro Cafetería y Panadería is a very friendly spot for breakfast, hot chocolate, tea, coffee and fresh juice.

El Pueblo

$

Head to the very popular **El Pueblo** restaurant for a drink or a late-night bite to eat.

Angolo

$$

In the middle of the village of Quepos, a little shop on the corner presents an incongruous sight: an authentic Italian grocery, here, leagues away from the Boot! Pizza, pasta, bread, cheese (ricotta), cold cuts, marinades... everything necessary to concoct a gourmet meal! A few tables accommodate those who wish to linger.

Dos Locos

$$

☎777-1526
Quepos also has a Mexican restaurant! Dos Locos is located on a corner and is attractively designed. It serves all the typical dishes of its Latin neighbours to the north.

Gabriel's Pizza

$$

☎777-1085
At another intersection of little village streets, delectable aromas waft at all hours from Gabriel's Pizza. This often busy pizzeria prepares its classic fare with a large variety of toppings on a tasty crust. Wine is also served and meals are consumed at small wooden tables in simple surroundings.

La Marquesa

$$

☎777-1545
Thanks to unbeatable prices, the large *soda* La Marquesa attracts a heterogeneous crowd made up of both visitors and residents. Fish and seafood, as well as typical Costa Rican dishes, including breakfasts, are served in a strictly functional dining room with a scattering of wooden tables.

Hotel Kamuk

$$

on the main street across from the ocean
☎777-0379
On the ground floor of Hotel Kamuk is a beautiful little restaurant with a refined, attractive decor. The Kamuk has another **restaurant** (*$$$*) on the third floor, which is isolated from the town traffic and has a lovely view of the surroundings. International menu.

Restaurante Isabel

$$

near Buena Nota
Quiet and yet extremely popular, Restaurante Isabel is the perfect place for a tasty light seafood meal right in the heart of Quepos.

El Gran Escape

$$$

closed Tue
El Gran Escape is an inescapable presence in Quepos. Its two large dining rooms take up a

corner of the main street and its festive atmosphere overflows onto the sidewalk. A long bar in the back and a sizable number of wooden tables are interspersed with a series of decorative elements, including a fountain, that create a wonderful effect. Candles on the tables add a pleasant touch. Fish and seafood dishes appear on the menu, of course, but so do meat dishes, hamburgers and Mexican food. It's all very nourishing, thanks to generous portions. However, avoid the French fries. Couples are welcome here, as well as large groups with children.

Quepos to Manuel Antonio

Most of the restaurants at the hotels in this area are open to the public, but here is a list of places worth remembering.

Café Milagro
$
Manuel Antonio road
www.cafemilagro.com
Like its sister establishment in the village, the Café Milagro serves little treats to be devoured any time of day and, of course, coffee that you'd travel miles for! Muffins, cakes, bagels and sandwiches will provide sustenance, while the choice of beverages and coffees, some of them iced, will lift your spirits. In the morning, there's a breakfast buf-

fet that is well worth a special trip. At amore-than-reasonable price, you can eat as much as you like: pancakes, French toast, eggs, ham, bacon, granola, fresh juice, fruit and still more. Enough to last the whole day! There is also a small shop that sells handicrafts and… coffee!

Pickles Deli
$-$$
☎*777-1597*
What a great discovery this deli is! Is there anything more enjoyable than heading off for a picnic in the country with a basket chock-full of good things tucked under your arm? This is now possible in Manuel Antonio thanks to Pickles Deli which has everything you need to create a lunch that suits you. They even rent little coolers! Marinated meats and chicken, grilled vegetables and smoked fish go into sandwiches that anyone would happily sink their teeth into! The French bread submarine sandwich made with a large variety of cold cuts, the grilled veggie *foccacia*, the roast beef sandwich served *au jus*… everything is absolutely delightful! Accompany them with a salad or (why not?) homemade chocolate chip cookies! You can even come here for breakfast, as two or three tables make this possible, before setting off with your lunch!

Barba Roja
$-$$
Tue to Sun 7:30am to midnight
Diagonally across from Café Milagro, Barba Roja is simultaneously a very frequented restaurant and an art gallery. It serves North American cuisine (hamburgers, sandwiches, steaks, some seafood and so on), which is popular with people who like this type of food.

Del Mar
$$
on the beach just before Manuel Antonio park
The restaurant-bar Del Mar has a lively Costa Rican atmosphere and menu. The background music caters to the rather young, dynamic clientele that frequents the place in the late afternoon and evenings. *Tico* menu.

El Mono Loco
$$
The first restaurant after the exit from the Manuel Antonio park, El Mono Loco is set up under a high, spacious, thatched-palm roof. It provides a good opportunity to meet the urgent need for sustenance or liquids at the end of a long day! International cuisine is served on glass tables surrounded by wicker armchairs.

Mar y Sombra
$$
500m (1,640ft) from the entrance to Manuel Antonio park Mar y Sombra is a popular restaurant that's also right on the beach,

but is a bit larger than the Del Mar. Its decor, including the landscaping, is sightly better. Costa Rican cuisine.

Jardin Gourmet
$$-$$$
Part of the Casitas Eclipse complex (see p 333), the restaurant and bar Jardin Gourmet offers Mediterranean cuisine in a decor to match. Breakfast, lunch and dinner are served.

La Cantina
$$-$$$
starting at 4pm
☎777-0584
Across from and associated with the Costa Verde hotel, La Cantina features a vacation atmosphere. Under a roof that is open to the seasons, a large grill emits myriad enticing aromas. Around it are a few low tables surrounded by leather rocking chairs. In front of them is a small space where a group of musicians usually appears. Behind it, another room provides a more tranquil corner for diners who are more starved for brochettes than for music. Its centre is dominated by an antique railroad car, brought in to house a small Internet centre that provides a means of communicating with the world.

El Mono Azul
$$-$$$
every day 7am to 10pm
☎777-1548
The restaurant at the El Mono Azul hotel features international cui-

sine. In an open room, a few plastic tables with colourful tablecoths serve as a restaurant with a menu of pasta, pizzas, rice and similar dishes. The tasty pizzas are served on a board. Next to it, there's a small shop run by children who donate its profits to help save the tropical forest (see p 344). Delivery available.

Restaurante Karola
$$$
Thu to Tue
between Barba Roja and the road to Mariposa, on the Quepos-Manuel Antonio road
☎777-0424
Restaurante Karola opens for breakfast at 7am. Specialties include macadamia nut pies, eggs *ranchero*, steaks and enchiladas among other things.

Hotel Plinio
$$$
set back a few hundred m from the road, 1km (0.6mi) from Quepos
☎777-0055
≈777-0558
The restaurant at the Hotel Plinio is good and recommended. The atmosphere is very pleasant, and the homemade bread and daily specials are delicious. The Plinio makes a delicious *tiramisu*, which might well be the best in the country. It's a good idea to make advance reservations.

Gato Negro
$$$
☎777-0408
The restaurant at the Gato Negro hotel stands at the edge of the road, but since it's on the second storey of a building, noise is not a problem. It has an airy and restful decor, all in white, from the stucco walls to the wicker funiture. The lengthy menu offers a variety of Italian dishes and the reception is particularly pleasant.

Vela Bar
$$$
100m from the main Quepos-Manuel Antonio road, near the park entrance
☎777-0413
≈777-7071
The restaurant at the hotel Vela Bar is pleasantly nestled in greenery and serves vegetarian cuisine.

Hotel El Byblos
$$$$
on the Quepos-Manuel Antonio road
The French-managed restaurant at Hotel El Byblos offers authentic French cuisine in a subdued, distinguished environment. This is the place for shrimp Provençale and succulent *profiteroles*!

Richard's
$$$$
on the Quepos-Manuel Antonio road
Across from El Byblos, Richard's is a classy pasta and seafood restaurant.

Entertainment

South of Puntarenas

The Jacó Region

Bar El Zarpe
in the Jacó shopping centre
Bar El Zarpe really livens up at night. It's always busy and the staff is very friendly.

There are two nightclubs in Jacó:
La Discoteca los Toucanes and **La Central**, at the ends of the streets from downtown to the beach. La Central is perhaps more of a typical nightclub than the other and offers parking.

The Quepos Region

Pub Kamuk
on the main street, facing the ocean, Quepos
☎*777-0379*
Pub Kamuk, at the hotel of the same name, is a live music venue that is quite busy.

Bahía Azul
next door to the Quepos marina
Bahía Azul is a restaurant and dance bar that has pretty views of the port and the sea. An excellent spot for a refreshing cocktail and a breath of fresh air, since it's a bit cooler here than in the rest of the town.

Arco Iris
next to Bahía Azul, in the Quepos marina
Arco Iris is a nightclub that attracts twentysomethings.

Behind and adjacent to the El Gran Escape restaurant, **Epicentro** is a little place that generally attracts a large, youthful crowd. Darts and video games, rock music and television satisfy groups that come to chat over a drink in this bar. Its three large barn doors open onto the street.

A little farther on, **La Taberna de Tío Fernando** is an establishment owned by Fernand, a Quebecer. Behind the bar, in a tiny and interestingly decorated room, he serves a mixed clientele that stops by to sit on stools and chat with their neighbours over a brew. Fernand's *taberna* is one of the few places here that serves good draft beer.

To dance, young people turn out at **Bistro Tropical**, a two-storey nightclub that draws a large crowd.

La Boquita
on the second floor, across from the restaurant El Pueblo
La Boquita is also very popular. Pool tables and reggae musique.

El Banco Bar
across from the Ramus hotel in Quepos
El Banco Bar is a very friendly, attractive bar covered with souvenir photos and frequented by a laid-back clientele.

Shopping

The Southern Nicoya Peninsula

Montezuma

Montezuma has many little shops that sell clothing, jewellery and souvenirs of Costa Rica. Whether you're looking for a hammock, sandals, a hat or a wet suit for surfing, you'll find a large selection.

El Hamaquero
next door to Café Montezuma
El Hamaquero offers a large selection of clothing, some of which is made in Costa Rica. As in the rest of the country, you can also find clothing and jewellery from Indonesia, India and Guatemala.

South of Puntarenas

The Jacó Region

Jacó has a full-fledged shopping mall, **Plaza Jacó**, located across from the Jacó Best Western. Inside there is a branch of Banco de Costa Rica, of course.

Wine and spirits are available at **Licorería del Mar**, a short distance south of the restaurant Killer Munchies, in Jacó.

Garden Café Jacó Beach Gift Shop
☎*643-3404*
The Garden Café Jacó Beach Gift Shop sells cigars and souvenirs of all sorts. Surfing, fishing and snorkelling equipment are also available here.

Just next door to the Rioasis restaurant, the refinement of **Galería de Arte La Heliconia** piques the curiosity of passers-by. Unlike most of the souvenir shops in Jaco, La Heliconia sells high-quality handicrafts. Vividly coloured ceramics, silver jewellery, clothing... everything is in good taste. Worth a visit even if you have nothing to buy!

Jaco also has **Cofre de Tesoro**, which offers a good selection of hand-icrafts, as well as imports from almost everywhere in the world. Furniture, knick-knacks, candles, candlesticks and other items fill the large rooms.

The Quepos Region

You can buy some magazines at the **Botica Quepos** pharmacy, in Quepos, at the corner of Avenida 2 and Calle 2, across from the lagoon.

Beside the playground in Quepos is **Galería Costa Rica**, a shop that sells crafts and colour-ful summer clothing.

Very attractive and friendly.

Not far from here, **Galería Del Sol Gift Shop**, next to Cabinas Hellen, also sells souvenirs and colourful clothing.

Uluwatu is a shop similar to those above.

Motmot, next door to the Malinche hotel, is a very appealing shop that sells crafts, beautiful agendas, original clothing, charm bracelets, jewellery, tinted glasses and pretty greeting cards, as well as lovely postcards, which are not very common in Costa Rica.

Aventura
Calle Central, Avenida Central/1
Quepos
☎*777-1019 or 777-0429*
≈*777-0279*
The "multi-boutique" Aventura is Québec-owned and sells high-quality crafts.

Café Milagro
on the street that runs parallel to the estuary in Quepos proper
☎*777-1707*
and
on the Quepos-Manuel Antonio road
At the friendly Café Milagro you can buy such things as coffee, jam, syrup, coffee cups and cigars as well as pick up some popular North American magazines (*Mademoiselle*, *The Enquirer* and *Billboard*) and newspapers such as *USA Today*.

Quepos to Manuel Antonio

Amazing Arts Art Gallery
☎*777-2252*
www.amazingarts.org
On the Manuel Antonio road, a small shop is worth stopping at because of its original-ity. In the El Mono Azul hotel, Amazing Arts Art Gallery is a handicrafts store run by children. In the beginning, in January 1999, two nine-year-old children started to sell their cre-ations to the public to raise money to preserve parcels of the tropical forest. Today, the pro-ject has widened in scope and the shop benefits from the col-laboration of many children, including en-tire school classes. Young people from all over the world are in-vited to join this great fund raising effort for the environment. Don't expect a large, fully stocked showroom. Though the shop sells only a few items, some of them still made by children, many of them make lovely souvenirs.

La Buena Nota
every day 8am to 7pm
Located 1km (0.6mi) before the park, the little shop La Buena Nota sells newspapers, magazines, postcards and some summer and beach clothing in bright colours with appealing prints.

Café Milagro
(see above)

The South

Not many vacationers venture to the southern parts of Costa Rica, though it has more pristine areas than any of the other regions, providing ample opportunities to commune with nature.

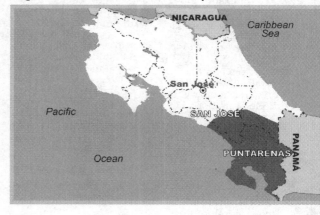

This chapter covers the region that extends from the Talamanca mountain range (in the middle of the country) to the Panamanian border in the south and the Pacific coast in the west. Many roads, including the Interamericana cross this region of striking contrasts. It has the country's highest peak (Cerro Chirripó), largest park (La Amistad), the Pacific coast's extreme heat and humidity and the country's coldest climatic zones! These factors have contributed to the diversity of the landscape: tundra-like vegetation caps the summits of the central mountains, whereas humid tropical forests flourish along the coast. The region's many charms include crystal-clear waterfalls, beaches ideal for surfing, rivers made for whitewater rafting, and tropical forests sheltering the exotic quetzal bird.

Southern Costa Rica also has a unique cultural and archeological heritage. Indigenous people descended from pre-Columbian tribes are reminders of the country's pre-colonial past.

In brief, southern Costa Rica offers many opportunities for discovery, relaxation, recreation, and learning.

Finding Your Way Around

By Plane

The Region's North

Palmar:The airport is located in Palmar Sur, south of the Río Grande de Térraba. Most arrivals are greeted by a fleet of taxis.

Golfito: **Sansa** *(Mon to Sat; $51 one way;* ☎*233-0397, 233-3258, 233-5330 or 255-2176)* and **Travelair** *(every day; $66 one way;* ☎*232-7883, 220-3054 or 220-0413)* offer regular service between Golfito and San José.

Osa Peninsula

Puerto Jiménez: **Sansa** *(*☎*221-9414)* and **Travelair** *(*☎*220-3054)* airlines offer daily service from San José to Puerto Jiménez. The flight takes nearly 1.5hrs, for about $150 return fare.

By Car

The Region's North

The **Costanera Sur**: the entire length of this highway was recently paved. Its impressive width certainly makes it one of the most pleasant roads in the country. Stay alert, however, as several villages are not far from the road. Surprisingly, they have no signs; a strange regulation prohibits putting signs along the road. So if you're looking for **Las Escaleras**, **Uvita** or **Ojochal**, you'll have to ask for directions. Keep in mind that all the villages are perched on the hill, to the north of the road, whereas the beaches with their small towns are found on the ocean side.

San Isidro de El General: Take the southbound Interamericana.

San Gerardo de Dota: Take the exit at Km 80 on the Interamericana.

Dominical: An asphalt road in fairly good condition runs from San Isidro de El General to Dominical in less than an hour. Drive cautiously, as this road snakes through the multitude of hills separating the two regions. You can also drive to Dominical from Quepos in 45min on a fairly decent road that travels inland via Savegre. This road joins the Costanera Sur.

Parque Nacional Chirripó

The 22km (13.7mi) between San Isidro and San Gerardo de Rivas take nearly 1.5hrs. From San Isidro, take the south-bound Interamericana. Cross the Río San Isidro bridge, then the Río Jilguero bridge, and turn left after a few hundred meters on an unmarked road. This small road is paved up until Rivas, where it becomes narrow and bumpy. Once you pass the small village of Canán, keep to your right for San Gerardo de Rivas (the left will take you to Herradura).

Osa Peninsula

Puerto Jiménez: To reach the Osa Peninsula, you can take the

Interamericana or the southbound coastal road to Palmar Norte. In the latter case, once you reach Chacarita (33km or 20.5mi south of Palmar Norte), keep your eyes open for a small sign (on the right, near the gas station) indicating the road that leads to the tip of the Osa peninsula. It takes about 2hrs to drive the 78km (48.5mi) to Puerto Jiménez on the Interamericana. The road is paved and in fairly good condition to Rincón (45km or 28mi), after which it deteriorates somewhat before arriving in Puerto Jiménez.

Bahía Drake: the bay is now accessible by car. Just past the village of Rincón, a road (unpaved of course) crosses the width of the peninsula and ends at the other side. Expect the drive to take about 2hrs.

Parque Nacional Corcovado (Carate)

Most visitors access the park via the La Leona entrance near Carate. From Puerto Jiménez, a small road leads to Carate (43km or 26.7mi, approx. 2hrs). All types of cars can make it to Cabo Matapalo (approx. 20km or 12.4mi), but you need a four-wheel drive to reach Carate. During our visit, we crossed 13 streams, three of which were fairly large. In Carate, which is less of a town than a stop-

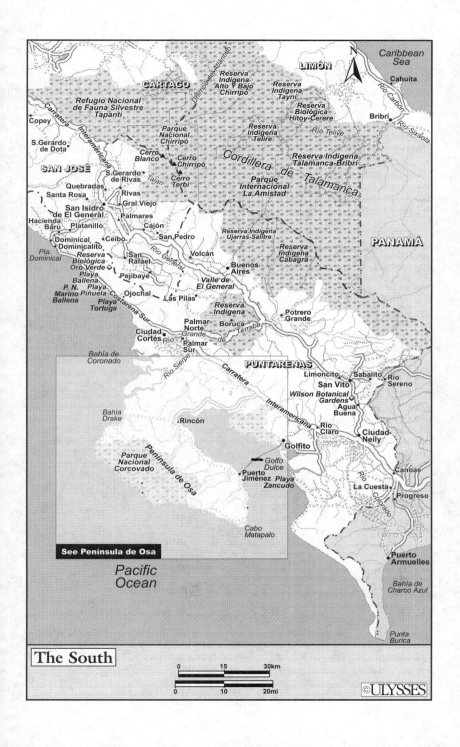

The South

ping place, the road ends near a small landing strip and a *pulpería*. Park your vehicle at the *pulpería* ($2/day) and walk 2km (1.2mi) along the beach to reach the park entrance.

The Region's South

To get to this sector, simply follow the Interamericana south from San Isidro de El General. This highway goes through most areas of interest, crossing the entire length of the Valle del General before turning off toward the lowlands along the coast to Panama. The Interamericana has turnoffs for two regional roads which lead to Playa Tortuga and Coto Brus (San Vito) respectively, completing the tour of the region.

Palmar: From San José or San Isidro de El General, follow the Interamericana to Palmar. Alternately, drive along the Pacific coast by way of the Costanera Sur, which passes through Dominical.

Sierpe: There is an access route to Sierpe on the Interamericana, close to Palma Sur. This road is poorly indicated so ask locals for directions.

Boruca: This reserve is set back from the Interamericana, reached via the road joining the Interamericana and Boruca, a few kilome-ters south of Curré. This road is quite rough and a four-wheel drive is necessary during the rainy season.

Golfito: Take the Interamericana from San José or San Isidro de El General. The exit for Golfito appears in Río Claro. Turn off the Interarmericana, onto a road that leads to the coast. From San José, it is about a 7hr drive.

Zancudo: The road from the Interamericana to Golfito branches to Zancudo. You will have to cross the Río Coto Colorado by ferry before continuing on to Zancudo. The road is not well indicated, so ask locals for directions.

Pavones: Situated some 10km (6.2mi) south of Zancudo.

San Vito: From San Isidro de El General, take the Interamericana to Paso Real. To get to the Coto Brus road (asphalted and in fairly good condition), turn left onto the bridge crossing the Río Grande de Térraba. It should take you just over 2hrs to get to San Vito. If you are coming from Golfito, head to Ciudad Neily and drive up the steep road located north of the city. The views of the mountains and coast are beautiful, but stay focussed on the road which, though mostly asphalted, is quite narrow and steep, with many hairpin turns. There are many potholes and thick fog is frequent at certain times of the year.

Wilson Botanical Garden: The Wilson Botanical Garden is 15min south of San Vito, on the road to Ciudad Neily.

By Bus

The Region's North

San Isidro de El General: The bus station for San José is situated on the Interamericana, between Calles 2 and 4. The Vargas Rojas bus company (*☎222-9763 in San José or 771-0419 in San Isidro*) offers four departures to San Isidro from San José (*$2; 6:30am, 9:30am, 12:30pm and 3:30pm*). The schedule is the same for the return trip.

San Gerardo de Dota: From San José, take the bus to San Isidro and ask the driver to let you off at the *Entrada* in San Gerardo, at Km 80 on the Interamericana.

Parque Nacional Chirripó

A bus from San Isidro (daily departures at 5am and 2pm) stops right in front of the park's administrative offices in San Gerardo de Rivas. The trip takes approximately 1.5hrs. Buses leave for San Isidro at 7am and 4pm.

Osa Peninsula

Puerto Jiménez: From San José, a bus *(daily departures at 6am and 12pm; corner of Calle 12 and Avenida 7)* goes directly to Puerto Jiménez, which is the main village on the Osa peninsula. The 9hr trip costs $6 *(Transportes Blanco-Lobo, ☎257-4121)*.

The Region's South

Boruca: Buses depart for Boruca twice a day from the Mercado Central in Buenos Aires. The trip takes 1.5hrs and costs a few dollars.

By Boat

Osa Peninsula

Golfito–Puerto Jiménez: A passenger ferry *(☎735-5017)* commutes between Golfito (daily departures at 11am) and Puerto Jiménez (daily departures at 6am). The crossing takes about 1.25hrs and costs $3. Depending on your destination, you can also take a taxi-boat *(Abocap, ☎775-0357)*.

Bahía Drake–Sierpe: It takes approximately 30min to drive from Palmar Norte to Sierpe (car, bus or taxi). If you have a reservation, most of the region's hotels provide boat transportation to and from Sierpe. Otherwise, taxi-boats can be hired at the dock. The Pulpería Fenix or the Pargo Hotel *(☎788-8111)* can assist you in finding a taxi-boat. The crossing takes about 1.5hrs and costs approximately $15 per person (each way).

The Region's South

Sierpe: (See above.)

Zancudo: Departures to Zancudo, from Muellecito de Golfito, are twice a day. Departure times are likely to change so enquire first.

Practical Information

In southern Costa Rica, the towns of San Isidro de El General, Golfito, Palmar Norte, Ciudad Neily, and San Vito provide basic services, such as banking (branch offices and ATM). Such services are rare in the Osa Peninsula, especially outside of Puerto Jiménez.

San Isidro de El General: The Banco del Commercio is located on the Avenida Central, between Calles 2 and 4. The Banco Popular is on the corner of Avenida 9 and Calle 1. The Banco Nacional de Costa Rica is situated on the corner of Avenida 1 and Calle Central. The Selvamar tourist reservations center is situated on the Calle Central, a little outside the downtown core, south of Avenida 10.

Palmar Norte: There is a branch office of the Banco Popular in a small shopping center, north of the Interamericana. The Banco Nacional is situated on the other side of the Interamericana, slightly to the east.

Ciudad Neily: Ciudad Neily centre has a modern and well-stocked Supermercado Loaiza, a *mercado*, a bus station, and a Banco Popular, Banco Nacional and Banco de Costa Rica.

San Vito: The Licorería La Cruz, in the northwest section of the town centre, sells English magazines. The Supermercado B&M is located close to the main intersection of the town centre. The Bancrecen, Popular, Nacional and Costa Rica banks all have branch offices in San Vito.

Golfito: The Banco de Costa Rica has a branch office in Golfito, close to the Muellecito. There is also a Banco Popular ATM at the Deposito Libre. Two reputable *supermercados*, Granados and Consucoop, are located side by side in the Pueblo Civil on Golfito's main boulevard.

Excursions

Selva Mar *(San Isidro de El General,* ☎ *771-4582,* ⇌ *771-8841)* is a major organization that arranges all kinds of outdoor activities in the south, and specializes in guided rafting trips for all levels. The agency can also help you plan horseback rides, boat trips and birdwatching excursions and, to top it off, is a reservation service that can help you arrange accommodations or car rentals. Some hotels on the coast between Uvita and Dominical will refer you to this organization to make reservations.

Exploring

The San Isidro de El General Region

The northern part of the region includes the alpine zone of the Talamanca mountain range, which you have to cross to get to San Isidro.

The change of climate and vegetation will become apparent as you drive along the Interamericana.

As the road rises to the **Cerro de la Muerte** ★★, the highest point before the descent to San Isidro, the lush forests that are common in other regions gradually give way to stunted tundra-like vegetation. The stunning panorama of green slopes plunging vertically into gorges far below can be admired from the *miradores*, or lookouts, along the way. The covered **Mirador Vista del Valle** is especially scenic.

Set out early in the morning to avoid the heavy fog that tends to encase these high-lying regions later in the day. And avoid driving at night! This narrow stretch of road, often devoid of a shoulder and protective railing, is made hazardous by fog (or rain), poor lighting, a heavy flow of trucks, and aggressive, erratic drivers.

Nestled in the Talamanca mountain range, Copey de Dota and San Gerardo de Dota are two lovely places from which to savor the landscape. The unique climate and topography of both moutainside towns will undoubtedly leave a lasting impression on you.

At an altitude of 2,000m (6,561ft), **Copey** (7km or 4.3mi below the Interamericana, at Km 58) grows apples, avocados, peaches, and plums. Lush forests, green pastures and a flowing river hemmed in by steep banks constitute the pastoral scenery of **San Gerardo de Dota** ★ (9km or 5.6mi below the Interamericana, at Km 85), a small town tucked into a valley. Myriad plant species flourish in the forest, including several types of colorful mushrooms. Oaks are over a hundred years old and thequetzal is often seen around. The area looks lovely, even when it rains (just remember that at this altitude, the rain can be quite cold).

However, to get there, you must drive down a very steep and narrow road (partially asphalt) that meanders down 9km (5.6mi) of mountainside. Four-wheel drive is highly recommended in this region. The **view** ★★ of San Isidro de El General and its valley from Dominical or the Cerro de la Muerte is gorgeous. As you drive through the area, you will catch glimpses of the vast expanse of green landscape surrounded by majestic mountains.

With a population 40,000, **San Isidro de El General**, is the southern region's capital and largest city. Although the city itself has no spectacular sights to offer, you can enjoy people-watching in the central park or explore the busy marketplace, which is always in full swing since San Isidro is a major centre for agricultural and other produce. The **Museo Regional del Sur** *(Mon to Fri 9am to noon and 1pm to 5pm; inside the cultural centre that formerly housed the municipal market, San Isidro, ☎/≈ 771-5273)* has several exhibits on Costa Rica's cultural and environmental issues.

San Isidro de El General is also the southern region's main point of departure for any destination. The city is an

Solidarity

Some stories are good to hear... In early 2000, citizens in the Rivas region won the battle they had been waging since 1995 against a large Spanish corporation. The story began that year when the company's engineers came to search Costa Rica for rivers that were powerful enough to produce hydroelectricity. When they ended up in the Rivas region, they were delighted, as this part of the country is irrigated by many tumultuous rivers. Hence, the Spaniards suggested to the Costa Rican government the building of a dam on the Chirripó River. The drawback, however insignificant to them, was enormous for others: they would have to expatriate a large number of the area's residents. Informed of this, the residents banded together and took the first measures in what would turn out to be a long war of attrition between a giant multi-national company and small local farmers. In the spring of 2000, huge strikes and demonstrations broke out in the country (or all over) against a government bill that would privatize the ICE, the national electricity company. One of the bill's clauses was aimed at making it easier for foreign countries to undertake major construction work in the field of electricity. But grassroots protests blocked the government's proposal and at the same time put an end to the hopes of the Spanish company in our story. So the citizens of Rivas can keep their land and the Chirripó River will continue its peaceful course in this spectacular region. It just goes to prove that war is sometimes worth waging, even if the forces involved don't seem evenly matched in the beginning...

important stop between San José and the neighbouring country further south, Panama. Thus, you have to pass through San Isidro to get to the Quebradas region, Cerro Chirripó, Dominical on the Pacific coast, and the southern sector of the region, which lies along the Interamericana.

Seven kilometres north of San Isidro, the **Las Quebradas Centre for Biology** ★ *(Tue to Thu 8am to 14pm, Sat to Sun 8am to 3pm, closed in Oct; Quebradas, ☎/≈771-4131)* is a protected nature reserve that promotes the conservation of the Río Quebradas basin, which is the principal source of drinking water for the El General region. Various nature-related activities are offered in this sector located at an altitude of 1,000m (3,280ft). Many varieties of plants and animals can be observed along the 2.5km (1.6mi) of paths. Picnicking and camping are permitted on site. During the rainy season (September and October), it is best to come here with a four-wheel drive.

The Rivas Region

The region of **Rivas** ★ is located 10km (6.2mi) northeast of San Isidro de El General. Not only is this region the gateway to Cerro Chirripó,

but it is also one of the country's most important archeological sites, where ongoing excavations are providing new insights into pre-Columbian societies. Eventually, when more objects will be uncovered, Rivas will become as archeologically significant as Turrialba and Guayabo (see p 126 and 129).

Take a day to visit the **Rancho La Botija** *(adults $5, children $3; Tue to Sun 7am to 8pm; 6 km or 3.7mi from San Isidro, on the road to Rivas, ☎382-3052, ≈771-1401)*, a small recreation center (playgrounds, game rooms, pool, etc.), located in what used to be a sugarcane refinery. The owners will give you a short tour of the property, stopping to examine objects from the past, such as an old *trapiche* (sugar mill), and a series of stones etched with glyphs (found all over Rivas) dating from the pre-Columbian period. You can also enjoy a light meal on site.

Like La Botija, **La Pradera** *(on the San Isidro–Rivas road, before reaching Albergue Talari, Rivas)* is a recreation centre where you can take part in all kinds of outdoor and sports activities (football, etc.). Or, stroll through the picturesque rolling countryside of Rivas, where you will come across many stones inscribed with glyphs.

A little farther down the road, just before the entrance to Parque Nacional Chirripó, is **San Gerardo de Rivas** ★★. Although most people drive straight through this little village on their way to the park, you might want to stop to better enjoy the beauty of the surroundings.

Hurricanes

We cannot fathom the power of hurricanes. Did you know that they can even move a riverbed? In southern Costa Rica in 1996, hurricane César transformed the landscape in a single night. Between 6pm and 6am on the Río El General, among other rivers, heavy rains and unbridled winds caused an accumulation of debris that forced the river, now a torrent, to leave its bed and forge a path 2km (1mi) away. It goes without saying that the river didn't return to its original course and that the region's inhabitants were forced to adapt to this new division of their land.

The road winds along, clinging to the mountains, and crosses the many rivers that irrigate the region. You will see small, colourful, wooden houses, sleepy villages, and small coffee depots perched beside the road, all amidst lush vegetation. A drive in the area will unquestionably present you with memorable moments and interesting discoveries. Among other places, stop at the Hotel Pelicano to view the **work of sculptor Don**

Rafael Elizondo. Here, skilfully carved wood puts on a surprising and amusing new face. You'll find his talent amazing!

What's more, just a kilometre from San Gerardo, on the road to **Herradura** (follow the 1km or 0.6mi path to the right of the road), you can take a dip in a hilltop **hot spring**. It costs $1, which you pay to the owner who lives beside the spring.

Parque Nacional Chirripó

With mountains over 3,000m (9,843ft) high, immense creased rock faces and a glacial lake, as well as shelters and marked trails for visitors, **Parque Nacional Chirripó ★ ★ ★** *($6; every day 5am to 12pm; ☎ 771-3297 or 771-3155, ≈ 771-3155, www.chirripo.com)* has something for everyone. Cerro Chirripó

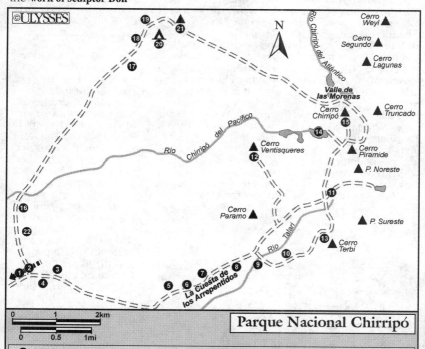

Parque Nacional Chirripó

0   1   2km

0   0.5   1mi

● **ATTRACTIONS**

1. Rivas
2. Canaán
3. San Gerardo de Rivas
4. Chirripó National Park Office
5. Llano Bonito Refuge
6. Monte Sin Fé
7. Refugio natural (Cave)
8. Cuesta de los Arrepentidos
9. Base Crestones Refuge
10. Los Crestones
11. Valle de los Conejos
12. Cerro Ventisqueres (3,810m or 12,500ft)
13. Cerro Terbi (3,760m or 12,336ft)
14. Lago San Juan
15. Cerro Chirripó (3,819m or 12,530ft)
16. Herradura
17. Cabaña de Rodolfo
18. Chirripó National Park entrance
19. Cordillère de Talamanca
20. Camping
21. Cerro Urán (3,800m or 12,467ft)
22. Hot Springs

(3,819m or 12,530ft) is the highest mountain in Costa Rica—and second highest in Central America. Thus, hikers will be impressed by the challenging trails through this alpine paradise amidst the tropical rainforest.

Covering 50,150ha (123,919 acres), Chirripó National Park is located 26km (16.1mi) northeast of San Isidro de El General and 150km (93.2mi) from San José. The park entrance is in the small village of San Gerardo de Rivas, at an altitude of 1,350m (4,429ft). The summit of Cerro Chirripó is some 2,500m (8,202ft) higher up—quite an exhausting climb! This hike takes at least three days (two nights). There are also other trails to the neighbouring mountaintops, which have wonderful views when the weather is good.

The park receives approximately 3.5m (11.5ft) of rain annually, and temperatures range between - 9°C (16°F) and 20°C (68°F). Since the weather is unpredictable, it is best to bring warm, sturdy, waterproof clothing. Also, since some 3,000 people visit this park every year, you should make advance reservations if you want to stay here overnight, especially on weekends, and above all during Easter when Costa Ricans flock here *en masse*. However, during the rainy season, you might well have the trails to yourself and have no problem finding a place to stay. It is best to come between January and April, during the Costa Rican summer, when it rains less.

Although most people spend at least a few days in the park, it also makes for a pleasant day-trip (*$6, no reservations, arrive as early as possible in the morning*).

You can stroll through the lovely pastures and the dense tropical rainforest with its epiphytic plants and majestic trees, and see some of the smaller animals or tracks of the larger, more elusive ones (Baird tapirs, pumas, etc.) as well as several species of birds, including the resplendent quetzal. If you only have a day, it is not recommend to climb higher than the first shelter, known as **Llano Bonito**, located about halfway between San Gerardo de Rivas and the main shelter.

The park also includes several distinct natural habitats. Thus, after passing through the tropical rainforest, you will come to a vast area of barren land swept by strong winds. The flora has adapted to this cold, wet habitat called the *páramo*, where there are many twisted trees whose growth has been stunted by the harsh climatic conditions. The Andean *páramo* stretches north to the Cerro Chirripó and the Cerro de la Muerte (along the Interamericana), a little further west.

The Cerro Chirripó rises over the Talamanca mountain range, which extends to the south. At the foot of the mountain lies a lovely, tranquil cold-water lake, **Lago San Juan**, which is a pleas-

Parque Nacional Chiiripó's entrance

ant place to take a break. Closer to the shelter is the magnificent mass of creased limestone and igneous rock, known as **Los Crestones**. Both sites are picture-postcard perfect and easily accessible from the **Base Crestones** shelter at the summit.

If you only come to Costa Rica for two or three weeks, you might not be able to arrange for all the equipment (parka, backpack, sleeping bag, camping stove, etc.) or make the necessary reservations (transportation, shelters, guides, horses, etc.) yourself. However, if you stay at the Talari (see p 377) mountain inn in Rivas, the owners can make all the arrangements required for your stay in the Parque Nacional Chirripó if you notify them a few days or weeks in advance. This way, you can enjoy your mountain hike without any last-minute hassles.

Horses can be rented to carry your belongings on treks during the dry season (usually from December to May). One horse can transport the baggage of three or four hikers, and costs about $10 per day. Outside the dry season, you can hire porters *($20/day)*. In addition, you usually have to hire one of the local guides *(approx. $20/day)*, many of whom speak English. A small guiding associa-

tion was established in the San Gerardo de Rivas and Herradura regions. The guides are reliable and friendly, and know the park trails like the backs of their hands.

Forest Fires

The Cerro Chirripó region has experienced a number of forest fires over the years, destroying thousands of hectares of forest, plain and savannah. Many were caused by careless hikers...

You must register at the park office *(every day 5am to 5pm)* when you arrive in San Gerardo de Rivas, whether you have a reservation or not. You can leave your car and extra luggage near the office for a few extra *colones*. The park warden will give you a very basic map of the park and inform you about the condition of the trails and the latest weather reports. There is a park admission fee, and additional charges to stay at the shelters *($3/person/night)* or camp *($1.25/person/ night)* near the Mount Uran summit, the only place in the park where it is permitted.

<h2 style="text-align:center">Climbing Cerro Chirripó</h2>

The first day is a long and steady (16km or 9.9mi) climb from San Gerardo de Rivas to the Base Crestones shelter, at about 2,200m (7,218ft). It is best to set out as early as possible, around 5am and 6am. Park wardens usually do not allow you to start this trek after 11am, since night falls around 6pm. Depending on your fitness level, your hiking experience, the weight of your backpack and the weather, allow yourself 7 to 12hrs to cover this distance.

The trail is well marked out and easy to follow. There are signs indicating the altitude reached and the number of kilometres remaining to the summit of Cerro Chirripó approximately every 2km (1.2mi). Remember to bring enough water, since the first source of drinkable water is almost halfway to the Base Crestones, at the Llano Bonito shelter. The trail passes through pastures, the lowland tropical rainforest and the dense upper rainforest. You will see and especially hear many birds along the way, and there are often monkeys around the first shelter.

Llano Bonito is the first shelter, but is really more of a rest station and emergency stop in case hikers experience serious difficulties, than a place to sleep. After this station, the trail climbs steadily to a small mountain known as **Monte Sin Fé**. The trees become smaller and the type of vegetation changes as the climate becomes drier.

A little farther on is a small cave known as a *refugio natural* that can accommodate about a dozen hikers for the night, should you run into major difficulties. From here, it is only a one to 2hr climb to the main shelter, after scaling the "Repentants' Hill" (*cuesta de los arrepentidos*). Finally, you will reach a huge rock face, pleated like an accordion: **Los Crestones**. The main shelter, **Base Crestones** (*$6 per person per night*), is so named because it is at the base of this cliff. It can accommodate sixty people in its four-bed rooms. Blankets can be rented. Note that camping is prohibited in this region.

The summit of Cerro Chirripó (3,819m or 12,530ft) is only 4km (2.5mi) from the shelter. It takes 1.5 to 2hrs to reach, and is 300m (984) higher up. Along the way, you will see the "Rabbits' Valley" (Valle de los Conejos), which was abandoned by these small creatures after a terrible fire in 1976. From the top of Cerro Chirripó, you will be able to see the Atlantic Ocean to the east and the Pacific Ocean to the west—if the sky is clear. Since it is often covered in clouds by early afternoon, we suggest that you wait for a clear morning before making this trek. If the weather is uncertain, you can hike along some of the other trails around the shelter, such as the **Valle de los Conejos**, **Cerro Ventisqueres** or **Cerro Terbi**.

Climbing Cerro Urán

Cerro Urán is located approximately 10km (6.2mi) northwest of the Cerro Chirripó. The trail up Cerro Urán starts in the tiny village of Herradura and passes through pastures before reaching the summit.

This climb leads you through exquisite valleys and a magnificent forest. You need a guide for this three-day hike, since the trails are not marked and cross privately owned farmland. You can either camp (*$1.25/person/night*) on the mountain range (over 3,000m (9,843ft) in altitude) or sleep in the small shelter (*$2/person/night*) known as **Cabaña de Rodolfo**, near the **Finca San Carlos**, about a 4hr walk from Herradura. We strongly recommend that you stay in the shelter, since the camp site is farther away and you will have to climb to it carrying all your equipment. Also, the area receives a lot of rain so camping is not always the most pleasant option.

The first day takes you along small trails through pastures from Herradura to the shelter. You will have spectacular views of the landscape, including the neighbouring valleys with their peacefully grazing cows. The view from the top of Cerro Urán is also incredible. However, protect yourself from the blazing sun, since the trail rarely ventures into the forest.

The next day is the steep climb to the summit. You should only take a small backpack on the trail that runs through superb tropical rainforest where moss, ferns and bromeliads abound. Farther on, the trail joins the Talamanca range. At this point, the lush vegetation gives way to small, sturdy trees that endure the strong winds that blow almost continuously. Since the cordillera is bordered by the mountain range, it also gets many clouds that bring fog and rain from the Atlantic. Thus, the weather can change quickly and with little warning. Cerro Urán's exact altitude is disputed: books and maps indicate it to be anywhere between 3,600m (11,811ft) and 3,800m (12,467ft) high, thus slightly lower than Cerro Chirripó (3,819m or 12,530ft).

The third day takes you back to Herradura, a small town where horseback is still the main means of transportation. It is therefore a perfect place to go horseback riding in the area (make reservations with your guide ahead of time) and discover the daily life of these proud and generous farmers. Our guide, René Robles Santamaría, cordially invited us to have dinner with him and his family, in a quaint house that is only accessible on horseback or by foot.

If you have any energy left, you can take a looping trail approximately 35km (21.7mi) long that passes through Herradura, Cerro Urán, Cerro Chirripó and San Gerardo de Rivas. This hike takes four to five days and is very difficult, especially since you have to carry your heavy backpack. You can also hire a guide to take you from Herradura to the entrance of the Chirripó National Park, located between the shelter (Cabaña de Rodolfo) and the cordillera. You must reserve in advance (at the San Gerardo de Rivas park office) for the Base Crestones shelter, and pay admission to the park.

The Dominical Region

If you are heading towards Dominical from San Isidro de El General, stop at the magnificent waterfalls **Cataratas Nauyaca** ★ or Santo Cristo *(midway between San Isidro and Dominical,* ☎ *771-3187,* ⇆ *787-0006)*. Situated in the mountains that separate the coastal region of Dominical and the San Isidro valley, the falls are 20m (65.6ft) and 45m (147ft) high, respectively, and feed a basin that is 6m (19.7ft) deep and has a surface of 1,000m² (10,764 sq ft). A truly superb spot! Because there is no road to the falls, you have to get there on horseback. The owners of the property organize daily tours that include the ride to and from the falls on forest paths, meals before and after the expedition, a visit to a small zoo and, of course, the falls themselves. It is possible to swim in the crystal-clear water. The Centro Turístico Nauyaca has a small inn and a campground.

Begin exploring the coastal region of Dominical by visiting the **Hacienda Barú** ★★ (see p 357), which is on the coast, 1km (0.6mi) north of the village of Dominical.

The **Cataratas Terciopelo** ★ *(access on horseback; make reservations with Selva Mar,* ☎ *771-4582,* ⇆ *771-8841)* is located inland from Dominical, north of the Hacienda Barú . With the surrounding jungle as its backdrop, this lovely three-tiered waterfall cascades into emerald green waters 40m (131ft) below. Paradise can't be much better than this!

The beach and surf attract throngs of young people to **Dominical.** In fact, many of the town's hotels and restaurants are owned by these surf lovers who have left their own country, for a time, or perhaps forever, to live out their dream. In Dominical, the best surf is on the village beach at the mouth of the Río Barú, or a little further south in **Punta Dominical**. The **Escuelita Dominical** even offers Spanish courses right on the beach.

Hacienda Barú

The **Hacienda Barú** ★★ *($2; every day;* ☎ *787-0003,* ⇆ *787-0004, www. haciendabaru.com)* is a magnificent 336ha (830 acres) private wildlife reserve, stretching west and northwest of Dominical. It encompasses many different habitats, including primary and secondary forest, pastures, mangroves, a former cocoa plantation and a superb beach on the Pacific with numerous trees and different types of vegetation.

The South

For the past twenty years, Jack and Diane Ewing have owned the park. Jack first came here in 1972 to run a 150-head cattle farm. Then, in 1978, he moved here permanently with Diane and their two children. At the time, the farm had no electricity, and the road was nothing but a small path. The Ewing family tried to grow rice, beans, soya beans and cocoa, but without any commercial success. In the late 1980s, the farm's main activity changed from farming to preserving the surrounding environment, and educating visitors about these natural riches. Now, the area is a park where you can stay one or more days in *cabinas* and tents in the jungle.

Steve Stroud teamed up with the Ewings in 1992 to help turn the area into a real ecotourist site with *cabinas* (see p 381), a restaurant and many possible activities. You can spend a few hours or a whole day on the trails, learning about the plant and animal life and the history of this model park.

The park has a total of 6km (3.7mi) of hiking trails. You will receive a small leaflet outlining the trails, which lead to a teak plantation, a canal, the mangrove, the beach and the mouth of the Río Barú.

For a more detailed description of the park (history, flora, fauna, etc.), we recommend buying the small book entitled *Trails & Tales* ($4.25; published by the Hacienda Barú, 1997, 74 pages), written by Jack Ewing and illustrated by his wife Diane.

You can also hire one of the six guides (*$15 to $25/person, depending on the trail*) to explore the park's rich variety of animals and plants. There are an estimated 311 species of birds, 62 species of mammals, 50 species of amphibians and reptiles and hundreds of species of plants, including 75 types of orchids. This area is home to white-faced capuchin monkeys, sloths, coyotes, pumas, ocelots, caimans, crocodiles and 22 species of bats.

Puma

Some of the activities available in the area include the popular canopy tour (*$35*), where visitors (3 people at a time) are hoisted up to an observation platform suspended from a tree 34m (112ft) in the air.

You can also spend the night camping out in the jungle (*$60*), where you will wake up to the typical noises of the rainforest. There are also horseback riding excursions along the beach and through the mangrove (*$25/ 3 hours*), and kayaking through the mangrove at high tide (*$35/3 hours*).

The national Hacienda Barú wildlife reserve is bound to become one of the most popular ecotourist destinations in Costa Rica.

La Costanera Sur

Hermosa and **Ballena** are among the best swimming beaches in Costa Rica's southern region. They are 20km (12.4mi) south of Dominical, along the Costanera Sur, towards Palmar and Ciudad Cortés.

The drive along the **Costanera Sur** ★ from Dominical to other picturesque coastal sites is very pleasant in itself. This relatively new route crosses undulating valleys. A few kilometers south of Dominical, **Las Escaleras** (The Stairs) is a new sector slowly developing in the hills above the seashore. The **view** ★★ is certainly worth the steep drive up to the neighbourhood's few hotels.

Close to Dominicalito, south of Dominical,

Poza Azul is an enjoyable place to visit. Set in the forest, it features a natural deep blue pool (*poza* is loosely translated as "swimming basin") fed by a waterfall. Accessible by car.

The Costanera Sur separates the coast from the hinterland. Here, you must decide whether to drive along the coast or turn inland into wooded areas. In San Josecito de Uvita, the **Reserva Biológica Oro Verde** *(20$/person; guided visit and light meal; a few kilometers from Uvita; make reservations with Selva Mar, ☎ 771-4582, ≈ 771-8841)* is situated in the mountains, 3km (1.9mi) from the Costerana Sur. Having owned the land for over 35 years, "Macho" Duarte has turned to tourism as a means of preserving the humid tropical forest covering his property. This very remote terrain is perched high in the mountains overlooking the Pacific coast, and is accessible on foot or horseback. Needless to say, the view at this altitude (600m or 1,969ft) is breathtaking! Selva Mar can arrange for you to meet members of the Duarte family, and possibly even share a meal with them. You can also learn the art of sugar making. Overnight stays are possible in one of two small *cabinas*.

Between the ocean and the Costanera Sur, a little south of the road to Oro Verde, the **Rancho La Merced** *($10 to 55$/person; make reservations with Selva Mar, ☎ 771-4582, ≈ 771-8841)* is a sanctuary for wild animals as well as a livestock ranch. You can visit for the day or spend the night in a rustic setting dining on *campesino* fare (see p 380). Activities include horseback riding, mountain climbing, and local tours. An addition to the ranch, the **Profelis Center** reintroduces endangered feline species to the wilderness. Reserve in advance as this site is very popular, even in low season.

A little farther south is **Uvita**, an unremarkable town on the route to the **Parque Nacional Marino Ballena** ★ (see p 360).

A little further still, the **Playa Tortuga** ★ region is about 25km (15.5mi) west of Palmar and has only recently begun to be developed, since the Costanera Sur made it easier to reach. The Playa Tortuga meets up with the Pacific coast, which is not possible farther east because of the Río Grande de Térraba delta.

Ojochal ★ is located near Playa Tortuga, nestled in the hills of the back country a few kilometres from the beach. This small village, no different from

others at first, has a surprise in store for Francophiles: a large French-speaking community made up of people from Europe, Québec and the Caribbean. As you stroll along the unpaved roads, you'll occasionally come across signs in French! True to their culture, these francophones have opened an impressive series of every sort of restaurant! Some are just passing through, but several have been here for a long time and can steer you towards hikes to take in the surrounding area. There is one deplorable aspect, however: this foreign community has attracted a number of investors who are trying to exploit the region's charm for all it's worth. Witness the huge shopping centre just before the village on the Costanera Sur. Enormous, it's a permanent scar on the otherwise magnificent landscape.

If you go just a bit further west on the Costanera Sur, you will come to **Playa Piñuela**. This is where the **Parque Nacional Marino Ballena** ★ (see p 360) begins. The **Piñuela** Beach is not especially attractive, since it is quite stony, particularly at its northern end, but it is the best place in the area for swimming, along with Ballena and Uvita further north.

The South

Parque Nacional Marino Ballena

Just 20km (12.4mi) south of Dominical, the **Parque Nacional Marino Ballena** ★ (*$6; every day 8am to 4pm;* ☎ *735-5036,* ≈ *735-5282*) was created in 1990 to protect the largest coral reef on the country's Pacific coast. This 4,500ha (11,119 acres) park lies between Punta Uvita and Punta Piñuela, stretching along 13km (8mi) of beach, rocks and mangroves.

This ocean park takes its name from the many humpback whales (rorquals) who come to the area between December and April. The humpback whale (*Megaptera novaeangliae*) is unquestionably the most spectacular of all whales, since its tail emerges each time it dives, and it can jump quite high out of the water. Also, this whale will often dramatically slap the water with its flippers, as though in a fit of anger. It can grow up to 16m (52.5ft) long and weigh as much as 36,000kg (79,365lbs). With an average life span of around 40 years, it sometimes lives alone, but is often found in groups or pairs.

The **Isla Ballena** is found in the middle of the park and is the perfect spot for observing frigates, brown boobies and ibises, as well as green iguanas and basilisks. Ridley (*Lepidochelys olivacea*) and Hawksbill (*Eretmochelys imbricata*) turtles come to the beach to lay their eggs between May and November, especially in September and October.

The park currently has few visitor services (the information centre is in Bahía, beside Uvita). However, it will probably become more popular due to the road along the coast, which now links Dominical and Palmar Norte. Camping is permitted, and the park's waters and coral reefs are great places for scuba diving and snorkelling.

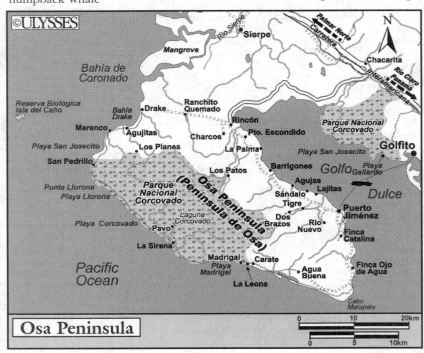

Osa Peninsula

You can also go scuba diving around Isla Ballena and **Rocas Las Tres Hermanas** (The Three Sisters' rocks), off Playa Ballena. You can swim in the natural pools that form in the rocks at low tide.

The Osa Peninsula

The **Osa Peninsula** ★ ★ juts out into the Pacific Ocean from Costa Rica's southwest. This region has been largely ignored by tourists, who tend to stay close to San José and thus prefer the Central Pacific coast and Guanacaste regions. However, the number of visitors who come to explore the Osa Peninsula looking for adventure grows every year, especially since the region has become easier to access by car or bus (about 8hrs from San José), and is only 1.5hrs away by plane.

This beautiful, isolated peninsula has one of the only tropical rainforests along the Pacific coast, and became home to an incredible variety of plants and animals over the centuries. However, because this area was unprotected, a large logging company bought it for next to nothing and set up shop here, along with dozens of settlers. Hunting and logging threatened the survival of much of the wildlife, which had already become extinct in other parts of the country.

The government did not want the Osa Peninsula to undergo the same environmental degradation as Guanacaste, where deforestation caused the wildlife to disappear and even led to a dramatic change in temperature that turned the region into a desert. Thus, the Corcovado region (41,788ha or 103,257 acres) of the peninsula was made a protected national park.

The Parque Nacional Corcovado has remained wild and difficult to access, and is thus a favourite destination for adventure-seeking tourists. In fact, most tourists come to Puerto Jiménez, Cabo Matapalo, Carate and Bahía Drake to visit this extraordinary national park, with its tropical forest and paradisiacal beaches, where you might spot a jaguar, a majestic scarlet macaw (*Ara macao*) or a keel-billed toucan (*Ramphastos sulfuratus*). The scarcely populated peninsula is a wonderful place to observe wildlife, with over 125 species of mammals and 367 species of birds.

Although it is wild and isolated, different tour packages of the Osa Peninsula are available to fit all tastes and budgets. The small village of Puerto Jiménez and the Parque Nacional Corcovado are ideal for visitors on a tight budget, while the more comfortable luxury hotels between Puerto Jiménez and Carate or in the superb Bahía Drake cater to travellers prepared to splurge a little.

The Puerto Jiménez Region

Puerto Jiménez ★ is the only real town on the peninsula, with many hotels and restaurants, public phones, transportation networks (buses, ferries, taxis, airplanes), grocery stores, a post office, tourist information offices, tour operators, a medical clinic, a national bank, a gas station and the administrative offices of the Parque Nacional Corcovado (near the airport).

With quiet roads, and a tranquil way of life, Puerto Jiménez has a certain charm, and seems far removed from San José—which it is! Even the dogs are happy and content, playing in the streets, sleeping on the sidewalks, or sometimes right in the middle of the road. Tourists wander through the streets, despite the oppressive heat, planning their activities for the next day (fishing, kayaking, scuba diving, hiking, visiting the gold mine, horseback riding, mountain biking, etc.) or making inquiries about how to get to the national park. The **municipal beach** northeast of the city is the perfect

The South

place to take a late-afternoon dip in the **Golfo Dulce**.

Early one morning (around 6am), we were treated to an amazing spectacle: dozens of scarlet macaws, some large, brightly coloured parakeets (red, blue and yellow and 80cm or 31.5in long), and hundreds of green parakeets flew overhead, each uttering their loud and distinctive cries—like the squeaking wheels of an old cart—before settling in the treetops!

The tourist information office at **Proyecto Osa Natural** *(Main Street* ☎/≈ *735-5440)* lists the region's many tourist agencies, most of which are local and specalize in tours of the peninsula's natural riches. Across the road, in the Carolina Restaurant, **Escondido Trex** *(☎/≈ 735-5210)* is a good place to get information about excursions, hotels, restaurants, beaches and other activities around Puerto Jiménez. The friendly and helpful staff speaks English.

If you want to visit the Parque Nacional Corcovado but do not have a four-wheel drive vehicle, go to the *minimercado* **El Tigre** *(every day 6am to 7pm; Main Street;* ☎ *735-5075)*, where one or more all-terrain taxis shuttle people between Puerto Jiménez and Carate every day at 6am. The

trip takes approximately 2hrs and costs $6 (one way). Return trips leave from Carate every morning at 8:30am. The trip to Cabo Matapalo costs about half the   price. You can take a taxi to the park at other times of the day, but be prepared to pay about $40 (a good price for groups).

The Cabo Matalpo Region

South of Puerto Jiménez, the magnificent **Cabo Matapalo** region covers the south-eastern part of the peninsula. This area has a beautiful beach lined with dense tropical forest. There is a pretty 25m (82ft) waterfall—a great place for watching monkeys, coatis, and sloths, as well as toucans, macaws and many other exotic birds. Cabo Matapalo also has some of the most luxurious hotels, each beautifully landscaped to blend in with the surrounding environment.

After Cabo Matapalo, the road narrows and begins its ascent up the mountain. You need a four-wheel drive vehicle to travel along it, since it crosses twelve rivers, some of which are several metres wide and is usually in muddy condition. Along the way, there are pastures and a few houses and small farms. The road finally ends in **Carate**, on the Pacific Ocean.

Carate basically consists of a *pulpería* and a landing strip, but is the entrance to the trail to the **Corcovado Lodge Tent Camp** (1.5km or 0.9mi; managed by the Costa Rica Expeditions agency), and La Leona of the Parque Nacional Corcovado (2km or 1.2mi).

★★
Bahía Drake

Bahía Drake is wonderfully nestled in Osa Peninsula, isolated from the rest of the country. You can thus imagine the tranquil solitude that permeates this area, which nevertheless has many comfortable hotels offering a wide range of activities. We strongly recommend that you stay here for at least three nights (four days) to allow enough time to leisurely explore the bay's surroundings or take a break and relax in a hammock by the Pacific Ocean, listening to the birds and the crashing of the waves.

The bay is very large, and bathed by the warm, tranquil Pacific Ocean. The coast has sections of rich tropical rainforest that extend right to the waters's edge. Offshore, the **Reserva Biológica Isla del Caño** ★★ (see p 366) harbours natural and historical treasures, and is a favourite spot for scuba divers. On the bay itself, the small village of **Agujitas** has a *pulpería*, a public telephone, a school and reasonably priced accommodations (see p 385).

The hotels dotting Bahía Drake coast all have boats, which can take you to Sierpe and on other excursions, like to the Parque Nacional Corcovado and the Reserva Biológica Isla del Caño, situated 10km (6.2mi) south of the Río Sierpe. You can also enjoy such activities as hiking, horseback riding, birdwatching, scuba diving, snorkelling, kayaking, fishing and swimming. In short, there are plenty of ways to fill up the days!

The bay can is now accessible via a little dirt road. If you travel over land, however, you will miss the pleasure of travelling down the Río Sierpe. The

number of flowers in the mangroves along this very wide, boggy river are dazzling, and the entire journey from Sierpe to Bahía Drake is very scenic. You might even spot caimans, monkeys, sloths, herons, trogons, egrets and parakeets. Upon arriving in Bahía Drake on the Pacific, you will be greeted by pelicans and sometimes even dolphins.

The **Marenco** biological reserve (☎221-1594, ⇌255-1346) is located southwest of Bahía Drake, and 5km (3.1mi) north of the Parque Nacional Corcovado. This 500ha (1,235 acres) private reserve can only be reached by boat (about 10min from the bay). Since the reserve is right next to the national park, its flora and fauna are very similar. Many kilo-

metres of trails crisscross the area, and biologists come here to study the complex and fascinating eco-diversity. The plant and animal life varies dramatically in this relatively small area as you go from the tropical forest to the rivers and their mouths and to the shores of the Pacific Ocean. The reserve provides its own accommodations (see p 386) and offers various excursions, including outings to the Parque Nacional Corcovado and the Isla del Caño.

Parque Nacional Corcovado

The **Parque Nacional Corcovado** ★ ★ ★ (*$6; every day 8am to 4pm;* ☎735-5036, ⇌735-5282) is unquestionably one of the most captivating in Costa Rica. Its 41,788ha (103,256 acres) protect a large part of the Osa Peninsula's tropical rainforest, and are endowed with eight different natural habitats. There are an additional 12,751ha (31,507 acres) of forest on the other side of the Golfo Dulce (Piedras Blancas sector), just west of Golfito. The park is a bird-watchers' paradise, with 367 species of birds including the magnificent scarlet macaw and the keel-billed toucan. Moreover, 140 species of mammals, 117 species of amphibians and reptiles, 40

Sir Francis Drake

Bahía Drake is named after the well-known English navigator Sir Francis Drake (1540-1596) who dropped anchor in the bay in 1579. Drake also visited the coasts of Chile and Peru during his travels in the south from 1577 to 1580. He fought several battles against

Spain, and is credited with having played a major role in dispersing the "Invincible Spanish Armada," a fleet of 130 ships that Philippe II of Spain sent to England in 1588 to avenge the execution of Marie Stuart and re-establish Catholic rule.

species of freshwater fish and 6,000 species of insects have been identified here!

With an annual rainfall of 5.5m (18ft), this tropical rainforest has an incredibly rich plant life that includes nearly 500 kinds of trees, some of which can grow from 40m (131ft) to 50m (164ft) tall! The largest is the *ceiba pentandra*, which can even reach heights of 70m (230ft). You can completely lose your sense of reality in the stifling heat among these giant trees covered in moss, epiphytic plants and vines.

We should point out, however, that this park is not to everyone's liking. We met several visitors (especially older travellers) who had visited the park on their own and complained about the heat and humidity, and especially the long distances between the park's different points of interest. Thus, you might want to take one of the many guided boat tours with numerous stops as well as hikes lasting from a few minutes to several hours. These are available from Puerto Jiménez, Cabo Matapalo or Bahía Drake.

On the other hand, if you like long hikes and sleeping under the stars or in rustic shelters, you will probably enjoy the Parque Nacional

Corcovado. It is one of the only parks to offer a large network of trails, as well as some tourist infrastructure (campsites, shelters, meals, etc.). However, you should first visit the administrative office in Puerto Jiménez (near the airport) before venturing into the park, to obtain the latest information and reserve a spot in one of the shelters (also called "stations" or "watch houses") and plan out your meals. Note that you can make these reservations over the phone well in advance, as long as you know your schedule.

There are five shelters in the park, four of which are very popular with hikers (La Leona, La Sirena, San Pedrillo and Los Patos). However, during the dry season (from December to April), the trails are especially busy and it is quite common for up to thirty hikers to converge in one spot, especially at the busy La Sirena shelter. All shelters have very basic accommodations, but cost only $2 per person per night. You have to bring your own sleeping bag, and should also bring a mosquito net. If you plan on camping instead (*$1.25/person/night*), make sure you have all the equipment you need (tents and other camping gear can be rented from the tourist information office in

Puerto Jiménez). Meals are available if you reserve in advance. If you plan on preparing your own meals, you must bring your own equipment (stove, dishes and utensils).

Various Itineraries

The Parque Nacional Corcovado has numerous hiking trails and three main entrances (**La Leona**, **Los Patos** and **San Pedrillo**), the busiest being La Leona. Over 60km (37.3mi) of trails, most of which run along the beach, link the different shelters or stations. There are also other trails leading to the forest, beaches or vistas around the shelters. You can map out your own itinerary, depending on how many days you plan on staying and the number of kilometres you are ready to walk in the heat and humidity while carrying your backpack.

Getting to the park is not a problem, since all kinds of transportation is available. All-terrain taxis run from Puerto Jiménez (*$6; depart at 6am from Minimercado El Tigre; 2 hours travel time; ☎735-5075*) to Carate, 2km (1.2mi) from La Leona station. There is also a small plane from Puerto Jiménez that can drop you off or pick you up from La Sirena station (*approx. $200 for 5 passengers; ☎735-5178*). From La Palma, all-terrain taxis can take you the 3km (1.9mi) to Los Patos station. From Bahía Drake (Agujitas), it is relatively easy to find a boat that goes to San Pedrillo station.

Although most hikers spend three or four nights in the park, some decide to spend only the day (generally around La Leona), whereas others stay for over a week, to leisurely discover the park's plant and wildlife. If you are planning a long hike in the park, we strongly recommend that you join a group (see p 374) for safety reasons and also to benefit from the knowledge of an experienced guide. We don't want to alarm you, but the park is very big it is easy to get lost. Moreover, there are many poisonous snakes, including the formidable "fer-de-lance." Not to mention the roaming packs of peccaries, a type of boar, which sometimes charge at hikers (if this happens, climb a tree quickly!) and, of course, the voracious insects (remember your insecticide).

The **La Sirena** sector is by far the most popular place for hikers, since the trails from the other sectors meet here. It also has a biological station where scientists study the tropical rainforest's flora and fauna. The itineraries described later in this chapter all lead to this sector, so you can eas-ily compare the relative distances. For instance, you can choose either a round trip (i.e.: Carate–La Sirena–Carate; 36km or 22.3mi) or a one-way excursion (i.e.: Los Patos–La Sirena–Carate; 41km or 25.5mi). Small brooks provide drinking water along the trails, but everyone should also have 2L of water on hand, since it can get very hot and humid.

To get to the park's entrance, you must travel 2km (1.2mi) along the beach, from Carate to La Leona sta-tion. If you spend the night at this station, or even if you're just there for the day, we recom-mend taking a trail called the **Río Madrigal**. This very narrow path starts near the station, climbs into the tropical forest, and then de-scends to the Río Mad-rigal. From there, you can kick off your shoes and walk down to the water, follow this in-credible river to the mouth of the Pacific, and return to the beach. If you walk qui-etly along the refresh-ing waters of the Río Madrigal, you can ob-serve a number of birds, and perhaps even some animals.

La Leona to La Sirena (16km or 9.9mi): The trail from La Leona (information, shelter, camping, meals, etc.) to La Sirena is 16km (9.9mi) long and fol-lows the shoreline along the beach. At some points, you will have to cross shallow sections of rivers, or turn off into the forest when rocks make it difficult to walk along the ocean. Five second-ary trails also run along the beach, but go through the forest. You should also be wary of the tide (ask the park warden at the La Leona station), since certain portions of the trails, especially between Chancha and Salsiquedes, are im-passable at high tide. About 2km (1.2mi) before La Sirena, the Río Claro can be diffi-cult to cross at high tide. If you find the water too high, head up the river about 200m (656ft). The river is shallower there (1m or 3.3ft at most), and you can cross it safely.

Los Patos to La Sirena (20km or 12.4mi): If you decide to drive to Los Patos with a four-wheel drive vehicle, be warned that the narrow road is difficult to ma-noeuvre, and you will have to ford several waterways. The **Los Patos** station is about 13km (8mi) from **La Palma**. After a 30min drive, you will have to walk another 45min to get to the station. Out-side of the dry season, rivers and the numer-ous other waterways can become major ob-stacles. A safer way is to hitch a ride with one of the tractors that go to los Patos. Ask at the bar in La Palma.

The area around the Los Patos station once saw a number of *oreros*, or gold-diggers, who searched the peninsula's rivers for this precious yellow metal. Only a few of these prospectors struck it rich, although many did manage to make a modest living from their finds. Apparently, the region was so overrun with *oreros* in the mid-1980s that the park's rivers and *laguna* were in danger of silting up. Two kilometres from the Los Patos entrance, the **Cerro de Oro** saw intense mining activity, which was very common in this area of the park before it was prohibited. The abandoned machinery of the **Coope Unioro** mining cooperative, which used to mine gold from this mountain, can still be seen, along with the hills of gravel by the river. With their detailed knowledge of the tropical rainforest, these *oreros* make excellent guides. Puerto Jiménez offers a variety of guided tours that centre around the gold mining that took place in the area (see p 376).

From the Los Patos station, the **El Mirador** trail (14km or 8.7mi round trip) leads to a wonderful view of the Parque Nacional Corcovado plains. This path cuts through virgin forest, and climbs to a maximum altitude of 225m (738ft). Expect to spend more than one night at this station if you choose this trail, since distances are quite long and the hike to the La Sirena station takes a whole day.

The trail to La Sirena station is 20km or 12mi (one way) and takes 6hrs to complete, not including stops to watch animals and plants, or simply to rest. The trail first goes through virgin forest, followed by a less dense secondary forest. Most of the trail is flat, and it never goes higher than 140m (459ft). The trail is well marked and easy to follow, and is not particularly difficult, except where it crosses two rivers. Depending on the season, you might encounter swarms of mosquitoes, so insecticide is a definite must. You can spot many species of birds, butterflies, frogs and monkeys along the trail, and it is not unusual to see the tracks of a Baird's tapir or ocelot.

San Pedrillo to La Sirena (24km or 14.9mi): San Pedrillo station is located northwest of the Parque Nacional Corcovado, and is only 10km (6.2mi) or so from Bahía Drake. Therefore, you can get there on foot, although most people take a boat to the station or to Playa Llorona. This trail, which links San Pedrillo to La Sirena, is closed during the rainy season (May to December).

The 24km (14.9mi) trail (one way) takes over 7hrs to complete, not including stops for swimming, eating, or resting. Set aside an entire day for this trek, and leave as early as possible so that you can proceed at a leisurely pace, enjoying the stops along the way. You will have to cross three rivers, so be wary of the tide (ask the park warden about the tide schedule). The first 7km (4.3mi) go through the forest along the shore, culminating at the beach. There is a magnificent 30m (98ft) waterfall at **Playa Llorona**, right on the beach. Farther south, a small trail branches off to a river where you can go for a refreshing swim. Further along, you will have to cross the Llorona, Corcovado and Sirena rivers. The Río Sirena, about 2hrs from the Río Corcovado, is the deepest of these. Since the current tends to be quite strong, and there are sometimes sharks and crocodiles at the mouth of the river, it is best to cross as far inland as possible. After the Río Sirena, it is only about 1km (0.6mi) to the La Sirena station.

Reserva Biológica Isla del Caño

You can spend a very pleasant day making all sorts of discoveries at the **Reserva Biológica Isla del Caño** ★★ (*$6; every* *day 8am to 4pm;* ☎ *735-5036,* ⚏ *735-5282),* near Bahía Drake, less than 20km (12.4mi) from the Osa Peninsula. This 300ha (741 acres) island is a real paradise, bordered by lush vegetation and small beaches, no more than 100m (328ft) long, and surrounded by rocks, coral reefs and warm, relaxing waters. It is thus not surprising that the Isla del Caño has quickly become a major tourist site! Fortunately, no large luxury resorts have been built on the island to date—so you can still visit this biological reserve without having a major impact on its ecosystem.

Following the creation of the Reserva Biológica Isla del Caño in 1978, 2,700ha (6,672 acres) of ocean around the island were also protected. The 15 species of coral and other interesting underwater features make this a perfect place for scuba diving—and especially for snorkelling, since the turquoise water is so incredibly clear that the ocean's splendours can be admired without even going deep underwater! Most hotels on the Osa Peninsula, and especially around Bahía Drake, offer excursions to the Isla del Caño, which are not to be missed! Not only will you have the chance to do some snorkelling and swimming, but you can also discover the entrancing wonders of this island.

The Reserva Biológica Isla del Caño (3km by 1.5km or 1.9mi by 0.9mi) is part of the Department of National Parks and has coasts rising almost 70m (230ft) out of the ocean. Although the highest point of the island lies at 110m (361ft), most of it is an immense plateau covered by dense tropical rainforest, which lies at an altitude of approximately 90m (295ft) and receives an annual rainfall of 4 to 5m (13.1 to 16.4ft). Trees grow to great heights, generally over 50m (164ft), and include the *vaco,* or "milk tree," which gets its name from its milky and edible liquid (latex). Other trees in the area include figs, wild coconuts and rubber trees, as well as fruit trees such as mango, orange, and banana trees, which are not indigenous to the island and were most likely introduced by early settlers. There are also 158 species of plants and ferns.

The island's forest is home to 10 species of birds, including cattle herons (*Bubulcus ibis*), black falcons (*Buteogallus anthracinus*) and ospreys (*Pandion haliaetus*). There is not much animal life, but small rodents, bats, lizards, frogs, small snakes and the boa constrictors, have been sighted.

The Isla del Caño is known for its pre-Columbian cemetery and stones carved into perfect spheres that are also seen in Palmar. Apparently, these round stones, which range from 10cm to 2m (3.9in to 6.6ft) in diameter, were used to indicate the social status of the dead, although their exact significance is unknown. Archeologists believe that these rocks were made in the communities of the Osa Peninsula, and then transported to the island by boat before finally being rolled to the cemetery. Many pieces of pottery from the Aguas Buenas (3rd to 9th centuries) and Chiriquí (9th to 16th centuries) have been excavated.

A reserve warden station, which also serves as the reception and information office, is located on the northwest part of the island and has washrooms, showers, drinking water and picnic areas on the beach. There are two trails running through the forest on the island: **Sitio Arqueológico** (2km or 1.2mi round trip), leads to the pre-Columbian cemetery and the rock spheres, and **El Mirador** (3km or 1.9mi round trip) takes you to a beautiful area from which you can admire the sea, the towering trees and the different species of birds.

The South

North of Palmar

While driving along the Interamericana towards Palmar, you will have the opportunity to admire the spectacle of the **Río Ceibo** between Buenos Aires and San Isidro de El General, which blends two differently coloured kinds of water: the water near the surface carries volcanic earth, while the deeper water is more clear.

A bit further downstream, as you pass the Paso Real, 8km (5mi) in the mountains, you can visit the reserve of the **Borucas** Indians who are well-known for their handicrafts (wooden masks, cotton place mats and belts, gourds). Visitors are welcome to explore the surroundings (which is not always the case on reserves). The Borucas subsist on agriculture. There is a **museum** on the reserve which has several displays, including native architecture, crafts and plants used to make textiles and medicine. Be careful, as the road is often washed out after it rains.

Around New Year's Day, the Borucas celebrate the three-day **Fiesta de los Diablitos** (The Festival of the Little Devils), which includes a dramatic re-enactment of a battle between the Spanish conquistadors and the native people, in which the natives emerged victorious. The actors wear flamboyant costumes and masks.

The Palmar Region

Although the Diquis Valley region's only airport is located in Palmar Sur, **Palmar**'s immediate surroundings are quite uninteresting, except for its many large, mysterious **rock spheres** ★. These boulders date back to pre-Columbian times, and their perfectly round shape has yet to be satisfactorily explained. The rocks are similar to those found on the Isla del Caño and vary in size, some measuring over 1m (3.3ft) in diameter! Palmar spheres are found in different parts of the city, and even in the courtyards of some houses. Ask around to see a few of them.

Palmar is where the new road, the Costanera Sur, begins. This route borders the Pacific Coast to the northwest and crosses the Playa Tortuga region before reaching Dominical. Thus, you can visit the entire area by starting your tour in Dominical.

On the road to Playa Tortuga, take a few minutes to stop in **Ciudad Cortés** ★, which is prettier than Palmar.

Part of it was built all at once at the beginning of the 20th century, so its rather simple architecture is quite unified, and gives the city a definite character. Many of the buildings are made of wood and are painted in colours that blend in wonderfully with the vegetation, as colonial architecture of the late 19th and early 20th century often does. Even the roads are picturesque (which is quite rare in this country). If this tiny village were developed, it would definitely have a lot to offer tourists who want to experience a different way of life for a short time.

South of Palmar, the Interamericana runs through the hot, humid region of the Diquis Valley, to reach the Osa Peninsula, Golfito, Ciudad Neily, and finally the Panamanian border. Although you can get to San Vito via the Coto Brus Valley and Palmar, it can also be reached from Ciudad Neily in the north. We recommend taking the latter route.

The Diquis Valley illustrates the damaging impact that intensive agricultural exploitation can have on the landscape. Many of the large tracts of deforested land along the Interamericana are used for farming and grazing. In the summer, they are yellow and dry (sometimes even during the rainy season),

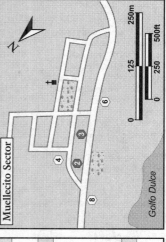

Golfito

Refugio Nacional de Fauna Silvestre Golfito

Golfo Dulce

Interamericana

71012

0   500   1,000m

0   1,500   3,000ft

See inset

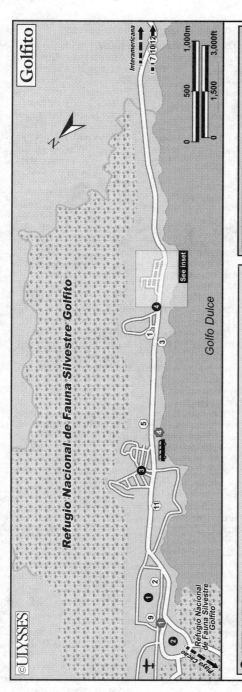

© ULYSSES

Refugio Nacional
de Fauna Silvestre
Golfito

Playa Cacao

Muellecito Sector

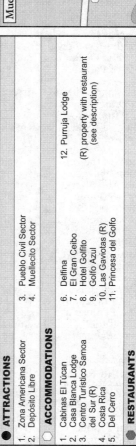

N

Golfo Dulce

0   125   250m

0   250   500ft

● **ATTRACTIONS**

1. Zona Americana Sector
2. Depósito Libre

3. Pueblo Civil Sector
4. Muellecito Sector

⬡ **ACCOMMODATIONS**

1. Cabinas El Túcan
2. Casa Blanca Lodge
3. Centro Turístico Samoa
   del Sur (R)
4. Costa Rica
5. Del Cerro

6. Delfina
7. El Gran Ceibo
8. Hotel Golfito
9. Golfo Azul
10. Las Gaviotas (R)
11. Princesa del Golfo

12. Puruja Lodge

(R) property with restaurant
    (see description)

● **RESTAURANTS**

1. La Cazuelita
2. La Dama del Delfín

3. La Eurekita
4. Soda El Barco

and it is hard to imagine the lush jungle that used to cover the area. We can only rejoice that the authorities have decided to protect the remaining land in the region by creating the Parque Nacional Corcovado, on the Osa Peninsula.

Sierpe (see p 370) is a particularly interesting region if you are interested in plant and animal life, with its **mangroves** *(Selva Mar offers hiking tours,* ☎ *771-4582,* ⇌ *771-8841)* at the mouth of the Río Sierpe on the Pacific Ocean, just south of Palmar.

Most tourists travelling to Bahía Drake go via Sierpe, on the Sierpe River. It has a park, a general store, public phones, a few hotels (many are on the outskirts of the village) and piers. The Sierpe region is becoming increasingly popular with birdwatchers and sports fishing enthusiasts, because of its location near many rivers and the Pacific Ocean.

Just before Piedras Blancas, a trail leading to the Osa Peninsula branches off the Interamericana, to the right.

The Golfito Region

The city of Golfito is also located at the end of a road that splits off to the right from the Interamericana, but which starts in Río

Claro. The road is well indicated, and you will know you are definitely on the right track when you pass the numerous palm tree plantations and the many billboards advertising the merchandise available at the Depósito Libre de Golfito (see further below).

Golfito ★ can be described as a "gulf within a gulf". The city lies at the end of a small gulf which opens into the larger Golfo Dulce, separated from the ocean by the Osa Peninsula. The waters in the two gulfs are very calm, making this area a good location for a port. Thus, Golfito is a seaport more than anything else. During the boom period of the United Fruit company, it was the main shipping centre for the company's fruit, especially for bananas exported from Costa Rica. However, the company shut down in the mid-1980s due to production-related problems that had developed over the years (increased export taxes, union problems, price drops, plant diseases, etc.). The city is still feeling the effects of the company's demise, which put an end to its period of prosperity.

The city's problems were partially solved with the establishment of a "free trade zone" (Depósito Libre) at the outskirts of the city and the growing tourist

industry with people coming from Costa Rica and abroad to visit Corcovado, the Wilson Botanical Gardens, etc. In fact, tourism has increased to the point where you will have to reserve your accommodations in advance—especially during the high season and on weekends.

Despite its decline, Golfito remains an important city in the region. Its airport is convenient for anyone travelling to the southern part of the country.

The city is built on a relatively narrow strip of land between the bay and the green forested mountains, and contains three main sectors: The Zona Americana (American Zone) in the north was home to the heads of the United Fruit company; the Pueblo Civil in the centre boasts Golfito's main pier *(muelle)*; and the *muellecito* sector (with a small pier) is a bit farther on. All in all, the city is almost 7km (4.3mi) long, and is divided by a main street that links all of its neighbourhoods. There is a large taxi fleet in addition to the regular bus service that runs every 15min during the day.

It is no surprise that the **Zona Americana** is the most elegant part of Golfito, since the United Fruit company's executives used to live here. The houses look sophisticated and are beautifully landscaped, bestowing a certain elegance on the entire sector, even if they are no longer as well maintained now that their original owners have left. The Zona Americana also encompasses the airport and the **Depósito Libre**. Since 1990, the Depósito Libre has been a free trade zone where consumer goods (from jeans to appliances) cost a little less than in other regions of Costa Rica. This Depósito Libre is very lively, especially on weekends. However, it is better to go there during the week when it is less crowded with Costa Ricans looking for discount prices. There is an entrance fee of a few dollars.

If the Zona American is where the upper classes lived, **Pueblo Civil** is for the working class. The architecture is less impressive, but the neighbourhood and the abundant restaurants are still very appealing. Many houses are made of wood.

The *muellecito* sector is not quite as frequented, but you can still find quaint little hotels and places to eat.

Most of Golfito's surroundings now belong to a wildlife reserve which you can access via several paths (many from the Zona Americana) which lead to hiking trails of varying lengths.

If you want to go out on the bay or the ocean, you can rent a boat from the *muelle* in Pueblo Civil or near the old United Fruit pier, or go with one of the tourist expeditions organized by local companies. You can also get to the beaches of Pavones, Zancudo and Cacao with boats that leave from Golfito's piers. Lastly, Golfito is a popular place for pleasure boats coming from other areas.

There are also some beaches where you can enjoy the bay waters along the edge of the peninsula across from Golfito. The best of these is **Cacao** beach, which has a great view of Golfito. **Gallardo** and **San Josecito** beaches to the west are also lovely.

Zancudo is a black-sand beach that stretches over many kilometres southwest of Golfito. Located on the point formed by the Río Coto Colorado, a river that flows into the Pacific Ocean, it is a very popular beach during the high season, but calm during the rainy season. It's a good place for swimmers and novice surfers, and even seems popular among the local fishers.

Also southeast of Golfito, **Pavones Beach** is one of the favourites with serious surfers, and most of its visitors come for the waves. Thus, you will rub shoulders with surf experts and fanatics, whether you like it or not—there can be a lot of them around, especially during the rainy season when the waves are at their highest.

The Ciudad Neily Region

Though it is the last big city before Panama, **Ciudad Neily** is not that popular with tourists. Rather, people visit it because it serves as an alternative to the Coto Brus route (located east of Palmar) to San Vito. However, the city is quite attractive, particularly along the two lively main thoroughfares in the downtown area. The Ricardo Neilly Park, in the heart of the city, is a perfect refuge from the heat that is prevalent in the area. There are many benches where you can socialize and get to know the locals a little.

The San Vito Region

To drink in a magnificent panorama before you leave the Pacific coast region, don't miss the **view ★★** from the road just outside of Ciudad Neily, towards San Vito. The road climbs more than 1,000m (3,280ft), and the hot and humid temperature of Ciudad Neily rapidly gives way to the cooler and foggy

The South

climate of the San Vito region. However the road is winding and has some very sharp 90-degree turns! And although it is paved, the road is very narrow, has no shoulder, and has a few potholes that you won't see until the last minute. These conditions make it difficult to admire the scenery while driving!

The **Wilson Botanical Garden** ★★★ (*$5 half day, $8 full day, children 6 to 12 years half price; 2-hour guided tours $35; closed Mon; 5 km or 3.1mi from San Vito on the Ciudad Neily-San Vito road,* ☎*240-6696,* ⇌*240-6783)* at the Las Cruces biological station is owned by the Organization for Tropical Studies (OTS). Its mission is to teach people about the tropical vegetation (particularly that of the mountain forest) found in its garden, which has the largest botanical collection in Central America. The station preserves endangered plant species from being destroyed in their natural habitat, and studies new plant species, especially for horticultural purposes.

This site was created by two Americans, Robert and Catherine Wilson, in the early 1960s, and was taken over by OTS ten years later. As one of the three sites belonging to this organization, the Wilson Botanical Garden is a centre for research and

education. At the beginning of the 1980s it was even recognized by UNESCO as part of the vast protected spaces that make up the Parque Internacional La Amistad (see below) and its appendages (472,000ha or 1,166,296 acres of land!). You can learn about the several thousand plant species (including 700 types of palm trees), as well as the hundreds of birds, reptiles and mammals at the garden. It is said that over 3,000 species of butterflies live here.

Red lavender

Using the literature sold at the centre, you can plan out your visit around one of the many thematic itineraries (the Wilson Botanical Garden, the trees of the Wilson Botanical Garden, a tour of the palm trees, the birds of Las Cruces, the orchid trail, the hummingbird gardens, medicinal plants, etc.), or take a guided tour. Some guides speak English and the staff is very friendly and helpful. Some of the literature is available in English. A

guided tour can be organized for handicapped visitors. You can also spend the night at the Wilson Botanical Garden (see p 391).

A few kilometres northeast of the Wilson Botanical Garden, towards San Vito, is the **Finca Cántaros**, bought and developed by the management of the Wilson Garden in 1994. This site is open to the public and will soon operate as an educational reforestation centre. With its splendid, peaceful rolling hills, the area is also being developed for recreational use (picnic tables, lake, and observation tower).

A few kilometres north of the Wilson Garden and Finca Cántaros is **San Vito** ★, a small town founded in the 1950s by Italian immigrants wanting to improve their lot. Today, the town has close to 40,000 inhabitants and is slowly losing its strictly Italian character with the influx of Spanish-speaking people from the rest of the country. Pictures and text about San Vito's settlement are on display at Catubrus (☎/⇌ *773-3570)*, the Cámara de Turismo (the tourist office) of Coto Brus, located in the centre of the city at the main intersection. You can have a good Italian meal at some of the area's restaurants.

The city itself is beautiful and cool, which is a welcome change after the heat along the coast. San Vito is often shrouded in very distinctive fog, thick as pea soup, and should therefore, in our view, be renamed San Vito-of-the-clouds! Lastly, the Parque Internacional La Amistad can be accessed from San Vito via Las Mellizas, on the Panamanian border.

Parque Internacional La Amistad

The **Parque Internacional La Amistad** *($6; every day 6am to 5pm;* ☎ *771-3297,* ≈ *771-3155)* is more of an immense protected zone than a park. There is no infrastructure for receiving visitors or for outdoor activities. With 193,929ha (479,192 acres), this is the largest park in Costa Rica, extending from Parque Nacional Chirripó to the Panamanian border. It protects much of the Cordillera de Talamanca, where mountains soar to heights of over 3,000m (9,843ft), as well as the forest of south-central Costa Rica. Since it extends into Panama (more than 400,000ha or 988,386 acres), it is considered an international park and one of the largest protected areas in Central America.

Parque Internacional La Amistad (Friendship) belongs to the **La**

Amistad Biosphere Reserve, whose total area of 248,337ha (613,632 acres) also comprises the Tapantí and Chirripó national parks, Reserva Biológica Hitoy Cerere, and several forest reserves and indigenous communities. This immense expanse of wilderness contains eight natural habitats, has one of the most impressive ecosystems in Central America, and was declared a biosphere reserve by UNESCO in 1982.

The Parque Internacional La Amistad is also home to diverse wildlife that includes over 400 species of birds and 263 species of amphibians and reptiles. It is estimated that 60% of all the vertebrate and invertebrate life found in Costa Rica lives in the park. This immense territory is one of the only in the country that is big enough for big cats such as jaguars, pumas and ocelots to hunt and reproduce. Jaguars, for examples, can weigh about 150kg (331lbs), and need hundreds of hectares to roam for hunting agoutis, pecari and deer.

The park currently has very little in the way of hiking trails and other visitor facilities. It is nevertheless a magical place where the most adventurous tourists (accompanied by local guides) used to long

treks in dense tropical rainforest can scale the 3,000m-high (9,843ft) mountains to observe animals that are rarely seen anywhere else in the country. Birdwatchers stand a good chance of spotting a quetzal in this pristine environment. The protected region of **Las Tablas**, northeast of San Vito next to the Panamanian border, is a favourite with many visitors, especially since there are hotels and guide services nearby.

Before visiting any of the park's three sectors (Tres Colinas, Estación Pittier and Altamira), we strongly recommended that you contact the National Park Service *(☎283-8004, ≈283-7343)* or the Fundación de Parques Nacionales *(☎257-2239, ≈222-4732)*, both located in San José, to get the most current information. When we were there, no detailed maps of the parks' regions or other information brochures were available yet.

Outdoor Activities

Hiking

The hike to the top of Cerro Chirripó (3,819m or 12,530ft), the highest peak in Costa Rica, is spectacular. The mountain is in the magnificent **Parque Nacional Chirripó** (see p 353), just north of San Isidro de El General. A brand-new shelter that has been built on the mountain can accommodate some 60 hikers overnight. In addition to the trail leading to the main summit, there are several others for experienced hikers who have the necessary equipment for camping in high mountains.

Hacienda Barú (see p 357) has 6km (3.7mi) of trails that run through the tropical forest and along a magnificent beach.

Quite close to the village of Ojochal, on the southern Pacific coast, a new ecological project is just getting off the ground. **Syntonia** (≈ 788-8351, embrujodel pacifico@yahoo.com) promises wonderful experiences in direct contact with nature. You can already take part in one of their mountain hikes with a guide who will introduce you to the fauna and flora, including various species of medicinal plants and trees. They also offer a day at sea with local fishers and a day at the Boruca Amerindian reserve.

Parque Nacional Corcovado (see p 363) has more than 80km (49.7mi) of paths, most of which are along the beach and connect the park's various shelters. Only experienced hikers who are knowledgeable about tropical wet forests should tackle the long hikes (overnighting in the shelters) in this isolated region with dense vegetation and extreme heat. You can easily hire a guide through an agency: **Escondido Trex** (☎/≈ 735-5210); **Proyecto Osa Natural** (☎/≈ 735-5440); **Corcovado Tours** (☎735-5062, ≈735-5043); **The True Local Guide Organizer** (Fernando and Carlos Quintero, ☎ 735-5216, ≈735-5414).

Situated less than 20km (12.4mi) from the Osa Peninsula, near Bahía Drake, the **Reserva Biológica Isla del Caño** (see p 366) has two short paths through the forest.

Scuba Diving and Snorkelling

There are excellent places for scuba diving and snorkelling in and around **Parque Nacional Marino Ballena** (see p 360). The **FDW Tres Marinos** (☎771-1903) agency offers snorkelling expeditions from a boat, and **Gino Salotti** (☎256-9996, ≈ 788-8210) in Ojochal offers a course in scuba diving.

The **Osa Peninsula** in general, and the Golfo Dulce in particular, are magnificent places to scuba dive and snorkel. All tours in this region are organized by the following agencies: **Osatours** (☎786-6534, ≈ 786-6335), **Osa Tropical** (☎735-5063, ≈735-5043), **Aquatic Tours** (☎735-5262, ≈735-5121) and **Proyecto Osa Natural** (☎/≈ 735-5440).

Bahía Drake (see p 362) and the **Reserva Biológica Isla del Caño** (see p 366) northwest of the Osa Peninsula are known for their scuba diving and snorkelling. The reserve's turquoise water is remarkably clear, and contains 15 different species of coral. Most hotels in Bahía Drake arrange scuba diving and snorkelling excursions.

Sport Fishing

Some of the fishermen in **Uvita** (☎771-1903) will take you deep-sea fishing around Parque Nacional Marino Ballena.

Jeff Lantz and Stig Hanson from **Iguana Lodge** (Puerto Jiménez, ☎/≈ 735-5205) have an international reputation for organizing sport fishing excursions around the Osa Peninsula. Bob Baker and Jerry Cooper of **Golfito Sportfishing** (☎/≈382-2716) are just as well-known. Other agencies such as **Osatours** (☎786-6534, ≈786-6335), **Osa Tropical** (☎735-5062,

☞ *735-5043)*, **Aquatic Tours** (☎ *735-5262*, ☞ *735-5121)* and **Proyecto Osa Natural** (☎/☞ *735-5440)* also organize fishing trips.

Kayaking

Hacienda Barú (see p 357) offers kayak excursions through the mangroves.

South of Parque Nacional Marino Ballena, **Kayak Joe** (☞ *788-8210)* will take you on a tour of the coast and its numerous caves in a sea kayak.

For an excursion of one or more days around the Osa Peninsula, contact **Escondido Trex** (*Puerto Viejo*, ☎/☞ *735-5210)*. **Osa Tropical** (☎ *735-5062*, ☞ *735-5043)* and **Iguana Lodge** (*Puerto Jiménez*, ☎/☞ *735-5205)* also organize trips on the river or ocean.

Surfing

Dominical is considered one of the best places on the Pacific coast for surfing: the waves here are incredible and break very close to the beach. Unfortunately, however, the current has a very strong undertow, and several people drown here each year. The bar-restaurant San Clement is

the place to go to find out about surfing conditions in the area and to meet other surfers from around the world.

Surfers should not miss **Playa Pavones**, south of Golfito. It is renowned for its "left-brake" waves, which are considered among the longest in the world.

Bahía Drake and **Cabo Matapalo**, the southeastern tip of the Osa Peninsula, also have superb waves for surfing.

Horseback Riding

In the **Uvita** region, the **Duarte family** organizes guided tours in the Oro Verde private reserve and the neighbouring areas. The nearby **Rancho La Merced** also arranges rides, and lets you play "cowboy for a day" by helping out with some of the different chores around the farm. For information or to reserve, call the **Selva Mar** (☎/☞ *771-1903)* agency in Dominical.

On the Osa Peninsula, **Osatours** (☎ *78-6534*, ☞ *786-6335)*, **Corcovado Tours** (☎ *735-5062*, ☞ *735-5043)* and **True Local Guide Organizer** (☎ *735-5216*, ☞ *735-5414)* arrange guided trips of one or more days. You can also rent horses by the hour or by the day at many other places. The **Proyecto Osa Natural** (☎/☞ *735-5440)* tourist

information bureau in the centre of Puerto Jiménez can give you more information.

Mountain Biking

The Osa Peninsula is a marvellous place for mountain biking! From Puerto Jiménez, you can go south as far as Carate and Parque Nacional Corcovado (43km or 26.7mi). Heading north, the road is narrow, unpaved and quiet as far as Rincón (35km or 21.7mi), where some smaller roads lead inland to the regions of Dos Brazos and Los Patos, among others. **La Llanta Picante** (☎/☞ *735-5414)* organizes mountain biking trips around the Río Tigre (Puerto Jiménez), and also rents high-quality, well-maintained mountain bikes.

Water Sports

In Golfito, boats can be moored at **Eagle's Roost Marina** (☎ *775-0838, or by radio VHF 12)* or **Sanbar Marina** (☎ *775-0735 or 775-0874*, ☞ *775-0321)*.

Rafting and Excursions

Selva Mar (see p 350) organizes rafting excursions in the region.

Canopy Tours

Hacienda Barú (see p 357) offers tours of the canopy from high observation platforms in the jungle.

Visits to Gold Mines

For many years, and until quite recently, the **Osa Peninsula** attracted gold prospectors, called *oreros*, who came and settled there. You can visit the areas around Puerto Jiménez and Dos Brazos, and even become something of a prospector yourself, by learning all about this business. Guided tours are arranged in Puerto Jiménez: **Escondido Trex** *(☎/≈ 735-5210)*; **Proyecto Osa Natural** *(☎/≈ 735-5440)*; **Corcovado Tours** *(☎ 735-5062, ≈ 735-5043)*; **The True Local Guide Organizer** *(Fernando and Carlos Quintero, ☎ 735-5216, ≈ 735-5414).*

Accommodations

The San Isidro de El General Region

The temperatures in these sub-regions are much cooler than on the coast, so it is important to bring warm clothing, especially if you are staying at the higher altitudes (in the San Gerardo de Dota area, for example).

Cerro de la Muerte and San Gerardo de Dota

Paradero Lacustre Los Ranchos
$
San Gerardo de Dota
☎771-2376
Just past Albergue de Montaña Savegre (see further below), in San Gerardo de Dota, is Paradero Lacustre Los Ranchos, a campground with electricity and hot water in the bathrooms. Some sites have cooking facilities. This waterside property has rowboats for boating and fishing, hiking trails, barbecue areas and a *mirador* for birdwatching.

El Toucanet Lodge
$$$ bkfst incl.
hw, pb, ℜ
exit at Km 58 from the Interamericana, near El Cañon de Guarco, then go 7km (4.3mi) to Copey de Dota
As you enter the more alpine atmosphere on

the way to Cerro de la Muerte from the Central Valley, El Toucanet Lodge is one of the first places that offers accommodations. This family- style lodge on a mountainside in the village of Copey de Dota has six rooms built completely of wood, with private terraces. There is also a little restaurant with a fireplace that serves country-style food.

Trogón Lodge
$$$$
pb, hw, ℜ
San Gerardo de Dota
☎771-1266 or 223-2421
≈222-5463
Situated on the banks of a river, the very attractive Trogón Lodge belongs to the Mawamba group, which has most of its hotels on the Caribbean coast. The wooden buildings blend well with this pastoral setting. The lodge is somewhat removed from the area's other hotel establishments, and is located at the beginning of the road that runs from San Gerardo to the Interamericana Highway. It is ideal if you want some privacy in a natural setting that has retained some aspects of wilderness. The restaurant is open for breakfast, lunch and dinner. Heated.

Albergue de Montaña Savegre
$$$$$ fb
hw, pb, ℜ
exit at Km 80 on the Interamericana, then descend 9km (5.6mi) to San Gerardo de Dota
☎/↔ *771-1732*
On a lovely hillside next to a mountain stream, with landscaping well-suited to its surroundings, Albergue de Montaña Savegre has very clean, large, simple rooms with extra heaters and a shared terrace. Three meals per day are included in the rate, and are served in the attractive and and inviting dining room. With all the activities offered at the *albergue* (birdwatching, fishing, hiking, boating and horseback riding), and San Gerardo de Dota's cool, green valley, who could ask for more?

San Isidro de El General

El Jardin
$
☎ *771-0349*
The most inexpensive hotel in San Isidro, El Jardin rents clean little rustic rooms on a large wooden platform. They have a somewhat closed-in feel to them.

El Valle
$$
⊗, *pb, hw, tv*
above the Núñez hardware store
☎ *771-0246*
El Valle is a hotel with clean, simple rooms with televisions.

Small provincial hotels, **Chirripó** (*$$; hw, pb;* ☎ *771-0529*) and **Amaneli** (*$$; hw, pb,* ⊗, *tv;* ☎ *771-0352*) rent simple, clean rooms. Amaneli has a restaurant on the main floor.

Iguazu
$$
⊗, *hw, pb/sb, tv*
above the Super Lido store
☎ *771-2571*
The small-town Iguazu hotel rents plain, but tasteful little rooms. Its cleanliness makes it a good choice if you are staying in San Isidro. The disadvantage is its noisy location right next to the Interamericana.

Hotel del Sur
$$$
pb, hw, tv, ⊗, ≡, ℜ, ≈
6km (3.7mi) south of San Isidro on the Interamericana
☎ *771-3033*
↔ *771-0527*
Hotel del Sur is a better quality hotel than those available in San Isidro proper. The rooms and cottages with living- and dining-rooms are modern, and there are conference rooms, gardens, a pool and sports facilities (volleyball, basketball and tennis courts). The extensive grounds isolate the hotel from traffic noise fairly well.

San Gerardo de Rivas

Cabinas Uran
$
sb, ℜ
Situated 50m (164ft) from the entrance to the trail that climbs the Cerro Chirripó, these *cabinas*, at more than affordable rates, will allow you an early morning start or a rest as soon as you get back! The Cabinas Uran were completed just recently, so they're new, clean and functional. Ten cement—floored rooms line both sides of the hallway and offer double beds, two single beds or one single bed. At the end of the hall are two showers and two bathrooms that are shared by everyone. You may have guessed that their decor is minimal, but with such an incredible setting outdoors, who cares? There's also a small cottage with four beds that can accommodate five people. Don't forget to visit Don Ulysses' *soda* (see p 392).

Talari Albergue de Montaña
$$$
pb, hw, ⊗, ℝ, ≈, ℜ
☎/↔ *771-0341*
On a lovely 8ha (12.8 acres) estate beside the Río El General, 30min from Parque Nacional Chirripó, Talari Albergue de Montaña is a great place for peace and quiet. The eight

rooms are subdued, clean and comfortable. Surrounding the inn is the forest (partly new growth) that is criss-crossed by paths leading through dozens of varieties of fruit trees, plants and flowers. The natural surroundings have also attracted a multitude of birds: 143 different species have been spotted to date. The charming owners, Pilar and Jan, prepare the meals: delicious dishes made with fresh ingredients and served in the cozy dining room. A small souvenir shop sells items made by the Boruca Indians. The inn is helpful in organizing visits to Parque Nacional Chirripó for its guests (reservations, transportation, guide, food, equipment, advice, etc.). Jan and Pilar love the region that they have made their home and they are very involved in its community life. Ask them more about it.

Dominical Region

Dominical

Cabinas San Clemente
$$
pb, hw, ≈
on the beach at Dominical
☎*787-0026*
⚎*787-0055*
Like those at the San Clemente Bar & Grill (see p 392), Cabinas San Clemente are perfect for hip tourists who come here for surfing and relaxation. The owner is from the United States and also has several beach houses for rent.

Cabinas Escondidas
$$$ bkfst incl.
pb, hw, ℜ
3.5km (2.1mi) south of Punta Dominical on Costanera Sur
The Cabinas Escondidas are a lovely retreat and study centre in a private natural park setting. The *cabinas* are airy and situated quite far apart to insure privacy. The jungle, with its many delights (streams, fauna and flora), has been preserved for guests to enjoy. Therapeutic massage is only one of the numerous activities offered. The beach has some secluded areas for swimmers. The restaurant serves Asian vegetarian cuisine. Kayaking and horseback riding are available.

Cabinas Punta Dominical
$$$
hw, pb, ⊗, ℜ
4km (2.5mi) south of Dominical
☎*787-0016*
Cabinas Punta Dominical is a warm, welcoming place on a spit of land jutting into the sea. The rustic and very clean cottages open to the outdoors on all four sides. This location has a wonderful view of the sea on two sides, with panoramic vistas and the impressive sound of the surf. The hotel is located some distance from Dominical, which is an advantage if you prefer tranquillity to the lively surfer crowd. The Punta Dominical restaurant (see p 392) is next to the cabinas.

Casitas de Puertocito
$$$
hw, pb, ⊗, ℜ
9km (5.6mi) south of Dominical
reservations through Selva Mar
☎*771-4582*
⚎*771-8841*
Casitas de Puertocito is where movie makers have come to film tropical paradise. Thatched-palm roofs cover "tropics-style" *cabinas* that are tucked away in the foliage along 1,200m (3,937ft) of oceanfront property. The *cabinas* are spacious, clean and charming, with large porches. The grounds have been kept in a natural state, and they are replete with streams, waterfalls, and luxuriant vegetation.

Villas Río Mar
$$$$$
hw, pb, ⊗, ≈
on a road indicated at the entrance to Dominical, look for the sign just after the Río Barú bridge
☎*787-0052 or 787-0053*
⚎*787-0054*
reservations in Selva Mar
☎*771-4582*
⚎*771-8841*
Villas Río Mar has 40 attractive bungalows for rent on a large, beautifully landscaped property. Each one has a lovely roomy terrace protected by mosquito nets making them really comfortable. There are

tennis courts and a restaurant (local and international cuisine).

La Costanera Sur

Las Escaleras

The following hotels are located in Las Escaleras, a small mountainous region just south of Dominical. The region has really wonderful views of the surrounding countryside and pleasantly cool evenings. However, the roads to its high-elevation hotels are often so bad that you should only attempt them with a four-wheel drive vehicle. The road conditions change according to the season, and they can deteriorate completely over the course of a day.

Pacific Edge
$$$
hw, pb, K
Dominicalito
reservations in Selva Mar
☎ *771-4582*
⇆ *771-8841*
Pacific Edge is a great place for a picture-perfect vacation. The sea lies 200m (656ft) below the property, and the tropical rainforest with its bird and animal calls is situated behind the comfortable wood *cabinas*. Each cottage has a living room, kitchenette, bedroom and balcony (hammock included, of course!).

Take the road indicated by a sign, 100m (328ft) south of the bridge in Dominical.

Villa Cabeza de Mono
$$$$$
hw, pb, K, ≈
reservations through Selva Mar
☎ *771-4582*
⇆ *771-8841*
Villa Cabeza de Mono is a luxurious villa surrounded by jungle. It has a living room and a dining room in addition to the kitchen and two large, attractive bedrooms. It can accommodate a party of five in the privacy afforded by the lush vegetation all around it.

Villas Escaleras
☎ / ⇆ *787-0031*
The former Escaleras Inn has been transformed into Villas Escaleras, which rents fully equipped villas. The main villa, which used to be the inn, costs $300 per night, and houses up to eight people. It has three bedrooms, five (!) bathrooms, a living room, library, pool, porch and terrace with a panoramic view. The friends' villa, a small cottage in its own garden, has a bedroom, living room, bathroom, balcony and terrace (*$125 for two people*). The newer two-storey stone-and-wood Villa ll (*$200/night, max. four people*) has two bedrooms, two bathrooms, a sitting room and a private swimming pool.

The owners, originally from the United States, provide cleaning service, coffee and bed linen.

Uvita

Uvita itself has very few comfortable places to stay. **Cocotico Lodge** and **Cabinas Los Laureles** (*$$; sb/pb, ≈; on a road that leads into farmland from the Uvita-Dominical national hwy*) are located at the limits of Uvita's residential area. The rooms are very simply furnished. The owner of Cabinas Los Laureles prepares home-cooked meals. Horseback rides in the nearby tropical rainforest go to waterfalls and are great opportunities for birdwatching.

Cabinas Flamingo
$$
pb, hw
on the coast opposite Parque Nacional Marino Ballena
☎ *771-8078 or 380-5948*
South of Uvita, in a completely natural setting on Costanera Sur, Cabinas Flamingo is a little restaurant with a separate, two-storey building containing two large bedrooms that can sleep six. They are furnished only with beds, but are comfortable and clean. Flamingo has direct access to the beach at Parque Nacional Marino Ballena.

The South

Rancho La Merced
$$$
Uvita
reservations through Selva Mar
☎ *771-4582*
⇆ *771-8841*
Between the sea and Costanera Sur, slightly south of the road to Oro Verde, Rancho La Merced operates both as a wildlife refuge and cattle ranch (see p 359). It offers rustic accommodations and country-style meals.

Ojochal

Communications in Ojochal are still somewhat difficult. All hotel owners and residents use one fax number and a single Internet address. If you wish to make a reservation at one of the hotels in the village, you can send a message by fax via ⇆ *786-6358* or by E-mail to *sindys@racsa.co.cr*.

Casa Papagayos
$$$
pb, hw, ⊗, ≈
Ojochal
Casa Papagayos is run by Canadians who rent a few rooms. Clean, bright and very well ventilated (a *must* in this weather), they are arranged around a swimming pool, and tennis and basketball courts. Hats off to anyone who can do these sports in the intense heat that is normal for this area! The owners organize all sorts of excursions, including a trip through the mangroves.

El Parezoso
$$$ bkfst incl.
pb, hw
Ojochal
El Parezoso is a Québec-owned inn. To get there, take the road off the Costanera Sur to Ojochal, and a little before Cabinas Papagayo to the right is the road that leads to the inn. Be careful fording the little river!

Paraíso del Pacífico
$$$
pb, hw, ℜ, ≈
Ojochal
Paraíso del Pacífico is situated in the Ojochal hills. Little buildings that are fairly close together each have two bedrooms with a living room area (good for long stays) and a semi-private terrace. It is relatively basic, but there is a pleasant view of the surroundings from the complex's hilltop location. A shuttle transports vacationers to the beach. Full board is available.

Rancho Soluna
$$$
⇆ *788-8210*
Rancho Soluna is like a family-style inn, owned by Leo and Michele from Québec. They rent two pleasant rooms with a shared terrace. Campsites are available with water and electricity, *($7/person under a thatched hut, $2.50/person without thatched hut)*. Michele runs the warm, intimate restaurant on the premises (see p 393).

Ultimo Refugio
$$$
500m (1,640ft) south of the Ojochal village primary school Ultimo Refugio is simultaneously a restaurant, a souvenir shop and a place to stay. While the grounds are relatively small, foliage hides the building from the street and improves the appearance of the setting. The owners, from Québec, have created a friendly atmosphere and the building is tastefully decorated.

Playa Tortuga

🏖 **Posada Playa Tortuga**
$$$ bkfst incl.
pb, hw, ⊗, ≈
ptortuga@racsa.co.cr
Overlooking the Playa Tortuga from above, the inn that bears its name also echoes its atmosphere. The ocean and beach that are visible from each room set a vacation-like tempo. The place is spectacular and the surrounding vegetation is gorgeous. The 10 simply decorated but comfortable rooms are lined up, motel style, on two storeys. They are decently sized, and windows on both sides of the building ensure good ventilation. The hotel was recently purchased by a friendly couple from the United States who have owned the famous pizzeria Gringo Mike's (see p 393) for many years. They know the area well and they love it! They do everything possible to make your

stay enjoyable, beginning with a generous breakfast buffet, and a warm welcome assisted by their two cats and two enormous dogs, who are ever eager to play with the guests! If you're at all musically inclined, ask the owner to show you her treasures. To get here, take the road that ascends on your left when you turn off the Costanera Sur towards Playa Tortuga.

Villas Gaia
$$$$
hw, pb, ⊗, ≈, ℜ
Playa Tortuga
☎*256-9956*
At Villas Gaia, individual *cabinas* are tastefully decorated in warm, tropical colours and have private balconies. The raised pool has a splendid view of the ocean. The look of the place in general, the style and comfort of the *cabinas*, the resaurant's cuisine and the quality of the service are all impeccable. There are all sorts of organized guided tours in the area.

Spider monkey

Hacienda Barú

Hacienda Barú
$$$ bkfst incl.
hw, pb, ⊗, K
on the right, just before the village of Dominical, coming from Quepos
☎*787-0003*
⇋*787-0004*
reservations through Selva Mar
☎*771-4582*
⇋*771-8841*
www.haciendabaru.com
On the Pacific coast, Hacienda Barú lets you visit a noteworthy private reserve and stay in one of the fine cottages not too far from the beach. The cottages have living rooms and kitchenettes, with a small, secluded porch. There are guided tours, and self-guided trails crisscross the area between the cottages and the ocean.

The Osa Peninsula

Bear in mind that the Osa Peninsula is one of the most isolated places in the country. Everything is scarcer and more expensive. Make sure you have a hotel reservation before coming and note the directions carefully, to ensure that you wind up at the right place. But the road is usually in fairly good condition, especially for a four-wheel-drive vehicle. Be aware too that the rainy season here is more intense than elsewhere.

The Puerto Jiménez Region

La Palma

Centro Turístico Playa Blanca
$2/tent
Centro Turístico Playa Blanca rents campsites with shared bathroom and shower facilities, as well as *cabinas* near the beach with an unbeatable view of the Golfo Dulce. There is also a bar, and a restaurant *(open at 11am)* that serves mainly fish and seafood. Different kinds of boats can be rented for fishing or boat rides.

Cabinas El Tucán
$
pb
In the centre of the village of La Palma, Cabinas El Tucán rents simple rooms at a modest price.

Cabinas Corcovado
$
sb/pb, ℜ
☎*775-0433*
⇋*775-0033*
Five kilometres from La Palma, and 500m (1,640ft) from the entrance to Parque Nacional Corcovado, Cabinas Corcovado also has campsites *($4 for two persons)*. The restaurant serves guests three typical Costa Rican meals for only $10 per day. The owner, Luis Angulo, is an experienced guide who can take you to visit the Guyami community.

The South

Cooperativa CoopeUnioro
$$ fb
sb, #
☎/≈775-0033
Cooperativa
CoopeUnioro is an
interesting place, cre-
ated some years ago by
gold prospectors who
found refuge in what is
now Parque Nacional
Corcovado. Members of
the cooperative take
part in the conservation
and reforestation of
their 30ha (74.1 acres)
property. It is a good
place to learn all about
tropical biology: over
80 species of medicinal
plants are cultivated
here! A rustic little
house with two bed-
rooms is available for
groups. Another build-
ing has six very simple
rooms for rent.

Cañaza

Cañaza Lodge
$$$$ fb/pers.
sb
≈735-5045
www.canaza.com
The two cottages at
Cañaza Lodge are nes-
tled, like the rest of the
property and, in fact,
the entire peninsula, in
abundant and fascinat-
ing vegetation. These
are actually open-air
camp sites that allow
you uninterrupted con-
tact with nature! Two
wooden walls meet in
an A-frame roof with
palm thatches that were
gathered a little further
off in the garden. You
are invited to the
larger, main house for
three meals each day,
shared with your hosts
in a very convivial at-
mosphere. The owners,
Franco-Quebecers,

have been in love with
this region for ages and
work furiously at study-
ing and cultivating its
trees, plants and flow-
ers. As a result, the
grounds are full of de-
lightful discoveries to
be made while taking a
pleasant stroll. There
are quite a few possible
activities here, espe-
cially since the gulf is
so close, just on the
other side of the fruit
tree plantation.

Dos Brazos

Bosque de Río Tigre Sanctuary & Lodge
$$
sb/pb
≈735-5045
Near the Río Tigre,
Bosque de Río Tigre
Sanctuary & Lodge is a
paradise for birders.
The hiking trails in the
area allow for tranquil
exploration of the sur-
roundings, and lead to
a 15m-high (49.2ft)
waterfall. The property
has several different
buildings set up to ac-
commodate visitors,
including the main
building where there
are four rooms for rent
on the second floor

Ecological Corcovado Guest House
$$ bkfst incl.
☎775-1422
≈735-5045
Ecological Corcovado is
a bed and breakfast at
the edge of the village
of Dos Brazos. It has
well-ventilated, com-
fortable, simple rooms.
The owner, Tali
Cantena, can suggest
various outdoor activi-
ties in the area.

La Llanta Picante
$$$ fb
pb, hw
☎/≈735-5414
Near Río Tigre, La
Llanta Picante special-
izes in mountain bike
excursions. It rents
comfortable *cabinas*,
mountain bikes and
kayaks.

Puerto Jiménez

You can camp at **El
Bambú**, 1km (0.6mi)
north of Puerto
Jiménez, and at **Bosque
Mar**, a few kilometres
south of the village.
Guests of the friendly
Costa Rican owners of
the latter can roam in
the magnificent gardens
and admire the fruit
trees. A short path
leads to the beach.

Cabinas Carolina
$
pb, ℜ
☎735-5185
Also in the centre of
the village, Cabinas
Carolina rents five
clean, fairly spacious
rooms. Right next door
is its namesake, a very
popular restaurant
which is a good place
to find out about the
area.

Cabinas Eylin
$
pb, tv
☎735-5011
Slightly outside the
village, about 300m
(984ft) south of the
service station, Cabinas
Eylin rents three lovely,
inexpensive rooms.
Two of them can ac-
commodate up to four
people, while the third
is large enough for one

or two. The atmosphere is very familial and cordial. You can have coffee or meals with the owner, William, and his family.

Cabinas Marcelina
$
pb, ⊗
☎*735-5007*
⇌*735-5045*
In the village centre, Cabinas Marcelina rents plain, but clean rooms. The owner, Lidiette Franceschi, organizes horseback riding and walking excursions.

Cabinas Puerto Jiménez
$
pb, ⊗
☎*735-5090*
Near the bar-restaurant El Rancho, Cabinas Puerto Jiménez has inexpensive, clean rooms, but gets noisy on weekends.

Hotel Oro Verde
$$
pb, hw, ⊗
☎/⇌*735-5241*
In the village centre, the Hotel Oro Verde has 10 large, clean, inviting rooms. Located on the second floor, they catch whatever breeze there happens to be.

Cabinas Agua Luna
$$-$$$
pb, hw, ≡, ℝ, tv, ℜ
☎/⇌*735-5034*
One of the more luxurious places in Puerto Jiménez, Cabinas Agua Luna is the only one to provide air-conditioning. It is right next to the landing for the ferry from Golfito, and faces the ocean. The rooms

are clean and inviting. Its restaurant is 100m (328ft) towards the village centre.

🦎 Doña Leta's Bungalows
$$$
pb, hw, ⊗, K, ℜ
☎/⇌*735-5180*
Doña Leta's Bungalows are near the airport, a few minutes from the village on foot. These *cabinas* are right on the beach, near mangroves that are teeming with life. Spacious and clean, they are also equipped for cooking. A bar-restaurant, volleyball court and kayaks round out the ensemble. The guide Juan Carlos can suggest several nature discovery activities.

🦎 Iguana Lodge
$$$
pb, ⊗, ℜ
☎*735-5205*
⇌*735-5436*
www.iguana-lodge.com
Iguana Lodge rents comfortable *cabinas* near the superb Platanares beach. They are just far enough away from the bustle of Puerto Jiménez to ensure peace and quiet. The wood *cabinas* are elevated to catch the ocean breeze and have a lovely view of the seascape. The water pump, lights and fans all run on solar energy. The owners, Jeff Lantz and Stig Hanson, came here from southern California to set up a hotel for fishing and nature discovery activities. Fishing is their passion, and they will

be glad to lead excursions to all the beautiful spots around the Osa Peninsula and the Golfo Dulce on their luxurious, modern and well-equipped boat. Full board, with excellent buffet-style meals is available.

Playa Preciosa Lodge
$$$$
pb, ⊗, ℜ
☎*735-5062*
⇌*735-5043*
Six kilometres east of the airport, Playa Preciosa Lodge rents eight attractive *cabinas* that have terraces with hammocks. There is a restaurant, an orchard and a hiking trail right outside the door. The lodge organizes several types of excursions.

Cabo Matapalo

Tierra de Milagros
$$
sb
☎*233-0233*
⇌*735-5045*
About 20km (12.4mi) from Puerto Jiménez, Tierra de Milagros is a place where all sorts of "new age" activities are practiced (yoga, tai chi, etc.). The facilities are very rudimentary, which suits the owners' lifestyle. Everyone helps to prepare the vegetarian meals.

🦎 Bosque del Cabo
$$$$ fb
pb, ≈, ℜ, #
☎/⇌*735-5206*
735-5043
boscabo@racsa.co.cr
At the southern end of the peninsula, where the Pacific Ocean and

the Golfo Dulce meet, Bosque del Cabo has one of the region's most beautiful natural settings: it is lush and tranquil, and the vast grounds are superbly maintained. Lots of grass, and many flowers, plants and trees beautify the area. Hiking trails in the forest lead to a waterfall, and to the Pacific and gulf coasts. The Bosque del Cabo is well-known as a place where you can see various mammals, birds and reptiles. The seven *cabinas* are tastefully arranged, comfortable and airy. The most luxurious have solar-generated electricity and extra-large beds. The standard *cabinas* have double beds and are candle lit. All of them have views of the ocean. There is also a charming house for rent; the Casa Blanca has two bedrooms and a fully equipped kitchen. The restaurant serves local and international cuisine. Full board is available.

Hacienda Bahía Esmeralda
$$$$$ fb
pb, ⊗, ≈, ℜ
☎*381-8521*
⇌*735-5045*
francisx@racsa.co.cr
This establishment is hidden away in the tropical rainforest, on a site that looks out over the Golfo Dulce. Behind the hacienda is a stone swimming pool filled with cool water from a mountain stream. The main building has three luxurious,

large bedrooms with private bathrooms and big, orthopaedic beds. Right beside it are three comfortable *cabinas* with terraces from which you can take in the magnificent view. The cuisine is reputedly excellent and varied: Italian, Spanish, Thai, Indian, Mexican, Chinese and French dishes are on the menu, along with foods cooked on the restaurant's grill. Full board is available, including transportation to and from Puerto Jiménez.

Lapa Ríos
$$$$$ fb
pb, hw, ⊗, ≈, ℜ, #
☎*735-5130*
⇌*735-5179*
www.laparios.com
Perched more than 100m (328ft) above sea level, the 14 bungalows at Lapa Ríos provide a worry-free vacation in the middle of primary and secondary tropical rainforest. The Minnesotan couple, John and Karen Lewis, came up with the idea of Lapa Ríos, and demonstrated that ecotourism and luxury could sometimes go together! Each bungalow has a romantic atmosphere, with its thatched roof and ocean view. The main building has a circular staircase that provides a magnificent view of the Golfo Dulce. Paths in the surrounding forest allow you to experience the flora and fauna up close. Many guided tours are available.

The Carate Region

Cabins Carate Jungle Camp
$-$$
sb, #
☎*735-5211*
Cabins Carate Jungle Camp is located in the forest near Carate. This establishment rents a *cabina* with an outdoor shower and three very modest rooms that consist of double beds surrounded by mosquito netting. Full board is available, but guests are permitted to bring their own food if they wish.

Corcovado Lodge Tent Camp
$$$$ fb
sb, ℜ
☎*257-0766*
⇌*257-1655*
costaric@expeditions.co.cr
Owned by Costa Rica Expeditions, Corcovado Lodge Tent Camp is only a few minutes from Parque Nacional Corcovado on foot. Staying here is a unique experience that permits you to enter into the pristine protected natural surroundings. Significant efforts are being made to respect the environment, and the establishment in no way intrudes on its surroundings. Arriving in Carate by plane or all-terrain vehicle, guests walk along the beach for 30 or 40min to get to the camp (while a horse-drawn cart carries the luggage). Corcovado Lodge has 20 large tents (3m by 3m or 9.8ft by 9.8ft) mounted on wooden platforms

within sight of the ocean. Each airy tent contains two single beds and a small table. The platform extends onto a terrace with two chairs. Only candles are used at night, so campers are encouraged to bring flashlights for getting around after sundown. The bathrooms are a short distance away. There is no hot water for the showers, but it is hardly missed, given the stifling heat of the region.

The outdoor dining room has long tables where everyone gets together to share their day's adventures. The food is excellent, healthy and varied, although there is no menu. In the recreation hall, you can relax in hammocks, chat at the bar, or simply enjoy the view from the terrace. There are slide shows featuring the region's flora and fauna on some nights. Behind the recreation hall, a trail climbs up into the rich, dense tropical rainforest, where it is quite common to see howler monkeys, agoutis, coatis, butterflies and numerous species of birds.

You can have the experience of a lifetime in this forest: to be raised up to the top of a 40m-high (131ft) tree! Well secured to the platform, and following the directions of an experienced guide, you can observe life in the forest canopy. You can

also experience the canopy at night. The guided tour in the tropical rainforest at Parque Nacional Corcovado follows a narrow trail that goes to Río Madrigal. Experienced riders can also go horseback riding in the park.

The Lookout Inn
$$$$ fb
pb, hw, ℜ
the office is next to the Puerto Jiménez bakery
☎**735-5205**
In the mountains, just a few minutes from the Carate airport by car, The Lookout Inn rents three rooms with private bathrooms and hot water. Each room has its own balcony with a view of the Pacific, and is furnished with a large bed, a dresser and table and chairs. There is a common living room upstairs with a stereo, cassette player, tv and library. Guests have free use of kayaks, canoes, fishing gear, mountain bikes and exercise equipment.

Bahía Drake

For anyone travelling on a tight budget, **Cabinas Cecilia** *($$ fb; sb; leave a message at* ☎*771-2336)*, **Cabinas y Restaurante Jade Mar** *($$$ fb;* ☎*284-6681,* ⇝*786-6358)* and **Mirador Lodge** *($$$ fb; pb;* ☎*494-4337)* are among the least expensive accommodationsto be found.

Rancho Corcovado
$$-$$$ fb
pb, ℜ
☎**788-8111**
Rancho Corcovado rents very simple rooms near the beach. Campsites are also available for $6 per person per day, dinner included.

Cabinas Las Caletas
$$-$$$ fb
sb/pb, ℜ
☎**381-4052**
⇝**786-6291**
Cabinas Las Caletas has such a calm atmosphere that it will make you forget about the stress of daily life. Owners David and Yolanda only accept a few visitors at a time. Guests can stay in a room in the owners' house or in a *cabina* with a private bathroom and a little terrace. The menu includes Costa Rican and European specialties, and the food is prepared using fresh, homegrown ingredients.

Corcovado Adventures Tent Camp
$$$ fb
sb, ℜ
☎**223-2770**
⇝**257-4201**
Forty-five minutes on foot from Bahía Drake, Corcovado Adventures Tent Camp rents tents that have thatched roofs and are mounted on wooden platforms. Each contains a small bed, a large bed, and a small terrace. The shared bathrooms are in a separate building. Swimming, fishing, sea kayaking and surfing

are some of the activities. There is also a short trail about 30min long that goes to Río Claro close to the Marenco Lodge and Parque Nacional Corcovado.

Marenco Lodge
$$$ fb
pb, ℜ
☎ *258-1919*
⇌ *255-1346*
www.marencolodge.com
Almost mid-way between Bahía Drake and Parqe Nacional Corcovado, Marenco Lodge has been turned into a private reserve dedicated to the preservation of the tropical rainforest. It rents rustic *cabinas* and bungalows, and has a dining room and a small library. Many excursions are organized from here, which are mostly nature-oriented.

Albergue Jinetes de Osa
$$$ fb
sb/pb, ℜ
☎ *788-8111*
⇌ *253-6909*
Albergue Jinetes de Osa is located on the west coast of the bay, above the black sand beach. The inn is surrounded by fruit trees and many different flowers that attract parrots. It has nine rooms with shared or private bathrooms. Costa Rica Adventure Divers organizes various scuba diving excursions for guests here.

Cocalito Lodge
$$-$$$$
sb/pb, ℜ
☎/⇌ *786-6150*
in Canada
☎ *519-782-3978*
Cocalito Lodge is owned by Canadians Marna and Mike Berry. They have set up their establishment to live in harmony with nature. One example of this is their organic garden, where herbs and all sorts of vegetables are grown and attract many different animals. Simple, but very clean, rooms and *cabinas* are available for guests, which are lit by candles at night. There are also three fully equipped tents, and campsites (*$*). The nearby beach is completely safe for swimming. The restaurant (*5:30pm to 9pm*) has a varied menu featuring grilled foods, seafood and organic vegetables, seasoned with fresh herbs from the garden.

Casa Corcovado Jungle Lodge
$$$-$$$$ fb
sb/pb, hw, ⊗*,* ℜ*, #*
☎ *256-3181*
⇌ *256-7409*
corcovdo@racsa.co.cr
Casa Corcovado Jungle Lodge, perched high above the beach, was built by a naturalist from the United States and is close to Parque Nacional Corcovado. The rooms are attractive and comfortable, allowing for a thoroughly enjoyable stay in the tropical rainforest. There are many trails throughout the area: one of them goes to the San Pedrillo entrance of Parque Nacional Corcovado, a half-hour away. This is a wonderful place for birdwatching, photography, fishing, kayaking and scuba diving. There are organized guided tours of the national park on Isla del Caño.

Drake Bay Wilderness Camp
$$$-$$$$ fb
sb/pb, hw, ⊗*,* ℜ
☎ *284-4107*
☎/⇌ *770-8012*
Drake Bay Wilderness Camp is on the Pacific Ocean and borders on Río Agujitas. Guests can enjoy the treasures of Bahía Drake here in a convivial family atmosphere. The site has 20 attractively decorated *cabinas* with double beds, private bathrooms, and terraces overlooking the bay and the tropical rainforest. Also available are four large tents with single beds, electricity, fans and shared bathrooms. Situated right by the Pacific, the restaurant serves excellent seafood, as well as homemade breads and desserts. Many guided tours are available: forest hiking, canoeing, kayaking, scuba diving, birdwatching and fishing. The swimming pool is in a natural rock formation.

La Poloma Lodge
$$$$ fb
pb, hw, ≈, ℜ, #
☎ *239-2801*
☎/⇌ *239-0954*
gladys@lapalomalodge.com
There is a spectacular view at La Poloma Lodge. Each *cabina* with thatched roof, balcony and hammocks overlooks the ocean and enjoys the sea breezes. Larger *ranchos* that can accommodate up to five guests are also available. The hosts Sue and Mike Kalmbach offer personalized service to their clientele. Naturalist guides are pleased to share their knowledge on organized tours. Snorkelling and scuba diving are just some of the favourite activities.

Aguila de Osa Inn
$$$$ fb
pb, hw, ⊗, ℜ
☎ *296-2190*
☎/⇌ *232-7722*
www.aguiladeosa.com
The Aguila de Osa Inn claims to be the most luxurious inn on Bahía Drake. The rooms are spacious, tastefully decorated and comfortable. The restaurant is reputed for its fine international cuisine thanks to the talents of chef Edgar Coolson, nicknamed *Cookie*. Snorkeling, fishing and other organized aquatic activities are available.

The Palmar Region

Palmar Norte

Casa Amarilla
$$
pb, ⊗
Palmar Norte, in front of the soccer field
☎ *786-6251*
The best bet in Palmar is Casa Amarilla in the middle of the village. The upstairs rooms have balconies. Because it is the best place to stay in the village, it is often full. Even in low season, reservations are a good idea.

Sierpe

Hotel Pargo
$$
pb, hw, ⊗, ≡, ℜ
☎ *788-8111*
⇌ *788-8251*
Hotel Pargo in Sierpe is a good place to stay near Bahía Drake. Parking is free for guests who are spending a few days at the bay. All the rooms at the hotel have both a single and a double bed. Those on the second floor have a view of the village and the river. The hotel has boats for all sorts of aquatic activities, as well as for transportation.

Río Sierpe Lodge
$$$$ fb
pb, hw, ⊗, ℜ
☎ *284-5595*
Like Mapache Lodge (see below), Río Sierpe Lodge is only accessible by boat. This place is also situated right in the middle of the area's

hiking trails. There are some 20 large, plain rooms, and lots of organized activities, including everything from fishing and scuba diving to hiking in Parque Nacional Corcovado and horseback riding. The birdwatching excursions to the Caño and Violines Islands are especially popular. Full board is available including transportation to and from Sierpe.

Eco-Manglares Lodge
$$$$ bkfst incl.
pb, hw, ℜ
☎ *296-1362 or 778-8111*
Two kilometres before the village of Sierpe, on the banks of Río Estero Azul, Eco-Manglares Lodge rents truly charming rustic *cabinas*. They are well ventilated, comfortable and have little terraces. The restaurant serves Italian food. There are hiking trails throughout the neighbouring forest. The lodge also organizes river excursions.

Estero Azul Lodge
$$$$ fb
pb, hw, ⊗, ℜ
☎ *788-8111*
⇌ *788-8251*
Very close to Eco-Manglares Lodge, Estero Azul Lodge also rents attractive wooden *cabinas* that are well set up and can accommodate up to four people. The restaurant near the *cabinas* serves local fish and seafood dishes. A 6m-long (19.7ft) boat takes guests on excursions on the river and to the Pacific coast.

Mapache Lodge
$$$$$ fb
sb, pb, tv, ≈, ℜ
☎ *786-6565 or 788-8111*
⇆ *768-6358*
mapache@greenarrow.com
Located about 12km (7.5mi) from Sierpe and only accessible by boat, Mapache Lodge is on 45ha (111 acres) of unspoiled land at the mouth of Río Toboga. Three types of lodgings are available: two rooms with private bathroom in the owners', Guilio and Giuseppina's, house; three rooms with shared bath; and large tents on wooden platforms. The restaurant serves Italian dishes, including pasta and seafood. Guests can stroll on the little trails and observe some of the 160 identified bird species. Among the suggested activities are horseback riding, kayaking and hiking. Full board includes transportation to and from Sierpe.

The Golfito Region

Casa Blanca Lodge
$
pb
300m (984ft) south of Depósito Libre, Golfito
☎ *775-0124*
Casa Blanca Lodge rents little rooms that are only furnished with a bed, on the second floor of a house that is set back from the road by its grounds, somewhat like the Princesa del Golfo (see further below). There are also some rental units in a motel-style building on the property, which are more modern and more expensive. This is a peaceful, shady place.

Cabinas Isabel
$
pb, ⊗
downtown Golfito
☎ *775-1774*
Cabinas Isabel rents small rooms with nothing more than beds in them, but the little building itself has charm. There is a cozy common living room on the second floor. The rooms are on both floors of the building, but all the windows open onto an indoor hallway.

Cabinas y Restaurante Mar y Luna
$
sb
where Golfito begins
☎ *775-0192*
⇆ *775-1049*
Cabinas y Restaurante Mar y Luna rents little rooms that only have beds in them and a common terrace, in a building on the gulf.

Cabinas El Tucán
$
pb, ⊗
across from the Los Bruncas stadium, Golfito
☎ *775-0553*
Cabinas El Tucán rents small rooms with a bathroom and a window with a view. They are pretty basic, but clean. In fact, the place prides itself on the cleanliness of its rooms!

Delfina
$
200m (656ft) south of the quay, Pueblo Civil, Golfito
Delfina is another of the many small-town hotels in the Golfito region. It has small rooms on the upper floor of a wooden building. The hotel looks out onto the gulf, but some of the surrounding buildings block the view from certain rooms.

Hotel Golfito
$
pb, ⊗
25m (82ft) south of the municipal dock, Golfito
The rooms at Hotel Golfito are laid out along the perimeter of a wooden building on the gulf, but you can't see much through the frosted glass windows. Only the bathroom window has a view! Also, the bedrooms contain nothing more than a bed and the reception is lukewarm.

Princesa del Golfo
$
pb, ⊗
diagonally across from the Banco Nacional building, Golfito
The rooms at Princesa del Golfo are in the owners' home, former residents of the United States. What makes this place so special is that it is located on extensive grounds that remove it from the rest of town. Rooms on the main floor have private entrances. The furnishings are minimal: a bed and a bathroom.

Purruja Lodge
$$
pb, ℜ
Golfito
☎/⇌ 775-1054
Purruja Lodge has a family-like atmosphere. The two small rooms are nothing spectacular, but they are in a separate *casita* with a shared terrace. The landscaping is attractive, and there is a restaurant on the premises.

Hotel Costa Rica
$$
hw, sb/pb, ≡, ⊗
Pueblo Civil, Golfito
☎/⇌ 775-0034
Hotel Costa Rica is another of those small-town hotels where rooms open onto an inside corridor. However, some of the rooms have air-conditioning, which is something to keep in mind in Golfito's heat.

El Gran Ceibo
$$$
pb, hw, ≡, ⊗, ℜ, *tv*, ≈
on the way into Golfito
☎/⇌ 775-0403
El Gran Ceibo is one of the few hotels in the city of Golfito that has a swimming pool and other modern comforts that make it appropriate for a stay of more than one day. The rooms are clean and reasonably well arranged.

Cabinas Los Cocos
$$$
hw, pb, K, ⊗
Playa Zancudo
☎ 776-0012
Cabinas Los Cocos rents four *cabinas* with small gardens that have

the ocean as a front yard. These cottages have covered verandas with hammocks. They offer many guided tours in the region. A taxi-boat picks up guests in Golfito.

Cabinas Sol y Mar
$$$
pb, hw, ⊗
25min on foot south of Playa Zancudo
☎ 776-0014
⇌ 776-0015
Cabinas Sol y Mar consists of four seaside *cabinas*. There is also a little three-storey house, with a kitchen that can accommodate six people.

Golfo Azul
$$$
hw, pb, ℜ
Depósito Libre, Golfito
☎ 775-0871
⇌ 775-1849
Golfo Azul is a hotel-restaurant. The rooms are in a modern, motel-style building behind the large restaurant. The landscaping looks like a parking lot. The rooms are standard in size and share a common porch along the front of the building.

Centro Turístico Samoa del Sur
$$$
pb, tv, ℜ
Golfito
☎ 775-0233 or 775-0573
The French-owned Centro Turístico Samoa del Sur is a tourist centre and hotel, located on the banks of the gulf. The rooms share terraces and are in a motel-style building that extends out over

the water. The building is above average in quality for this area: it is very clean, and the furniture is modern. The grounds are quite large (considering that this is the most urbanized area of Golfito). The buildings are set back from the street and are well spaced amid tasteful landscaping. This is a good place to stay compared to others in the area, and its restaurant adds a lot to its value (see p 395).

Las Gaviotas
$$$
hw, pb, tv, ≡, ≈, *K*, ℜ
at the beginning of Golfito
☎ 775-0062
⇌ 775-0544
Las Gaviotas is one of the best places to stay in Golfito. There are three bungalows (with kitchenettes) and 18 rooms on a well-landscaped, shady lot. While the rooms are in a long, motel-style building, each has a large, private terrace, which is a plus. Need we say how much the swimming pools were appreciated? The restaurant is also one of the best in town (see p 395).

☘ Esquinas Lodge
$$$$$ *fb*
pb, hw, ⊗, ℜ
La Gamba, 4km (2.5mi) from Km 37 on the Interamericana, near Golfito
☎ 775-0631
⇌ 775-0131
Esquinas Lodge is a genuine ecotourism resort. The lodge was developed by the Aus-

trian government as an experiment combining research, nature conservation and sustainable development. All profits from the resort go towards environmental conservation and back into the community. It is in a beautiful setting, with wood architecture and landscaping that blends perfectly into the natural surroundings. The main building is open on all sides, and the restaurant and common areas are very relaxing. The *cabinas* access a veranda with a bamboo rocking chair. The menu is international with a slight emphasis on Viennese cuisine. The swimming pool is fed by a clear, natural pond and a stream, and there are also some orchards on the property. A network of trails leads to caves and waterfalls hidden away in the tropical rainforest. There is free airport pick-up for guests, but reservations must be made for this in advance. If you are driving, note that the road is not always in good condition, but a four-wheel drive vehicle is not necessary. The room rate includes an excursion to Piedras Blancas.

The Ciudad Neily Region

Andrea
$$$
⊗, ≡ , *pb*
Ciudad Neily
☎/⇋ **783-3784 or 783-5240**
If it weren't for the lack of a swimming pool (a necessity in this region), Andrea would be the best hotel in Ciudad Neily. The rooms are clean and pretty, with a bright, fresh look, in a building with front porches that extend along the entire length of both floors. The grounds are spacious and well maintained. There is one other disadvantage, however: only two of the rooms have hot water (a slight problem) and air-conditioning (disastrous!).

Centro Turístico Neily
$$$
≈, ≡, ℜ
Ciudad Neily
☎ **783-3301**
Centro Turístico Neily rents 20 motel-style units in a rather ordinary building: average-sized rooms, view of the back of the property, not much of a terrace. However, the well landscaped, shady grounds include two swimming pools (a blessing!), a restaurant and a night club.

The San Vito Region

Centro Turístico Las Huacas
$
hw, pb
on the way into San Vito, on the Coto Brus road
☎ **773-3115**
Centro Turístico Las Huacas is a community centre that functions as a bar and night club on weekends and has rooms for rent as well. The typically Costa Rican-style rooms are relatively clean; but the only furniture in the bedrooms is the bed.

Hotel Rino
$
hw, pb
Al Pizar commercial centre, downtown, San Vito
☎ **773-3071**
Hotel Rino is a tiny hotel with clean rooms.

El Ceibo
$$
pb, hw, ctv, ℜ
a few steps away from the municipal hall, San Vito
☎ **773-3025**
One of the best hotels in San Vito is the Italian-owned El Ceibo. The rooms open onto a small wooded area in back of the property (via a very small door), and have little, Italian-style balconies. They are very simply set up and not overly large, but clean. The hotel is partially hidden by a screen of vegetation (on the road that runs east of the main intersection), so be careful not to miss it.

Wilson Botanical Garden
$$$$$ fb
pb, hw
reservations through the "Organization for Tropical Studies"
☎*240-6696*
⇆*240-6783*
You can stay overnight at the Wilson Botanical Garden. In fact, it is one of the best places to stay in the area. The *cabinas* are lovely and impeccably clean, and the view from their windows is magnificent. A peaceful stay in the middle of the garden, and good food are guaranteed. In short, it's paradise! There are even two rooms specially equipped for disabled travellers. Reservations must be made early in the season, because this place is very popular.

La Amistad Lodge
$$$$$ fb
sb/pb, hw
about 3km (1.9mi) from Las Mellizas, northeast of San Vito
☎*233-8228 or 773-3193*
La Amistad Lodge is probably the hotel most off the tourist-beaten path in Costa Rica. It is near the Panamanian border northwest of San Vito, near the little village of Las Mellizas. If you don't have a four-wheel drive vehicle, you might have to walk part of the way there. La Amistad is a family-owned lodge that was established to integrate ecotourism into the park. Thanks to the many trails and excellent guides, this is a great place to learn more about the flora

and fauna that grows at this altitude of the primary forest. In fact, full board includes a guided tour. Part of the land is used to grow organic coffee. The combination of these two activities makes for an interesting and pleasant stay. The rooms are clean and simple.

Restaurants

The San Isidro de El General Region

Cerro de la Muerte

Los Chespiritos
$$
in the neighbourhood of Ojo de Agua, about 2km (1.2mi) north of the road to San Gerardo de Dota, Cerro La Muerte
Los Chespiritos is a cafeteria that also serves as an *abastecedor* (convenience store). Its fruits and ready-to-eat treats (candies, marinated and conserved foods, etc.) are greatly appreciated by anyone stopping here between the Central Valley and San Isidro de El General. You can also buy souvenirs here. This clean and lively place is particularly welcoming in the chilly heights of Cerro de la Muerte.

Mirador Vista del Valle
$$
Km 119 on the Interamericana Hwy., Cerro de la Muerte
☎*284-4685*
⇆*771-2003*
In addition to having a unique view of the Valle del General, Mirador Vista del Valle serves typical Costa Rican food, and fresh trout is on the menu every day. You can also do some birdwatching, contemplate the restaurant's orchids, or shop for handicrafts.

San Gerardo de Dota

Los Lagos
$$
☎*771-2077*
At San Gerardo de Dota, Los Lagos is a charming restaurant whose menu features fresh trout from the area's many rivers. Breakfast is also served. Although the large dining room is quite plain, the restaurant's surroundings are spectacular, with the Río Savegre running right next to it. A fountain completes the attractive setting.

San Isidro de El General

Soda El Jardín
$
San Isidro
☎*771-0349*
Soda El Jardín has the same name as the hotel, and serves good fast food, Costa Rican-style. You will recognize the restaurant by

its orange tables and chairs.

The Rivas Region

San Gerardo de Rivas

Soda Don Ulysses
$
Almost at the foot of the trail that comes tumbling down from the Cerro Chirripó, this little *soda* can be a godsend! In a breathtaking setting at the end of an impossible road, this little snack bar with its shared tables with flower-printed, plastic tablecloths makes for a marvellous stop. Don Ulysses, with many years and several ascents of the *cerro* behind him, adds authenticity to the setting. He will regale you with his stories, if you're so inclined and can follow his accent. Since the *soda* doubles as a *pulperia*, you can also pick up some supplies here. Should you come by car, you can park it in front for a small fee during your ramble in the park.

The Dominical Region

Kardigui
$
Kardigui is an inviting *tico*-style restaurant-bar situated on the ocean between Uvita and Dominical. It serves Costa Rican dishes at reasonable prices. The building has large open spaces with a red metal roof over the bar.

Soda Nanyoa
$
Dominical
Soda Nanyoa serves inexpensive *tico* food. The setting is also typically Costa Rican.

Thrusters
$$
The favourite hangout of the many surfers who camp in the region, bar-restaurant Thrusters's food is designed to satisfy them. The menu lists Mexican dishes, side-by-side with the ubiquitous hamburger. Yet all of it tastes quite good.

Punta Dominical
$$
4km (2.5mi) south of Dominical
☎787-0016
≈787-0017
Right beside the cabinas of the same name, the restaurant-bar Punta Dominical is a great place to go at sundown to savour Costa Rican or international food, or simply for a drink. The stereo-like sound of the sea lapping against the shores of the narrow point on which the restaurant is built is especially soothing and distinct at night.

San Clemente Bar & Grill
$$
every day, 7am to 9pm
Dominical
With the same owners as the Cabinas San Clemente, which are on the sea, this place serves *tico* and North American cuisine, with grilled food as the house specialty. On Saturdays, the restaurant turns into a bar and nightclub. The atmosphere is very relaxed, with board games and billiards and a satellite television that shows all kinds of sports. Together with Thrusters, the San Clemente Bar & Grill is the place to go in the evenings in Dominical.

La Campanna
$$-$$$
☎787-0072
Seemingly in the middle of nowhere, where you'd hardly expect to have a feast, La Campanna comes as a pleasant surprise. This Italian restaurant, run by three friendly Italian travellers, who have drifted all the way here, is not to be missed if you are staying near Dominical. A thatched-palm roof shelters a few wooden tables set up in front of an open kitchen. Candles burn, melting into different shapes beside pretty napkin holders on the tables. The atmosphere here leads to relaxed conversation and stretching out the evening. Behind the kitchen counter, the chef Fabio creates carefully prepared and tastefully presented cuisine: pizza, fish, meats—including delicious scallopini—and pasta—including divine vegetarian lasagne with *pesto* sauce—that will delight your tastebuds. There are even small

pieces of garlic *pita* to munch on.

La Costanera Sur

Ojochal

As previously mentioned, Ojochal harbours a large community of French-speakers from Europe, Québec and the Caribbean. Imagine what happens when all these people decide to open restaurants! You'll find such a high density of good restaurants in this small village that you should already be planing to stay here for a few days...

Ask residents to reveal the location of the **Frank Bakery**, a great place to buy bread.

El Gringo Mike's Pizza & Café
$$
El Gringo Mike's Pizza & Café is where vacationers from around Playa Tortuga go in the evenings. You've guessed it, Gringo Mike's serves pizza and other typical North American fast food. Mike, the owner, has lived in the area for years and can tell you what there is to see.

Rancho Soluna
$$
Ojochal
☎ **788-8210**
The little Rancho Soluna is both a restaurant and a small inn (see p 380) to which the owners, Léo and Michèle originally from

Québec, devote much time and energy. The cozy, relaxed restaurant serves spaghetti, pizza, hamburgers, and even *poutine*, as well as delicious North American desserts prepared by Michèle. An ideal place to feel at home away from home!

Chez Elle
$$
The owner, originally from Brittany, makes lovely, thin crepes that are browned to perfection and delicious, despite the absence of buckwheat flour. Savoury (*à la florentine*, *forestière*, seafood) or sweet (caramelized fruit, *flambé* with rum, and so on) all will brighten up your day. Especially since the *crêperie's* few tables are set in extraordinary surroundings, overlooking a small stream in the middle of a luxuriant garden. Moreover, it's in this garden that the cook's husband gathers the condiments used to make the presentation of your meal as beautiful as it is fragrant.

Dulce Lucy
$$
Located beside the road, Quebecer Robert Gravel's establishment in Ojochal attracts a lot of people. Of course, the location and the Internet services he provides for the customers have something to do with this, but people come here mainly because of the appetizing menu. This

very small establishment, consisting of a counter and three or four tables on the terrace, serves an extensive selection. *Baguette* sandwiches served with chips (fries), pita sandwiches, thin-crust pizza and even hot dishes— everything displays originality and, above all, precision in choosing the perfect ingredient to improve the taste. And you'll be amazed by the variety of these ingredients! Have a good, cold Belgian beer to go with whatever you choose, and *Bon appétit!*

🍴 Exo-Tica
$$$
Like many establishments in Ojochal, El Complejo Diquis recently changed hands. In this case, it was a very lucky transaction, since it has brought the restaurant, Exo-Tica, a remarkable chef: Marcella, a multinational who has worked in many different places around the world. You'd never suspect from the restaurant's decor and location that such a gem is hiding here. Seated on plastic furniture set up beside the pool, you'll be served dishes whose composition will delight you. These dishes, inspired both by the local ingredients and by ideas that Marcella has collected in her travels, reveal a great deal of finesse. Spicy tomato–mango *gaspacho*, avocado–pineapple salad, chicken breasts with

prunes and cream sauce, fish fillets served in various ways (such as covered with a banana curry sauce), bouillabaisse seasoned with a touch of coconut milk—all are a real treat! Expect some difficulty limiting your order to the amount you can eat, but very likely, none of the dishes will disappoint you. Service is also very thoughtful.

Último Refugio
$$$
500m (1,640ft) south of the elementary school in Ojochal
☏**786-6358**
The Québec-run Último Refugio comprises rooms, a restaurant and a souvenir shop. A very pleasant and charming place tucked away amidst the greenery.

The Osa Peninsula

Because getting around is rather difficult on the Osa Peninsula, most hotels, inns and *cabinas* have their own dining rooms for their guests, and sometimes for people just travelling through, as well. Most restaurants, as well as several excellent, inexpensive small *sodas*, are found in Puerto Jiménez.

Puerto Jiménez Region

Ventana al Golfo
$
On the road just before Rincón, when coming from the mainland, there is a house high on your right. This is

the location of the friendly and very aptly named restaurant, Ventana al Golfo (gulf window), with a beautiful view of the gulf from its terrace. It serves the usual Costa Rican *soda* fare.

Sabores del Golfo
$
every day, 6am to 9pm
South of La Palma, towards Puerto Jiménez, Sabores del Golfo serves excellent and inexpensive local food in a family atmosphere.

Puerto Jiménez

Jardín del Buho
$
At the entrance to the village, Jardín del Buho is tucked away in a house at the end of an alley. Its appeal is enhanced by white wicker furniture and plants. The menu (presented on file folders!) features meat and fish dishes prepared in typical Costa Rican style.

Agua Luna
$-$$
☏**735-5034**
Agua Luna is situated opposite the Golfo Dulce, right beside the Cacao stream, near where the ferry from Golfito lands. Excellent local and international food is prepared at this very large, airy restaurant; the seafood is especially good.

Carolina
$-$$
every day, 7am to 8pm
In the heart of Puerto Jiménez, the Carolina

restaurant-bar is rarely empty. Drop by for a soft drink, a coffee or a beer, to chat with friends or simply pass the time. The Escondido Trex tourist agency is situated at the back of the restaurant. The food is excellent, varied and reasonably priced.

Jossette
$-$$
☏**735-5227**
Also on the main street, Jossette is a *soda* and restaurant that serves grilled food, seafood and Chinese food, as well as fast food dishes.

The Palmar Region

There are two reasonably priced restaurants at the crossroads of the Interamericana Highway and the road to Puerto Jiménez, on the way from Palmar to Golfito or Ciudad Neily: **Corcovado** and **Carratera Chacarita**.

The Golfito Region

La Dama del Delfín
☏**775-0235**
☏**775-0042**
At Golfito, good daily specials for under $5 are served at La Dama del Delfín restaurant and souvenir shop. The place has a good view of Golfito's Pueblo Civil district and of the gulf itself. The owner can give you all kinds of information about the area.

El Barco

$

Golfito

El Barco is a friendly little *soda*, with *tico* prices.

La Cazuelita

$$

200m (656ft) west of Depósito Libre, Golfito

☎775-1621

La Cazuelita serves Chinese food in a simple, friendly setting.

La Eurekita

$$

Golfito

☎775-1616

The little La Eurekita restaurant is open on two sides, so it has views of both the gulf and the main streets of Golfito's Pueblo Civil. Costa Rican dishes and fast food are served in a friendly atmosphere. One of the largest restaurants in Pueblo Civil, it is also one of the busiest at noon.

Las Gaviotas

$$

as you enter Golfito

☎775-0062

≈775-0544

The restaurant of the hotel Las Gaviotas is a very good seafood restaurant. Built outside but with an overhead covering, its open-air setting is very pleasant, and the view of the bay is marvellous.

Centro Turístico Samoa del Sur

$$$

Golfito

☎775-0233

≈775-0573

Centro Turístico Samoa del Sur is a restaurant-bar next to the hotel of the same name (see p 389). The food here is very good (pizza, seafood and *tico* dishes; try the *ceviche* or the *patacones con frijoles molidos*). The atmosphere under the large, inviting shelter is lively in the evenings, and you can have a drink while the TV and video compete for your attention. This is also a good place to sip delicious fruit juices in the late afternoon.

The Ciudad Neily Region

Soda La Cuchara de Margoth

$

Ciudad Neily

On the banks of a small river running through the city, Soda La Cuchara de Margoth is a very pretty, pleasant place for a light meal.

Soda El Parque

$

Cuidad Neily

Soda El Parque is a little closer to the centre of town than La Cuchara de Margoth. A clean place where the beautiful white tablecloths are covered with plastic. Costa Rican cuisine.

La Moderna

$$

Ciudad Neily

☎783-3097

La Moderna is one of the best restaurants in Ciudad Neily, with a varied menu that lists both *tico* and international dishes.

The San Vito Region

There are two prosperous and highly respected Italian restaurants in San Vito: **Mamma Mia** (*$$*) and **Liliana** (*$$*). Both are good, with slightly Italian decor.

Restaurant Neily

$$

San Vito

For *tico* cooking, Restaurant Neily is highly recommended by the citizens of San Vito. The dining room is very clean, and its layout is simple but inviting.

Jimar

$$

San Vito

Jimar is a similar restaurant that is also very popular. The animated little terrace has a beautiful view of the surrounding area.

El Ceibo

$$

near the municipal building, San Vito

☎773-3025

The restaurant of the hotel El Ceibo is owned by an Italian and serves decent Italian and *tico* food in a plain setting—with a television droning in the background, of course!

Entertainment

Bars and Nightclubs

The Dominical Region

Dominical

Thrusters bar-restaurant serves as a rallying point for the region's surfers, who come to have a drink while chatting at the bar or playing pool. You can encounter the species here every night, recounting the feats of the day.

Shopping

The Dominical Region

Dominical

Dos Hermanos
right at the exit to town from the hwy. going to Uvita
In Dominical, Dos Hermanos is a supermarket located in the Plaza Pacifica shopping centre that is perched on top of a little hill.

Bowing to the requirements of the village's vocation, the **Funky Orchid** is basically a surf shop. You'll also find a variety of souvenirs here.

La Costanera Sur

Ojochal

Ultimo Refugio
500m (1,640ft) south of the elementary school in Ojochal
In Ojochal, Ultimo Refugio is the place to buy yourself presents from this region.

The Palmar Region

Tonio is a little *abastecedor* (a kind of convenience store) in Palmar Norte, not far from the Interamericana Highway. The owners of the inns and restaurants in the area shop here for supplies. Tonio sells different and exotic local products.

The Golfito Region

Southern Costa Rica has a zone known as "free port" where you can buy all kinds of consumer goods for a little less than elsewhere in the country.

This area was established in 1990, in Golfito's **Depósito Libre** district. However, there is an entrance fee to shop in the district. It is best to visit the Depósito Libre during the week, because the place— including hotels—becomes very crowded on weekends, when many Costa Ricans go there to shop, lured by the discounts. All sorts of products are sold in the Depósito Libre, and you will notice more and more billboards advertising the merits of this or that product as you approach the city of Golfito.

The San Vito Region

English-language magazines are available at **Librería La Cruz**, in the centre of San Vito.

Mangrove

Glossary

CONSONANTS

b   Is pronounced b or sometimes a soft v, depending on the region or the person: *bizcocho* (biz-koh-choh or viz-koh-choh).

c   As in English, c is pronounced as s before *i* and *e*: *cerro* (seh-rroh). When it is placed in front of other vowels, it is hard and pronounced as k: *carro* (kah-rroh). The c is also hard when it comes before a consonant, except before an *h* (see further below).

d   Is pronounced like a soft d: *dar* (dahr). *D* is usually not pronounced when at the end of a word.

g   As with the *c*, *g* is soft before an *i* or an *e*, and is pronounced like a soft h: *gente* (hente). In front of other vowels and consonants, the *g* is hard: *golf* (pronounced the same way as in English).

ch   Pronounced ch, as in English: *leche* (le-che). Like the *ll*, this combination is considered a single letter in the Spanish alphabet, listed separately in dictionaries and telephone directories.

h   Is not pronounced: *hora* (oh-ra).

j   Is pronounced like a guttural h, as in "him."

ll   Is pronounced like a hard y, as in "yes": *llamar* (yah-mar). In some regions, such as central Colombia, *ll* is pronounced as a soft g, as in "mirage" (*Medellín* is pronounced Medegin). Like the *ch*, this combination is considered a single letter in the Spanish alphabet, and is listed separately in dictionaries and telephone directories.

ñ   Is pronounced like the ni in "onion," or the ny in "canyon": *señora* (seh-nyo-rah).

qu   Is pronounced k: *aquí* (ah-kee).

r   Is rolled, as the Irish or Italian pronunciation of r.

s   Is always pronounced s like "sign": *casa* (cah-ssah).

v   Is pronounced like a b: *vino* (bee-noh).

z   Is pronounced like s: *paz* (pahss).

VOWELS

a   Is always pronounced ah as in "part", and never *ay* as in "day": *faro* (fah-roh).

e   Is pronounced eh as in "elf," and never *ey* as in "grey or "ee" as in "key": *helado* (eh-lah-doh].

i   Is always pronounced ee: *cine* (see-neh).

o   Is always pronounced oh as in "cone": *copa* (koh-pah).

u   Is always pronounced oo: *universidad* (oo-nee-ver-see-dah).

All other letters are pronounced the same as in English.

STRESSING SYLLABLES

In Spanish, syllables are differently stressed. This stress is very important, and emphasizing the right syllable might even be necessary to make yourself understood. If a vowel has an accent, this syllable is the one that should be stressed. If there is no accent, follow this rule:

Stress the second-last syllable of any word that ends with a vowel: *amigo*.

Stress the last syllable of any word that ends in a consonant, except for s (plural of nouns and adjectives) or n (plural of nouns): *usted* (but *amigos, hablan*).

GREETINGS

Goodbye	*adiós, hasta luego*
Good afternoon and good evening	*buenas tardes*
Hi (casual)	*hola*
Good morning	*buenos días*
Good night	*buenas noches*
Thank-you	*gracias*
Please	*por favor*
You are welcome	*de nada*
Excuse me	*perdone/a*
My name is...	*mi nombre es...*
What is your name?	*¿cómo se llama usted?*
no/yes	*no/sí*
Do you speak English?	*¿habla usted inglés?*
Slower, please	*más despacio, por favor*
I am sorry, I don't speak Spanish	*Lo siento, no hablo español*
How are you?	*¿qué tal?*
I am fine	*estoy bien*
I am American (male/female)	*Soy estadounidense*
I am Australian	*Soy autraliano/a*
I am Belgian	*Soy belga*
I am British (male/female)	*Soy británico/a*
I am Canadian	*Soy canadiense*
I am German (male/female)	*Soy alemán/a*
I am Italian (male/female)	*Soy italiano/a*
I am Swiss	*Soy suizo*
I am a tourist	*Soy turista*
single (m/f)	*soltero/a*
divorced (m/f)	*divorciado/a*
married (m/f)	*casado/a*
friend (m/f)	*amigo/a*
child (m/f)	*niño/a*
husband, wife	*esposo/a*
mother, father	*madre, padre*
brother, sister	*hermano/a*
widower widow	*viudo/a*
I am hungry	*tengo hambre*
I am ill	*estoy enfermo/a*

| I am thirsty | tengo sed |

DIRECTIONS

beside	al lado de
to the right	a la derecha
to the left	a la izquierda
here, there	aquí, allí
into, inside	dentro
outside	fuera
behind	detrás
in front of	delante
between	entre
far from	lejos de
Where is ... ?	¿dónde está ... ?
To get to ...?	¿para ir a...?
near	cerca de
straight ahead	todo recto

MONEY

money	dinero / plata
credit card	tarjeta de crédito
exchange	cambio
traveller's cheque	cheque de viaje
I don't have any money	no tengo dinero
The bill, please	la cuenta, por favor
receipt	recibo

SHOPPING

store	tienda
market	mercado
open, closed	abierto/a, cerrado/a
How much is this?	¿cuánto es?
to buy, to sell	comprar, vender
the customer	el / la cliente
salesman	vendedor
saleswoman	vendedora
I need...	necesito...
I would like...	yo quisiera...
batteries	pilas
blouse	blusa
cameras	cámaras
cosmetics and perfumes	cosméticos y perfumes
cotton	algodón
dress jacket	saco
eyeglasses	lentes, gafas
fabric	tela
film	película
gifts	regalos
gold	oro
handbag	bolsa
hat	sombrero
jewellery	joyería
leather	cuero, piel
local crafts	artesanía
magazines	revistas
newpapers	periódicos
pants	pantalones

records, cassettes	discos, casetas
sandals	sandalias
shirt	camisa
shoes	zapatos
silver	plata
skirt	falda
sun screen products	productos solares
T-shirt	camiseta
watch	reloj
wool	lana

MISCELLANEOUS

a little	poco
a lot	mucho
good (m/f)	bueno/a
bad (m/f)	malo/a
beautiful (m/f)	hermoso/a
pretty (m/f)	bonito/a
ugly	feo
big	grande
tall (m/f)	alto/a
small (m/f)	pequeño/a
short (length) (m/f)	corto/a
short (person) (m/f)	bajo/a
cold (m/f)	frío/a
hot	caliente
dark (m/f)	oscuro/a
light (colour)	claro
do not touch	no tocar
expensive (m/f)	caro/a
cheap (m/f)	barato/a
fat (m/f)	gordo/a
slim, skinny (m/f)	delgado/a
heavy (m/f)	pesado/a
light (weight) (m/f)	ligero/a
less	menos
more	más
narrow (m/f)	estrecho/a
wide (m/f)	ancho/a
new (m/f)	nuevo/a
old (m/f)	viejo/a
nothing	nada
something (m/f)	algo/a
quickly	rápidamente
slowly (m/f)	despacio/a
What is this?	¿qué es esto?
when?	¿cuando?
where?	¿dónde?

TIME

in the afternoon, early evening	por la tarde
at night	por la noche
in the daytime	por el día
in the morning	por la mañana
minute	minuto
month	mes
ever	jamás

never	*nunca*
now	*ahora*
today	*hoy*
yesterday	*ayer*
tomorrow	*mañana*
What time is it?	*¿qué hora es?*
hour	*hora*
week	*semana*
year	*año*
Sunday	*domingo*
Monday	*lunes*
Tuesday	*martes*
Wednesday	*miércoles*
Thursday	*jueves*
Friday	*viernes*
Saturday	*sábado*
January	*enero*
February	*febrero*
March	*marzo*
April	*abril*
May	*mayo*
June	*junio*
July	*julio*
August	*agosto*
September	*septiembre*
October	*octubre*
November	*noviembre*
December	*diciembre*

WEATHER

It is cold	*hace frío*
It is warm	*hace calor*
It is very hot	hace mucho calor
sun	*sol*
It is sunny	hace sol
It is cloudy	*está nublado*
rain	*lluvia*
It is raining	*está lloviendo*
wind	*viento*
It is windy	*hay viento*
snow	*nieve*
damp	*húmedo*
dry	*seco*
storm	*tormenta*
hurricane	*huracán*

COMMUNICATION

air mail	*correos aéreo*
collect call	*llamada por cobrar*
dial the number	*marcar el número*
area code, country code	*código*
envelope	*sobre*
long distance	*larga distancia*
post office	*correo*
rate	*tarifa*
stamps	*estampillas*
telegram	*telegrama*

| telephone book | un guia telefónica |
| wait for the tone | esperar la señal |

ACTIVITIES

beach	playa
museum or gallery	museo
scuba diving	buceo
to swim	bañarse
to walk around	pasear
hiking	caminata
trail	pista, sendero
cycling	ciclismo
fishing	pesca

TRANSPORTATION

arrival, departure	llegada, salida
on time	a tiempo
cancelled (m/f)	anulado/a
one way ticket	ida
return	regreso
round trip	ida y vuelta
schedule	horario
baggage	equipajes
north, south	norte, sur
east, west	este, oeste
avenue	avenida
street	calle
highway	carretera
expressway	autopista
airplane	avión
airport	aeropuerto
bicycle	bicicleta
boat	barco
bus	bus
bus stop	parada
bus terminal	terminal
train	tren
train crossing	crucero ferrocarril
station	estación
neighbourhood	barrio
collective taxi	colectivo
corner	esquina
express	rápido
safe	seguro/a
be careful	cuidado
car	coche, carro
To rent a car	alquilar un auto
gas	gasolina
gas station	gasolinera
no parking	no estacionar
no passing	no adelantar
parking	parqueo
pedestrian	peaton
road closed, no through traffic	no hay paso
slow down	reduzca velocidad
speed limit	velocidad permitida
stop	alto

stop! (an order)
traffic light

pare
semáforo

ACCOMMODATION
cabin, bungalow
accommodation
double, for two people
single, for one person
high season
low season
bed
floor (first, second...)
main floor
manager
double bed
cot
bathroom
with private bathroom
hot water
breakfast
elevator
air conditioning
fan
pool
room

cabaña
alojamiento
doble
sencillo
temporada alta
temporada baja
cama
piso
planta baja
gerente, jefe
cama matrimonial
camita
baños
con baño privado
agua caliente
desayuno
ascensor
aire acondicionado
ventilador, abanico
piscina, alberca
habitación

NUMBERS

1	uno	30	treinta
2	dos	31	treinta y uno
3	tres	32	treinta y dos
4	cuatro	40	cuarenta
5	cinco	50	cincuenta
6	seis	60	sesenta
7	siete	70	setenta
8	ocho	80	ochenta
9	nueve	90	noventa
10	diez	100	cien
11	once	101	ciento uno
12	doce	102	ciento dos
13	trece	200	doscientos
14	catorce	300	trescientos
15	quince	400	quatrocientoa
16	dieciséis	500	quinientos
17	diecisiete	600	seiscientos
18	dieciocho	700	sietecientos
19	diecinueve	800	ochocientos
20	veinte	900	novecientos
21	veintiuno	1,000	mil
22	veintidós	1,100	mil cien
23	veintitrés	1,200	mil doscientos
24	veinticuatro	2000	dos mil
25	veinticinco	3000	tres mil
26	veintiséis	10,000	diez mil
27	veintisiete	100,000	cien mil
28	veintiocho	1,000,000	un millón
29	veintinueve		

Glossary

Index

Index

Index

Index

Index

Order Form

Ulysses Travel Guides

☐ Atlantic Canada .... $24.95 CAN $17.95 US	☐ Louisiana .... $29.95 CAN $21.95 US
☐ Bahamas .... $24.95 CAN $17.95 US	☐ Martinique .... $24.95 CAN $17.95 US
☐ Beaches of Maine .... $12.95 CAN $9.95 US	☐ Montréal .... $19.95 CAN $14.95 US
☐ Bed & Breakfasts .... $14.95 CAN in Québec $10.95 US	☐ New Orleans .... $17.95 CAN $12.95 US
☐ Belize .... $16.95 CAN $12.95 US	☐ New York City .... $19.95 CAN $14.95 US
☐ Calgary .... $17.95 CAN $12.95 US	☐ Nicaragua .... $24.95 CAN $16.95 US
☐ Canada.............. $29.95 CAN $21.95 US	☐ Ontario's Best Hotels .... $16.95 CAN and Restaurants $12.95US
☐ Chicago .... $19.95 CAN $14.95 US	☐ Ontario .... $27.95 CAN $19.95US
☐ Chile .... $27.95 CAN $17.95 US	☐ Ottawa .... $17.95 CAN $12.95 US
☐ Colombia .... $29.95 CAN $21.95 US	☐ Panamá .... $24.95 CAN $17.95 US
☐ Costa Rica .... $27.95 CAN $19.95 US	☐ Peru .... $27.95 CAN $19.95 US
☐ Cuba .... $24.95 CAN $17.95 US	☐ Phoenix .... $16.95 CAN $12.95 US
☐ Dominican .... $24.95 CAN Republic $17.95 US	☐ Portugal .... $24.95 CAN $16.95 US
☐ Ecuador and .... $24.95 CAN Galápagos Islands $17.95 US	☐ Provence - .... $29.95 CAN Côte d'Azur $21.95US
☐ El Salvador .... $22.95 CAN $14.95 US	☐ Puerto Rico .... $24.95 CAN $17.95 US
☐ Guadeloupe .... $24.95 CAN $17.95 US	☐ Québec .... $29.95 CAN $21.95 US
☐ Guatemala .... $24.95 CAN $17.95 US	☐ Québec City .... $17.95 CAN $12.95 US
☐ Hawaii .... $29.95 CAN $21.95 US	☐ Québec and Ontario ...... $9.95 CAN with Via $7.95 US
☐ Honduras .... $24.95 CAN $17.95 US	☐ Seattle .... $17.95 CAN $12.95 US
☐ Islands of the .... $24.95 CAN Bahamas $17.95 US	☐ Toronto .... $18.95 CAN $13.95 US
☐ Las Vegas $17.95 $12.95	☐ Tunisia .... $27.95 CAN $19.95 US
☐ Lisbon .... $18.95 CAN $13.95 US	☐ Vancouver .... $17.95 CAN $12.95 US
	☐ Washington D.C. .... $18.95 CAN $13.95 US
	☐ Western Canada .... $29.95 CAN $21.95 US

Ulysses Due South

☐ Acapulco .... $14.95 CAN $9.95 US	☐ Cancun Cozumel .... $17.95 CAN $12.95 US
☐ Belize .... $16.95 CAN $12.95 US	☐ Huatulco - .... $17.95 CAN Puerto Escondido $12.95 US
☐ Cartagena .... $12.95 CAN (Colombia) $9.95 US	

☐ Los Cabos and La Paz . . . . $14.95 CAN
$7.99 US
☐ Puerto Plata - Sosua . . . . . $14.95 CAN
$9.95 US

☐ Puerto Vallarta . . . . $14.95 CAN
$9.95 US
☐ St. Martin and . . . . $16.95 CAN
St. Barts $12.95 US

Ulysses Travel Journals

☐ Ulysses Travel Journal . . $9.95 CAN
(Blue, Red, Green, Yellow, Sextant)
$7.95 US

☐ Ulysses Travel Journal . . . $14.95 CAN
(80 Days) $9.95 US

Ulysses Green Escapes

☐ Cycling in France . . . . $22.95 CAN
$16.95 US
☐ Cycling in Ontario . . . . . $22.95 CAN
$16.95 US

☐ Hiking in the . . . . $19.95 CAN
Northeastern U.S. $13.95 US
☐ Hiking in Québec . . . . $19.95 CAN
$13.95 US

Ulysses Conversation Guides

☐ French for Better Travel . . $9.95 CAN
$6.50 US

☐ Spanish for Better Travel . . $9.95 CAN
in Latin America $6.50 US

Title	Qty	Price	Total

Name:		Subtotal	
		Shipping	$4 CAN $3 US
Address:		Subtotal	
		GST in Canada 7%	
		Total	

Tel: Fax:

E-mail:

Payment: ☐ Cheque ☐ Visa ☐ MasterCard

Card number_____ Expiry date_____

Signature_____

ULYSSES TRAVEL GUIDES

4176 St-Denis,
Montréal, Québec, H2W 2M5
(514) 843-9447
fax (514) 843-9448

305 Madison Avenue,
Suite 1166,
New York, NY 10165
Toll free: 1-877-542-7247

www.ulyssesguides.com
info@ulysses.ca